Arbitrage Theory in Continuous Time

Third Edition

Arbitrage Theory in Continuous Time

THIRD EDITION

TOMAS BJÖRK
Stockholm School of Economics

OXFORD
UNIVERSITY PRESS

Great Clarendon Street, Oxford OX2 6DP

Oxford University Press is a department of the University of Oxford.
It furthers the University's objective of excellence in research, scholarship,
and education by publishing worldwide in

Oxford New York

Auckland Cape Town Dar es Salaam Hong Kong Karachi
Kuala Lumpur Madrid Melbourne Mexico City Nairobi
New Delhi Shanghai Taipei Toronto

With offices in

Argentina Austria Brazil Chile Czech Republic France Greece
Guatemala Hungary Italy Japan Poland Portugal Singapore
South Korea Switzerland Thailand Turkey Ukraine Vietnam

Oxford is a registered trade mark of Oxford University Press
in the UK and in certain other countries

Published in the United States
by Oxford University Press Inc., New York

© Tomas Björk 2009

The moral rights of the author have been asserted
Database right Oxford University Press (maker)

First published 2009

British Library Cataloguing in Publication Data

Data available

Library of Congress Cataloging in Publication Data

Data available

Typeset by SPI Publisher Services, Pondicherry, India
Printed in Great Britain
on acid-free paper by
Clays Ltd., St Ives plc

ISBN 978-0-19-957474-2

4

To Agneta, Kajsa, and Stefan

PREFACE TO THE THIRD EDITION

The third edition differs from the second edition by the fact that I have added chapters on the following subjects.

- The martingale approach to optimal investment problems.
- Optimal stopping theory with applications to American options.
- Positive interest models and their connection to potential theory and stochastic discount factors.

Apart from this I have changed the previous definition of arbitrage in Chapter 3 into the standard one. This leads to slightly more complicated mathematics but it has the advantage that martingale measures will be equivalent to the objective measure instead of merely absolutely continuous.

I have corrected a large number of typos from the second edition. In all probability there are still some typos left. If you find any of these, I would be very grateful if you could inform me by e-mail < tomas.bjork@hhs.se >. I will try to keep an updated typo list on my home page, which is clickable from "http://www.hhs.se/Finance".

I am extremely grateful for very helpful comments from, among others, Axel Andre, Damir Filipovic, Karunarathna Panagamuwa Gamage, Chih Ying Hsiao, Martin Groth, Gunther Hahn, Lane Hughston, Edward Kao, Nuutti Kuosa, Koichi Maekawa, Axel Mjøs, Christina Nikitopoulos Sklibosios, Trygve Nilsen, Ragnar Norberg, Sabbir Rahman, Walter Schachermayer, Josef Teichmann, Ubbo Wiersema, Min Zheng.

For many years I have benefited immensely from discussions with all my PhD students in mathematical finance at SSE: Magnus Blix, Mikael Elhouar, Raquel Gaspar, Mia Hinnerich, Magnus Hyll, Linus Kaisajuntti, Agatha Murgoci and Irina Slinko. My warmest thanks to all of you.

Special thanks are due to Mark Davis and Camilla Landén for letting me use some of our joint work in Chapter 20. My good friend and colleague Camilla Landén is also the single most important contributor of good advice for this book. For many years she has provided me with so much input that it is impossible to mention each item. For this I am truly grateful.

Tomas Björk

Stockholm
January 17 2009

PREFACE TO THE SECOND EDITION

One of the main ideas behind the first edition of this book was to provide a reasonably honest introduction to arbitrage theory without going into abstract measure and integration theory. This approach, however, had some clear drawbacks: Some topics, like the change of numeraire theory and the recently developed LIBOR and swap market models, are very hard to discuss without using the language of measure theory, and an important concept like that of a martingale measure can only be fully understood within a measure theoretic framework.

For the second edition I have therefore decided to include also some more advanced material but in order to keep the book accessible for the reader who does not want to study measure theory, I have organized the text as follows.

- The more advanced parts of the book are marked with a star *.
- The main parts of the book are virtually unchanged and kept on an elementary level (i.e. marked without a star).
- The reader who is looking for an elementary treatment can simply skip the starred chapters and sections. The non-starred sections thus constitute a self-contained course on arbitrage theory.

The organization and contents of the new parts are as follows.

- I have added appendices on measure theory, probability theory and martingale theory. These appendices can be used for a lighthearted but honest introductory course on the corresponding topics, and they define the prerequisites for the advanced parts of the main text. In the appendices there is an emphasis on building intuition for basic concepts, such as measurability, conditional expectation, and measure changes. Most results are given formal proofs but for some results the reader is referred to the literature.
- There is a new chapter on the martingale approach to arbitrage theory, where we discuss (in some detail) the First and Second Fundamental Theorems of mathematical finance, i.e. the connections between absence of arbitrage, the existence of martingale measures, and completeness of the market. The full proofs of these results are very technical but I have tried to provide a fairly detailed guided tour through the theory, including the Delbaen–Schachermayer proof of the First Fundamental Theorem.
- Following the chapter on the general martingale approach there is a separate chapter on martingale representation theorems and Girsanov transformations in a Wiener framework. Full proofs are given and I have also added a section on maximum likelihood estimation for diffusion processes.

- As the obvious application of the machinery developed above, there is a chapter where the Black–Scholes model is discussed in detail from the martingale point of view. There is also an added chapter on the martingale approach to multidimensional models, where these are investigated in some detail. In particular we discuss stochastic discount factors and derive the Hansen–Jagannathan bounds.
- The old chapter on changes of numeraire always suffered from the restriction to a Markovian setting. It has now been rewritten and placed in its much more natural martingale setting.
- I have added a fairly extensive chapter on the LIBOR and swap market models which have become so important in interest rate theory.

Acknowledgements

Since the publication of the first edition I have received valuable comments and help from a large number of people. In particular I am very grateful to Raquel Medeiros Gaspar who, apart from pointing out errors and typos, has done a splendid job in providing written solutions to a large number of the exercises. I am also very grateful to Åke Gunnelin, Mia Hinnerich, Nuutti Kuosa, Roger Lee, Trygve Nilsen, Ragnar Norberg, Philip Protter, Rolf Poulsen, Ping Wu, and K.P. Gamage.

Special thanks are due to Kjell Johansson and Andrew Sheppard for providing important and essential input at crucial points.

Tomas Björk

Stockholm
April 30 2003

PREFACE

The purpose of this book is to present arbitrage theory and its applications to pricing problems for financial derivatives. It is intended as a textbook for graduate and advanced undergraduate students in finance, economics, mathematics, and statistics and I also hope that it will be useful for practitioners.

Because of its intended audience, the book does not presuppose any previous knowledge of abstract measure theory. The only mathematical prerequisites are advanced calculus and a basic course in probability theory. No previous knowledge in economics or finance is assumed.

The book starts by contradicting its own title, in the sense that the second chapter is devoted to the binomial model. After that, the theory is exclusively developed in continuous time.

The main mathematical tool used in the book is the theory of stochastic differential equations (SDEs), and instead of going into the technical details concerning the foundations of that theory I have focused on *applications*. The object is to give the reader, as quickly and painlessly as possible, a solid working knowledge of the powerful mathematical tool known as Itô calculus. We treat basic SDE techniques, including Feynman–Kač representations and the Kolmogorov equations. Martingales are introduced at an early stage. Throughout the book there is a strong emphasis on concrete computations, and the exercises at the end of each chapter constitute an integral part of the text.

The mathematics developed in the first part of the book is then applied to arbitrage pricing of financial derivatives. We cover the basic Black–Scholes theory, including delta hedging and "the greeks", and we extend it to the case of several underlying assets (including stochastic interest rates) as well as to dividend paying assets. Barrier options, as well as currency and quanto products, are given separate chapters. We also consider, in some detail, incomplete markets.

American contracts are treated only in passing. The reason for this is that the theory is complicated and that few analytical results are available. Instead I have included a chapter on stochastic optimal control and its applications to optimal portfolio selection.

Interest rate theory constitutes a large part of the book, and we cover the basic short rate theory, including inversion of the yield curve and affine term structures. The Heath–Jarrow–Morton theory is treated, both under the objective measure and under a martingale measure, and we also present the Musiela parametrization. The basic framework for most chapters is that of a multifactor model, and this allows us, despite the fact that we do not formally use measure theory, to give a fairly complete treatment of the general change of numeraire technique which is so essential to modern interest rate theory. In particular we treat forward neutral measures in some detail. This allows us to present the Geman–El Karoui–Rochet formula for option pricing, and we apply it to the general Gaussian forward rate model, as well as to a number of particular cases.

Concerning the mathematical level, the book falls between the elementary text by Hull (1997), and more advanced texts such as Duffie (1996) or Musiela and Rutkowski (1997). These books are used as canonical references in the present text.

In order to facilitate using the book for shorter courses, the pedagogical approach has been that of first presenting and analyzing a simple (typically one-dimensional) model, and then to derive the theory in a more complicated (multidimensional) framework. The drawback of this approach is of course that some arguments are being repeated, but this seems to be unavoidable, and I can only apologize to the technically more advanced reader.

Notes to the literature can be found at the end of most chapters. I have tried to keep the reference list on a manageable scale, but any serious omission is unintentional, and I will be happy to correct it. For more bibliographic information the reader is referred to Duffie (1996) and to Musiela and Rutkowski (1997) which both contain encyclopedic bibliographies.

On the more technical side the following facts can be mentioned. I have tried to present a reasonably honest picture of SDE theory, including Feynman–Kač representations, while avoiding the explicit use of abstract measure theory. Because of the chosen technical level, the arguments concerning the construction of the stochastic integral are thus forced to be more or less heuristic. Nevertheless I have tried to be as precise as possible, so even the heuristic arguments are the "correct" ones in the sense that they can be completed to formal proofs. In the rest of the text I try to give full proofs of all mathematical statements, with the exception that I have often left out the checking of various integrability conditions.

Since the Girsanov theory for absolutely continuous changes of measures is outside the scope of this text, martingale measures are introduced by the use of locally riskless portfolios, partial differential equations (PDEs) and the Feynman–Kač representation theorem. Still, the approach to arbitrage theory presented in the text is basically a probabilistic one, emphasizing the use of martingale measures for the computation of prices.

The integral representation theorem for martingales adapted to a Wiener filtration is also outside the scope of the book. Thus we do not treat market completeness in full generality, but restrict ourselves to a Markovian framework. For most applications this is, however, general enough.

Acknowledgements

Bertil Näslund, Staffan Viotti, Peter Jennergren and Ragnar Lindgren persuaded me to start studying financial economics, and they have constantly and generously shared their knowledge with me.

Hans Bühlman, Paul Embrechts and Hans Gerber gave me the opportunity to give a series of lectures for a summer school at Monte Verita in Ascona 1995. This summer school was for me an extremely happy and fruitful time, as well as the start of a partially new career. The set of lecture notes produced for that occasion is the basis for the present book.

Over the years of writing, I have received valuable comments and advice from a large number of people. My greatest debt is to Camilla Landén who has given me more good advice (and pointed out more errors) than I thought was humanly possible. I am also highly indebted to Flavio Angelini, Pia Berg, Nick Bingham, Samuel Cox, Darrell Duffie, Otto Elmgart, Malin Engström, Jan Ericsson, Damir Filipović, Andrea Gombani, Stefano Herzel, David Lando, Angus MacDonald, Alexander Matros, Ragnar Norberg, Joel Reneby, Wolfgang Runggaldier, Per Sjöberg, Patrik Säfvenblad, Nick Webber and Anna Vorwerk.

The main part of this book has been written while I have been at the Finance Department of the Stockholm School of Economics. I am deeply indebted to the school, the department and the staff working there for support and encouragement.

Parts of the book were written while I was still at the mathematics department of KTH, Stockholm. It is a pleasure to acknowledge the support I got from the department and from the persons within it.

Finally I would like to express my deeply felt gratitude to Andrew Schuller, James Martin and Kim Roberts, all at Oxford University Press, and Neville Hankins, the freelance copy-editor who worked on the book. The help given (and patience shown) by these people has been remarkable and invaluable.

Tomas Björk

Stockholm
July 1998

CONTENTS

1

INTRODUCTION

1.1 Problem Formulation

The main project in this book consists in studying theoretical pricing models for those financial assets which are known as **financial derivatives**. Before we give the formal definition of the concept of a financial derivative we will, however, by means of a concrete example, introduce the single most important example: the European call option.

Let us thus consider the Swedish company $C\&H$, which today (denoted by $t = 0$) has signed a contract with an American counterpart $ACME$. The contract stipulates that $ACME$ will deliver 1000 computer games to $C\&H$ exactly six months from now (denoted by $t = T$). Furthermore it is stipulated that $C\&H$ will pay 1000 US dollars per game to $ACME$ at the time of delivery (i.e. at $t = T$). For the sake of the argument we assume that the present spot currency rate between the Swedish krona (SEK) and the US dollar is 8.00 SEK/\$.

One of the problems with this contract from the point of view of $C\&H$ is that it involves a considerable **currency risk**. Since $C\&H$ does not know the currency rate prevailing six months from now, this means that it does not know how many SEK it will have to pay at $t = T$. If the currency rate at $t = T$ is still 8.00 SEK/\$ it will have to pay 8,000,000 SEK, but if the rate rises to, say, 8.50 it will face a cost of 8,500,000 SEK. Thus $C\&H$ faces the problem of how to guard itself against this currency risk, and we now list a number of natural strategies.

1. The most naive stratgey for $C\&H$ is perhaps that of buying \$1,000,000 **today** at the price of 8,000,000 SEK, and then keeping this money (in a Eurodollar account) for six months. The advantage of this procedure is of course that the currency risk is completely eliminated, but there are also some drawbacks. First of all the strategy above has the consequence of tying up a substantial amount of money for a long period of time, but an even more serious objection may be that $C\&H$ perhaps does not have access to 8,000,000 SEK today.

2. A more sophisticated arrangement, which does not require any outlays at all today, is that $C\&H$ goes to the forward market and buys a **forward contract** for \$1,000,000 with delivery six months from now. Such a contract may, for example, be negotiated with a commercial bank, and in the contract two things will be stipulated.

   • The bank will, at $t = T$, deliver \$1,000,000 to $C\&H$.
   • $C\&H$ will, at $t = T$, pay for this delivery at the rate of K SEK/\$.

The exchange rate K, which is called the **forward price**, (or forward exchange rate) at $t = 0$, for delivery at $t = T$, is determined at $t = 0$. By the definition of a forward contract, the cost of entering the contract equals zero, and the forward rate K is thus determined by supply and demand on the forward market. Observe, however, that even if the price of entering the forward contract (at $t = 0$) is zero, the contract may very well fetch a nonzero price during the interval $[0, T]$.

Let us now assume that the forward rate today for delivery in six months equals 8.10 SEK/\$. If *C&H* enters the forward contract this simply means that there are no outlays today, and that in six months it will get \$ 1,000,000 at the predetermined total price of 8,100,000 SEK. Since the forward rate is determined today, *C&H* has again completely eliminated the currency risk.

However, the forward contract also has some drawbacks, which are related to the fact that a forward contract is a **binding** contract. To see this let us look at two scenarios.

- Suppose that the spot currency rate at $t = T$ turns out to be 8.20. Then *C&H* can congratulate itself, because it can now buy dollars at the rate 8.10 despite the fact that the market rate is 8.20. In terms of the million dollars at stake *C&H* has thereby made an indirect profit of 8,200,000 $-8,100,000 = 100,000$ SEK.
- Suppose on the other hand that the spot exchange rate at $t = T$ turns out to be 7.90. Because of the forward contract this means that *C&H* is forced to buy dollars at the rate of 8.10 despite the fact that the market rate is 7.90, which implies an indirect loss of $8,100,000 - 7,900,000 = 200,000$ SEK.
3. What *C&H* would like to have of course is a contract which guards it against a high spot rate at $t = T$, while still allowing it to take advantage of a low spot rate at $t = T$. Such contracts do in fact exist, and they are called **European call options**. We will now go on to give a formal definition of such an option.

Definition 1.1 *A* **European call option** *on the amount of X US dollars, with* **strike price** *(exercise price) K SEK/\$ and* **exercise date** *T is a contract written at $t = 0$ with the following properties.*

- *The holder of the contract has, exactly at the time $t = T$, the* **right** *to buy X US dollars at the price K SEK/\$.*
- *The holder of the option has no obligation to buy the dollars.*

Concerning the nomenclature, the contract is called an option precisely because it gives the holder the option (as opposed to the obligation) of buying some **underlying** asset (in this case US dollars). A **call** option gives the holder the right to buy, wheareas a **put** option gives the holder the right to sell the underlying object at a prespecified price. The prefix **European** means that the option can only be exercised at exactly the date of expiration. There also exist **American** options, which give the holder the right to exercise the option at any time before the date of expiration.

Options of the type above (and with many variations) are traded on options markets all over the world, and the underlying objects can be anything from foreign currencies to stocks, oranges, timber or pig stomachs. For a given underlying object there are typically a large number of options with different dates of expiration and different strike prices.

We now see that *C&H* can insure itself against the currency risk very elegantly by buying a European call option, expiring six months from now, on a million dollars with a strike price of, for example, 8.00 SEK/\$. If the spot exchange rate at T exceeds the strike price, say that it is 8.20, then *C&H* exercises the option and buys at 8.00 SEK/\$. Should the spot exchange rate at T fall below the strike price, it simply abstains from exercising the option.

Note, however, that in contrast to a forward contract, which by definition has the price zero at the time at which it is entered, an option will always have a nonnegative price, which is determined on the existing options market. This means that our friends in *C&H* will have the rather delicate problem of determining exactly which option they wish to buy, since a higher strike price (for a call option) will reduce the price of the option.

One of the main problems in this book is to see what can be said from a theoretical point of view about the market price of an option like the one above. In this context it is worth noting that the European call has some properties which turn out to be fundamental.

- Since the value of the option (at T) depends on the future level of the spot exchange rate, the holding of an option is equivalent to a **future stochastic claim**.
- The option is a **derivative asset** in the sense that it is **defined** in terms of some **underlying** financial asset.

Since the value of the option is contingent on the evolution of the exchange rate, the option is often called a **contingent claim**. Later on we will give a precise mathematical definition of this concept, but for the moment the informal definition above will do. An option is just one example of a financial derivative, and a far from complete list of commonly traded derivatives is given below.

- European calls and puts
- American options
- Forward rate agreements
- Convertibles
- Futures
- Bonds and bond options
- Caps and floors
- Interest rate swaps

Later on we will give precise definitions of (most of) these contracts, but at the moment the main point is the fact that financial derivatives exist in a great variety and are traded in huge volumes. We can now formulate the two main problems which concern us in the rest of the book.

Main Problems: Take a fixed derivative as given.

- What is a "fair" price for the contract?
- Suppose that we have sold a derivative, such as a call option. Then we have exposed ourselves to a certain amount of financial risk at the date of expiration. How do we protect ("hedge") ourselves against this risk?

Let us look more closely at the pricing question above. There exist two natural and mutually contradictory answers.

Answer 1: "Using standard principles of operations research, a reasonable price for the derivative is obtained by computing the expected value of the discounted future stochastic payoff."

Answer 2: "Using standard economic reasoning, the price of a contingent claim, like the price of any other commodity, will be determined by market forces. In particular it will be determined by the supply and demand curves for the market for derivatives. Supply and demand will in their turn be influenced by such factors as aggregate risk aversion, liquidity preferences, etc., so it is impossible to say anything concrete about the theoretical price of a derivative."

The reason that there is such a thing as a theory for derivatives lies in the following fact.

Main Result: *Both answers above are incorrect! It* **is** *possible (given, of course, some assumptions) to talk about the "correct" price of a derivative, and this price is* **not** *computed by the method given in Answer 1 above.*

In the succeeding chapters we will analyze these problems in detail, but we can already state the basic philosophy here. The main ideas are as follows.

Main Ideas

- A financial derivative is **defined in terms of** some underlying asset which already exists on the market.
- The derivative cannot therefore be priced arbitrarily **in relation to the underlying prices** if we want to **avoid mispricing between the derivative and the underlying price**.
- We thus want to price the derivative in a way that is **consistent** with the underlying prices given by the market.
- We are **not** trying to compute the price of the derivative in some "absolute" sense. The idea instead is to determine the price of the derivative **in terms of the market prices of the underlying assets**.

2

THE BINOMIAL MODEL

In this chapter we will study, in some detail, the simplest possible nontrivial model of a financial market—the binomial model. This is a discrete time model, but despite the fact that the main purpose of the book concerns continuous time models, the binomial model is well worth studying. The model is very easy to understand, almost all important concepts which we will study later on already appear in the binomial case, the mathematics required to analyze it is at high school level, and last but not least the binomial model is often used in practice.

2.1 The One Period Model

We start with the one period version of the model. In the next section we will (easily) extend the model to an arbitrary number of periods.

2.1.1 *Model Description*

Running time is denoted by the letter t, and by definition we have two points in time, $t = 0$ ("today") and $t = 1$ ("tomorrow"). In the model we have two assets: a **bond** and a **stock**. At time t the price of a bond is denoted by B_t, and the price of one share of the stock is denoted by S_t. Thus we have two price processes B and S.

The bond price process is deterministic and given by

$$B_0 = 1,$$
$$B_1 = 1 + R.$$

The constant R is the spot rate for the period, and we can also interpret the existence of the bond as the existence of a bank with R as its rate of interest.

The stock price process is a stochastic process, and its dynamical behaviour is described as follows.

$$S_0 = s,$$
$$S_1 = \begin{cases} s \cdot u, & \text{with probability } p_u. \\ s \cdot d, & \text{with probability } p_d. \end{cases}$$

It is often convenient to write this as

$$\begin{cases} S_0 = s, \\ S_1 = s \cdot Z, \end{cases}$$

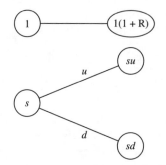

FIG. 2.1. Price dynamics

where Z is a stochastic variable defined as

$$Z = \begin{cases} u, & \text{with probability } p_u. \\ d, & \text{with probability } p_d. \end{cases}$$

We assume that today's stock price s is known, as are the positive constants u, d, p_u and p_d. We assume that $d < u$, and we have of course $p_u + p_d = 1$. We can illustrate the price dynamics using the tree structure in Fig. 2.1.

2.1.2   Portfolios and Arbitrage

We will study the behaviour of various **portfolios** on the (B, S) market, and to this end we define a portfolio as a vector $h = (x, y)$. The interpretation is that x is the number of bonds we hold in our portfolio, whereas y is the number of units of the stock held by us. Note that it is quite acceptable for x and y to be positive as well as negative. If, for example, $x = 3$, this means that we have bought three bonds at time $t = 0$. If on the other hand $y = -2$, this means that we have sold two shares of the stock at time $t = 0$. In financial jargon we have a **long** position in the bond and a **short** position in the stock. It is an important assumption of the model that short positions are allowed.

Assumption 2.1.1 *We assume the following institutional facts.*

- *Short positions, as well as fractional holdings, are allowed. In mathematical terms this means that every $h \in R^2$ is an allowed portfolio.*
- *There is no bid-ask spread, i.e. the selling price is equal to the buying price of all assets.*
- *There are no transactions costs of trading.*
- *The market is completely liquid, i.e. it is always possible to buy and/or sell unlimited quantities on the market. In particular it is possible to borrow unlimited amounts from the bank (by selling bonds short).*

Consider now a fixed portfolio $h = (x, y)$. This portfolio has a deterministic market value at $t = 0$ and a stochastic value at $t = 1$.

Definition 2.1 *The* **value process** *of the portfolio h is defined by*

$$V_t^h = xB_t + yS_t, \quad t = 0, 1,$$

or, in more detail,

$$V_0^h = x + ys,$$
$$V_1^h = x(1 + R) + ysZ.$$

Everyone wants to make a profit by trading on the market, and in this context a so called arbitrage portfolio is a dream come true; this is one of the central concepts of the theory.

Definition 2.2 *An* **arbitrage** *portfolio is a portfolio h with the properties*

$$V_0^h = 0,$$
$$V_1^h > 0, \quad \text{with probability 1.}$$

An arbitrage portfolio is thus basically a deterministic money making machine, and we interpret the existence of an arbitrage portfolio as equivalent to a serious case of mispricing on the market. It is now natural to investigate when a given market model is arbitrage free, i.e. when there are no arbitrage portfolios.

Proposition 2.3 *The model above is free of arbitrage if and only if the following conditions hold:*

$$d \leq (1 + R) \leq u. \tag{2.1}$$

Proof The condition (2.1) has an easy economic interpretation. It simply says that the return on the stock is not allowed to dominate the return on the bond and vice versa. To show that absence of arbitrage implies (2.1), we assume that (2.1) does in fact not hold, and then we show that this implies an arbitrage opportunity. Let us thus assume that one of the inequalities in (2.1) does not hold, so that we have, say, the inequality $s(1 + R) > su$. Then we also have $s(1 + R) > sd$ so it is always more profitable to invest in the bond than in the stock. An arbitrage strategy is now formed by the portfolio $h = (s, -1)$, i.e. we sell the stock short and invest all the money in the bond. For this portfolio we obviously have $V_0^h = 0$, and as for $t = 1$ we have

$$V_1^h = s(1 + R) - sZ,$$

which by assumption is positive.

Now assume that (2.1) is satisfied. To show that this implies absence of arbitrage let us consider an arbitrary portfolio such that $V_0^h = 0$. We thus have $x + ys = 0$, i.e. $x = -ys$. Using this relation we can write the value of the portfolio at $t = 1$ as

$$V_1^h = \begin{cases} ys\,[u - (1 + R)], & \text{if } Z = u. \\ ys\,[d - (1 + R)], & \text{if } Z = d. \end{cases}$$

Assume now that $y > 0$. Then h is an arbitrage strategy if and only if we have the inequalities

$$u > 1 + R,$$
$$d > 1 + R,$$

but this is impossible because of the condition (2.1). The case $y < 0$ is treated similarly. □

At first glance this result is perhaps only moderately exciting, but we may write it in a more suggestive form. To say that (2.1) holds is equivalent to saying that $1 + R$ is a convex combination of u and d, i.e.

$$1 + R = q_u \cdot u + q_d \cdot d,$$

where $q_u, q_d \geq 0$ and $q_u + q_d = 1$. In particular we see that the weights q_u and q_d can be interpreted as probabilities for a new probability measure Q with the property $Q(Z = u) = q_u$, $Q(Z = d) = q_d$. Denoting expectation w.r.t. this measure by E^Q we now have the following easy calculation

$$\frac{1}{1+R}E^Q\,[S_1] = \frac{1}{1+R}\,[q_u su + q_d sd] = \frac{1}{1+R} \cdot s(1 + R) = s.$$

We thus have the relation

$$s = \frac{1}{1+R}E^Q\,[S_1],$$

which to an economist is a well-known relation. It is in fact a **risk neutral** valuation formula, in the sense that it gives today's stock price as the discounted expected value of tomorrow's stock price. Of course we do not assume that the agents in our market are risk neutral—what we have shown is only that if we use the Q-probabilities instead of the objective probabilities then we have in fact a risk neutral valuation of the stock (given absence of arbitrage). A probability measure with this property is called a **risk neutral measure**, or alternatively a **risk adjusted measure** or a **martingale measure**. Martingale measures will play a dominant role in the sequel so we give a formal definition.

Definition 2.4 *A probability measure Q is called a* **martingale measure** *if the following condition holds:*

$$S_0 = \frac{1}{1+R} E^Q [S_1].$$

We may now state the condition of no arbitrage in the following way.

Proposition 2.5 *The market model is arbitrage free if and only if there exists a martingale measure Q.*

For the binomial model it is easy to calculate the martingale probabilities. The proof is left to the reader.

Proposition 2.6 *For the binomial model above, the martingale probabilities are given by*

$$\begin{cases} q_u = \dfrac{(1+R) - d}{u - d}, \\[2mm] q_d = \dfrac{u - (1+R)}{u - d}. \end{cases}$$

2.1.3 *Contingent Claims*

Let us now assume that the market in the preceding section is arbitrage free. We go on to study pricing problems for contingent claims.

Definition 2.7 *A* **contingent claim** *(financial derivative) is any stochastic variable X of the form $X = \Phi(Z)$, where Z is the stochastic variable driving the stock price process above.*

We interpret a given claim X as a contract which pays X SEK to the holder of the contract at time $t = 1$. See Fig. 2.2, where the value of the claim at each node is given within the corresponding box. The function Φ is called the **contract function**. A typical example would be a European call option on the stock with strike price K. For this option to be interesting we assume that $sd < K < su$. If $S_1 > K$ then we use the option, pay K to get the stock and

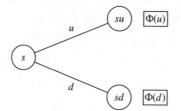

FIG. 2.2. Contingent claim

then sell the stock on the market for su, thus making a net profit of $su - K$. If $S_1 < K$ then the option is obviously worthless. In this example we thus have

$$X = \begin{cases} su - K, & \text{if } Z = u, \\ 0, & \text{if } Z = d, \end{cases}$$

and the contract function is given by

$$\Phi(u) = su - K,$$
$$\Phi(d) = 0.$$

Our main problem is now to determine the "fair" price, if such an object exists at all, for a given contingent claim X. If we denote the price of X at time t by $\Pi(t; X)$, then it can be seen that at time $t = 1$ the problem is easy to solve. In order to avoid arbitrage we must (why?) have

$$\Pi(1; X) = X,$$

and the hard part of the problem is to determine $\Pi(0; X)$. To attack this problem we make a slight detour.

Since we have assumed absence of arbitrage we know that we cannot make money out of nothing, but it is interesting to study what we **can** achieve on the market.

Definition 2.8 *A given contingent claim X is said to be* **reachable** *if there exists a portfolio h such that*
$$V_1^h = X,$$
with probability 1. In that case we say that the portfolio h is a **hedging** *portfolio or a* **replicating** *portfolio. If all claims can be replicated we say that the market is* **complete**.

If a certain claim X is reachable with replicating portfolio h, then, from a financial point of view, there is no difference between holding the claim and holding the portfolio. No matter what happens on the stock market, the value of the claim at time $t = 1$ will be exactly equal to the value of the portfolio at $t = 1$. Thus the price of the claim should equal the market value of the portfolio, and we have the following basic pricing principle.

Pricing principle 1 *If a claim X is reachable with replicating portfolio h, then the only reasonable price process for X is given by*

$$\Pi(t; X) = V_t^h, \quad t = 0, 1.$$

The word "reasonable" above can be given a more precise meaning as in the following proposition. We leave the proof to the reader.

Proposition 2.9 *Suppose that a claim X is reachable with replicating portfolio h. Then any price at $t = 0$ of the claim X, other than V_0^h, will lead to an arbitrage possibility.*

We see that in a complete market we can in fact price all contingent claims, so it is of great interest to investigate when a given market is complete. For the binomial model we have the following result.

Proposition 2.10 *Assume that the general binomial model is free of arbitrage. Then it is also complete.*

Proof   We fix an arbitrary claim X with contract function Φ, and we want to show that there exists a portfolio $h = (x, y)$ such that

$$V_1^h = \Phi(u), \quad \text{if } Z = u,$$
$$V_1^h = \Phi(d), \quad \text{if } Z = d.$$

If we write this out in detail we want to find a solution (x, y) to the following system of equations

$$(1 + R)x + suy = \Phi(u),$$
$$(1 + R)x + sdy = \Phi(d).$$

Since by assumption $d < u$, this linear system has a unique solution, and a simple calculation shows that it is given by

$$x = \frac{1}{1 + R} \cdot \frac{u\Phi(d) - d\Phi(u)}{u - d}, \tag{2.2}$$

$$y = \frac{1}{s} \cdot \frac{\Phi(u) - \Phi(d)}{u - d}. \tag{2.3}$$

$\square$

2.1.4 *Risk Neutral Valuation*

Since the binomial model is shown to be complete we can now price any contingent claim. According to the pricing principle of the preceding section the price at $t = 0$ is given by

$$\Pi(0; X) = V_0^h,$$

and using the explicit formulas (2.2)–(2.3) we obtain, after some reshuffling of terms,

$$\Pi(0; X) = x + sy$$
$$= \frac{1}{1 + R} \left\{ \frac{(1 + R) - d}{u - d} \cdot \Phi(u) + \frac{u - (1 + R)}{u - d} \cdot \Phi(d) \right\}.$$

Here we recognize the martingale probabilities q_u and q_d of Proposition 2.6. If we assume that the model is free of arbitrage, these are true probabilities (i.e. they are nonnegative), so we can write the pricing formula above as

$$\Pi(0; X) = \frac{1}{1+R} \left\{ \Phi(u) \cdot q_u + \Phi(d) \cdot q_d \right\}.$$

The right-hand side can now be interpreted as an expected value under the martingale probability measure Q, so we have proved the following basic pricing result, where we also add our old results about hedging.

Proposition 2.11 *If the binomial model is free of arbitrage, then the arbitrage free price of a contingent claim X is given by*

$$\Pi(0; X) = \frac{1}{1+R} E^Q [X]. \tag{2.4}$$

Here the martingale measure Q is uniquely determined by the relation

$$S_0 = \frac{1}{1+R} E^Q [S_1], \tag{2.5}$$

and the explicit expression for q_u and q_d are given in Proposition 2.6. Furthermore the claim can be replicated using the portfolio

$$x = \frac{1}{1+R} \cdot \frac{u\Phi(d) - d\Phi(u)}{u - d}, \tag{2.6}$$

$$y = \frac{1}{s} \cdot \frac{\Phi(u) - \Phi(d)}{u - d}. \tag{2.7}$$

We see that the formula (2.4) is a "risk neutral" valuation formula, and that the probabilities which are used are just those for which the stock itself admits a risk neutral valuation. The main economic moral can now be summarized.

Moral
- The only role played by the objective probabilities is that they determine which events are possible and which are impossible. In more abstarct probabilistic terminology they thus determine the class of *equivalent probability measures*. See Chapter 10.
- When we compute the arbitrage free price of a financial derivative we carry out the computations **as if** we live in a risk neutral world.
- This does **not** mean that we *de facto* live (or believe that we live) in a risk neutral world.
- The valuation formula holds for all investors, regardless of their attitude towards risk, as long as they prefer more deterministic money to less.

- The formula above is therefore often referred to as a "preference free" valuation formula.

We end by studying a concrete example.

Example 2.12 We set $s = 100$, $u = 1.2$, $d = 0.8$, $p_u = 0.6$, $p_d = 0.4$ and, for computational simplicity, $R = 0$. By convention, the monetary unit is the US dollar. Thus we have the price dynamics

$$S_0 = 100,$$

$$S_1 = \begin{cases} 120, & \text{with probability } 0.6. \\ 80, & \text{with probability } 0.4. \end{cases}$$

If we compute the discounted expected value (under the objective probability measure P) of tomorrow's price we get

$$\frac{1}{1+R} E^P [S_1] = 1 \cdot [120 \cdot 0.6 + 80 \cdot 0.4] = 104.$$

This is higher than the value of today's stock price of 100, so the market is risk averse. Since condition (2.1) obviously is satisfied we know that the market is arbitrage free. We consider a European call with strike price $K = 110$, so the claim X is given by

$$X = \begin{cases} 10, & \text{if } S_1 = 120. \\ 0, & \text{if } S_1 = 80. \end{cases}$$

Using the method of computing the price as the discounted expected values under the objective probabilities, i.e. "Answer 1" in Section 1.1, this would give the price as

$$\Pi(0; X) = \frac{1}{1+0} [10 \cdot 0.6 + 0 \cdot 0.4] = 6.$$

Using the theory above it is easily seen that the martingale probabilities are given by $q_u = q_d = 0.5$, thus giving us the theoretical price

$$\Pi(0; X) = \frac{1}{1+0} [10 \cdot 0.5 + 0 \cdot 0.5] = 5.$$

We thus see that the theoretical price differs from the naive approach above. If our theory is correct we should also be able to replicate the option, and from the proposition above the replicating portfolio is given by

$$x = \frac{1.2 \cdot 0 - 0.8 \cdot 10}{1.2 - 0.8} = -20,$$

$$y = \frac{1}{100} \cdot \frac{10 - 0}{1.2 - 0.8} = \frac{1}{4}.$$

In everyday terms this means that the replicating portfolio is formed by borrowing \$20 from the bank, and investing this money in a quarter of a share in the stock. Thus the net value of the portfolio at $t = 0$ is five dollars, and at $t = 1$ the value is given by

$$V_1^h = -20 + \frac{1}{4} \cdot 120 = 10, \quad \text{if } S_1 = 120,$$

$$V_1^h = -20 + \frac{1}{4} \cdot 80 = 0, \quad \text{if } S_1 = 80,$$

so we see that we have indeed replicated the option. We also see that if anyone is foolish enough to buy the option from us for the price \$6, then we can make a riskless profit. We sell the option, thereby obtaining six dollars. Out of these six we invest five in the replicating portfolio and invest the remaining one in the bank. At time $t = 1$ the claims of the buyer of the option are completely balanced by the value of the replicating portfolio, and we still have one dollar invested in the bank. We have thus made an arbitrage profit. If someone is willing to sell the option to us at a price lower than five dollars, we can also make an arbitrage profit by selling the portfolio short.

We end this section by making some remarks.

First of all we have seen that in a complete market, like the binomial model above, there is indeed a unique price for any contingent claim. The price is given by the value of the replicating portfolio, and a negative way of expressing this is as follows. There exists a theoretical price for the claim precisely because of the fact that, strictly speaking, the claim is superfluous—it can equally well be replaced by its hedging portfolio.

Secondly we see that the structural reason for the completeness of the binomial model is the fact that we have two financial instruments at our disposal (the bond and the stock) in order to solve two equations (one for each possible outcome in the sample space). This fact can be generalized. A model is complete (in the generic case) if the number of underlying assets (including the bank account) equals the number of outcomes in the sample space.

If we would like to make a more realistic multiperiod model of the stock market, then the last remark above seems discouraging. If we make a (non-recombining) tree with 20 time steps this means that we have $2^{20} \sim 10^6$ elementary outcomes, and this number exceeds by a large margin the number of assets on any existing stock market. It would therefore seem that it is impossible to construct an interesting complete model with a reasonably large number of time steps. Fortunately the situation is not at all as bad as that; in a multiperiod model we will also have the possibility of considering **intermediary trading**, i.e. we can allow for portfolios which are rebalanced over time. This will give us much more degrees of freedom, and in the next section we will in fact study a complete multiperiod model.

2.2   The Multiperiod Model

2.2.1   *Portfolios and Arbitrage*

The multiperiod binomial model is a discrete time model with the time index t running from $t = 0$ to $t = T$, where the horizon T is fixed. As before we have two underlying assets, a bond with price process B_t and a stock with price process S_t.

We assume a constant deterministic short rate of interest R, which is interpreted as the simple period rate. This means that the bond price dynamics are given by

$$B_{n+1} = (1 + R)B_n,$$
$$B_0 = 1.$$

The dynamics of the stock price are given by

$$S_{n+1} = S_n \cdot Z_n,$$
$$S_0 = s.$$

here $Z_0, \ldots, Z_{T-1}$ are assumed to be i.i.d. (independent and identically distributed) stochastic variables, taking only the two values u and d with probabilities

$$P(Z_n = u) = p_u,$$
$$P(Z_n = d) = p_d.$$

We can illustrate the stock dynamics by means of a tree, as in Fig. 2.3. Note that the tree is **recombining** in the sense that an "up"-move followed by a "down"-move gives the same result as a "down"-move followed by an "up"-move.

We now go on to define the concept of a dynamic portfolio strategy.

Definition 2.13 *A* **portfolio strategy** *is a stochastic process*

$$\{h_t = (x_t, y_t); \quad t = 1, \ldots, T\}$$

such that h_t is a function of $S_0, S_1, \ldots, S_{t-1}$. For a given portfolio strategy h we set $h_0 = h_1$ by convention. The **value process** *corresponding to the portfolio h is defined by*

$$V_t^h = x_t(1 + R) + y_t S_t.$$

The interpretation of the formal definition is that x_t is the amount of money which we invest in the bank at time $t - 1$ and keep until time t. We interpret y_t as the number of shares that we buy at time $t - 1$ and keep until time t. We allow the portfolio strategy to be a contingent strategy, i.e. the portfolio we buy at t is allowed to depend on all information we have collected by observing the evolution of the stock price up to time t. We are, however, not allowed to

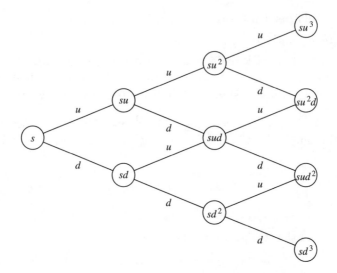

FIG. 2.3. Price dynamics

look into the future. The entity V_t^h above is of course the market value of the portfolio (x_t, y_t) (which has been held since $t - 1$) at time t.

The portfolios which primarily interest us are the **self-financing** portfolios, i.e. portfolios without any exogenous infusion or withdrawal of money. In practical terms this means that in a self-financing portfolio strategy the accession of a new asset has to be financed through the sale of some other asset. The mathematical definition is as follows.

Definition 2.14 *A portfolio strategy h is said to be* **self financing** *if the following condition holds for all $t = 0, \ldots, T - 1$*

$$x_t(1 + R) + y_t S_t = x_{t+1} + y_{t+1} S_t.$$

The condition above is simply a budget equation. It says that, at each time t, the market value of the "old" portfolio (x_t, y_t) (which was created at $t - 1$) equals the purchase value of the new portfolio (x_{t+1}, y_{t+1}), which is formed at t (and held until $t + 1$).

We can now define the multiperiod version of an arbitrage possibility.

Definition 2.15 *An* **arbitrage** *possibility is a self-financing portfolio h with the properties*

$$V_0^h = 0,$$
$$P\left(V_T^h \geq 0\right) = 1,$$
$$P\left(V_T^h > 0\right) > 0.$$

We immediately have the following necessary condition for absence of arbitrage.

Lemma 2.16 *If the model is free of arbitrage then the following conditions necessarily must hold.*

$$d \leq (1 + R) \leq u. \tag{2.8}$$

The condition above is in fact also sufficient for absence of arbitrage, but this fact is a little harder to show, and we will prove it later. In any case we assume that the condition holds.

Assumption 2.2.1 *Henceforth we assume that $d < u$, and that the condition (2.8) holds.*

As in the one period model we will have use for "martingale probabilities" which are defined and computed exactly as before.

Definition 2.17 *The martingale probabilities q_u and q_d are defined as the probabilities for which the relation*

$$s = \frac{1}{1+R} E^Q [S_{t+1} | S_t = s]$$

holds.

Proposition 2.18 *The martingale probabilities are given by*

$$
\begin{cases}
q_u = \dfrac{(1 + R) - d}{u - d}, \\[2mm]
q_d = \dfrac{u - (1 + R)}{u - d}.
\end{cases}
$$

2.2.2 Contingent Claims

We now give the formal definition of a contingent claim in the model.

Definition 2.19 *A **contingent claim** is a stochastic variable X of the form*

$$X = \Phi (S_T),$$

*where the **contract function** Φ is some given real valued function.*

The interpretation is that the holder of the contract receives the stochastic amount X at time $t = T$. Notice that we are only considering claims that are "simple", in the sense that the value of the claim only depends on the value S_T of the stock price at the final time T. It is also possible to consider stochastic payoffs which depend on the entire path of the price process during the interval $[0, T]$, but then the theory becomes a little more complicated, and in particular the event tree will become nonrecombining.

Our main problem is that of finding a "reasonable" price process

$$\{\Pi(t; X); \ t = 0, \ldots, T\}$$

for a given claim X, and as in the one period case we attack this problem by means of replicating portfolios.

Definition 2.20 *A given contingent claim X is said to be* **reachable** *if there exists a self-financing portfolio h such that*

$$V_T^h = X,$$

with probability 1. In that case we say that the portfolio h is a **hedging** *portfolio or a* **replicating** *portfolio. If all claims can be replicated we say that the market is (dynamically)* **complete**.

Again we have a natural pricing principle for reachable claims.

Pricing principle 2 *If a claim X is reachable with replicating (self-financing) portfolio h, then the only reasonable price process for X is given by*

$$\Pi(t; X) = V_t^h, \quad t = 0, 1, \ldots, T$$

Let us go through the argument in some detail. Suppose that X is reachable using the self-financing portfolio h. Fix t and suppose that at time t we have access to the amount V_t^h. Then we can invest this money in the portfolio h, and since the portfolio is self-financing we can rebalance it over time without any extra cost so as to have the stochastic value V_T^h at time T. By definition $V_T^h = X$ with probability 1, so regardless of the stochastic movements of the stock price process the value of our portfolio will, at time T, be equal to the value of the claim X. Thus, from a financial point of view, the portfolio h and the claim X are equivalent so they should fetch the same price.

The "reasonableness" of the pricing formula above can be expressed more formally as follows. The proof is left to the reader.

Proposition 2.21 *Suppose that X is reachable using the portfolio h. Suppose furthermore that, at some time t, it is possible to buy X at a price cheaper than (or to sell it at a price higher than) V_t^h. Then it is possible to make an arbitrage profit.*

We now turn to the completeness of the model.

Proposition 2.22 *The multiperiod binomial model is complete, i.e. every claim can be replicated by a self-financing portfolio.*

It is possible, and not very hard, to give a formal proof of the proposition, using mathematical induction. The formal proof will, however, look rather messy with lots of indices, so instead we prove the proposition for a concrete example, using a binomial tree. This should (hopefully) convey the idea of the proof, and the mathematically inclined reader is then invited to formalize the argument.

Example 2.23 We set $T = 3$, $S_0 = 80$, $u = 1.5$, $d = 0.5$, $p_u = 0.6$, $p_d = 0.4$ and, for computational simplicity, $R = 0$.

The dynamics of the stock price can now be illustrated using the binomial tree in Fig. 2.4, where in each node we have written the value of the stock price.

We now consider a particular contingent claim, namely a European call on the underlying stock. The date of expiration of the option is $T = 3$, and the strike price is chosen to be $K = 80$. Formally this claim can be described as

$$X = \max\left[S_T - K, 0\right].$$

We will now show that this particular claim can be replicated, and it will be obvious from the argument that the result can be generalized to any binomial model and any claim.

The idea is to use induction on the time variable and to work backwards in the tree from the leaves at $t = T$ to the root at $t = 0$. We start by computing the price of the option at the date of expiration. This is easily done since obviously (why?) we must have, for any claim X, the relation

$$\Pi(T; X) = X.$$

This result is illustrated in Fig. 2.5, where the boxed numbers indicate the price of the claim. Just to check, we see that if $S_3 = 90$, then we exercise the option,

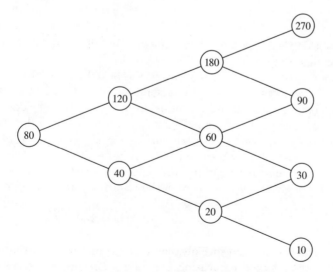

FIG. 2.4. Price dynamics

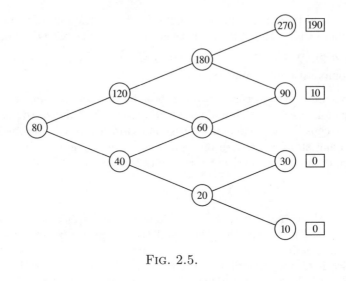

FIG. 2.5.

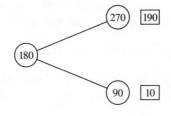

FIG. 2.6.

pay 80 to obtain the stock, and then immediately sell the stock at market price 90, thus making a profit of 10.

Our problem is thus that of replicating the boxed payoff structure at $t = 3$. Imagine for a moment that we are at some node at $t = 2$, e.g. at the node $S_2 = 180$. What we then see in front of us, from this particular node, is a simple one period binomial model, given in Fig. 2.6, and it now follows directly from the one period theory that the payoff structure in Fig. 2.6 can indeed be replicated from the node $S_2 = 180$. We can in fact compute the cost of this replicating portfolio by risk neutral valuation, and since the martingale probabilities for this example are given by $q_u = q_d = 0.5$ the cost of the replicating portfolio is

$$\frac{1}{1+0} \left[190 \cdot 0.5 + 10 \cdot 0.5 \right] = 100.$$

In the same way we can consider all the other nodes at $t = 2$, and compute the cost of the corresponding replicating portfolios. The result is the set of boxed numbers at $t = 2$ in Fig. 2.7.

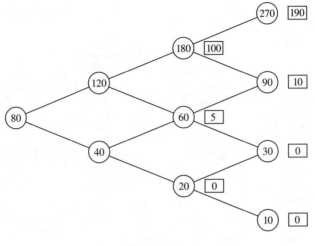

FIG. 2.7.

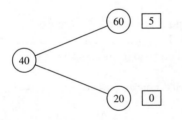

FIG. 2.8.

What we have done by this procedure is to show that if we can find a self-financing portfolio which replicates the boxed payoff structure at $t = 2$, then it is in fact possible to replicate the original claim at $t = 3$. We have thus reduced the problem in the time variable, and from now on we simply reproduce the construction above, but this time at $t = 1$. Take, for example, the node $S_1 = 40$. From the point of view of this node we have a one period model given by Fig. 2.8, and by risk neutral valuation we can replicate the payoff structure using a portfolio, which at the node $S_1 = 40$ will cost

$$\frac{1}{1 + 0} [5 \cdot 0.5 + 0 \cdot 0.5] = 2.5.$$

In this manner we fill the nodes at $t = 1$ with boxed portfolio costs, and then we carry out the same construction again at $t = 0$. The result is given in Fig. 2.9.

We have thus proved that it is in fact possible to replicate the European call option at an initial cost of 27.5. To check this let us now follow a possible price path forward through the tree.

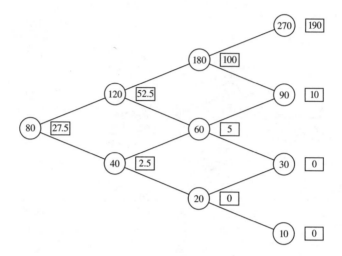

FIG. 2.9.

We start at $t = 0$, and since we want to reproduce the boxed claim $(52.5, 2.5)$ at $t = 1$, we can use Proposition 2.4 to compute the hedging portfolio as $x_1 = -22.5, y_1 = 5/8$. The reader should check that the cost of this portfolio is exactly 27.5.

Suppose that the price now moves to $S_1 = 120$. Then our portfolio is worth

$$-22.5 \cdot (1 + 0) + \frac{5}{8} \cdot 120 = 52.5.$$

Since we now are facing the claim $(100, 5)$ at $t = 2$ we can again use Proposition 2.4 to calculate the hedging portfolio as $x_2 = -42.5, y_2 = 95/120$, and the reader should again check that the cost of this portfolio equals the value of our old portfolio, i.e. 52.5. Thus it is really possible to rebalance the portfolio in a self-financing manner.

We now assume that the price falls to $S_2 = 60$. Then our portfolio is worth

$$-42.5 \cdot (1 + 0) + \frac{95}{120} \cdot 60 = 5.$$

Facing the claim $(10, 0)$ at $t = 3$ we use Proposition 2.4 to calculate the hedging portfolio as $x_3 = -5, y_3 = 1/6$, and again the cost of this portfolio equals the value of our old portfolio.

Now the price rises to $S_3 = 90$, and we see that the value of our portfolio is given by

$$-5 \cdot (1 + 0) + \frac{1}{6} \cdot 90 = 10,$$

which is exactly equal to the value of the option at that node in the tree. In Fig. 2.10 we have computed the hedging portfolio at each node.

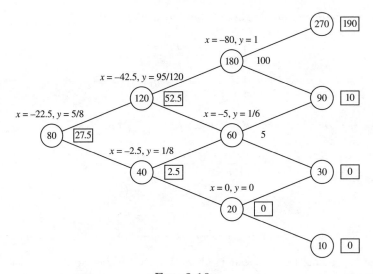

FIG. 2.10.

If we think a bit about the computational effort we see that all the value computations, i.e. all the boxed values, have to be calculated off-line. Having done this we have of course not only computed the arbitrage free price at $t = 0$ for the claim, but also computed the arbitrage free price, at every node in the tree.

The dynamic replicating portfolio does not have to be computed off-line. As in the example above, it can be computed on-line as the price process evolves over time. In this way we only have to compute the portfolio for those nodes that we actually visit.

We now go on to give the general binomial algorithm. In order to do this we need to introduce some more notation to help us keep track of the price evolution. It is clear from the construction that the value of the price process at time t can be written as

$$S_t = su^k d^{t-k}, \quad k = 0, \ldots, t$$

where k denotes the number of up-moves that have occurred. Thus each node in the binomial tree can be represented by a pair (t, k) with $k = 0, \ldots, t$.

Proposition 2.24 (Binomial algorithm) *Consider a T-claim $X = \Phi(S_T)$. Then this claim can be replicated using a self-financing portfolio. If $V_t(k)$ denotes the value of the portfolio at the node (t, k) then $V_t(k)$ can be computed recursively by the scheme*

$$\begin{cases} V_t(k) = \dfrac{1}{1+R} \left\{ q_u V_{t+1}(k+1) + q_d V_{t+1}(k) \right\}, \\ V_T(k) = \Phi\left(su^k d^{T-k}\right). \end{cases}$$

where the martingale probabilities q_u and q_d are given by

$$\begin{cases} q_u = \dfrac{(1+R) - d}{u - d}, \\[4mm] q_d = \dfrac{u - (1+R)}{u - d}. \end{cases}$$

With the notation as above, the hedging portfolio is given by

$$\begin{cases} x_t(k) = \dfrac{1}{1+R} \cdot \dfrac{uV_t(k) - dV_t(k+1)}{u - d}, \\[4mm] y_t(k) = \dfrac{1}{S_{t-1}} \cdot \dfrac{V_t(k+1) - V_t(k)}{u - d}. \end{cases}$$

In particular, the arbitrage free price of the claim at $t = 0$ is given by $V_0(0)$.

From the algorithm above it is also clear that we can obtain a risk neutral valuation formula.

Proposition 2.25 *The arbitrage free price at $t = 0$ of a T-claim X is given by*

$$\Pi(0; X) = \frac{1}{(1+R)^T} \cdot E^Q[X],$$

where Q denotes the martingale measure, or more explicitly

$$\Pi(0; X) = \frac{1}{(1+R)^T} \cdot \sum_{k=0}^{T} \binom{T}{k} q_u^k q_d^{T-k} \Phi\left(su^k d^{T-k}\right).$$

Proof The first formula follows directly from the algorithm above. If we let Y denote the number of up-moves in the tree we can write

$$X = \Phi(S_T) = \Phi\left(su^Y d^{T-Y}\right),$$

and now the second formula follows from the fact that Y has a binomial distribution. □

We end this section by proving absence of arbitrage.

Proposition 2.26 *The condition*

$$d < (1+R) < u$$

is a necessary and sufficient condition for absence of arbitrage.

Proof The necessity follows from the corresponding one period result. Assume that the condition is satisfied. We want to prove absence of arbitrage, so let us assume that h (a potential arbitrage portfolio) is a self-financing portfolio satisfying the conditions

$$P(V_T^h \geq 0) = 1,$$
$$P(V_T^h > 0) > 0.$$

From these conditions, and from the risk neutral valuation formula, it follows that

$$V_0^h = \frac{1}{(1+R)^T} \cdot E^Q\left[V_T^h\right] > 0,$$

which shows that h is not an arbitrage portfolio.   □

2.3   Exercises

Exercise 2.1

(a) Prove Proposition 2.6.
(b) Show, in the one period binomial model, that if $\Pi(1; X) = X$ with probability 1, then you can make a riskless profit.

Exercise 2.2 Prove Proposition 2.21.

Exercise 2.3 Consider the multiperiod example in the text. Suppose that at time $t = 1$ the stock price has gone up to 120, and that the market price of the option turns out to be 50.0. Show explictly how you can make an arbitrage profit.

Exercise 2.4 Prove Proposition 2.24, by using induction on the time horizon T.

2.4   Notes

For the origins of the binomial model, see Cox *et al.* (1979) and Rendleman and Bartter (1979). The textbook Cox and Rubinstein (1992) has become a standard reference.

3

A MORE GENERAL ONE PERIOD MODEL

In this chapter we will investigate absence of arbitrage and completeness in slightly more general terms than in the binomial model. To keep things simple we will be content with a one period model, but the financial market and the underlying sample space will be more general than for the binomial model. The point of this investigation of a simple case is that it highlights some very basic and important ideas, and our main results will in fact be valid for much more general models.

3.1 The Model

We consider a financial market with N different financial assets. These assets could in principle be almost anything, like bonds, stocks, options or whatever financial instrument that is traded on a liquid market. The market only exists at the two points in time $t = 0$ and $t = 1$, and the price per unit of asset No. i at time t will be denoted by S_t^i. We thus have a price vector process S_t, $t = 0, 1$ and we will view the price vector as a *column* vector, i.e.

$$ S_t = \begin{bmatrix} S_t^1 \\ \vdots \\ S_t^N \end{bmatrix} $$

The randomness in the system is modeled by assuming that we have a finite sample space $\Omega = \{\omega_1, \ldots, \omega_M\}$ and that the probabilities $p_j = P(\omega_j)$, $j = 1, \ldots, N$ are all strictly positive. The price vector S_0 is assumed to be deterministic and known to us, but the price vector at time $t = 1$ depends upon the outcome $\omega \in \Omega$, and $S_1^i(\omega_j)$ denotes the price per unit of asset No. i at time $t = 1$ if ω_j has occured.

We may therefore define the matrix D by

$$ D = \begin{bmatrix} S_1^1(\omega_1) & S_1^1(\omega_2) & \cdots & S_1^1(\omega_M) \\ S_1^2(\omega_1) & S_1^2(\omega_2) & \cdots & S_1^2(\omega_M) \\ \vdots & \vdots & & \vdots \\ S_1^N(\omega_1) & S_1^N(\omega_2) & \cdots & S_1^N(\omega_M) \end{bmatrix} $$

We can also write D as

$$D = S_t = \begin{bmatrix} | & & | \\ d_1 & \cdots & d_M \\ | & & | \end{bmatrix}$$

where $d_1, \ldots, d_M$ are the columns of D. We will need one important but very mild assumption.

Assumption 3.1.1 *We assume that asset price process S^1 is strictly positive or, more precisely,*

$$S_0^1 > 0,$$
$$S_1^1(\omega_j) > 0, \quad \text{J} = 1, \ldots, M.$$

3.2 Absence of Arbitrage

We now define a **portfolio** as an N dimensional row vector $h = \begin{bmatrix} h^1, \ldots, h^N \end{bmatrix}$ with the interpretation that h^i is the number of units of asset No. i that we buy at time $t = 0$ and keep until time $t = 1$.

Since we are buying the assets with deterministic prices at time $t = 0$ and selling them at time $t = 1$ at stochastic prices, the **value process** of our portfolio will be a stochastic process V_t^h defined by

$$V_t^h = \sum_{i=1}^{N} h^i S_t^i = h S_t, \quad t = 0, 1, \tag{3.1}$$

and in more detail we can write this as

$$V_t^h(\omega_i) = h S_t(\omega_i) = h d_i = (hD)_i.$$

There are various similar, but not equivalent, variations of the concept of an arbitrage portfolio. The standard one is the following.

Definition 3.1 *The portfolio h is an* **arbitrage** *portfolio if it satisfies the conditions*

$$V_0^h = 0,$$
$$P\left(V_1^h \geq 0\right) = 1,$$
$$P\left(V_1^h > 0\right) > 0.$$

In more detail we can write this as

$$V_0^h < 0,$$
$$V_1^h(\omega_i) \geq 0, \quad \text{for all } i = 1, \ldots, M,$$
$$V_1^h(\omega_i) > 0, \quad \text{for some } i = 1, \ldots, M.$$

We now go on to investigate when the market model above is free of arbitrage possibilities, and the main technical tool for this investigation is the Farkas' Lemma.

Lemma 3.2 (Farkas' Lemma) *Suppose that* $d_0, d_1, \ldots d_K$ *are column vectors in* R^N. *Then exactly one of the two following problems possesses a solution.*

Problem 1: *Find* **nonnegative** *numbers* $\lambda_1, \ldots, \lambda_K$ *such that*

$$d_0 = \sum_{j=1}^{K} \lambda_j d_j.$$

Problem 2: *Find a row vector* $h \in R^N$ *such that*

$$hd_0 < 0,$$
$$hd_j \geq 0, \quad j = 1, \ldots, M.$$

Proof   Let K be the set of all nonnegative linear combinations of $d_1, \ldots, d_M$. It is easy to see that K is a closed convex cone containing the origin. Exactly one of the following cases can hold:

- The vector d_0 belongs to K. This means that Problem 1 above has a solution.
- The vector d_0 does not belong to K. Then, by the separation theorem for convex sets, there exists a hyperplane H such that d_0 is strictly on one side of H whereas K is on the other side. Letting h be defined as a normal vector to H pointing in the direction where K lies, this means that Problem 2 has a solution.   □

We now go on to investigate absence of arbitrage for our model, and in order to see more clearly what is going on we will consider not only the **nominal price system** $S^1, \ldots, S^N$, but also the **normalized price system** $Z^1, \ldots, Z^N$, **under the numeraire** S^1, defined by

$$Z_t^i(\omega_j) = \frac{S_t^i(\omega_j)}{S_t^1(\omega_j)}, \quad i = 1, \ldots, N, \quad j = 1, \ldots, M.$$

The economist will immediately recognize the Z price vector as the vector of relative prices under the numeraire S^1, so if the nominal prices are in dollars and the numeraire is the ACME stock, then the relative prices are given in terms of ACME. More precisely, if a given asset TBINC is quoted at the price 150 dollars, and ACME is quoted at 100 dollars, then the price of TBINC in terms of ACME will be 1.5. The reason for changing from the nominal prices to relative prices is simply that the relative price system is so much easier to analyze. If we obtain a number of results for the relative price system we can then easily translate these results back to the nominal system. To make this translation between the two price systems, we note that a given portfolio h can be viewed as a portfolio in the S system and as a portfolio in the Z system. It will thus generate two different (but equivalent) value processes: The S value process, defined by $V_t^h = hS_t$, and the Z value process, defined by $V_t^{h,Z} = hZ_t$.

We now note the following simple results.

Lemma 3.3 *With notation as above, the following hold.*

1. *The Z value process is related to the S value process by*

$$V_t^{h,Z} = \frac{1}{S_t^1} V_t^h.$$

2. *A portfolio is an arbitrage in the S economy if and only if it is an arbitrage in the Z economy.*

3. *In the Z price system, the numeraire asset Z^1 has unit constant price, i.e.*

$$Z_0^1 = 1,$$
$$Z_1^1(\omega_j) = 1, \quad j = 1, \ldots, M.$$

Proof   Obvious. $\square$

The economic interpretation of the fact that $Z^1 \equiv 1$ is that **in the normalized price system, the numeraire asset is risk free** corresponding to a bank with **zero interest rate**. This is the main reason why the normalized prices system is so much easier to analyze than the nominal one.

We can now formulate our first main result.

Proposition 3.4 *The market is arbitrage free if and only if there exists strictly positive real numbers $q_1, \ldots, q_M$ with*

$$q_1 + \ldots + q_j = 1, \tag{3.2}$$

such that the following vector equality holds

$$Z_0 = \sum_{j=1}^{M} Z_1(\omega_j) q_j, \tag{3.3}$$

or, on component form,

$$Z_0^i = \sum_{j=1}^{M} Z_1^i(\omega_j) q_j, \quad i = 1, \ldots, N.$$

Proof   Define the matrix D^Z by

$$D^Z = \begin{bmatrix} Z_1^1(\omega_1) & Z_1^1(\omega_2) & \cdots & Z_1^1(\omega_M) \\ Z_1^2(\omega_1) & Z_1^2(\omega_2) & \cdots & Z_1^2(\omega_M) \\ \vdots & \vdots & & \vdots \\ Z_1^N(\omega_1) & Z_1^N(\omega_2) & \cdots & Z_1^N(\omega_M) \end{bmatrix}$$

which we can also write as

$$
D^Z = \begin{bmatrix}
1 & 1 & \cdots & 1 \\
Z_1^2(\omega_1) & Z_1^2(\omega_2) & \cdots & Z_1^2(\omega_M) \\
\vdots & \vdots & & \vdots \\
Z_1^N(\omega_1) & Z_1^N(\omega_2) & \cdots & Z_1^N(\omega_M)
\end{bmatrix}
\tag{3.4}
$$

From the definition of arbitrage, and from Lemma 3.3 it is clear that the market is arbitrage free if and only if the following system of equations has no solution, $h \in R^N$, where $(D^Z)_j$ is component No j of the row vector hD^Z.

$$
hZ_0 = 0,
$$
$$
(hD^Z)_j \geq 0, \quad \text{for all } j = 1, \ldots, M
$$
$$
(hD^Z)_j > 0, \quad \text{for some } j = 1, \ldots, M
$$

We now want to apply Farkas' Lemma to this system and in order to do this we define the column vector p in R^M by

$$
p = \begin{bmatrix}
p_1 \\
p_2 \\
\vdots \\
p_M
\end{bmatrix}
$$

We can now rewrite the system above as

$$
hZ_0 = 0,
$$
$$
hD^Z \geq 0,
$$
$$
hD^Z p > 0,
$$

where the second inequality is interpreted component wise. (We remark that we could in fact have replaced the vector p by any vector in R^M with strictly positive components.) We finally rewrite the first equality as a double inequality to obtain

$$
hZ_0 \geq 0,
$$
$$
h(-Z_0) \geq 0,
$$
$$
hD^Z \geq 0,
$$
$$
-hD^Z p < 0.
$$

The point of all this is that if we define the vector $\hat{d}_0$ and the block matrix $\hat{D}$ by

$$\hat{d}_0 = -D^Z p,$$
$$\hat{D} = [D^Z, \ Z_0, \ -Z_0]$$

we see that the market is free of arbitrage if and only if the system

$$h\hat{d}_0 < 0,$$
$$h\hat{D} \geq 0,$$

has no solution $h \in R^N$, where the last inequality is interpreted component wise. Applying Farkas' Lemma to this system we thus see that absence of arbitrage is equivalent to the existence of non negative real numbers $\lambda_1, \lambda_2, \ldots, \lambda_M, \lambda_{N+1}, \lambda_{N+2}$ such that (with obvious notation)

$$\hat{d}_0 = \hat{D}\lambda.$$

If we now define the vector $\beta \in R^M$ by

$$\beta = \begin{bmatrix} \lambda_1 \\ \lambda_2 \\ \vdots \\ \lambda_M \end{bmatrix}$$

and define the real number α by $\alpha = \lambda_{N+2} - \lambda_{N+1}$ we can write the relation $\hat{d}_0 = \hat{D}\lambda$ as

$$-D^Z p = D^Z \beta - \alpha Z_0$$

or as

$$\alpha Z_0 = D^Z (p + \beta). \tag{3.5}$$

Here $\beta \geq 0$ but we do not know the sign of α.

If we focus on the first component of the vector equality (3.5), and recall that $Z_0^1 = 1$ and that the first row of D^Z has the unit 1 in all positions, we obtain

$$\alpha = \sum_{j=1}^{M} (p_j + \beta_j).$$

From this we see that $\alpha > 0$, and if we define the column vector $q \in R^M$ by

$$q = \frac{1}{\alpha} (p + \beta)$$

we see that

$$q_j > 0, \quad j = 1, \ldots, M, \tag{3.6}$$

and that

$$\sum_{i=1}^{M} q_j = 1. \tag{3.7}$$

Rewriting eqn 3.5 as

$$Z_0 = D^Z q,$$

gives us 3.3. □

3.3 Martingale Measures

In this section we will discuss the result from the previous section from a more probabilistic and economic perspective, and also express the results in a way which can be extended to a much more general situation.

Definition 3.5 *Given the objective probability measure P above, we say that another probability measure Q defined on the same Ω is* **equivalent** *to P if*

$$P(A) = 0 \iff Q(A) = 0,$$

or equivalently

$$P(A) = 1 \iff Q(A) = 1.$$

Two probability measures are thus equivalent if they agree on the events with probability zero and the events which have probability one. In our setting above where $P(\omega_j) > 0$ for $j = 1, \ldots, M$, it is clear that $Q \sim P$ if and only if $Q(\omega_j) > 0$ for $j = 1, \ldots, M$.

We now come to a very important probabilistic concept.

Definition 3.6 *A discrete time random process $\{X_n : n = 0, 1, \ldots\}$ is a* **martingale** *if*

$$E[X_m | \mathcal{F}_n] = X_n, \quad \text{for all } n \le m,$$

where $\mathcal{F}_n$ denotes the information available at time n.

A martingale is thus a process which is constant in conditional mean. See Appendix C for details. We note that in the rather trivial setting when we have a process X defined only for time $t = 0, 1$, then the martingale definition trivializes to the condition

$$E[X_1] = X_0.$$

We now go on to define one of the central concepts of arbitrage pricing.

Definition 3.7 *Consider the market model above, and fix the asset S^1 as the numeraire asset. We say that a probability measure Q defined on Ω is a* **martingale measure** *if it satisfies the following conditions.*

1. Q is equivalent to P, i.e.

$$Q \sim P$$

2. For every $i = 1, \ldots, N$, the normalized asset price process

$$Z_t^i = \frac{S_t^i}{S_t^1},$$

is a martingale under the measure Q.

We can now restate Proposition 3.4 as the following result, which in its far reaching generalizations is known as "the first fundamental theorem of mathematical finance".

Theorem 3.8 (First Fundamental Theorem) *Given a fixed numeraire, the market is free of arbitrage possibilities if and only if there exists a martingale measure Q.*

Proof   From Proposition 3.4 we know that absence of arbitrage is equivalent to the existence of strictly positive constants $q_1, \ldots, q_M$ with $q_1 + \ldots + q_N = 1$ such that (3.3) is satisfied. We may thus define a probability measure Q by setting $Q(\omega_j) = q_j$ and since $q_j > 0$ for all j we see that $Q \sim P$. With this definition of Q, the relation (3.3) takes the form

$$Z_0 = E^Q [Z_1], \qquad (3.8)$$

which is precisely the stated martingale condition.   □

The martingale condition above will allow for a particularly nice economic interpretation if we assume that the numeraire asset S^1 is a **risk free** asset, in the sense that the asset price S_1^1 at time $t = 1$ is constant as a function of ω. By scaling we may assume that $S_0^1 = 1$, and since S_1^1 does not depend on ω we may write

$$S_1^1(\omega_j) = 1 + R, \quad \text{for all } j = 1, \ldots, M,$$

where we can interpret R as the **short interest rate**. We now have the following variation of Theorem 3.8.

Theorem 3.9 (First Fundamental Theorem) *Assume that there exists a risk free asset, and denote the corresponding risk free interest rate by R. Then the market is arbitrage free if and only if there exists a measure $Q \sim P$ such that*

$$S_0^i = \frac{1}{1 + R} E^Q [S_1^i], \quad \text{for all } i = 1, \ldots, N. \qquad (3.9)$$

The economic interpretation is thus that today's asset prices are obtained as the expected value of tomorrow's asset prices, discounted with the risk free rate. The formula is also referred to as a "risk-neutral pricing formula". Note that the expectation above is **not** taken under the objective probability measure P but under the martingale measure Q.

3.4 Martingale Pricing

In this section we will study how to price *financial derivatives* or, in technical terms *contingent claims*. We take the previously studied market model as given and we assume for simplicity that there exists a risk free asset. In order to highlight the role of the risk free asset we denote its price process by B_t and we may thus regard B_t as a bank account, where our money (or our debts) grow at the risk free rate. (In the previous section we thus had $B = S^1$.)

Definition 3.10 *A* **contingent claim** *is any random variable X, defined on Ω.*

The interpretation is that a contingent claim X represents a stochastic amount of money which we will obtain at time $t = 1$. Our main problem is now to determine a "reasonable" price $\Pi(0; X)$, at time $t = 0$ for a given claim X, and in order to do this we must give a more precise meaning to the word "reasonable" above.

More precisely we would like to price the claim X **consistently** with the underlying a priori given assets $S^1, \ldots, S^N$, or put in other words, we would like to price the claim X in such a way that there are **no arbitrage opportunities** on the extended market consisting of $\Pi, S^1, \ldots, S^N$. This problem is, however, easily solved by applying the First Fundamental Theorem to the extended market. We thus see that the extended market is arbitrage free if and only if there exists some martingale measure Q such that

$$\Pi(0; X) = \frac{1}{1 + R} E^Q [\Pi(1; X)],$$

and

$$S_0 = \frac{1}{1 + R} E^Q [S_1].$$

Thus, in particular, Q is a martingale measure for the underlying assets. At time $t = 1$ the value of the claim X is known, so in order to avoid arbitrage we must have $\Pi(1; X) = X$. Plugging this into the equation above we have the following result.

Proposition 3.11 *Consider a given claim X. In order to avoid arbitrage, X must then be priced according to the formula*

$$\Pi(0; X) = \frac{1}{1 + R} E^Q [X], \tag{3.10}$$

where Q is a martingale measure for the underlying market.

We see that this formula extends the corresponding risk neutral pricing formula (3.9) for the underlying assets. Again we have the economic interpretation that the price at $t = 0$ of the claim X is obtained by computing the expected value of X, discounted by the risk free interest rate, and we again emphasize that the expectation is **not** taken under the objective measure P but under the martingale measure Q.

The pricing formula (3.10) looks very nice, but there is a problem: If there exists several different martingale measures then we will have several possible arbitrage free prices for a given claim X. This has to do with the (possible lack of) **completeness** of the market.

3.5   Completeness

In this section we will discuss how it is possible to generate payment streams at $t = 1$ by forming portfolios in the underlying.

Assumption 3.5.1 *We assume that the market $S^1, \ldots, S^N$ is arbitrage free and that there exists a risk free asset.*

Definition 3.12 *Consider a contingent claim X. If there exists a portfolio h, based on the underlying assets, such that*

$$V_1^h = X, \quad \text{with probability 1.} \tag{3.11}$$

i.e.

$$V_1^h(\omega_j) = X(\omega_j), \quad j = 1, \ldots, M, \tag{3.12}$$

then we say that X is **replicated**, *or* **hedged** *by h. Such a portfolio h is called a replicating, or hedging portfolio. If every contingent claim can be replicated, we say that the market is* **complete**.

It is easy to characterize completeness in our market, and we have the following result.

Proposition 3.13 *The market is complete if and only if the rows of the matrix D span R^M, i.e. if and only if D has rank M.*

Proof   For any portfolio h, we view the random variable V_1^h as a row vector $[V_1^h(\omega_1), \ldots, V_1^h(\omega_M)]$ and with this notation we have

$$V_1^h = hD.$$

The market is thus complete if and only if, for every random variable X, (viewed as a row vector in R^M) the equation

$$hD = X$$

has a solution. But hD is exactly a linear combination of the rows of D with the components of h as coefficients. $\square$

The concept of a replicating portfolio gives rise to an alternative way of pricing contingent claims. Assume that the claim X can be replicated by the portfolio h. Then there is an obvious candidate as the price (at time $t = 0$)

for X, namely the market price, at $t = 0$, of the replicating portfolio. We thus propose the natural pricing formula

$$\Pi(0; X) = V_0^h. \tag{3.13}$$

We also note that any other price would produce an arbitrage possibility, since if for example $V_0^h = 7$ and the price of the claim is given by $\Pi(0; X) = 10$ then we would sell the claim, obtain 10 units of money, and use 7 of these to buy the replicating portfolio. The remaining 3 units of money would be invested safely in the bank. At time $t = 1$ our obligations $(-X)$ would be exactly matched by our assets $V_1^h = X$ and we would still have our money in the bank.

Here there is a possibility that may get us into trouble. There may very well exist two different hedging portfolios f and g, and it could in principle happen that $V_0^f = V_0^g$. It is, however, easy to see that this would lead to an arbitrage possibility (how?) so we may disregard that possibility.

The pricing formula (3.13) can also be written in another way, so let us assume that h replicates X. Then, by definition, we have

$$X = hS_1, \tag{3.14}$$

and from (3.13) we obtain

$$\Pi(0; X) = hS_0. \tag{3.15}$$

However, on our arbitrage free market we also have the pricing formula (3.9)

$$S_0 = \frac{1}{1+R} E^Q [S_1]. \tag{3.16}$$

combining this with (3.14)–(3.15) we obtain the pricing formula

$$\Pi(0; X) = \frac{1}{1+R} E^Q [X]. \tag{3.17}$$

which is exactly the formula given by Proposition 3.11. Thus the two pricing approaches coincide on the set of hedgable claims.

In Proposition 3.13 we obtained one characterization of complete markets. There is another characterization which connects completeness to martingale measures. This result, which we give below in our simple setting, is known as "the second fundamental theorem of mathematical finance".

Proposition 3.14 (Second Fundamental Theorem) *Assume that the model is arbitrage free. Then the market is complete if and only if the martingale measure is unique.*

Proof From Proposition 3.13 we know that the market is complete if and only if the rows of D span the whole of R^M, i.e. if and only if

$$Im [D^\star] = R^M,$$

where we view the transpose matrix $D^\star$ as a mapping from R^N to R^M. On the other hand, from Proposition 3.4 and the assumption of absence of arbitrage we know that there exists a solution (even a strictly positive one) to the equation

$$Z_0 = D^Z q.$$

This solution is unique if and only if the kernel (null space) of D^Z is trivial, i.e. if and only if

$$Ker\left[D^Z\right] = 0,$$

and it is easy to see that this is equivalent to the condition

$$Ker\left[D\right] = 0.$$

We now recall the following well known duality result:

$$(Im\left[D^\star\right])^\perp = Ker\left[D\right].$$

Thus $Ker\left[D\right] = 0$ if and only if $Im\left[D^\star\right] = R^M$, i.e. the market is complete if and only if the martingale measure is unique. □

We may now summarize our findings.

Proposition 3.15 *Using the risk free asset as the numeraire, the following hold.*

- *The market is arbitrage free if and only if there exists a martingale measure Q.*

- *The market is complete if and only if the martingale measure is unique.*

- *For any claim X, the only prices which are consistent with absence of arbitrage are of the form*

$$\Pi\left(0; X\right) = \frac{1}{1+R} E^Q\left[X\right], \qquad (3.18)$$

where Q is a martingale measure for the underlying market.

- *If the market is incomplete, then different choices of martingale measures Q in the formula (3.18) will generically give rise to different prices.*

- *If X is replicable then, even in an incomplete market, the price in (3.18) will not depend upon the particular choice of martingale measure Q. If X is replicable, then*

$$V_0^h = \frac{1}{1+R} E^Q\left[X\right],$$

for all martingale measures Q and for all replicating portfolios h.

3.6   Stochastic Discount Factors

In the previous sections we have seen that we can price financial derivatives by using martingale measures and the formula

$$\Pi(0; X) = \frac{1}{1+R} E^Q [X].$$

In some applications of the theory (in particular in asset pricing) it is common to write this expected value directly under the objective probability measure P instead of under Q.

Recalling the notation $p_i = P(\omega_i)$ and $q_i = Q(\omega_i)$, $i = 1, \ldots, M$, and the assumption that $p_i > 0$ for $i = 1, \ldots, M$, we may define a new random variable on Ω.

Definition 3.16 *The random variable L on Ω is defined by*

$$L(\omega_i) = \frac{q_i}{p_i}, \quad i = 1, \ldots, M.$$

Thus L gives us the *likelihood ratio* between the measures P and Q, and in more general situations it is known as the *Radon-Nikodym derivative* of Q w.r.t. P.

Definition 3.17 *Assume absence of arbitrage, and fix a martingale measure Q. With notations a above, the* **stochastic discount factor** *(or "state price deflator") is the random variable Λ on Ω defined by*

$$\Lambda(\omega) = \frac{1}{1+R} \cdot L(\omega). \tag{3.19}$$

We can now express our arbitrage free pricing formulas in a slightly different way.

Proposition 3.18 *The arbitrage free price of any claim X is given by the formula*

$$\Pi(0; X) = E^P [\Lambda \cdot X] \tag{3.20}$$

where Λ is a stochastic discount factor.

Proof   Exercise for the reader.   □

We see that there is a one-to-one correspondence between stochastic discount factors and martingale measures, and it is largely a matter of taste if you want to work with Λ or with Q. The advantage of working with Λ is that you formally stay with the objective measure P. The advantage with working under Q is that the decomposition of Λ in (3.19) gives us important structural information, and in more complicated situations there exists a deep theory (see "Girsanov transformations" later in the text) which allows us to have complete control over the class of martingale measures.

From an economic point of view, the stochastic discount factor is precisely an Arrow–Debreu state price system, which gives the price $\Lambda(\omega_i)$ to the primitive claim X_i which pays 1 if ω_i occurs, and zero otherwise.

3.7 Exercises

Exercise 3.1 Prove that Q in Proposition 3.11 is a martingale measure also for the price process $\Pi(t; X)$, i.e. show that

$$\frac{\Pi(0; X)}{B_0} = E^Q \left[\frac{\Pi(1; X)}{B_1} \right].$$

where B is the risk free asset.

Exercise 3.2 Prove the last item in Proposition 3.15.

Exercise 3.3 Prove Proposition 3.18.

4

STOCHASTIC INTEGRALS

4.1 Introduction

The purpose of this book is to study asset pricing on financial markets in continuous time. We thus want to model asset prices as continuous time stochastic processes, and the most complete and elegant theory is obtained if we use **diffusion processes** and **stochastic differential equations** as our building blocks. What, then, is a diffusion?

Loosely speaking we say that a stochastic process X is a diffusion if its local dynamics can be approximated by a stochastic difference equation of the following type.

$$X(t + \Delta t) - X(t) = \mu(t, X(t)) \Delta t + \sigma(t, X(t)) Z(t). \tag{4.1}$$

Here $Z(t)$ is a normally distributed disturbance term which is independent of everything which has happened up to time t, while μ and σ are given deterministic functions. The intuitive content of (4.1) is that, over the time interval $[t, t + \Delta t]$, the X-process is driven by two separate terms.

- A locally deterministic velocity $\mu(t, X(t))$.
- A Gaussian disturbance term, amplified by the factor $\sigma(t, X(t))$.

The function μ is called the (local) **drift** term of the process, whereas σ is called the **diffusion** term. In order to model the Gaussian disturbance terms we need the concept of a Wiener process.

Definition 4.1 *A stochastic process W is called a* **Wiener process** *if the following conditions hold.*

1. *$W(0) = 0$.*
2. *The process W has independent increments, i.e. if $r < s \leq t < u$ then $W(u) - W(t)$ and $W(s) - W(r)$ are independent stochastic variables.*
3. *For $s < t$ the stochastic variable $W(t) - W(s)$ has the Gaussian distribution $N\left[0, \sqrt{t - s}\,\right]$.*
4. *W has continuous trajectories.*

Remark 4.1.1 Note that we use a somewhat old fashioned notation, where $N[\mu, \sigma]$ denotes a Gaussian distribution with expected value μ and standard deviation σ.

In Fig. 4.1 a computer simulated Wiener trajectory is shown.

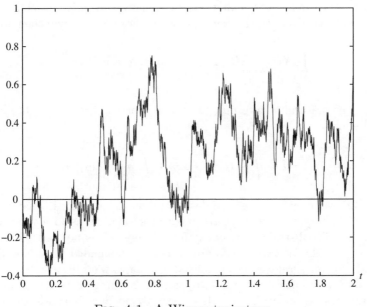

FIG. 4.1. A Wiener trajectory

We may now use a Wiener process in order to write (4.1) as

$$X(t + \Delta t) - X(t) = \mu\left(t, X(t)\right)\Delta t + \sigma\left(t, X(t)\right)\Delta W(t), \qquad (4.2)$$

where $\Delta W(t)$ is defined by

$$\Delta W(t) = W(t + \Delta t) - W(t).$$

Let us now try to make (4.2) a bit more precise. It is then tempting to divide the equation by Δt and let Δt tend to zero. Formally we would obtain

$$\dot{X}(t) = \mu\left(t, X(t)\right) + \sigma\left(t, X(t)\right)v(t), \qquad (4.3)$$
$$X(0) = a, \qquad (4.4)$$

where we have added an initial condition and where

$$v(t) = \frac{dW}{dt}$$

is the formal time derivative of the Wiener process W.

If v were an ordinary (and well defined) process we would now in principle be able to solve (4.3) as a standard ordinary differential equation (ODE) for each v-trajectory. However, it can be shown that with probability 1 a Wiener trajectory is nowhere differentiable (cf. Fig. 4.1), so the process v cannot even be defined. Thus this is a dead end.

Another possibility of making eqn (4.2) more precise is to let Δt tend to zero without first dividing the equation by Δt. Formally we will then obtain the expression

$$\begin{cases} dX(t) = \mu\left(t, X(t)\right) dt + \sigma\left(t, X(t)\right) dW(t), \\ X(0) = a, \end{cases} \tag{4.5}$$

and it is now natural to interpret (4.5) as a shorthand version of the following integral equation

$$X(t) = a + \int_0^t \mu\left(s, X(s)\right) ds + \int_0^t \sigma\left(s, X(s)\right) dW(s). \tag{4.6}$$

In eqn (4.6) we may interpret the ds-integral as an ordinary Riemann integral. The natural interpretation of the dW-integral is to view it as a Riemann–Stieltjes integral for each W-trajectory, but unfortunately this is not possible since one can show that the W-trajectories are of locally unbounded variation. Thus the stochastic dW-integral cannot be defined in a naive way.

As long as we insist on giving a precise meaning to eqn (4.2) **for each** W**-trajectory separately**, we thus seem to be in a hopeless situation. If, however, we relax our demand that the dW-integral in eqn (4.6) should be defined trajectorywise we can still proceed. It is in fact possible to give a global (L^2-)definition of integrals of the form

$$\int_0^t g(s)dW(s) \tag{4.7}$$

for a large class of processes g. This new integral concept—the so called Itô integral—will then give rise to a very powerful type of stochastic differential calculus—the Itô calculus. Our program for the future thus consists of the following steps.

1. Define integrals of the type

$$\int_0^t g(s)dW(s).$$

2. Develop the corresponding differential calculus.
3. Analyze stochastic differential equations of the type (4.5) using the stochastic calculus above.

4.2 Information

Let X be any given stochastic process. In the sequel it will be important to define "the information generated by X" as time goes by. To do this in a rigorous fashion is outside the main scope of this book, but for most practical purposes the following heuristic definitions will do nicely. See the appendices for a precise treatment.

Definition 4.2 *The symbol $\mathcal{F}_t^X$ denotes "the information generated by X on the interval $[0, t]$", or alternatively "what has happened to X over the interval $[0, t]$". If, based upon observations of the trajectory $\{X(s);\ 0 \leq s \leq t\}$, it is possible to decide whether a given event A has occurred or not, then we write this as*

$$A \in \mathcal{F}_t^X,$$

or say that "A is $\mathcal{F}_t^X$-measurable".

  If the value of a given stochastic variable Z can be completely determined given observations of the trajectory $\{X(s);\ 0 \leq s \leq t\}$, then we also write

$$Z \in \mathcal{F}_t^X.$$

If Y is a stochastic process such that we have

$$Y(t) \in \mathcal{F}_t^X$$

for all $t \geq 0$ then we say that Y is **adapted** *to the* **filtration** $\left\{\mathcal{F}_t^X\right\}_{t \geq 0}$. *For brevity of notation, we will sometimes write the filtration as $\left\{\mathcal{F}_t^X\right\}_{t \geq 0} = \mathbf{F}$.*

The above definition is only intended to have an intuitive content, since a precise definition would take us into the realm of abstract measure theory (see Appendix B for details). Nevertheless it is usually extremely simple to use the definition, and we now give some fairly typical examples.

1. If we define the event A by $A = \{X(s) \leq 3.14,\ \text{for all}\ s \leq 9\}$ then we have $A \in \mathcal{F}_9^X$.
2. For the event $A = \{X(10) > 8\}$ we have $A \in \mathcal{F}_{10}^X$. Note, however, that we do not have $A \in \mathcal{F}_9^X$, since it is impossible to decide if A has occurred or not on the basis of having observed the X-trajectory only over the interval $[0, 9]$.
3. For the stochastic variable Z, defined by

$$Z = \int_0^5 X(s)\,ds,$$

   we have $Z \in \mathcal{F}_5^X$.
4. If W is a Wiener process and if the process X is defined by

$$X(t) = \sup_{s \leq t} W(s),$$

   then X is adapted to the W-filtration.

5. With W as above, but with X defined as

$$X(t) = \sup_{s \leq t+1} W(s),$$

X is not adapted (to the W-filtration).

4.3 Stochastic Integrals

We now turn to the construction of the stochastic integral. For that purpose we consider as given a Wiener process W, and another stochastic process g. In order to guarantee the existence of the stochastic integral we have to impose some kind of integrability conditions on g, and the class $\pounds^2$ turns out to be natural.

Definition 4.3

(i) *We say that the process g belongs to the class $\pounds^2[a,b]$ if the following conditions are satisfied.*

- $\int_a^b E\left[g^2(s)\right] ds < \infty.$
- *The process g is adapted to the $\mathcal{F}_t^W$-filtration.*

(ii) *We say that the process g belongs to the class $\pounds^2$ if $g \in \pounds^2[0,t]$ for all $t > 0$.*

Our object is now to define the stochastic integral $\int_a^b g(s)dW(s)$, for a process $g \in \pounds^2[a,b]$, and this is carried out in two steps.

Suppose to begin with that the process $g \in \pounds^2[a,b]$ is **simple**, i.e. that there exist deterministic points in time $a = t_0 < t_1 < \cdots < t_n = b$, such that g is constant on each subinterval. In other words we assume that $g(s) = g(t_k)$ for $s \in [t_k, t_{k+1})$. Then we define the stochastic integral by the obvious formula

$$\int_a^b g(s)dW(s) = \sum_{k=0}^{n-1} g(t_k)\left[W(t_{k+1}) - W(t_k)\right]. \tag{4.8}$$

Remark 4.3.1 Note that in the definition of the stochastic integral we take so called **forward** increments of the Wiener process. More specifically, in the generic term $g(t_k)\left[W(t_{k+1}) - W(t_k)\right]$ of the sum the process g is evaluated at the **left** end t_k of the interval $[t_k, t_{k+1}]$ over which we take the W-increment. This is essential to the following theory both from a mathematical and (as we shall see later) from an economical point of view.

For a general process $g \in \pounds^2[a,b]$ which is not simple we may schematically proceed as follows.

1. Approximate g with a sequence of simple processes g_n such that

$$\int_a^b E\left[\{g_n(s) - g(s)\}^2\right] ds \to 0.$$

2. For each n the integral $\int_a^b g_n(s)dW(s)$ is a well defined stochastic variable Z_n, and it is possible to prove that there exists a stochastic variable Z such that $Z_n \to Z$ (in L^2) as $n \to \infty$.
3. We now define the stochastic integral by

$$\int_a^b g(s)dW(s) = \lim_{n\to\infty} \int_a^b g_n(s)dW(s). \tag{4.9}$$

The most important properties of the stochastic integral are given by the following proposition. In particular we will use the property (4.12) over and over again.

Proposition 4.4 *Let g be a process satisfying the conditions*

$$\int_a^b E\left[g^2(s)\right] ds < \infty, \tag{4.10}$$

g is adapted to the $\mathcal{F}_t^W$-filtration. $\tag{4.11}$

Then the following relations hold

$$E\left[\int_a^b g(s)dW(s)\right] = 0. \tag{4.12}$$

$$E\left[\left(\int_a^b g(s)dW(s)\right)^2\right] = \int_a^b E\left[g^2(s)\right] ds. \tag{4.13}$$

$$\int_a^b g(s)dW(s) \text{ is } \mathcal{F}_b^W\text{-measurable.} \tag{4.14}$$

Proof   A full proof is outside the scope of this book, but the general strategy is to start by proving all the assertions above in the case when g is simple. This is fairly easily done, and then it "only" remains to go to the limit in the sense of (4.9). We illustrate the technique by proving (4.12) in the case of a simple g. We obtain

$$E\left[\int_a^b g(s)dW(s)\right] = E\left[\sum_{k=0}^{n-1} g(t_k)\left[W(t_{k+1}) - W(t_k)\right]\right]$$

$$= \sum_{k=0}^{n-1} E\left[g(t_k)\left[W(t_{k+1}) - W(t_k)\right]\right].$$

Since g is adapted, the value $g(t_k)$ only depends on the behavior of the Wiener process on the interval $[0, t_k]$. Now, by definition W has independent increments, so $[W(t_{k+1}) - W(t_k)]$ (which is a **forward** increment) is independent of $g(t_k)$. Thus we have

$$E\left[g(t_k)\left[W(t_{k+1}) - W(t_k)\right]\right] = E\left[g(t_k)\right] \cdot E\left[W(t_{k+1}) - W(t_k)\right]$$
$$= E\left[g(t_k)\right] \cdot 0 = 0.$$

□

Remark 4.3.2 It is possible to define the stochastic integral for a process g satisfying only the weak condition

$$P\left(\int_a^b g^2(s)ds < \infty\right) = 1. \tag{4.15}$$

For such a general g we have no guarantee that the properties (4.12) and (4.13) hold. Property (4.14) is, however, still valid.

4.4 Martingales

The theory of stochastic integration is intimately connected to the theory of martingales, and the modern theory of financial derivatives is in fact based mainly on martingale theory. Martingale theory, however, requires some basic knowledge of abstract measure theory, and a formal treatment is thus outside the scope of the more elementary parts of this book.

Because of its great importance for the field, however, it would be unreasonable to pass over this important topic entirely, and the object of this section is to (informally) introduce the martingale concept. The more advanced reader is referred to the appendices for details.

Let us therefore consider a given filtration ("flow of information") $\{\mathcal{F}_t\}_{t\geq 0}$, where, as before, the reader can think of $\mathcal{F}_t$ as the information generated by all observed events up to time t. For any stochastic variable Y we now let the symbol

$$E\left[Y | \mathcal{F}_t\right]$$

denote the "expected value of Y, given the information available at time t". A precise definition of this object requires measure theory, so we have to be content with this informal description. Note that for a fixed t, the object $E\left[Y | \mathcal{F}_t\right]$ is a stochastic variable. If, for example, the filtration is generated by a single observed process X, then the information available at time t will of course depend upon the behaviour of X over the interval $[0, t]$, so the conditional expectation $E\left[Y | \mathcal{F}_t\right]$ will in this case be a function of all past X-values $\{X(s) : s \leq t\}$. We will need the following two rules of calculation.

Proposition 4.5

- If Y and Z are stochastic variables, and Z is $\mathcal{F}_t$-measurable, then

$$E\left[Z \cdot Y | \mathcal{F}_t\right] = Z \cdot E\left[Y | \mathcal{F}_t\right].$$

- *If Y is a stochastic variable, and if s < t, then*

$$E\left[E\left[Y|\mathcal{F}_t\right]|\mathcal{F}_s\right] = E\left[Y|\mathcal{F}_s\right].$$

The first of these results should be obvious: in the expected value $E\left[Z \cdot Y|\mathcal{F}_t\right]$ we condition upon all information available at time t. If now $Z \in \mathcal{F}_t$, this means that, given the information $\mathcal{F}_t$, we know exactly the value of Z, so in the conditional expectation Z can be treated as a constant, and thus it can be taken outside the expectation. The second result is called the "law of iterated expectations", and it is basically a version of the law of total probability.

We can now define the martingale concept.

Definition 4.6 *A stochastic process X is called an $(\mathcal{F}_t)$-**martingale** if the following conditions hold.*

- *X is adapted to the filtration $\{\mathcal{F}_t\}_{t\geq0}$.*
- *For all t*

$$E\left[|X(t)|\right] < \infty.$$

- *For all s and t with $s \leq t$ the following relation holds*

$$E\left[X(t)|\mathcal{F}_s\right] = X(s).$$

A process satisfying, for all s and t with $s \leq t$, the inequality

$$E\left[X(t)|\mathcal{F}_s\right] \leq X(s),$$

*is called a **supermartingale**, and a process satisfying*

$$E\left[X(t)|\mathcal{F}_s\right] \geq X(s),$$

*is called a **submartingale**.*

The first condition says that we can observe the value $X(t)$ at time t, and the second condition is just a technical condition. The really important condition is the third one, which says that the expectation of a future value of X, given the information available today, equals today's observed value of X. Another way of putting this is to say that a martingale has no systematic drift.

It is possible to prove the following extension of Proposition 4.4.

Proposition 4.7 *For any process $g \in \mathcal{L}^2\left[s,t\right]$ the following hold:*

$$E\left[\left.\int_s^t g(u)dW(u)\right|\mathcal{F}_s^W\right] = 0.$$

As a corollary we obtain the following important fact.

Corollary 4.8 *For any process $g \in \pounds^2$, the process X, defined by*

$$X(t) = \int_0^t g(s)dW(s),$$

is an $(\mathcal{F}_t^W)$-martingale. In other words, modulo an integrability condition, **every stochastic integral is a martingale.**

Proof   Fix s and t with $s < t$. We have

$$
\begin{aligned}
E\left[\left.X(t)\right|\mathcal{F}_s^W\right] &= E\left[\left.\int_0^t g(\tau)dW(\tau)\right|\mathcal{F}_s^W\right] \\
&= E\left[\left.\int_0^s g(\tau)dW(\tau)\right|\mathcal{F}_s^W\right] + E\left[\left.\int_s^t g(\tau)dW(\tau)\right|\mathcal{F}_s^W\right].
\end{aligned}
$$

The integral in the first expectation is, by Proposition 4.4, measurable w.r.t. $\mathcal{F}_s^W$, so by Proposition 4.5 we have

$$E\left[\left.\int_0^s g(\tau)dW(\tau)\right|\mathcal{F}_s^W\right] = \int_0^s g(\tau)dW(\tau),$$

From Proposition 4.4 we also see that $E\left[\left.\int_s^t g(\tau)dW(\tau)\right|\mathcal{F}_s^W\right] = 0$, so we obtain

$$E\left[\left.X(t)\right|\mathcal{F}_s^W\right] = \int_0^s g(\tau)dW(\tau) + 0 = X(s).$$

$\square$

We have in fact the following stronger (and very useful) result.

Lemma 4.9 *Within the framework above, and assuming enough integrability, a stochastic process X (having a stochastic differential) is a martingale if and only if the stochastic differential has the form*

$$dX(t) = g(t)dW(t),$$

i.e. X has no dt-term.

Proof   We have already seen that if dX has no dt-term then X is a martingale. The reverse implication is much harder to prove, and the reader is referred to the literature cited in the notes below. $\square$

4.5   Stochastic Calculus and the Itô Formula

Let X be a stochastic process and suppose that there exists a real number a and two adapted processes μ and σ such that the following relation holds for all $t \geq 0$.

$$X(t) = a + \int_0^t \mu(s)ds + \int_0^t \sigma(s)dW(s), \qquad (4.16)$$

where a is some given real number. As usual W is a Wiener process. To use a less cumbersome notation we will often write eqn (4.16) in the following form

$$dX(t) = \mu(t)dt + \sigma(t)dW(t), \qquad (4.17)$$

$$X(0) = a. \qquad (4.18)$$

In this case we say that X has a **stochastic differential** given by (4.17) with an **initial condition** given by (4.18). Note that the formal string $dX(t) = \mu(t)dt + \sigma(t)dW(t)$ has no independent meaning. It is simply a shorthand version of the expression (4.16) above. From an intuitive point of view the stochastic differential is, however, a much more natural object to consider than the corresponding integral expression. This is because the stochastic differential gives us the "infinitesimal dynamics" of the X-process, and as we have seen in Section 4.1 both the drift term $\mu(s)$ and the diffusion term $\sigma(s)$ have a natural intuitive interpretation.

Let us assume that X indeed has the stochastic differential above. Loosely speaking we thus see that the infinitesimal increment $dX(t)$ consists of a locally deterministic drift term $\mu(t)dt$ plus an **additive Gaussian** noise term $\sigma(t)dW(t)$. Assume furthermore that we are given a $C^{1,2}$-function

$$f : R_+ \times R \to R$$

and let us now define a new process Z by

$$Z(t) = f(t, X(t)).$$

We may now ask what the local dynamics of the Z-process look like, and at first it seems fairly obvious that, except for the case when f is linear in x, Z will not have a stochastic differential. Consider, for example, a discrete time example where X satisfies a stochastic difference equation with additive Gaussian noise in each step, and suppose that $f(t,x) = e^x$. Then it is clear that Z will not be driven by additive Gaussian noise—the noise will in fact be multiplicative and log-normal. It is therefore extremely surprising that for continuous time models the stochastic differential structure with a drift term plus additive Gaussian noise will in fact be preserved even under nonlinear transformations. Thus the process Z **will** have a stochastic differential, and the form of dZ is given explicitly by the famous Itô formula below. Before turning to the Itô formula we have to take a closer look at some rather fine properties of the trajectories of the Wiener process.

As we saw earlier the Wiener process is defined by a number of very simple probabilistic properties. It is therefore natural to assume that a typical Wiener trajectory is a fairly simple object, but this is not at all the case. On the contrary—one can show that, with probability 1, the Wiener trajectory will be a continuous function of time (see the definition above) which is nondifferentiable at every point. Thus a typical trajectory is a continuous curve consisting entirely of corners and it is of course quite impossible to draw a figure of such an object (it is in fact fairly hard to prove that such a curve actually exists). This lack of smoothness gives rise to an odd property of the quadratic variation of the Wiener trajectory, and since the entire theory to follow depends on this particular property we now take some time to study the Wiener increments a bit closer.

Let us therefore fix two points in time, s and t with $s < t$, and let us use the handy notation

$$\Delta t = t - s,$$
$$\Delta W(t) = W(t) - W(s).$$

Using well known properties of the normal distribution it is fairly easy to obtain the following results, which we will use frequently.

$$E\left[\Delta W\right] = 0, \tag{4.19}$$

$$E\left[(\Delta W)^2\right] = \Delta t, \tag{4.20}$$

$$Var[\Delta W] = \Delta t, \tag{4.21}$$

$$Var[(\Delta W)^2] = 2\left(\Delta t\right)^2. \tag{4.22}$$

We see that the squared Wiener increment $(\Delta W(t))^2$ has an expected value which equals the time increment Δt. The really important fact, however, is that, according to (4.22), the variance of $[\Delta W(t)]^2$ is negligible compared to its expected value. In other words, as Δt tends to zero $[\Delta W(t)]^2$ will of course also tend to zero, but the variance will approach zero much faster than the expected value. Thus $[\Delta W(t)]^2$ will look more and more "deterministic" and we are led to believe that in the limit we have the purely formal equality

$$[dW(t)]^2 = dt. \tag{4.23}$$

The reasoning above is purely heuristic. It requires a lot of hard work to turn the relation (4.23) into a mathematically precise statement, and it is of course even harder to prove it. We will not attempt either a precise formulation or a precise proof. In order to give the reader a flavor of the full theory we will, however, give another argument for the relation (4.23).

Let us therefore fix a point in time t and subdivide the interval $[0, t]$ into n equally large subintervals of the form $\left[k\frac{t}{n}, (k+1)\frac{t}{n}\right]$, where $k = 0, 1, \ldots, n-1$. Given this subdivision, we now define the quadratic variation of the Wiener process by S_n, i.e.

$$S_n = \sum_{i=1}^{n} \left[W\left(i\frac{t}{n}\right) - W\left((i-1)\frac{t}{n}\right) \right]^2, \qquad (4.24)$$

and our goal is to see what happens to S_n as the subdivision becomes finer, i.e. as $n \to \infty$. We immediately see that

$$E\left[S_n\right] = \sum_{i=1}^{n} E\left[\left[W\left(i\frac{t}{n}\right) - W\left((i-1)\frac{t}{n}\right) \right]^2 \right]$$
$$= \sum_{i=1}^{n} \left[i\frac{t}{n} - (i-1)\frac{t}{n} \right] = t.$$

Using the fact that W has independent increments we also have

$$Var[S_n] = \sum_{i=1}^{n} Var\left[\left[W\left(i\frac{t}{n}\right) - W\left((i-1)\frac{t}{n}\right) \right]^2 \right]$$
$$= \sum_{i=1}^{n} 2\left[\frac{t^2}{n^2} \right] = \frac{2t^2}{n}.$$

Thus we see that $E\left[S_n\right] = t$ whereas $Var[S_n] \to 0$ as $n \to \infty$. In other words, as $n \to \infty$ we see that S_n tends to the **deterministic** limit t. This motivates us to write

$$\int_0^t [dW]^2 = t, \qquad (4.25)$$

or, equivalently,

$$[dW]^2 = dt. \qquad (4.26)$$

Note again that all the reasoning above has been purely motivational. In this text we will have to be content with accepting (4.26) as a dogmatic truth, and now we can give the main result in the theory of stochastic calculus—the Itô formula.

Theorem 4.10 (Itô's formula) *Assume that the process X has a stochastic differential given by*

$$dX(t) = \mu(t)dt + \sigma(t)dW(t), \qquad (4.27)$$

where μ and σ are adapted processes, and let f be a $C^{1,2}$-function. Define the process Z by $Z(t) = f(t, X(t))$. Then Z has a stochastic differential given by

$$df(t, X(t)) = \left\{ \frac{\partial f}{\partial t} + \mu\frac{\partial f}{\partial x} + \frac{1}{2}\sigma^2\frac{\partial^2 f}{\partial x^2} \right\} dt + \sigma\frac{\partial f}{\partial x}dW(t). \qquad (4.28)$$

Remark 4.5.1 In the statement of the theorem above we have, for readability reasons, suppressed a lot of variables. The term $\mu\frac{\partial f}{\partial x}$, for example, is shorthand notation for

$$\mu(t)\frac{\partial f}{\partial x}(t, X(t))$$

and correspondingly for the other terms.

Proof   A full formal proof is outside the scope of this text, so we only give a heuristic proof. (See Remark 4.5.2 below.) If we make a Taylor expansion including second order terms we obtain

$$df = \frac{\partial f}{\partial t}dt + \frac{\partial f}{\partial x}dX + \frac{1}{2}\frac{\partial^2 f}{\partial x^2}(dX)^2 + \frac{1}{2}\frac{\partial^2 f}{\partial t^2}(dt)^2 + \frac{\partial^2 f}{\partial t \partial x}dtdX. \qquad (4.29)$$

By definition we have

$$dX(t) = \mu(t)dt + \sigma(t)dW(t),$$

so, at least formally, we obtain

$$(dX)^2 = \mu^2(dt)^2 + 2\mu\sigma(dt)(dW) + \sigma^2(dW)^2.$$

The term containing $(dt)^2$ above is negligible compared to the dt-term in (4.27), and it can also be shown that the $(dt)(dW)$-term is negligible compared to the dt-term. Furthermore we have $(dW)^2 = dt$ from (4.23), and plugging in all this into the Taylor expansion (4.29) gives us the result.   □

It may be hard to remember the Itô formula, so for practical purposes it is often easier to copy our "proof" above and make a second order Taylor expansion.

Proposition 4.11 (Itô's formula) *With assumptions as in Theorem 4.10, df is given by*

$$df = \frac{\partial f}{\partial t}dt + \frac{\partial f}{\partial x}dX + \frac{1}{2}\frac{\partial^2 f}{\partial x^2}(dX)^2 \qquad (4.30)$$

where we use the following formal multiplication table.

$$\begin{cases} (dt)^2 = 0, \\ dt \cdot dW = 0, \\ (dW)^2 = dt. \end{cases}$$

Remark 4.5.2 As we have pointed out, the "proof" of the Itô formula above does not at all constitute a formal proof. We end this section by giving an outline of the full proof. What we have to prove is that, for all t, the following relation holds with probability one.

$$f(t, X(t)) - f(0, X(0)) = \int_0^t \left(\frac{\partial f}{\partial t} + \mu\frac{\partial f}{\partial x} + \frac{1}{2}\sigma^2\frac{\partial^2 f}{\partial x^2}\right)ds + \int_0^t \sigma\frac{\partial f}{\partial x}dW(s).$$

$$(4.31)$$

We therefore divide the interval $[0, t]$ as $0 = t_0 < t_1 < \ldots < t_n = t$ into n equal subintervals. Then we have

$$f(t, X(t)) - f(0, X(0)) = \sum_{k=0}^{n-1} f\left(t_{k+1}, X(t_{k+1})\right) - f\left(t_k, X(t_k)\right). \qquad (4.32)$$

Using Taylor's formula we obtain, with subscripts denoting partial derivatives and obvious notation,

$$\begin{aligned}
f\left(t_{k+1}, X(t_{k+1})\right) &- f\left(t_k, X(t_k)\right) \\
&= f_t\left(t_k, X(t_k)\right) \Delta t + f_x\left(t_k, X(t_k)\right) \Delta X_k \qquad (4.33) \\
&\quad + \frac{1}{2} f_{xx}\left(t_k, X(t_k)\right) \left(\Delta X_k\right)^2 + Q_k,
\end{aligned}$$

where Q_k is the remainder term. Furthermore we have

$$\begin{aligned}
\Delta X_k = X(t_{k+1}) - X(t_k) &= \int_{t_k}^{t_{k+1}} \mu(s)ds + \int_{t_k}^{t_{k+1}} \sigma(s)dW(s) \\
&= \mu(t_k)\Delta t + \sigma(t_k)\Delta W_k + S_k, \qquad (4.34)
\end{aligned}$$

where S_k is a remainder term. From this we obtain

$$\left(\Delta X_k\right)^2 = \mu^2(t_k)\left(\Delta t\right)^2 + 2\mu(t_k)\sigma(t_k)\Delta t \Delta W_k + \sigma^2(t_k)\left(\Delta W_k\right)^2 + P_k, \qquad (4.35)$$

where P_k is a remainder term. If we now substitute (4.34)–(4.35) into (4.32) we obtain, in shorthand notation,

$$f(t, X(t)) - f(0, X(0)) = I_1 + I_2 + I_3 + \frac{1}{2}I_4 + \frac{1}{2}K_1 + K_2 + R,$$

where

$$\begin{aligned}
I_1 &= \sum_k f_t(t_k)\Delta t, & I_2 &= \sum_k f_x(t_k)\mu(t_k)\Delta t, \\
I_3 &= \sum_k f_x(t_k)\sigma(t_k)\Delta W_k, & I_4 &= \sum_k f_{xx}(t_k)\sigma^2(t_k)\left(\Delta W_k\right)^2, \\
K_1 &= \sum_k f_{xx}(t_k)\mu^2(t_k)\left(\Delta t\right)^2, & K_2 &= \sum_k f_{xx}(t_k)\mu(t_k)\sigma(t_k)\Delta t \Delta W_k, \\
R &= \sum_k \left\{Q_k + S_k + P_k\right\}.
\end{aligned}$$

Letting $n \to \infty$ we have, more or less by definition,

$$\begin{aligned}
I_1 &\to \int_0^t f_t\left(s, X(s)\right) ds, & I_2 &\to \int_0^t f_x\left(s, X(s)\right)\mu(s)ds, \\
I_3 &\to \int_0^t f_x\left(s, X(s)\right)\sigma(s)dW(s).
\end{aligned}$$

Very much as when we proved earlier that $\sum\left(\Delta W_k\right)^2 \to t$, it is possible to show that

$$I_4 \to \int_0^t f_{xx}\left(s, X(s)\right)\sigma^2(s)ds,$$

and it is fairly easy to show that K_1 and K_2 converge to zero. The really hard part is to show that the term R, which is a large sum of individual remainder terms, also converges to zero. This can, however, also be done and the proof is finished.

4.6 Examples

In order to illustrate the use of the Itô formula we now give some examples. All these examples are quite simple, and the results could have been obtained as well by using standard techniques from elementary probability theory. The full force of the Itô calculus will be seen in the following chapters.

The first two examples illustrate a useful technique for computing expected values in situations involving Wiener processes. Since arbitrage pricing to a large extent consists of precisely the computation of certain expected values this technique will be used repeatedly in the sequel.

Suppose that we want to compute the expected value $E\left[Y\right]$ where Y is some stochastic variable. Schematically we will then proceed as follows.

1. Try to write Y as $Y = Z(t_0)$ where t_0 is some point in time and Z is a stochastic process having an Itô differential.
2. Use the Itô formula to compute dZ as, for example,

$$dZ(t) = \mu(t)dt + \sigma(t)dW(t),$$
$$Z(0) = z_0.$$

3. Write this expression in integrated form as

$$Z(t) = z_0 + \int_0^t \mu(s)ds + \int_0^t \sigma(s)dW(s).$$

4. Take expected values. Using Proposition 4.4 we see that the dW-integral will vanish. For the ds-integral we may move the expectation operator inside the integral sign (an integral is "just" a sum), and we thus have

$$E\left[Z(t)\right] = z_0 + \int_0^t E\left[\mu(s)\right]ds.$$

Now two cases can occur.
   (a) We may, by skill or pure luck, be able to calculate the expected value $E\left[\mu(s)\right]$ explicitly. Then we only have to compute an ordinary Riemann integral to obtain $E\left[Z(t)\right]$, and thus to read off $E\left[Y\right] = E\left[Z(t_0)\right]$.
   (b) If we cannot compute $E\left[\mu(s)\right]$ directly we have a harder problem, but in some cases we may convert our problem to that of solving an ordinary differential equation (ODE).

Example 4.12 Compute $E\left[W^4(t)\right]$.

Solution: Define Z by $Z(t) = W^4(t)$. Then we have $Z(t) = f(t, X(t))$ where $X = W$ and f is given by $f(t, x) = x^4$. Thus the stochastic differential of X is trivial, namely $dX = dW$, which, in the notation of the Itô formula (4.28), means that $\mu = 0$ and $\sigma = 1$. Furthermore we have $\frac{\partial f}{\partial t} = 0$, $\frac{\partial f}{\partial x} = 4x^3$ and $\frac{\partial^2 f}{\partial x^2} = 12x^2$. Thus the Itô formula gives us

$$dZ(t) = 6W^2(t)dt + 4W^3(t)dW(t),$$
$$Z(0) = 0.$$

Written in integral form this reads

$$Z(t) = 0 + 6 \int_0^t W^2(s)ds + 4 \int_0^t W^3(s)dW(s).$$

Now we take the expected values of both members of this expression. Then, by Proposition 4.4, the stochastic integral will vanish. Furthermore we may move the expectation operator inside the ds-integral, so we obtain

$$E\left[Z(t)\right] = 6 \int_0^t E\left[W^2(s)\right]ds.$$

Now we recall that $E\left[W^2(s)\right] = s$, so in the end we have our desired result

$$E\left[W^4(t)\right] = E\left[Z(t)\right] = 6 \int_0^t sds = 3t^2.$$

Example 4.13 Compute $E\left[e^{\alpha W(t)}\right]$.

Solution: Define Z by $Z(t) = e^{\alpha W(t)}$. The Itô formula gives us

$$dZ(t) = \frac{1}{2}\alpha^2 e^{\alpha W(t)}dt + \alpha e^{\alpha W(t)}dW(t),$$

so we see that Z satisfies the **stochastic differential equation** (SDE)

$$dZ(t) = \frac{1}{2}\alpha^2 Z(t)dt + \alpha Z(t)dW(t),$$
$$Z(0) = 1.$$

In integral form this reads

$$Z(t) = 1 + \frac{1}{2}\alpha^2 \int_0^t Z(s)(ds) + \alpha \int_0^t Z(s)dW(s).$$

Taking expected values will make the stochastic integral vanish. After moving the expectation within the integral sign in the ds-integral and defining m by $m(t) = E\left[Z(t)\right]$ we obtain the equation

$$m(t) = 1 + \frac{1}{2}\alpha^2 \int_0^t m(s)(ds).$$

This is an integral equation, but if we take the t-derivative we obtain the ODE

$$\begin{cases} \dot{m}(t) = \frac{\alpha^2}{2}m(t), \\ m(0) = 1. \end{cases}$$

Solving this standard equation gives us the answer

$$E\left[e^{\alpha W(t)}\right] = E\left[Z(t)\right] = m(t) = e^{\alpha^2 t/2}.$$

$\square$

It is natural to ask whether one can "compute" (in some sense) the value of a stochastic integral. This is a fairly vague question, but regardless of how it is interpreted, the answer is generally no. There are just a few examples where the stochastic integral can be computed in a fairly explicit way. Here is the most famous one.

Example 4.14 Compute

$$\int_0^t W(s)dW(s).$$

Solution: A natural guess is perhaps that $\int_0^t W(s)dW(s) = \frac{W^2(t)}{2}$. Since Itô calculus does not coincide with ordinary calculus this guess cannot possibly be true, but nevertheless it seems natural to start by investigating the process $Z(t) = W^2(t)$. Using the Itô formula on the function $f(t,x) = x^2$ and with $X = W$ we get

$$dZ(t) = dt + 2W(t)dW(t).$$

In integrated form this reads

$$W^2(t) = t + 2\int_0^t W(s)dW(s),$$

so we get our answer

$$\int_0^t W(s)dW(s) = \frac{W^2(t)}{2} - \frac{t}{2}.$$

$\square$

We end with a useful lemma.

Lemma 4.15 *Let* $\sigma(t)$ *be a given* **deterministic** *function of time and define the process* X *by*

$$X(t) = \int_0^t \sigma(s)dW(s). \tag{4.36}$$

Then $X(t)$ *has a normal distribution with zero mean, and variance given by*

$$Var[X(t)] = \int_0^t \sigma^2(s)ds.$$

This is of course an expected result because the integral is "just" a linear combination of the normally distributed Wiener increments with deterministic coefficients. See the exercises for a hint of the proof.

4.7 The Multidimensional Itô Formula

Let us now consider a vector process $X = (X_1, \ldots, X_n)^\star$, where the component X_i has a stochastic differential of the form

$$dX_i(t) = \mu_i(t)dt + \sum_{j=1}^{d} \sigma_{ij}(t)dW_j(t)$$

and $W_1, \ldots, W_d$ are d **independent** Wiener processes.

Defining the drift vector μ by

$$\mu = \begin{bmatrix} \mu_1 \\ \vdots \\ \mu_n \end{bmatrix},$$

the d-dimensional vector Wiener process W by

$$W = \begin{bmatrix} W_1 \\ \vdots \\ W_d \end{bmatrix},$$

and the $n \times d$-dimensional **diffusion matrix** σ by

$$\sigma = \begin{bmatrix} \sigma_{11} & \sigma_{12} & \cdots & \sigma_{1d} \\ \sigma_{21} & \sigma_{22} & \cdots & \sigma_{2d} \\ \vdots & \vdots & \ddots & \vdots \\ \sigma_{n1} & \sigma_{n2} & \cdots & \sigma_{nd} \end{bmatrix},$$

we may write the X-dynamics as

$$dX(t) = \mu(t)dt + \sigma(t)dW(t).$$

Let us furthermore define the process Z by

$$Z(t) = f(t, X(t)),$$

where $f : R_+ \times R^n \to R$ is a $C^{1,2}$ mapping. Then, using arguments as above, it can be shown that the stochastic differential df is given by

$$df(t, X(t)) = \frac{\partial f}{\partial t} dt + \sum_{i=1}^{n} \frac{\partial f}{\partial x_i} dX_i + \frac{1}{2} \sum_{i=1}^{n} \sum_{j=1}^{n} \frac{\partial^2 f}{\partial x_i \partial x_j} dX_i dX_j, \qquad (4.37)$$

with the extended multiplication rule (see the exercises)

$$(dW_i)(dW_j) = 0, \quad \text{for } i = j.$$

Written out in full (see the exercises) this gives us the following result.

Theorem 4.16 (Itô's formula) *Let the n-dimensional process X have dynamics given by*

$$dX(t) = \mu(t)dt + \sigma(t)dW(t),$$

with notation as above. Then the following hold.

- *The process $f(t, X(t))$ has a stochastic differential given by*

$$df = \left\{ \frac{\partial f}{\partial t} + \sum_{i=1}^{n} \mu_i \frac{\partial f}{\partial x_i} + \frac{1}{2} \sum_{i,j=1}^{n} C_{ij} \frac{\partial^2 f}{\partial x_i \partial x_j} \right\} dt + \sum_{i=1}^{n} \frac{\partial f}{\partial x_i} \sigma_i dW.$$

Here the row vector σ_i is the ith row of the matrix σ, i.e.

$$\sigma_i = [\sigma_{i1}, \dots, \sigma_{id}],$$

and the matrix C is defined by

$$C = \sigma\sigma^\star,$$

where $\star$ denotes transpose.

- *Alternatively, the differential is given by the formula*

$$df(t, X(t)) = \frac{\partial f}{\partial t} dt + \sum_{i=1}^{n} \frac{\partial f}{\partial x_i} dX_i + \frac{1}{2} \sum_{i,j=1}^{n} \frac{\partial^2 f}{\partial x_i \partial x_j} dX_i dX_j,$$

with the formal multiplication table

$$\begin{cases} (dt)^2 = 0, \\ dt \cdot dW = 0, \\ (dW_i)^2 = dt, \quad i = 1, \dots, d, \\ dW_i \cdot dW_j = 0, \quad i = j. \end{cases}$$

Remark 4.7.1 (Itô's formula) The Itô formula can also be written as

$$df = \left\{ \frac{\partial f}{\partial t} + \sum_{i=1}^{n} \mu_i \frac{\partial f}{\partial x_i} + \frac{1}{2} tr \left[\sigma^\star H \sigma \right] \right\} dt + \sum_{i=1}^{n} \frac{\partial f}{\partial x_i} \sigma_i dW,$$

where H denotes the Hessian matrix

$$H_{ij} = \frac{\partial^2 f}{\partial x_i \partial x_j},$$

and tr denotes the **trace** of a matrix. The trace is defined, for any square matrix A, as the sum of the diagonal elements, i.e.

$$trA = \sum_i A_{ii}.$$

See the exercises for details.

4.8 Correlated Wiener Processes

Up to this point we have only considered independent Wiener processes, but sometimes it is convenient to build models based upon Wiener processes which are correlated. In order to define such objects, let us therefore consider d independent standard (i.e. unit variance) Wiener processes $\bar{W}_1, \ldots, \bar{W}_d$. Let furthermore a (deterministic and constant) matrix

$$\delta = \begin{bmatrix} \delta_{11} & \delta_{12} & \ldots & \delta_{1d} \\ \delta_{21} & \delta_{22} & \ldots & \delta_{2d} \\ \vdots & \vdots & \ddots & \vdots \\ \delta_{n1} & \delta_{n2} & \ldots & \delta_{nd} \end{bmatrix}$$

be given, and consider the n-dimensional processes W, defined by

$$W = \delta \bar{W}$$

where

$$W = \begin{bmatrix} W_1 \\ \vdots \\ W_n \end{bmatrix}.$$

In other words

$$W_i = \sum_{j=1}^{d} \delta_{ij} \bar{W}_j, \quad i = 1, \ldots, n.$$

Let us now **assume that the rows of** δ **have unit length**, i.e.

$$||\delta_i|| = 1, \quad i = 1, \ldots, n,$$

where the Euclidean norm is defined as usual by

$$||x|| = \sqrt{\sum_{i=1}^{d} x_i^2}.$$

Then it is easy to see (how?) that each of the components $W_1, \ldots, W_n$ separately are standard (i.e. unit variance) Wiener processes. Let us now define the (instantaneous) **correlation matrix** ρ of W by

$$\rho_{ij} dt = Cov[dW_i, dW_j].$$

We then obtain

$$\rho_{ij} dt = E[dW_i \cdot dW_j] - E[dW_i] \cdot E[dW_j] = E[dW_i \cdot dW_j]$$

$$= E \left[\sum_{k=1}^{d} \delta_{ik} d\bar{W}_k \cdot \sum_{l=1}^{d} \delta_{jl} d\bar{W}_l \right] = \sum_{kl} \delta_{ik} \delta_{jl} E[d\bar{W}_k \cdot d\bar{W}_l]$$

$$= \sum_{k=1}^{d} \delta_{ik} \delta_{jk} = \delta_i \delta_j^\star dt,$$

i.e.

$$\rho = \delta \delta^\star.$$

Definition 4.17 *The process* W, *constructed as above, is called a vector of* **correlated** *Wiener processes, with* **correlation matrix** ρ.

Using this definition we have the following Itô formula for correlated Wiener processes.

Proposition 4.18 (Itô's formula) *Take a vector Wiener process* $W = (W_1, \ldots, W_n)$ *with correlation matrix* ρ *as given, and assume that the vector process* $X = (X_1, \ldots, X_k)^\star$ *has a stochastic differential. Then the following hold.*

- *For any* $C^{1,2}$ *function* f, *the stochastic differential of the process* $f(t, X(t))$ *is given by*

$$df(t, X(t)) = \frac{\partial f}{\partial t} dt + \sum_{i=1}^{n} \frac{\partial f}{\partial x_i} dX_i + \frac{1}{2} \sum_{i,j=1}^{n} \frac{\partial^2 f}{\partial x_i \partial x_j} dX_i dX_j,$$

with the formal multiplication table

$$\begin{cases} (dt)^2 = 0, \\ dt \cdot dW_i = 0, \quad i = 1, \ldots, n, \\ dW_i \cdot dW_j = \rho_{ij} dt. \end{cases}$$

- *If, in particular, $k = n$ and dX has the structure*

$$dX_i = \mu_i dt + \sigma_i dW_i, \quad i = 1, \ldots, n,$$

where $\mu_1, \ldots, \mu_n$ and $\sigma_1, \ldots, \sigma_n$ are scalar processes, then the stochastic differential of the process $f(t, X(t))$ is given by

$$df = \left\{ \frac{\partial f}{\partial t} + \sum_{i=1}^{n} \mu_i \frac{\partial f}{\partial x_i} + \frac{1}{2} \sum_{i,j=1}^{n} \sigma_i \sigma_j \rho_{ij} \frac{\partial^2 f}{\partial x_i \partial x_j} \right\} dt + \sum_{i=1}^{n} \sigma_i \frac{\partial f}{\partial x_i} dW_i.$$

We end this section by showing how it is possible to translate between the two formalisms above. Suppose therefore that the n-dimensional process X has a stochastic differential of the form

$$dX(t) = \mu(t)dt + \sigma(t)dW(t), \tag{4.38}$$

i.e.

$$dX_i(t) = \mu_i(t)dt + \sum_{j=1}^{d} \sigma_{ij}(t)dW_i(t), \quad i = 1, \ldots, n. \tag{4.39}$$

Thus the drift vector process μ is given by

$$\mu = \begin{bmatrix} \mu_1 \\ \vdots \\ \mu_n \end{bmatrix},$$

and the diffusion matrix process σ by

$$\sigma = \begin{bmatrix} \sigma_{11} & \sigma_{12} & \cdots & \sigma_{1d} \\ \sigma_{21} & \sigma_{22} & \cdots & \sigma_{2d} \\ \vdots & \vdots & \ddots & \vdots \\ \sigma_{n1} & \sigma_{n2} & \cdots & \sigma_{nd} \end{bmatrix}.$$

W is assumed to be d-dimensional standard vector Wiener process (i.e. with independent components) of the form

$$W = \begin{bmatrix} W_1 \\ \vdots \\ W_d \end{bmatrix}.$$

The system (4.38) can also be written as

$$dX_i(t) = \mu_i(t)dt + \sigma_i(t)dW(t),$$

where, as usual, σ_i is the ith row of the matrix σ. Let us now define n new scalar Wiener processes $\bar{W}_1, \ldots, \bar{W}_n$ by

$$\bar{W}_i = \frac{1}{\|\sigma_i\|}\sigma_i W, \quad i = 1, \ldots, n.$$

We can then write the X-dynamics as

$$dX_i(t) = \mu_i(t)dt + \|\sigma_i(t)\|d\bar{W}_i(t), \quad i = 1, \ldots, n. \tag{4.40}$$

As is easily seen, each $\bar{W}_i$ is a standard scalar Wiener process, but $\bar{W}_1, \ldots, \bar{W}_d$ are of course correlated. The local correlation is easily calculated as

$$\rho_{ij}dt = E\left[d\bar{W}_i d\bar{W}_j\right] = \frac{1}{\|\sigma_i\| \cdot \|\sigma_j\|} \sum_{k=1}^{d} \sigma_{ik}\sigma_{jk}dt = \frac{\sigma_i\sigma_j^{\star}}{\|\sigma_i\| \cdot \|\sigma_j\|}dt.$$

Summing up we have the following result.

Proposition 4.19 *The system*

$$dX_i(t) = \mu_i(t)dt + \sum_{j=1}^{d}\sigma_{ij}(t)dW_i(t), \quad i = 1, \ldots, n, \tag{4.41}$$

where $W_1, \ldots, W_d$ are independent, may equivalently be written as

$$dX_i(t) = \mu_i(t)dt + \delta_i(t)d\bar{W}_i(t), \quad i = 1, \ldots, n, \tag{4.42}$$

where $\bar{W}_1, \ldots, \bar{W}_d$ have the local correlation matrix ρ. The connections between (4.41) and (4.42) are given by the following expressions.

$$\begin{cases} \bar{W}_i = \frac{1}{\|\sigma_i\|}\sigma_i W, & i = 1, \ldots, n, \\ \delta_i = \|\sigma_i\|, & i = 1, \ldots, n, \\ \rho_{ij} = \frac{\sigma_i\sigma_j^{\star}}{\|\sigma_i\| \cdot \|\sigma_j\|}, & i, j = 1, \ldots, n. \end{cases}$$

4.9 Exercises

Exercise 4.1 Compute the stochastic differential dZ when

(a) $Z(t) = e^{\alpha t}$,

(b) $Z(t) = \int_0^t g(s)dW(s)$, where g is an adapted stochastic process.

(c) $Z(t) = e^{\alpha W(t)}$

(d) $Z(t) = e^{\alpha X(t)}$, where X has the stochastic differential

$$dX(t) = \mu dt + \sigma dW(t)$$

(μ and σ are constants).

(e) $Z(t) = X^2(t)$, where X has the stochastic differential

$$dX(t) = \alpha X(t)dt + \sigma X(t)dW(t).$$

Exercise 4.2 Compute the stochastic differential for Z when $Z(t) = \frac{1}{X(t)}$ and X has the stochastic differential

$$dX(t) = \alpha X(t)dt + \sigma X(t)dW(t).$$

By using the definition $Z = X^{-1}$ you can in fact express the right-hand side of dZ entirely in terms of Z itself (rather than in terms of X). Thus Z satisfies a stochastic differential equation. Which one?

Exercise 4.3 Let $\sigma(t)$ be a given deterministic function of time and define the process X by

$$X(t) = \int_0^t \sigma(s)dW(s). \qquad (4.43)$$

Use the technique described in Example 4.13 in order to show that the characteristic function of $X(t)$ (for a fixed t) is given by

$$E\left[e^{iuX(t)}\right] = \exp\left\{-\frac{u^2}{2}\int_0^t \sigma^2(s)ds\right\}, \quad u \in R, \qquad (4.44)$$

thus showing that $X(t)$ is normally distibuted with zero mean and a variance given by

$$Var[X(t)] = \int_0^t \sigma^2(s)ds.$$

Exercise 4.4 Suppose that X has the stochastic differential

$$dX(t) = \alpha X(t)dt + \sigma(t)dW(t),$$

where α is a real number whereas $\sigma(t)$ is any stochastic process. Use the technique in Example 4.13 in order to determine the function $m(t) = E[X(t)]$.

Exercise 4.5 Suppose that the process X has a stochastic differential

$$dX(t) = \mu(t)dt + \sigma(t)dW(t),$$

and that $\mu(t) \geq 0$ with probability one for all t. Show that this implies that X is a submartingale.

Exercise 4.6 A function $h(x_1, \ldots, x_n)$ is said to be **harmonic** if it satisfies the condition

$$\sum_{i=1}^{n} \frac{\partial^2 h}{\partial x_i^2} = 0.$$

It is **subharmonic** if it satisfies the condition

$$\sum_{i=1}^{n} \frac{\partial^2 h}{\partial x_i^2} \geq 0.$$

Let $W_1, \ldots, W_n$ be independent standard Wiener processes, and define the process X by $X(t) = h(W_1(t), \ldots, W_n(t))$. Show that X is a martingale (submartingale) if h is harmonic (subharmonic).

Exercise 4.7 The object of this exercise is to give an argument for the formal identity

$$dW_1 \cdot dW_2 = 0,$$

when W_1 and W_2 are independent Wiener processes. Let us therefore fix a time t, and divide the interval $[0, t]$ into equidistant points $0 = t_0 < t_1 < \cdots < t_n = t$, where $t_i = \frac{i}{n} \cdot t$. We use the notation

$$\Delta W_i(t_k) = W_i(t_k) - W_i(t_{k-1}), \quad i = 1, 2.$$

Now define Q_n by

$$Q_n = \sum_{k=1}^{n} \Delta W_1(t_k) \cdot \Delta W_2(t_k).$$

Show that $Q_n \to 0$ in L^2, i.e. show that

$$E[Q_n] = 0,$$
$$Var[Q_n] \to 0.$$

Exercise 4.8 Let X and Y be given as the solutions to the following system of stochastic differential equations.

$$dX = \alpha X dt - Y dW, \quad X(0) = x_0,$$
$$dY = \alpha Y dt + X dW, \quad Y(0) = y_0.$$

Note that the initial values x_0, y_0 are deterministic constants.

(a) Prove that the process R defined by $R(t) = X^2(t) + Y^2(t)$ is deterministic.

(b) Compute $E[X(t)]$.

Exercise 4.9 For a $n \times n$ matrix A, the **trace** of A is defined as

$$tr(A) = \sum_{i=1}^{n} A_{ii}.$$

(a) If B is $n \times d$ and C is $d \times n$, then BC is $n \times n$. Show that

$$tr(BC) = \sum_{ij} B_{ij} C_{ji}.$$

(b) With assumptions as above, show that

$$tr(BC) = tr(CB).$$

(c) Show that the Itô formula in Theorem 4.16 can be written

$$df = \left\{ \frac{\partial f}{\partial t} + \sum_{i=1}^{n} \mu_i \frac{\partial f}{\partial x_i} + \frac{1}{2} tr\left[\sigma^\star H \sigma\right] \right\} dt + \sum_{i=1}^{n} \frac{\partial f}{\partial x_i} \sigma_i dW_i,$$

where H denotes the Hessian matrix

$$H_{ij} = \frac{\partial^2 f}{\partial x_i \partial x_j}.$$

Exercise 4.10 Prove all claims in Section 4.8.

4.10   Notes

As (far reaching) introductions to stochastic calculus and its applications, Øksendal (1998) and Steele (2001) can be recommended. Standard references on a more advanced level are Karatzas and Shreve (2008), and Revuz and Yor (1991). The theory of stochastic integration can be extended from the Wiener framework to allow for semimartingales as integrators, and a classic in this field is Meyer (1976). Standard references are Jacod and Shiryaev (1987), Elliott (1982), Dellacherie and Meyer (1972), and Protter (2004).

5

DIFFERENTIAL EQUATIONS

5.1 Stochastic Differential Equations

Let $M(n, d)$ denote the class of $n \times d$ matrices, and consider as given the following objects.

- A d-dimensional (column-vector) Wiener process W.
- A (column-vector valued) function $\mu : R_+ \times R^n \to R^n$.
- A function $\sigma : R_+ \times R^n \to M(n, d)$.
- A real (column) vector $x_0 \in R^n$.

We now want to investigate whether there exists a stochastic process X which satisfies the **stochastic differential equation** (SDE)

$$dX_t = \mu(t, X_t)\, dt + \sigma(t, X_t)\, dW_t, \tag{5.1}$$

$$X_0 = x_0. \tag{5.2}$$

To be more precise we want to find a process X satisfying the integral equation

$$X_t = x_0 + \int_0^t \mu(s, X_s)\, ds + \int_0^t \sigma(s, X_s)\, dW_s, \quad \text{for all } t \geq 0. \tag{5.3}$$

The standard method for proving the existence of a solution to the SDE above is to construct an iteration scheme of Cauchy–Picard type. The idea is to define a sequence of processes $X^0, X^1, X^2, \ldots$ according to the recursive definition

$$X_t^0 \equiv x_0, \tag{5.4}$$

$$X_t^{n+1} = x_0 + \int_0^t \mu(s, X_s^n)\, ds + \int_0^t \sigma(s, X_s^n)\, dW_s. \tag{5.5}$$

Having done this one expects that the sequence $\{X^n\}_{n=1}^{\infty}$ will converge to some limiting process X, and that this X is a solution to the SDE. This construction can in fact be carried out, but as the proof requires some rather hard inequalities we only give the result.

Proposition 5.1 *Suppose that there exists a constant K such that the following conditions are satisfied for all x, y and t.*

$$\|\mu(t, x) - \mu(t, y)\| \leq K\|x - y\|, \tag{5.6}$$

$$\|\sigma(t, x) - \sigma(t, y)\| \leq K\|x - y\|, \tag{5.7}$$

$$\|\mu(t, x)\| + \|\sigma(t, x)\| \leq K(1 + \|x\|). \tag{5.8}$$

Then there exists a unique solution to the SDE (5.1)–(5.2). The solution has the properties

1. *X is $\mathcal{F}_t^W$-adapted.*
2. *X has continuous trajectories.*
3. *X is a Markov process.*
4. *There exists a constant C such that*

$$E\left[\|X_t\|^2\right] \le Ce^{Ct}\left(1 + \|x_0\|^2\right). \tag{5.9}$$

The fact that the solution X is $\mathcal{F}_t^W$-adapted means that for each fixed t the process value X_t is a functional of the Wiener trajectory on the interval $[0, t]$, and in this way an SDE induces a transformation of the space $C[0, \infty)$ into itself, where a Wiener trajectory $W.(\omega)$ is mapped to the corresponding solution trajectory $X.(\omega)$. Generically this transformation, which takes a Wiener trajectory into the corresponding X-trajectory, is enormously complicated and it is extremely rare that one can "solve" an SDE in some "explicit" manner. There are, however, a few nontrivial interesting cases where it is possible to solve an SDE, and the most important example for us is the equation below, describing the so-called geometric Brownian motion (GBM).

5.2   Geometric Brownian Motion

Geometric Brownian motion will be one of our fundamental building blocks for the modeling of asset prices, and it also turns up naturally in many other places. The equation is one of two natural generalizations of the simplest linear ODE and looks as follows.

Geometric Brownian motion:

$$dX_t = \alpha X_t dt + \sigma X_t dW_t, \tag{5.10}$$
$$X_0 = x_0. \tag{5.11}$$

Written in a slightly sloppy form we can write the equation as

$$\dot{X}_t = \left(\alpha + \sigma \dot{W}_t\right) X_t$$

where $\dot{W}$ is "white noise", i.e. the (formal) time derivative of the Wiener process. Thus we see that GBM can be viewed as a linear ODE, with a stochastic coefficient driven by white noise. See Fig. 5.1, for a computer simulation of GBM with $\alpha = 1$, $\sigma = 0.2$ and $X(0) = 1$. The smooth line is the graph of the expected value function $E[X_t] = 1 \cdot e^{\alpha t}$. For small values of σ, the trajectory will (at least initially) stay fairly close to the expected value function, whereas a large value of σ will give rise to large random deviations. This can clearly be seen when we compare the simulated trajectory in Fig. 5.1 to the three simulated trajectories in Fig. 5.2 where we have $\sigma = 0.4$.

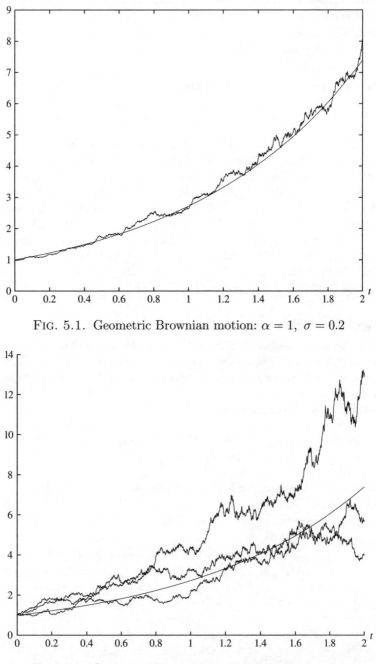

FIG. 5.1. Geometric Brownian motion: $\alpha = 1$, $\sigma = 0.2$

FIG. 5.2. Geometric Brownian motion: $\alpha = 1$, $\sigma = 0.4$

Inspired by the fact that the solution to the corresponding deterministic linear equation is an exponential function of time we are led to investigate the process Z, defined by $Z_t = \ln X_t$, where we **assume** that X is a solution and that X is strictly positive (see below). The Itô formula gives us

$$dZ = \frac{1}{X}dX + \frac{1}{2}\left\{-\frac{1}{X^2}\right\}[dX]^2$$

$$= \frac{1}{X}\left\{\alpha X dt + \sigma X dW\right\} + \frac{1}{2}\left\{-\frac{1}{X^2}\right\}\sigma^2 X^2 dt$$

$$= \left\{\alpha dt + \sigma dW\right\} - \frac{1}{2}\sigma^2 dt.$$

Thus we have the equation

$$dZ_t = \left(\alpha - \frac{1}{2}\sigma^2\right)dt + \sigma dW_t,$$

$$Z_0 = \ln x_0.$$

This equation, however, is extremely simple: since the right-hand side does not contain Z it can be integrated directly to

$$Z_t = \ln x_0 + \left(\alpha - \frac{1}{2}\sigma^2\right)t + \sigma W_t,$$

which means that X is given by

$$X_t = x_0 \cdot \exp\left\{\left(\alpha - \frac{1}{2}\sigma^2\right)t + \sigma W_t\right\}. \tag{5.12}$$

Strictly speaking there is a logical flaw in the reasoning above. In order for Z to be well defined we have to assume that there actually exists a solution X to eqn (5.10) and we also have to assume that the solution is positive. As for the existence, this is covered by Proposition 5.1, but the positivity seems to present a bigger problem. We may actually avoid both these problems by regarding the calculations above as purely heuristic. Instead we **define** the process X by the formula (5.12). Then it is an easy exercise to show that X thus defined actually satisfies the SDE (5.10)–(5.11). Thus we really have proved the first part of the following result, which will be used repeatedly in the sequel. The result about the expected value is an easy exercise, which is left to the reader.

Proposition 5.2 *The solution to the equation*

$$dX_t = \alpha X_t dt + \sigma X_t dW_t, \tag{5.13}$$

$$X_0 = x_0, \tag{5.14}$$

is given by

$$X(t) = x_0 \cdot \exp\left\{\left(\alpha - \frac{1}{2}\sigma^2\right)t + \sigma W(t)\right\}. \tag{5.15}$$

The expected value is given by

$$E[X_t] = x_0 e^{\alpha t}. \tag{5.16}$$

5.3   The Linear SDE

In this section we will study the linear SDE, which in the scalar case has the form

$$\begin{cases} dX_t = aX_t dt + \sigma dW_t, \\ X_0 = x_0. \end{cases} \qquad (5.17)$$

This equation turns up in various physical applications, and we will also meet it below in connection with interest rate theory.

In order to get some feeling for how to solve this equation we recall that the linear ODE

$$\frac{dx_t}{dt} = ax_t + u_t,$$

where u is a deterministic function of time, has the solution

$$x_t = e^{at}x_0 + \int_0^t e^{a(t-s)}u_s ds. \qquad (5.18)$$

If we, for a moment, reason heuristically, then it is tempting to formally divide eqn (5.17) by dt. This would (formally) give us

$$\frac{dX_t}{dt} = aX_t + \sigma\frac{dW_t}{dt},$$

and, by analogy with the ODE above, one is led to conjecture the formal solution

$$X_t = e^{at}X_0 + \sigma\int_0^t e^{a(t-s)}\frac{dW_s}{ds}ds = e^{at}X_0 + \sigma\int_0^t e^{a(t-s)}dW_s.$$

Generally speaking, tricks like this will not work, since the solution of the ODE is based on ordinary calculus, whereas we have to use Itô calculus when dealing with SDEs. In this case, however, we have a linear structure, which means that the second order term in the Itô formula does not come into play. Thus the solution of the linear SDE is indeed given by the heuristically derived formula above. We formulate the result for a slightly more general situation, where we allow X to be vector-valued.

Proposition 5.3 *Consider the n-dimensional linear SDE*

$$\begin{cases} dX_t = (AX_t + b_t)\,dt + \sigma_t dW_t, \\ X_0 = x_0 \end{cases} \qquad (5.19)$$

where A is an $n \times n$ matrix, b is an R^n-valued deterministic function (in column vector form), σ is a deterministic function taking values in $M(n,d)$, and W an d-dimensional Wiener process. The solution of this equation is given by

$$X_t = e^{At}x_0 + \int_0^t e^{A(t-s)}b_s ds + \int_0^t e^{A(t-s)}\sigma_s dW_s. \qquad (5.20)$$

Here we have used the matrix exponential e^{At}, defined by

$$e^{At} = \sum_{k=0}^{\infty} \frac{A^k}{k!} t^k.$$

Proof   Defining the process X by (5.20) and using the Itô formula, it is easily seen that X satisfies the SDE (5.19). See the exercises for some details.   □

In the exercises you will find results about the moments of X_t as well as details about the matrix exponential.

5.4   The Infinitesimal Operator

Consider, as in Section 5.1, the n-dimensional SDE

$$dX_t = \mu(t, X_t)\, dt + \sigma(t, X_t)\, dW_t. \tag{5.21}$$

Through the Itô formula, the process above is closely connected to a partial differential operator $\mathcal{A}$, defined below. The next two sections are devoted to investigating the connections between, on the one hand, the analytical properties of the operator $\mathcal{A}$, and on the other hand the probabilistic properties of the process X above.

Definition 5.4 *Given the SDE in (5.21), the partial differential operator $\mathcal{A}$, referred to as the* **infinitesimal operator** *of X, is defined, for any function $h(x)$ with $h \in C^2(R^n)$, by*

$$\mathcal{A}h(t, x) = \sum_{i=1}^{n} \mu_i(t, x) \frac{\partial h}{\partial x_i}(x) + \frac{1}{2} \sum_{i,j=1}^{n} C_{ij}(t, x) \frac{\partial^2 h}{\partial x_i \partial x_j}(x),$$

where as before

$$C(t, x) = \sigma(t, x)\sigma^{\star}(t, x).$$

This operator is also known as the **Dynkin operator**, the **Itô operator**, or the **Kolmogorov backward operator**. We note that, in terms of the infinitesimal generator, the Itô formula takes the form

$$df(t, X_t) = \left\{ \frac{\partial f}{\partial t} + \mathcal{A}f \right\} dt + [\nabla_x f] \sigma dW_t$$

where the gradient ∇_x is defined for $h \in C^1(R^n)$ as

$$\nabla_x h = \left[\frac{\partial h}{\partial x_1}, \dots, \frac{\partial h}{\partial x_n} \right].$$

5.5 Partial Differential Equations

In this section we will explore the intimate connection which exists between stochastic differential equations and certain parabolic partial differential equations. Consider for example the following so called **Cauchy problem.**

We are given three scalar functions $\mu(t, x)$, $\sigma(t, x)$ and $\Phi(x)$. Our task is to find a function F which satisfies the following **boundary value problem** on $[0, T] \times R$:

$$\frac{\partial F}{\partial t}(t, x) + \mu(t, x)\frac{\partial F}{\partial x} + \frac{1}{2}\sigma^2(t, x)\frac{\partial^2 F}{\partial x^2}(t, x) = 0, \qquad (5.22)$$

$$F(T, x) = \Phi(x). \qquad (5.23)$$

Now, instead of attacking this problem using purely analytical tools, we will produce a so called **stochastic representation formula**, which gives the solution to (5.22)–(5.23) in terms of the solution to an SDE which is associated to (5.22)–(5.23) in a natural way. Thus we assume that there actually exists a solution F to (5.22)–(5.23). Let us now fix a point in time t and a point in space x. Having fixed these we **define** the stochastic process X on the time interval $[t, T]$ as the solution to the SDE

$$dX_s = \mu(s, X_s)ds + \sigma(s, X_s)dW_s, \qquad (5.24)$$

$$X_t = x, \qquad (5.25)$$

and the point is that the infinitesimal generator $\mathcal{A}$ for this process is given by

$$\mathcal{A} = \mu(t, x)\frac{\partial}{\partial x} + \frac{1}{2}\sigma^2(t, x)\frac{\partial^2}{\partial x^2},$$

which is exactly the operator apearing in the PDE above. Thus we may write the boundary value problem as

$$\frac{\partial F}{\partial t}(t, x) + \mathcal{A}F(t, x) = 0, \qquad (5.26)$$

$$F(T, x) = \Phi(x). \qquad (5.27)$$

Applying the Itô formula to the process $F(s, X(s))$ gives us

$$F(T, X_T) = F(t, X_t) + \int_t^T \left\{ \frac{\partial F}{\partial t}(s, X_s) + \mathcal{A}F(s, X_s) \right\} ds$$

$$+ \int_t^T \sigma(s, X_s)\frac{\partial F}{\partial x}(s, X_s)dW_s. \qquad (5.28)$$

Since, by assumption, F actually satisfies eqn (5.26), the time integral above will vanish. If furthermore the process $\sigma(s, X_s)\frac{\partial F}{\partial x}(s, X_s)$ is sufficiently integrable and we take expected values, the stochastic integral will also vanish. The initial value $X_t = x$ and the boundary condition $F(T, x) = \Phi(x)$ will eventually leave us with the formula

$$F(t, x) = E_{t,x}\left[\Phi\left(X_T\right)\right],$$

where we have indexed the expectation operator in order to emphasize that the expected value is to be taken given the initial value $X_t = x$. Thus we have proved the following result, which is known as the **Feynman–Kač stochastic representation formula**.

Proposition 5.5 (Feynman–Kač) *Assume that F is a solution to the boundary value problem*

$$\frac{\partial F}{\partial t}(t, x) + \mu(t, x)\frac{\partial F}{\partial x} + \frac{1}{2}\sigma^2(t, x)\frac{\partial^2 F}{\partial x^2}(t, x) = 0,$$
$$F(T, x) = \Phi(x).$$

Assume furthermore that the process

$$\sigma(s, X_s)\frac{\partial F}{\partial x}(s, X_s)$$

is in $\pounds^2$ (see Definition 4.3), where X is defined below. Then F has the representation

$$F(t, x) = E_{t,x}\left[\Phi\left(X_T\right)\right], \tag{5.29}$$

where X satisfies the SDE

$$dX_s = \mu(s, X_s)ds + \sigma(s, X_s)dW_s, \tag{5.30}$$
$$X_t = x. \tag{5.31}$$

Note that we need the integrability assumption $\sigma(s, X_s)\frac{\partial F}{\partial x}(s, X_s) \in \pounds^2$ in order to guarantee that the expected value of the stochastic integral in (5.28) equals zero. In fact the generic situation is that a boundary value problem of the type above—a so called **parabolic** problem—will have infinitely many solutions, (see John 1982). It will, however, only have one "nice" solution, the others being rather "wild", and the proposition above will only give us the "nice" solution.

We may also consider the closely related boundary value problem

$$\frac{\partial F}{\partial t}(t, x) + \mu(t, x)\frac{\partial F}{\partial x} + \frac{1}{2}\sigma^2(t, x)\frac{\partial^2 F}{\partial x^2}(t, x) - rF(t, x) = 0, \tag{5.32}$$
$$F(T, x) = \Phi(x), \tag{5.33}$$

where r is a given real number. Equations of this type appear over and over again in the study of pricing problems for financial derivatives. Inspired by the ODE technique of integrating factors we are led to multiply the entire eqn (5.32) by the factor e^{rs}, and if we then consider the process $Z(s) = e^{-rs}F(s, X(s))$, where X as before is defined by (5.30)–(5.31), we obtain the following result.

Proposition 5.6 (Feynman–Kač) *Assume that F is a solution to the boundary value problem*

$$\frac{\partial F}{\partial t}(t,x) + \mu(t,x)\frac{\partial F}{\partial x}(t,x) + \frac{1}{2}\sigma^2(t,x)\frac{\partial^2 F}{\partial x^2}(t,x) - rF(t,x) = 0, \qquad (5.34)$$

$$F(T,x) = \Phi(x). \qquad (5.35)$$

Assume furthermore that the process $e^{-rs}\sigma(s, X_s)\frac{\partial F}{\partial x}(s, X_s)$ is in $\pounds^2$, where X is defined below. Then F has the representation

$$F(t,x) = e^{-r(T-t)}E_{t,x}\left[\Phi\left(X_T\right)\right], \qquad (5.36)$$

where X satisfies the SDE

$$dX_s = \mu(s, X_s)ds + \sigma(s, X_s)dW_s, \qquad (5.37)$$

$$X_t = x. \qquad (5.38)$$

Example 5.7 Solve the PDE

$$\frac{\partial F}{\partial t}(t,x) + \frac{1}{2}\sigma^2\frac{\partial^2 F}{\partial x^2}(t,x) = 0,$$

$$F(T,x) = x^2,$$

where σ is a constant.

Solution: From Proposition 5.5 we immediately have

$$F(t,x) = E_{t,x}\left[X_T^2\right],$$

where

$$dX_s = 0 \cdot ds + \sigma dW_s,$$

$$X_t = x.$$

This equation can easily be solved, and we have

$$X_T = x + \sigma\left[W_T - W_t\right],$$

so X_T has the distribution $N[x, \sigma\sqrt{T - t}]$. Thus we have the solution

$$F(t, x) = E\left[X_T^2\right] = Var[X_T] + \{E\left[X_T\right]\}^2$$
$$= \sigma^2(T - t) + x^2.$$

□

Up to now we have only treated the scalar case, but exactly the same arguments as above will give us the following result.

Proposition 5.8 *Take as given*

- *A (column-vector valued) function $\mu : R_+ \times R^n \to R^n$.*
- *A function $C : R_+ \times R^n \to M(n, n)$, which can be written in the form*

$$C(t, x) = \sigma(t, x)\sigma^\star(t, x),$$

for some function $\sigma : R_+ \times R^n \to M(n, d)$.
- *A real valued function $\Phi : R^n \to R$.*
- *A real number r.*

Assume that $F : R_+ \times R^n \to R$ is a solution to the boundary value problem

$$\frac{\partial F}{\partial t}(t, x) + \sum_{i=1}^n \mu_i(t, x)\frac{\partial F}{\partial x_i}(t, x) + \frac{1}{2}\sum_{i,j=1}^n C_{ij}(t, x)\frac{\partial^2 F}{\partial x_i \partial x_j}(t, x) - rF(t, x) = 0,$$

$$F(T, x) = \Phi(x).$$

Assume furthermore that the process

$$e^{-rs}\sum_{i=1}^n \sigma_i(s, X_s)\frac{\partial F}{\partial x_i}(s, X_s)$$

is in $\pounds^2$ (see Definition 4.3), where X is defined below. Then F has the representation

$$F(t, x) = e^{-r(T-t)}E_{t,x}\left[\Phi\left(X_T\right)\right], \tag{5.39}$$

where X satisfies the SDE

$$dX_s = \mu(s, X_s)dt + \sigma(s, X_s)dW_s, \tag{5.40}$$
$$X_t = x. \tag{5.41}$$

We end this section with a useful result. Given Lemma 4.9 the proof is easy and left to the reader.

Proposition 5.9 *Consider as given a vector process X with generator $\mathcal{A}$, and a function $F(t, x)$. Then, modulo some integrability conditions, the following hold.*

- *The process $F(t, X_t)$ is a martingale relative to the filtration $\mathcal{F}^X$ if and only if F satisfies the PDE*

$$\frac{\partial F}{\partial t} + \mathcal{A}F = 0.$$

- *The process $F(t, X_t)$ is a martingale relative to the filtration $\mathcal{F}^X$ if and only if, for every (t, x) and $T \geq t$, we have*

$$F(t, x) = E_{t,x}\left[F(T, X_T)\right].$$

5.6 The Kolmogorov Equations

We will now use the results of the previous section in order to derive some classical results concerning the transition probabilities for the solution to an SDE. The discussion has the nature of an overview, so we allow ourselves some latitude as to technical details.

Suppose that X is a solution to the equation

$$dX_t = \mu(t, X_t)dt + \sigma(t, X_t)dW_t, \qquad (5.42)$$

with infinitesimal generator $\mathcal{A}$ given by

$$(\mathcal{A}f)(s, y) = \sum_{i=1}^{n} \mu_i(s, y)\frac{\partial f}{\partial y_i}(s, y) + \frac{1}{2}\sum_{i,j=1}^{n} C_{ij}(s, y)\frac{\partial^2 f}{\partial y_i \partial y_j}(s, y),$$

where as usual

$$C(t, x) = \sigma(t, x)\sigma^\star(t, x).$$

Now consider the boundary value problem

$$\left(\frac{\partial u}{\partial s} + \mathcal{A}u\right)(s, y) = 0, \quad (s, y) \in (0, T) \times R^n,$$

$$u(T, y) = I_B(y), \quad y \in R^n,$$

where I_B is the indicator function of the set B. From Proposition 5.8 we immediately have

$$u(s, y) = E_{s,y}\left[I_B(X_T)\right] = P\left(X_T \in B \mid X_s = y\right),$$

where X is a solution of (5.42). This argument can also be turned around, and we have thus (more or less) proved the following result.

Proposition 5.10 (Kolmogorov backward equation) *Let X be a solution to eqn (5.42). Then the transition probabilities $P(s, y; t, B) = P(X_t \in B \mid)$ $X(s) = y$ are given as the solution to the equation*

$$\left(\frac{\partial P}{\partial s} + \mathcal{A}P\right)(s, y; t, B) = 0, \quad (s, y) \in (0, t) \times R^n, \tag{5.43}$$

$$P(t, y; t, B) = I_B(y). \tag{5.44}$$

Using basically the same reasoning one can also prove the following corresponding result for transition densities.

Proposition 5.11 (Kolmogorov backward equation) *Let X be a solution to eqn (5.42). Assume that the measure $P(s, y; t, dx)$ has a density $p(s, y; t, x)dx$. Then we have*

$$\left(\frac{\partial p}{\partial s} + \mathcal{A}p\right)(s, y; t, x) = 0, \quad (s, y) \in (0, t) \times R^n, \tag{5.45}$$

$$p(s, y; t, x) \to \delta_x, \quad as \ s \to t. \tag{5.46}$$

The reason that eqns (5.43) and (5.45) are called backward equations is that the differential operator is working on the "backward variables" (s, y). We will now derive a corresponding "forward" equation, where the action of the differential operator is on the "forward" variables (t, x). For simplicity we consider only the scalar case.

We assume that X has a transition density. Let us then fix two points in time s and T with $s < T$. Now consider an arbitrary "test function", i.e. an infinite differentiable function $h(t, x)$ with compact support in the set $(s, T) \times R$. From the Itô formula we have

$$h(T, X_T) = h(s, X_s) + \int_s^T \left(\frac{\partial h}{\partial t} + \mathcal{A}h\right)(t, X_t)dt + \int_s^T \frac{\partial h}{\partial x}(t, X_t)dW_t.$$

Applying the expectation operator $E_{s,y}[\cdot]$, and using the fact that, because of the compact support, $h(T, x) = h(s, x) = 0$, we obtain

$$\int_{-\infty}^\infty \int_s^T p(s, y; t, x)\left(\frac{\partial}{\partial t} + \mathcal{A}\right)h(t, x)dxdt = 0.$$

Partial integration with respect to t (for $\frac{\partial}{\partial t}$) and with respect to x (for $\mathcal{A}$) gives us

$$\int_{-\infty}^\infty \int_s^T h(t, x)\left(-\frac{\partial}{\partial t} + \mathcal{A}^\star\right)p(s, y; t, x)dxdt = 0,$$

where the adjoint operator $\mathcal{A}^\star$ is defined by

$$(\mathcal{A}^\star f)(t, x) = -\frac{\partial}{\partial x}[\mu(t, x)f(t, x)] + \frac{1}{2}\frac{\partial^2}{\partial x^2}\left[\sigma^2(t, x)f(t, x)\right].$$

Since this equation holds for all test functions we have shown the following result.

Proposition 5.12 (Kolmogorov forward equation) *Assume that the solution X of eqn (5.42) has a transition density $p(s, y; t, x)$. Then p will satisfy the* **Kolmogorov forward equation**

$$\frac{\partial}{\partial t} p(s, y; t, x) = \mathcal{A}^\star p(s, y; t, x), \quad (t, x) \in (0, T) \times R, \quad (5.47)$$

$$p(s, y; t, x) \to \delta_y, \quad as \ t \downarrow s. \quad (5.48)$$

This equation is also known as the **Fokker–Planck equation**. The multi-dimensional version is readily obtained as

$$\frac{\partial p}{\partial t} p(s, y; t, x) = \mathcal{A}^\star p(s, y; t, x),$$

where the adjoint operator $\mathcal{A}^\star$ is defined by

$$\left(\mathcal{A}^\star f \right)(t, x) = -\sum_{i=1}^n \frac{\partial}{\partial x_i} \left[\mu_i(t, x) f(t, x) \right] + \frac{1}{2} \sum_{i,j=1}^n \frac{\partial^2}{\partial x_i \partial x_j} \left[C_{ij}(t, x) f(t, x) \right].$$

Example 5.13 Let us consider a standard Wiener process with constant diffusion coefficient σ, i.e. the SDE

$$dX_t = \sigma dW_t.$$

The Fokker–Planck equation for this process is

$$\frac{\partial p}{\partial t}(s, y; t, x) = \frac{1}{2} \sigma^2 \frac{\partial^2 p}{\partial x^2}(s, y; t, x),$$

and it is easily checked that the solution is given by the Gaussian density

$$p(s, y; t, x) = \frac{1}{\sigma \sqrt{2\pi(t - s)}} \exp \left[-\frac{1}{2} \frac{(x - y)^2}{\sigma^2 (t - s)} \right].$$

Example 5.14 Consider the GBM process

$$dX_t = \alpha X_t dt + \sigma X_t dW_t.$$

The Fokker–Planck equation for this process is

$$\frac{\partial p}{\partial t}(s, y; t, x) = \frac{1}{2} \frac{\partial^2}{\partial x^2} \left[\sigma^2 x^2 p(s, y; t, x) \right] - \frac{\partial}{\partial x} \left[\alpha x p(s, y; t, x) \right],$$

i.e.

$$\frac{\partial p}{\partial t} = \frac{1}{2}\sigma^2 x^2 \frac{\partial^2 p}{\partial x^2} + \left(2\sigma^2 - \alpha\right) x \frac{\partial p}{\partial x} + \left(\sigma^2 - \alpha\right) p.$$

A change of variables of the form $x = e^y$ reduces this equation to an equation with constant coefficients, which can be solved by Fourier methods. For us it is perhaps easier to get the transition density directly by solving the SDE above. See the exercises below.

5.7 Exercises

Exercise 5.1 Show that the scalar SDE

$$dX_t = \alpha X_t dt + \sigma dW_t,$$
$$X_0 = x_0,$$

has the solution

$$X(t) = e^{\alpha t} \cdot x_0 + \sigma \int_0^t e^{\alpha(t-s)} dW_s, \qquad (5.49)$$

by differentiating X as defined by eqn (5.49) and showing that X so defined actually satisfies the SDE.

Hint: Write eqn (5.49) as

$$X_t = Y_t + Z_t \cdot R_t,$$

where

$$Y_t = e^{\alpha t} \cdot x_0,$$
$$Z_t = e^{\alpha t} \cdot \sigma,$$
$$R_t = \int_0^t e^{-\alpha s} dW_s,$$

and first compute the differentials dZ, dY and dR. Then use the multidimensional Itô formula on the function $f(y, z, r) = y + z \cdot r$.

Exercise 5.2 Let A be an $n \times n$ matrix, and define the matrix exponential e^A by the series

$$e^A = \sum_{k=0}^{\infty} \frac{A^k}{k!}.$$

This series can be shown to converge uniformly.

(a) Show, by taking derivatives under the summation sign, that

$$\frac{de^{At}}{dt} = Ae^{At}.$$

(b) Show that
$$e^0 = I,$$

where 0 denotes the zero matrix, and I denotes the identity matrix.

(c) Convince yourself that if A and B commute, i.e. $AB = BA$, then

$$e^{A+B} = e^A \cdot e^B = e^B \cdot e^A.$$

Hint: Write the series expansion in detail.

(d) Show that e^A is invertible for every A, and that in fact

$$\left[e^A\right]^{-1} = e^{-A}.$$

(e) Show that for any A, t and s

$$e^{A(t+s)} = e^{At} \cdot e^{As}$$

(f) Show that

$$\left(e^A\right)^\star = e^{A^\star}$$

Exercise 5.3 Use the exercise above to complete the details of the proof of Proposition 5.3.

Exercise 5.4 Consider again the linear SDE (5.19). Show that the expected value function $m(t) = E[X(t)]$, and the covariance matrix $C(t) = \{Cov(X_i(t), X_j(t))\}_{i,j}$ are given by

$$m(t) = e^{At}x_0 + \int_0^t e^{A(t-s)}b(s)ds,$$

$$C(t) = \int_0^t e^{A(t-s)}\sigma(s)\sigma^\star(s)e^{A^\star(t-s)}ds,$$

where * denotes transpose.

Hint: Use the explicit solution above, and the fact that

$$C(t) = E\left[X_t X_t^\star\right] - m(t)m^\star(t).$$

Geometric Brownian motion (GBM) constitutes a class of processes which is closed under a number of nice operations. Here are some examples.

Exercise 5.5 Suppose that X satisfies the SDE

$$dX_t = \alpha X_t dt + \sigma X_t dW_t.$$

Now define Y by $Y_t = X_t^\beta$, where β is a real number. Then Y is also a GBM process. Compute dY and find out which SDE Y satisfies.

Exercise 5.6 Suppose that X satisfies the SDE

$$dX_t = \alpha X_t dt + \sigma X_t dW_t,$$

and Y satisfies

$$dY_t = \gamma Y_t dt + \delta Y_t dV_t,$$

where V is a Wiener process which is independent of W. Define Z by $Z = \frac{X}{Y}$ and derive an SDE for Z by computing dZ and substituting Z for $\frac{X}{Y}$ in the right hand side of dZ. If X is nominal income and Y describes inflation then Z describes real income.

Exercise 5.7 Suppose that X satisfies the SDE

$$dX_t = \alpha X_t dt + \sigma X_t dW_t,$$

and Y satisfies

$$dY_t = \gamma Y_t dt + \delta Y_t dW_t.$$

Note that now both X and Y are driven by the same Wiener process W. Define Z by $Z = \frac{X}{Y}$ and derive an SDE for Z.

Exercise 5.8 Suppose that X satisfies the SDE

$$dX_t = \alpha X_t dt + \sigma X_t dW_t,$$

and Y satisfies

$$dY_t = \gamma Y_t dt + \delta Y_t dV_t,$$

where V is a Wiener process which is independent of W. Define Z by $Z = X \cdot Y$ and derive an SDE for Z. If X describes the price process of, for example, IBM in US\$ and Y is the currency rate SEK/US\$ then Z describes the dynamics of the IBM stock expressed in SEK.

Exercise 5.9 Use a stochastic representation result in order to solve the following boundary value problem in the domain $[0, T] \times R$.

$$\frac{\partial F}{\partial t} + \mu x \frac{\partial F}{\partial x} + \frac{1}{2}\sigma^2 x^2 \frac{\partial^2 F}{\partial x^2} = 0,$$
$$F(T, x) = \ln(x^2).$$

Here μ and σ are assumed to be known constants.

Exercise 5.10 Consider the following boundary value problem in the domain $[0, T] \times R$.

$$\frac{\partial F}{\partial t} + \mu(t, x)\frac{\partial F}{\partial x} + \frac{1}{2}\sigma^2(t, x)\frac{\partial^2 F}{\partial x^2} + k(t, x) = 0,$$
$$F(T, x) = \Phi(x).$$

Here μ, σ, k and Φ are assumed to be known functions.

Prove that this problem has the stochastic representation formula

$$F(t, x) = E_{t,x}\left[\Phi(X_T)\right] + \int_t^T E_{t,x}\left[k(s, X_s)\right] ds,$$

where as usual X has the dynamics

$$dX_s = \mu(s, X_s)ds + \sigma(s, X_s)dW_s,$$
$$X_t = x.$$

Hint: Define X as above, assume that F actually solves the PDE and consider the process $Z_s = F(s, X_s)$.

Exercise 5.11 Use the result of the previous exercise in order to solve

$$\frac{\partial F}{\partial t} + \frac{1}{2}x^2\frac{\partial^2 F}{\partial x^2} + x = 0,$$
$$F(T, x) = \ln(x^2).$$

Exercise 5.12 Consider the following boundary value problem in the domain $[0, T] \times R$.

$$\frac{\partial F}{\partial t} + \mu(t, x)\frac{\partial F}{\partial x} + \frac{1}{2}\sigma^2(t, x)\frac{\partial^2 F}{\partial x^2} + r(t, x)F = 0,$$
$$F(T, x) = \Phi(x).$$

Here $\mu(t, x)$, $\sigma(t, x)$, $r(t, x)$ and $\Phi(x)$ are assumed to be known functions. Prove that this problem has a stochastic representation formula of the form

$$F(t, x) = E_{t,x}\left[\Phi(X_T)e^{\int_t^T r(s, X_s)ds}\right],$$

by considering the process $Z_s = F(s, X_s) \times \exp\left[\int_t^s r(u, X_u)du\right]$ on the time interval $[t, T]$.

Exercise 5.13 Solve the boundary value problem

$$\frac{\partial F}{\partial t}(t, x, y) + \frac{1}{2}\sigma^2\frac{\partial^2 F}{\partial x^2}(t, x, y) + \frac{1}{2}\delta^2\frac{\partial^2 F}{\partial y^2}(t, x, y) = 0,$$
$$F(T, x, y) = xy.$$

Exercise 5.14 Go through the details in the derivation of the Kolmogorov forward equation.

Exercise 5.15 Consider the SDE

$$dX_t = \alpha dt + \sigma dW_t,$$

where α and σ are constants.

(a) Compute the transition density $p(s, y; t, x)$, by solving the SDE.

(b) Write down the Fokker–Planck equation for the transition density and check the equation is indeed satisfied by your answer in (a).

Exercise 5.16 Consider the standard GBM

$$dX_t = \alpha X_t dt + \sigma X_t dW_t$$

and use the representation

$$X_t = X_s \exp\left\{\left[\alpha - \frac{1}{2}\sigma^2\right](t - s) + \sigma\left[W_t - W_s\right]\right\}$$

in order to derive the transition density $p(s, y; t, x)$ of GBM. Check that this density satisfies the Fokker-Planck equation in Example 5.14.

5.8 Notes

All the results in this chapter are standard and can be found in Karatzas and Shreve (2008), Revuz and Yor (1991) and Øksendal (1998). For an encyclopedic treatment of the probabilistic approach to parabolic PDEs see Doob (1984).

6

PORTFOLIO DYNAMICS

6.1 Introduction

Let us consider a financial market consisting of different assets such as stocks, bonds with different maturities, or various kinds of financial derivatives. In this chapter we will take the price dynamics of the various assets as given, and the main objetive is that of deriving the dynamics of (the value of) a so-called **self-financing** portfolio. In continuous time this turns out to be a fairly delicate task, so we start by studying a model in discrete time. We will then let the length of the time step tend to zero, thus obtaining the continuous time analogs. It is to be stressed that this entire section is only motivating and heuristic. The formal definitions and the corresponding theory will be given in the next section.

Let us thus study a financial market, where time is divided into periods of length Δt, and where trading only takes place at the discrete points in time $n\Delta t$, $n = 0, 1, \ldots$. We consider a fixed period $[t, t + \Delta t)$. This period (where of course $t = n\Delta t$ for some n) is henceforth referred to as "period t". In the sequel we will assume that all assets are stocks, but this is purely for linguistic convenience.

Definition 6.1

> $N =$ the number of different types of stocks.
>
> $h_i(t) =$ number of shares of type i held during the period $[t, t + \Delta t)$.
>
> $h(t) =$ the portfolio $[h_1(t), \ldots, h_N(t)]$ held during period t.
>
> $c(t) =$ the amount of money spent on consumption per unit time during the period $[t, t + \Delta t)$.
>
> $S_i(t) =$ the price of one share of type i during the period $[t, t + \Delta t)$.
>
> $V(t) =$ the value of the portfolio h at time t.

The information and the decisions in the model are structured as follows.

- At time t, i.e. at the **start** of period t, we bring with us an "old" portfolio $h(t - \Delta t) = \{h_i(t - \Delta t), i = 1, \ldots, N\}$ from the previous period $t - \Delta t$.
- At time t we can observe the price vector $S(t) = (S_1(t), \ldots, S_N(t))$.
- At time t, after having observed $S(t)$, we choose a new portfolio $h(t)$, to be held during period t. At the same time we also choose the consumption rate $c(t)$ for the period t. Both $h(t)$ and $c(t)$ are assumed to be constant over the period t.

Remark 6.1.1 Note that, so far, we only consider **nondividend paying** assets. The case of dividend paying assets is slightly more complicated, and since it will only be used in Chapter 16, we omit it from our main discussion. See Section 6.3 below for details.

We will only consider so called **self-financing** portfolio–consumption pairs (h, c), i.e. portfolios with no exogenous infusion or withdrawal of money (apart of course from the c-term). In other words, the purchase of a new portfolio, as well as all consumption, must be financed solely by selling assets already in the portfolio.

To start the analysis we observe that our wealth $V(t)$, i.e. the wealth at the **start** of period t, equals the value of the old portfolio $h(t - \Delta t)$. Thus we have

$$V(t) = \sum_{i=1}^{N} h_i(t - \Delta t) S_i(t) = h(t - \Delta t) S(t), \qquad (6.1)$$

where we have used the notation

$$xy = \sum_{i=1}^{N} x_i y_i$$

for the inner product in R^N. Equation (6.1) simply says that at the beginning of period t our wealth equals what we get if we sell our old portfolio at today's prices. We may now use the proceeds of this sale for two purposes.

- Reinvest in a new portfolio $h(t)$.
- Consume at the rate $c(t)$ over the period t.

The cost of the new portfolio $h(t)$, which has to be bought at today's prices, is given by

$$\sum_{i=1}^{N} h_i(t) S_i(t) = h(t) S(t),$$

whereas the cost for the consumption rate $c(t)$ is given by $c(t)\Delta t$. The budget equation for period t thus reads

$$h(t - \Delta t) S(t) = h(t) S(t) + c(t)\Delta t. \qquad (6.2)$$

If we introduce the notation

$$\Delta X(t) = X(t) - X(t - \Delta t),$$

for an arbitrary process X, we see that the budget equation (6.2) reads

$$S(t)\Delta h(t) + c(t)\Delta t = 0. \qquad (6.3)$$

Since our goal is to obtain the budget equation in continuous time it is now tempting to let $\Delta t \to 0$ in eqn (6.3) to obtain the formal expression

$$S(t)dh(t) + c(t)dt = 0.$$

This procedure is, however, **not** correct, and it is important to understand why that is so. The reasons are as follows.

- All stochastic differentials are to be interpreted in the Itô sense.
- The Itô integral $\int g(t)dW(t)$ was defined as the limit of sums of the type

$$\sum g(t_n) \left[W(t_{n+1}) - W(t_n) \right],$$

where it was essential that the W-increments were **forward** differences.
- In eqn (6.3) we have a **backward** h-difference.

In order to get Itô differentials we thus have to reformulate eqn (6.3). This is done by adding and subtracting the term $S(t - \Delta t)\Delta h(t)$ to the left-hand side, and the budget equation now reads

$$S(t - \Delta t)\Delta h(t) + \Delta S(t)\Delta h(t) + c(t)\Delta t = 0. \tag{6.4}$$

Now, at last, we may let $\Delta t \to 0$ in the budget eqn (6.4), giving us

$$S(t)dh(t) + dh(t)dS(t) + c(t)dt = 0. \tag{6.5}$$

Letting $\Delta t \to 0$ in eqn (6.1) gives us

$$V(t) = h(t)S(t), \tag{6.6}$$

and if we take the Itô differential of this expression we get

$$dV(t) = h(t)dS(t) + S(t)dh(t) + dS(t)dh(t). \tag{6.7}$$

To sum up, eqn (6.7) is the general equation for the dynamics of an arbitrary portfolio, and eqn (6.5) is the budget equation which holds for all self-financing portfolios. Substituting (6.5) into (6.7) thus gives us our desired object, namely the dynamics of (the wealth of) a self-financing portfolio.

$$dV(t) = h(t)dS(t) - c(t)dt. \tag{6.8}$$

In particular we see that in a situation without any consumption we have the following V-dynamics.

$$dV(t) = h(t)dS(t). \tag{6.9}$$

Remark 6.1.2 The natural economic interpretation of eqn (6.9) is of course that in a model without any exogenous income, all change of wealth is due to changes in asset prices. Thus (6.8) and (6.9) seem to be rather self-evident, and one may think that our derivation was rather unneccesary. This is, however, not the case, which we realize if we recall that the stochastic differentials in (6.8) and (6.9) are to be interpreted in the Itô sense, where it is important that the integrator increment $dS(t)$ is a **forward** increment. If we had chosen to define our stochastic integral in some other way, e.g. by using **backward** increments (this can actually be done), the formal **appearance** of (6.8)–(6.9) would have been quite different. The real **content**, on the other hand, would of course have been the same.

6.2 Self-financing Portfolios

Having gone through the derivations of the preceding section there are some natural questions.

1. In which sense (L^2, P-a.s., etc.) is the limiting procedure of letting $\Delta t \to 0$ to be interpreted?
2. Equation (6.8) is supposed to be describing the dynamics of a self-financing portfolio in continuous time, but what is "continuous time trading" supposed to mean "in reality"?

The answer to these questions is simply that the preceding reasoning has only been of a motivating nature. We now give a purely mathematical **definition** of the central concepts. The interpretations of the concepts are of course those of the preceding section.

Definition 6.2 *Let the N-dimensional price process $\{S(t); t \geq 0\}$ be given.*

1. *A **portfolio strategy** (most often simply called a portfolio) is any $\mathcal{F}_t^S$-adapted N-dimensional process $\{h(t); t \geq 0\}$.*
2. *The portfolio h is said to be **Markovian** if it is of the form*
$$h(t) = h(t, S(t)),$$
for some function $h : R_+ \times R^N \to R^N$.
3. *The **value process** V^h corresponding to the portfolio h is given by*
$$V^h(t) = \sum_{i=1}^{N} h_i(t) S_i(t). \tag{6.10}$$
4. *A **consumption process** is any $\mathcal{F}_t^S$-adapted one-dimensional process $\{c(t); t \geq 0\}$.*
5. *A portfolio–consumption pair (h, c) is called **self-financing** if the value process V^h satisfies the condition*
$$dV^h(t) = \sum_{i=1}^{N} h_i(t) dS_i(t) - c(t) dt, \tag{6.11}$$

i.e. if
$$dV^h(t) = h(t)dS(t) - c(t)dt.$$

Remark 6.2.1 Note that, in general, the portfolio $h(t)$ is allowed to depend upon the entire past price trajectory $\{S(u); u \le t\}$. In the sequel we will almost exclusively be dealing with Markovian portfolios, i.e. those portfolios for which the value at time t depends only on today's date t and today's value of the price vector $S(t)$.

For computational purposes it is often convenient to describe a portfolio in relative terms instead of in absolute terms as above. In other words, instead of specifying the absolute number of shares held of a certain stock, we specify the relative proportion of the total portfolio value which is invested in the stock.

Definition 6.3 *For a given portfolio h the corresponding* **relative portfolio** *u is given by*

$$u_i(t) = \frac{h_i(t)S_i(t)}{V^h(t)}, \quad i = 1, \dots, N, \tag{6.12}$$

where we have

$$\sum_{i=1}^{N} u_i(t) = 1.$$

The self-financing condition can now easily be given in terms of the relative portfolio.

Lemma 6.4 *A portfolio–consumption pair (h, c) is self-financing if and only if*

$$dV^h(t) = V^h(t) \sum_{i=1}^{N} u_i(t) \frac{dS_i(t)}{S_i(t)} - c(t)dt. \tag{6.13}$$

In the future we will need the following slightly technical result which roughly says that if a process **looks** as if it is the value process of a self-financing portfolio, then it actually **is** such a value process.

Lemma 6.5 *Let c be a consumption process, and assume that there exist a scalar process Z and a vector process $q = (q_1, \dots, q_N)$ such that*

$$dZ(t) = Z(t) \sum_{i=1}^{N} q_i(t) \frac{dS_i(t)}{S_i(t)} - c(t)dt, \tag{6.14}$$

$$\sum_{i=1}^{N} q_i(t) = 1. \tag{6.15}$$

Now define a portfolio h by

$$h_i(t) = \frac{q_i(t)Z(t)}{S_i(t)}. \tag{6.16}$$

Then the value process V^h is given by $V^h = Z$, the pair (h, c) is self-financing, and the corresponding relative portfolio u is given by $u = q$.

Proof By definition the value process V^h is given by $V^h(t) = h(t)S(t)$, so eqns (6.15) and (6.16) give us

$$V^h(t) = \sum_{i=1}^{N} h_i(t)S_i(t) = \sum_{i=1}^{N} q_i(t)Z(t) = Z(t)\sum_{i=1}^{N} q_i(t) = Z(t). \qquad (6.17)$$

Inserting (6.17) into (6.16) we see that the relative portfolio u corresponding to h is given by $u = q$. Inserting (6.17) and (6.16) into (6.14) we obtain

$$dV^h(t) = \sum_{i=1}^{N} h_i(t)dS_i(t) - c(t)dt,$$

which shows that (h, c) is self-financing. $\qquad \square$

6.3 Dividends

This section is only needed for Chapter 16. We again consider the setup and notation of Section 6.1, with the addition that the assets now may pay dividends.

Definition 6.6 *We take as given the processes $D_1(t), \ldots, D_N(t)$, where $D_i(t)$ denotes the* **cumulative dividends** *paid to the holder of one unit of asset i during the interval $(0, t]$. If D_i has the structure*

$$dD_i(t) = \delta_i(t)dt,$$

for some process δ_i, then we say that asset i pays a continuous **dividend yield***.*

The dividends paid to the holder of one unit of asset i during $(s, t]$ are thus given by $D_i(t) - D_i(s)$, and in the case of a dividend yield we have

$$D_i(t) = \int_0^t \delta_i(s)ds.$$

We assume that all the dividend processes have stochastic differentials.

We now go on to derive the dynamics of a self-financing portfolio, and as usual we define the value process V by

$$V(t) = h(t)S(t).$$

The difference between the present situation and the nondividend paying case is that the budget equation (6.2) now has to be modified. We have to take into account the fact that the money at our disposal at time t now consists of two terms.

- The value of our old portfolio, as usual given by

$$h(t - \Delta t)S(t).$$

- The dividends earned during the interval $(t - \Delta t, t]$. These are given by

$$\sum_{i=1}^{N} h_i(t - \Delta t)[D_i(t) - D_i(t - \Delta t)] = h(t - \Delta t)\Delta D(t).$$

The relevant budget equation is thus given by

$$h(t - \Delta t)S(t) + h(t - \Delta t)\Delta D(t) = h(t)S(t) + c(t)\Delta t. \tag{6.18}$$

Going through the same arguments as in Section 6.1 we end up with the following dynamics for a self-financing portfolio

$$dV(t) = \sum_{i=1}^{N} h_i(t)dS_i(t) + \sum_{i=1}^{N} h_i(t)dD_i(t) - c(t)dt,$$

and we write this as a formal definition.

Definition 6.7

1. *The* **value process** V^h *is given by*

$$V^h(t) = \sum_{i=1}^{N} h_i(t)S_i(t). \tag{6.19}$$

2. *The (vector valued)* **gain process** G *is defined by*

$$G(t) = S(t) + D(t). \tag{6.20}$$

3. *The portfolio–consumption pair* (h, c) *is called* **self-financing** *if*

$$dV^h(t) = \sum_{i=1}^{N} h_i(t)dG_i(t) - c(t)dt. \tag{6.21}$$

With notation as above we have the following obvious result.

Lemma 6.8 *In terms of the relative portfolio weights, the dynamics of a self-financing portfolio can be expressed as*

$$dV^h(t) = V(t) \cdot \sum_{i=1}^{N} u_i(t) \frac{dG_i(t)}{S_i(t)} - c(t)dt \qquad (6.22)$$

6.4   Exercises

Exercise 6.1 Work out the details in the derivation of the dynamics of a self-financing portfolio in the dividend paying case.

7

ARBITRAGE PRICING

7.1 Introduction

In this chapter we will study a special case of the general model set out in the previous chapter. We will basically follow the arguments of Merton (1973), which only require the mathematical machinery presented in the previous chpaters. For the full story see Chapter 10.

Let us therefore consider a financial market consisting of only two assets: a risk free asset with price process B, and a stock with price process S. What, then, is a risk free asset?

Definition 7.1 *The price process B is the price of a **risk free** asset if it has the dynamics*

$$dB(t) = r(t)B(t)dt, \qquad (7.1)$$

where r is any adapted process.

The defining property of a risk free asset is thus that it has no driving dW-term. We see that we also can write the B-dynamics as

$$\frac{dB(t)}{dt} = r(t)B(t),$$

so the B-process is given by the expression

$$B(t) = B(0)\exp\int_0^t r(s)ds.$$

A natural interpretation of a riskless asset is that it corresponds to a bank with the (possibly stochastic) **short rate of interest** r. An important special case appears when r is a deterministic constant, in which case we can interpret B as the price of a bond.

We assume that the stock price S is given by

$$dS(t) = S(t)\alpha\,(t, S(t))\,dt + S(t)\sigma\,(t, S(t))\,d\bar{W}(t), \qquad (7.2)$$

where $\bar{W}$ is a Wiener process and α and σ are given deterministic functions. The reason for the notation $\bar{W}$, instead of the simpler W, will become clear below. The function σ is known as the **volatility** of S, while α is the **local mean rate of return** of S.

Remark 7.1.1 Note the difference between the risky stock price S, as modeled above, and the riskless asset B. The rate of return of B is formally given by

$$\frac{dB(t)}{B(t) \cdot dt} = r(t)$$

This object is **locally deterministic** in the sense that, at time t, we have complete knowledge of the return by simply observing the prevailing short rate $r(t)$. Compare this to the rate of return on the stock S. This is formally given by

$$\frac{dS(t)}{S(t) \cdot dt} = \alpha\left(t, S(t)\right) + \sigma\left(t, S(t)\right) \frac{d\bar{W}(t)}{dt},$$

and this is **not** observable at time t. It consists of the terms $\alpha\left(t, S(t)\right)$ and $\sigma\left(t, S(t)\right)$, which both are observable at time t, plus the "white noise" term $d\bar{W}(t)/dt$, which is random. Thus: as opposed to the risk free asset, the stock has a **stochastic rate of return**, even on the infinitesimal scale.

The most important special case of the above model occurs when r, α and σ are deterministic constants. This is the famous **Black–Scholes model**.

Definition 7.2 *The* **Black–Scholes model** *consists of two assets with dynamics given by*

$$dB(t) = rB(t)dt, \tag{7.3}$$
$$dS(t) = \alpha S(t)dt + \sigma S(t)d\bar{W}(t), \tag{7.4}$$

where r, α and σ are deterministic constants.

7.2 Contingent Claims and Arbitrage

We take as given the model of a financial market given by eqns (7.1)–(7.2), and we now approach the main problem to be studied in this book, namely the pricing of financial derivatives. Later we will give a mathematical definition, but let us at once present the single most important derivative—the European call option.

Definition 7.3 *A* **European call option** *with* **exercise price** *(or strike price) K and* **time of maturity** *(exercise date) T on the* **underlying asset** *S is a contract defined by the following clauses.*

- *The holder of the option has, at time T, the right to buy one share of the underlying stock at the price K SEK from the underwriter of the option.*
- *The holder of the option is in no way obliged to buy the underlying stock.*
- *The right to buy the underlying stock at the price K can only be exercised at the precise time T.*

Note that the exercise price K and the time of maturity T are determined at the time when the option is written, which for us typically will be at $t = 0$. A **European put option** is an option which in the same way gives the holder the right to **sell** a share of the underlying asset at a predetermined strike price. For an **American call option** the right to buy a share of the underlying asset can be exercised at any time before the given time of maturity. The common factor of all these contracts is that they all are completely defined in terms of the underlying asset S, which makes it natural to call them **derivative instruments** or **contingent claims**. We will now give the formal definition of a contingent claim.

Definition 7.4 *Consider a financial market with vector price process S. A **contingent claim** with **date of maturity** (exercise date) T, also called a T-claim, is any stochastic variable $\mathcal{X} \in \mathcal{F}_T^S$. A contingent claim $\mathcal{X}$ is called a **simple claim** if it is of the form*

$$\mathcal{X} = \Phi(S(T)).$$ *The function Φ is called the **contract function**.*

The interpretation of this definition is that a contingent claim is a contract, which stipulates that the holder of the contract will obtain $\mathcal{X}$ SEK (which can be positive or negative) at the time of maturity T. The requirement that $\mathcal{X} \in \mathcal{F}_T^S$ simply means that, at time T, it will actually be possible to determine the amount of money to be paid out. We see that the European call is a simple contingent claim, for which the contract function is given by

$$\Phi(x) = \max\left[x - K, 0\right].$$

The graphs of the contract functions for European calls and puts can be seen in Figs 7.1–7.2. It is obvious that a contingent claim, e.g. like a European call option, is a financial asset which will fetch a price on the market. Exactly how much the option is worth on the market will of course depend on the time t and on the price $S(t)$ of the underlying stock. Our main problem is to determine a "fair" (in some sense) price for the claim, and we will use the standard notation

$$\Pi\left(t; \mathcal{X}\right), \tag{7.5}$$

for the price process of the claim $\mathcal{X}$, where we sometimes suppress the $\mathcal{X}$. In the case of a simple claim we will sometimes write $\Pi\left(t; \Phi\right)$.

If we start at time T the situation is simple. Let us first look at the particular case of a European call.

1. If $S(T) \geq K$ we can make a certain profit by exercising the option in order to buy one share of the underlying stock. This will cost us K SEK.

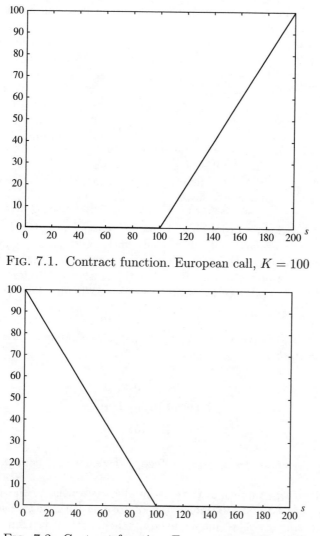

FIG. 7.1. Contract function. European call, $K = 100$

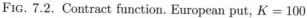

FIG. 7.2. Contract function. European put, $K = 100$

Then we immediately sell the asset on the stock exchange at the price $S(T)$, thus giving us a net profit of $S(T) - K$ SEK.

2. If $S(T) < K$ the option has no value whatsoever.

Thus we see that the only reasonable price $\Pi(T)$ for the option at time T is given by

$$\Pi(T) = \max[S(T) - K, 0]. \tag{7.6}$$

In exactly the same way we see that for a more general contingent claim $\mathcal{X}$ we have the relation

$$\Pi(T;\mathcal{X}) = \mathcal{X}, \tag{7.7}$$

and in the particular case of a simple claim

$$\Pi(T;\mathcal{X}) = \Phi(S(T)). \tag{7.8}$$

For any time $t < T$ it is, however, far from obvious what the correct price is for a claim $\mathcal{X}$. On the contrary it seems to be obvious that there is no such thing as a "correct" or "fair" price. The price of an option, like the price of any other asset, is of course determined on the (option) market, and should therefore be an extremely complex aggregate of, for example, the various attitudes to risk on the market and expectations about the future stock prices. It is therefore an extremely surprising fact that, given some fairly mild assumptions, there is a formula (the Black–Scholes formula) which gives the unique price of the option. The main assumption we will make is that the market is **efficient** in the sense that it is **free of arbitrage possibilities**. We now define this new and central concept.

Definition 7.5 *An* **arbitrage** *possibility on a financial market is a self-financed portfolio h such that*

$$V^h(0) = 0, \tag{7.9}$$
$$P\left(V^h(T) \geq 0\right) = 1. \tag{7.10}$$
$$P\left(V^h(T) > 0\right) > 0. \tag{7.11}$$

We say that the market is **arbitrage free** *if there are no arbitrage possibilities.*

An arbitrage possibility is thus essentially equivalent to the possibility of making a positive amount of money out of nothing without taking any risk. It is thus essentially a riskless money making machine or, if you will, a free lunch on the financial market. We interpet an arbitrage possibility as a serious case of mispricing in the market, and our main assumption is that the market is efficient in the sense that no arbitrage is possible.

Assumption 7.2.1 *We assume that the price process $\Pi(t)$ is such that there are no arbitrage possibilities on the market consisting of $(B(t),\ S(t),\ \Pi(t))$.*

A natural question now is how we can identify an arbitrage possibility. The general answer to this question requires quite a lot of fairly heavy probabilistic machinery which the more advanced reader will find in Chapter 10. Happily enough there is a partial result which is sufficient for our present purposes.

Proposition 7.6 *Suppose that there exists a self-financed portfolio* h, *such that the value process* V^h *has the dynamics*

$$dV^h(t) = k(t)V^h(t)dt, \qquad (7.12)$$

where k *is an adapted process. Then it must hold that* $k(t) = r(t)$ *for all* t, *or there exists an arbitrage possibility.*

Proof We sketch the argument, and assume for simplicity that k and r are constant and that $k > r$. Then we can borrow money from the bank at the rate r. This money is immediately invested in the portfolio strategy h where it will grow at the rate k with $k > r$. Thus the net investment at $t = 0$ is zero, whereas our wealth at any time $t > 0$ will be positive. In other words we have an arbitrage. If on the other hand $r > k$, we sell the portfolio h short and invest this money in the bank, and again there is an arbitrage. The cases with nonconstant and nondeterministic r and k are handled in the same way. □

The main point of the above is that if a portfolio has a value process whose dynamics contain no driving Wiener process, i.e. a **locally riskless porfolio**, then the rate of return of that portfolio must equal the short rate of interest. To put it in another way, the existence of a portfolio h is for practical purposes equivalent to the existence of a bank with k as its short rate of interest. We can then paraphrase the lemma above by saying that on an arbitrage free market there can only be one short rate of interest.

We now return to the question of how the price process $\Pi(t; \mathcal{X})$ for a contingent claim $\mathcal{X}$ can behave, and the main idea is the following. Since the claim is **defined** entirely in terms of the underlying asset(s), we ought to be able to **price** it in terms of the price of the underlying asset(s) if arbitrage possibilities are to be avoided. Thus we are looking for a way to price the derivative in a way which is **consistent** with the price process of the underlying asset.

To take a simple example, it is quite obvious that for a European call we must have the relation $\Pi(t) \leq S(t)$ in an arbitrage free market, because no one in their right mind will buy an option to buy a share at a later date at price K if the share itself can be bought cheaper than the option. For a more formal argument, suppose that at some time t we actually have the relation $\Pi(t) > S(t)$. Then we simply sell one option. A part of that money can be used for buying the underlying stock and the rest is invested in the bank (i.e. we buy the riskless asset). Then we sit down and do nothing until time T. In this way we have created a self-financed portfolio with zero net investment at time t. At time T we will owe $\max[S(T) - K, 0]$ to the holder of the option, but this money can be paid by selling the stock. Our net wealth at time T will thus be $S(T) - \max[S(T) - K, 0]$, which is positive, plus the money invested in the bank. Thus we have an arbitrage.

It is thus clear that the requirement of an arbitrage free market will impose some restrictions on the behavior of the price process $\Pi(t; \mathcal{X})$. This in itself is not terribly surprising. What is surprising is the fact that in the market specified by eqns (7.1)–(7.2) these restrictions are so strong as to completely specify, for any given claim $\mathcal{X}$, the unique price process $\Pi\,(t;\mathcal{X})$ which is consistent with absence of arbitrage. For the case of **simple** contingent claims the formal argument will be given in the next section, but we will now give the general idea.

To start with, it seems reasonable to assume that the price $\Pi\,(t;\mathcal{X})$ at time t in some way is determined by expectations about the future stock price $S(T)$. Since S is a Markov process such expectations are in their turn based on the present value of the price process (rather than on the entire trajectory on $[0,t]$). We thus make the following assumption.

Assumption 7.2.2 *We assume that*

1. *The derivative instrument in question can be bought and sold on a market.*
2. *The market is free of arbitrage.*
3. *The price process for the derivative asset is of the form*

$$\Pi\,(t;\mathcal{X}) = F(t, S(t)), \tag{7.13}$$

where F is some smooth function.

Our task is to determine what F might look like if the market consisting of $S(t)$, $B(t)$ and $\Pi\,(t;\mathcal{X})$ is arbitrage free. Schematically we will proceed in the following manner.

1. Consider α, σ, Φ, F and r as exogenously given.
2. Use the general results from Section 6.2 to describe the dynamics of the value of a hypothetical self-financed portfolio based on the derivative instrument and the underlying stock (nothing will actually be invested in or loaned by the bank).
3. It turns out that, by a clever choice, we can form a self-financed portfolio whose value process has a stochastic differential without any driving Wiener process. It will thus be of the form (7.12) above.
4. Since we have assumed absence of arbitrage we must have $k = r$.
5. The condition $k = r$ will in fact have the form of a partial differential equation with F as the unknown function. In order for the market to be efficient F must thus solve this PDE.
6. The equation has a unique solution, thus giving us the unique pricing formula for the derivative, which is consistent with absence of arbitrage.

7.3   The Black–Scholes Equation

In this section we will carry through the schematic argument given in the previous section. We assume that the a priori given market consists of two assets with dynamics given by

$$dB(t) = rB(t)dt, \tag{7.14}$$

$$dS(t) = S(t)\alpha\,(t, S(t))\,dt + S(t)\sigma\,(t, S(t))\,d\bar{W}(t), \tag{7.15}$$

where the short rate of interest r is a deterministic constant. We consider a simple contingent claim of the form

$$\mathcal{X} = \Phi(S(T)), \tag{7.16}$$

and we assume that this claim can be traded on a market and that its price process $\Pi(t) = \Pi(t; \Phi)$ has the form

$$\Pi(t) = F(t, S(t)), \tag{7.17}$$

for some smooth function F. Our problem is to find out what F must look like in order for the market $[S(t), B(t), \Pi(t)]$ to be free of arbitrage possibilities.

We start by computing the price dynamics of the derivative asset, and the Itô formula applied to (7.17) and (7.15) gives us

$$d\Pi(t) = \alpha_\pi(t)\Pi(t)\,dt + \sigma_\pi(t)\Pi(t)\,d\bar{W}(t), \tag{7.18}$$

where the processes $\alpha_\pi(t)$ and $\sigma_\pi(t)$ are defined by

$$\alpha_\pi(t) = \frac{F_t + \alpha S F_s + \frac{1}{2}\sigma^2 S^2 F_{ss}}{F}, \tag{7.19}$$

$$\sigma_\pi(t) = \frac{\sigma S F_s}{F}. \tag{7.20}$$

Here subscripts denote partial derivatives, and we have used a shorthand notation of the form

$$\frac{\sigma S F_s}{F} = \frac{\sigma(t, S(t))S(t)F_s(t, S(t))}{F(t, S(t))},$$

and similarly for the other terms above.

Let us now form a portfolio based on two assets: the underlying stock and the derivative asset. Denoting the relative portfolio by (u_s, u_π) and using eqn (6.13) we obtain the following dynamics for the value V of the portfolio.

$$dV = V\left\{u_s\left[\alpha dt + \sigma d\bar{W}\right] + u_\pi\left[\alpha_\pi dt + \sigma_\pi d\bar{W}\right]\right\} \tag{7.21}$$

where we have suppressed t. We now collect dt- and $d\bar{W}$-terms to obtain

$$dV = V\left[u_s\alpha + u_\pi\alpha_\pi\right]dt + V\left[u_s\sigma + u_\pi\sigma_\pi\right]d\bar{W}. \tag{7.22}$$

The point to notice here is that both brackets above are linear in the arguments u_s and u_π. Recall furthermore that the only restriction on the relative portfolio is that we must have

$$u_s + u_\pi = 1,$$

for all t. Let us thus define the relative portfolio by the linear system of equations

$$u_s + u_\pi = 1, \tag{7.23}$$
$$u_s\sigma + u_\pi\sigma_\pi = 0. \tag{7.24}$$

Using this portfolio we see that by its very definition the driving $d\bar{W}$-term in the V-dynamics of eqn (7.22) vanishes completely, leaving us with the equation

$$dV = V\left[u_s\alpha + u_\pi\alpha_\pi\right]dt. \tag{7.25}$$

Thus we have obtained a locally riskless portfolio, and because of the requirement that the market is free of arbitrage, we may now use Proposition 7.6 to deduce that we must have the relation

$$u_s\alpha + u_\pi\alpha_\pi = r. \tag{7.26}$$

This is thus the condition for absence of arbitrage, and we will now look more closely at this equation.

It is easily seen that the system (7.23)–(7.24) has the solution

$$u_s = \frac{\sigma_\pi}{\sigma_\pi - \sigma}, \tag{7.27}$$

$$u_\pi = \frac{-\sigma}{\sigma_\pi - \sigma}, \tag{7.28}$$

which, using (7.20), gives us the portfolio more explicitly as

$$u_s(t) = \frac{S(t)F_s(t, S(t))}{S(t)F_s(t, S(t)) - F(t, S(t))}, \tag{7.29}$$

$$u_\pi(t) = \frac{-F(t, S(t))}{S(t)F_s(t, S(t)) - F(t, S(t))}. \tag{7.30}$$

Now we substitute (7.19), (7.29) and (7.30) into the absence of arbitrage condition (7.26). Then, after some calculations, we obtain the equation

$$F_t(t, S(t)) + rS(t)F_s(t, S(t)) + \frac{1}{2}\sigma^2(t, S(t))S^2(t)F_{ss}(t, S(t)) - rF(t, S(t)) = 0.$$

Furthermore, from the previous section we must have the relation

$$\Pi(T) = \Phi(S(T)).$$

These two equations have to hold with probability 1 for each fixed t. Furthermore it can be shown that under very weak assumptions (which trivially are satisfied in the Black–Scholes model) the distribution of $S(t)$ for every fixed $t > 0$ has support on the entire positive real line. Thus $S(t)$ can take any value whatsoever, so F has to satisfy the following (deterministic) PDE.

$$F_t(t, s) + rsF_s(t, s) + \frac{1}{2}s^2\sigma^2(t, s)F_{ss}(t, s) - rF(t, s) = 0,$$

$$F(T, s) = \Phi(s).$$

Summing up these results we have proved the following proposition, which is in fact one of the most central results in the book.

Theorem 7.7 (Black–Scholes Equation) *Assume that the market is speci-fied by eqns (7.14)–(7.15) and that we want to price a contingent claim of the form (7.16). Then the only pricing function of the form (7.17) which is con-sistent with the absence of arbitrage is when F is the solution of the following boundary value problem in the domain $[0, T] \times R_+$.*

$$F_t(t, s) + rsF_s(t, s) + \frac{1}{2}s^2\sigma^2(t, s)F_{ss}(t, s) - rF(t, s) = 0, \qquad (7.31)$$

$$F(T, s) = \Phi(s). \qquad (7.32)$$

Before we go on to a closer study of the pricing equation (7.31) let us make a few comments.

Firstly it is important to stress the fact that we have obtained the price of the claim $\mathcal{X}$ in the form $\Pi(t; \mathcal{X}) = F(t, S(t))$, i.e. the price of the claim is given as a function of the price of the underlying asset S. This is completely in line with the basic idea explained earlier, that the pricing of derivative assets is a question of pricing the derivative in a way which is **consistent** with the price of the underlying asset. We are thus **not** presenting an **absolute** pricing formula for $\mathcal{X}$. On the contrary, derivative pricing is all about **relative** pricing, i.e. pricing the derivative asset **in terms of** the price of the underlying asset. In particular this means that in order to use the technique of arbitrage pricing at all we must have one or several underlying price processes given a priori.

Secondly a word of criticism. At a first glance our derivation of the pricing equation (7.31) seems to be fairly convincing, but in fact it contains some rather weak points. The logic of the argument was that we **assumed** that the price of the derivative was a function F of t and $S(t)$. Using this assumption we then showed that in an arbitrage free market F had to satisfy the Black–Scholes equation. The question now is if we really have good reasons to assume that the price is of the form $F(t, S(t))$. The Markovian argument given above sounds good, but it is not totally convincing.

A much more serious objection is that we assume that there actually exists a market for the derivative asset, and in particular that there exists a price process for the derivative. This assumption of an existing market for the derivative is crucial for the argument since we are actually constructing a portfolio based on the derivative (and the underlying asset). If the derivative is not traded then the portfolio cannot be formed and our argument breaks down. The assumption of an existing price for the derivative is of course innocent enough in the case of a standard derivative, like a European call option, which *de facto* is traded in large volumes. If, however, we want to price an OTC ("over the counter") instrument, i.e. an instrument which is not traded on a regular basis, then we seem to be in big trouble.

Happily enough there is an alternative argument for the derivation of the pricing equation (7.31), and this argument (which will be given below) is not open to the criticism above. The bottom line is that the reader can feel safe: equation (7.31) really is the "correct" equation.

Let us end by noting an extremely surprising fact about the pricing equation, namely that it does not contain the local mean rate of return $\alpha(t, s)$ of the underlying asset. In particular this means that, when it comes to pricing derivatives, the local rate of return of the underlying asset plays no role whatsoever. The only aspect of the underlying price process which is of any importance is the volatility $\sigma(t, s)$. Thus, for a given volatility, the price of a fixed derivative (like a European call option) will be exactly the same regardless of whether the underlying stock has a 10%, a 50%, or even a -50% rate of return. At a first glance this sounds highly counter-intuitive and one is tempted to doubt the whole procedure of arbitrage pricing. There is, however, a natural explanation for this phenomenon, and we will come back to it later. At this point we can only say that the phenomenon is closely connected to the fact that we are pricing the derivative in terms of the price of the underlying asset.

7.4   Risk Neutral Valuation

Let us again consider a market given by the equations

$$dB(t) = rB(t)dt, \tag{7.33}$$
$$dS(t) = S(t)\alpha\,(t, S(t))\,dt + S(t)\sigma\,(t, S(t))\,d\bar{W}(t), \tag{7.34}$$

and a contingent claim of the form $\mathcal{X} = \Phi(S(T))$. Then we know that the arbitrage free price is given by $\Pi\,(t; \Phi) = F(t, S(t))$ where the function F is the solution of the pricing equation (7.31)–(7.32). We now turn to the question of actually solving the pricing equation and we notice that this equation is precisely of the form which can be solved using a stochastic representation formula à la Feynman–Kač. Using the results from Section 5.5 we see that the solution is given by

$$F(t, s) = e^{-r(T-t)}E^{t,s}\left[\Phi(X(T))\right], \tag{7.35}$$

where the X process is defined by the dynamics

$$dX(u) = rX(u)d(u) + X(u)\sigma(u, X(u))dW(u), \tag{7.36}$$
$$X(t) = s, \tag{7.37}$$

where W is a Wiener process. The important point to note here is that the SDE (7.36) is of precisely the same form as that of the price process S. The only, but important, change is that whereas S has the local rate of return α, the X-process has the short rate of interest r as its local rate of return.

The X-process above is logically just a technical tool, defined for the moment, and in particular we can name it as we please. In view of the resemblance between X and S it is rather tempting to call it S instead of X. This is perfectly acceptable as long as we do not confuse the "real" S-process of (7.34) with the "new" S-process, and one way to achieve this goal is by the following procedure.

Let us agree to denote the "objective" probability measure which governs our real model (7.33)–(7.34) by the letter P. Thus we say that the P-dynamics of the S-process are that of (7.34). We now define another probability measure Q under which the S-process has a different probability distribution. This is done by defining the Q-dynamics of S as

$$dS(t) = rS(t)dt + S(t)\sigma\left(t, S(t)\right) dW(t), \tag{7.38}$$

where W is a Q-Wiener process. In order to distinguish the measure under which we take expectations we introduce some notational conventions.

Notational convention 7.4.1 *For the rest of the text, the following conventions will be used.*

- *We identify the expectation operator by letting E denote expectations taken under the P-measure whereas E^Q denotes expectations taken under the Q-measure.*

- *We identify the Wiener process. Thus $\bar{W}$ will denote a P-Wiener process, whereas W will denote a Q-Wiener process.*

The convention on W has the advantage that it is possible, at a glance, to decide under which measure a certain SDE is given. We will work much more often under Q than under P, and this is the reason why the Q-Wiener process W has a simpler notation than the P-Wiener process $\bar{W}$. Using this notation we may now state the following central result for derivative pricing.

Theorem 7.8 (Risk Neutral Valuation) *The arbitrage free price of the claim $\Phi(S(T))$ is given by $\Pi(t; \Phi) = F(t, S(t))$, where F is given by the formula*

$$F(t,s) = e^{-r(T-t)} E^Q_{t,s}\left[\Phi(S(T))\right], \tag{7.39}$$

where the Q-dynamics of S are those of (7.38).

There is a natural economic interpretation of the formula (7.39). We see that the price of the derivative, given today's date t and today's stock price s, is computed by taking the expectation of the final payment $E^Q_{t,s}\left[\Phi(S(T))\right]$ and then discounting this expected value to present value using the discount factor $e^{-r(T-t)}$. The important point to note is that when we take the expected value we are **not** to do this using the objective probability measure P. Instead we shall use the Q-measure defined in (7.38). This Q-measure is sometimes called the **risk adjusted measure** but most often it is called the **martingale measure**, and this will be our terminology. The reason for the name is that under Q the normalized process $\frac{S(t)}{B(t)}$ turns out to be a Q-martingale. In the deeper investigation of arbitrage pricing, which will be undertaken in Chapter 10, the Q-measure is the fundamental object of study. We formulate the martingale property as a separate result.

Proposition 7.9 (The Martingale Property) *In the Black–Scholes model, the price process $\Pi(t)$ for every traded asset, be it the underlying or derivative asset, has the property that the normalized price process*

$$Z(t) = \frac{\Pi(t)}{B(t)}$$

is a martingale under the measure Q.

Proof   See the exercises.   □

The formula (7.39) is sometimes referred to as the formula of **risk neutral valuation**. Suppose that all agents are risk neutral. Then all assets will command a rate of return equal to the short rate of interest, i.e. in a risk neutral world the stock price will actually have the Q-dynamics above (more precisely, in this case we will have $Q = P$). Furthermore, in a risk neutral world the present value of a future stochastic payout will equal the expected value of the net payments discounted to present value using the short rate of interest. Thus formula (7.39) is precisely the kind of formula which would be used for valuing a contingent claim in a risk neutral world. Observe, however, that we do **not** assume that the agents in our model are risk neutral. The formula only says that the value of the contingent claim can be calculated **as if** we live in a risk neutral world. In particular the agents are allowed to have any attitude to risk whatsoever, as long as they all prefer a larger amount of (certain) money to a lesser amount. Thus the valuation formula above is **preference free** in the sense that it is valid regardless of the specific form of the agents' preferences.

7.5   The Black–Scholes Formula

In this section we specialize the model of the previous section to the case of the Black–Scholes model,

$$dB(t) = rB(t)dt, \tag{7.40}$$
$$dS(t) = \alpha S(t)dt + \sigma S(t)d\bar{W}(t), \tag{7.41}$$

where α and σ are constants. From the results of the previous section we know that the arbitrage free price of a simple claim $\Phi(S(T))$ is given by

$$F(t, s) = e^{-r(T-t)} E_{t,s}^{Q} \left[\Phi(S(T)) \right], \tag{7.42}$$

where the Q-dynamics of S are given by

$$dS(u) = rS(u)du + \sigma S(u)dW(u), \qquad (7.43)$$
$$S(t) = s. \qquad (7.44)$$

In this SDE we recognize our old friend geometric Brownian motion from Section 5.2. Using the results from section 5.2 we can thus write $S(T)$ explicitly as

$$S(T) = s \exp \left\{ \left(r - \frac{1}{2}\sigma^2 \right) (T - t) + \sigma \left(W(T) - W(t) \right) \right\}. \qquad (7.45)$$

Thus we have the pricing formula

$$F(t, s) = e^{-r(T-t)} \int_{-\infty}^{\infty} \Phi \left(se^z \right) f(z)dz, \qquad (7.46)$$

where f is the density of a random variable Z with the distribution

$$N \left[\left(r - \frac{1}{2}\sigma^2 \right) (T - t), \sigma\sqrt{T - t} \right].$$

Formula (7.46) is an integral formula which, for a general choice of contract function Φ, must be evaluated numerically. There are, however, a few particular cases where we can evaluate (7.46) more or less analytically, and the best known of these is the case of a European call option, where Φ has the form $\Phi(x) = \max[x - K, 0]$. In this case we obtain

$$E_{t,s}^Q \left[\max \left[se^Z - K, 0 \right] \right] = 0 \cdot Q \left(se^Z \leq K \right) + \int_{\ln\left(\frac{K}{s}\right)}^{\infty} \left(se^z - K \right) f(z)dz. \qquad (7.47)$$

After some standard calculations we are left with the following famous result which is known as the **Black–Scholes formula**.

Proposition 7.10 *The price of a European call option with strike price K and time of maturity T is given by the formula $\Pi(t) = F(t, S(t))$, where*

$$F(t, s) = sN[d_1(t, s)] - e^{-r(T-t)}KN[d_2(t, s)]. \qquad (7.48)$$

Here N is the cumulative distribution function for the $N[0, 1]$ distribution and

$$d_1(t, s) = \frac{1}{\sigma\sqrt{T - t}} \left\{ \ln \left(\frac{s}{K} \right) + \left(r + \frac{1}{2}\sigma^2 \right) (T - t) \right\}, \qquad (7.49)$$
$$d_2(t, s) = d_1(t, s) - \sigma\sqrt{T - t}. \qquad (7.50)$$

Shown in Fig. 7.3 is the graph of the Black–Scholes pricing function (the unit of time is chosen to be one year).

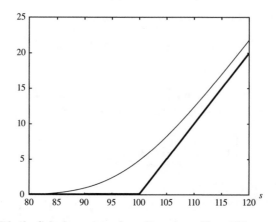

FIG. 7.3. The Black–Scholes price of a call option: $K = 100, \sigma = 0.2, T-t = 0.25$

7.6 Options on Futures

The purpose of this section is to derive the Black formulas for options written on a futures contract. Our discussion here will be rather brief, and for more institutional and technical information the reader is referred to Chapter 29 (and the Notes), where the contracts are discussed in more detail.

7.6.1 Forward Contracts

Consider a standard Black–Scholes model, a simple T-claim $\mathcal{X} = \Phi(S_T)$, and assume that we are standing at time t. A **forward contract** on $\mathcal{X}$, made at t, is a contract which stipulates that the holder of the contract pays the deterministic amount K at the **delivery date** T, and receives the stochastic amount $\mathcal{X}$ at T. Nothing is paid or received at the time t, when the contract is made. Note that **forward price** K is determined already at time t. It is customary to use the notation $K = f(t; T, \mathcal{X})$, and our primary concern is to compute $f(t; T, \mathcal{X})$.

   This is, however, easily done. We see that the entire forward contract is a contingent T-claim Y of the form

$$Y = \mathcal{X} - K,$$

and, by definition, the value of Y at the time t when the contract is made equals zero. Thus we have

$$\Pi\left(t; \mathcal{X} - K\right) = 0,$$

which leads to

$$\Pi\left(t; \mathcal{X}\right) = \Pi\left(t; K\right).$$

Using risk neutral valuation we immediately have $\Pi(t;K) = e^{-r(T-t)}K$ and $\Pi(t;\mathcal{X}) = e^{-r(T-t)} \times E^Q_{t,s}[\mathcal{X}]$, so we have proved the first part of the following result. The second part is left as an exercise.

Proposition 7.11 *The forward price $f(t;T,\mathcal{X})$, contracted at t, on the T-claim $\mathcal{X}$ is given by*

$$f(t;T,\mathcal{X}) = E^Q_{t,s}[\mathcal{X}]. \tag{7.51}$$

In particular, if $\mathcal{X} = S_T$ the corresponding forward price, denoted by $f(t;T)$, is given by

$$f(t;T) = e^{r(T-t)}S_t. \tag{7.52}$$

Remark 7.6.1 Note the difference between the forward price $f(t;T,\mathcal{X})$ which is a sum to be paid at T, for a forward contract entered at time t, and the spot price of the entire forward contract. This latter price is zero at the time t when the contract is made, but at any subsequent time $s > t$ it will typically have a nonzero value.

7.6.2 Futures Contracts and the Black Formula

With the same setup as the previous section we will now discuss a **futures contract** on $\mathcal{X}$. This contract is very close to the corresponding forward contract in the sense that it is still a contract for the delivery of $\mathcal{X}$ at T. The difference is that all the payments, from the holder of the contract to the underwriter, are no longer made at T. Let us denote the futures price by $F(t;T,\mathcal{X})$; the payments are delivered continuously over time, such that the holder of the contract over the time interval $[s, s + \Delta s]$ receives the amount

$$F(s + \Delta s;T,\mathcal{X}) - F(s;T,\mathcal{X})$$

from the underwriter. Finally the holder will receive $\mathcal{X}$, and pay $F(T;T,\mathcal{X})$, at the **delivery date** T. By definition, the (spot) price (at any time) of the entire futures contract equals zero. Thus the cost of entering or leaving a futures contract is zero, and the only contractual obligation is the payment stream described above. See Chapter 29 for more details, and for a proof of the following result.

Proposition 7.12 *If the short rate is deterministic, then the forward and the futures price processes coincide, and we have*

$$F(t;T,\mathcal{X}) = E^Q_{t,s}[\mathcal{X}]. \tag{7.53}$$

We will now study the problem of pricing a European call option, with exercise date T, and exercise price K, on an underlying futures contract. The futures contract is a future on S with delivery date T_1, with $T < T_1$. Options of this kind are traded frequently, and by definition the holder of this option will, at the exercise time T, obtain a long position in the futures contract, plus the stochastic amount

$$\mathcal{X} = \max[F(T;T_1) - K, 0]. \tag{7.54}$$

Since the spot price of the futures contract equals zero, we may, for pricing purposes, forget about the long futures position embedded in the option, and identify the option with the claim in (7.54).

We now go on to price the futures option, and we start by using Proposition 7.12 and eqn (7.52) in order to write

$$\mathcal{X} = e^{r(T_1 - T)} \max[S_T - e^{-r(T_1 - T)} K, 0].$$

Thus we see that the futures option consists of $e^{r(T_1-T)}$ call options on the underlying asset S, with exercise date T and exercise price $e^{-r(T_1-T)}K$. Denoting the price at T of the futures option by c, the stock price at t by s, and the futures price $F(t;T_1)$ by F, we thus have, from the Black–Scholes formula,

$$c = e^{r(T_1 - T)} \left[sN[d_1] - e^{-r(T-t)} e^{-r(T_1 - T)} KN[d_2] \right]$$

where d_1 and d_2 are obtained from the Black–Scholes d_1 and d_2 by replacing k with $e^{-r(T_1-T)}K$. Finally we may substitute $s = Fe^{-r(T_1-t)}$, and simplify, to obtain the so called "Black-76 formula".

Proposition 7.13 (Black's formula) *The price, at t, of a European call option, with exercise date T and exercise price K, on a futures contract (on an underlying asset price S) with delivery date T_1 is given by*

$$c = e^{-r(T-t)} \left[FN[d_1] - KN[d_2] \right], \tag{7.55}$$

where F is the futures price $F = F(T;T_1)$, and

$$d_1 = \frac{\ln\left(\frac{F}{K}\right) + \frac{1}{2}\sigma^2(T-t)}{\sigma\sqrt{T-t}},$$
$$d_2 = d_1 - \sigma\sqrt{T-t}.$$

7.7   Volatility

In order to be able to use the theory derived above in a concrete situation, we need to have numerical estimates of all the input parameters. In the Black–Scholes model the input data consists of the string s, r, T, t and σ. Out of these five parameters, s, r, T and t can be observed directly, which leaves us with the problem of obtaining an estimate of the volatility σ. Here there are two basic approaches, namely to use "historic volatility" or "implied volatility".

7.7.1 *Historic Volatility*

Suppose that we want to value a European call with six months left to maturity. An obvious idea is to use historical stock price data in order to estimate σ. Since, in real life, the volatility is not constant over time, one standard practice is to use historical data for a period of the same length as the time to maturity, which in our case means that we use data for the last six months.

In order to obtain an estimate of σ we assume that we have the standard Black–Scholes GBM model (7.4) under the objective measure P. We sample (observe) the stock price process S at $n + 1$ discrete equidistant points $t_0, t_1, \ldots, t_n$, where Δt denotes the length of the sampling interval, i.e. $\Delta t = t_i - t_{i-1}$.

We thus observe $S(t_0), \ldots, S(t_n)$, and in order to estimate σ we use the fact that S has a log-normal distribution. Let us therefore define $\xi_1, \ldots, \xi_n$ by

$$\xi_i = \ln\left(\frac{S(t_i)}{S(t_{i-1})}\right).$$

From (5.15) we see that $\xi_1, \ldots, \xi_n$ are independent, normally distributed random variables with

$$E\left[\xi_i\right] = \left(\alpha - \frac{1}{2}\sigma^2\right)\Delta t,$$

$$Var[\xi_i] = \sigma^2 \Delta t.$$

Using elementary statistical theory we see that an estimate of σ is given by

$$\sigma^\star = \frac{S_\xi}{\sqrt{\Delta t}},$$

where the sample variance S_ξ^2 is given by

$$S_\xi^2 = \frac{1}{n-1}\sum_{i=1}^{n}\left(\xi_i - \bar{\xi}\right)^2,$$

$$\bar{\xi} = \frac{1}{n}\sum_{i=1}^{n}\xi_i.$$

The standard deviation, D, of the estimate $\sigma^\star$ is approximatively given by

$$D(\sigma^\star) \approx \frac{\sigma^\star}{\sqrt{2n}}.$$

7.7.2 *Implied Volatility*

Suppose again that we want to value a European call with six months left to maturity. An argument against the use of historical volatility is that in real life volatility is not constant, but changes over time, and thus we want an estimate of the volatility for the coming six months. Using historical volatility we will, however, only obtain an estimate for the volatility over the past six months. If, furthermore, our objective is to price our option **consistently** with respect to other assets which are already priced by the market, then we really should use the **market expectation** of the volatility for the next six months.

One way of finding the market expectation of the volatility is by getting market price data for another six month "benchmark" option, written on the same underlying stock as the option which we want to value. Denoting the price of the benchmark option by p, the strike price by K, today's observed value of the underlying stock by s, and writing the Black–Scholes pricing formula for European calls by $c(s, t, T, r, \sigma, K)$, we then solve the following equation for σ

$$p = c(s, t, T, r, \sigma, K).$$

In other words, we try to find the value of σ which the market has implicitly used for valuing the benchmark option. The value of σ is called the **implied volatility**, and we then use the implied volatility for the benchmark in order to price our original option. Put another way, we price the original option in terms of the benchmark.

We note that implied volatilities can be used to test (in a nonstandard way) the Black–Scholes model. Suppose, for example, that we observe the market prices of a number of European calls with the same exercise date on a single underlying stock. If the model is correct (with a constant volatility) then, if we plot implied volatility as a function of the exercise price, we should obtain a horizontal straight line. Contrary to this, it is often empirically observed that options far out of the money or deep into the money are traded at higher implied volatilities than options at the money. The graph of the observed implied volatility function thus often looks like the smile of the Cheshire cat, and for this reason the implied volatility curve is termed the **volatility smile**.

Remark 7.7.1 A call option is said to be "in the money" at time t if $S_t > K$, and "out of the money" if $S_t < K$. For put options the inequalities are reversed. If $S_t = K$ the option is said to be "at the money".

7.8 American Options

Up to now we have assumed that a contract, like a call option, can only be exercised exactly at the exercise time T. In real life a large number of options can in fact be exercised at **any time prior to T**. The choice of exercise time is thus left to the holder of the contract, and a contract with this feature is called an **American** contract.

To put it more formally, let us fix a final exercise date T and a contract function Φ. The European version of this contract will, as usual, pay the amount $\Phi(S_T)$ at time T to the holder of the contract. If the contract, on the other hand, is of the American type, then the holder will obtain the amount $\Phi(S_t)$ if he/she chooses to exercise the contract at time t. The situation is complicated further by the fact that the exercise time t does not have to be chosen a priori (i.e. at $t = 0$). It can be chosen on the basis of the information generated by the stock price process, and thus the holder will in fact choose a **random exercise time** τ. The exercise time (or rather exercise strategy) τ has to be chosen such that the decision on whether to exercise the contract at time t or not, depends only upon the information generated by the price process up to time t. The mathematical formulation of this property is in terms of so called "stopping times", but we will not go further into this subject.

American contracts are thus more complicated to analyze than their European counterparts, since the holder of the contract has to decide on an **optimal exercise strategy**. Mathematically this means that we have to solve the "optimal stopping problem"

$$\max_{\tau} \; E^Q \left[e^{-r\tau} \Phi(S_\tau) \right],$$

where τ is allowed to vary over the class of stopping times. Problems of this kind are quite hard to solve, and analytically they lead to so called "free boundary value problems" (or variational inequalities) instead of the corresponding parabolic PDEs for the European counterparts. For details, see Chapter 21 where we give an introduction to the theory of optimal stopping. For the moment we note that for American contracts practically no analytical formulas are at hand. See the Notes below for references.

One situation, however, is very easy to analyze, even for American contracts, and that is the case of an American call option on a nondividend paying underlying stock. Let us consider an American call option with final exercise date T and exerise price K. We denote the pricing function for the American option by $C(t,s)$ and the pricing function for the corresponding European option (with the same T and K) by $c(t,s)$.

Firstly we note that we have (why?) the trivial inequality

$$C(t,s) \geq c(t,s). \tag{7.56}$$

Secondly we have, for all $t < T$, the less obvious inequality.

$$c(t,s) \geq s - Ke^{-r(T-t)}. \tag{7.57}$$

To see why this inequality holds it is sufficient to consider two portfolios, A and B. A consists of a long position in the European option, whereas B consists of a long position in the underlying stock and a loan expiring at T, with face value K.

Denoting the price of A and B at any time t by A_t and B_t respectively, it is easily seen that $A_T \geq B_T$ regardless of the value of S_T (analyze the two cases $S_T \geq K$ and $S_T < K$). In order to avoid arbitrage possibilities we then must have $A_t \geq B_t$ for all $t \leq T$, which is precisely the content of (7.57).

Furthermore, assuming a positive rate of interest, we have the trivial inequality

$$s - Ke^{-r(T-t)} > s - K, \quad \forall t < T,$$

so we end up with the inequality

$$C(t,s) > s - K, \quad \forall t < T. \tag{7.58}$$

On the left-hand side we have the value of the American option at time t, whereas the right-hand side gives us the value of actually exercising the option at time t. Since the value of the option is strictly greater than the value of exercising the option, it can thus not be optimal to exercise the option at time t. Since this holds for all $t < T$, we see that it is in fact never optimal to exercise the option before T, and we have the following result.

Proposition 7.14 *Assume that $r > 0$. For an American call option, written on an underlying stock without dividends, the optimal exercise time τ is given by $\tau = T$. Thus the price of the American option coincides with the price of the corresponding European option.*

For American call options with discrete dividends, the argument above can be extended to show that it can only be optimal to exercise the option either at the final time T or at one of the dividend times. The American put option (even without dividends) presents a hard problem without an analytical solution. See the Notes below.

7.9   Exercises

Exercise 7.1 Consider the standard Black–Scholes model and a T-claim $\mathcal{X}$ of the form $\mathcal{X} = \Phi(S(T))$. Denote the corresponding arbitrage free price process by $\Pi(t)$.

   (a) Show that, under the martingale measure Q, $\Pi(t)$ has a local rate of return equal to the short rate of interest r. In other words show that $\Pi(t)$ has a differential of the form

$$d\Pi(t) = r \cdot \Pi(t)\, dt + g(t)dW(t).$$

   Hint: Use the Q-dynamics of S together with the fact that F satisfies the pricing PDE.

   (b) Show that, under the martingale measure Q, the process $Z(t) = \frac{\Pi(t)}{B(t)}$ is a **martingale**. More precisely, show that the stochastic differential for Z

has zero drift term, i.e. it is of the form

$$dZ(t) = Z(t)\sigma_Z(t)dW(t).$$

Determine also the diffusion process $\sigma_Z(t)$ (in terms of the pricing function F and its derivatives).

Exercise 7.2 Consider the standard Black–Scholes model. An innovative company, $F\&H\ INC$, has produced the derivative "the Golden Logarithm", henceforth abbreviated as the GL. The holder of a GL with maturity time T, denoted as $GL(T)$, will, at time T, obtain the sum $\ln S(T)$. Note that if $S(T) < 1$ this means that the holder has to pay a positive amount to $F\&H\ INC$. Determine the arbitrage free price process for the $GL(T)$.

Exercise 7.3 Consider the standard Black–Scholes model. Derive the Black–Scholes formula for the European call option.

Exercise 7.4 Consider the standard Black–Scholes model. Derive the arbitrage free price process for the T-claim $\mathcal{X}$ where $\mathcal{X}$ is given by $\mathcal{X} = \{S(T)\}^{\beta}$. Here β is a known constant.

Hint: For this problem you may find Exercises 5.5 and 4.4 useful.

Exercise 7.5 A so called **binary option** is a claim which pays a certain amount if the stock price at a certain date falls within some prespecified interval. Otherwise nothing will be paid out. Consider a binary option which pays K SEK to the holder at date T if the stock price at time T is in the interval $[\alpha, \beta]$. Determine the arbitrage free price. The pricing formula will involve the standard Gaussian cumulative distribution function N.

Exercise 7.6 Consider the standard Black–Scholes model. Derive the arbitrage free price process for the claim $\mathcal{X}$ where $\mathcal{X}$ is given by $\mathcal{X} = \frac{S(T_1)}{S(T_0)}$. The times T_0 and T_1 are given and the claim is paid out at time T_1.

Exercise 7.7 Consider the American corporation $ACME\ INC$. The price process S for $ACME$ is of course denoted in US\$ and has the P-dynamics

$$dS = \alpha S dt + \sigma S d\bar{W}_1,$$

where α and σ are known constants. The currency ratio SEK/US\$ is denoted by Y and Y has the dynamics

$$dY = \beta Y dt + \delta Y d\bar{W}_2,$$

where $\bar{W}_2$ is independent of $\bar{W}_1$. The broker firm $F\&H$ has invented the derivative "Euler". The holder of a T-Euler will, at the time of maturity T, obtain the sum

$$\mathcal{X} = \ln\left[\{Z(T)\}^2\right]$$

in SEK. Here $Z(t)$ is the price at time t in SEK of the $ACME$ stock.

Compute the arbitrage free price (in SEK) at time t of a T-Euler, given that the price (in SEK) of the $ACME$ stock is z. The Swedish short rate is denoted by r.

Exercise 7.8 Prove formula (7.52).

Exercise 7.9 Derive a formula for the value, at s, of a forward contract on the T-claim X, where the forward contract is made at t, and $t < s < T$.

7.10 Notes

The classics in the field are Black and Scholes (1973), and Merton, 1973. The modern martingale approach to arbitrage pricing was developed in Harrison and Kreps (1979), and Harrison and Pliska (1981). A deep study of the connections between (various formulations of) absence of arbitrage and the existence of a martingale measure can be found in Delbaen and Schachermayer (1994).

For a wealth of information on forward and futures contracts, see Hull, 2003 and Duffie (1989). Black's formula was derived in Black (1976). For American options see Barone-Adesi and Elliott (1991), Geske and Johnson (1984), and Musiela and Rutkowski (1997). The standard references for optimal stopping problems are Shiryaev (2008) and Peskir and Shiryaev (2006). A very readable exposition of optimal stopping theory can be found in Øksendal (1998). Option pricing with stochastic volatility is discussed in Hull and White (1987), and Leland (1995) studies the consequences of introducing transaction costs.

8

COMPLETENESS AND HEDGING

8.1 Introduction

In the previous chapter we noticed that our derivation of the pricing equation (7.31) was somewhat unsatisfactory, and a major criticism was that we were forced to assume that the derivative asset a priori possessed a price process and actually was traded on the market. In this chapter we will look at arbitrage pricing from a somewhat different point of view, and this alternative approach will have two benefits. Firstly it will allow us to dispose of the annoying assumption above that the derivative is actually traded, and secondly it will provide us with an explanation of the surprising fact that the simple claims investigated earlier can be given a unique price. For a more detailed discussion see Chapters 10, 12 and 15.

We start with a fairly general situation by considering a financial market with a price vector process $S = (S^1, \ldots, S^N)$, governed by an objective probability measure P. The process S is as usual interpreted as the price process of the exogenously given underlying assets and we now want to price a contingent T-claim $\mathcal{X}$. We assume that all the underlying assets are traded on the market, but we do not assume that there exists an a priori market (or a price process) for the derivative. To avoid trivialities we also assume that the underlying market is arbitrage free.

Definition 8.1 *We say that a T-claim $\mathcal{X}$ can be* **replicated**, *alternatively that it is* **reachable** *or* **hedgeable**, *if there exists a self-financing portfolio h such that*

$$V^h(T) = \mathcal{X}, \quad P - a.s. \tag{8.1}$$

In this case we say that h is a **hedge** *against $\mathcal{X}$. Alternatively, h is called a* **replicating** *or* **hedging** *portfolio. If every contingent claim is reachable we say that the market is* **complete**.

Let us now consider a fixed T-claim $\mathcal{X}$ and let us assume that $\mathcal{X}$ can be replicated by a portfolio h. Then we can make the following mental experiment:

1. Fix a point in time t with $t \leq T$.
2. Suppose that we, at time t, possess $V^h(t)$ SEK.
3. We can then use this money to buy the portfolio $h(t)$. If furthermore we follow the portfolio strategy h on the time interval $[t, T]$ this will cost us nothing, since h is self-financing. At time T the value of our portfolio will then be $V^h(T)$ SEK.

4. By the replication assumption the value, at time T, of our portfolio will thus be exactly $\mathcal{X}$ SEK, regardless of the stochastic price movements over the interval $[t, T]$.

5. From a purely financial point of view, holding the portfolio h is thus equivalent to the holding of the contract $\mathcal{X}$.

6. The "correct" price of $\mathcal{X}$ at time t is thus given by $\Pi(t; \mathcal{X}) = V^h(t)$.

For a hedgeable claim we thus have a natural price process, $\Pi(t; \mathcal{X}) = V^h(t)$, and we may now ask if this has anything to do with absence of arbitrage.

Proposition 8.2 *Suppose that the claim $\mathcal{X}$ can be hedged using the portfolio h. Then the only price process $\Pi(t; \mathcal{X})$ which is consistent with no arbitrage is given by $\Pi(t; \mathcal{X}) = V^h(t)$. Furthermore, if $\mathcal{X}$ can be hedged by g as well as by h then $V^g(t) = V^h(t)$ holds for all t with probability 1.*

Proof If at some time t we have $\Pi(t; \mathcal{X}) < V^h(t)$ then we can make an arbitrage by selling the portfolio short and buying the claim, and vice versa if $\Pi(t; \mathcal{X}) > V^h(t)$. A similar argument shows that we must have $V^g(t) = V^h(t)$. $\square$

8.2 Completeness in the Black–Scholes Model

We will now investigate completeness for the generalized Black–Scholes model given by

$$dB(t) = rB(t)dt, \tag{8.2}$$
$$dS(t) = S(t)\alpha(t, S(t)) \, dt + S(t)\sigma(t, S(t)) \, d\bar{W}(t), \tag{8.3}$$

where we assume that $\sigma(t, s) > 0$ for all (t, s). The main result is the following.

Theorem 8.3 *The model (8.2)–(8.3) is complete.*

The proof of this theorem requires some fairly deep results from probability theory and is thus outside the scope of this book. We will prove a weaker version of the theorem, namely that every **simple** claim can be hedged. This is often quite sufficient for practical purposes, and our proof of the restricted completeness also has the advantage that it gives the replicating portfolio in explicit form. We will use the notational convention $h(t) = \left[h^0(t), h^\star(t)\right]$ where h^0 is the number of bonds in the portfolio, whereas $h^\star$ denotes the number of shares in the underlying stock. We thus fix a simple T-claim of the form $\mathcal{X} = \Phi(S(T))$ and we now want to show that this claim can be hedged. Since the formal proof is of the form "consider the following odd construction", we will instead start by presenting a purely heuristic (but good) argument. This argument is, from a formal point of view, only of motivational nature and the logic of it is rather unclear. Since the argument is only heuristic the logical flaws do not matter, since in the end we will in fact present a rigorous statement and a rigorous proof. Before we start the heuristics, let us make more precise what we are looking for. Using Lemma 6.5 we immediately have the following result.

Lemma 8.4 *Suppose that there exists an adapted process V and an adapted process $u = \begin{bmatrix} u^0, u^\star \end{bmatrix}$ with*

$$u^0(t) + u^\star(t) = 1, \qquad (8.4)$$

such that

$$\begin{cases} dV(t) = V(t) \left\{ u^0(t)r + u^\star(t)\alpha(t, S(t)) \right\} dt + V(t)u^\star(t)\sigma(t, S(t))d\bar{W}(t), \\ V(T) = \Phi(S(T)). \end{cases}$$

$$(8.5)$$

Then the claim $\mathcal{X} = \Phi(S(T))$ can be replicated using u as the relative portfolio. The corresponding value process is given by the process V and the absolute portfolio h is given by

$$h^0(t) = \frac{u^0(t)V(t)}{B(t)}, \qquad (8.6)$$

$$h^\star(t) = \frac{u^\star(t)V(t)}{S(t)}. \qquad (8.7)$$

Our strategy now is to look for a process V and a process u satisfying the conditions above.

Begin Heuristics

We assume what we want to prove, namely that $\mathcal{X} = \Phi(S(T))$ is indeed replicable, and then we ponder on what the hedging strategy u might look like. Since the S-process and (trivially) the B-process are Markov processes it seems reasonable to assume that the hedging portfolio is of the form $h(t) = h(t, S(t))$ where, with a slight misuse of notation, the h in the right member of the equality is a deterministic function. Since, furthermore, the value process V (we suppress the superscript h) is defined as $V(t) = h^0(t)B(t) + h^\star(t)S(t)$ it will also be a function of time and stock price as

$$V(t) = F(t, S(t)), \qquad (8.8)$$

where F is some real valued deterministic function which we would like to know more about.

Assume therefore that (8.8) actually holds. Then we may apply the Itô formula to V in order to obtain the V-dynamics as

$$dV = \left\{ F_t + \alpha S F_s + \frac{1}{2}\sigma^2 S^2 F_{ss} \right\} dt + \sigma S F_s d\bar{W}, \qquad (8.9)$$

where we have suppressed the fact that V and S are to be evaluated at time t, whereas α, σ and F are to be evaluated at $(t, S(t))$. Now, in order to make (8.9) look more like (8.5) we rewrite (8.9) as

$$dV = V \left\{ \frac{F_t + \alpha S F_s + \frac{1}{2}\sigma^2 S^2 F_{ss}}{V} \right\} dt + V \frac{S F_s}{V}\sigma d\bar{W}. \qquad (8.10)$$

Since we have assumed that $\mathcal{X}$ is replicated by V we see from (8.10) and (8.5) that $u^\star$ must be given by

$$u^\star(t) = \frac{S(t)F_s(t, S(t))}{F(t, S(t))}, \qquad (8.11)$$

(remember that we have assumed that $V(t) = F(t, S(t))$), and if we substitute (8.11) into (8.10) we get

$$dV = V \left\{ \frac{F_t + \frac{1}{2}\sigma^2 S^2 F_{ss}}{rF} r + u^\star \alpha \right\} dt + V u^\star \sigma d\bar{W}. \qquad (8.12)$$

Comparing this expression to (8.5) we see that the natural choice for u^0 is given by

$$u^0 = \frac{F_t + \frac{1}{2}\sigma^2 S^2 F_{ss}}{rF}, \qquad (8.13)$$

but we also have to satisfy the requirement $u^0 + u^\star = 1$ of (8.4). Using (8.11) and (8.13) this gives us the relation

$$\frac{F_t + \frac{1}{2}\sigma^2 S^2 F_{ss}}{rF} = \frac{F - SF_s}{F}, \qquad (8.14)$$

which, after some manipulation, turns out to be the familiar Black–Scholes equation

$$F_t + rSF_s + \frac{1}{2}\sigma^2 S^2 F_{ss} - rF = 0. \qquad (8.15)$$

Furthermore, in order to satisfy the relation $F(T, S(T)) = \Phi(S(T))$ of (8.5) (remember that we assume that $V(t) = F(t, S(t))$) we must have the boundary value

$$F(T, s) = \Phi(s), \quad \text{for all } s \in R_+. \qquad (8.16)$$

End Heuristics

Since at this point the reader may well be somewhat confused as to the logic of the reasoning, let us try to straighten things out. The logic of the reasoning above is basically as follows.

- We **assumed** that the claim $\mathcal{X}$ was replicable.
- Using this and some further (reasonable) assumptions we showed that they **implied** that the value process of the replicating portfolio was given as $V(t) = F(t, S(t))$ where F is a solution of the Black–Scholes equation.

This is of course not at all what we wish to achieve. What we want to do is to **prove** that $\mathcal{X}$ really can be replicated. In order to do this we put the entire argument above within a logical parenthesis and formally disregard it. We then have the following result.

Theorem 8.5 *Consider the market (8.2)–(8.3), and a contingent claim of the form $\mathcal{X} = \Phi(S(T))$. Define F as the solution to the boundary value problem*

$$\begin{cases} F_t + rsF_s + \frac{1}{2}\sigma^2 s^2 F_{ss} - rF = 0, \\ \qquad\qquad\qquad\qquad F(T,s) = \Phi(s). \end{cases} \tag{8.17}$$

Then $\mathcal{X}$ can be replicated by the relative portfolio

$$u^0(t) = \frac{F(t, S(t)) - S(t)F_s(t, S(t))}{F(t, S(t))}, \tag{8.18}$$

$$u^\star(t) = \frac{S(t)F_s(t, S(t))}{F(t, S(t))}. \tag{8.19}$$

The corresponding absolute portfolio is given by

$$h^0(t) = \frac{F(t, S(t)) - S(t)F_s(t, S(t))}{B(t)}, \tag{8.20}$$

$$h^\star(t) = F_s(t, S(t)), \tag{8.21}$$

and the value process V^h is given by

$$V^h(t) = F(t, S(t)). \tag{8.22}$$

Proof   Applying the Itô formula to the process $V(t)$ defined by (8.22) and performing exactly the same calculations as in the heuristic argument above, will show that we can apply Lemma 8.4. □

The result above gives us an explanation of the surprising facts that there actually exists a **unique** price for a derivative asset in the Black–Scholes model and that this price does not depend on any particular assumptions about individual preferences. The arbitrage free price of a derivative asset is uniquely determined simply because in this model the derivative is superfluous. It can always be replaced by a corresponding "synthetic" derivative in terms of a replicating portfolio.

Since the replication is done with P-probability 1, we also see that if a contingent claim $\mathcal{X}$ is replicated under P by a portfolio h and if $P^\star$ is some other probability measure such that P and $P^\star$ assign probability 1 to exactly the same events (such measures P and $P^\star$ are said to be **equivalent**), then h will replicate $\mathcal{X}$ also under the measure $P^\star$. Thus the pricing formula for a certain claim will be exactly the same for all measures which are equivalent to P. It is a well known fact (the Girsanov theorem) in the theory of SDEs that if we change the measure from P to some other equivalent measure, this will change the drift in the SDE, but the diffusion term will be unaffected. Thus the drift will play no part in the pricing equation, which explains why α does not appear in the Black–Scholes equation.

Let us now list some popular claims and see which of them will fall into the framework above.

$$\mathcal{X} = \max\left[S(T) - K, 0\right] \quad \text{(European call option)} \tag{8.23}$$

$$\mathcal{X} = S(T) - K \quad \text{(Forward contract)} \tag{8.24}$$

$$\mathcal{X} = \max\left[\frac{1}{T}\int_0^T S(t)dt - K, 0\right] \quad \text{(Asian option)} \tag{8.25}$$

$$\mathcal{X} = S(T) - \inf_{0 \leq t \leq T} S(t) \quad \text{(Lookback contract)} \tag{8.26}$$

We know from Theorem 8.3 that in fact all of the claims above can be replicated. For general claims this is, however, only an abstract existence result and we have no guarantee of obtaining the replicating portfolio in an explicit form. The point of Theorem 8.5 is precisely that, by restricting ourselves to **simple** claims, i.e. claims of the form $\mathcal{X} = \Phi(S(T))$, we obtain an explicit formula for the hedging portfolio.

It is clear that the European call as well as the forward contract above are simple claims, and we may thus apply Theorem 8.5. The Asian option (also called a mean value option) as well as the lookback present harder problems since neither of these claims is simple. Instead of just being functions of the value of S at time T we see that the claims depend on the entire S-trajectory over the interval $[0, T]$. Thus, while we know that there exist hedging portfolios for both these claims, we have presently no obvious way of determining the shape of these portfolios.

It is in fact quite hard to determine the hedging portfolio for the lookback, but the Asian option belongs to a class of contracts for which we can give a fairly explicit representation of the replicating portfolio, using very much the same technique as in Theorem 8.5.

Proposition 8.6 *Consider the model*

$$dB(t) = rB(t)dt, \tag{8.27}$$

$$dS(t) = S(t)\alpha\left(t, S(t)\right)dt + S(t)\sigma\left(t, S(t)\right)d\bar{W}(t), \tag{8.28}$$

and let $\mathcal{X}$ be a T-claim of the form

$$\mathcal{X} = \Phi\left(S(T), Z(T)\right), \tag{8.29}$$

where the process Z is defined by

$$Z(t) = \int_0^t g(u, S(u))du, \tag{8.30}$$

for some choice of the deterministic function g. Then $\mathcal{X}$ can be replicated using a relative portfolio given by

$$u^0(t) = \frac{F(t, S(t), Z(t)) - S(t)F_s(t, S(t), Z(t))}{F(t, S(t), Z(t))}, \tag{8.31}$$

$$u^\star(t) = \frac{S(t)F_s(t, S(t), Z(t))}{F(t, S(t), Z(t))}, \tag{8.32}$$

where F is the solution to the boundary value problem

$$\begin{cases} F_t + srF_s + \frac{1}{2}s^2\sigma^2 F_{ss} + gF_z - rF = 0, \\ \qquad\qquad F(T, s, z) = \Phi(s, z). \end{cases} \tag{8.33}$$

The corresponding value process V is given by $V(t) = F(t, S(t), Z(t))$, and F has the stochastic representation

$$F(t, s, z) = e^{-r(T-t)} E_{t,s,z}^Q \left[\Phi(S(T), Z(T)) \right], \tag{8.34}$$

where the Q-dynamics are given by

$$dS(u) = rS(u)du + S(u)\sigma(u, S(u))dW(u), \tag{8.35}$$

$$S(t) = s, \tag{8.36}$$

$$dZ(u) = g(u, S(u))du, \tag{8.37}$$

$$Z(t) = z. \tag{8.38}$$

Proof   The proof is left as an exercise for the reader. Use the same technique as in the proof of Theorem 8.5.   □

Again we see that the arbitrage free price of a contingent claim is given as the expected value of the claim discounted to the present time. Here, as before, the expected value is to be calculated using the martingale measure Q instead of the objective probability measure P. As we have said before, this general structure of arbitrage free pricing holds in much more general situations, and as a rule of thumb one can view the martingale measure Q as being defined by the property that all **traded** underlying assets have r as the rate of return under Q. It is important to stress that it is only traded assets which will have sr as the rate of return under Q. For models with nontraded underlying objects we have a completely different situation, which we will encounter below.

8.3   Completeness—Absence of Arbitrage

In this section we will give some general rules of thumb for quickly determining whether a certain model is complete and/or free of arbitrage. The arguments will be purely heuristic.

Let us consider a model with M traded underlying assets **plus** the risk free asset (i.e. totally $M + 1$ assets). We assume that the price processes of the underlying assets are driven by R "random sources". We cannot give a precise definition of what constitutes a "random source" here, but the typical example is a driving Wiener process. If, for example, we have five independent Wiener processes driving our prices, then $R = 5$. Another example of a random source would be a counting process such as a Poisson process. In this context it is important to note that if the prices are driven by a point process with different jump sizes then the appropriate number of random sources equals the number of different jump sizes.

When discussing completeness and absence of arbitrage it is important to realize that these concepts work in opposite directions. Let the number of random sources R be fixed. Then every new underlying asset added to the model (without increasing R) will of course give us a potential opportunity of creating an arbitrage portfolio, so in order to have an arbitrage free market the number M of underlying assets must be small in comparison to the number of random sources R.

On the other hand we see that every new underlying asset added to the model gives us new possibilities of replicating a given contingent claim, so completeness requires M to be great in comparison to R.

We cannot formulate and prove a precise result here, but the following rule of thumb, or "meta-theorem", is nevertheless extremely useful. In concrete cases it can in fact be given a precise formulation and a precise proof. See Chapters 10 and 14. We will later use the meta-theorem when dealing with problems connected with nontraded underlying assets in general and interest rate theory in particular.

Meta-theorem 8.3.1 *Let M denote the number of underlying* **traded** *assets in the model* **excluding** *the risk free asset, and let R denote the number of random sources. Generically we then have the following relations:*

1. *The model is arbitrage free if and only if $M \leq R$.*
2. *The model is complete if and only if $M \geq R$.*
3. *The model is complete and arbitrage free if and only if $M = R$.*

As an example we take the Black–Scholes model, where we have one underlying asset S plus the risk free asset so $M = 1$. We have one driving Wiener process, giving us $R = 1$, so in fact $M = R$. Using the meta-theorem above we thus expect the Black–Scholes model to be arbitrage free as well as complete and this is indeed the case.

8.4 Exercises

Exercise 8.1 Consider a model for the stock market where the short rate of interest r is a deterministic constant. We focus on a particular stock with price process S. Under the objective probability measure P we have the following dynamics for the price process.

$$dS(t) = \alpha S(t)dt + \sigma S(t)dW(t) + \delta S(t-)dN(t).$$

Here W is a standard Wiener process whereas N is a Poisson process with intensity λ. We assume that α, σ, δ and λ are known to us. The dN term is to be interpreted in the following way:

- Between the jump times of the Poisson process N, the S-process behaves just like ordinary geometric Brownian motion.
- If N has a jump at time t this induces S to have a jump at time t. The size of the S-jump is given by

$$S(t) - S(t-) = \delta \cdot S(t-).$$

Discuss the following questions.

(a) Is the model free of arbitrage?
(b) Is the model complete?
(c) Is there a unique arbitrage free price for, say, a European call option?
(d) Suppose that you want to replicate a European call option maturing in January 1999. Is it posssible (theoretically) to replicate this asset by a portfolio consisting of bonds, the underlying stock and European call option maturing in December 2001?

Exercise 8.2 Use the Feynman–Kač technique in order to derive a risk neutral valuation formula in connection with Proposition 8.6.

Exercise 8.3 The fairly unknown company $F\&H\ INC.$ has blessed the market with a new derivative, "the Mean". With "effective period" given by $[T_1, T_2]$ the holder of a Mean contract will, at the date of maturity T_2, obtain the amount

$$\frac{1}{T_2 - T_1} \int_{T_1}^{T_2} S(u)du.$$

Determine the arbitrage free price, at time t, of the Mean contract. Assume that you live in a standard Black–Scholes world, and that $t < T_1$.

Exercise 8.4 Consider the standard Black–Scholes model, and n different simple contingent claims with contract functions $\Phi_1, \ldots, \Phi_n$. Let

$$V = \sum_{i=1}^{n} h_i(t)S_i(t)$$

denote the value process of a self-financing, Markovian (see Definition 6.2) portfolio. Because of the Markovian assumption, V will be of the form $V(t, S(t))$. Show that V satisfies the Black–Scholes equation.

8.5 Notes

Completeness is mathematically closely related to rather deep results about the possibility of representing martingales as sums of stochastic integrals. Using this connection, it can be shown that the market is complete if and only if the martingale measure is unique. This is developed in some detail in Chapters 10 and 14. See also Harrison and Pliska (1981) and Musiela and Rutkowski (1997).

9

PARITY RELATIONS AND DELTA HEDGING

9.1 Parity Relations

Consider the standard Black–Scholes model. As we know from general theory (Theorem 8.3) this model allows us to replicate any contingent claim using a portfolio based on the underlying asset and the risk free asset. For a nontrivial claim the structure of the hedging portfolio is typically quite complicated, and in particular it is a portfolio which is continuously rebalanced. For practical purposes this continuous rebalancing presents a problem because in real life trading does have a cost. For managerial purposes it would be much nicer if we could replicate a given claim with a portfolio which did not have to be rebalanced, in other words a portfolio which is **constant** over time. Such a portfolio is known as a **buy-and-hold** portfolio.

If we insist on using only B and S in our replicating portfolio we cannot replicate any interesting claims using constant portfolios, but if we allow ourselves to include some derivative, like a European call option, in our hedging portfolio, then life becomes much simpler, and the basic result we will use is the following trivial linear property of pricing.

Proposition 9.1 *Let* Φ *and* Ψ *be contract functions for the* T*-claims* $\mathcal{X} = \Phi(S(T))$ *and* $Y = \Psi(S(T))$. *Then for any real numbers* α *and* β *we have the following price relation.*

$$\Pi\left(t; \alpha\Phi + \beta\Psi\right) = \alpha\Pi\left(t; \Phi\right) + \beta\Pi\left(t; \Psi\right). \tag{9.1}$$

Proof This follows immediately from the risk neutral valuation formula (7.39) and the linear property of mathematical expectation. □

To set notation let $c(t, s; K, T, r, \sigma)$ and $p(t, s; K, T, r, \sigma)$ denote the price at time t given $S(t) = s$ of a European call option and a European put option respectively. In both cases T denotes the time of maturity, K the strike price, whereas r and σ indicate the dependence on model parameters. From time to time we will freely suppress one or more of the variables (t, s, K, T, r, σ). Let us furthermore consider the following "basic" contract functions.

$$\Phi_S(x) = x, \tag{9.2}$$
$$\Phi_B(x) \equiv 1, \tag{9.3}$$
$$\Phi_{C,K}(x) = \max\left[x - K, 0\right]. \tag{9.4}$$

The corresponding claims at the time of maturity give us one share of the stock, \$1, and one European call with strike price K respectively. For these claims the prices are given by

$$\Pi\left(t;\Phi_S\right) = S(t), \tag{9.5}$$

$$\Pi\left(t;\Phi_B\right) = e^{-r(T-t)}, \tag{9.6}$$

$$\Pi\left(t;\Phi_{C,K}\right) = c(t, S(t); K, T). \tag{9.7}$$

Let us now fix a time of maturity T and a T-claim $\mathcal{X}$ of the form $\mathcal{X} = \Phi(S(T))$, i.e. a simple claim. It is now clear that if Φ is a linear combination of the basic contracts above, i.e. if we have

$$\Phi = \alpha\Phi_S + \beta\Phi_B + \sum_{i=1}^{n}\gamma_i\Phi_{C,K_i}, \tag{9.8}$$

then we may price Φ in terms of the prices of the basic contracts as

$$\Pi\left(t;\Phi\right) = \alpha\Pi\left(t;\Phi_S\right) + \beta\Pi\left(t;\Phi_B\right) + \sum_{i=1}^{n}\gamma_i\Pi\left(t;\Phi_{C,K_i}\right). \tag{9.9}$$

Note also that in this case we may replicate the claim Φ using a portfolio consisting of basic contracts that is **constant** over time, i.e. a "buy-and hold" portfolio. More precisely the replicating portfolio consists of

- α shares of the underlying stock,
- β zero coupon T-bonds with face value \$1,
- γ_i European call options with strike price K_i, all maturing at T.

The result above is of course interesting only if there is a reasonably large class of contracts which in fact can be written as linear combinations of the basic contracts given by (9.2), (9.3) and (9.4). This is indeed the case, and as a first example we consider the European put option with strike price K, for which the contract function $\Phi_{P,K}$ is defined by

$$\Phi_{P,K}(x) = \max\left[K - x, 0\right]. \tag{9.10}$$

It is now easy to see (draw a figure!) that

$$\Phi_{P,K} = K\Phi_B + \Phi_{C,K} - \Phi_S,$$

so we have the following so called put–call parity relation.

Proposition 9.2 (Put–call parity) *Consider a European call and a European put, both with strike price K and time of maturity T. Denoting the corresponding pricing functions by $c(t, s)$ and $p(t, s)$, we have the following relation.*

$$p(t, s) = Ke^{-r(T-t)} + c(t, s) - s. \tag{9.11}$$

In particular the put option can be replicated with a constant (over time) portfolio consisting of a long position in a zero coupon T-bond with face value K, a long position in a European call option and a short position in one share of the underlying stock.

It is now natural to pose the following more general question. Which contracts can be replicated in this way using a constant portfolio consisting of bonds, call options and the underlying stock? The answer is very pleasing.

Proposition 9.3 *Fix an arbitrary continuous contract function* Φ *with compact support. Then the corresponding contract can be replicated with arbitrary precision (in sup-norm) using a constant portfolio consisting only of bonds, call options and the underlying stock.*

Proof It is easily seen that any affine function can be written as a linear combination of the basic contract functions. The result now follows from the fact that any continuous function with compact support can be approximated uniformly by a piecewise linear function. □

9.2 The Greeks

Let $P(t, s)$ denote the pricing function at time t for a portfolio based on a **single underlying asset** with price process S_t. The portfolio can thus consist of a position in the underlying asset itself, as well as positions in various options written on the underlying asset. For practical purposes it is often of vital importance to have a grip on the sensitivity of P with respect to the following.

1. Price changes of the underlying asset.
2. Changes in the model parameters.

In case 1 above we want to obtain a measure of our risk exposure, i.e. how the value of our portfolio (consisting of stock and derivatives) will change given a certain change in the underlying price. At first glance case 2 seems self-contradictory, since a model parameter is by definition a given constant, and thus it cannot possibly change within the given model. This case is therefore not one of risk exposure but rather one of sensitivity with respect to misspecifications of the model parameters.

We introduce some standard notation.

Definition 9.4

$$\Delta = \frac{\partial P}{\partial s}, \tag{9.12}$$

$$\Gamma = \frac{\partial^2 P}{\partial s^2}, \tag{9.13}$$

$$\rho = \frac{\partial P}{\partial r}, \tag{9.14}$$

$$\Theta = \frac{\partial P}{\partial t}, \tag{9.15}$$

$$\mathcal{V} = \frac{\partial P}{\partial \sigma}. \tag{9.16}$$

All these sensitivity measures are known as "the greeks". This includes $\mathcal{V}$, which in this case is given the Anglo-Hellenic pronounciation "vega". A portfolio which is insensitive w.r.t. small changes in one of the parameters above is said to be **neutral**, and formally this means that the corresponding greek equals zero. A portfolio with zero delta is said to be **delta neutral**, and correspondingly for the other greeks. In the next section we will study various hedging schemes, based upon the greeks, but first we present the basic formulas for the case of a call option. See Figs 9.1–9.5 for graphs of the greeks as functions of the underlying stock price.

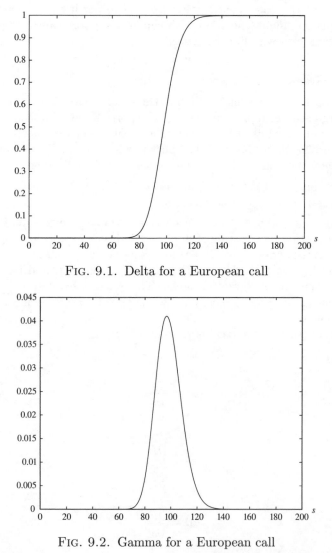

FIG. 9.1. Delta for a European call

FIG. 9.2. Gamma for a European call

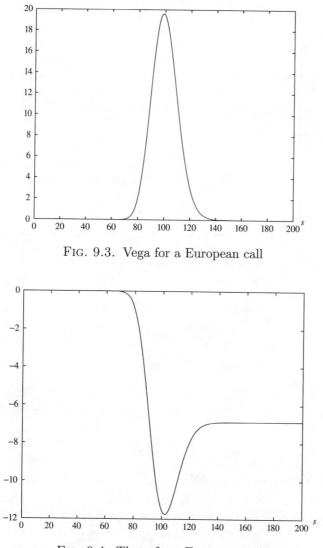

FIG. 9.3. Vega for a European call

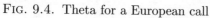

FIG. 9.4. Theta for a European call

Proposition 9.5 *For a European call with strike price K and time of maturity T we have the following relations, with notation as in the Black–Scholes formula. The letter φ denotes the density function of the $N[0,1]$ distribution.*

$$\Delta = N(d_1), \tag{9.17}$$

$$\Gamma = \frac{\varphi(d_1)}{s\sigma\sqrt{T-t}}, \tag{9.18}$$

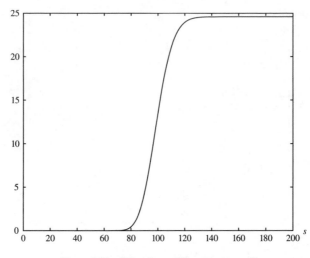

FIG. 9.5. Rho for a European call

$$\rho = K(T - t)e^{-r(T-t)}N(d_2), \tag{9.19}$$

$$\Theta = -\frac{s\varphi(d_1)\sigma}{2\sqrt{T - t}} - rKe^{-r(T-t)}N(d_2), \tag{9.20}$$

$$\mathcal{V} = s\varphi(d_1)\sqrt{T - t}. \tag{9.21}$$

Proof   Use the Black–Scholes formula (7.48) and take derivatives. The (brave) reader is invited to carry this out in detail. The calculations are sometimes quite messy.   □

9.3   Delta and Gamma Hedging

As in the previous section, let us consider a given portfolio with pricing function $P(t, s)$. The object is to immunize this portfolio against small changes in the underlying asset price s. If the portfolio already is delta neutral, i.e. if

$$\Delta_P = \frac{\partial P}{\partial s} = 0,$$

then we are done, but what can we do in the more interesting case when $\Delta_P = 0$? One possibility is of course to sell the entire portfolio, and invest the sum thus obtained in the bank, but this is in most cases neither practically feasible, nor preferable.

A more interesting idea is to add a derivative (e.g. an option or the underlying asset itself) to the portfolio. Since the price of a derivative is perfectly correlated with the underlying asset price, we should be able to balance the derivative against the portfolio in such a way that the adjusted portfolio becomes delta neutral. The reader will recognize this argument from the derivation of the Black–Scholes PDE, and the formal argument is as follows.

We denote the pricing function of the chosen derivative by $F(t, s)$, and x denotes the number of units of the derivative which we will add to the a priori given portfolio. The value V of the adjusted portfolio is then given by

$$V(t, s) = P(t, s) + x \cdot F(t, s). \tag{9.22}$$

In order to make this portfolio delta neutral we have to choose x such that $\frac{\partial V}{\partial s} = 0$, and this gives us the equation

$$\frac{\partial P}{\partial s} + x \frac{\partial F}{\partial s} = 0,$$

which, with obvious notation, has the solution

$$x = -\frac{\Delta_P}{\Delta_F}. \tag{9.23}$$

Example 9.6 Let us assume that we have sold a particular derivative with pricing function $F(t, s)$, and that we wish to hedge it using the underlying asset itself. In (9.22) we now have $P = -1 \cdot F$, whereas F is replaced by s, and we get the equation

$$\frac{\partial}{\partial s} [-F(t, s) + x \cdot s] = 0,$$

with the solution

$$x = \Delta_F = \frac{\partial F(t, s)}{\partial s}.$$

We thus see that the delta of a derivative gives us the number of units of the underlying stock that is needed in order to hedge the derivative.

It is important to note that a delta hedge only works well for small changes in the underlying price, and thus only for a short time. In Example 9.6 above, what we did was to approximate the pricing function $F(t, s)$ with its tangent, and in Fig. 9.6 this is illustrated for the case when F is the pricing function of a European call option. Δ_F equals the slope of the tangent. In Fig. 9.1 we have a graph of the delta of a European call, as a function of the underlying stock price. As time goes by the value of s (and t) will change, and thus we will be using an old, incorrect value of Δ. What is done in practice is to perform a **discrete rebalanced delta hedge**, which for the example above can be done along the following lines:

- Sell one unit of the derivative at time $t = 0$ at the price $F(0, s)$.
- Compute Δ and buy Δ shares. Use the income from the sale of the derivative, and if necessary borrow money from the bank.

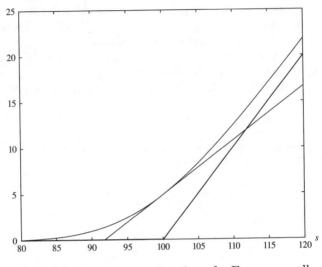

FIG. 9.6. Linear approximation of a European call

- Wait one day (week, minute, second). The stock price has now changed and your old Δ is no longer correct.
- Compute the new value of Δ and adjust your stock holdings accordingly. Balance your account by borrowing from or lending to the bank.
- Repeat this procedure until the exercise time T.
- In this way the value of your stock and money holdings will approximately equal the value of the derivative.

It is in fact not hard to prove (see the exercises) the following asymptotic result.

Proposition 9.7 *In a continuously rebalanced delta hedge, the value of the stock and money holdings will replicate the value of the derivative.*

In a (discrete) scheme of the kind above we face a dilemma concerning the frequency of the rebalancing points in time. If we rebalance often, we will have a very good hedge, but we will also suffer from high transaction costs. The reason why we have to rebalance is that delta changes as the underlying price changes, and a measure of the sensitivity of Δ with respect to s is of course given by $\Gamma = \frac{\partial \Delta}{\partial s} = \frac{\partial^2 P}{\partial s^2}$. See Fig. 9.2 for a graph of the gamma of a European call. If gamma is high we have to rebalance often, whereas a low gamma will allow us to keep the delta hedge for a longer period. It is thus preferable to form a portfolio which, apart from being delta neutral, is also **gamma neutral**.

In order to analyze this in some generality, let us again consider an a priori given portfolio with price function $P(t, s)$. For future use we state the following trivial but important facts.

Lemma 9.8 *For the underlying stock, the delta and gamma are given by*

$$\Delta_S = 1,$$
$$\Gamma_S = 0.$$

From the fact that the gamma of the underlying stock equals zero, it follows that we cannot use the stock itself in order to change the gamma of the portfolio. Since we want the adjusted portfolio to be both delta and gamma neutral, it is also obvious that we need two different derivatives in the hedge. Let us thus fix two derivatives, e.g. two call options with different exercise prices or different times of maturity, with pricing functions F and G. We denote the number of units of the derivatives by x_F and x_G respectively, and the value of the hedged portfolio is now given by

$$V = P(t,s) + x_F \cdot F(t,s) + x_G \cdot G(t,s).$$

In order to make this portfolio both delta and gamma neutral we have to choose x_F and x_G such that the equations

$$\frac{\partial V}{\partial s} = 0,$$
$$\frac{\partial^2 V}{\partial s^2} = 0,$$

are satisfied. With obvious notation we thus obtain the system

$$\Delta_P + x_F \cdot \Delta_F + x_G \cdot \Delta_G = 0, \tag{9.24}$$
$$\Gamma_P + x_F \cdot \Gamma_F + x_G \cdot \Gamma_G = 0, \tag{9.25}$$

which can easily be solved.

It is natural, and very tempting, to construct a delta and gamma neutral hedge by the following two step procedure.

1. Choose x_F such that the portfolio consisting of P and F is delta neutral. This portfolio will generally not be gamma neutral.

2. Now add the derivative G in order to make the portfolio gamma neutral.

The problem with this scheme is that the second step in general will destroy the delta neutrality obtained by the first step. In this context we may, however, use the fact that the stock itself has zero gamma and we can thus modify the scheme as follows:

1. Choose x_F such that the portfolio consisting of P and F is gamma neutral. This portfolio will generally not be delta neutral.

2. Now add the underlying stock in order to make the portfolio delta neutral.

Formally the value of the hedged portfolio will now be given by

$$V = P + x_F \cdot F + x_S \cdot s$$

and, using the lemma above, we obtain the following system.

$$\Delta_P + x_F \cdot \Delta_F + x_S = 0, \tag{9.26}$$
$$\Gamma_P + x_F \cdot \Gamma_F = 0. \tag{9.27}$$

This system is triangular, and thus much simpler than the system (9.24)–(9.25). The solution is given by

$$x_F = -\frac{\Gamma_P}{\Gamma_F},$$
$$x_S = \frac{\Delta_F \cdot \Gamma_P}{\Gamma_F} - \Delta_P.$$

Using the technique described above one can easily derive hedging schemes in order to make a given portfolio neutral with respect to any of the greeks above. This is, however, left to the reader.

9.4 Exercises

Exercise 9.1 Consider the standard Black–Scholes model. Fix the time of maturity T and consider the following T-claim $\mathcal{X}$.

$$\mathcal{X} = \begin{cases} K & \text{if } S(T) \leq A \\ K + A - S(T) & \text{if } A < S(T) < K + A \\ 0 & \text{if } S(T) > K + A. \end{cases} \tag{9.28}$$

This contract can be replicated using a portfolio, consisting solely of bonds, stock and European call options, which is constant over time. Determine this portfolio as well as the arbitrage free price of the contract.

Exercise 9.2 The setup is the same as in the previous exercise. Here the contract is a so-called **straddle**, defined by

$$\mathcal{X} = \begin{cases} K - S(T) & \text{if } 0 < S(T) \leq K \\ S(T) - K & \text{if } K < S(T). \end{cases} \tag{9.29}$$

Determine the constant replicating portfolio as well as the arbitrage free price of the contract.

Exercise 9.3 The setup is the same as in the previous exercises. We will now study a so-called "bull spread" (see Fig. 9.7). With this contract we can, to a

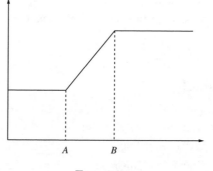

FIG. 9.7.

limited extent, take advantage of an increase in the market price while being protected from a decrease. The contract is defined by

$$\mathcal{X} = \begin{cases} B & \text{if } S(T) > B \\ S(T) & \text{if } A \leq S(T) \leq B \\ A & \text{if } S(T) < A. \end{cases} \tag{9.30}$$

We have of course the relation $A < B$. Determine the constant replicating portfolio as well as the arbitrage free price of the contract.

Exercise 9.4 The setup and the problem are the same as in the previous exercises. The contract is defined by

$$\mathcal{X} = \begin{cases} 0 & \text{if } S(T) < A \\ S(T) - A & \text{if } A \leq S(T) \leq B \\ C - S(T) & \text{if } B \leq S(T) \leq C \\ 0 & \text{if } S(T) > C. \end{cases} \tag{9.31}$$

By definition the point C divides the interval $[A, C]$ in the middle, i.e $B = \frac{A+C}{2}$.

Exercise 9.5 Suppose that you have a portfolio P with $\Delta_P = 2$ and $\Gamma_P = 3$. You want to make this portfolio delta and gamma neutral by using two derivatives F and G, with $\Delta_F = -1$, $\Gamma_F = 2$, $\Delta_G = 5$ and $\Gamma_G = -2$. Compute the hedge.

Exercise 9.6 Consider the same situation as above, with the difference that now you want to use the underlying S instead of G. Construct the hedge according to the two step scheme descibed in Section 9.3.

Exercise 9.7 Prove Proposition 9.7 by comparing the stock holdings in the continuously rebalanced portfolio to the replicating portfolio in Theorem 8.5 of the previous chapter.

Exercise 9.8 Consider a self-financing Markovian portfolio (in continuous time) containing various derivatives of the single underlying asset in the Black–Scholes model. Denote the value (pricing function) of the portfolio by $P(t, s)$. Show that the following relation must hold between the various greeks of P.

$$\Theta_P + rs\Delta_P + \frac{1}{2}\sigma^2 s^2 \Gamma_P = rP.$$

Hint: Use Exercise 8.4.

Exercise 9.9 Use the result in the previous exercise to show that if the portfolio is both delta and gamma neutral, then it replicates the risk free asset, i.e. it has a risk free rate of return which is equal to the short rate r.

Exercise 9.10 Show that for a European put option the delta and gamma are given by

$$\Delta = N[d_1] - 1,$$
$$\Gamma = \frac{\varphi(d_1)}{s\sigma\sqrt{T-t}}.$$

Hint: Use put–call parity.

Exercise 9.11 Take as given the usual portfolio P, and investigate how you can hedge it in order to make it both delta and vega neutral.

10

THE MARTINGALE APPROACH
TO ARBITRAGE THEORY*

In this chapter, we consider a market model consisting of $N + 1$ a priori given asset price processes $S_0, S_1, \ldots, S_N$. Typically we specify the model by giving the dynamics of the asset price processes under the objective probability measure P, and the main problems are as follows.

Fundamental Problems 10.1

1. Under what conditions is the market arbitrage free?
2. Under what conditions is the market complete?

We attack the fundamental problems above by presenting the "martingale approach" to financial derivatives. This is, so far, the most general approach existing for arbitrage pricing, and it is also extremely efficient from a computational point of view. The answers to the problems above are given by the famous so-called **First** and **Second Fundamental Theorems** of Mathematical Finance, which will be treated below. However; while these results are extremely general and powerful, they are also quite deep, necessarily involving hard results from functional analysis, so at some points we only present the main structural ideas of the proofs. For full proofs the reader is directed to the references in the Notes. For the benefit of the reader who does not want to go deeply into the theory, we give a summary of the results in Section 10.7. That section can be read without reading the rest of the chapter.

10.1 The Case with Zero Interest Rate

We will start by considering the special case when one of the assets on the market is a risk free asset with zero rate of return. This may sound very restrictive, but we will later show how the general case easily can be reduced to this special case.

As the basic setup we thus consider a financial market consisting of N exogenously given risky traded assets, and the asset price vector is as usual denoted by

$$S(t) = \begin{bmatrix} S_1(t) \\ \vdots \\ S_N(t) \end{bmatrix} \tag{10.1}$$

We also assume that there exists a risk free asset with price process $S_0(t)$. This will be our numeraire, and in this section we assume that in fact it is constant, i.e. it has zero rate of return.

Assumption 10.1.1 *We assume that*

$$S_0(t) = 1, \quad for\ all\ t \geq 0. \tag{10.2}$$

The S_0 asset can thus be interpreted as a money account in a bank with zero short rate. In the most general version of the theory, the risky price processes are allowed to be general semimartingales, but for our purposes it will be enough to assume that all price processes possess stochastic differentials with a finite number of driving Wiener processes. Our fundamental problems are to find out under what conditions the market described above is free of arbitrage possibilities, and under what conditions it is complete.

Before starting a formal discussion of this project we have to be a bit more precise about the set of admissible portfolios. Let us on a preliminary basis define a **naive** portfolio process as *any* adapted process $h(t) = [h_0(t), h_1(t), \ldots, h_N(t)]$. It then turns out that in order to construct a reasonable theory, the class of naive self financing portfolios is simply too big, and we have in fact the following strongly negative result.

Theorem 10.1 *If at least one of the assets $S_1, \ldots S_N$ has a diffusion term which is nonzero at all times, and if naive portfolio strategies are admitted, then the model admits arbitrage.*

Proof   The idea of the proof is based upon the so called "doubling strategy" for the roulette. In this strategy you start by investing one dollar on black. If you win you stop, having won one dollar. If you lose, you bet another two dollars, and if you win in this bet your total gain is again one dollar. If you lose again you bet another four dollars, etc. Thus; as soon as you win you stop, and as long as you lose you double your bet. In this way, and as long as the roulette has positive probability for black coming up (it does not have to be evenly balanced), you will eventually (i.e. with probability one) win, and your net profit will be one dollar.

This is an arbitrage on the roulette, and the reason that this does not work well in practice, like in Monte Carlo, is that it requires you to have unlimited credit, since at some points in the game you will have lost an enormous amount of money before eventually winning one dollar. Also, the time spent until you win is a priori unbounded although it is finite with probability one. Thus the probability is high that the sun (and you) has died until you get your dollar.

In real life you do not have unlimited credit, but within our theoretical framework credit **is** unlimited, and it is in fact quite simple to use our market model to imitate the Monte Carlo roulette wheel and the doubling strategy above in *finite time*. If you want the play to be over at $t = 1$ you simply invest at the discrete times $1 - 1/n;\ n = 1, 2, \ldots$. You start by investing one dollar in the risky asset, financing by a bank loan, and then you stop as soon as you gain on the investment and you double your investment as long as you lose (all the time financing by a bank loan). It is then easy to see that you can in fact repeat this arbitrage strategy an infinite number of times on any bounded interval, so with probability one you will become infinitely rich.   □

In order to have a reasonable theory we must thus restrict the class of admissible strategies to a smaller class where these doubling strategies are excluded. There are many ways of doing this and a commonly used one is given below. In order to have a compact notation we will use $h_S(t)$ as shorthand for the part of the portfolio which is connected to the risky assets, i.e. $h_S(t) = [h_1(t), \ldots, h_N(t)]$, and we can thus write the entire portfolio h as $h = [h_0, h_S]$.

Definition 10.2

- For any process $h = [h_0, h_S]$, its **value process** $V(t; h)$ is defined by

$$V(t; h) = h_0(t) \cdot 1 + \sum_{i=1}^{N} h_i(t) S_i(t), \qquad (10.3)$$

or in compact form

$$V(t; h) = h_0(t) \cdot 1 + h_S(t) S(t) \qquad (10.4)$$

- An adapted process h_S is called **admissible** if there exists a nonnegative real number α (which may depend on the choice of h_S) such that

$$\int_0^t h_S(u) dS(u) \geq -\alpha, \quad \text{for all } t \in [0, T]. \qquad (10.5)$$

A process $h(t) = [h_0(t), h_S(t)]$, is called an **admissible portfolio** process if h_S is admissible.

- An admissible portfolio is said to be **self-financing**, if

$$V(t; h) = V(0, h) + \int_0^t h_S(u) dS(u), \qquad (10.6)$$

i.e. if

$$dV(t; h) = h_S(t) dS(t). \qquad (10.7)$$

Comparing with Definition 6.2, we note that formally the self-financing condition should be

$$dV(t; h) = h_0(t) dS_0(t) + h_S(t) dS(t),$$

but since in our case $S_0 \equiv 1$, we have $dS_0 \equiv 0$ so the self-financing condition reduces to (10.7). This is a simple but important fact, which is highlighted by the following result.

Lemma 10.3 *For any adapted process h_S satisfying the admissibility condition (10.5), and for any real number x, there exists a unique adapted process h_0, such that:*

- *The portfolio h defined by $h = [h_0, h_S]$ is self financing.*
- *The value process is given by*

$$V(t; h) = x + \int_0^t h_S(u) dS(u).$$ (10.8)

In particular, the space $\mathcal{K}_0$ of portfolio values, reachable at time T by means of a self-financing portfolio with zero initial cost is given by

$$\mathcal{K}_0 = \left\{ \int_0^T h_S(t) dS(t) \middle| h_S \text{ is admissible} \right\}$$ (10.9)

Proof   Define h_0 by

$$h_0(t) = x + \int_0^t h_S(u) dS(u) - h_S(t) S(t).$$

Then, by the definition of the value process, we obviously have

$$V(t; h) = h_0(t) + h_S(t) S(t) = x + \int_0^t h_S(u) dS(u)$$

and from this we obtain directly

$$dV(t; h) = h_S(t) dS(t),$$

which shows that h is self financing. The last item is now obvious.   □

We stress the fact that the simple characterization of the zero cost reachable claims in (10.9) depends crucially on our assumption that $S_0 \equiv 1$.

10.2   Absence of Arbitrage

We consider the market model (10.1) over the finite time interval $[0, T]$, still with the assumption that $S_0 \equiv 1$.

We now give the formal definition of a martingale measure.

Definition 10.4 *A probability measure Q on $\mathcal{F}_T$ is called an* **equivalent martingale measure** *for the market model (10.1), the numeraire S_0, and the time interval $[0, T]$, if it has the following properties.*

- *Q is equivalent to P on $\mathcal{F}_T$.*
- *All price processes $S_0, S_1, \ldots, S_N$ are martingales under Q on the time interval $[0, T]$.*

An equivalent martingale measure will often be referred to as just "a martingale measure" or as "an EMM". If $Q \sim P$ has the property that $S_0, S_1, \ldots, S_N$ are local martingales, then Q is called a **local martingale measure.**

We note that by our assumption above, S_0 is trivially always a martingale. From an informal point of view, the main result of the entire arbitrage theory is the following not very precisely formulated Theorem.

Theorem 10.5 (The First Fundamental Theorem) *The model is arbitrage free essentially if and only if there exists a (local) martingale measure Q.*

This widely quoted result has the nature of a "Folk Theorem" in the sense that it is known to everyone and that, apart from the diffuse term "essentially", it is correct. Below we will discuss exactly what we mean with "essentially" in the formulation above, and we will also give more exact formulations of it. A full proof of a precise version of the First Fundamental Theorem is very hard and technical, and thus to a large extent outside the scope of the book. The main ideas, however, are quite simple and straightforward. We will present these ideas and we will also point out where the technical problems appear. The reader interested in the full story is referred to the Notes.

10.2.1 *A Rough Sketch of the Proof*

In this section we will informally discuss the main ideas of the proof of the First Fundamental Theorem, and we will also point out the problems encountered. The proof consists of two parts:

- Existence of an EMM implies absence of arbitrage.
- Absence of arbitrage implies existence of an EMM.

The first part is rather easy, whereas the second part is very hard.

I: Existence of an EMM implies absence of arbitrage. This part is in fact surprisingly easy. To see this, let us assume that there does indeed exist a martingale measure Q. In our Wiener driven world this implies (see the Girsanov Theorem in Chapter 11 below) that all price processes have zero drift under Q, i.e. their Q dynamics are of the form

$$dS_i(t) = S_i(t)\sigma_i(t)dW^Q(t), \quad i = 1, \ldots, N, \tag{10.10}$$

where W^Q is some multidimensional Q-Wiener process and σ_i is some adapted row vector process.

We now want to prove that there exist no arbitrage possibilities, so we assume that for some self-financing process h, which we for the moment assume to be uniformly bounded, the corresponding value process satisfies the relations

$$P\left(V(T;h) \geq 0\right) = 1, \qquad (10.11)$$
$$P\left(V(T;h) > 0\right) > 0. \qquad (10.12)$$

We are thus viewing h as a potential arbitrage portfolio, and in order to prove absence of arbitrage we thus want to show that $V(0,h) > 0$.

Since $Q \sim P$ we see that we also have the relations

$$Q\left(V(T;h) \geq 0\right) = 1, \qquad (10.13)$$
$$Q\left(V(T;h) > 0\right) > 0, \qquad (10.14)$$

Since h is self financing we have (remember that $dS_0 = 0$)

$$dV(t;h) = \sum_{i=1}^{N} h_i(t)S_i(t)\sigma_i(t)dW^Q(t),$$

and thus (by the boundedness assumptions) we see that $V(t;h)$ is a Q-martingale. In particular we then have

$$V(0;h) = E^Q\left[V(T;h)\right].$$

However, (10.13)–(10.14) imply that $E^Q\left[V(T;h)\right] > 0$, so $V(0;h) > 0$. We have thus shown that (10.11)–(10.12) implies $V(0;h) > 0$, thereby proving the nonexistence of a bounded arbitrage portfolio.

For the case of a possibly unbounded, but of course still admissible, portfolio we have to resort to more delicate arguments. One can then show that, since the value process is bounded from below it is in fact a supermartingale. Thus

$$V(0;h) \geq E^Q\left[V(T;h)\right] > 0,$$

and the proof of this part is finished.   ☐

II: Absence of arbitrage implies existence of an EMM. This is the really difficult part of the first fundamental theorem. It requires several hard results from functional analysis, but the basic ideas are as follows.

In order to avoid integrability problems we assume that all asset price processes are bounded and we interpret "arbitrage" as "bounded arbitrage". We thus assume absence of arbitrage and we want to prove the existence of an EMM, or in more technical terms we would like to prove the existence of a Radon–Nikodym derivative L on $\mathcal{F}_T$ which will transform the P-measure into a martingale measure Q. Inspired from the simple one period model discussed in Chapter 3 it is natural to look for some sort of convex separation theorem, and to this end we need to put our problem within a more functional analytical setting. Since the Radon–Nikodym derivative L should be in L^1, it is natural to try to utilize duality between L^∞ and L^1 so therefore we define the following sets, with L^1 denoting $L^1(\Omega, \mathcal{F}_T, P)$ and L^∞ denoting $L^\infty(\Omega, \mathcal{F}_T, P)$. (Recall that $\mathcal{K}_0$ is the space of all claims which can be reached by a self financed portfolio at zero initial cost.)

$$\mathcal{K} = \mathcal{K}_0 \cap L^\infty, \tag{10.15}$$
$$L^\infty_+ = \text{the nonnegative random variables in } L^\infty, \tag{10.16}$$
$$\mathcal{C} = \mathcal{K} - L^\infty_+. \tag{10.17}$$

The space $\mathcal{K}$ thus consists of all bounded claims which are reachable by a self-financing portfolio at zero initial cost. The set $\mathcal{C}$ are those claims which are dominated by the claims in $\mathcal{K}$, so every claim in $\mathcal{C}$ can be reached by self-financing portfolio with zero initial cost if you also allow yourself to throw away money.

Since we have assumed absence of arbitrage we deduce that

$$\mathcal{C} \cap L^\infty_+ = \{0\}. \tag{10.18}$$

Now, both $\mathcal{C}$ and L^∞_+ are convex sets in L^∞ with only one point in common, so at this point (which is the crucial point of the argument, see below) one would like to refer to a convex separation theorem to guarantee the existence of a nonzero random variable $L \in L^1$ such that

$$E^P[LX] \geq 0, \quad \text{for all } X \in L^\infty_+, \tag{10.19}$$
$$E^P[LX] \leq 0, \quad \text{for all } X \in \mathcal{C}. \tag{10.20}$$

Assume for the moment that this part of the argument can be carried out. From (10.19) we can then deduce that in fact $L \geq 0$, and by scaling we can choose L such that $E^P[L] = 1$. We can thus use L as a Radon–Nikodym derivative to define a new measure Q by $dQ = LdP$ on $\mathcal{F}_T$, and Q is now our natural candidate as a martingale measure. □

Although the main ideas above are good, there are two hard technical problems which must be dealt with:

- Since L^1 is **not** the dual of L^∞ (in the norm topologies) we can not use a standard convex separation theorem. An application of a standard Banach space separation theorem would provide us with a linear functional $L \in (L^\infty)^*$ such that $\langle X, L \rangle \geq 0$ for all $X \in L^\infty_+$ and $\langle X, L \rangle \leq 0$ for all X in $\mathcal{C}$, but since L^1 is strictly included in $(L^\infty)^*$ we have no guarantee that L can be represented by an element in L^1. We thus need a stronger separation theorem than the standard one.
- Supposing that the duality problem above can be resolved, it remains to prove that L is strictly positive (not only nonnegative), since otherwise we may only have $Q << P$ but not $Q \sim P$.

10.2.2 Precise Results

We now move on to a more formal discussion of the various versions the First Fundamental Theorem. For the main proof we follow Delbaen and Schachermayer (1994). This will force us to use some results and concepts from functional analysis which are outside the present text, and the reader is referred to Rudin (1991) for general information. The new ingredients of the full proof are as follows:

- We introduce a variation of the concept of no arbitrage, namely "No Free Lunch with Vanishing Risk".
- In order to obtain a duality between L^1 and L^∞ we consider the weak* topologies instead of the norm topologies.
- We use the Kreps–Yan separation Theorem.

As a first step, it turns out that the standard definition of absence of arbitrage is a bit too restrictive to allow us to deduce the existence of an EMM, so we need to modify this concept slightly.

Definition 10.6 *With notation as in the previous section, we say that the model admits*

- **No Arbitrage** *(NA) if*

$$\mathcal{C} \cap L^\infty_+ = \{0\}\,, \tag{10.21}$$

- **No Free Lunch with Vanishing Risk** *(NFLVR) if*

$$\bar{\mathcal{C}} \cap L^\infty_+ = \{0\}\,, \tag{10.22}$$

where $\bar{\mathcal{C}}$ denotes the closure of $\mathcal{C}$ in L^∞.

The no arbitrage condition is the same as before, whereas NFLVR is a slightly wider concept. If NFLVR does not hold then there will exist a nonzero claim $X \in L^\infty_+$ and a sequence $X_n \in \mathcal{C}$ such that $|X_n - X| < 1/n$ for all n, so in particular $X_n > -1/n$. Thus; for each n there exists a self-financing (zero initial cost) portfolio generating a claim which is closer than $1/n$ to the arbitrage claim X, while the downside risk is less than $1/n$. This is almost an arbitrage.

As a second step we consider the weak* topology on L^∞ generated by L^1. It is well known (see Rudin (1991)) that with the weak* topology, the dual of L^∞ is L^1 so we are now in a nice position to apply a separation theorem. More precisely we will need the following deep result.

Theorem 10.7 (Kreps–Yan Separation Theorem) *If $\mathcal{C}$ is weak* closed, and if*

$$\mathcal{C} \cap L^\infty_+ = \{0\}\,,$$

then there exists a random variable $L \in L^1$ such that L is P almost surely strictly positive, and

$$E^P\left[L \cdot X\right] \le 0, \quad \text{for all } X \in \mathcal{C}.$$

Proof For a proof and references see Schachermayer (1994). □

We are now almost in business, and we see that in order for the Kreps–Yan Theorem to work we need to assume No Arbitrage and we also need assumptions which guarantee that $\mathcal{C}$ is weak* closed. Happily enough we have the following surprising result from Delbaen-Schachermayer (1994) which shows that the closedness of $\mathcal{C}$ in fact follows from NFLVR. The proof is very hard and therefore omitted.

Proposition 10.8 *If the asset price processes are uniformly bounded, then the condition NFLVR implies that $\mathcal{C}$ is weak* closed.*

We can now state and prove the main result.

Theorem 10.9 (First Fundamental Theorem) *Assume that the asset price process S is bounded. Then there exists an equivalent martingale measure if and only if the model satisfies NFLVR.*

Proof The *only if* part is the easy one, and the proof is already given in Section 10.2.1. Before going on we recall the definitions of $\mathcal{K}$ and $\mathcal{C}$ and from (10.15)–(10.17). For the *if* part we assume NFLVR. This implies that $\mathcal{C}$ is weak* closed and it also (trivially) implies No Arbitrage, i.e. $\mathcal{C} \cap L_+^\infty = \{0\}$. We may thus apply the Kreps–Yan Separation to deduce the existence of a random variable $L \in L^1$ such that L is P almost surely strictly positive, and

$$E^P[L \cdot X] \leq 0, \quad \text{for all } X \in \mathcal{C}. \tag{10.23}$$

By scaling we can choose L such that $E^P[L] = 1$. We may thus use L as a Radon–Nikodym derivative to define a new measure Q by $dQ = LdP$ on $\mathcal{F}_T$, and Q is now our natural candidate as a martingale measure. It follows from (10.23) and the definition of $\mathcal{K}$ that $E^P[LX] \leq 0$ for all $X \in \mathcal{K}$. Since $\mathcal{K}$ is a linear subspace this implies that in fact $E^Q[X] = E^P[LX] = 0$ for all $X \in \mathcal{K}$. In order to prove the martingale property of S_i for a fixed i, we choose fixed s and t with $s \leq t$, as well as an arbitrary event $A \in \mathcal{F}_s$. Now consider the following self-financing portfolio strategy:

- Start with zero wealth and do nothing until time s.
- At time s buy I_A units of asset No. i. Finance this by a loan in the bank.
- At time t sell the holdings of asset No. i and repay the loan. Put any surplus in the bank and keep it there until time T.

Since the short rate equals zero, the initial loan (at time s) in the bank is payed back (at time t) by the same amount, so at time t the value of our portfolio is given by $V(t; h) = I_A[S_i(t) - S_i(s)]$. Since the short rate equals zero this will also be the value of our portfolio at time T. Thus we have $I_A(S_i(t) - S_i(s)) \in \mathcal{K}$ so we must have $E^Q[I_A(S_i(t) - S_i(s))] = 0$, and since this holds for all s, t and $A \in \mathcal{F}_s$ we have proved that S_i is a Q martingale. □

In most applications, the assumption of a bounded S process is far too restrictive. The Delbaen–Schachermayer Theorem can however easily be extended to a
more general case.

Theorem 10.10 *Assume that the asset price process S is locally bounded. Then
there exists an equivalent local martingale measure if and only if the model
satisfies NFLVR.*

Remark 10.2.1 We note that in particular the result above will hold if the
S process has continuous trajectories. It will also hold for an S process with
jumps as long as the jumps are bounded. The case of an S process which is
not locally bounded such as for example a process with lognormally distributed
jumps at exponentially distributed times is much more difficult, and in such
a case NFLVR is only equivalent to the existence of an equivalent measure Q
such that S becomes a so-called "sigma-martingale" under Q. See the Notes for
references.

10.3   The General Case

We now relax the assumption that $S_0 \equiv 1$, and go on to consider a market model
consisting of the price processes

$$S_0, S_1, \ldots, S_N,$$

where we make the following assumption.

Assumption 10.3.1 *We assume that $S_0(t) > 0$ P-a.s. for all $t \geq 0$.*

The main problem is to give conditions for absence of arbitrage in this model,
and these are easily obtained by moving to the "normalized" economy where we
use S_0 as a numeraire.

Thus: instead of looking at the price vector process $S = [S_0, S_1, \ldots, S_N]$ we
look at the *relative price vector process* $S(t)/S_0(t)$, where we have used S_0 as the
numeraire price. This object will be studied in more detail in Chapter 26.

Definition 10.11 *The* **normalized economy** *(also referred to as the
"Z-economy") is defined by the price vector process Z, where*

$$Z(t) = \frac{S(t)}{S_0(t)},$$

i.e.

$$Z(t) = [Z_0(t), \ldots, Z_N(t)] = \left[1, \frac{S_1(t)}{S_0(t)}, \frac{S_2(t)}{S_0(t)}, \ldots, \frac{S_N(t)}{S_0(t)} \right]. \tag{10.24}$$

The point of this is that in the Z economy we have a risk free asset $Z_0 \equiv 1$,
with zero rate of return, so the simple idea is to apply the results from the
previous sections to the Z economy.

First, however, we have two price systems to keep track of: the S-system and
the Z-system, and before going on we have to clarify the relations between these

systems. In particular, for any portfolio process h there will be associated two value processes, one in the S system and one in the Z system, and we thus need to introduce some notation.

Definition 10.12

- *A* **portfolio strategy** *is any adapted* $(N+1)$*-dimensional process*

$$h(t) = [h_0(t), h_1(t), \ldots, h_N(t)]$$

- *The* **S-value process** $V^S(t; h)$ *corresponding to the portfolio h is given by*

$$V^S(t; h) = \sum_{i=0}^{N} h_i(t) S_i(t). \tag{10.25}$$

- *The* **Z-value process** $V^Z(t; h)$ *corresponding to the portfolio h is given by*

$$V^Z(t; h) = \sum_{i=0}^{N} h_i(t) Z_i(t). \tag{10.26}$$

- *A portfolio is said to be* **admissible** *if it is admissible in the sense of Definition 10.2 as a Z portfolio.*
- *An admissible portfolio is said to be* **S-self-financing** *if*

$$dV^S(t; h) = \sum_{i=0}^{N} h_i(t) dS_i(t). \tag{10.27}$$

- *An admissible portfolio is said to be* **Z-self-financing** *if*

$$dV^Z(t; h) = \sum_{i=0}^{N} h_i(t) dZ_i(t). \tag{10.28}$$

We can also make the obvious definitions of a given T-claim being S-reachable and Z-reachable respectively.

The intuitive feeling is that the concept of a self-financing portfolio should not depend upon the particular choice of numeraire. That this is indeed the case is shown by the following "Invariance Lemma".

Lemma 10.13 (Invariance lemma) *With assumptions and notation as above, the following hold:*

(i) A portfolio h is S-self-financing if and only if it is Z-self-financing.
(ii) The value processes V^S and V^Z are connected by

$$V^Z(t; h) = \frac{1}{S_0(t)} \cdot V^S(t; h).$$

(iii) A claim $\mathcal{Y}$ is S-reachable if and only if the claim

$$\frac{\mathcal{Y}}{S_0(T)}$$

is Z-reachable.

- *The model is S arbitrage free if and only if it is S arbitrage free.*

Proof   Items (ii) and (iii) are obvious. Thus it only remains to prove the self-financing result, and for simplicity we assume that all processes possess stochastic differentials driven by a finite number of Wiener processes. Assume therefore that the portfolio h is S-self-financing. Denoting the scalar product between vectors by the "scalar dot" $\cdot$, using the notation $\beta = S_0$, and suppressing the t-variable, we have from this assumption that

$$Z = \beta^{-1}S, \tag{10.29}$$
$$V^S = h \cdot S, \tag{10.30}$$
$$V^Z = \beta^{-1}V^S, \tag{10.31}$$
$$dV^S = h \cdot dS. \tag{10.32}$$

We now want to prove that in fact

$$dV^Z = h \cdot dZ.$$

Using the Itô formula on $Z = \beta^{-1}S$, we thus want to prove that

$$dV^Z = \beta^{-1}h \cdot dS + h \cdot S d\beta^{-1} + h \cdot dS d\beta^{-1}. \tag{10.33}$$

Now, from (10.31) we have

$$dV^Z = \beta^{-1}dV^S + V^S d\beta^{-1} + d\beta^{-1}dV^S.$$

Substituting (10.30) and (10.32) into this equation gives

$$dV^Z = \beta^{-1}h \cdot dS + h \cdot S d\beta^{-1} + d\beta^{-1}h \cdot dS,$$

which is what we wanted to prove.   □

We may now formulate and prove the main result concerning absence of arbitrage.

Theorem 10.14 (The First Fundamental Theorem)   *Consider the market model $S_0, S_1, \ldots, S_N$ where we assume that $S_0(t) > 0$, P-a.s. for all $t \geq 0$. Assume furthermore that $S_0, S_1, \ldots, S_N$ are locally bounded. Then the following conditions are equivalent:*

- *The model satisfies NFLVR.*
- *There exists a measure $Q \sim P$ such that the processes*

$$Z_0, Z_1, \ldots, Z_N,$$

defined through (10.24), are local martingales under Q.

Proof This follows directly from the Invariance Lemma and from Theorem 10.10.   □

Remark 10.3.1 It is important to note that the martingale measure Q above is connected to the particular choice of numeraire S_0, and that different numeraires will produce different martingale measures. A more precise notation for the martingale measure should therefore perhaps be Q^0, in order to emphasize the dependence upon the chosen numeraire.

From now on we will, for a given numeraire, use the term "martingale measure" to denote the (not necessarily unique) local martingale measure of Theorem 10.14.

10.4 Completeness

In this section we assume absence of arbitrage, i.e. we assume that there exists a (local) martingale measure. We now turn to the possibility of replicating a given contingent claim in terms of a portfolio based on the underlying assets. This problem is most conveniently carried out in terms of normalized prices, and we have the following useful lemma, which shows that hedging is equivalent to the existence of a stochastic integral representation of the normalized claim.

Lemma 10.15 *Consider a given T-claim X. Fix a martingale measure Q and assume that the normalized claim $X/S_0(T)$ is integrable. If the Q-martingale M, defined by*

$$M(t) = E^Q \left[\frac{X}{S_0(T)} \middle| \mathcal{F}_t \right],$$ (10.34)

admits an integral representation of the form

$$M(t) = x + \sum_{i=1}^{N} \int_0^t h_i(s) dZ_i(s),$$ (10.35)

then X can be hedged in the S-economy. Furthermore, the replicating portfolio $(h_0, h_1, \ldots, h_N)$ is given by (10.35) for $(h_1, \ldots, h_K)$, whereas h_0 is given by $h_0(t) = M(t) - \sum_{i=1}^{N} h_i(t) Z_i(t)$.

Proof We want to hedge X in the S economy, i.e. we want to hedge $X/S_0(T)$ in the Z economy. In terms of normalized prices, and using the Invariance

Lemma, we are thus looking for a process $h = (h_0, h_1, \ldots, h_N)$ such that

$$V^Z(T; h) = \frac{X}{S_0(T)}, \quad P - a.s. \tag{10.36}$$

$$dV^Z = \sum_{i=1}^{N} h_i dZ_i, \tag{10.37}$$

where the normalized value process is given by

$$V^Z(t; h) = h_0(t) \cdot 1 + \sum_{i=1}^{N} h_i(t) Z_i(t). \tag{10.38}$$

A reasonable guess is that $M = V^Z$, so we let M be defined by (10.34). Furthermore we define $(h_1, \ldots, h_N)$ by (10.35), and we define h_0 by

$$h_0(t) = M(t) - \sum_{i=1}^{N} h_i(t) Z_i(t). \tag{10.39}$$

Now, from (10.38) we obviously have $M = V^Z$, and from (10.35) we get

$$dV^Z = dM = \sum_{i=1}^{N} h_i dZ_i,$$

which shows that the portfolio is self financing. Furthermore we have

$$V^Z(T; h) = M(T) = E^Q\left[\frac{X}{S_0(T)}\bigg|\mathcal{F}_T\right] = \frac{X}{S_0(T)},$$

which shows that X is replicated by h.   □

We thus see that, modulo some integrability considerations, completeness is equivalent to the existence of a martingale representation theorem for the discounted price process. Thus we may draw on the deep results of Jacod (1979) from semimartingale theory which connect martingale representation properties for Z with the extremal points of the set of martingale measures.

Theorem 10.16 (Jacod) *Let $\mathcal{M}$ denote the (convex) set of equivalent martingale measures. Then, for any fixed $Q \in \mathcal{M}$, the following statements are equivalent.*

- *Every Q local martingale M has dynamics of the form*

$$dM(t) = \sum_{i=1}^{N} h_i(t) dZ_i(t).$$

- *Q is an extremal point of $\mathcal{M}$.*

We then have the second fundamental theorem of mathematical finance.

Theorem 10.17 (The Second Fundamental Theorem) *Assume that the market is arbitrage free and consider a fixed numeraire asset S_0. Then the market is complete if and only if the martingale measure Q, corresponding to the numeraire S_0, is unique.*

Proof If the martingale measure Q is unique then $\mathcal{M}$ is a singleton $\mathcal{M} = \{Q\}$ so Q is trivially an extremal point of $\mathcal{M}$. Thus the Jacod Theorem provides us with a stochastic integral representation of every Q martingale, and it then follows from Lemma 10.15 that the model is complete. The other implication follows easily from (10.56) of Proposition 10.25 below. □

Remark 10.4.1 The reader may find the proof given above rather abstract, and we provide two alternatives:

- A more functional analytic proof of the Second Fundamental Theorem would be roughly as follows: The market is unique if and only if the set $\mathcal{C}$ of reachable claims at zero initial cost has codimension one, i.e. if

$$L^\infty = \mathcal{C} \oplus R \cdot Y$$

for some $Y \in L^\infty$. This implies that the separating hyperplane implied by the Kreps–Yan Theorem 10.7 is unique and thus that the martingale measure is unique.

- In Section 14.3 we provide a self-contained and complete proof of the Second Fundamental Theorem for the special case of purely Wiener driven models.

10.5 Martingale Pricing

We now turn to the pricing problem for contingent claims. In order to do this, we consider the "primary" market $S_0, S_1, \ldots, S_N$ as given a priori, and we fix a T-claim X. Our task is that of determining a "reasonable" price process $\Pi(t; X)$ for X, and we assume that the primary market is arbitrage free. There are two main approaches:

- The derivative should be priced in a way that is **consistent** with the prices of the underlying assets. More precisely we should demand that the extended market $\Pi(\ ; X), S_0, S_1, \ldots, S_N$ is free of arbitrage possibilities.
- If the claim is **attainable**, with hedging portfolio h, then the only reasonable price is given by $\Pi(t; X) = V(t; h)$.

In the first approach above, we thus demand that there should exist a martingale measure Q for the extended market $\Pi(X), S_0, S_1, \ldots, S_N$. Letting Q denote such a measure, assuming enough integrability, and applying the definition of a martingale measure we obtain

$$\frac{\Pi(t; X)}{S_0(t)} = E^Q\left[\left.\frac{\Pi(T; X)}{S_0(T)}\right|\mathcal{F}_t\right] = E^Q\left[\left.\frac{X}{S_0(T)}\right|\mathcal{F}_t\right] \tag{10.40}$$

We thus have the following result.

Theorem 10.18 (General Pricing Formula) *The arbitrage free price process for the T-claim X is given by*

$$\Pi\left(t; X\right) = S_0(t) E^Q \left[\left. \frac{X}{S_0(T)} \right| \mathcal{F}_t \right], \tag{10.41}$$

where Q is the (not necessarily unique) martingale measure for the a priori given market $S_0, S_1, \ldots, S_N$, with S_0 as the numeraire.

Note that different choices of Q will generically give rise to different price processes.

In particular we note that if we assume that if S_0 is the money account

$$S_0(t) = S_0(0) \cdot e^{\int_0^t r(s)ds},$$

where r is the short rate, then (10.41) reduced to the familiar "risk neutral valuation formula".

Theorem 10.19 (Risk Neutral Valuation Formula) *Assuming the existence of a short rate, the pricing formula takes the form*

$$\Pi\left(t; X\right) = E^Q \left[\left. e^{-\int_t^T r(s)ds} X \right| \mathcal{F}_t \right]. \tag{10.42}$$

where Q is a (not necessarily unique) martingale measure with the money account as the numeraire.

For the second approach to pricing let us assume that X can be replicated by h. Since the holding of the derivative contract and the holding of the replicating portfolio are equivalent from a financial point of view, we see that price of the derivative must be given by the formula

$$\Pi\left(t; X\right) = V(t; h). \tag{10.43}$$

One problem here is what will happen in a case when X can be replicated by two different portfolios, and one would also like to know how this formula is connected to (10.41).

Defining $\Pi\left(t; X\right)$ by (10.43) see that $\Pi\left(t; X\right)/S_0(t) = V^Z(t)$ and since, assuming enough integrability, V^Z is a Q-martingale, we see that also $\Pi\left(t; X\right)/S_0(t)$ is a Q-martingale. Thus we again obtain the formula (10.41) and for an attainable claim we have in particular the formula

$$V(t; h) = S_0(t) E^Q \left[\left. \frac{X}{S_0(T)} \right| \mathcal{F}_t \right], \tag{10.44}$$

which will hold for any replicating portfolio and for any martingale measure Q. Thus we see that the two pricing approaches above do in fact coincide on the set of attainable claims. In Section 10.7 we will summarize our results.

10.6 Stochastic Discount Factors

In the previous sections we have seen that we can price a contingent T-claim X by using the formula

$$\Pi(t; X) = E^Q \left[e^{-\int_t^T r(s)ds} X \,\middle|\, \mathcal{F}_t \right], \tag{10.45}$$

where Q is a martingale measure with the money account as a numeraire. In some applications of the theory (in particular in asset pricing) it is common to write this expected value directly under the objective probability measure P instead of under Q. This can easily be obtained by using the likelihood process L, where a usual L is defined on the interval $[0, T]$ through

$$L(t) = \frac{dQ}{dP}, \quad \text{on } \mathcal{F}_t. \tag{10.46}$$

Using the Abstract Bayes' Formula we can now write (10.45) as

$$\Pi(t; X) = \frac{E^P \left[e^{-\int_t^T r(s)ds} L(T) X \,\middle|\, \mathcal{F}_t \right]}{L(t)} = E^P \left[e^{-\int_t^T r(s)ds} \frac{L(T)}{L(t)} X \,\middle|\, \mathcal{F}_t \right],$$

which naturally leads us to the following definition.

Definition 10.20 *Assume the existence of a short rate r. For any fixed martingale measure Q, let the likelihood process L be defined by (10.46). The* **stochastic discount factor** *(SDF) process Λ, corresponding to Q, is defined as*

$$\Lambda(t) = e^{-\int_0^t r(s)ds} L(t). \tag{10.47}$$

We thus see that there is a one-to-one correspondence between martingale measures and stochastic discount factors. We have now more or less proved the following result.

Proposition 10.21 *Assume absence of arbitrage. With notation as above, the following hold:*

- *For any sufficiently integrable T-claim X, the arbitrage free price is given by*

$$\Pi(t; X) = E^P \left[\frac{\Lambda(T)}{\Lambda(t)} X \,\middle|\, \mathcal{F}_t \right]. \tag{10.48}$$

- *For any arbitrage free asset price process S (derivative or underlying) the process*

$$\Lambda(t)S(t) \tag{10.49}$$

is a (local) P-martingale.
- *The P-dynamics of Λ is given by*

$$d\Lambda(t) = -r(t)\Lambda(t)dt + \frac{1}{B(t)}dL(t). \tag{10.50}$$

Proof   The remaining details of the proof are left to the reader.   □

Although SDFs and martingale measures are logically equivalent, it is often convenient to be able to switch from one to the other. The main advantage of using the martingale measure formalism is that it provides us with a canonical decomposition of the SDF as the (inverse) bank account multiplied by the likelihood process L, and we can then use the deep and well established theory for likelihood processes (see Chapter 11).

We may also, in the obvious way, define stochastic discount factors for other choices of the numeraire than the money account.

An alternative approach to SDFs is to **define** an SDF as any nonnegative random process Λ possessing the property that $S(t)\Lambda(t)$ is a (local) P-martingale for every asset price process S. The First Fundamental Theorem can then be restated as the equivalence between absence of arbitrage and the existence of an SDF.

10.7   Summary for the Working Economist

In this section we summarize the results for the martingale approach. We consider a market model consisting of the asset price processes $S_0, S_1, \ldots, S_N$ on the time interval $[0, T]$. The "numeraire process" S_0 is assumed to be strictly positive. Modulo some technicalities we then have the following results. The first provides conditions for absence of arbitrage.

Theorem 10.22 (First Fundamental Theorem) *The market model is free of arbitrage if and only if there exists a* **martingale measure**, *i.e. a measure $Q \sim P$ such that the processes*

$$\frac{S_0(t)}{S_0(t)}, \frac{S_1(t)}{S_0(t)}, \ldots, \frac{S_N(t)}{S_0(t)}$$

are (local) martingales under Q.

For the case when the numeraire is the money account we have an alternative characterization of a martingale measure. The proof is a simple application of the Itô formula.

Proposition 10.23 *If the numeraire S_0 is the money account, i.e.*

$$S_0(t) = e^{\int_0^t r(s)ds},$$

where r is the (possibly stochastic) short rate, and if we assume that all processes are Wiener driven, then a measure $Q \sim P$ is a martingale measure if and only if all assets $S_0, S_1, \ldots, S_N$ have the short rate as their local rates of return, i.e. if the Q-dynamics are of the form

$$dS_i(t) = S_i(t)r(t)dt + S_i(t)\sigma_i(t)dW^Q(t), \tag{10.51}$$

where W^Q is a (multidimensional) Q-Wiener process.

The second result gives us conditions for market completeness.

Theorem 10.24 (Second Fundamental Theorem) *Assuming absence of arbitrage, the market model is complete if and only if the martingale measure Q is unique.*

As far as pricing of contingent claims is concerned the theory can be summarized as follows.

Proposition 10.25

1. *In order to avoid arbitrage, X must be priced according to the formula*

$$\Pi(t; X) = S_0(t) E^Q \left[\left. \frac{X}{S_0(T)} \right| \mathcal{F}_t \right], \qquad (10.52)$$

where Q is a martingale measure for $[S_0, S_1, \ldots, S_N]$, with S_0 as the numeraire.
2. *In particular, we can choose the bank account $B(t)$ as the numeraire. Then B has the dynamics*

$$dB(t) = r(t) B(t) dt, \qquad (10.53)$$

where r is the (possibly stochastic) short rate process. In this case the pricing formula above reduces to

$$\Pi(t; X) = E^Q \left[\left. e^{-\int_t^T r(s) ds} X \right| \mathcal{F}_t \right]. \qquad (10.54)$$

3. *Different choices of Q will generically give rise to different price processes for a fixed claim X. However, if X is attainable then all choices of Q will produce the same price process, which then is given by*

$$\Pi(t; X) = V(t; h), \qquad (10.55)$$

where h is the hedging portfolio. Different choices of hedging portfolios (if such exist) will produce the same price process.
4. *In particular, for every replicable claim X it holds that*

$$V(t; h) = E^Q \left[\left. e^{-\int_t^T r(s) ds} X \right| \mathcal{F}_t \right]. \qquad (10.56)$$

Summing up we see that in a complete market the price of any derivative will be **uniquely** determined by the requirement of absence of arbitrage. The price is unique precisely because the derivative is in a sense superfluous—it can equally well be replaced by its replicating portfolio. In particular we see that the price does not depend on any assumptions made about the risk-preferences of the agents in the market. The agents can have any attitude towards risk, as long as they prefer more (deterministic) money to less.

In an incomplete market the requirement of no arbitrage is no longer sufficient to determine a unique price for the derivative. We have several martingale measures, all of which can be used to price derivatives in a way consistent with no arbitrage. The question which martingale measure one should use for pricing has a very simple answer: The martingale measure is chosen by the market.

Schematically speaking the price of a derivative is thus determined by two major factors.

1. We require that the derivative should be priced in such a way as to not introduce arbitrage possibilities into the market. This requirement is reflected by the fact that all derivatives must be priced by formula (10.52) where the same Q is used for all derivatives.

2. In an incomplete market the price is also partly determined by aggregate supply and demand on the market. Supply and demand for a specific derivative are in turn determined by the aggregate risk aversion on the market, as well as by liquidity considerations and other factors. All these aspects are aggregated into the particular martingale measure used by the market.

Let us now assume that we have specified some model under the objective probability measure P. This means that we have specified the P-dynamics of all asset prices in the primary market. We may also have specified the P-dynamics of some processes which are not price processes, like the inflation rate, the unemployment rate, or the outside temperature (which influences the demand for electric energy).

In order to be able to apply the theory developed above, it is then clear that we need the following tools:

• We need to have full control of the class of equivalent measure transformations that can be made from a given objective measure P.
• Given an equivalent measure Q (a potential martingale measure), we must be able to write down the Q-dynamics of all processes under consideration.
• We need theorems which allow us to write certain stochastic variables (typically contingent claims) as stochastic integrals of some given processes (typically normalized asset prices).

All these tools are in fact provided by the following mathematical results which are the objects under study in the next chapter.

• The Martingale Representation Theorem for Wiener processes.
• The Girsanov Theorem.

10.8   Notes

The martingale approach to arbitrage pricing was developed in Harrison and Kreps (1979), Kreps (1981), and Harrison and Pliska (1981). It was then extended by, among others, Duffie and Huang (1986), Delbaen (1992), (Schachermayer 1994), and Delbaen and Schachermayer (1994). In this chapter we follow closely Delbaen and Schachermayer (1994) for the case of locally bounded price processes. The general case of unbounded price processes and its connection to sigma-martingales was finally resolved in Delbaen and Schachermayer (1998), which also contains further bibliographic information on this subject. Rudin (1991) is a standard reference on functional analysis, which is also treated in Royden (1988).

Stochastic discount factors are treated in Duffie (2001), and in most modern textbooks on asset pricing such as Cochrane (2001).

11

THE MATHEMATICS OF THE
MARTINGALE APPROACH*

In this chapter we will present the two main workhorses of the martingale approach to arbitrage theory. These are:

- The Martingale Representation Theorem, which shows that in a Wiener world every martingale can be written as a stochastic integral w.r.t. the underlying Wiener process.
- The Girsanov Theorem, which gives us complete control of all absolutely continuous measure transformations in a Wiener world.

11.1 Stochastic Integral Representations

Let us consider a fixed time interval $[0, T]$, a probability space $(\Omega, \mathcal{F}, P)$, with some filtration $\{\mathcal{F}_t\}_{t \geq 0}$, and an adapted vector Wiener process $W = (W_1, \ldots, W_d)^\star$. Now fix a vector process $h = (h_1, \ldots, h_d)$ which is "integrable enough" (for example $h \in \mathcal{L}^2$ is enough) and a real number x_0. If we now define the process M by

$$M(t) = x_0 + \sum_{i=1}^{d} \int_0^t h_i(s) dW_i(s), \quad t \in [0, T], \qquad (11.1)$$

then we know that M is a martingale. In other words: under mild integrability conditions, every stochastic integral w.r.t a Wiener process is an $\mathcal{F}_t$-martingale. A very natural and important question is now whether the converse holds, i.e. if every $\mathcal{F}_t$-adapted martingale M can be written in the form (11.1). If this is indeed the case, then we say that M has a **stochastic integral representation** w.r.t the Wiener process W.

It is not hard to see that in the completely general case, there is no hope for a stochastic integral representation w.r.t W for a general martingale M. As a counterexample, let W be scalar (i.e. $d = 1$) and consider, apart from W, also a Poisson process N, with constant intensity λ, where N is independent of W. Now define the filtration by $\mathcal{F}_t = \mathcal{F}_t^{W,N}$, i.e. $\mathcal{F}_t$ contains all the information generated by W and N over the interval $[0, t]$.

It is now very easy to see that the process M defined by

$$M(t) = N(t) - \lambda t,$$

is an $\mathcal{F}_t$-martingale. If we look at the trajectories of M, they consist of straight lines with downward slope λ, interrupted at exponentially distributed points in time by positive jumps of unit size. From this it is obvious that M can possess no stochastic integral representation of the form (11.1), since any such representation implies that M has continuous trajectories. The intuitive reason is of course that since M is independent of W, we cannot use W in order to represent M.

From this example it is clear that we can only hope for a stochastic integral representation result in the case when $\{\mathcal{F}_t\}_{t\geq 0}$ is the *internal filtration* generated by the Wiener process W itself. We start with the following basic representation for Wiener functionals, which in turn will give us our martingale representation result.

Theorem 11.1 (Representation of Wiener Functionals) *Let W be a d-dimensional Wiener process, and let X be a stochastic variable such that*

- $X \in \mathcal{F}_T^W$,
- $E\left[|X|\right] < \infty$.

Then there exist uniquely determined $\mathcal{F}_t^W$-adapted processes $h_1, \ldots, h_d$, such that X has the representation

$$X = E\left[X\right] + \sum_{i=1}^{d} \int_0^T h_i(s)dW_i(s) \tag{11.2}$$

Under the additional assumption

$$E\left[X^2\right] < \infty,$$

then $h_1, \ldots, h_d$ are in $\mathcal{L}^2$

Proof We only give the proof for the L^2 case, where we present the main ideas of a particularly nice proof from Steele (2001). For notational simplicity we only consider the scalar case.

We start by recalling that the GBM equation

$$dX_t = \sigma X_t dW_t,$$
$$X_0 = 1,$$

has the solution

$$X_t = e^{-\frac{1}{2}\sigma^2 t + \sigma W_t}. \tag{11.3}$$

Writing the SDE on integral form as

$$X_t = 1 + \int_0^t \sigma X_s dW_s \tag{11.4}$$

and plugging (11.3) into (11.4) we obtain, after some reshuffling of terms,

$$e^{\sigma W_t} = e^{\frac{1}{2}\sigma^2 t} + \sigma \int_0^t e^{-\frac{1}{2}\sigma^2(u-t)+\sigma W_u} dW_u$$

Using the same argument we easily obtain, for $s \leq t$,

$$e^{\sigma(W_t - W_s)} = e^{\frac{1}{2}\sigma^2(t-s)} + \sigma \int_s^t e^{-\frac{1}{2}\sigma^2(u-t+s)+\sigma W_u} dW_u, \qquad (11.5)$$

where the important point is that the integral is only over the interval $[s, t]$. Thus any stochastic variable Z of the form

$$Z = \exp\{\sigma(W_t - W_s)\}$$

will have a representation of the form

$$Z = E[Z] + \int_0^T h_u dW_u,$$

where $h \equiv 0$ outside $[s, t]$. From this it follows easily (see the exercises) that any variable Z of the form

$$Z = \prod_{k=1}^n \exp\{\sigma_k (W_{t_k} - W_{t_{k-1}})\} \qquad (11.6)$$

where $0 \leq t_0 \leq t_1 \leq \ldots \leq t_n \leq T$, has a representation of the form

$$Z = E[Z] + \int_0^T h_u dW_u. \qquad (11.7)$$

It is now fairly straightforward to see that also any variable of the form

$$Z = \prod_{k=1}^n \exp\{i\sigma_k (W_{t_k} - W_{t_{k-1}})\} \qquad (11.8)$$

where i is the imaginary unit, has a representation of the form (11.7). At this point we may use Fourier techniques to see that the set of variables of the form (11.8) is dense in the (complex) space $L^2(\mathcal{F}_T)$, and from this one can deduce that in fact every $Z \in L^2(\mathcal{F}_T)$ has a representation of the form (11.7). See Steele (2001) for the details.   □

From this result we now easily obtain the martingale representation theorem.

Theorem 11.2 (The Martingale Representation Theorem) *Let W be a d-dimensional Wiener process, and assume that the filtration $\underline{\mathcal{F}}$ is defined as*

$$\mathcal{F}_t = \mathcal{F}_t^W, \quad t \in [0, T].$$

Let M be any $\mathcal{F}_t$-adapted martingale. Then there exist uniquely determined $\mathcal{F}_t$-adapted processes $h_1, \ldots, h_d$ such that M has the representation

$$M(t) = M(0) + \sum_{i=1}^{d} \int_0^t h_i(s)dW_i(s), \quad t \in [0, T]. \tag{11.9}$$

If the martingale M is square integrable, then $h_1, \ldots, h_d$ are in $\mathcal{L}^2$.

Proof From Theorem 11.1 we have

$$M(T) = M(0) + \sum_{i=1}^{d} \int_0^T h_i(s)dW_i(s).$$

The result now follows by taking conditional expectations and using the fact that M as well as the stochastic integral is a martingale. $\square$

It is worth noticing that the martingale representation theorem above is an abstract existence result. It guarantees the existence of the processes $h_1, \ldots, h_d$, but it does not tell us what the h process looks like. In fact, in the general case we know very little about what exact form of h. The most precise description of h obtained so far is via the so-called Clarc–Ocone formula (see the Notes), but that requires the use and language of Malliavin calculus so it is outside the present text.

In one special case, however, we have a rather explicit description of the integrand h. Let us therefore assume that we have some a priori given n-dimensional process X with dynamics of the form

$$dX(t) = \mu(t)dt + \sigma(t)dW(t), \tag{11.10}$$

where W is as above, whereas μ and σ are adapted processes taking values in R^n and $M(n, d)$ respectively. Let us now assume that the martingale M is of the very particular form $M(t) = f(t, X(t))$ for some deterministic smooth function $f(t, x)$. From the Itô formula we then have

$$df(t, X(t)) = \left\{ \frac{\partial f}{\partial t}(t, X(t)) + \mathcal{A}f(t, X(t)) \right\} dt + (\nabla_x f)(t, X(t))\sigma(t)dW(t)$$

where $\mathcal{A}$ is the usual Ito operator. Now; since $f(t, X_t)$ was assumed to be a martingale, the drift must vanish, so in fact we have

$$df(t, X(t)) = (\nabla_x f)(t, X(t))\,\sigma(t)dW(t).$$

Written out in more detail this becomes

$$df(t, X_t) = \sum_{i=1}^{n} \frac{\partial f}{\partial x_i}(t, X(t))\sigma^i(t)dW_i(t),$$

where σ^i is the i:th row of σ. In this particular case we thus have the explicit description of the integrand h as

$$h_i(t) = \frac{\partial f}{\partial x_i}(t, X(t))\sigma^i(t), \quad i = 1, \ldots d.$$

11.2   The Girsanov Theorem: Heuristics

We now start a discussion of the effect that an absolutely continuous measure transformation will have upon a Wiener process. This discussion will lead us to the Girsanov Theorem which is the central result of the next section.

Assume therefore that our space $(\Omega, \mathcal{F}, P, \underline{\mathcal{F}})$ carries a scalar P-Wiener process W^P, and that for some fixed T we have changed to a new measure Q on $\mathcal{F}_T$ by choosing a nonnegative random variable $L_T \in \mathcal{F}_T$ and defining Q by

$$dQ = L_T dP, \quad \text{on } \mathcal{F}_T.$$

This measure transformation will generate a likelihood process (see section C.3) $\{L_t; \ t \geq 0\}$ defined by

$$L_t = \frac{dQ}{dP}, \quad \text{on } \mathcal{F}_t,$$

and from Proposition C.12 we know that L is a P-martingale.

Since L is a nonnegative P-martingale, and since any (suitably integrable) stochastic integral w.r.t. W is a martingale, it is natural to define L as the solution of the SDE

$$dL_t = \varphi_t L_t dW_t^P, \tag{11.11}$$

$$L_0 = 1. \tag{11.12}$$

for some choice of the process φ.

It thus seems that we can generate a large class of natural measure transformations from P to a new measure Q by the following prescription:

- Choose an arbitrary adapted process φ.
- Define a likelihood process L by

$$dL_t = \varphi_t L_t dW_t^P, \tag{11.13}$$

$$L_0 = 1. \tag{11.14}$$

- Define a new measure Q by setting

$$dQ = L_t dP, \qquad (11.15)$$

on $\mathcal{F}_t$ for all $t \in [0, T]$.

By applying the Itô formula we easily see that we can express L as

$$L_t = e^{\int_0^t \varphi_s dW_s^P - \frac{1}{2} \int_0^t \varphi_s^2 ds},$$

so L is nonnegative, which is necessary if it is going to act as a likelihood process. If φ is integrable enough (see the Novikov condition below) it is also clear (why?) that L is a martingale and the initial condition $L_0 = 1$ guarantees that $E^P[L_t] = 1$.

To see what the dynamics of W^P are under Q, let us first recall that if a process X has the dynamics

$$dX_t = \mu_t dt + \sigma_t dW_t^P,$$

then the drift μ and (squared) diffusion σ has the interpretation of being the conditional drift and quadratic variation processes respectively. A bit more precisely, but still heuristically, we have

$$E^P[dX_t| \mathcal{F}_t] = \mu_t dt,$$
$$E^P\left[(dX_t)^2 \middle| \mathcal{F}_t\right] = \sigma_t^2 dt,$$

where we have the informal interpretation $dX_t = X_{t+dt} - X_t$. Let us now define the process X by $X = W^P$, i.e. we have $\mu = 0$ and $\sigma = 1$ under P. Our task is to compute the drift and diffusion under Q and for that we will use the Abstract Bayes' Theorem (B.41). Using the fact that L is a P-martingale, and recalling that $dX_t \in \mathcal{F}_{t+dt}$ (see definition above), we obtain

$$E^Q[dX_t| \mathcal{F}_t] = \frac{E^P[L_{t+dt} dX_t| \mathcal{F}_t]}{E^P[L_{t+dt}| \mathcal{F}_t]} = \frac{E^P[L_{t+dt} dX_t| \mathcal{F}_t]}{L_t}$$

$$= \frac{E^P[L_t dX_t + dL_t dX_t| \mathcal{F}_t]}{L_t}$$

$$= \frac{E^P[L_t dX_t| \mathcal{F}_t]}{L_t} + \frac{E^P[dL_t dX_t| \mathcal{F}_t]}{L_t}.$$

Since L is adapted (so $L_t \in \mathcal{F}_t$) and X has zero drift under P, we have

$$\frac{E^P[L_t dX_t| \mathcal{F}_t]}{L_t} = L_t \cdot \frac{E^P[dX_t| \mathcal{F}_t]}{L_t} = E^P[dX_t| \mathcal{F}_t] = 0 \cdot dt.$$

Furthermore we have

$$dL_t dX_t = L_t \varphi_t dW_t^P \left(0 \cdot dt + 1 \cdot dW_t^P\right) = L_t \varphi_t \left(dW_t^P\right)^2 = L_t \varphi_t dt.$$

Using this and the fact that $L_t \varphi_t \in \mathcal{F}_t$ we get

$$\frac{E^P \left[dL_t dX_t \mid \mathcal{F}_t\right]}{L_t} = \frac{L_t \varphi_t}{L_t} dt = \varphi_t dt.$$

Using the fact that under P we have $dX_t^2 = dt$ we can also easily compute the quadratic variation of X under Q as

$$E^Q \left[(dX_t)^2 \Big| \mathcal{F}_t\right] = \frac{E^P \left[L_{t+dt} \cdot (dX_t)^2 \Big| \mathcal{F}_t\right]}{L_t} = \frac{E^P \left[L_{t+dt} \cdot dt \mid \mathcal{F}_t\right]}{L_t}$$
$$= \frac{E^P \left[L_{t+dt} \mid \mathcal{F}_t\right]}{L_t} dt = \frac{L_t}{L_t} dt = dt.$$

Summing up we have thus obtained the formal relations

$$E^Q \left[dX_t \mid \mathcal{F}_t\right] = \varphi_t dt,$$
$$E^Q \left[(dX_t)^2 \Big| \mathcal{F}_t\right] = 1 \cdot dt.$$

or in other words:

- The process $X = W^P$ was, under P, a standard Wiener process with unit diffusion term and zero drift.
- Under the probability measure Q defined above, the drift process for X has changed from zero to φ, while the diffusion term remains the same as under P (i.e. unit diffusion).

11.3   The Girsanov Theorem

Rephrasing the results of the previous discussion, we thus see that we should be able to write the P-Wiener process W^P as

$$dW_t^P = \varphi_t dt + dW_t^Q,$$

where W^Q is a Q-Wiener process. This is precisely the content of the Girsanov Theorem, which we now formulate.

Theorem 11.3 (The Girsanov Theorem) *Let W^P be a d-dimensional standard P-Wiener process on $(\Omega, \mathcal{F}, P, \underline{F})$ and let φ be any d-dimensional* *adapted column vector process. Choose a fixed T and define the process L on $[0, T]$ by*

$$dL_t = \varphi_t^\star L_t dW_t^P, \qquad (11.16)$$
$$L_0 = 1, \qquad (11.17)$$

i.e.

$$L_t = e^{\int_0^t \varphi_s^\star dW_s^P - \frac{1}{2} \int_0^t \|\varphi_s\|^2 ds}.$$

Assume that

$$E^P[L_T] = 1, \qquad (11.18)$$

and define the new probability measure Q on $\mathcal{F}_T$ by

$$L_T = \frac{dQ}{dP}, \quad on \ \mathcal{F}_T. \qquad (11.19)$$

Then

$$dW_t^P = \varphi_t dt + dW_t^Q,$$

where W^Q is a Q-Wiener process

Remark 11.3.1 An equivalent, but perhaps less suggestive, way of formulating the conclusion of the Girsanov Theorem is to say that the process W^Q, defined by

$$W_t^Q = W_t^P - \int_0^t \varphi_s ds \qquad (11.20)$$

is a standard Q-Wiener process.

Proof   We only give the proof in the scalar case, the multidimensional case being a straightforward extension. Using the formulation in Remark 11.3.1 we thus have to show that, for $s < t$ and under Q, the increment $W_t^Q - W_s^Q$ is independent of $\mathcal{F}_s$, and normally distributed with zero mean and variance $t - s$. We start by considering the special case when $s = 0$ and we thus want to show that, for any t, W_t^Q is normal with zero mean and variance t under Q. Using characteristic functions it is thus enough to show that for all $t \in R_+$ and $u \in R$ we have

$$E^Q\left[e^{iuW_t^Q}\right] = e^{-\frac{u^2}{2}t},$$

i.e.

$$E^P\left[L_t \cdot e^{iuW_t^Q}\right] = e^{-\frac{u^2}{2}t}.$$

To show this, let us choose any fixed u, and define the process Z by

$$Z_t = L_t \cdot e^{iuW_t^Q}.$$

The dynamics of Z are given by

$$dZ_t = L_t \cdot d\left(e^{iuW_t^Q}\right) + e^{iuW_t^Q}dL_t + d\left(e^{iuW_t^Q}\right) \cdot dL_t. \qquad (11.21)$$

From the definitions we have

$$dL_t = \varphi_t L_t dW_t^P,$$
$$dW_t^Q = dW_t^P - \varphi_t dt,$$

so, remembering that W^P is P-Wiener, the Itô formula gives us

$$d\left(e^{iuW_t^Q}\right) = iue^{iuW_t^Q}dW_t^Q - \frac{u^2}{2}e^{iuW_t^Q}\left(dW_t^Q\right)^2$$

$$= iue^{iuW_t^Q}dW_t^P - iue^{iuW_t^Q}\varphi_t dt - \frac{u^2}{2}e^{iuW_t^Q}dt.$$

Plugging this, and the L-dynamics above into (11.21), we obtain

$$dZ_t = iuZ_t dW_t^P - iuZ_t\varphi_t dt - \frac{u^2}{2}Z_t dt + \varphi_t Z_t dW_t^P + iu\varphi_t Z_t dt$$

$$= \{iuZ_t + \varphi_t Z_t\}\, dW_t^P - \frac{u^2}{2}Z_t dt.$$

Since W^P is P-Wiener, standard technique gives us

$$E^P[Z_t] = e^{-\frac{u^2}{2}\cdot t},$$

which finishes the proof in the special case when $s = 0$.

In the general case we want to prove that for any $s \leq t$

$$E^Q\left[e^{iu(W_t^Q - W_s^Q)}\bigg|\, \mathcal{F}_s\right] = e^{-\frac{u^2}{2}\cdot(t-s)}$$

and this is equivalent (why?) to proving that

$$E^Q\left[I_A \cdot e^{iu(W_t^Q - W_s^Q)}\right] = Q(A)e^{-\frac{u^2}{2}\cdot(t-s)}, \qquad (11.22)$$

for every $A \in \mathcal{F}_s$. To prove (11.22) we define, for fixed s and $A \in \mathcal{F}_s$, the process $\{Z_t; t \geq s\}$ by

$$Z_t = L_t \cdot I_A \cdot e^{iu(W_t^Q - W_s^Q)},$$

and then we can proceed exactly as above.   □

Remark 11.3.2 *The process φ above will often be referred to as the* **Girsanov kernel** *of the measure transformation.*

Remark 11.3.3 *In the formulation above we have used vector notation. Written on component form, and with obvious notation, the L dynamics will have the form*

$$dL(t) = L(t) \sum_{i=1}^{d} \varphi_i(t) dW_i^P(t),$$

and explicit form of L will be given by

$$L(t) = \exp \left\{ \sum_{i=1}^{d} \int_0^t \varphi_i(s) dW_i^P(s) - \frac{1}{2} \int_0^t \sum_{i=1}^{d} \varphi_i^2(s) ds \right\}$$

Since this process is so important it has a name of its own:

Definition 11.4 *For any Wiener process W and any kernel process φ, the* **Doleans exponential** *process $\mathcal{E}$ is defined by*

$$\mathcal{E}\left(\varphi \star W\right)(t) = \exp \left\{ \int_0^t \varphi^\star(s) dW(s) - \frac{1}{2} \int_0^t \|\varphi\|^2(s) ds \right\} \qquad (11.23)$$

With notation as above we thus have

$$L(t) = \mathcal{E}\left(\varphi \star W\right)(t). \qquad (11.24)$$

Remark 11.3.4 *Note that in the Girsanov Theorem we have to assume* ad hoc *that φ is such that $E^P[L_T] = 1$ or, in other words, that L is a martingale. The problem is one of integrability on the process $L\varphi$, since otherwise we have no guarantee that L will be a true martingale and in the general case it could in fact happen that $E^P[L_T] < 1$. A sufficient condition for $E^P[L_T] = 1$ is of course that the process $L \cdot \varphi$ is in $\mathcal{L}^2$ but it is not easy to give a general* **a priori** *condition on φ only, which guarantees the martingale property of L. This problem used to occupy a minor industry, and the most general result so far is the "Novikov Condition" below.*

Lemma 11.5 (The Novikov Condition) *Assume that the Girsanov kernel φ is such that*

$$E^P \left[e^{\frac{1}{2} \int_0^T \|\varphi_t\|^2 dt} \right] < \infty. \qquad (11.25)$$

Then L is a martingale and in particular $E^P[L_T] = 1$.

There are counter examples which show that the exponent $\frac{1}{2}$ in the Novikov condition cannot be improved.

11.4   The Converse of the Girsanov Theorem

If we start with a measure P and perform a Girsanov transformation, according to (11.16)–(11.20), to define a new measure Q, then we know that $Q << P$. A natural question to ask is now whether **all** absolutely continuous measure transformations are obtained in this way, i.e. by means of a Girsanov transformation.

It is clear that in a completely general situation, this cannot possibly be true, since the Girsanov transformation above is completely defined in terms of the Wiener process W^P whereas there could be many other processes living on $(\Omega, \mathcal{F}, P, \underline{\mathcal{F}})$. However, in the case where the filtration $\{\mathcal{F}_t\}_{t \geq 0}$ is the one generated by the Wiener process itself, i.e. in the case when we have no other sources of randomness apart from W^P, then we have a converse result of the Girsanov Theorem.

Theorem 11.6 (The Converse of the Girsanov Theorem) *Let W^P be a d-dimensional standard (i.e. zero drift and unit variance independent components) P-Wiener process on $(\Omega, \mathcal{F}, P, \underline{\mathcal{F}})$ and assume that*

$$\mathcal{F}_t = \mathcal{F}_t^{W^p}, \forall t.$$

Assume that there exists a probability measure Q such that $Q << P$ on $\mathcal{F}_T$. Then there exists an adapted process φ such that the likelihood process L has the dynamics

$$dL_t = L_t \varphi_t^\star dW_t^P,$$
$$L_0 = 1.$$

Proof   We know from Theorem C.12 that the likelihood process L is a P martingale. Since the filtration is the one generated by W^P we deduce from the Martingale Representation Theorem 11.2 that there exists a process g such that

$$dL_t = g_t^\star dW_t^P.$$

Now we simply define φ by

$$\varphi_t = \frac{1}{L_t} \cdot g_t$$

and the proof is basically finished. There remains a small problem, namely what happens when $L_t = 0$ but also this can be handled and we omit it.   □

This converse result is very good news, since it implies that for the case of a Wiener filtration we have complete control of the class of absolutely continuous measure transformations.

11.5   Girsanov Transformations and Stochastic Differentials

We will now discuss the effect that a Girsanov transformation has on the dynamics of a more general Itô process. Suppose therefore that, under the original measure P, we have a process X with P-dynamics

$$dX_t = \mu_t dt + \sigma_t dW_t^P,$$

where W^P is a (possible multidimensional) standard P-Wiener process, and where μ and σ are adapted and suitably integrable. Suppose furthermore that we perform a Girsanov transformation with kernel process φ and transform from P to a new measure Q. The problem is to find out what the Q dynamics of X look like.

This problem is easily solved, since from the Girsanov Theorem we know that we can write

$$dW_t^P = \varphi_t dt + dW_t^Q$$

where W^Q is Q-Wiener. We now simply plug this expression into the X dynamics above, collect the dt-terms and obtain

$$dX_t = \{\mu_t + \sigma_t \varphi_t\} \, dt + \sigma_t dW_t^Q dt.$$

The moral of this is as follows:

- The diffusion term is unchanged.
- The drift term is changed from μ to $\mu + \sigma\varphi$.

11.6 Maximum Likelihood Estimation

In this section we give a brief introduction to maximum likelihood (ML) estimation for Itô processes. It is a bit outside the main scope of the book, but since ML theory is such an important topic and we already have developed most of the necessary machinery, we include it.

We need the concept of a statistical model.

Definition 11.7 *A dynamic* **statistical model** *over a finite time interval* $[0, T]$ *consists of the following objects:*

- *A measurable space* $(\Omega, \mathcal{F})$.
- *A flow of information on the space, formalized by a filtration* $\underline{\mathcal{F}} = \{\mathcal{F}_t\}_{t \geq 0}$.
- *An indexed family of probability measures* $\{P_\alpha; \ \alpha \in A\}$, *defined on the space* $(\Omega, \mathcal{F})$, *where* A *is some index set and where all measures are assumed to be absolutely continuous on* $\mathcal{F}_T$ *w.r.t. some base measure* P_{α_0}.

In most concrete applications (see examples below) the parameter α will be a real number or a finite dimensional vector, i.e. A will be the real line or some finite dimensional Euclidian space. The filtration will typically be generated by some observation process X.

The interpretation of all this is that the probability distribution is governed by some measure P_α, but we do not know which. We do have, however, access to a flow of information over time, and this is formalized by the filtration above, so at time t we have the information contained in $\mathcal{F}_t$. Our problem is to try to estimate α given this flow of observations, or more precisely: for every t we want an estimate α_t of α, based upon the information contained in $\mathcal{F}_t$, i.e. based on the observations over the time interval $[0, t]$. The last requirement is formalized by requiring that the estimation process should be adapted to $\underline{\mathcal{F}}$, i.e. that $\alpha_t \in \mathcal{F}_t$.

One of the most common techniques used in this context is that of finding, for each t, the **maximum likelihood** estimate of α. Formally the procedure works as follows.

- Compute, for each α the corresponding Likelihood process $L(\alpha)$ defined by

$$L_t(\alpha) = \frac{dP_\alpha}{dP_{\alpha_0}}, \quad \text{on } \mathcal{F}_t.$$

- For each fixed t, find the value of α which maximizes the likelihood ratio $L_t(\alpha)$.
- The optimal α is denoted by $\hat{\alpha}_t$ and is called the **maximum likelihood estimate** of α based on the information gathered over $[0, t]$.

As the simplest possible example let us consider the problem of estimating the constant but unknown drift of a scalar Wiener process. In elementary terms we could naively formulate the model by saying that we can observe a process X with dynamics given by

$$dX_t = \alpha dt + dW_t,$$
$$X_0 = 0.$$

Here W is assumed to be Wiener under some given measure P and the drift α is some unknown real number. Since this example is so simple, we do in fact have an obvious candidate (why?) for the estimator process, namely

$$\hat{\alpha}_t = \frac{X_t}{t}.$$

In a naive formulation like this, we have a single underlying Wiener process, W under a single given probability measure P, and we see that for different choices of α we have different X-processes. In order to apply the ML techniques we must reformulate our problem, so that we instead have a single X process and a family of measures. This is done as follows.

- Fix a process X which is Wiener under some probability measure P_0. In other words: under P_0, the process X has the dynamics

$$dX_t = 0 \cdot dt + dW_t^0,$$

where W^0 is P_0-Wiener.

- We assume that the information flow is the one generated by observations of X,
  so we define the filtration by setting $\mathcal{F}_t = \mathcal{F}_t^X$. For every real number α, we then define a Girsanov transformation to a new measure P_α by defining the likelihood process $L(\alpha)$ through

$$dL_t(\alpha) = \alpha L_t(\alpha) dX_t, \tag{11.26}$$

$$L_0(\alpha) = 1. \tag{11.27}$$

- From Girsanov's Theorem it now follows immediately that we can write $dW_t^0 = \alpha dt + dW_t^\alpha$, where W^α is be a P_α Wiener process. Thus X will have the P_α dynamics

$$dX_t = \alpha dt + dW_t^\alpha$$

We now have a statistical model along the general lines above, and we notice that, as opposed to the case in the naive formulation, we have a single process X, but the driving Wiener processes are different for different values of α.

To obtain the ML estimation process for α, we need to compute the likelihood process explicitly, i.e. we have to solve (11.26)–(11.27). This is easily done and we have

$$L_t(\alpha) = e^{\alpha \cdot X_t - \frac{1}{2}\alpha^2 \cdot t}.$$

We may of course maximize $\ln\left[L_t(\alpha)\right]$ instead of maximize $L_t(\alpha)$ so our problem is to maximize (over α) the expression

$$\alpha \cdot X_t - \frac{1}{2}\alpha^2 \cdot t.$$

This trivial quadratic optimization problem can be solved by setting the α derivative equal to zero, and we obtain the optimal α as

$$\hat{\alpha}_t = \frac{X_t}{t}.$$

Thus we see that in this example the ML estimator actually coincides with our naive guess above. The point of using the ML technique is of course that in a more complicated situation (see the exercises) we may have no naive candidate, whereas the ML technique in principle is always applicable.

11.7   Exercises

Exercise 11.1 Complete an argument in the proof of Theorem 11.1 by proving that if X and Y are random variables of the form

$$X = x_0 + \int_0^T g_s dW_s,$$

$$Y = y_0 + \int_0^T h_s dW_s,$$

and if g and h have disjoint support on the time axis, i.e. if

$$g_t h_t = 0, \quad P - a.s. \quad 0 \leq t \leq T$$

then

$$XY = x_0 y_0 + \int_0^T [X_s h_s + Y_s g_s]\, dW_s.$$

Hint: Define the processes X_t and Y_t by $X_t = x_0 + \int_0^t g_s dW_s$ and correspondingly for Y and use the Itô formula.

Exercise 11.2 Consider the following SDE.

$$dX_t = \alpha f(X_t)dt + \sigma(X_t)dW_t,$$
$$X_0 = x_0.$$

Here f and σ are known functions, whereas α is an unknown parameter. We assume that the SDE possesses a unique solution for every fixed choice of α.

Construct a dynamical statistical model for this problem and compute the ML estimator process $\hat{\alpha}_t$ for α, based upon observations of X.

11.8   Notes

The results in this chapter can be found in any textbook on stochastic analysis such as Karatzas and Shreve (2008), Øksendal (1998), and Steele (2001).

12

BLACK–SCHOLES FROM A MARTINGALE
POINT OF VIEW*

In this chaper we will discuss the standard Black–Scholes model from the martingale point of view. We thus choose a probability space $(\Omega, \mathcal{F}, P, \underline{\mathcal{F}})$ carrying a P-Wiener proces $\bar{W}$, where the filtration $\underline{\mathcal{F}}$ is the one generated by $\bar{W}$, i.e. $\mathcal{F}_t = \mathcal{F}_t^{\bar{W}}$. On this space we define the model by

$$dS_t = \alpha S_t dt + \sigma S_t d\bar{W}_t, \tag{12.1}$$
$$dB_t = r B_t dt. \tag{12.2}$$

Note that for ease of notation the P-Wiener process is denoted by $\bar{W}$ rather than by W^P.

12.1 Absence of Arbitrage

We now want to see whether the model is arbitrage free on a finite interval $[0, T]$, and for that purpose we use the First Fundamental Theorem (10.22) which says that we have absence of arbitrage if and only if there exists a martingale measure Q for our model. We then use the Girsanov Theorem to look for a Girsanov kernel process h such that the induced measure Q is a martingale measure. Defining, as usual, the likelihood process L by

$$dL_t = h_t L_t d\bar{W}_t,$$

and setting $dQ = L_T dP$ on $\mathcal{F}_T$, we know from Girsanov's Theorem that

$$d\bar{W}_t = h_t dt + dW_t,$$

where W is Q-Wiener. (For ease of notation we write W instead of the earlier W^Q.) Inserting the above expression into the stock price dynamics we obtain, after a collection of terms, the Q-dynamics of S as

$$dS_t = S_t \{\alpha + \sigma h_t\} dt + \sigma S_t dW_t.$$

In order for Q to be a martingale measure, we know from (10.51) that the local rate of return under Q must equal the short rate. Thus we want to determine the process h such that

$$\alpha + \sigma h_t = r. \tag{12.3}$$

This equation has the simple solution

$$h_t = -\frac{\alpha - r}{\sigma},$$

and we see that the Girsanov kernel process h is in fact deterministic and constant.

Furthermore, h has an important economic interpretation: In the quotient

$$\frac{\alpha - r}{\sigma},$$

the numerator $\alpha - r$, commonly known as the "risk premium" of the stock, denotes the excess rate return of the stock over the risk free rate of return on the market. In the denominator we have the volatility of the stock, so the quotient above has an interpretation as "risk premium per unit volatility" or "risk premium per unit risk". This important concept will be discussed in some detail later on, and it is known in the literature as "the market price of risk". It is commonly denoted by λ, so we have the following result.

Lemma 12.1 *The Girsanov kernel h is given by*

$$h = -\lambda$$

where the market price of risk λ is defined by

$$\lambda = \frac{\alpha - r}{\sigma}.$$

We have thus proved the existence of a martingale measure and from the First Fundamnetal Theorem we then have the following basic result for the Black–Scholes model.

Theorem 12.2 *The Black–Scholes model above is arbitrage free.*

We note in passing that instead of the standard Black–Scholes model above we could have considered a much more general model of the form

$$dS_t = \alpha_t S_t dt + \sigma_t S_t d\bar{W}_t, \tag{12.4}$$
$$dB_t = r_t B_t dt. \tag{12.5}$$

where α, σ and r are allowed to be arbitrary adapted (but suitably integrable) processes with $\sigma_t = 0$ P-a.s. and for all t. The analysis of this more complicated model would be completely parallell to the one carried out above, with the only difference that the Girsanov kernel h would now be a stochastic process given by the formula

$$h_t = -\frac{\alpha_t - r_t}{\sigma_t}. \tag{12.6}$$

As long as this h satisfies the Novikov condition, the market would still be arbitrage free.

Remark 12.1.1 The formal reason for the condition $\sigma_t = 0$ is that otherwise the quotient in (12.6) is undefined. Being a bit more precise, and going back to the fundamental equation

$$\alpha_t + h_t \sigma_t = r_t,$$

we see that we can in fact solve this equation (and thus guarantee absence of arbitrage) as long as the condition

$$\sigma_t = 0 \quad \Rightarrow \quad \alpha_t = r_t.$$

is valid. The economic interpretation of this condition is that if $\sigma_t = 0$, then the stock price is locally riskless with dynamics $dS_t = S_t \alpha_t dt$, so in order to avoid arbitrage with the money account B we must have $\alpha_t = r_t$.

12.2 Pricing

Consider the standard Black–Scholes model and a fixed T-claim X. From Proposition 10.25 we immediately have the usual "risk-neutral" pricing formula

$$\Pi(t; X) = e^{-r(T-t)} E^Q[X|\mathcal{F}_t], \tag{12.7}$$

where the Q dynamics of S are given as usual by

$$dS_t = rS_t dt + \sigma S_t dW_t.$$

For a general claim we can not say so much more, but for the case of a simple claim of the form

$$X = \Phi(S_T),$$

we can, of course, write down the Kolmogorov backward equation for the expectation and express the price as

$$\Pi(t; X) = F(t, S_t),$$

where the pricing function F solves the Black–Scholes equation.

$$\begin{cases} \frac{\partial F}{\partial t} + rs\frac{\partial F}{\partial x} + \frac{1}{2}\sigma^2 s^2 \frac{\partial^2 F}{\partial s^2} - rF = 0, \\ \qquad\qquad\qquad\qquad F(T, s) = \Phi(s) \end{cases} \tag{12.8}$$

The moral of all this is that the fundamental object is the risk neutral valuation formula (12.7), which is valid for all possible claims, whereas the Black–Scholes PDE is only valid for the case of simple claims.

12.3   Completeness

We now go on to investigate the completeness of the Black–Scholes model, and to this end we will use the Second Fundamental Theorem (10.24) which says that the market is complete if and only if the martingale measure is unique. We have seen in the previous section that there exists a martingale measure and the remaining question is whether this is the only martingale measure.

In the present setting, where the filtration is the one generated by $\bar{W}$ we know from Theorem 11.6 that **every** absolutely continuous measure transformation is obtained from a Girsanov transformation, and since the basic equation (12.3) has a unique solution, we see that the martingale measure is in fact unique. The same argument is valid for the more general model above, and we have thus proved the following result.

Theorem 12.3 *The Black–Scholes model (12.1)–(12.2) is complete. This also holds for the more general model (12.4)–(12.5).*

From an abstract point of view, the theorem above settles the completeness question, but since it is based on the second fundamental theorem, which in turn relies on rather abstract martingale theory, the argument is perhaps not overly instructive. We will therefore provide a more self contained completeness proof, which more clearly shows the use and central importance of the Martingale Representation Theorem 11.2.

We will carry out the argument for the standard Black–Scholes model (12.1)–(12.2), but the argument goes through with very small changes also for the more general model above. We will use the technique in Lemma 10.15 and in terms of the notation of that lemma we identify the numeraire S_0 with the money account B, and S_1 with the stock price S. We then define the normalized processes Z_0 and Z_1 by

$$Z_0(t) = \frac{B(t)}{B(t)}, \quad Z_1(t) = \frac{S(t)}{B(t)}.$$

Let Q be the (unique) martingale measure derives above, and consider an arbitrary T-claim X with

$$E^Q\left[\frac{X}{B(T)}\right] < \infty$$

(For the standard Black–Scholes model we may of course take the factor $1/B(T)$ out of the expectation.) We then define the Q martingale M by

$$M(t) = E^Q\left[\frac{X}{B(T)}\bigg|\mathcal{F}_t\right], \tag{12.9}$$

and it now follows from Lemma 10.15 that the model is complete if we can find a process $h_1(t)$ such that

$$dM(t) = h_1(t)dZ_1(t). \tag{12.10}$$

In order to prove the existence of such a process h_1 we use the Martingale Representation Theorem 11.2 (under Q), which says that there exists a process $g(t)$ such that

$$dM(t) = g(t)dW(t) \tag{12.11}$$

where W is the Q-Wiener process defined earlier. With the purpose of connecting (12.11) to (12.10) we now use the Itô formula and the fact that Q is a martingale measure for the numeraire B to derive the Q dynamics of Z_1 as

$$dZ_1(t) = Z_1(t)\sigma dW(t). \tag{12.12}$$

We thus have

$$dW(t) = \frac{1}{Z_1(t)\sigma}dZ_1(t),$$

and plugging this into (12.11) we see that we in fact have (12.10) satisfied with h_1 defined by

$$h_1(t) = \frac{g(t)}{\sigma Z_1(t)}.$$

Again using Lemma 10.15, have thus proved the following result.

Theorem 12.4 *In the Black–Scholes model (standard as well as extended), every T-claim X satisfying*

$$E^Q\left[\frac{X}{B(T)}\right] < \infty$$

can be replicated. The replicating portfolio is given by

$$h_1(t) = \frac{g(t)}{\sigma Z_1(t)}, \tag{12.13}$$

$$h_0(t) = M(t) - h_1(t)Z_1(t), \tag{12.14}$$

where M is defined by (12.9) and g is defined by (12.11).

This completeness result is much more general than the one derived in Chapter 8. The price that we have to pay for the increased generality is that we have to rely on the Martingale Representation Theorem which is an abstract existence result. Thus, for a general claim it is very hard (or virtually impossible) to compute the hedging portfolio in a reasonably explicit way. However, for the case of a simple claim of the form

$$X = \Phi(S_T),$$

the situation is of course more manageable. In this case we have

$$M(t) = E^Q\left[e^{-rT}\Phi(S(T))\big|\,\mathcal{F}_t\right],$$

and from the Kolmogorov backward equation (or from a Feynman–Kač representation) we have $M(t) = f(t, S(t))$ where f solves the boundary value problem

$$
\begin{cases}
\dfrac{\partial f}{\partial t}(t, s) + rs \dfrac{\partial f}{\partial s}(t, s) + \dfrac{1}{2}\sigma^2 s^2 \dfrac{\partial^2 f}{\partial s^2}(t, s) = 0, \\
\\
\qquad\qquad\qquad\qquad\qquad\qquad f(T, s) = e^{-rT}\Phi(s).
\end{cases}
$$

Itô's formula now gives us

$$
dM(t) = \sigma S(t)\frac{\partial f}{\partial s}(t, S(t)),
$$

so in terms of the notation above we have

$$
g(t) = \sigma S(t) \cdot \frac{\partial f}{\partial s}(t, S(t)),
$$

which gives us the replicating portfolio h as

$$
\begin{aligned}
h_0(t) &= f(t, S(t)) - S(t)\frac{\partial f}{\partial s}(t, S(t)), \\
h_1(t) &= B(t)\frac{\partial f}{\partial s}(t, S(t)).
\end{aligned}
$$

We have the interpretation $f(t, S(t)) = V^Z(t)$, i.e. f is the value of the normalized hedging portfolio, but it is natural to express everything in terms of the unnormalized value process $V(t)$ rather than in terms of V^Z. Therefore we define $F(t, s)$ by $F(t, s) = e^{rt}f(t, s)$ which gives us the following result which we recognize from Chapter 8.

Proposition 12.5 *Consider the Black–Scholes model and a T-claim of the form* $X = \Phi(S(T))$. *Then* X *can be replicated by the portfolio*

$$
\begin{cases}
h_0(t) = \dfrac{F(t, S(t)) - S(t)\frac{\partial F}{\partial s}(t, S(t))}{B(t)}, \\
h_1(t) = \dfrac{\partial F}{\partial s}(t, S(t)),
\end{cases}
\tag{12.15}
$$

where F *solves the* **Black–Scholes equation**

$$
\begin{cases}
\frac{\partial F}{\partial t} + rs\frac{\partial F}{\partial s} + \frac{1}{2}\sigma^2 s^2 \frac{\partial^2 F}{\partial s^2} - rF = 0, \\
\qquad\qquad\qquad\qquad\quad F(T, s) = \Phi(s)
\end{cases}
\tag{12.16}
$$

Furthermore the value process for the replicating portfolio is given by

$$
V(t) = F(t, S(t)).
$$

13

MULTIDIMENSIONAL MODELS: CLASSICAL APPROACH

13.1 Introduction

In this chapter we will generalize the Black–Scholes model to the case where, apart from the risk free asset, we have several underlying risky assets. In the present chapter we will carry out the analysis using the "classical" delta-hedging approach. In Chapter 14 we will then provide a more complete analysis using the martingale methods of Chapter 10.

We assume that we have n a priori given risky assets ("stocks") with price processes $S_1(t), \ldots, S_n(t)$. The entire asset price vector is denoted by $S(t)$, and in matrix notation we will write it as a column vector

$$S(t) = \begin{bmatrix} S_1(t) \\ \vdots \\ S_n(t) \end{bmatrix}.$$

The main problems are those of pricing and hedging contingent claims of the form

$$\mathcal{X} = \Phi\left(S(T)\right),$$

where T as usual is a fixed exercise time.

In the first sections we will analyze this problem in some detail using the "classical approach" developed in Chapters 7 and 8. In Chapter 14 we will then use the martingale machinery developed in Chapter 10 to extend the analysis considerably. However, while from a formal point of view, all results obtained by the elementary approach in the present chapter are special cases of the results of Chapter 14, there is a substantial amount of economic intuition to be gathered from the classical approach, so the present chpater is not redundant even for the mathematically advanced reader.

The first problem to be attacked is how to construct a "reasonable" mathematical model for the dynamics of the asset price vector S, and in this context we have two demands. We of course want the model to be free of arbitrage possibilities, and we also want the model to be such that we have a unique arbitrage free price process $\Pi(t; \mathcal{X})$ for any given claim $\mathcal{X}$.

From the meta-theorem 8.3.1 we know that we may generically expect absence of arbitrage if we have at least as many sources of randomness as we have underlying assets, so it is natural to demand that the price vector S should be driven by at least n independent Wiener processes.

If, on the other hand, we want a unique price process for every claim, then we need a complete market model, and according to meta-theorem 8.3.1 this will only occur if we have at least as many assets as we have sources of randomness. In order to obtain a nicely behaved model we are thus forced to model the stock price dynamics using exactly n independent Wiener processes, and we now go on to specify the formal model.

Assumption 13.1.1 *We assume the following.*

- *Under the objective probability measure P, the S-dynamics are given by*

$$dS_i(t) = \alpha_i S_i(t)dt + S_i(t)\sum_{j=1}^{n}\sigma_{ij}d\bar{W}_j(t), \qquad (13.1)$$

for $i = 1,\ldots,n$. Here $\bar{W}_1,\ldots,\bar{W}_n$ are independent P-Wiener processes.
- *The coefficients α_i and σ_{ij} above are assumed to be known constants.*
- *The* **volatility matrix**

$$\sigma = \{\sigma_{ij}\}_{i,j=1}^{n}$$

is nonsingular.
- *We have the standard risk free asset with price process B, where*

$$dB(t) = rB(t)dt. \qquad (13.2)$$

The assumption that the coefficients are constants is made for ease of exposition. Later on we will see that we may allow the coefficients to be functions of current time and current stock prices, i.e. $\alpha_i = \alpha_i(t, S(t))$, $\sigma_{ij} = \sigma_{ij}(t, S(t))$.

In the sequel we will let $\bar{W}(t)$ denote the column vector

$$\bar{W}(t) = \begin{bmatrix} \bar{W}_1(t) \\ \vdots \\ \bar{W}_n(t) \end{bmatrix}$$

and it will be convenient to define the row vector σ_i as the ith row of the volatility matrix σ, i.e.

$$\sigma_i = [\sigma_{i1},\ldots,\sigma_{in}].$$

With this notation we may write the stock price dynamics more compactly as

$$dS_i(t) = \alpha_i S_i(t)dt + S_i(t)\sigma_i d\bar{W}(t). \qquad (13.3)$$

It is in fact possible to write the S-dynamics even more compactly. For any n-vector $x = (x_1,\ldots,x_n)$ we let $D[x]$ denote the diagonal matrix

$$D[x] = \begin{bmatrix} x_1 & 0 & \ldots & 0 \\ 0 & x_2 & \ldots & 0 \\ \vdots & \vdots & \ddots & \vdots \\ 0 & 0 & \ldots & x_n \end{bmatrix} \qquad (13.4)$$

and we let α denote the column vector

$$\alpha = \begin{bmatrix} \alpha_1 \\ \vdots \\ \alpha_n \end{bmatrix}. \tag{13.5}$$

Using this notation we can write the S-dynamics as

$$dS(t) = D[S(t)]\alpha dt + D[S(t)]\sigma d\bar{W}(t). \tag{13.6}$$

13.2 Pricing

We take the market model above as given and we consider a fixed T-claim of the form

$$\Phi(S(T)).$$

The problem is to find the arbitrage free price process $\Pi(t; \mathcal{X})$ for $\mathcal{X}$, and we will do this by using a slight variation of the technique for the one-dimensional case. As before we start by assuming that there actually **is** a market price process for the claim, and that the price process is of the form

$$\Pi(t; \mathcal{X}) = F(t, S(t)),$$

for some deterministic function

$$F : R_+ \times R^n \to R.$$

Our problem is to find out what F must look like, in order not to introduce any arbitrage possibilities, if we are allowed to trade in the derivative as well as in the underlying assets. More precisely, we want the market $[S_1(t), \ldots, S_n(t), \Pi(t; \mathcal{X})]$ to be free of arbitrage, and the basic scheme is as follows.

- Take the model for the underlying assets, the contract function Φ, and the pricing function F as given.
- Form a self-financing portfolio, based on $S_1, \ldots, S_n, B$ and F. Since we have $n + 2$ assets, and the portfolio weights must add to unity, this will give us $n + 1$ degrees of freedom in our choice of weights.
- Choose the portfolio weights such that the driving Wiener processes are canceled in the portfolio, thus leaving us with portfolio dynamics of the form

$$dV(t) = V(t)k(t)dt.$$

Since we have n driving Wiener processes this will "use up" n degrees of freedom.

- Use the remaining degree of freedom in order to force the value dynamics to be of the form

$$dV(t) = (r + \beta) V(t)dt,$$

where β is some fixed nonzero real number. In the equation above we think of β as being a positive real number, so we are in effect trying to "beat the risk free asset" B by constructing a synthetic risk free asset with higher rate of return than the money account. It turns out that this is technically possible if and only if a certain matrix is nonsingular.

- Since we assume that the market is free of arbitrage possibilities, it is impossible to beat the risk free asset in the way described above. Therefore, the matrix mentioned above has to be singular.

- The singularity condition of the matrix leads to a PDE for the pricing function F, and the solution of this PDE is thus the unique arbitrage free pricing function for the claim $\mathcal{X}$.

To put these ideas into action we start by computing the price dynamics of the derivative. The multidimensional Itô formula gives us (see Remark 4.7.1), after some reshuffling,

$$dF = F \cdot \alpha_F dt + F \cdot \sigma_F d\bar{W}, \tag{13.7}$$

where

$$\alpha_F(t) = \frac{1}{F} \left[F_t + \sum_1^n \alpha_i S_i F_i + \frac{1}{2} tr \left\{ \sigma^\star D[S] F_{ss} D[S] \sigma \right\} \right], \tag{13.8}$$

$$\sigma_F(t) = \frac{1}{F} \sum_1^n S_i F_i \sigma_i. \tag{13.9}$$

Here the arguments t and $S(t)$ have been suppressed, and we have used the notation

$$F_t = \frac{\partial F}{\partial t}(t, S(t)),$$

$$F_i = \frac{\partial F}{\partial s_i}(t, S(t)),$$

$$F_{ss} = \left\{ \frac{\partial^2 F}{\partial s_i \partial s_j}(t, S(t)) \right\}_{i,j=1}^n.$$

Note that F_t and F_i are scalar functions, whereas F_{ss} is an $n \times n$ matrix-valued function.

We now form a portfolio based on $S_1, \ldots, S_n, B$ and F. For $S_1, \ldots, S_n$ and F we use the notation $u_1, \ldots, u_n$ and u_F for the corresponding portfolio weights, which gives us the weight u_B for the money account as

$$u_B = 1 - \left(\sum_1^n u_i + u_F \right).$$

The dynamics of the value process for the corresponding self-financing portfolio are given by

$$dV = V \left[\sum_1^n u_i \frac{dS_i}{S_i} + u_F \frac{dF}{F} + u_B \frac{dB}{B} \right],$$

and substituting the expression for u_B above, as well as inserting the dynamics of the processes involved, gives us

$$dV = V \cdot \left[\sum_1^n u_i \left(\alpha_i - r \right) + u_F \left(\alpha_F - r \right) + r \right] dt + V \cdot \left[\sum_1^n u_i \sigma_i + u_F \sigma_F \right] d\bar{W}.$$

We now try to choose the weights so that, first of all, the value process is locally risk free, i.e. it has no driving Wiener process. This means that we want to solve the equation

$$\sum_1^n u_i \sigma_i + u_F \sigma_F = 0.$$

Supposing for the moment that this can be done, we now have value dynamics of the form

$$dV = V \cdot \left[\sum_1^n u_i \left(\alpha_i - r \right) + u_F \left(\alpha_F - r \right) + r \right] dt,$$

and now we try to beat the market by choosing the weights such that we obtain a rate of return on the portfolio equaling $r + \beta$. Mathematically this means that we want to solve the equation

$$\sum_1^n u_i \left(\alpha_i - r \right) + u_F \left(\alpha_F - r \right) + r = r + \beta.$$

In order to see some structure, we now write these equations in matrix form as

$$\begin{bmatrix} \alpha_1 - r \ldots \alpha_n - r & \alpha_F - r \\ \sigma_1^\star & \cdots & \sigma_n^\star & \sigma_F^\star \end{bmatrix} \begin{bmatrix} u_S \\ u_F \end{bmatrix} = \begin{bmatrix} \beta \\ 0 \end{bmatrix}, \tag{13.10}$$

(note that $\sigma_i^\star$ is a column vector) where we have used the notation

$$u_S = \begin{bmatrix} u_1 \\ u_2 \\ \vdots \\ u_n \end{bmatrix}.$$

Let us now take a closer look at the coefficient matrix in eqn (13.10). Denoting this matrix by H, we see that it is an $(n+1) \times (n+1)$ matrix, and we have two possibilities to consider, namely whether H is invertible or not.

If H is invertible, then the system (13.10) has a unique solution for every choice of β. In economic terms this means that we are able to form a self-financing portfolio with the dynamics

$$dV(t) = (r + \beta)V(t)dt,$$

which in turn means that we have constructed a "synthetic bank" with $r + \beta$ as its rate of interest. This will of course lead to arbitrage opportunities. We just solve the system for, say, $\beta = 0.10$, then we borrow a (large) amount of money from the bank and invest it in the portfolio. By this arrangement our net outlays at $t = 0$ are zero, our debt to the bank will increase at the rate r, whereas the value of our portfolio will increase at a rate which is 10% higher.

Since we assume absence of arbitrage we thus see that H must be singular, and in order to see the implications of this we choose, for readability reasons, to study its transpose $H^\star$, given by

$$H^\star = \begin{bmatrix} \alpha_1 - r & \sigma_1 \\ \vdots & \vdots \\ \alpha_n - r & \sigma_n \\ \alpha_F - r & \sigma_F \end{bmatrix} \qquad (13.11)$$

(recall that σ_i is a row vector). We can write this somewhat more compactly by defining the n-dimensional column vector 1_n as

$$1_n = \begin{bmatrix} 1 \\ \vdots \\ 1 \end{bmatrix}. \qquad (13.12)$$

With this notation we have

$$H^\star = \begin{bmatrix} \alpha - r1_n & \sigma \\ \alpha_F - r & \sigma_F \end{bmatrix}.$$

Since $H^\star$ is singular this means that the columns are linearly dependent, and since the matrix σ was assumed to be nonsingular we draw the conclusion that the first column of H^* can be written as a linear combination of the other columns. Thus there exist real numbers $\lambda_1, \ldots, \lambda_n$ such that

$$\alpha_i - r = \sum_{j=1}^{n} \sigma_{ij}\lambda_j, \quad i = 1, \ldots, n, \tag{13.13}$$

$$\alpha_F - r = \sum_{j=1}^{n} \sigma_{Fj}\lambda_j, \tag{13.14}$$

where σ_{Fj} denotes the jth component of the row vector σ_F.

There is an economic interpretation of the multipliers $\lambda_1, \ldots, \lambda_n$ as so-called "market prices of risk" (cf. standard CAPM theory), and later on we will discuss this in some detail. For the moment the main logical point is that eqn (13.14) is the equation which will determine the derivative pricing function F. In order to use this equation we need, however, to get hold of the λ-vector, and as we shall see, this vector is determined by the system (13.13).

Writing (13.13) in vector form we see that the vector

$$\lambda = \begin{bmatrix} \lambda_1 \\ \vdots \\ \lambda_n \end{bmatrix}$$

is the solution of the $n \times n$ linear system

$$\alpha - r\mathbf{1}_n = \sigma\lambda,$$

and since σ by assumption is nonsingular we see that λ is in fact uniquely determined as

$$\lambda = \sigma^{-1}\left[\alpha - r\mathbf{1}_n\right]. \tag{13.15}$$

We now want to substitute this expression for λ into (13.14), but first we rewrite (13.14) in vector form as

$$\alpha_F - r = \sigma_F\lambda, \tag{13.16}$$

and from the definition of σ_F in (13.9) we see that we may write σ_F more compactly as

$$\sigma_F = \frac{1}{F} \cdot [S_1 F_1, \ldots, S_n F_n]\,\sigma. \tag{13.17}$$

Inserting (13.15) and (13.17) into (13.16) and using $\sigma\sigma^{-1} = I$, we obtain the relation

$$\alpha_F - r = \frac{1}{F} \cdot [S_1 F_1, \ldots, S_n F_n]\left[\alpha - r\mathbf{1}_n\right], \tag{13.18}$$

and finally we insert the expression for α_F from (13.8) into (13.18) to obtain, after some calculations,

$$F_t + \sum_{i=1}^{n} rS_i F_i + \frac{1}{2} tr \left\{ \sigma^\star D[S] F_{ss} D[S] \sigma \right\} - rF = 0. \qquad (13.19)$$

Note that this equation is a stochastic equation. For ease of reading we have suppressed most of the arguments, but if we backtrack we will see that, for example, the term $rS_i F_i$ in the equation above is just shorthand for the expression

$$rS_i(t) \frac{\partial F}{\partial s_i} (t, S(t)).$$

Thus eqn (13.19) must hold, at each t, with probability 1 for every possible value of the price vector $S(t)$. Now, in our model for the price process it can be shown that the support (the set of possible values) for the vector $S(t)$ is the entire set R_+^n, and thus eqn (13.19) must also hold for each deterministic t and s. By a standard argument we must also have $F(T, S(T)) = \Phi(S(T))$, so we have proved our main pricing result.

Theorem 13.1 *Consider the contract $\mathcal{X} = \Phi(S(T))$. In order to avoid arbitrage possibilities, the pricing function $F(t, s)$ must solve the boundary value problem*

$$\begin{cases} F_t(t, s) + \sum_{i=1}^{n} rs_i F_i(t, s) + \frac{1}{2} tr \left\{ \sigma^\star D[s] F_{ss} D[s] \sigma \right\} - rF(t, s) = 0, \\ \qquad\qquad\qquad\qquad\qquad\qquad\qquad\qquad\qquad F(T, s) = \Phi(s). \end{cases} \qquad (13.20)$$

Remark 13.2.1 To be more explicit we recall that we can write the quadratic term above as

$$tr \left\{ \sigma^\star D[S] F_{ss} D[S] \sigma \right\} = \sum_{i,j=1}^{n} s_i s_j \frac{\partial^2 F}{\partial s_i \partial s_j} (t, s) C_{ij},$$

where

$$C_{ij} = [\sigma \sigma^\star]_{ij}.$$

Remark 13.2.2 As in the one-dimensional case we notice that the drift vector α, of the price process, does not appear in the pricing equation. Again we see that the only part of the underlying price process which influences the price of a financial derivative is the diffusion matrix σ. The reason for this phenomenon is the same as in the scalar case and we refer the reader to our earlier discussion on the subject. A deeper understanding involves the Girsanov Theorem. See next chapter.

Remark 13.2.3 In the derivation of the result above we have assumed that the drift vector α and the volatility matrix σ in the price dynamics eqn (13.1) are constant. Going through the arguments it is, however, easily seen that we may allow the coefficients to be functions of current time and current stock price, i.e. they may be of the form

$$\alpha = \alpha(t, S(t)),$$
$$\sigma = \sigma(t, S(t)).$$

If we assume that the volatility matrix $\sigma(t, s)$ is invertible for each (t, s), then Theorem 13.1 will still hold, the only difference being that the term

$$tr\left\{\sigma^{\star}D[S]F_{ss}D[S]\sigma\right\}$$

in the pricing equation is replaced by the term

$$tr\left\{\sigma^{\star}(t, s)D[s]F_{ss}(t, s)D[s]\sigma(t, s)\right\}.$$

13.3 Risk Neutral Valuation

As in the scalar case there is a natural economic interpretation of Theorem 13.1 in terms of risk neutral valuation. From the Feynman–Kač representation theorem 5.8 we may immediately obtain a probabilistic formula for the solution to the pricing equation.

Theorem 13.2 *The pricing function $F(t, s)$ of Theorem 13.1 has the following representation.*

$$F(t, s) = e^{-r(T-t)}E_{t,s}^{Q}\left[\Phi\left(S(T)\right)\right].$$

Here the expectation is to be taken with respect to the martingale measure Q, defined by the fact that the Q-dynamics of the price process S are given by

$$dS_i = rS_idt + S_i\sigma_idW, \quad i = 1, \ldots, n.$$

Adhering to the notational convention 7.4.1 the expression $E_{t,s}^{Q}\left[\right]$ indicates, as usual, that the expectation shall be taken under Q, given the initial condition $S(t) = s$. By the same convention, W is a Q-Wiener process.

Again we see that the arbitrage free price of a derivative is given as the discounted expected value of the future cash flow, and again the main moral is that the expected value is **not** to be taken with respect to the objective probability measure P. Instead we must use the **martingale measure** Q. This martingale measure, or **risk adjusted measure**, is characterized by the following equivalent facts. The proof is left as an exercise to the reader.

Proposition 13.3 *The martingale measure Q is characterized by any of the following equivalent conditions.*

1. *Under Q every price process $\Pi(t)$, be it underlying or derivative, has the risk neutral valuation property*

$$\Pi(t) = e^{-r(T-t)} E_{t,s}^Q [\Pi(T)].$$

2. *Under Q every price process $\Pi(t)$, be it underlying or derivative, has the short rate of interest as its local rate of return, i.e. the Q-dynamics are of the form*

$$d\Pi(t) = r\Pi(t)\, dt + \Pi(t)\, \sigma_\Pi(t) dW,$$

where the volatility vector σ_Π is the same under Q as under P.

3. *Under Q every price process $\Pi(t)$, be it underlying or derivative, has the property that the normalized price process*

$$\frac{\Pi(t)}{B(t)}$$

is a martingale, i.e. it has a vanishing drift coefficient.

As before we may summarize the moral as follows:

- When we compute arbitrage free prices of derivative assets, we can carry out the computations **as if** we live in a risk neutral world.
- This does **not** mean that we *de facto* live, or think that we live, in a risk neutral world.
- The formulas above hold regardless of the investor's preferences, and attitude towards risk, as long as he/she prefers more deterministic money to less.

13.4   Reducing the State Space

From Theorem 13.1 we see that in order to compute the price of a financial derivative based on n underlying assets, we have to solve a PDE with n state variables, and for a general case this has to be done by numerical methods. Sometimes it is, however, possible to reduce the dimension of the state space, and this can lead to a drastic simplification of the computational work, and in some cases even to analytical formulas. We will now present a theory which will allow us to obtain analytical pricing formulas for some nontrivial multidimensional claims which quite often occur in practice. The theory presented here is based on an analysis of the pricing PDE, but there also exists a corresponding probabilistic theory. See Chapter 26 below.

Let us assume that we have the model

$$dS_i(t) = \alpha_i S_i(t) dt + S_i(t) \sum_{j=1}^n \sigma_{ij} d\bar{W}_j(t), \quad i = 1, \ldots, n. \tag{13.21}$$

We consider a T-claim of the form $\mathcal{X} = \Phi(S(T))$, and the crucial assumptions are the following.

Assumption 13.4.1

- *For the rest of the section we assume that the contract function Φ is homogeneous of degree 1, i.e. that*

$$\Phi(t \cdot s) = t \cdot \Phi(s),$$

for all $t > 0$ and for all $s \in R^n$.
- *The volatility matrix σ is constant.*

For a homogeneous Φ we see that, by choosing $t = s_n^{-1}$, we have the relation

$$\Phi(s_1, \ldots, s_n) = s_n \Phi\left(\frac{s_1}{s_n}, \ldots, \frac{s_{n-1}}{s_n}, 1\right).$$

This naturally gives us the idea that perhaps also the corresponding pricing function F has the same homogeneity property, so we try the **ansatz**

$$F(t, s_1, \ldots, s_n) = s_n G\left(t, \frac{s_1}{s_n}, \ldots, \frac{s_{n-1}}{s_n}\right) \tag{13.22}$$

where G is some function

$$G : R_+ \times R^{n-1} \to R.$$

First of all, if there is a solution to the pricing PDE of the form (13.22), then it has to satisfy the boundary condition

$$F(T, s) = \Phi(s), \quad \forall s,$$

and translated into G this gives the boundary condition

$$G(T, z) = \Psi(z), \quad \forall z, \tag{13.23}$$

where the function $\Psi : R^{n-1} \to R$ is defined by

$$\Psi(z_1, \ldots, z_{n-1}) = \Phi(z_1, \ldots, z_{n-1}, 1). \tag{13.24}$$

The main problem is now to see whether there is a function G such that the ansatz (13.22) satisfies the pricing PDE. We therefore compute the various partial derivatives of F in terms of G, and substitute the result into the PDE.

After some tedious calculations we have the following relations, where for brevity z denotes the vector $z = (\frac{s_1}{s_n}, \ldots, \frac{s_{n-1}}{s_n})$. Subscripts denotes partial derivatives.

$$F_t(t, s) = s_n G_t(t, z),$$

$$F_i(t, s) = G_i(t, z), \quad i = 1, \ldots, n - 1,$$

$$F_n(t, s) = G(t, z) - \sum_{j=1}^{n-1} \frac{s_j}{s_n} G_j(t, z),$$

$$F_{ij}(t, s) = \frac{1}{s_n} G_{ij}(t, z), \quad i, j = 1, \ldots, n - 1,$$

$$F_{in}(t, s) = F_{ni}(t, s) = - \sum_{j=1}^{n-1} \frac{s_j}{s_n^2} G_{ij}(t, z), \quad i = 1, \ldots, n - 1,$$

$$F_{nn} = - \sum_{i,j=1}^{n-1} \frac{s_i s_j}{s_n^3} G_{ij}(t, z).$$

As in Remark 13.2.1 we write the pricing PDE as

$$F_t(t, s) + \sum_{i=1}^{n} r s_i F_i(t, s) + \frac{1}{2} \sum_{i,j=1}^{n} s_i s_j F_{ij}(t, s) C_{ij} - r F(t, s) = 0. \qquad (13.25)$$

Substituting the expressions above for the partial derivatives of F into eqn (13.25) may look fairly forbidding, but in fact there will be many cancelations, and we end up with the following PDE for G.

$$G_t(t, z) + \frac{1}{2} \sum_{i,j=1}^{n-1} z_i z_j G_{ij}(t, z) D_{ij} = 0, \qquad (13.26)$$

where

$$D_{ij} = C_{ij} + C_{nn} + C_{in} + C_{nj}. \qquad (13.27)$$

We have thus proved the following result.

Proposition 13.4 *Assume that the contract function Φ is homogeneous of degree 1, and that the volatility matrix σ is constant. Then the pricing function F is given by*

$$F(t, s) = s_n G\left(t, \frac{s_1}{s_n}, \ldots, \frac{s_{n-1}}{s_n}\right),$$

where $G(t, z_1, \ldots, z_{n-1})$ solves the boundary value problem

$$\begin{cases} G_t(t, z) + \frac{1}{2} \sum_{i,j=1}^{n-1} z_i z_j G_{ij}(t, z) D_{ij} = 0, \\ \\ \qquad\qquad\qquad G(T, z) = \Psi(z). \end{cases} \qquad (13.28)$$

Here the matrix D is defined in (13.27), where C is given by Remark 13.2.1. The function Ψ is defined in (13.24).

The point of this result is that, instead of having to solve a PDE with n state variables (and one time variable), we have reduced the problem to that of solving a PDE with only $n-1$ state variables.

Remark 13.4.1 The crucial assumption in Proposition 13.4 is of course the homogeneity of the contract function, but one may wonder where we used the assumption of a constant volatility matrix. The point is that, with a state dependent σ, the PDE (13.26) is no longer a PDE in only the $n-1$ state variables $z_1, \ldots, z_{n-1}$, because the matrix D now depends on the entire price vector $s_1, \ldots, s_n$.

It is interesting to note that the PDE satisfied by G is of parabolic type. By inspection we see that it can in fact be interpreted as the pricing PDE, in a world with zero interest rate, for a claim of the form $Y = \Psi(Z(T))$, where the $n-1$ underlying price processes satisfy an SDE of the form

$$dZ(t) = D[Z]\mu(t)dt + D[Z]\tilde{\sigma}d\tilde{W}(t),$$

where the drift vector μ is as usual of no importance, the process $\tilde{W}$ is an $(n-1)$-dimensional standard P-Wiener process, and the covariance matrix satisfies

$$\tilde{\sigma}\tilde{\sigma}^\star = D.$$

Example 13.5 We illustrate the technique of state space reduction by a simple example of some practical importance. We consider a model with two underlying price processes S_1 and S_2, satisfying (under P) the following system of SDEs:

$$dS_1 = S_1\alpha_1 dt + S_1\sigma_1 d\tilde{W}_1,$$
$$dS_2 = S_2\alpha_2 dt + S_2\sigma_2 d\tilde{W}_2.$$

As usual $\tilde{W}_1$ and $\tilde{W}_2$ are independent, so in this model the price processes are also independent, but this is just for notational simplicity.

The claim to be studied is an **exchange option**, which gives the holder the right, but not the obligation, to exchange one S_2 share for one S_1 share at time T. Formally this means that the claim is defined by $\mathcal{X} = \max[S_1(T) - S_2(T), 0]$, and we see that we have indeed a contract function which is homogeneous of degree 1. A straightforward application of Theorem 13.1 would give us the PDE

$$\begin{cases} F_t + rs_1F_1 + rs_2F_2 + \frac{1}{2}s_1^2\sigma_1^2F_{11} + \frac{1}{2}s_2^2\sigma_2^2F_{22} - rF = 0, \\ F(T, s_1, s_2) = \max[s_1 - s_2, 0]. \end{cases}$$

Using Proposition 13.4 we can instead write

$$F(t, s_1, s_2) = s_2 \cdot G\left(t, \frac{s_1}{s_2}\right),$$

where $G(t, z)$ satisfies

$$\begin{cases} G_t(t, z) + \frac{1}{2}z^2 G_{zz}(t, z)(\sigma_1^2 + \sigma_2^2) = 0, \\ G(T, z) = \max\left[z - 1, 0.\right] \end{cases}$$

We see that this is the pricing equation, in a world with short rate $r = 0$, for a European call option with strike price $K = 1$ written on a single stock with volatility $\sqrt{\sigma_1^2 + \sigma_2^2}$. Thus G can be obtained directly from the Black–Scholes formula, and after some minor calculations we get

$$F(t, s_1, s_2) = s_1 N\left[d_1(t, z)\right] - s_2 N\left[d_2(t, z)\right],$$

where $z = \frac{s_1}{s_2}$. N is as usual the cumulative distribution function for the $N[0, 1]$ distribution and

$$d_1(t, z) = \frac{1}{\sqrt{(\sigma_1^2 + \sigma_2^2)(T - t)}} \left\{ \ln z + \frac{1}{2}(\sigma_1^2 + \sigma_2^2)(T - t) \right\},$$

$$d_2(t, z) = d_1(t, z) - \sqrt{(\sigma_1^2 + \sigma_2^2)(T - t)}.$$

13.5 Hedging

When we introduced the model

$$dS_i(t) = \alpha_i S_i(t)dt + S_i(t)\sigma_i d\bar{W}(t) \tag{13.29}$$

for the price vector process, one reason for the assumption of an invertible volatility matrix was that we wanted a complete market, and the goal of this section is to show that our model is in fact complete. From Chapter 8 we recall the following definition.

Definition 13.6 *We say that a T-claim $\mathcal{X}$ can be **replicated**, alternatively that it is **reachable** or **hedgeable**, if there exists a self financing portfolio h such that*

$$V^h(T) = \mathcal{X}, \quad P - a.s. \tag{13.30}$$

*In this case we say that h is a **hedge** against $\mathcal{X}$, alternatively a **replicating portfolio** for $\mathcal{X}$. If every contingent claim is reachable we say that the market is **complete**.*

Since we are not using the full probabilistic machinery in this chpater, we will not be able to show that we can hedge **every** contingent T-claim $\mathcal{X}$. As in the scalar case, we will "only" be able to prove completeness for simple claims, i.e. we will prove that every claim of the form

$$\mathcal{X} = \Phi\left(S(T)\right),$$

can be replicated. For the full story see next chapter.

Let us thus fix a date of delivery T, and a claim $\mathcal{X} = \Phi\left(S(T)\right)$. We denote portfolio weights by $u^0, u^1, \ldots, u^n$, where u^i is the weight on asset i for $i = 1, \ldots, n$, whereas u^0 is the weight on the risk free asset. From Lemma 6.5 it is clear that if we can find a process V, and weight processes $u^0, u^1, \ldots, u^n$ such that

$$V(T) = \Phi\left(S(T)\right), \quad P - a.s. \tag{13.31}$$

$$dV = V\left\{u^0\frac{dB}{B} + \sum_{i=1}^{n} u^i\frac{dS_i}{S_i}\right\}, \tag{13.32}$$

$$\sum_{i=0}^{n} u^i = 1, \tag{13.33}$$

then $u^0, u^1, \ldots, u^n$ is a replicating portfolio for $\mathcal{X}$, and V is the corresponding value process. For future use we note that eqns (13.32)–(13.33) can be written as

$$dV = V \cdot \left\{r\left(1 - \sum_{i=1}^{n} u^i\right) + \sum_{i=1}^{n} u^i\alpha_i\right\} dt + V \cdot \sum_{i=1}^{n} u^i\sigma_i d\bar{W}. \tag{13.34}$$

The structure of the proof is that we will make an educated guess about the nature of the value process V, so we will make an ansatz. Given this ansatz we then compute the stochastic differential dV, and at last, comparing the expression thus obtained to (13.34), we identify the portfolio weights by inspection.

We now go on to produce a natural candidate for the role as value process, and to this end we recall from Section 8.1 that, for a hedgeable claim, we should have the relation $\Pi\left(t; \mathcal{X}\right) = V(t)$.

Thus the obvious candidate as the value process for the replicating portfolio (if it exists at all) is the price process $\Pi\left(t; \mathcal{X}\right)$ for the claim. On the other hand we have already computed the price process as

$$\Pi\left(t; \mathcal{X}\right) = F\left(t, S(t)\right),$$

where F solves the pricing PDE of Theorem 13.1.

Let us thus **define** F as the solution to the pricing PDE, and then **define** the process V by $V(t) = F\left(t, S(t)\right)$. Our task is to show that V in fact is the value process of a replicating portfolio, i.e. to show that the relation (13.31) is satisfied, and that the dynamics for V can be written in the form (13.34). Equation (13.31) is obviously (why?) satisfied, and using the identity (by definition) $F = V$, we obtain from (13.7)

$$dV = F\alpha_F dt + F\sigma_F d\bar{W}.$$

So, from (13.8)–(13.9)

$$dV = V \cdot \frac{F_t + \sum_1^n \alpha_i S_i F_i + \frac{1}{2} tr\left(\sigma^\star D[S] F_{ss} D[S] \sigma\right)}{F} dt + V \cdot \sum_1^n \frac{S_i F_i}{F} \sigma_i d\bar{W}.$$

(13.35)

Comparing the diffusion part of (13.35) to that of (13.34) we see that the natural candidates as $u^1, \ldots, u^n$ are given by

$$u^i(t) = \frac{S_i F_i}{F}, \quad i = 1, \ldots, n.$$

(13.36)

Substituting these expressions into (13.35) gives us

$$dV = V \cdot \left\{ \sum_1^n u^i \alpha_i + \frac{F_t + \frac{1}{2} tr\left(\sigma^\star D[S] F_{ss} D[S] \sigma\right)}{F} \right\} dt + V \cdot \sum_1^n u^i \sigma_i d\bar{W},$$

and, using the fact that F satisfies the pricing PDE, we obtain

$$dV = V \cdot \left\{ \sum_1^n u^i \alpha_i + \frac{-\sum_1^n r S_i F_i + rF}{F} \right\} dt + V \cdot \sum_1^n u^i \sigma_i d\bar{W}.$$

Again using the definition (13.36), this reduces to

$$dV = V \cdot \left\{ \left(1 - \sum_1^n u^i\right) r + \sum_1^n u^i \alpha_i \right\} dt + V \cdot \sum_1^n u^i \sigma_i d\bar{W},$$

(13.37)

which is exactly eqn (13.34). We have thus proved the second part of the following theorem.

Theorem 13.7 *Assume that the volatility matrix σ is invertible. Then the following hold:*

- *The market is complete, i.e. every claim can be replicated.*
- *For a T-claim $\mathcal{X}$ of the form $\mathcal{X} = \Phi(S(T))$, the weights in the replicating portfolio are given by*

$$u^i(t) = \frac{S_i(t) F_i(t, S(t))}{F(t, S(t))}, \quad i = 1, \ldots, n,$$

$$u^0(t) = 1 - \sum_{i=1}^n u^i(t),$$

where F by definition is the solution of the pricing PDE in Theorem 13.1.

We have only proved that every **simple** contingent claim can be replicated, so we have not proved the first item above in full generality. It can in fact be proved that every (sufficiently integrable) claim can be replicated, but this requires the use of more advanced probabilistic tools (the martingale representation theorem for Wiener filtrations) and is treated in the next section.

13.6   Exercises

Exercise 13.1 Prove Proposition 13.3.

Exercise 13.2 Check all calculations in the derivation of the PDE in Proposition 13.4.

Exercise 13.3 Consider again the exchange option in Example 13.5. Now assume that $\bar{W}_1$ and $\bar{W}_2$ are no longer independent, but that the local correlation is given by $d\bar{W}_1 \cdot d\bar{W}_2 = \rho dt$. (We still assume that both Wiener processes have unit variance parameter, i.e. that $d\bar{W}_1^2 = d\bar{W}_2^2 = dt$.) How will this affect the Black–Scholes-type formula given in the example?

Exercise 13.4 Consider the stock price model in Example 13.5. The T-contract $\mathcal{X}$ to be priced is defined by

$$\mathcal{X} = \max\left[aS_1(T), bS_2(T)\right],$$

where a and b are given positive numbers. Thus, up to the scaling factors a and b, we obtain the maximum of the two stock prices at time T. Use Proposition 13.4 and the Black–Scholes formula in order to derive a pricing formula for this contract. See Johnson (1987).

Hint: You may find the following formula (for $x > 0$) useful.

$$\max[x, 1] = 1 + \max[x - 1, 0].$$

Exercise 13.5 Use the ideas in Section 13.4 to analyze the pricing PDE for a claim of the form $\mathcal{X} = \Phi(S(T))$ where we now assume that Φ is homogeneous of degree β, i.e.

$$\Phi(t \cdot s) = t^{\beta}\Phi(s), \quad \forall t > 0.$$

14

MULTIDIMENSIONAL MODELS: MARTINGALE APPROACH*

In this chapter we will now change our point of view and use the martingale machinery of Chapter 10 to analyze a multidimensional model which is more general than the one discussed in the previous chapter. This will give more general results than those obtained earlier and it will also provide us with an enhanced understanding of the pricing and hedging problems for Wiener driven models. In particular we will, for the special case of Wiener driven models, produce a self-contained proof of the Second Fundamental Theorem.

Let us thus consider a filtered probability space $(\Omega, \mathcal{F}, P, \underline{\mathcal{F}})$ carrying a k-dimensional standard Wiener process $\bar{W}$. The basic setup is as follows.

Assumption 14.0.1 *We assume the following:*

- *There are n risky asset $S_1, \ldots, S_n$ given a priori.*
- *Under the objective probability measure P, the S-dynamics are given by*

$$dS_i(t) = \alpha_i(t)S_i(t)dt + S_i(t)\sum_{j=1}^{k}\sigma_{ij}(t)d\bar{W}_j(t), \tag{14.1}$$

for $i = 1, \ldots, n$.
- *The coefficients processes α_i and σ_{ij} above are assumed to be adapted.*
- *We have the standard risk free asset with price process B, where*

$$dB(t) = r(t)B(t)dt. \tag{14.2}$$

The short rate is allowed to be a stochastic adapted process.

With notation as above we can write this on compact form as

$$dS(t) = D\left[S(t)\right]\alpha(t)dt + D\left[S(t)\right]\sigma(t)d\bar{W}(t), \tag{14.3}$$

where D is the diagonal matrix defined in (13.4).

Note that at this point we do **not** assume that we have the same number of driving Wiener processes as the number of risky assets. Also note that the probability space is allowed to carry also other processes than the Wiener process $\bar{W}$, and thus that the filtration could be generated by other processes beside $\bar{W}$. For example, we make no assumptions about the distribution of the short rate process r or of the processes α_i and σ_{ij}— we only assume that they are adapted.

In particular this allows for models where these processes are path dependent upon the Wiener process, or that they are driven by some other "hidden" state variable processes. See below for a particular case.

Remark 14.0.1 In many applications there are, beside S, other non financial variables which may influence r, α, and σ or the claims under consideration. A common situation is when these non financial variables are modeled through some (vector) process X with P-dynamics of the form

$$dX(t) = \mu_X(t)dt + \sigma_X(t)d\bar{W}(t). \tag{14.4}$$

Note that we assume that the same P-Wiener process $\bar{W}$ is driving both S and X. This is no serious restriction, since if for example S is driven by $\bar{W}^1$ and X is driven by $\bar{W}^2$ then we define $\bar{W}$ as $(\bar{W}^1, \bar{W}^2)$. Note that it is important that we assume that the vector process X does **not** contain any **price process**. Any price component of X should instead be included in S.

14.1 Absence of Arbitrage

Our first task is to investigate when our model is free of arbitrage, and to this end we use the First Fundamental Theorem 10.22 and look for a martingale measure Q with B as the numeraire. Using the Girsanov Theorem 11.16 we define a prospective likelihood process L by

$$dL(t) = L(t)\varphi^\star(t)d\bar{W}(t), \tag{14.5}$$
$$L(0) = 1, \tag{14.6}$$

where φ is some adapted k-dimensional (column-vector) process, and we recall from (11.24) that L is given by the Doleans exponential as

$$L(t) = \mathcal{E}\left(\varphi \star \bar{W}\right)(t) = \exp\left\{\int_0^t \varphi^\star(s)d\bar{W}(s) - \frac{1}{2}\int_0^t \|\varphi\|^2(s)ds\right\}.$$

We now define our candidate martingale measure Q by setting $dQ = L(T)dP$ on $\mathcal{F}_T$, and from the Girsanov Theorem we know that we can write

$$d\bar{W}(t) = \varphi(t)dt + dW(t), \tag{14.7}$$

where W is a standard Q-Wiener process. Plugging (14.7) into the P-dynamics (14.3) we obtain the following Q-dynamics of S.

$$dS(t) = D\left[S(t)\right]\left[\alpha(t) + \sigma(t)\varphi(t)\right]dt + D\left[S(t)\right]\sigma(t)dW(t). \tag{14.8}$$

From (10.51) we know that, disregarding integrability problems, Q is a martingale measure if and only if the local rate of return of each asset equals the short rate, i.e. if and only if the equality

$$\alpha(t) + \sigma(t)\varphi(t) = \mathbf{r}(t) \tag{14.9}$$

holds with probability one for each t, where $\mathbf{r}$ is defined by

$$\mathbf{r} = \begin{bmatrix} r \\ \vdots \\ r \end{bmatrix}.$$

In this equation, which we write as

$$\sigma(t)\varphi(t) = \mathbf{r}(t) - \alpha(t), \tag{14.10}$$

α, σ, and r are given a priori and we want to solve for φ. Thus, for each t, and P-a.s., the n-dimensional vector $\mathbf{r}(t) - \alpha(t)$ must be in the image of the diffusion matrix $\sigma(t)$ so we have the following result.

Proposition 14.1 *A necessary condition for absence of arbitrage is that*

$$\mathbf{r}(t) - \alpha(t) \in Im\,[\sigma(t)] \tag{14.11}$$

with probability one for each t. A sufficient condition for absence of arbitrage is that there exists a process φ which solves (14.10) and such that $\mathcal{E}\left(\varphi \star \bar{W}\right)$ is a martingale.

Note that it is not enough for φ to solve (14.10). We also need enough integrability to ensure that L is a true martingale (and not just a local one). Hence the following definition.

Definition 14.2 *A Girsanov kernel φ is said to be **admissible** if it generates a martingale measure, i.e. it solves (14.10) and $\mathcal{E}\left(\varphi \star \bar{W}\right)$ is a martingale.*

The integrability problem for L will be discussed further below, as in Proposition 14.10. However, the main focus will be on equation (14.10) and we will thus often carry out the arguments "modulo integrability problems".

Proposition 14.1 is quite general, but it also covers "pathological" models, such as those where all assets $S_1, \ldots, S_n$ are identical. In order not to be distracted by silly models like that we make the following definition which will guarantee that the concept of no arbitrage is structurally stable.

Definition 14.3 *The model above is said to be **generically arbitrage free** if it is arbitrage free for every (sufficiently integrable) choice of α.*

We then have the following central result.

Proposition 14.4 *Disregarding integrability problems the model is generically arbitrage free if and only if, for each $t \leq T$ and P-a.s., the mapping*

$$\sigma(t) : R^k \to R^n$$

is surjective, i.e. if and only if the volatility matrix $\sigma(t)$ has rank n.

rom this result it follows in particular that for absence of arbitrage we must
n the generic case necessarily have $n \leq k$, i.e. we must have at least as many
ndependent Wiener processes as we have risky assets. This is quite in accordance
vith the informal reasoning in the meta-theorem 8.3.1.

We note that the martingale measure equation (14.10) only involves the
S-dynamics, and **not** the dynamics of the extra factor process X (if the model
ncludes such a factor). This is of course because the no arbitrage restrictions
only concern **prices of traded assets**.

If our (or the market's) choice of Q is generated by the Girsanov kernel φ, then
he Q dynamics of X are of course determined by this Girsanov transformation,
o we have complete control of the distribution of X under Q. We summarize
his as a separate result.

Proposition 14.5 *Assuming absence of arbitrage, consider a fixed martingale
measure Q generated by φ, and denote the corresponding Q-Wiener process by
V. Then the following hold:*

- *The Q dynamics of S are*

$$dS(t) = r(t)D\left[S(t)\right]dt + D\left[S(t)\right]\sigma(t)dW(t). \qquad (14.12)$$

- *If the model contains an extra factor process X with P-dynamics given by
(14.4), then the Q-dynamics of X are given by*

$$dX(t) = \{\mu_X(t) + \sigma_X(t)\varphi(t)\}\,dt + \sigma_X(t)dW(t), \qquad (14.13)$$

14.2 Completeness

We now go on to obtain conditions for the model to be complete, and in order
o avoid pathological cases we assume that the model is generically arbitrage
free. From the Second Fundamental Theorem 10.24 we know that the model is
complete if and only if the martingale measure is unique, so it is tempting to
draw the conclusion that we have completeness if and only if equation (14.10)
has a unique solution, i.e. if and only if the condition

$$Ker\left[\sigma(t)\right] = \{0\}, \qquad (14.14)$$

s satisfied for all t and with probability one. This is, however, not quite true
and the reason is that, in case of a general filtered probability space, there is no
guarantee that *all* equivalent measure transformations are of the Girsanov type
above. In a general situation, where there are other sources of randomness beside
the Wiener process $\bar{W}$, like say an independent Poisson process N, the Girsanov
transformation above will only change the measure for the Wiener process, but
t will not affect the Poisson process. Thus; even if equation (14.10) has a unique
solution we do not have a unique martingale measure, since we have no restriction
on how we are allowed to change the measure for the Poisson process. Put into
more economic terms it is fairly obvious that if we consider a claim $\mathcal{X}$ of the

type $\mathcal{X} = \Phi(N(T))$, then it is impossible to hedge this claim if the asset prices are driven by the Wiener process alone.

In order to obtain sharp results we are therefore forced to make the assumption that all randomness in our model is generated by the Wiener process $\bar{W}$ We then have the following basic result.

Proposition 14.6 *Assume that the model is generically arbitrage free and that the filtration $\underline{\mathcal{F}}$ is defined by*

$$\mathcal{F}_t = \mathcal{F}_t^{\bar{W}}. \tag{14.15}$$

Then, disregarding integrability problems, the model is complete if and only if $k = n$ and the volatility matrix $\sigma(t)$ is invertible P-a.s. for each $t \leq T$.

Proof From the Converse of the Girsanov Theorem 11.6, we know that under the assumption that the filtration is the one generated by the Wiener process, *every* equivalent measure transformation is obtained by a Girsanov transformation of the type above. Hence the martingale measure is unique if and only if the solution of the "martingale measure equation" (14.10) is unique, and this occurs if and only if $\sigma(t)$ is injective, which implies $k \leq n$. Since we have assumed generic absence of arbitrage, we know that $n \geq k$ and that $\sigma(t)$ is surjective Thus $k = n$ and $\sigma(t)$ is invertible.   □

14.3 Hedging

In this section we will discuss the completeness question from the more concrete perspective of actually producing hedging strategies for an arbitrary T-claim $\mathcal{X}$ This has independent interest and it will also provide us with a new proof (within the framework of the present chapter) for the Second Fundamental Theorem. The advantage of this alternative proof is that it is much more concrete than the rather abstract one given in Section 10.4. The drawback is that we only provide the proof for Wiener driven models, whereas the Second Fundamental Theorem in fact holds in much more general situations.

Let us thus again consider the model from (14.3)

$$dS(t) = D\left[S(t)\right]\alpha(t)dt + D\left[S(t)\right]\sigma(t)d\bar{W}(t). \tag{14.16}$$

Assumption 14.3.1 *We assume that the model is generically free of arbitrage, i.e. that*

$$Im\left[\sigma(t)\right] = R^n, \tag{14.17}$$

for all t and with probability one. We also assume that the model is purely Wiener driven, i.e. that $\mathcal{F}_t = \mathcal{F}_t^{\bar{W}}$.

Since we have assumed absence of arbitrage there exists some (not necessarily unique) martingale measure and we choose a particular one, denote it by Q and keep it fixed for the rest of the argument.

We then choose an arbitrary T-claim $\mathcal{X}$ in $L^1(Q)$, and the problem is to find a hedging portfolio for $\mathcal{X}$. From Lemma 10.15 we know that $\mathcal{X}$ can be hedged if and only if the martingale M, defined by

$$M(t) = E^Q \left[\left. \frac{\mathcal{X}}{B(T)} \right| \mathcal{F}_t \right],\qquad(14.18)$$

admits dynamics of the form

$$dM(t) = h(t)dZ(t),\qquad(14.19)$$

where as usual $Z = S/B$, and where h is an adapted (row vector) process in R^n. Given our assumption of a purely Wiener driven system it follows from the Martingale Representation Theorem 11.2 that there exists an adapted k-dimensional (row vector) process g such that

$$dM(t) = g(t)dW(t).\qquad(14.20)$$

On the other hand, since the Z process is a (local) martingale under Q, it follows easily from Itô that the Q-dynamics are given by

$$dZ(t) = D\left[Z(t)\right] \sigma(t)dW(t).\qquad(14.21)$$

Plugging (14.21) into (14.19) gives us

$$dM(t) = h(t)D\left[Z(t)\right] \sigma(t)dW(t).\qquad(14.22)$$

Comparing (14.22) with (14.20) we see that we can hedge $\mathcal{X}$ if and only if we can solve (at each t and for every ω) the equation

$$h(t)D\left[Z(t)\right] \sigma(t) = g(t),$$

or, alternatively the equation

$$\sigma^\star(t)D\left[Z(t)\right] h^\star(t) = g^\star(t).\qquad(14.23)$$

In this equation, g is generated by the claim $\mathcal{X}$ and we want to solve the equation for h. Since $D\left[Z(t)\right]$ is nondegenerate diagonal, the equation can be solved if and only if

$$g^\star(t) \in Im\left[\sigma^\star(t)\right],$$

and we have the following result.

Proposition 14.7 *Under Assumption 14.3.1 the model is complete if and only if*

$$Im\left[\sigma^\star(t)\right] = R^k.\qquad(14.24)$$

If the model is complete then, using the notation of Chapter 10, the replicating portfolio $[h_0, h_S]$ *is given by*

$$h_S(t) = g(t)\sigma^{-1}(t)D^{-1}[Z(t)], \tag{14.25}$$
$$h_0(t) = M(t) - h(t)Z(t). \tag{14.26}$$

Proof   Follows immediately from Lemma 10.15.   □

Note that $D^{-1}[Z(t)]$ is just a diagonal matrix with $Z_1^{-1}(t), \ldots, Z_n^{-1}(t)$ on the diagonal.

We can now easily provide an alternative proof of a restricted version of the Second Fundamental Theorem.

Theorem 14.8 (The Second Fundamental Theorem)   *Under Assumption 14.3.1 the model is complete if and only if the martingale measure is unique.*

Proof   Using Proposition 14.7 and the standard duality result

$$\{Im [\sigma^\star(t)]\}^\perp = Ker [\sigma(t)]$$

we see that the model is complete if and only if

$$Ker [\sigma(t)] = \{0\}. \tag{14.27}$$

This is, however, precisely the condition for the uniqueness of the martingale measure obtained earlier.   □

It is instructive to compare these duality arguments with those given in the simple setting of Chapter 3, and in particular to the proof of Theorem 3.14, to see how much of the structure that is carried over from the simple one period model to the present general setting. From the discussion above we see that the "martingale measure equation" (14.10) and the "hedging equation" (14.23) are adjoint equations. Thus absence of arbitrage and completeness are truly dual concepts from a functional analytical point of view.

14.4   Pricing

Assuming absence of arbitrage, the general pricing formula is, as always, given by the risk neutral valuation formula

$$\Pi(t; \mathcal{X}) = e^{-r(T-t)}E^Q[\mathcal{X}|\mathcal{F}_t], \tag{14.28}$$

where Q is some choice of martingale measure, where the Q dynamics of S are given by

$$dS(t) = D[S(t)]r(t)dt + D[S(t)]\sigma(t)dW^Q(t), \tag{14.29}$$

and where W^Q is Q-Wiener.

14.5 Markovian Models and PDEs

We now apply the martingale approach to the Markovian model discussed in the previous chapter. Thus we again introduce Assumption 13.1.1, i.e. we assume that $k = n$, that the vector of returns α as well as the volatility matrix σ are deterministic and constant over time, that σ is invertible and that the filtration is the one generated by the Wiener process. Thus S will be a Markov process. The general pricing formula is, as always,

$$\Pi\left(t;\mathcal{X}\right) = e^{-r(T-t)}E^{Q}\left[\mathcal{X}\mid\mathcal{F}_t\right], \tag{14.30}$$

where the Q-dynamics of S are given by

$$dS(t) = D\left[S(t)\right]rdt + D\left[S(t)\right]\sigma dW(t).$$

If we now assume that $\mathcal{X}$ is a *simple* claim, i.e. of form $\mathcal{X} = \Phi\left(S(T)\right)$, then, since S is Markovian we have

$$e^{-r(T-t)}E^{Q}\left[\mathcal{X}\mid\mathcal{F}_t\right] = e^{-r(T-t)}E^{Q}\left[\mathcal{X}\mid S(t)\right],$$

and thus (exactly why?) the pricing process must be of the form $\Pi\left(t;\mathcal{X}\right) = F(t, S(t))$ for some pricing function F. We can then apply the Kolmogorov backward equation to the expectation above and we immediately see that the pricing function must solve the PDE

$$\begin{cases} F_t(t,s) + \displaystyle\sum_{i=1}^{n} rs_i F_i(t,s) + \frac{1}{2}tr\left\{\sigma^{\star}D[S]F_{ss}D[S]\sigma\right\} -rF(t,s) = 0, \\ \qquad\qquad\qquad\qquad\qquad\qquad\qquad\qquad F(T,s) \ = \Phi(s). \end{cases} \tag{14.31}$$

We have thus recovered our old pricing result from Theorem 13.1.

Turning to hedging, we know from the uniqueness of the martingale measure that the market is complete, and thus that there exists a hedging portfolio $h = (h_0, h_1, \ldots, h_n)$. The value process dynamics are of course given by

$$dV(t;h) = h_0(t)dB(t) + \sum_{i=1}^{n} h_i(t)dS_i(t),$$

but we also have $V(t;h) = F(t, S(t))$ where F solves the PDE above. Applying the Itô formula, this gives us

$$dV(t;h) = \sum_{i=1}^{n} F_i(t, S(t))dS_i(t) + (\text{second order terms})dt.$$

Comparing these two equations we can identify $h_1, \ldots, h_n$ from the dS_i terms and we see that the hedging portfolio is given by

$$h_i(t) = \frac{\partial F}{\partial S_i}(t, S(t)), \quad i = 1, \ldots, n, \tag{14.32}$$

$$h_0(t) = \frac{1}{B(t)} \left\{ F(t, S(t)) - \sum_{i=1}^{n} \frac{\partial F}{\partial S_i}(t, S(t)) S_i(t) \right\}. \tag{14.33}$$

If we express the portfolio in terms of relative weights, this will once again give us the hedge of Theorem 13.7.

14.6   Market Prices of Risk

Going back to the general model of Section 14.1 let us assume that the model is generically free of arbitrage possibilities, then we know that the "martingale measure equation"

$$\sigma(t)\varphi(t) = \mathbf{r}(t) - \alpha(t), \tag{14.34}$$

always possesses a (not necessarily unique) solution $\varphi = (\varphi_1, \ldots, \varphi_k)^\star$, where φ is the Girsanov kernel used in the transition from P to Q. If we now define the vector process λ by $\lambda = -\varphi$, then we can write (14.34) as

$$\alpha(t) - \mathbf{r}(t) = \sigma(t)\lambda(t), \tag{14.35}$$

and on component form this becomes

$$\alpha_i(t) - r(t) = \sum_{i=1}^{k} \sigma_{ij}(t)\lambda_j(t), \quad i = 1, \ldots, n. \tag{14.36}$$

As in the simpler setting of Section 13.2 we have an economic interpretation of this equation. On the left-hand side we have the excess rate of return over the risk free rate for asset No. i, and on the right-hand side we have a linear combination of the volatilities σ_{ij} of asset No. i with respect to the individual Wiener processes $\bar{W}_1, \ldots, \bar{W}_k$. Thus λ_j is the "factor loading" for the individual risk factor $\bar{W}_j$, and this object is often referred to as the "market price of risk for risk factor No. j". Roughly speaking one can then say that λ_j gives us a measure of the aggregate risk aversion in the market towards risk factor No. j. The main point to notice here is that *the same* λ is used for *all* assets. We can summarize the situation as follows:

- Under absence of arbitrage there will exist a market price of risk vector process λ satisfying (14.35).
- The market price of risk λ is related to the Girsanov kernel φ through

$$\varphi(t) = -\lambda(t).$$

- In a complete market the market price of risk, or alternatively the martingale measure Q, is uniquely determined and there is thus a unique price for every derivative.
- In an incomplete market there are several possible market prices of risk processes and several possible martingale measures, all of which are consistent with no arbitrage.
- In an incomplete market, φ, λ, and Q are thus not determined by absence of arbitrage alone. Instead they will be determined by supply and demand on the actual market, i.e. by the agents on the market.

14.7 Stochastic Discount Factors

Consider again the model in Section 14.1, assume absence of arbitrage, and choose a fixed martingale measure Q with corresponding Girsanov kernel φ. In Section 10.6 we defined the stochastic discount factor Λ by

$$\Lambda(t) = e^{-\int_0^t r(s)ds} L(t),$$

where L is the likelihood process for the measure transformation from P to Q. In the special case of a Wiener driven model we can compute L explicitly as

$$L(t) = \mathcal{E}\left(\varphi \star \bar{W}\right)(t) = e^{\int_0^t \varphi^\star(s)d\bar{W}(s) - \frac{1}{2}\int_0^t \|\varphi(s)\|^2 ds}$$

so in this model we have an explicit expression for Λ as

$$\Lambda(t) = e^{\int_0^t \varphi^\star(s)d\bar{W}(s) - \frac{1}{2}\int_0^t \left\{\|\varphi(s)\|^2 + r(s)\right\}ds}, \tag{14.37}$$

we can of course also express Λ in terms of the market price of risk process as

$$\Lambda(t) = e^{-\int_0^t \lambda^\star(s)d\bar{W}(s) - \frac{1}{2}\int_0^t \left\{\|\lambda(s)\|^2 + r(s)\right\}ds}. \tag{14.38}$$

14.8 The Hansen–Jagannathan Bounds

Assume that we have generic absence of arbitrage, i.e. that $\sigma(t)$ is surjective, so the martingale measure equation

$$\sigma(t)\varphi(t) = \mathbf{r}(t) - \alpha(t), \tag{14.39}$$

always possesses a solution. As noted above, this is not enough to ensure absence of arbitrage, since we must also have a guarantee that there exists an *admissible* solution φ, i.e. a φ such that the induced likelihood process $L = \mathcal{E}\left(\varphi \star \bar{W}\right)$ is a true martingale (and not just a local one). Recalling, from Lemma 11.5, the Novikov condition

$$E^P \left[e^{\frac{1}{2} \int_0^T \|\varphi(t)\|^2 dt} \right] < \infty,$$

it is then natural to look for a solutions φ to (14.39) with minimal Euclidian norm at every t.

We recall the following result from elementary linear algebra.

Proposition 14.9 *Assume that the $n \times k$ matrix A is surjective as a mapping $A : R^k \to R^n$. For any $y \in R^n$, consider the optimization problem*

$$\min_{x \in R^k} \quad \|x\|^2,$$
$$s.t. \quad Ax = y.$$

Then the following hold:

- *$A^\star$ is injective and $A^\star A$ is invertible.*
- *The unique optimal solution of the minimum norm problem is given by*

$$\hat{x} = (A^\star A)^{-1} A^\star y. \tag{14.40}$$

Proof   Left to the reader as an exercise.   □

From this we have the following obvious result.

Proposition 14.10 *Assume that the volatility matrix $\sigma(t)$ is surjective P-a.s. for all t. Then the process $\hat{\varphi}$ defined by*

$$\hat{\varphi} = [\sigma^\star \sigma]^{-1} \sigma^\star [\mathbf{r} - \alpha], \tag{14.41}$$

has the property that,

$$\|\hat{\varphi}(t)\| \leq \|\varphi(t)\| \tag{14.42}$$

for all t and for every φ which satisfies (14.39). If in particular $\hat{\varphi}$ satisfies the Novikov condition, then the model is free of arbitrage.

We may of course use the correspondence $\lambda = -\varphi$ between the Girsanov kernel φ and the market price of risk λ to formulate a parallel result for market prices of risk. We define the minimal market price of risk process as

$$\hat{\lambda} = [\sigma^\star \sigma]^{-1} \sigma^\star [\alpha - \mathbf{r}], \tag{14.43}$$

and we have the inequality

$$\|\hat{\lambda}(t)\| \leq \|\lambda(t)\|$$

for all admissible λ.

These simple facts are more or less the essence of what in discrete time asset pricing is known as the "Hansen–Jagannathan bounds" (see the Notes). To obtain these bounds we consider the price process $\pi(t)$ of any asset in the model (underlying or derivative), write its P-dynamics on the form

$$d\pi(t) = \pi(t)\alpha_\pi(t)dt + \pi(t)\sigma_\pi(t)d\bar{W}(t)$$

and define its **Sharpe Ratio** process by the expression

$$\frac{\alpha_\pi(t) - r(t)}{\|\sigma_\pi(t)\|}.$$

Denoting the P-variance by Var^P we have the informal interpretation

$$\|\sigma_\pi(t)\|^2 dt = Var^P\left[d\pi(t)/\pi(t)|\,\mathcal{F}_t\right]$$

so the Sharpe Ratio gives us the conditional mean excess rate of return per unit of total volatility.

We now have the following simple but interesting result.

Proposition 14.11 (The Hansen–Jagannathan Bounds)
Assume generic absence of arbitrage and define $\hat{\lambda}$ by (14.43). Then the following holds for all assets, underlying or derivative, and for all admissible market prices of risk λ.

$$\left|\frac{\alpha_\pi(t) - r(t)}{\|\sigma_\pi(t)\|}\right| \leq \|\hat{\lambda}(t)\| \leq \|\lambda(t)\|. \tag{14.44}$$

Proof The second inequality is already proved so we only have to prove the first. Fix any λ generating a martingale measure. We then have

$$\sigma_\pi(t)\lambda(t) = \alpha_\pi(t) - r(t),$$

so

$$\frac{\alpha_\pi(t) - r(t)}{\|\sigma_\pi(t)\|} = \frac{\sigma_\pi(t)}{\|\sigma_\pi(t)\|}\lambda(t),$$

and from the Cauchy–Schwartz inequality in finite dimensional space we obtain

$$\left|\frac{\alpha_\pi(t) - r(t)}{\|\sigma_\pi(t)\|}\right| \leq \left\|\frac{\sigma_\pi(t)}{\|\sigma_\pi(t)\|}\right\| \cdot \|\lambda(t)\| = \|\lambda(t)\|.$$

Since this holds for every λ, it holds in particular for $\hat{\lambda}$. $\qquad\square$

We can now connect this result to the stochastic discount factor Λ by noting that, for our model class, the dynamics of Λ are given by

$$d\Lambda(t) = -r(t)\Lambda(t)dt + \Lambda(t)\varphi^\star(t)d\bar{W}(t), \tag{14.45}$$

or alternatively

$$d\Lambda(t) = -r(t)\Lambda(t)dt - \Lambda(t)\lambda^*(t)d\bar{W}(t). \qquad (14.46)$$

λ (and φ) also has the interpretation as the volatility vector of the stochastic discount factor. The point of this from an economic perspective is that we can either view the Hansen–Jagannathan bounds as a lower bound for the stochastic discount factor volatility for a given (observed) Sharpe ratio, or as an upper bound on the Sharpe ratio for a given (observed) stochastic discount factor volatility.

14.9   Exercises

Exercise 14.1 Derive (14.46).

Exercise 14.2 Assume generic absence of arbitrage and prove that any market price of risk process λ generating a martingale measure must be of the form

$$\lambda(t) = \hat{\lambda}(t) + \mu(t)$$

where $\mu(t)$ is orthogonal to the rows of $\sigma(t)$ for all t.

14.10   Notes

The results in this chapter are fairly standard. The Hansen–Jagannathan bounds were first derived (in discrete time) in Hansen and Jagannathan (1991). They have since then become the subject of a large literature. See the textbook Cochrane (2001) for an exposition of (mostly discrete time) asset pricing, including a detailed discussion of the discrete time HJ bounds, connections to the "equity premium puzzle" and an extensive bibliography on the subject.

15

INCOMPLETE MARKETS

15.1 Introduction

In this chapter we will investigate some aspects of derivative pricing in incomplete markets. We know from the meta-theorem that markets generically are incomplete when there are more random sources than there are traded assets, and this can occur in an infinite number of ways, so there is no "canonical" way of writing down a model of an incomplete market. We will confine ourselves to study a particular type of incomplete market, namely a "factor model", i.e. a market where there are some nontraded underlying objects. Before we go on to the formal description of the models let us briefly recall what we may expect in an incomplete model.

- Since, by assumption, the market is incomplete we will not be able to hedge a generic contingent claim.
- In particular there will not be a unique price for a generic derivative.

15.2 A Scalar Nonpriced Underlying Asset

We will start by studying the simplest possible incomplete market, namely a market where the only randomness comes from a scalar stochastic process which is **not** the price of a traded asset. We will then discuss the problems which arise when we want to price derivatives which are written in terms of the underlying object. The model is as follows.

Assumption 15.2.1 *The only objects which are a priori given are the following.*

- *An empirically observable stochastic process X, which is **not** assumed to be the price process of a traded asset, with P-dynamics given by*

$$dX(t) = \mu\left(t, X(t)\right) dt + \sigma\left(t, X(t)\right) d\bar{W}(t). \tag{15.1}$$

Here $\bar{W}$ is a standard scalar P-Wiener process.
- *A risk free asset (money account) with the dynamics*

$$dB(t) = rB(t)dt, \tag{15.2}$$

where r as usual is the deterministic short rate of interest.

We now consider a given contingent claim, written in terms of the process X. More specifically we define the T-claim $\mathcal{Y}$ by

$$\mathcal{Y} = \Phi\left(X(T)\right), \tag{15.3}$$

where Φ is some given deterministic function, and our main problem is that of studying the price process $\Pi(t; \mathcal{Y})$ for this claim.

In order to give some substance to the discussion, and to understand the difference between the present setting and that of the previous chapters, let us consider a specific concrete, interpretation of the model. We may, for example, interpret the process X as the temperature at some specific point on the earth, say the end of the Palace Pier in Brighton. Thus $X(t)$ is the temperature (in centigrade) at time t at the Palace Pier. Suppose now that you want to go to Brighton for a holiday, but that you fear that it will be unpleasantly cold at the particular time T when you visit Brighton. Then it may be wise to buy "holiday insurance", i.e. a contract which pays you a certain amount of money if the weather is unpleasant at a prespecified time in a prespecified place. If the monetary unit is the pound sterling, the contract function Φ above may have the form

$$\Phi(x) = \begin{cases} 100, & \text{if } x \le 20, \\ 0, & \text{if } x > 20. \end{cases}$$

In other words, if the temperature at time T is below 20°C (degrees centigrade) you will obtain 100 pounds from the insurance company, whereas you will get nothing if the temperature exceeds 20°C.

The problem is now that of finding a "reasonable" price for the contract above, and as usual we interpret the word "reasonable" in the sense that there should be no arbitrage possibilities if we are allowed to trade the contract. This last sentence contains a hidden assumption which we now formalize.

Assumption 15.2.2 *There is a liquid market for every contingent claim.*

If we compare this model with the standard Black–Scholes model, we see many similarities. In both cases we have the money account B, and in both cases we have an a priori given underlying process. For the Black–Scholes model the underlying process is the stock price S, whereas we now have the underlying process X, and in both models the claim to be priced is a deterministic function Φ of the underlying process, evaluated at time T.

In view of these similarities it is now natural to assume that the results from the Black–Scholes analysis will carry over to the present case, i.e. we are (perhaps) led to believe that the price process for the claim $\mathcal{Y}$ is uniquely determined by the P-dynamics of the underlying process X. It is, however, very important to understand that this is, most emphatically, **not** the case, and the reasons are as follows:

1. If we consider the a priori given market, which only consists of the money account B, we see that the number R of random sources in this case equals one (one driving Wiener process), while the number M of traded assets (always excluding the money account B) equals zero. From the meta-theorem it now follows that the market is incomplete. The incompleteness

can also be seen from the obvious fact that in the a priori given market there are no interesting ways of forming self-financing portfolios. The only strategy that is allowed is to invest all our money in the bank, and then we can only sit down and passively watch our money grow at the rate r. In particular we have no possibility to replicate any interesting derivative of the form $\Phi(X(T))$. We thus conclude that, since we cannot replicate our claim, we cannot expect to obtain a unique arbitrage free price process.

2. One natural strategy to follow in order to obtain a unique price for the claim X is of course to imitate the scheme for the Black–Scholes model. We would assume that the price process $\Pi(t; \mathcal{Y})$ is of the form $\Pi(t; \mathcal{Y}) = F(t, X(t))$, and then we would form a portfolio based on the derivative F and the underlying X. Choosing the portfolio weights such that the portfolio has no driving Wiener process would give us a riskless asset, the rate of return on which would have to equal the short rate r, and this last equality would finally have the form of a PDE for the pricing function F. This approach is, however, completely nonsensical, since in the present setting the process X is (by assumption) **not the price of a traded asset**, and thus it is meaningless to talk about a "portfolio based on X". In our concrete interpretation this is eminently clear. Obviously you can buy any number of insurance contracts and put them in your portfolio, but it is also obvious that you cannot meaningfully add, for example, 15^oC to that portfolio.

We can summarize the situation as follows:

- The price of a particular derivative will **not** be completely determined by the specification (15.1) of the X-dynamics and the requirement that the market $[B(t), \Pi(t; \mathcal{Y})]$ is free of arbitrage.
- The reason for this fact is that arbitrage pricing is always a case of pricing a derivative **in terms of** the price of some underlying assets. In our market we do not have sufficiently many underlying assets.

Thus we will not obtain a unique price of a particular derivative. This fact does not mean, however, that prices of various derivatives can take any form whatsoever. From the discussion above we see that the reason for the incompleteness is that we do not have enough underlying assets, so if we adjoin one more asset to the market, without introducing any new Wiener processes, then we expect the market to be complete. This idea can be expressed in the following ways.

Idea 15.2.1

- We **cannot** say anything about the price of any **particular** derivative.
- The requirement of an arbitrage free derivative market implies that **prices of different derivatives** (i.e. claims with different contract functions or different times of expiration) will have to satisfy certain **internal consistency relations** in order to avoid arbitrage possibilities on the bond

market. In terms of our concrete interpretation this means that even if we are unable to produce a unique price for a fixed weather insurance contract, say the "20°C contract"

$$\Phi(x) = \begin{cases} 100, & \text{if } x \leq 20, \\ 0, & \text{if } x > 20, \end{cases}$$

for the fixed date T, there must be internal consistency requirements between the price of this contract and the price of the following "25°C contract"

$$\Gamma(x) = \begin{cases} 100, & \text{if } x \leq 25, \\ 0, & \text{if } x > 25, \end{cases}$$

with some expiration date T' (where of course we may have $T = T'$).

- In particular, if we take the price of **one** particular "benchmark" derivative as a priori given, then the prices of all other derivatives will be uniquely determined by the price of the benchmark. This fact is in complete agreement with the meta-theorem, since in an a priori given market consisting of one benchmark derivative plus the risk free asset we will have $R = M = 1$, thus guaranteeing completeness. In our concrete interpretation we expect that the prices of all insurance contracts should be determined by the price of any fixed benchmark contract. If, for example, we choose the 20°C contract above as our benchmark, and take its price as given, then we expect the 25°C contract to be priced uniquely in terms of the benchmark price.

To put these ideas into action we now take as given two fixed T-claims, $\mathcal{Y}$ and $\mathcal{Z}$, of the form

$$\mathcal{Y} = \Phi\left(X(T)\right),$$
$$\mathcal{Z} = \Gamma\left(X(T)\right),$$

where Φ and Γ are given deterministic real valued functions. The project is to find out how the prices of these two derivatives must be related to each other in order to avoid arbitrage possibilities on the derivative market. As above we assume that the contracts are traded on a frictionless market, and as in the Black–Scholes analysis we make an assumption about the structure of the price processes.

Assumption 15.2.3 *We assume that*

- *There is a liquid, frictionless market for each of the contingent claims $\mathcal{Y}$ and $\mathcal{Z}$.*
- *The market prices of the claims are of the form*

$$\Pi\left(t; \mathcal{Y}\right) = F\left(t, X(t)\right),$$
$$\Pi\left(t; \mathcal{Z}\right) = G\left(t, X(t)\right),$$

where F and G are smooth real valued functions.

We now proceed exactly as in the Black–Scholes case. We form a portfolio based on F and G, and choose the weights so as to make the portfolio locally riskless. The rate of return of this riskless portfolio has to equal the short rate of interest, and this relation will give us some kind of equation, which we then have to analyze in detail.

From the assumption above, the Itô formula, and the X-dynamics we obtain the following price dynamics for the price processes $F(t, X(t))$ and $G(t, X(t))$.

$$dF = \alpha_F F dt + \sigma_F F d\bar{W}, \tag{15.4}$$

$$dG = \alpha_G G dt + \sigma_G G d\bar{W}. \tag{15.5}$$

Here the processes α_F and σ_F are given by

$$\alpha_F = \frac{F_t + \mu F_x + \frac{1}{2}\sigma^2 F_{xx}}{F},$$

$$\sigma_F = \frac{\sigma F_x}{F},$$

and correspondingly for α_G and σ_G. As usual we have suppressed most arguments, so in more detail we have, for example,

$$\mu F_x = \mu(t, X(t))\frac{\partial F}{\partial x}(t, X(t)).$$

We now form a self-financing portfolio based on F and G, with portfolio weights denoted by u_F and u_G respectively. According to (6.13), the portfolio dynamics are given by

$$dV = V \left\{ u_F \cdot \frac{dF}{F} + u_G \cdot \frac{dG}{G} \right\},$$

and using the expressions above we get

$$dV = V \left\{ u_F \cdot \alpha_F + u_G \cdot \alpha_G \right\} dt + V \left\{ u_F \cdot \sigma_F + u_G \cdot \sigma_G \right\} d\bar{W}. \tag{15.6}$$

In order to make this portfolio locally riskless we must choose u_F and u_G such that $u_F \cdot \sigma_F + u_G \cdot \sigma_G = 0$, and we must also remember that they must add to unity. Thus we define u_F and u_G as the solution to the following system of equations.

$$\begin{cases} u_F + u_G = 1, \\ u_F \cdot \sigma_F + u_G \cdot \sigma_G = 0. \end{cases}$$

The solution to this system is given by

$$\begin{cases} u_F = \dfrac{-\sigma_G}{\sigma_F - \sigma_G}, \\ u_G = \dfrac{\sigma_F}{\sigma_F - \sigma_G}, \end{cases}$$

and inserting this into the portfolio dynamics equation (15.6) gives us

$$dV = V \cdot \left\{ \frac{\alpha_G \cdot \sigma_F - \alpha_F \cdot \sigma_G}{\sigma_F - \sigma_G} \right\} dt.$$

We have thus created a locally riskless asset, so using Proposition 7.6, absence of arbitrage must imply the equation

$$\frac{\alpha_G \cdot \sigma_F - \alpha_F \cdot \sigma_G}{\sigma_F - \sigma_G} = r.$$

After some reshuffling we can rewrite this equation as

$$\frac{\alpha_F - r}{\sigma_F} = \frac{\alpha_G - r}{\sigma_G}.$$

The important fact to notice about this equation is that the left-hand side does not depend on the choice of G, while the right-hand side does not depend upon the choice of F. The common quotient will thus depend neither on the choice of F nor on the choice of G, and we have proved the following central result.

Proposition 15.1 *Assume that the market for derivatives is free of arbitrage. Then there exists a universal process $\lambda(t)$ such that, with probability 1, and for all t, we have*

$$\frac{\alpha_F(t) - r}{\sigma_F(t)} = \lambda(t), \qquad (15.7)$$

regardless of the specific choice of the derivative F.

There is a natural economic interpretation of this result, and of the process λ. In eqn (15.7) the numerator is given by $\alpha_F - r$, and from (15.4) we recognize α_F as the local mean rate of return on the derivative F. The numerator $\alpha_F - r$ is thus the local mean excess return on the derivative F over the riskless rate of return r, i.e. the risk premium of F. In the denominator we find the volatility σ_F of the F process, so we see that λ has the dimension "risk premium per unit of volatility". This is a concept well known from CAPM theory, so λ is commonly called "the market price of risk". Proposition 15.1 can now be formulated in the following, slightly more flashy, form:

- In a no arbitrage market all derivatives will, regardless of the specific choice of contract function, have the same market price of risk.

We can obtain more explicit information from eqn (15.7) by substituting our earlier formulas for α_F and σ_F into it. After some algebraic manipulations we then end up with the following PDE.

$$F_t + \{\mu - \lambda\sigma\} F_x + \frac{1}{2}\sigma^2 F_{xx} - rF = 0.$$

This is really shorthand notation for an equation which must hold with probability 1, for each t, when all terms are evaluated at the point $(t, X(t))$. Assuming for the moment that the support of X is the entire real line, we can then draw the conclusion that the equation must also hold identically when we evaluate it at an arbitrary deterministic point (t, x). Furthermore it is clear that we must have the boundary condition

$$F(T, x) = \Phi(x), \quad \forall x \in R,$$

so we finally end up with the following result.

Proposition 15.2 (Pricing equation) *Assuming absence of arbitrage, the pricing function $F(t, x)$ of the T-claim $\Phi(X(T))$ solves the following boundary value problem.*

$$F_t(t, x) + \mathcal{A}F(t, x) - rF(t, x) = 0, \quad (t, x) \in (0, T) \times R, \qquad (15.8)$$
$$F(T, x) = \Phi(x), \quad x \in R, \qquad (15.9)$$

where

$$\mathcal{A}F(t, x) = \{\mu(t, x) - \lambda(t, x)\sigma(t, x)\} F_x(t, x) + \frac{1}{2}\sigma^2(t, x)F_{xx}(t, x).$$

At first glance this result may seem to contradict the moral presented above. We have stressed earlier the fact that, because of the incompleteness of the market, there will be **no** unique arbitrage free price for a particular derivative. In Proposition 15.2, on the other hand, we seem to have arrived at a PDE which, when solved, will give us precisely the unique pricing function for any simple claim. The solution to this conundrum is that the pricing equation above is indeed very nice, but in order to solve it we have to know the short rate of interest r, as well as the functions $\mu(t, x)$, $\sigma(t, x)$, $\Phi(x)$ and $\lambda(t, x)$. Of these, only r, $\mu(t, x)$, $\sigma(t, x)$ and $\Phi(x)$ are specified exogenously. The market price of risk λ, on the contrary, is **not** specified within the model. We can now make Idea 15.2.1 above more precise.

Firstly we see that, even though we cannot determine a unique price for a particular derivative, prices of different derivatives must satisfy internal consistency requirements. This requirement is formulated precisely in Proposition 15.1, which says that all derivatives must have the same market price of risk. Thus, if we consider two different derivative assets with price processes F and G, these may have completely different local mean rates of return (α_F and α_G), and they may also have completely different volatilities (σ_F and σ_G). The consistency relation which has to be satisfied in order to avoid arbitrage between the derivatives is that, at all times, the quotient

$$\frac{\alpha_F - r}{\sigma_F}$$

must equal

$$\frac{\alpha_G - r}{\sigma_G}.$$

Secondly, let us assume that we take the price process of one particular derivative as given. To be concrete let us fix the "benchmark" claim $\Gamma(X(T))$ above and assume that the pricing function $G(t,x)$, for $\Gamma(X(T))$, is specified exogenously. Then we can compute the market price of risk by the formula

$$\lambda(t,x) = \frac{\alpha_G(t,x) - r}{\sigma_G(t,x)}. \tag{15.10}$$

Let us then consider an arbitrary pricing function, say the function F for the claim $\Phi(X(T))$. Since the market price of risk is the same for all derivatives we may now take the expression for λ obtained from (15.10) and insert this into the pricing equation (15.8)–(15.9) for the function F. Now everything in this equation is well specified, so we can (in principle) solve it, in order to obtain F. Thus we see that the price F of an arbitrary claim is indeed uniquely determined by the price G of any exogenously specified benchmark claim.

We can obtain more information from the pricing equation by applying the Feynman–Kač representation. The result can be read off immediately and is as follows.

Proposition 15.3 (Risk neutral valuation) *Assuming absence of arbitrage, the pricing function* $F(t,x)$ *of the* T*-claim* $\Phi(X(T))$ *is given by the formula*

$$F(t,x) = e^{-r(T-t)} E_{t,x}^{Q} \left[\Phi(X(T)) \right], \tag{15.11}$$

where the dynamics of X *under the martingale measure* Q *are given by*

$$dX(t) = \{\mu(t, X(t)) - \lambda(t, X(t))\sigma(t, X(t))\} \, dt + \sigma(t, X(t)) \, dW(t).$$

Here W *is a* Q*-Wiener process, and the subscripts* t, x *indicate as usual that* $X(t) = x$.

Again we have an "explicit" risk neutral valuation formula for the pricing function. The arbitrage free price of the claim is given as the discounted value of the mathematical expectation of the future claim. As before the expectation is, however, not to be taken under the objective measure P, but under the martingale ("risk adjusted") measure Q. Note that there is a one-to-one correspondence between the martingale measure and the market price of risk. Thus, choosing a particular λ is equivalent to choosing a particular Q. The characterization of Q is just the same as in Proposition 13.3. The proof is left to the reader.

Proposition 15.4 *The martingale measure Q is characterized by any of the following equivalent facts.*

- *The local mean rate of return of any derivative price process $\Pi(t)$ equals the short rate of interest, i.e. the $\Pi(t)$-dynamics have the following structural form under Q*

$$d\Pi(t) = r\Pi(t)dt + \sigma_\Pi \Pi(t)(t)dW,$$

  where W is a Q-Wiener process, and σ_Π is the same under Q as under P.
- *With Π as above, the process $\Pi(t)/B(t)$ is a Q-martingale, i.e. it has a zero drift term.*

As for the pricing equation above, we have to know λ in order to compute the expected value in the risk neutral valuation formula. Thus, in the present context, and in contrast to the Black–Scholes case, the martingale measure Q is not (generically) determined within the model.

It is instructive to see how the standard Black–Scholes model can be interpreted within the present model. Let us therefore assume, in contrast to our earlier assumptions, that X **is** in fact the price of a stock in a Black–Scholes model. This of course means that the P-dynamics of X are given by

$$dX = \alpha G dt + \sigma G d\bar{W},$$

for some constants α and σ. Thus, in terms of the notation in (15.1), $\mu(t,x) = x \cdot \alpha$ and $\sigma(t,x) = x \cdot \sigma$. Our project is still that of finding the arbitrage free price for the claim $\Phi(X(T))$, and to this end we follow the arguments given above, which of course are still valid, and try to find a suitable benchmark claim Γ. In the present setting we can make a particularly clever choice of $\Gamma(X(T))$, and in fact we define the claim by

$$\Gamma(X(T)) = X(T).$$

This is the claim which at time T gives us exactly one share of the underlying stock, and the point is that the price process $G(t, X(t))$ for this claim is particularly simple. We have in fact $G(t, X(t)) = X(t)$, the reason being that the claim can be trivially replicated using a buy-and-hold strategy which consists of one unit of the stock itself. Note that for this argument to hold we use critically our new assumption that X really is the price of a traded asset. Using the identity $dG = dX$ we now trivially obtain the G-dynamics as

$$dG = \alpha X dt + \sigma X d\bar{W}.$$

Thus, in terms of our earlier discussion we have $\alpha_G(t,x) = \alpha$ and $\sigma_G(t,x) = \sigma$. We can now determine the market price of risk as

$$\lambda(t,x) = \frac{\alpha_G - r}{\sigma_G} = \frac{\alpha - r}{\sigma},$$

and the point to note is that, because of our tradability assumption, λ is now determined **within** the model. We now go on to the pricing PDE, into which we substitute λ given as above. The critical part, $\mathcal{A}F$, of the PDE now becomes

$$\mathcal{A}F(t,x) = \{\mu(t,x) - \lambda(t,x)\sigma(t,x)\}\, F_x(t,x) + \frac{1}{2}\sigma^2(t,x)F_{xx}(t,x)$$

$$= \left\{\alpha x - \frac{\alpha - r}{\sigma}\cdot \sigma x\right\} F_x + \frac{1}{2}x^2\sigma^2 F_{xx}$$

$$= rxF_x + \frac{1}{2}x^2\sigma^2 F_{xx},$$

so we end up (as expected) with the Black–Scholes equation

$$\begin{cases} F_t + rxF_x + \frac{1}{2}x^2\sigma^2 F_{xx} - rF = 0, \\ \qquad\qquad\qquad\qquad F(T,x) = \Phi(x), \end{cases}$$

and in the risk neutral valuation formula we will get the old Black–Scholes Q-dynamics

$$dX = rX\,dt + \sigma X\,dW.$$

15.3   The Multidimensional Case

We will now go on to study pricing in a model with more than one non-priced underlying asset. The model is as follows.

Assumption 15.3.1 *The only objects which are a priori given are the following.*

• *An empirically observable k-dimensional stochastic process*

$$X = (X_1,\ldots,X_k),$$

which is **not** *assumed to be the price process of a traded asset, with P-dynamics given by*

$$dX_i(t) = \mu_i\,(t,X(t))\,dt + \delta_i\,(t,X(t))\,d\bar{W}(t), \quad i = 1,\ldots,k, \qquad (15.12)$$

where $\bar{W} = (\bar{W}_1,\ldots,\bar{W}_n)^\star$ *is a standard n-dimensional P-Wiener process.*
• *A risk free asset (money account) with the dynamics*

$$dB(t) = rB(t)dt. \qquad (15.13)$$

The object is to find an arbitrage free price process for a T-claim $\mathcal{Y}$ of the form

$$\mathcal{Y} = \Phi(X(T)).$$

Drawing on our experiences from the previous two sections we expect the following.

• We cannot say anything precise about the price process of any particular contingent claim.

- Different claims will, however, have to satisfy certain internal consistency requirements in order to avoid arbitrage on the derivative market.
- More precisely, since we now have n sources of randomness we can (generically) specify the price processes of n different "benchmark" claims. The price processes of all other claims will then be uniquely determined by the prices of the benchmarks.

As usual we assume that there is a liquid market for all contingent claims, and in order to use the ideas above we fix exactly n claims $\mathcal{Y}_1, \ldots, \mathcal{Y}_n$ of the form

$$\mathcal{Y}_i = \Phi_i(t, X(T)), \quad i = 1, \ldots, n.$$

We furthermore assume that the price processes, $[\Pi^1(t), \ldots, \Pi^n(t)]$, for these claims exist, and that they are of the form

$$\Pi^i(t) = F^i(t, X(t)), \quad i = 1, \ldots, n.$$

Remark 15.3.1 Note that we use superscripts to distinguish between the various pricing functions. This is done in order to allow us to use subscripts to denote partial derivatives.

These claims are our "benchmarks", and we now study the claim

$$\mathcal{Y} = \Phi(X(T))$$

above, the price of which is assumed to have the form

$$\Pi(t) = F(t, X(t)).$$

Using the same notational conventions as in Section 13.2, the price dynamics of the various derivatives are given by

$$dF = \alpha_F F dt + \sigma_F F d\bar{W},$$
$$dF^i = \alpha_i F^i dt + \sigma_i F^i d\bar{W}, \quad i = 1, \ldots, n,$$

where

$$\alpha_i = \frac{F_t^i + \sum_{j=1}^{k} F_j^i \mu_j + \frac{1}{2} tr \left\{ \delta^\star F_{xx}^i \delta \right\}}{F^i}, \tag{15.14}$$

$$\sigma_i = \frac{\sum_{j=1}^{k} F_j^i \delta_j}{F^i}, \tag{15.15}$$

$$\alpha_F = \frac{F_t + \sum_{j=1}^{k} F_j \mu_j + \frac{1}{2} tr \left\{ \delta^\star F_{xx} \delta \right\}}{F}, \tag{15.16}$$

$$\sigma_F = \frac{\sum_{j=1}^{k} F_j \delta_j}{F}. \tag{15.17}$$

We can now follow the reasoning of Section 13.2 word for word. To recapitulate, we form a self-financing portfolio based on the price processes $[B, F, F^1, \ldots, F^n]$. We then choose the weights so as to make the portfolio locally riskless, and finally we try to "beat the bank" by forcing the portfolio to have a higher rate of return than the short rate r.

The conclusion will once again be that, in order to have an arbitrage free market, the matrix

$$H^\star = \begin{bmatrix} \alpha_1 - r & \sigma_1 \\ \vdots & \vdots \\ \alpha_n - r & \sigma_n \\ \alpha_F - r & \sigma_F \end{bmatrix} \tag{15.18}$$

must be singular (recall that σ_i is a row vector). Assuming that the $n \times n$ matrix

$$\sigma = \begin{bmatrix} \sigma_1 \\ \vdots \\ \sigma_n \end{bmatrix}$$

is invertible (with probability 1 for each t) we thus deduce the existence of multiplier processes $\lambda_1(t, X(t)), \ldots, \lambda_n(t, X(t))$ such that

$$\alpha_i - r = \sum_{j=1}^n \sigma_{ij}\lambda_j, \quad i = 1, \ldots, n,$$

and

$$\alpha_F - r = \sum_{j=1}^n \sigma_{Fj}\lambda_j. \tag{15.19}$$

Since the claim $\Phi(X(T))$ was chosen arbitrarily we see that the risk premium, $\alpha_F - r$, of any asset can be written as a linear combination of the volatility components, σ_{Fj}, of the asset, the important point being that the multipliers are the same for all assets. The vector process $\lambda(t, X(t))$ is (see Sections 13.2 and 15.2) known as the **market price (vector) of risk** (cf. CAPM), and we see that the individual component λ_j has the dimension "risk premium per unit of j-type volatility".

Using the notational conventions of Section 13.2, the λ-vector is determined by the equation

$$\alpha - r1_n = \sigma\lambda,$$

i.e.

$$\lambda = \sigma^{-1} [\alpha - r1_n]. \tag{15.20}$$

This is precisely eqn (13.15), but in the present setting the volatility matrix σ and the vector of returns α are no longer given a priori, so λ is not determined within the model. We can summarize this as follows:

- If the derivatives are traded in a no arbitrage market, then there will exist a market price of risk vector which is the same for all assets.
- The market price of risk is not determined within the a priori specified model.
- If we exogenously specify the prices of any n assets such that the corresponding volatility matrix process σ is nonsingular with probability 1 for all t, then the market price of risk will be uniquely determined by this specification and by eqn (15.20). Thus all derivatives will be priced **in terms of** the benchmark prices.

Note that we can choose the (smooth) benchmark pricing functions above in any way whatsoever, subject only to the following conditions.

- The boundary conditions $F^i(T, x) = \Phi_i(x), i = 1, \ldots, n$ are satisfied.
- The volatility matrix $\sigma(t, x)$ is invertible for all (t, x).

The first condition is obvious. The second is the mathematical formulation of the requirement that the family of benchmark derivatives is rich enough to span the entire space of derivatives.

We can easily obtain a PDE for derivative pricing, by writing out eqn (15.19) in detail. Using (15.16)–(15.17) we obtain, after some simplification, the following result.

Proposition 15.5 (Pricing equation) *If the market is arbitrage free, then the arbitrage free price process $\Pi(t; \Phi)$ is given by $\Pi(t; \Phi) = F(t, X(t))$, where F solves the boundary value problem*

$$
\begin{cases}
F_t + \sum_{i=1}^{k} \left(\mu_i - \sum_{j=1}^{n} \delta_{ij} \lambda_j \right) F_i + \frac{1}{2} tr\left\{ \delta^{\star} F_{xx} \delta \right\} - rF = 0, \\
\qquad\qquad\qquad\qquad\qquad\qquad\qquad\qquad F(T, x) = \Phi(x),
\end{cases}
$$

where $\lambda_1, \ldots, \lambda_n$ are universal in the sense that they do not depend on the specific choice of derivative.

A standard application of the Feynman–Kač technique gives us a risk neutral valuation formula.

Proposition 15.6 (Risk neutral valuation) *If the market is arbitrage free, then there exists a martingale measure Q, such that the pricing function F in the proposition above can be represented as*

$$
F(t, x) = e^{-r(T-t)} E_{t,x}^{Q} \left[\Phi(X(T)) \right], \tag{15.21}
$$

where the Q-dynamics of the process X are given by

$$dX^i = \{\mu_i - \delta_i \lambda\} \, dt + \delta_i dW, \quad i = 1, \ldots, k.$$

where $\lambda_1, \ldots, \lambda_n$ are universal.

We have the usual characterization of the martingale measure Q.

Proposition 15.7 *The martingale measure Q has the following properties.*

1. *Under Q every price process $\Pi(t)$, be it underlying or derivative, has the risk neutral valuation property*

$$\Pi(t) = e^{-r(T-t)} E^Q_{t,s} [\Pi(T)].$$

2. *Under Q every price process $\Pi(t)$, be it underlying or derivative, has the short rate of interest as its local rate of return, i.e. the Q-dynamics are of the form*

$$d\Pi(t) = r\Pi(t) \, dt + \Pi(t) \, \sigma_\Pi(t) dW,$$

   where the volatility vector σ_Π is the same under Q as under P.

3. *Under Q every price process $\Pi(t)$, be it underlying or derivative, has the property that the normalized price process*

$$\frac{\Pi(t)}{B(t)}$$

   is a martingale, i.e. it has a vanishing drift coefficient.

Remark 15.3.2 The model formulation above also includes the case when some, or all, of the X-components, say $X_1, \ldots, X_m$, are traded assets (e.g. exogenously given stock prices), whereas the remaining components (if any) are nontraded state variables. As a special case we see that if $m = k = n$, then we are back in the case of a complete market treated in Chapter 13.

15.4   A Stochastic Short Rate

In the theory derived above we have assumed a constant short rate of interest r. Let us now assume that we have exactly the same situation as in Section 15.3 with the following difference.

Assumption 15.4.1 *The short rate of interest is assumed to be a deterministic function of the factors, i.e.*

$$r(t) = r(X(t)). \tag{15.22}$$

Here we have used a slightly sloppy notation: the r on the left-hand side denotes a stochastic process, whereas the r appearing on the right-hand side denotes a deterministic function. We have thus assumed that the factor vector X completely determines the short rate, and as a special case we can of course have one of the factors equal to the short rate itself.

For this model, we can now go through all our earlier arguments once again, and we will easily obtain the following version of Proposition 15.5.

Proposition 15.8 (Pricing equation) *The arbitrage free price process* $\Pi(t;\Phi)$ *is given by* $\Pi(t;\Phi) = F(t, X(t))$, *where* F *solves the boundary value problem*

$$
\begin{cases}
F_t + \sum_{i=1}^{k} \left(\mu_i - \sum_{1}^{n} \delta_{ij}\lambda_j \right) F_i + \frac{1}{2}tr\left\{ \delta^\star F_{xx}\delta \right\} - r(x)F = 0, \\
\qquad\qquad\qquad\qquad\qquad\qquad\qquad\qquad F(T, x) = \Phi(x),
\end{cases}
$$

where $\lambda_1, \ldots, \lambda_n$ *are the same for all derivatives.*

Again a standard application of the Feynman–Kač technique gives us a risk neutral valuation formula.

Proposition 15.9 (Risk neutral valuation) *There exists a martingale measure* Q, *such that the pricing function* F *in the proposition above can be represented as*

$$
F(t, x) = E_{t,x}^{Q}\left[e^{-\int_t^T r(X(u))du} \cdot \Phi(X(T)) \right], \tag{15.23}
$$

where the Q-dynamics of the process X are given by

$$
dX^i = \{\mu_i - \delta_i\lambda\}\, dt + \delta_i dW, \quad i = 1, \ldots, k,
$$

and $\lambda_1, \ldots, \lambda_n$ *are the same for all derivatives.*

15.5   The Martingale Approach*

From the martingale point of view the setup and results of this entire chapter are in fact already covered (in more generality) in Chapter 14. Let us, however, briefly recollect some main points.

- Since we have assumed that the only asset given a priori is B and that X is **not** the price vector of traded assets, the normalized price process Z is one dimensional with $Z = Z_0 = B/B \equiv 1$. Now: the constant process $Z_0(t) \equiv 1$ is a martingale regardless of the choice of measure, so **every** equivalent measure Q will be a martingale measure

- From Proposition 10.25 we *always* have the risk neutral valuation formula

$$
\Pi(t; \mathcal{Y}) = E^Q\left[e^{-\int_t^T r(s)ds} \cdot \mathcal{Y} \,\middle|\, \mathcal{F}_t \right] \tag{15.24}
$$

for *any* T-claim $\mathcal{Y}$ and *any* specification of the short rate process r. In particular, r does not have to be of the form $r(t, X(t))$.

- Denoting a fixed choice of martingale measure by Q, where φ is the corresponding Girsanov kernel and $\lambda = -\varphi$ the market price of risk, the Q dynamics of X are

$$dX(t) = \{\mu(t, X(t)) - \delta(t, X(t))\lambda(t)\}\, dt + \delta(t, X(t))dW(t) \qquad (15.25)$$

- In general, the market price of risk process λ is just an adapted (possibly path dependent) process, so generically X will **not** be a Markov process under Q.
- If we **assume** that the market prices of risk is of the form $\lambda(t, X(t))$, then X will be Markovian under the corresponding Q. In this special case we can use the PDE methods discussed earlier in the chapter for pricing.

15.6 Summing Up

We may now sum up our experiences from the preceding sections.

Result 15.6.1

- In an arbitrage free market, regardless of whether the market is complete or incomplete, there will exist a market price of risk process, $\lambda(t)$, which is common to all assets in the market. More precisely, let $\Pi(t)$ be any price process in the market, with P-dynamics

$$d\Pi(t) = \Pi(t)\alpha_\Pi(t)dt + \Pi(t)\sigma_\Pi(t)d\bar{W}(t).$$

Then the following holds, for all t, and P-a.s.

$$\alpha_\Pi(t) - r = \sigma_\Pi(t)\lambda(t).$$

- In a complete market the price of any derivative will be **uniquely** determined by the requirement of absence of arbitrage. In hedging terms this means that the price is unique because the derivative can equally well be replaced by its replicating portfolio. Phrased in terms of pricing PDEs and risk neutral valuation formulas, the price is unique because a complete market has the property that the martingale measure Q, or equivalently the market price of risk λ, is uniquely determined within the model.
- In an incomplete market the requirement of no arbitrage is no longer sufficient to determine a unique price for the derivative. We have several possible martingale measures, and several market prices of risk. The reason that there are several possible martingale measures simply means that there are several different price systems for the derivatives, all of which are consistent with absence of arbitrage.

Schematically speaking the price of a derivative is thus determined by two major factors.

- We require that the derivative should be priced in such a way so as to not introduce arbitrage possibilities into the market. This requirement is reflected by the fact that all derivatives must be priced by formula (15.11) where the same Q is used for all derivatives, or equivalently by the pricing PDE (15.8)–(15.9), where the same λ is used for all derivatives.

- In an incomplete market the price is also partly determined, in a nontrivial way, by aggregate supply and demand on the market. Supply and demand for a specific derivative are in turn determined by the aggregate risk aversion on the market, as well as by liquidity considerations and other factors. All these aspects are aggregated into the particular martingale measure used by the market.

When dealing with derivative pricing in an incomplete market we thus have to fix a specific martingale measure Q, or equivalently a λ, and the question arises as to how this is to be done.

Question:
Who chooses the martingale measure?

From the discussions above the answer should by now be fairly clear.

Answer:
The market!

The main implication of this message is that, within our framework, it is **not** the job of the theorist to determine the "correct" market price of risk. The market price of risk is determined on the market, by the agents in the market, and in particular this means that if we assume a particular structure of the market price of risk, then we have implicitly made an assumption about the preferences on the market. To take a simple example, suppose that in our computations we assume that $\lambda = 0$. This means in fact that we have assumed that the market is risk neutral (why?).

From this it immediately follows that if we have a concrete model, and we want to obtain information about the prevailing market price of risk, then we must go to the concrete market and get that information using empirical methods. It would of course be nice if we were able to go to the market and ask the question "What is today's market price of risk?", or alternatively "Which martingale measure are you using?", but for obvious reasons this cannot be done in real life. The information that **can** be obtained from the market is **price** data, so a natural idea is to obtain implicit information about the market price of risk using the existing prices on the market. This method, sometimes called "calibrating the model to market data", "backing out the parameters", or "computing the implied parameter values", can schematically be described as follows.

Let us take a concrete model as given, say the one defined by eqn (15.1). We assume that we know the exact form of μ and σ. Our problem is that of pricing a fixed claim $\Phi(X(T))$, and in order to do this we need to know the market price of risk $\lambda(t, x)$, and we have to consider two possible scenarios for the derivative market, which we are trying to model.

The first case occurs if there is no existing market for any derivative product with X as its underlying object, i.e. no weather insurance contracts for Brighton are traded. Then we are stuck. Since the market price of risk is determined by the market, then if there is no market, there is no market price of risk.

The second case occurs if some contracts are already traded. Let us thus assume that there exists a market for the claims $\Phi_i(X(T))$, $i = 1, \ldots, n$. Let us furthermore assume that we want to choose our market price of risk from a parameterized family of functions, i.e. we assume a priori that λ is of the form

$$\lambda = \lambda(t, x; \beta), \quad \beta \in R^k.$$

We have thus a priori specified the functional form of λ but we do not know which parameter vector β we should use. We then carry out the following scheme. We are standing at time $t = 0$.

- Compute the theoretical pricing functions $F^i(t, x)$ for the claims $\Phi_1, \cdots, \Phi_n$. This is done by solving the pricing PDE for each contract, and the result will of course depend on the parameter β, so the pricing functions will be of the form

$$F^i = F^i(t, x; \beta), \quad i = 1, \ldots, n.$$

- In particular, by observing today's value of the underlying process, say $X(0) = x_0$, we can compute today's **theoretical prices** of the contracts as

$$\Pi^i(0; \beta) = F^i(0, x_0; \beta).$$

- We now go to the concrete market and observe the actually traded prices for the contracts, thus obtaining the **observed prices**

$$\Pi^{i\star}(0),$$

where the superscript $\star$ indicates an observed value.
- We now choose the "implied" parameter vector $\beta^\star$ in such a way that the theoretical prices are "as close as possible" to the observed prices, i.e. such that

$$\Pi^{i\star}(0) \approx \Pi^i(0; \beta^\star), \quad i = 1, \ldots, n.$$

One way, out of many, of formalizing this step is to determine $\beta^\star$ by solving the least squares minimization problem

$$\min_{\beta \in R^k} \left[\sum_{i=1}^{n} \left\{ \Pi^i(0; \beta) - \Pi^{i\star}(0) \right\}^2 \right].$$

In the theory of interest rates, this procedure is widely used under the name of "the inversion of the yield curve" and in that context we will study it in some detail.

As we have repeatedly stressed, the problem of determining the market price of risk is not a theoretical one, but an empirical one. It should, however, be pointed out that the truth of this statement depends on our particular framework, where we have not specified individual preferences at all. An alternative framework is that of a general equilibrium model, where we have specified the utility functions of a number of individuals, and the production functions of a number of firms. In such a model all prices, derivative or underlying, as well as the market price of risk, will be determined endogenously within the model, so we no longer have to go to the market to find λ. The price we have to pay for a general equilibrium approach is that we must then specify the individual preferences, which in turn is essentially equivalent to a specification of the market price of risk.

15.7 Exercises

Exercise 15.1 Consider a claim $\Phi(X(T))$ with pricing function $F(t, x)$. Prove Proposition 15.4, i.e. prove that dF under Q has the form

$$dF = rF dt + \{\cdots\} dW,$$

where W is a Q-Wiener process.

Hint: Use Itô's formula on F, using the Q-dynamics of X. Then use the fact that F satisfies the pricing PDE.

Exercise 15.2 Convince yourself, either in the scalar or in the multidimensional case, that the market price of risk process λ really is of the form

$$\lambda = \lambda(t, X(t)).$$

Exercise 15.3 Prove Proposition 15.7.

Exercise 15.4 Consider the scalar model in Section 15.2 and a fixed claim $\Gamma(X(T))$. Take as given a pricing function $G(t, x)$, for this claim, satisfying the boundary condition $G(T, x) = \Gamma(x)$, and assume that the corresponding volatility function $\sigma_G(t, x)$ is nonzero. We now expect the market $[B, G]$ to be complete. Show that this is indeed the case, i.e. show that every simple claim of the form $\Phi(X(T))$ can be replicated by a portfolio based on B and G.

Exercise 15.5 Consider the multidimensional model in Section 15.3 and a fixed family of claims $\Phi_i(X(T))$, $i = 1, \ldots, n$. Take as given a family of pricing functions $F^i(t, x)$, $i = 1, \ldots, n$, for these claims, satisfying the boundary condition $F^i(T, x) = \Phi_i(x)$, $i = 1, \ldots, n$, and assume that the corresponding volatility matrix $\sigma(t, x)$ is nonzero. Show that the market $[B, F^1, \ldots, F^n]$ is complete, i.e. show that every simple claim of the form $\Phi(X(T))$ can be replicated by a portfolio based on $[B, F^1, \ldots, F^n]$.

Exercise 15.6 Prove the propositions in Section 15.4.

15.8 Notes

As we have seen, in an incomplete market there is generically not a unique price for a given claim, and it is impossible to hedge perfectly. A natural idea is then to try to find an approximate hedge, and the obvious first choice is to use a quadratic loss function. This line of ideas was first investigated by Föllmer and Sondermann (1986) and then generalized in Schweizer (1991) and many other papers. The quadratic hedging approach has subsequently been the object of intensive research and has led to a large and deep literature. For a recent overview with an extensive bibliography see Schweizer (2001). One possibility of pricing in an incomplete market is to choose, based on some given principle, one particular member of the infinite set of possible martingale measures. In the quadratic hedging theory one thus ecounters the "minimal martingale measure" as well as the "variance optimal measure". The "minimal entropy measure" is another canonical choice of a martingale measure where an entropy related distance between the objective measure and the martingale measure is minimized. This approach was introduced by Miyahara (1976) and developed by Frittelli in several papers such as Frittelli (2000). The "Esscher transformation", discussed in Gerber and Shiu (1994), is related to actuarial mathematics. For a utility approach to pricing in incomplete markets see Davis (1997). For textbook treatments of incomplete markets, see Bingham and Kiesel (2004) and Dana and Jeanblanc (2003).

16

DIVIDENDS

The object of the present chapter is to study pricing problems for contingent claims which are written on dividend paying underlying assets. In real life the vast majority of all traded options are written on stocks having at least one dividend left before the date of expiration of the option. Thus the study of dividends is important from a practical point of view. Furthermore, it turns out that the theory developed in this chapter will be of use in the study of currency derivatives and we will also need it in connection with futures contracts. In the main part of the chapter we will use classical delta hedging arguments, but in Section 16.3 we will also study dividend paying price processes using the martingale approach.

16.1 Discrete Dividends

16.1.1 *Price Dynamics and Dividend Structure*

We consider an underlying asset ("the stock") with price process S, over a fixed time interval $[0, T]$. We take as given a number of deterministic points in time, $T_1, \ldots, T_n$, where

$$0 < T_n < T_{n-1} < \ldots < T_2 < T_1 < T.$$

The interpretation is that at these points in time dividends are paid out to the holder of the stock. We now go on to construct a model for the stock price process as well as for the dividend structure, and we assume that, under the objective probability measure P, the stock price has the following dynamics, **between dividends**.

$$dS = \alpha S dt + \sigma S d\bar{W}. \tag{16.1}$$

To be quite precise we assume that the S-process satisfies the SDE above on each half open interval of the form $[T_{i+1}, T_i)$, $i = 1, \ldots, n-1$, as well as on the intervals $[0, T_n)$ and $[T_1, T]$.

The first conceptual issue that we have to deal with concerns the interpretation of S_t as "the price of the stock at time t", and the problem to be handled is the following: do we regard S_t as the price immediately **after**, or immediately **before**, the payment of a dividend? From a logical point of view we can choose any interpretation—nothing is affected in real terms, but our choice of interpretation will affect the notation below. We will in fact choose the first interpretation, i.e. we view the stock price as the price **ex dividend**. If we think of the model on an infinitesimal time scale we have the interpretation that, if t is a dividend point, dividends are paid out, not at the time point t, but rather at $t - dt$ or, if you will, at $t-$.

Next we go on to model the size of the dividends.

Assumption 16.1.1 *We   assume   as   given   a   deterministic   continuous function $\delta[s]$*

$$\delta : R \to R.$$

The dividend δ, at a dividend time t, is assumed to have the form

$$\delta = \delta[S_{t-}].$$

Note that the assumption above guarantees that the size of the dividend δ at a dividend time t is already determined at $t-$. The reason that we are using the bracket notation $\delta[S_{t-}]$ instead of the more standard $\delta(S_{t-})$ is that in this way we avoid some hard-to-read formulas with repeated parenthesis signs later on.

Our next problem concerns the behavior of the stock price at a dividend point t, and an easy (but slightly heuristic) arbitrage argument (see the exercises) gives us the following result.

Proposition 16.1 (Jump condition) *In order to avoid arbitrage possibilities the following jump condition must hold at every dividend point t:*

$$S_t = S_{t-} - \delta[S_{t-}]. \tag{16.2}$$

The stock price structure can now be summarized as follows:

- Between dividend points the stock price process satisfies the SDE

$$dS = \alpha S dt + \sigma S d\bar{W}.$$

- Immediately before a dividend time t, i.e. at $t- = t - dt$, we observe the stock price S_{t-}.
- Given the stock price above, the size of the dividend is determined as $\delta[S_{t-}]$.
- "Between" $t - dt$ and t the dividend is paid out.
- At time t the stock price has a jump, determined by

$$S_t = S_{t-} - \delta[S_{t-}].$$

16.1.2   *Pricing Contingent Claims*

As usual we consider a fixed contingent T-claim of the form

$$\mathcal{X} = \Phi(S_T),$$

where Φ is some given deterministic function, and our immediate problem is to find the arbitrage free price process $\Pi(t; \mathcal{X})$ for the claim $\mathcal{X}$. We will solve this problem by a recursive procedure where, starting at T and then working backwards in time, we will compute $\Pi(t; \mathcal{X})$ for each intra-dividend interval separately.

$T_1 \leq t \leq T$:

We start by computing $\Pi(t; \mathcal{X})$ for $t \in [T_1, T]$. Since our interpretation of the stock price is ex dividend, this means that we are actually facing a problem without dividends over this interval. Thus, for $T_1 \leq t \leq T$, we have $\Pi(t; \mathcal{X}) = F(t, S_t)$ where F solves the usual Black–Scholes equation

$$\begin{cases} \dfrac{\partial F}{\partial t} + rs\dfrac{\partial F}{\partial s} + \dfrac{1}{2}s^2\sigma^2\dfrac{\partial^2 F}{\partial s^2} - rF = 0, \\ \qquad\qquad\qquad\qquad\qquad F(T, s) = \Phi(s). \end{cases}$$

In particular, the pricing function at T_1 is given by $F(T_1, s)$.

$T_2 \leq t < T_1$:

Now we go on to compute the price of the claim for $T_2 \leq t \leq T_1$. We start by computing the pricing function F at the time immediately before T_1, i.e. at $t = T_1-$. Suppose therefore that we are holding one unit of the contingent claim, and let us assume that the price at time T_1- is $S_{T_1-} = s$. This is the price cum dividend, and in the next infinitesimal interval the following will happen.

- The dividend $\delta[s]$ will be paid out to the shareholders.
- At time T_1 the stock price will have dropped to $s - \delta[s]$.
- We are now standing at time T_1, holding a contract which is worth $F(T_1, s - \delta[s])$. The value of F at T_1 has, however, already been computed in the previous step, so we have the **jump condition**

$$F(T_1-, s) = F(T_1, s - \delta[s]). \tag{16.3}$$

It now remains to compute F for $T_2 \leq t < T_1$, but this turns out to be quite easy. We are holding a contingent claim on an underlying asset which over the interval $[T_2, T_1)$ is not paying dividends. Thus the standard Black–Scholes argument applies, which means that F has to solve the usual Black–Scholes equation

$$\frac{\partial F}{\partial t} + rs\frac{\partial F}{\partial s} + \frac{1}{2}s^2\sigma^2\frac{\partial^2 F}{\partial s^2} - rF = 0,$$

over this interval. The boundary value is now given by the jump condition (16.3) above. Another way of putting this is to say that, over the *half-open* interval $[T_2, T_1)$, we have $F(t, s) = F^1(t, s)$ where F^1 solves the following boundary value problem over the *closed* interval $[T_2, T_1]$.

$$\begin{cases} \dfrac{\partial F^1}{\partial t} + rs\dfrac{\partial F^1}{\partial s} + \dfrac{1}{2}s^2\sigma^2\dfrac{\partial^2 F^1}{\partial s^2} - rF^1 = 0, \\ \qquad\qquad\qquad\qquad\qquad F^1(T, s) = F(T_1, s - \delta[s]). \end{cases}$$

Thus we have determined F on $[T_2, T_1)$.

$T_3 \leq t < T_2$:

Now the story repeats itself. At T_2 we will again have the jump condition

$$F(T_2-, s) = F(T_2, s - \delta[s]),$$

and over the half-open interval $[T_3, T_2)$ F has to satisfy the Black–Scholes equation.

We may summarize our results as follows.

Proposition 16.2 (Pricing equation) *The pricing function $F(t,s)$ is determined by the following recursive procedure.*

- *On the interval $[T_1, T]$ F solves the boundary value problem*

$$\begin{cases} \dfrac{\partial F}{\partial t} + rs\dfrac{\partial F}{\partial s} + \dfrac{1}{2}s^2\sigma^2\dfrac{\partial^2 F}{\partial s^2} - rF = 0, \\ \qquad\qquad\qquad\qquad F(T, s) = \Phi(s). \end{cases} \qquad (16.4)$$

- *At each dividend point T_i, F has to satisfy the jump condition*

$$F(T_i-, s) = F(T_i, s - \delta[s]). \qquad (16.5)$$

- *On every half-open interval of the form $[T_{i+1}, T_i)$, $i = 1, 2, \ldots n-1$, as well as on the interval $[0, T_n)$, F solves the Black–Scholes equation*

$$\frac{\partial F}{\partial t} + rs\frac{\partial F}{\partial s} + \frac{1}{2}s^2\sigma^2\frac{\partial^2 F}{\partial s^2} - rF = 0. \qquad (16.6)$$

Another way of formulating this result in order to stress the recursive nature of the procedure is as follows.

Proposition 16.3

- *On the interval $[T_1, T]$ we have $F(t, s) = F^0(t, s)$, where F^0 solves the boundary value problem*

$$\begin{cases} \dfrac{\partial F^0}{\partial t} + rs\dfrac{\partial F^0}{\partial s} + \dfrac{1}{2}s^2\sigma^2\dfrac{\partial^2 F^0}{\partial s^2} - rF^0 = 0, \\ \qquad\qquad\qquad\qquad F^0(T, s) = \Phi(s). \end{cases} \qquad (16.7)$$

- *On each half-open interval $[T_{i+1}, T_i)$ we have $F(t, s) = F^i(t, s)$ for $i = 1, 2, \ldots$, where F^i, over the closed interval $[T_{i+1}, T_i]$, solves the boundary value problem*

$$\begin{cases} \dfrac{\partial F^i}{\partial t} + rs\dfrac{\partial F^i}{\partial s} + \dfrac{1}{2}s^2\sigma^2\dfrac{\partial^2 F^i}{\partial s^2} - rF^i = 0, \\ \qquad\qquad\qquad\qquad F^i(T_i, s) = F^{i-1}(T_i, s - \delta[s]) \end{cases} \qquad (16.8)$$

Throughout the entire section we have assumed the standard Black–Scholes price dynamics (16.1) between dividends. It is easy to see that we also have the following more general result.

Proposition 16.4 *Assume that the stock price dynamics between dividends are of the form*

$$dS_t = S_t \alpha(t, S_t)dt + S_t \sigma(t, S_t)d\bar{W}_t. \tag{16.9}$$

Assume furthermore that the dividend structure as before is given by

$$\delta = \delta[S_{t-}].$$

Then the results of Propositions 16.2 and 16.3 still hold, provided that the constant σ is replaced by the function $\sigma(t, s)$ in the PDEs.

We now turn to the possibility of obtaining a probabilistic "risk neutral valuation" formula for the contingent claim above, and as in the PDE approach this is done in a recursive manner.

For $T_1 \leq t \leq T$ the situation is simple. Since we have no dividend points left we may use the old risk neutral valuation formula to obtain

$$F^0(t, s) = e^{-r(T-t)} E_{t,s}^Q \left[\Phi(S_T) \right]. \tag{16.10}$$

Here the Q-dynamics of the stock price are given by

$$dS = rSdt + \sigma SdW,$$

and we have used the notation F^0 to emphasize that in this interval there are zero dividend points left. Note that the Q-dynamics of S above are only defined for the interval $[T_1, T]$.

For $T_2 \leq t < T_1$ the situation is slightly more complicated. From Proposition 16.3 we know that the pricing function, which on this interval is denoted by F^1, solves the PDE

$$\begin{cases} \dfrac{\partial F^1}{\partial t} + rs\dfrac{\partial F^1}{\partial s} + \dfrac{1}{2}s^2\sigma^2\dfrac{\partial^2 F^1}{\partial s^2} - rF^1 = 0, \\ \qquad\qquad F^1(T_1, s) = F^0(T_1, s - \delta[s]). \end{cases}$$

We may now apply the Feynman–Kač Theorem 5.6 to obtain the stochastic representation

$$F^1(t, s) = e^{-r(T_1-t)} E_{t,s} \left[F^0(T_1, X_{T_1} - \delta[X_{T_1}]) \right] \tag{16.11}$$

where the process X, which at this point only acts as a computational dummy, is defined by

$$dX = rXdt + \sigma XdW. \tag{16.12}$$

Notice that the dummy process X is defined by (16.12) over the entire **closed** interval $[T_2, T_1]$ (whereas the pricing function F^1 is the relevant pricing function only over the half-open interval $[T_2, T_1)$). This implies that X has continuous trajectories over the closed interval $[T_2, T_1]$, so in particular we see that $X_{T_1-} = X_{T_1}$. We may thus rewrite (16.11) as

$$F^1(t, s) = e^{-r(T_1-t)} E_{t,s} \left[F^0(T_1, X_{T_1-} - \delta[X_{T_1-}]) \right], \qquad (16.13)$$

still with the X-dynamics (16.12) on the closed interval $[T_2, T_1]$.

Let us now define the Q-dynamics for S over the closed interval $[T_2, T_1]$ by writing

$$dS = rSdt + \sigma SdW,$$

for the half-open interval $[T_2, T_1)$ and adding the jump condition

$$S_{T_1} = S_{T_1-} - \delta[S_{T_1-}].$$

In this notation we can now write (16.13) as

$$F^1(t, s) = e^{-r(T_1-t)} E_{t,s}^Q \left[F^0(T_1, S_{T_1}) \right],$$

and, plugging in our old expression for F^0, we obtain

$$F^1(t, s) = e^{-r(T_1-t)} E_{t,s}^Q \left[e^{-r(T-T_1)} E_{T_1, S(T_1)}^Q \left[\Phi(S_T) \right] \right].$$

Taking the discount factor out of the expectation, and using standard rules for iterated conditional expectations, this formula can be reduced to

$$F^1(t, s) = e^{-r(T-t)} E_{t,s}^Q \left[\Phi(S_T) \right].$$

We may now iterate this procedure for each intra-dividend interval to obtain the following risk neutral valuation result, which we formulate in its more general version.

Proposition 16.5 (Risk neutral valuation) *Consider a T-claim of the form $\Phi(S_T)$ as above. Assume that the price dynamics between dividends are given by*

$$dS_t = \alpha(t, S_t) S_t dt + \sigma(t, S_t) S_t d\bar{W},$$

and that the dividend size at a dividend point t is given by

$$\delta = \delta[S_{t-}].$$

Then the arbitrage free pricing function $F(t, s)$ has the representation

$$F(t, s) = e^{-r(T-t)} E_{t,s}^Q \left[\Phi(S_T) \right], \qquad (16.14)$$

where the Q-dynamics of S between dividends are given by

$$dS_t = rS_t dt + \sigma(t, S_t)S_t dW, \tag{16.15}$$

with the jump condition

$$S_t = S_{t-} - \delta[S_{t-}] \tag{16.16}$$

at each dividend point, i.e. at $t = T_1, T_2, \ldots, T_n$.

We end this section by specializing to the case when we have the standard Black–Scholes dynamics

$$dS = \alpha S dt + \sigma S d\bar{W} \tag{16.17}$$

between dividends, and the dividend structure has the particularly simple form

$$\delta[s] = s\delta, \tag{16.18}$$

where δ on the right-hand side denotes a positive constant.

As usual we consider the T-claim $\Phi(S_T)$ and, in order to emphasize the role of the parameter δ, we let $F_\delta(t, s)$ denote the pricing function for the claim Φ. In particular we observe that F_0 is our standard pricing function for Φ in a model with no dividends at all. Using the risk neutral valuation formula above, it is not hard to prove the following result.

Proposition 16.6 *Assume that the P-dynamics of the stock price and the dividend structure are given by (16.17)–(16.18). Then the following relation holds.*

$$F_\delta(t, s) = F_0(t, (1 - \delta)^n \cdot s), \tag{16.19}$$

where n is the number of dividend points in the interval $(t, T]$.

Proof See the exercises. □

The point of this result is of course that in the simple setting of (16.17)–(16.18) we may use our "old" formulas for no dividend models in order to price contingent claims in the presence of dividends. In particular we may use the standard Black–Scholes formula for European call options in order to price call options on a dividend paying stock. Note, however, that in order to obtain these nice results we must assume both (16.17) and (16.18).

16.2 Continuous Dividends

In this section we consider the case when dividends are paid out continuously in time. As usual S_t denotes the price of the stock at time t, and by $D(t)$ we denote the cumulative dividends over the interval $[0, t]$. Put in differential form this means that over the infinitesimal interval $(t, t + dt]$ the holder of the stock receives the amount $dD(t) = D(t + dt) - D(t)$.

16.2.1   Continuous Dividend Yield

We start by analyzing the simplest case of continuous dividends, which is when we have a **continuous dividend yield**.

Assumption 16.2.1 *The price dynamics, under the objective probability measure, are given by*

$$dS_t = S_t \cdot \alpha(S_t)dt + S_t \cdot \sigma(S_t)d\bar{W}_t. \tag{16.20}$$

The dividend structure is assumed to be of the form

$$dD(t) = S_t \cdot \delta[S_t]dt, \tag{16.21}$$

where δ is a continuous deterministic function.

The most common special case is of course when the functions α and σ above are deterministic constants, and when the function δ is a deterministic constant. We note that, since we have no discrete dividends, we do not have to worry about the interpretation of the stock price as being ex dividend or cum dividend.

The problem to be solved is again that of determining the arbitrage free price for a T-claim of the form $\Phi(S_T)$. This turns out to be quite easy, and we can in fact follow the strategy of Chapter 7. More precisely we recall the following scheme:

1. Assume that the pricing function is of the form $F(t, S_t)$.
2. Consider α, σ, Φ, F, δ and r as exogenously given.
3. Use the general results from Section 6.2 to describe the dynamics of the value of a hypothetical self-financed portfolio based on the derivative instrument and the underlying stock.
4. Form a self-financed portfolio whose value process V has a stochastic differential without any driving Wiener process, i.e. it is of the form

$$dV(t) = V(t)k(t)dt.$$

5. Since we have assumed absence of arbitrage we must have $k = r$.
6. The condition $k = r$ will in fact have the form of a partial differential equation with F as the unknown function. In order for the market to be efficient F must thus solve this PDE.
7. The equation has a unique solution, thus giving us the unique pricing formula for the derivative, which is consistent with absence of arbitrage.

We now carry out this scheme and, since the calculations are very close to those in Chapter 7, we will be rather brief.

Denoting the relative weights of the portfolio invested in the stock and in the derivative by u_S and u_F respectively we obtain (see Section 6.3) the value process dynamics as

$$dV = V \cdot \left\{ u_S \frac{dG_S}{S} + u_F \frac{dF}{F} \right\},$$

where the gain differential dG_S for the stock is given by

$$dG_S = dS + dD,$$

i.e.

$$dG_S = S(\alpha + \delta)dt + \sigma S d\bar{W}.$$

From the Itô formula we have the usual expression for the derivative dynamics

$$dF = \alpha_F F dt + \sigma_F F d\bar{W},$$

where

$$\alpha_F = \frac{1}{F} \left\{ \frac{\partial F}{\partial t} + \alpha S \frac{\partial F}{\partial s} + \frac{1}{2}\sigma^2 S^2 \frac{\partial^2 F}{\partial s^2} \right\},$$

$$\sigma_F = \frac{1}{F} \cdot \sigma S \frac{\partial F}{\partial s}.$$

Collecting terms in the value equation gives us

$$dV = V \cdot \{u_S(\alpha + \delta) + u_F \alpha_F\} \, dt + V \cdot \{u_S \sigma + u_F \sigma_F\} \, d\bar{W},$$

and we now determine the portfolio weights in order to obtain a value process without a driving Wiener process, i.e. we define u_S and u_F as the solution to the system

$$u_S \sigma + u_F \sigma_F = 0,$$
$$u_S + u_F = 1.$$

This system has the solution

$$u_S = \frac{\sigma_F}{\sigma_F - \sigma},$$

$$u_F = \frac{-\sigma}{\sigma_F - \sigma},$$

and leaves us with the value dynamics

$$dV = V \cdot \{u_S(\alpha + \delta) + u_F \alpha_F\} \, dt.$$

Absence of arbitrage now implies that we must have the equation

$$u_S(\alpha + \delta) + u_F \alpha_F = r,$$

with probability 1, for all t, and, substituting the expressions for u_F, u_S, α_F and σ_F into this equation, we get the equation

$$\frac{\partial F}{\partial t} + (r - \delta)S\frac{\partial F}{\partial s} + \frac{1}{2}\sigma^2 S^2 \frac{\partial^2 F}{\partial s^2} - rF = 0.$$

The boundary value is obvious, so we have the following result.

Proposition 16.7 *The pricing function $F(t, s)$ of the claim $\Phi(S_T)$ solves the boundary value problem*

$$\begin{cases} \dfrac{\partial F}{\partial t} + (r - \delta)s\dfrac{\partial F}{\partial s} + \dfrac{1}{2}\sigma^2 s^2 \dfrac{\partial^2 F}{\partial s^2} - rF = 0, \\ \hspace{5cm} F(T, s) = \Phi(s). \end{cases} \qquad (16.22)$$

Applying the Feynman–Kač representation theorem immediately gives us a risk neutral valuation formula.

Proposition 16.8 (Pricing equation) *The pricing function has the representation*

$$F(t, s) = e^{-r(T-t)} E^Q_{t,s}\left[\Phi(S_T)\right], \qquad (16.23)$$

where the Q-dynamics of S are given by

$$dS_t = (r - \delta[S_t])S_t dt + \sigma(S_t)S_t dW_t. \qquad (16.24)$$

In contrast with the case of discrete dividends we see that the appropriate martingale measure in the dividend case differs from that of the no dividend case. It is left as an exercise to prove the following result.

Proposition 16.9 (Risk neutral valuation) *Under the martingale measure Q, the* **normalized gain process**

$$G^Z(t) = \frac{S_t}{B_t} + \int_0^t \frac{1}{B_\tau} dD(\tau),$$

is a Q-martingale.

Note that this property is quite reasonable from an economic point of view: in a risk neutral world today's stock price should be the expected value of all future discounted earnings which arise from holding the stock. In other words, we expect that

$$S(0) = E^Q \left[\int_0^t e^{-r\tau} dD(\tau) + e^{-rt} S(t)\right], \qquad (16.25)$$

and in the exercises the reader is invited to prove this "cost of carry" formula.

As in the discrete case it is natural to analyze the pricing formulas for the special case when we have the standard Black–Scholes dynamics

$$dS = \alpha S dt + \sigma S d\bar{W}, \tag{16.26}$$

where α and σ are constants. We also assume that the dividend function δ is a deterministic constant. This implies that the martingale dynamics are given by

$$dS = (r - \delta)S dt + \sigma S dW, \tag{16.27}$$

i.e. S is geometric Brownian motion also under the risk adjusted probabilities. Again we denote the pricing function by F_δ in order to highlight the dependence upon the parameter δ. It is now easy to prove the following result, which shows how to price derivatives for a dividend paying stock in terms of pricing functions for a nondividend case.

Proposition 16.10 *Assume that the functions σ and δ are constant. Then, with notation as above, we have*

$$F_\delta(t, s) = F_0(t, se^{-\delta(T-t)}). \tag{16.28}$$

16.2.2 The General Case

We now consider a more general dividend structure, which we will need when dealing with futures contracts in Chapter 29 below.

Assumption 16.2.2 *The price dynamics, under the objective probability measure, are given by*

$$dS_t = S_t \cdot \alpha(S_t)dt + S_t \cdot \sigma(S_t)d\bar{W}_t. \tag{16.29}$$

The dividend structure is assumed to be of the form

$$dD(t) = S_t \cdot \delta[S_t]dt + S_t\gamma[S_t]d\bar{W}_t, \tag{16.30}$$

where δ and γ are continuous deterministic functions.

We again consider the pricing problem for a contingent T-claim of the form

$$\mathcal{X} = \Phi(S_T),$$

and the only difference from the continuous yield case is that now we have to assume that the pricing function for the claim is a function of D as well as S. We thus assume a claim price process of the form

$$\Pi(t; \mathcal{X}) = F(t, S_t, D_t),$$

and then we carry out the standard program 1–7 of the previous section.

After a large number of simple, but messy and extremely boring, calculations which (needless to say) are left as an exercise, we end up with the following result.

Proposition 16.11 (Pricing equation) *The pricing function $F(t, s, D)$ for the claim $\mathcal{X} = \Phi(S_T)$ solves the boundary value problem*

$$
\begin{cases}
\dfrac{\partial F}{\partial t} + \mathcal{A}F - rF = 0, \\
\quad F(T, s, D) = \Phi(s),
\end{cases}
\tag{16.31}
$$

where

$$
\mathcal{A}F = \left(\frac{\alpha\gamma + \sigma r - \delta\sigma}{\sigma + \gamma} \right) s\frac{\partial F}{\partial s} + \left(\frac{\delta\sigma + \gamma r - \gamma\alpha}{\sigma + \gamma} \right) s\frac{\partial F}{\partial D}
$$

$$
+ \frac{1}{2}\sigma^2 s^2 \frac{\partial^2 F}{\partial s^2} + \frac{1}{2}\gamma^2 s^2 \frac{\partial^2 F}{\partial D^2} + \sigma\gamma s^2 \frac{\partial^2 F}{\partial s \partial D}.
$$

Using the Feynman–Kač technique we have the following risk neutral valuation result.

Proposition 16.12 (Risk neutral valuation) *The pricing function has the representation*

$$
F(t, s, D) = e^{-r(T-t)} E^Q_{t,s,D} \left[\Phi(S_T) \right],
$$

where the Q-dynamics of S and D are given by

$$
dS_t = S_t \left(\frac{\alpha\gamma + \sigma r - \delta\sigma}{\sigma + \gamma} \right) dt + S_t \sigma dW_t,
$$

$$
dD_t = S_t \left(\frac{\delta\sigma + \gamma r - \gamma\alpha}{\sigma + \gamma} \right) dt + S_t \gamma dW_t.
$$

Remark 16.2.1 In the expressions of the propositions above we have suppressed S_t and s in the functions $\alpha, \sigma, \delta, \gamma$.

The role of the martingale measure is the same as in the previous section.

Proposition 16.13 *The martingale measure Q is characterized by the following facts:*

- *There exists a market price of risk process λ such that the Q-dynamics are in the form*

$$
dS = S(\alpha - \lambda\sigma)dt + S\sigma dW,
$$
$$
dD = S(\delta - \lambda\gamma)dt + S\gamma dW.
$$

- *The normalized gains process G_Z, defined by*

$$G^Z(t) = \frac{S_t}{B_t} + \int_0^t \frac{1}{B_\tau} dD(\tau),$$

is a Q-martingale.

This result has extensions to multidimensional factor models. We will not go into details, but are content with stating the main result.

Proposition 16.14 *Consider a general factor model of the form in Sections 15.3–15.4. If the market is free of arbitrage, then there will exist universal market price of risk processes $\lambda = (\lambda_1, \ldots, \lambda_k)^\star$ such that*

- *For any T-claim $\mathcal{X}$ the pricing function F has the representation*

$$F(t,x) = E_{t,x}^Q \left[e^{-\int_t^T r(X(u))du} \cdot \Phi(X(T)) \right]. \qquad (16.32)$$

- *The Q-dynamics of the factor processes $X^1, \ldots, X^k$ are of the form*

$$dX^i = \{\mu_i - \delta_i \lambda\} dt + \delta_i dW, \quad i = 1, \ldots, k.$$

- *For any price process S (underlying or derivative) with dividend process D, the normalized gains process*

$$Z_t = \frac{S_t}{B_t} + \int_0^t \frac{1}{B_\tau} dD(\tau)$$

is a Q-martingale.

16.3 The Martingale Approach*

As we saw in Proposition 16.9, the natural martingale property of a price dividend pair (S, D) with continuous dividend process, is that the gain process

$$G_t^Z = \frac{S_t}{B_t} + \int_0^t \frac{1}{B_u} dD_u$$

is a martingale under the risk neutral martingale measure with the bank account as numeraire. This result was derived within a simple Markovian framework using delta hedging and PDE techniques, but it should of course be possible to derive this result directly from the First Fundamental Theorem, and we would also like to understand the effect of using another numeraire than the bank account.

16.3.1 *The Bank Account as Numeraire*

We start by using the bank account as numeraire, so we consider an arbitrage free market consisting of the bank account B and an asset with price process S and cumulative dividend process D. Our program is now as follows:

- Consider the self-financing portfolio where we hold exactly one unit of the asset S, and invest all dividends in the bank account. Denote the value process of this portfolio by V.
- The point is now that the portfolio V can be viwed as a **nondividend paying** asset.
- Thus the process V_t/B_t should be a martingale under the risk neutral martingale measure Q with the numeraire B.

To carry out this program we have to derive the dynamics of the portfolio V, and to do this we denote by X_t the (so far unknown) number of units of the risk free asset B at time t, so the amount of money in the bank at time t is X_tB_t. Since we are holding exactly one unit of the underlying asset, the market value of the portfolio at time t will be given by

$$V_t = 1 \cdot S_t + X_t B_t. \tag{16.33}$$

We can now use the Itô formula to calculate the V dynamics as

$$dV_t = dS_t + X_t dB_t + B_t dX_t + dX_t dB_t = dS_t + X_t dB_t + B_t dX_t,$$

where we have used the fact that dB contains no dW term, so $dX_t dB_t = 0$. On the other hand, the self-financing condition says that

$$dV_t = 1 \cdot dS_t + 1 \cdot dD_t + X_t dB_t.$$

Comparing these two expression for dV we obtain

$$dS_t + X_t dB_t + B_t dX_t = dS_t + dD_t + X_t dB_t,$$

which gives us

$$dX_t = \frac{1}{B_t} dD_t,$$

or

$$X_t = \int_0^t \frac{1}{B_s} dD_s. \tag{16.34}$$

This result should not come as a big surprise. We can rewrite it as

$$X_t B_t = \int_0^t \frac{B_t}{B_s} dD_s$$

and it simply says that the amount of money in the bank at time t is the sum of all the capitalized dividends payments over the interval $[0, t]$.

Since V can be viewed as a nondividend paying asset we know from general theory that V must be a Q-martingale, so from (16.33) we conclude that the process

$$\frac{S_t}{B_t} + X_t,$$

is a Q-martingale. Using (16.34) we have thus again derived the main result, but now in much greater generality.

Proposition 16.15 *Under the risk neutral martingale measure Q, the* **normalized gain process**

$$G^Z(t) = \frac{S_t}{B_t} + \int_0^t \frac{1}{B_u} dD_u,$$

is a Q-martingale.

16.3.2 An Arbitrary Numeraire

In this section we again consider a price dividend pair but instead of using the bank account B as numeraire we now want to use the price process A of another (nondividend paying asset) as numeraire. From general theory we know that, given absence of arbitrage, there will exist a martingale measure Q^A with the property that for every nondividend paying asset price S, the normalized price process S_t/A_t is a Q^A martingale. From this result, and by comparing with Proposition 16.15, one is easily led to conjecture that for the dividend paying case, the process

$$\frac{S_t}{A_t} + \int_0^t \frac{1}{A_u} dD_u$$

should be a Q^A martingale but, as we will see below, this is **not** generally true.

We consider a price dividend pair (S, D) and the structure of the argument is exactly like in the previous section. We consider the portfolio where we hold exactly one unit of the asset S, and where all dividends are invested in the asset A. The value V of this portfolio can be viewed as the price process of a non-dividend paying asset, so from general theory we conclude that the normalized process V/A should be a Q^A martingale.

For a general numeraire asset A the derivation of the V dynamics is more complicated than it was in the previous case when we used B as numeraire. To facilitate the derivation we will need some new notation, which turns out to be very convenient.

Definition 16.16 *Let X and Y be Itô processes, with dynamics*

$$dX_t = \mu_X(t)dt + \sigma_X(t)dW_t,$$
$$dY_t = \mu_Y(t)dt + \sigma_Y(t)dW_t$$

The process $\langle X, Y \rangle$ is defined by

$$\langle X, Y \rangle_t = \int_0^t \sigma_X(s)\sigma_Y(s)ds, \tag{16.35}$$

or, equivalently by

$$d\langle X, Y \rangle_t = dX_t dY_t,$$

with the usual multiplication rules.

We now have some easy result concerning the angular bracket process.

Proposition 16.17 *For any real numbers α and β and any Itô processes X, Y and Z we have*

$$\langle X, Y \rangle_t = \langle Y, X \rangle_t,$$
$$\langle \alpha X + \beta Y, Z \rangle_t = \alpha \langle X, Z \rangle_t + \beta \langle Y, Z \rangle_t.$$
$$\langle X, \langle Y, Z \rangle \rangle \equiv 0.$$

Proof   The proof is easy and left to the reader.   □

A very important fact is that the angular bracket is also linear w.r.t stochastic integration. To formulate this we denote stochastic integration by $\star$ so that for two process h and X, the integrated process $h \star X$ is defined by

$$(h \star X)_t = \int_0^t h_s dX_s.$$

Proposition 16.18 *With notation as above we have*

$$\langle h \star X, Y \rangle = h \star \langle X, Y \rangle,$$

or equivalently

$$d\langle h \star X, Y \rangle_t = h_t d\langle X, Y \rangle_t.$$

Proof   Obvious from the definitions.   □

We now go back to the construction of the self-financing portfolio. We denote the value process for the portfolio by V, and we denote by X_t the number of units of asset A in the portfolio at time t. Since, by definition, the portfolio consists of exactly one unit of the dividend paying asset S, we have

$$V_t = S_t + X_t A_t. \tag{16.36}$$

Using Itô we obtain

$$dV_t = dS_t + X_t dA_t + A_t dX_t + d\langle X, A \rangle_t.$$

From the self-financing condition we have

$$dV_t = 1 \cdot dS_t + 1 \cdot dD_t + X_t dA_t,$$

and by comparing these expressions we obtain

$$dD_t = A_t dX_t + d\langle X, A \rangle_t. \tag{16.37}$$

In order to find an expression for dX we now multiply (16.37) by dA_t. This gives us

$$d\langle D, A \rangle_t = A_t d\langle X, A \rangle_t,$$

so

$$d\langle X, A \rangle_t = \frac{1}{A_t} d\langle D, A \rangle_t,$$

and from (16.37) we obtain

$$dX_t = \frac{1}{A_t} dD_t - \frac{1}{A_t^2} d\langle D, A \rangle_t,$$

or on integrated form

$$X_t = \int_0^t \frac{1}{A_s} dD_s - \int_0^t \frac{1}{A_s^2} d\langle D, A \rangle_s. \tag{16.38}$$

Applying the First Fundamental Theorem, we know that V/A should be a Q^A martingale, so from (16.36) and (16.38) we have the following result.

Proposition 16.19 *Assume that (S, D) is a price dividend pair and that A is the price process of a nondividend paying asset. Assuming absence of arbitrage we denote the martingale measure for the numeraire A by Q^A. Then the following hold.*

- *The normalized gain process G^Z defined by*

$$G_t^Z = \frac{S_t}{A_t} + \int_0^t \frac{1}{A_s} dD_s - \int_0^t \frac{1}{A_s^2} d\langle D, A \rangle_s \tag{16.39}$$

  is a Q^A martingale.
- *If the dividend process D has no driving Wiener component, or more generally if $d\langle D, A \rangle = 0$, then the gain process has the simpler form*

$$G_t^Z = \frac{S_t}{A_t} + \int_0^t \frac{1}{A_s} dD_s. \tag{16.40}$$

We see from this that the gain process G^Z above differs from the "naive" definition (16.40) by a term which is connected to the covariation $d\langle D, A \rangle$ between the dividend process D and the numeraire process A.

16.4   Exercises

Exercise 16.1 Prove Proposition 16.1. Assume that you are standing at $t-$ and that the conclusion of the theorem does not hold. Show that by trading at $t-$ and t you can then create an arbitrage. This is mathematically slightly imprecise, and the advanced reader is invited to provide a precise proof based on the martingale approach of Chapter 10.

Exercise 16.2 Prove the cost-of-carry formula (16.25).

Exercise 16.3 Derive a cost-of-carry formula for the case of discrete dividends.

Exercise 16.4 Prove Proposition 16.9.

Exercise 16.5 Prove Proposition 16.10.

Exercise 16.6 Consider the Black–Scholes model with a constant continuous dividend yield δ. Prove the following put–call parity relation, where c_δ (p_δ) denotes the price of a European call (put).

$$p_\delta = c_\delta - se^{-\delta(T-t)} + Ke^{-r(T-t)}.$$

Exercise 16.7 Consider the Black–Scholes model with a constant discrete dividend, as in eqns (16.17)–(16.18). Derive the relevant put–call parity for this case, given that there are n remaining dividend points.

Exercise 16.8 Consider the Black–Scholes model with a constant continuous dividend yield δ. The object of this exercise is to show that this model is complete. Take therefore as given a contingent claim $\mathcal{X} = \Phi(S(T))$. Show that this claim can be replicated by a self-financing portfolio based on B and S, and that the portfolios weights are given by

$$u^B(t, s) = \frac{F(t, s) - sF_s(t, s)}{F(t, s)},$$

$$u^S(t, s) = \frac{sF_s(t, s)}{F(t, s)},$$

where F is the solution of the pricing eqn (16.8).

Hint: Copy the reasoning from Chapter 8, while using the self-financing dynamics given in Section 6.3.

Exercise 16.9 Consider the Black–Scholes model with a constant continuous dividend yield δ. Use the result from the previous exercise in order to compute explicitly the replicating portfolio for the claim $\Phi(S(T)) = S(T)$.

Exercise 16.10 Check that, when $\gamma = 0$ in Section 16.2.2, all results degenerate into those of Section 16.2.1.

Exercise 16.11 Prove Propositions 16.11–16.13.

17

CURRENCY DERIVATIVES

In this chapter we will study a model which incorporates not only the usual domestic equity market, but also a market for the exchange rate between the domestic currency and a fixed foreign currency, as well as a foreign equity market. Financial derivatives defined in such situations are commonly known as **quanto products**. We will start by studying derivatives written directly on the exchange rate X, and then go on to study how to price (in the domestic currency) contracts written on foreign equity.

17.1 Pure Currency Contracts

Consider a situation where we have two currencies: the domestic currency (say pounds sterling), and the foreign currency (say US dollars). The spot exchange rate at time t is denoted by $X(t)$, and by definition it is quoted as

$$\frac{\text{units of the domestic currency}}{\text{unit of the foreign currency}},$$

i.e. in our example it is quoted as pounds per dollar. We assume that the domestic short rate r_d, as well as the foreign short rate r_f, are deterministic constants, and we denote the corresponding riskless asset prices by B_d and B_f respectively. Furthermore we assume that the exchange rate is modelled by geometric Brownian motion. We can summarize this as follows.

Assumption 17.1.1 *We take as given the following dynamics (under the objective probability measure P):*

$$dX = X\alpha_X dt + X\sigma_X d\bar{W}, \tag{17.1}$$

$$dB_d = r_d B_d dt, \tag{17.2}$$

$$dB_f = r_f B_f dt, \tag{17.3}$$

where α_X, σ_X are deterministic constants, and $\bar{W}$ is a scalar Wiener process.

Our problem is that of pricing a currency derivative, i.e. a T-claim $\mathcal{Z}$ of the form

$$\mathcal{Z} = \Phi(X(T)),$$

where Φ is some given deterministic function. To take a concrete and important example, we can consider the case when $\mathcal{Z} = \max[X(T) - K, 0]$, i.e. we have a

European call which gives the owner the option to buy one unit of the foreign currency at the price K (in the domestic currency).

At first glance it may perhaps seem that the problem of pricing the call option above is solved by use of the standard Black–Scholes formula, where we use domestic rate r_d as the short rate of interest, and the stock price S is replaced by the exchange rate X. It is, however, important to understand that this line of argument is incorrect, and the reason is as follows. When we buy a stock (without dividends), this means that we buy a piece of paper, which we keep until we sell it. When we buy a foreign currency (say US dollars) we will, on the contrary, not just keep the physical dollar bills until we sell them again. Instead we will typically put the dollars into an account where they will grow at a certain rate of interest. The obvious implication of this fact is that a foreign currency plays very much the same role as a **domestic stock with a continuous dividend**, and we will show below that this is indeed the case. First we formalize the institutional assumptions.

Assumption 17.1.2 *All markets are frictionless and liquid. All holdings of the foreign currency are invested in the foreign riskless asset, i.e. they will evolve according to the dynamics*

$$dB_f = r_f B_f dt.$$

Remark 17.1.1 Interpreted literally this means that, for example, US dollars are invested in a US bank. In reality this does not have to be the case—US dollars bought in Europe will typically be placed in a European so called **Eurodollar account** where they will command the Eurodollar rate of interest.

Applying the standard theory of derivatives to the present situation we have the usual risk neutral valuation formula

$$\Pi\left(t; \mathcal{Z}\right) = e^{-r_d(T-t)} E_{t,x}^Q \left[\Phi(X(T))\right],$$

and our only problem is to figure out what the martingale measure Q looks like. To do this we use the result from Proposition 13.3, that Q is characterized by the property that every **domestic** asset has the short rate r_d as its local rate of return under Q. In order to use this characterization we have to translate the possibility of investing in the foreign riskless asset into domestic terms. Since $B_f(t)$ units of the foreign currency are worth $B_f(t) \cdot X(t)$ in the domestic currency we immediately have the following result.

Lemma 17.1 *The possibility of buying the foreign currency, and investing it at the foreign short rate of interest, is equivalent to the possibility of investing in a* **domestic** *asset with price process $\tilde{B}_f$, where*

$$\tilde{B}_f(t) = B_f(t) \cdot X(t).$$

The dynamics of $\tilde{B}_f$ are given by

$$d\tilde{B}_f = \tilde{B}_f \left(\alpha_X + r_f\right) dt + \tilde{B}_f \sigma_X d\bar{W}.$$

Summing up we see that our currency model is equivalent to a model of a domestic market consisting of the assets B_d and $\tilde{B}_f$. It now follows directly from the general results that the martingale measure Q has the property that the Q-dynamics of $\tilde{B}_f$ are given by

$$d\tilde{B}_f = r_d \tilde{B}_f dt + \tilde{B}_f \sigma_X dW, \tag{17.4}$$

where W is a Q-Wiener process. Since by definition we have

$$X(t) = \frac{\tilde{B}_f}{B_f(t)}, \tag{17.5}$$

we can use Itô's formula, (17.3) and (17.4) to obtain the Q-dynamics of X as

$$dX = X(r_d - r_f)dt + X\sigma_X dW. \tag{17.6}$$

The basic pricing result follows immediately.

Proposition 17.2 (Pricing formulas) *The arbitrage free price $\Pi(t; \Phi)$ for the T-claim $\mathcal{Z} = \Phi(X(T))$ is given by $\Pi(t; \Phi) = F(t, X(t))$, where*

$$F(t, x) = e^{-r_d(T-t)} E_{t,x}^Q [\Phi(X(T))], \tag{17.7}$$

and where the Q-dynamics of X are given by

$$dX = X(r_d - r_f)dt + X\sigma_X dW. \tag{17.8}$$

Alternatively $F(t, x)$ can be obtained as the solution to the boundary value problem

$$\begin{cases} \dfrac{\partial F}{\partial t} + x(r_d - r_f)\dfrac{\partial F}{\partial x} + \dfrac{1}{2}x^2\sigma_X^2\dfrac{\partial^2 F}{\partial x^2} - r_d F = 0, \\ F(T, x) = \Phi(x). \end{cases} \tag{17.9}$$

Proof The risk neutral valuation formula (17.7)–(17.8) follows from the standard risk neutral valuation formula and (17.6). The PDE result then follows via Feynman–Kač. □

Comparing (17.8) to (16.27) we see that our original guess was correct: a foreign currency is to be treated exactly as a stock with a continuous dividend. We may thus draw upon the results from Section 16.2 (see Proposition 16.10), which allows us to use pricing formulas for stock prices (without dividends) to price currency derivatives.

Proposition 17.3 (Option pricing formula) *Let $F_0(t, x)$ be the pricing function for the claim $\mathcal{Z} = \Phi(X(T))$, in a world where we interpret X as the price of an ordinary stock without dividends. Let $F(t, x)$ be the pricing function* *of the same claim when X is interpreted as an exchange rate. Then the following relation holds*

$$F(t, x) = F_0(t, xe^{-r_f(T-t)}).$$

In particular, the price of the European call, $\mathcal{Z} = \max[X(T) - K, 0]$, on the foreign currency, is given by the modified Black–Scholes formula

$$F(t, x) = xe^{-r_f(T-t)} N[d_1] - e^{-r_d(T-t)} KN[d_2], \qquad (17.10)$$

where

$$d_1(t, x) = \frac{1}{\sigma_X \sqrt{T-t}} \left\{ \ln\left(\frac{x}{K}\right) + \left(r_d - r_f + \frac{1}{2}\sigma_X^2\right)(T-t) \right\},$$

$$d_2(t, x) = d_1(t, x) - \sigma_X \sqrt{T-t}.$$

17.2   Domestic and Foreign Equity Markets

In this section we will model a market which, apart from the objects of the previous section, also includes a domestic equity with (domestic) price S_d, and a foreign equity with (foreign) price S_f. The restriction to a single domestic and foreign equity is made for notational convenience, and in most practical cases it is also sufficient.

We model the equity dynamics as geometric Brownian motion, and since we now have three risky assets we use a three-dimensional Wiener process in order to obtain a complete market.

Assumption 17.2.1 *The dynamic model of the entire economy, under the objective measure P, is as follows.*

$$dX = X\alpha_X dt + X\sigma_X d\bar{W}, \qquad (17.11)$$

$$dS_d = S_d\alpha_d dt + S_d\sigma_d d\bar{W}, \qquad (17.12)$$

$$dS_f = S_f\alpha_f dt + S_f\sigma_f d\bar{W}, \qquad (17.13)$$

$$dB_d = r_d B_d dt, \qquad (17.14)$$

$$dB_f = r_f B_f dt, \qquad (17.15)$$

where

$$\bar{W} = \begin{bmatrix} \bar{W}_1 \\ \bar{W}_2 \\ \bar{W}_3 \end{bmatrix}$$

is a three-dimensional Wiener process (as usual with independent components). Furthermore, the (3×3)-dimensional matrix σ, given by

$$\sigma = \begin{bmatrix} \sigma_X \\ \sigma_d \\ \sigma_f \end{bmatrix} = \begin{bmatrix} \sigma_{X1} & \sigma_{X2} & \sigma_{X3} \\ \sigma_{d1} & \sigma_{d2} & \sigma_{d3} \\ \sigma_{f1} & \sigma_{f2} & \sigma_{f3} \end{bmatrix},$$

is assumed to be invertible.

Remark 17.2.1 The reason for the assumption about σ is that this is the necessary and sufficient condition for completeness. See Proposition 17.4 below.

Remark 17.2.2 It is also possible, and in many situations convenient, to model the market using three scalar correlated Wiener processes (one for each asset). See Remark 17.2.4 below.

Typical T-contracts which we may wish to price (in terms of the domestic currency) are given by the following list.

- A **foreign equity call, struck in foreign currency**, i.e. an option to buy one unit of the foreign equity at the strike price of K units of the foreign currency. The value of this claim at the date of expiration is, expressed in the foreign currency, given by

$$\mathcal{Z}^f = \max\left[S_f(T) - K, 0\right].$$ (17.16)

Expressed in terms of the domestic currency the value of the claim at T is

$$\mathcal{Z}^d = X(T) \cdot \max\left[S_f(T) - K, 0\right].$$ (17.17)

- A **foreign equity call, struck in domestic currency**, i.e. a European option to buy one unit of the foreign equity at time T, by paying K units of the domestic currency. Expressed in domestic terms this claim is given by

$$\mathcal{Z}^d = \max\left[X(T) \cdot S_f(T) - K, 0\right].$$ (17.18)

- An **exchange option** which gives us the right to exchange one unit of the domestic equity for one unit of the foreign equity. The corresponding claim, expressed in terms of the domestic currency, is

$$\mathcal{Z}^d = \max\left[X(T) \cdot S_f(T) - S_d(T), 0\right].$$ (17.19)

More generally we will study pricing problems for T-claims of the form

$$\mathcal{Z} = \Phi\left(X(T), S_d(T), S_f(T)\right),$$ (17.20)

where $\mathcal{Z}$ is measured in the domestic currency. From the general theory of Chapter 13 we know that the pricing function $F(t, x, s_d, s_f)$ is given by the risk neutral valuation formula

$$F(t, x, s_d, s_f) = e^{-r_d(T-t)} E^Q_{t,x,s_d,s_f}\left[\Phi(X(T))\right],$$

so we only have to find the correct risk adjusted measure Q. We follow the technique of the previous section and transform all foreign traded assets into domestic terms. The foreign bank account has already been taken care of, and it is obvious that one unit of the foreign stock, worth $S_f(t)$ in the foreign currency, is worth $X(t) \cdot S_f(t)$ in domestic terms. We thus have the following equivalent domestic model, where the asset dynamics follow from the Itô formula.

Proposition 17.4 *The original market (17.11)–(17.15) is equivalent to a market consisting of the price processes $S_d, \tilde{S}_f, \tilde{B}_f, B_d$, where*

$$\tilde{B}_f(t) = X(t)B_f(t),$$
$$\tilde{S}_f(t) = X(t)S_f(t).$$

The P-dynamics of this equivalent model are given by

$$dS_d = S_d\alpha_d dt + S_d\sigma_d d\bar{W}, \qquad (17.21)$$
$$d\tilde{S}_f = \tilde{S}_f\left(\alpha_f + \alpha_X + \sigma_f\sigma_X^\star\right)dt + \tilde{S}_f\left(\sigma_f + \sigma_X\right)d\bar{W}, \qquad (17.22)$$
$$d\tilde{B}_f = \tilde{B}_f\left(\alpha_X + r_f\right)dt + \tilde{B}_f\sigma_X d\bar{W}, \qquad (17.23)$$
$$dB_d = r_d B_d dt. \qquad (17.24)$$

Here we have used * to denote transpose, so

$$\sigma_f\sigma_X^\star = \sum_{i=1}^{3} \sigma_{fi}\sigma_{Xi}.$$

Note that, because of Assumption 17.2.1, the volatility matrix above is invertible, so the market is complete.

Since $S_d, \tilde{S}_f, \tilde{B}_f$ can be interpreted as prices of domestically traded assets, we can easily obtain the relevant Q-dynamics.

Proposition 17.5 *The Q-dynamics are as follows.*

$$dS_d = S_d r_d dt + S_d\sigma_d dW, \qquad (17.25)$$
$$d\tilde{S}_f = \tilde{S}_f r_d dt + \tilde{S}_f\left(\sigma_f + \sigma_X\right)dW, \qquad (17.26)$$
$$d\tilde{B}_f = \tilde{B}_f r_d dt + \tilde{B}_f\sigma_X dW, \qquad (17.27)$$
$$dX = X(r_d - r_f)dt + X\sigma_X dW, \qquad (17.28)$$
$$dS_f = S_f\left(r_f - \sigma_f\sigma_X^\star\right)dt + S_f\sigma_f dW. \qquad (17.29)$$

Proof Equations (17.25)–(17.27) follow from Proposition 13.3. The equation for X follows from (17.27), the relation $X = \tilde{B}_f/B_f$ and Itô's formula. A similar computation applied to the relation $S_f = \tilde{S}_f/X$ gives us (17.29). □

We can now immediately obtain the risk neutral valuation formula, and this can in fact be done in two ways. We can either use (X, S_d, S_f) as state variables, or use the equivalent (there is a one-to-one mapping) set $(X, S_d, \tilde{S}_f)$. Which set to use is a matter of convenience, depending on the particular claim under study, but in both cases the arbitrage free price is given by the discounted expected value of the claim under the Q-dynamics. (It is of course quite possible to use the set $(\tilde{B}_f, S_d, \tilde{S}_f)$ also, but there seems to be no point in doing so.)

Proposition 17.6 (Pricing formulas) *For a claim of the form*

$$\mathcal{Z} = \Phi(X(T), S_d(T), \tilde{S}_f(T))$$

the corresponding pricing function $F(t, x, s_d, \tilde{s}_f)$ is given by

$$F(t, x, s_d, \tilde{s}_f) = e^{-r_d(T-t)} E^Q_{t,x,s_d,\tilde{s}_f} \left[\Phi(X(T), S_d(T), \tilde{S}_f(T)) \right], \qquad (17.30)$$

where the Q-dynamics are given by Proposition 17.5.
   The pricing PDE is

$$\frac{\partial F}{\partial t} + x(r_d - r_f)\frac{\partial F}{\partial x} + s_d r_d \frac{\partial F}{\partial s_d} + \tilde{s}_f r_d \frac{\partial F}{\partial \tilde{s}_f}$$

$$+ \frac{1}{2}\left\{ x^2 \|\sigma_X\|^2 \frac{\partial^2 F}{\partial x^2} + s_d^2 \|\sigma_d\|^2 \frac{\partial^2 F}{\partial s_d^2} + \tilde{s}_f^2 \left(\|\sigma_f\|^2 + \|\sigma_X\|^2 + 2\sigma_f\sigma_X^\star \right) \frac{\partial^2 F}{\partial \tilde{s}_f^2} \right\}$$

$$+ s_d x \sigma_d \sigma_X^\star \frac{\partial^2 F}{\partial s_d \partial x} + \tilde{s}_f x \left(\sigma_f \sigma_X^\star + \|\sigma_X\|^2 \right) \frac{\partial^2 F}{\partial \tilde{s}_f \partial x}$$

$$+ s_d \tilde{s}_f \left(\sigma_d \sigma_f^\star + \sigma_d \sigma_X^\star \right) \frac{\partial^2 F}{\partial s_d \partial \tilde{s}_f} - r_d F = 0,$$

$$F(T, x, s_d, \tilde{s}_f) = \Phi(x, s_d, \tilde{s}_f).$$

Proposition 17.7 *For a claim of the form*

$$\mathcal{Z} = \Phi(X(T), S_d(T), S_f(T))$$

the corresponding pricing function $F(t, x, s_d, s_f)$ is given by

$$F(t, x, s_d, s_f) = e^{-r_d(T-t)} E^Q_{t,x,s_d,s_f} \left[\Phi(X(T), S_d(T), S_f(T)) \right], \qquad (17.31)$$

where the Q-dynamics are given by Proposition 17.5.
   The pricing PDE is

$$\frac{\partial F}{\partial t} + x(r_d - r_f)\frac{\partial F}{\partial x} + s_d r_d \frac{\partial F}{\partial s_d} + s_f \left(r_f - \sigma_f \sigma_X^\star \right) \frac{\partial F}{\partial s_f}$$

$$+ \frac{1}{2}\left(x^2 \|\sigma_X\|^2 \frac{\partial^2 F}{\partial x^2} + s_d^2 \|\sigma_d\|^2 \frac{\partial^2 F}{\partial s_d^2} + s_f^2 \|\sigma_f\|^2 \frac{\partial^2 F}{\partial s_f^2} \right)$$

$$+ s_d x \sigma_d \sigma_X^\star \frac{\partial^2 F}{\partial s_d \partial x} + s_f x \sigma_f \sigma_X^\star \frac{\partial^2 F}{\partial s_f \partial x} + s_d s_f \sigma_d \sigma_f^\star \frac{\partial^2 F}{\partial s_d \partial s_f} - r_d F = 0,$$

$$F(T, x, s_d, s_f) = \Phi(x, s_d, s_f).$$

Remark 17.2.3 In many applications the claim under study is of the restricted form

$$\mathcal{Z} = \Phi\left(X(T), S_f(T)\right).$$

In this case all partial derivatives w.r.t. s_d vanish from the PDEs above. A similar reduction will of course also take place for a claim of the form

$$\mathcal{Z} = \Phi\left(X(T), S_d(T)\right).$$

We end this section by pricing the contracts (17.16) and (17.18) above.

Example 17.8 (Foreign call, struck in foreign currency) We recall that the value of the claim, at time T, expressed in the foreign currency, is

$$\mathcal{Z}^f = \max\left[S_f(T) - K, 0\right].$$

Let us denote the pricing function, again in the foreign currency, for this claim at time t, by $F^f(t, s_f)$. (It will obviously not involve x.) Furthermore we denote value of the claim at time t, expressed in the domestic currency, by $F^d(t, x, s_f)$. Now an elementary arbitrage argument (which?) immediately gives us the relation

$$F^d(t, x, s_f) = x \cdot F^f(t, s_f),$$

so it only remains to compute $F^f(t, s_f)$. This, however, is just the value of a European call on a stock with volatility $\|\sigma_f\|$, in an economy with a short rate equal to r_f. Thus the value is given by the Black–Scholes formula, and the pricing formula in domestic terms is as follows.

$$F^d(t, x, s_f) = x s_f N[d_1] - x e^{-r_f(T-t)} K N[d_2],$$

where

$$d_1(t, s_f) = \frac{1}{\|\sigma_f\|\sqrt{T-t}}\left\{\ln\left(\frac{s_f}{K}\right) + \left(r_f + \frac{1}{2}\|\sigma_f\|^2\right)(T-t)\right\},$$

$$d_2(t, s_f) = d_1(t, s_f) - \|\sigma_f\|\sqrt{T-t}.$$

See also Remark 17.2.4 for another formalism.

Example 17.9 (Foreign call, struck in domestic currency) The claim, expressed in domestic terms, is given by

$$\mathcal{Z}^d = \max\left[X(T) \cdot S_f(T) - K, 0\right]$$

which we write as

$$\mathcal{Z}^d = \max\left[\tilde{S}_f(T) - K, 0\right].$$

As we have seen above, the process $\tilde{S}_f$ can be interpreted as the price process of a domestically traded asset, and from Proposition 17.5 we see that its volatility is given by $\|\sigma_f + \sigma_X\|$. Thus we may again use the Black–Scholes formula to obtain the pricing function $F(t, \tilde{s}_f)$ as

$$F(t, \tilde{s}_f) = \tilde{s}_f N[d_1] - e^{-r_d(T-t)} K N[d_2],$$

where

$$d_1(t, \tilde{s}_f) = \frac{1}{\|\sigma_f + \sigma_X\|\sqrt{T-t}}\left\{\ln\left(\frac{\tilde{s}_f}{K}\right) + \left(r_d + \frac{1}{2}\|\sigma_f + \sigma_X\|^2\right)(T-t)\right\},$$

$$d_2(t, \tilde{s}_f) = d_1(t, \tilde{s}_f) - \|\sigma_f + \sigma_X\|\sqrt{T-t}.$$

See also Remark 17.2.4 for another formalism.

Remark 17.2.4 In practical applications it may be more convenient to model the market, and easier to read the formulas above, if we model the market using correlated Wiener processes (see Section 4.8). We can formulate our basic model (under Q) as

$$dX = X\alpha_X dt + X\delta_X d\bar{V}_X,$$
$$dS_d = S_d\alpha_d dt + S_d\delta_d d\bar{V}_d,$$
$$dS_f = S_f\alpha_f dt + S_f\delta_f d\bar{V}_f,$$
$$dB_d = r_d B_d dt,$$
$$dB_f = r_f B_f dt,$$

where the three processes $\bar{V}_X, \bar{V}_d, \bar{V}_f$ are one-dimensional correlated Wiener processes. We assume that $\delta_X, \delta_d, \delta_f$ are positive. The instantaneuos correlation between $\bar{V}_X$ and $\bar{V}_f$ is denoted by ρ_{Xf} and correspondingly for the other pairs. We then have the following set of translation rules between the two formalisms

$$\|\sigma_i\| = \delta_i, \qquad i = X, d, f,$$
$$\sigma_i\sigma_j^\star = \delta_i\delta_j\rho_{ij}, \qquad i, j = X, d, f,$$
$$\|\sigma_i + \sigma_j\| = \sqrt{\delta_i^2 + \delta_j^2 + 2\delta_i\delta_j\rho_{ij}}, \quad i, j = X, d, f.$$

17.3 Domestic and Foreign Market Prices of Risk

This section constitutes a small digression in the sense that we will not deriv
any new pricing formulas. Instead we will take a closer look at the various mar
ket prices of risk. As will be shown below, we have to distinguish between th
domestic and the foreign market price of risk, and we will clarify the connectio
between these two objects. As a by-product we will obtain a somewhat deepe
understanding of the concept of risk neutrality.

Let us therefore again consider the international model X, S_d, S_f, B_d, B_f
with dynamics under the objective measure P given by (17.11)–(17.15). A
before we transform the international model into the domestically traded asset
$S_d, \tilde{S}_f, B_d, \tilde{B}_f$ with P-dynamics given by (17.21)–(17.24).

In the previous section we used the general results from Chapter 13 to infe
the existence of a martingale measure Q, under which all **domestically** trade
assets command the domestic short rate r_d as the local rate of return. Ou
first observation is that, from a logical point of view, we could just as wel
have chosen to transform (17.11)–(17.15) into equivalent assets traded on th
foreign market. Thus we should really denote our "old" martingale measure Q
by Q_d in order to emphasize its dependence on the domestic point of view. I
we instead take a foreign investor's point of view we will end up with a "foreig
martingale measure", which we will denote by Q_f, and an obvious project is t
investigate the relationship between these martingale measures. A natural gues
is perhaps that $Q_d = Q_f$, but as we shall see this is generically not the case
Since there is a one-to-one correspondence between martingale measures an
market prices of risk, we will carry out the project above in terms of marke
prices of risk.

We start by taking the domestic point of view, and applying Result 15.6.
to the domestic price processes (17.21)–(17.24), we infer the existence of th
domestic market price of risk process

$$\lambda_d(t) = \begin{bmatrix} \lambda_{d1}(t) \\ \lambda_{d2}(t) \\ \lambda_{d3}(t) \end{bmatrix}$$

with the property that if Π is the price process of any domestically traded asse
in the model, with price dynamics under P of the form

$$d\Pi(t) = \Pi(t)\alpha_\Pi(t)dt + \Pi(t)\sigma_\Pi(t)d\bar{W}(t),$$

then, for all t and P-a.s., we have

$$\alpha_\Pi(t) - r_d = \sigma_\Pi(t)\lambda_d(t).$$

Applying this to (17.21)–(17.23) we get the following set of equations:

$$\alpha_d - r_d = \sigma_d \cdot \lambda_d, \tag{17.32}$$

$$\alpha_f + \alpha_X + \sigma_f \sigma_X^\star - r_d = (\sigma_f + \sigma_X) \lambda_d, \tag{17.33}$$

$$\alpha_X + r_f - r_d = \sigma_X \cdot \lambda_d. \tag{17.34}$$

In passing we note that, since the coefficient matrix

$$\sigma = \begin{bmatrix} \sigma_d \\ \sigma_f + \sigma_X \\ \sigma_X \end{bmatrix}$$

is invertible by Assumption 17.2.1, λ_d is uniquely determined (and in fact constant). This uniqueness is of course equivalent to the completeness of the model.

We now go on to take the perspective of a foreign investor, and the first thing to notice is that the model (17.11)–(17.15) of the international market does not treat the foreign and the domestic points of view symmetrically. This is due to the fact that the exchange rate X by definition is quoted as

$$\frac{\text{units of the domestic currency}}{\text{unit of the foreign currency}}.$$

From the foreign point of view the exchange rate X should thus be replaced by the exchange rate

$$Y(t) = \frac{1}{X(t)}$$

which is then quoted as

$$\frac{\text{unit of the foreign currency}}{\text{units of the domestic currency}},$$

and the dynamics for X, S_d, S_f, B_d, B_f should be replaced by the dynamics for Y, S_d, S_f, B_d, B_f. In order to do this we only have to compute the dynamics of Y, given those of X, and an easy application of Itô's formula gives us

$$dY = Y\alpha_Y dt + Y\sigma_Y d\bar{W}, \tag{17.35}$$

where

$$\alpha_Y = -\alpha_X + \|\sigma_X\|^2, \tag{17.36}$$

$$\sigma_Y = -\sigma_X. \tag{17.37}$$

Following the arguments from the domestic analysis, we now transform the processes Y, S_d, S_f, B_d, B_f into a set of asset prices on the foreign market, namely $S_f, \tilde{S}_d, \tilde{B}_d$, where

$$\tilde{S}_d = Y \cdot S_d,$$
$$\tilde{B}_d = Y \cdot B_d.$$

If we want to obtain the P-dynamics of $S_f, \tilde{S}_d, \tilde{B}_d$ we now only have to use (17.21)–(17.24), substituting Y for X and d for f. Since we are not interested in these dynamics *per se*, we will, however, not carry out these computations. The object that we are primarily looking for is the foreign market price of risk λ_f and we can easily obtain that by writing down the foreign version of the system and substituting d for f and Y for X directly in (17.32)–(17.34). We get

$$\alpha_f - r_f = \sigma_f \cdot \lambda_f,$$
$$\alpha_d + \alpha_Y + \sigma_d \sigma_Y^\star - r_f = (\sigma_d + \sigma_Y)\lambda_f,$$
$$\alpha_Y + r_d - r_f = \sigma_Y \cdot \lambda_f,$$

and, inserting (17.36)–(17.37), we finally obtain

$$\alpha_f - r_f = \sigma_f \cdot \lambda_f, \tag{17.38}$$
$$\alpha_d - \alpha_X + \|\sigma_X\|^2 - \sigma_d \sigma_X^\star - r_f = (\sigma_d - \sigma_X)\lambda_f, \tag{17.39}$$
$$-\alpha_X + \|\sigma_X\|^2 + r_d - r_f = -\sigma_X \cdot \lambda_f. \tag{17.40}$$

After some simple algebraic manipulations, the two systems (17.32)–(17.34) and (17.38)–(17.40) can be written as

$$\alpha_X + r_f - r_d = \sigma_X \cdot \lambda_d,$$
$$\alpha_d - r_d = \sigma_d \cdot \lambda_d,$$
$$\alpha_f + \sigma_f \sigma_X^\star - r_f = \sigma_f \cdot \lambda_d,$$
$$\alpha_X - \|\sigma_X\|^2 + r_f - r_d = \sigma_X \cdot \lambda_f,$$
$$\alpha_d - \sigma_d \sigma_X^\star - r_d = \sigma_d \cdot \lambda_f,$$
$$\alpha_f - r_f = \sigma_f \cdot \lambda_f.$$

These equations can be written as

$$\delta = \sigma \lambda_d,$$
$$\varphi = \sigma \lambda_f,$$

where

$$\delta = \begin{bmatrix} \alpha_X + r_f - r_d \\ \alpha_d - r_d \\ \alpha_f + \sigma_f \sigma_X^\star - r_f \end{bmatrix}, \quad \varphi = \begin{bmatrix} \alpha_X - \|\sigma_X\|^2 + r_f - r_d \\ \alpha_d - \sigma_d \sigma_X^\star - r_d \\ \alpha_f - r_f \end{bmatrix}$$

so, since σ is invertible,

$$\lambda_d = \sigma^{-1}\delta,$$
$$\lambda_f = \sigma^{-1}\varphi.$$

Thus we have

$$\lambda_d - \lambda_f = \sigma^{-1}(\delta - \varphi),$$

and since

$$\delta - \varphi = \begin{bmatrix} \sigma_X \sigma_X^\star \\ \sigma_d \sigma_X^\star \\ \sigma_f \sigma_X^\star \end{bmatrix} = \sigma \sigma_X^\star,$$

we obtain

$$\lambda_d - \lambda_f = \sigma^{-1}(\delta - \varphi) = \sigma^{-1}\sigma\sigma_X^\star = \sigma_X^\star.$$

We have thus proved the following central result.

Proposition 17.10 *The foreign market price of risk is uniquely determined by the domestic market price of risk, and by the exchange rate volatility vector σ_X, through the formula*

$$\lambda_f = \lambda_d - \sigma_X^\star. \tag{17.41}$$

Remark 17.3.1 For the benefit of the probabilist we note that this result implies that the transition from Q_d to Q_f is effected via a Girsanov transformation, for which the likelihood process L has the dynamics

$$dL = L\sigma_X dW,$$
$$L(0) = 1.$$

Proposition 17.10 has immediate consequences for the existence of risk neutral markets. If we focus on the domestic market can we say that the market is (on the aggregate) risk neutral if the following valuation formula holds, where Π_d is the price process for any domestically traded asset.

$$\Pi_d(t) = e^{-r_d(T-t)} E^P \left[\Pi_d(T) \mid \mathcal{F}_t \right]. \tag{17.42}$$

In other words, the domestic market is risk neutral if and only if $P = Q_d$. In many scientific papers an assumption is made that the domestic market is in fact risk neutral, and this is of course a behavioral assumption, typically made in order to facilitate computations. In an international setting it then seems natural to assume that both the domestic market **and** the foreign market are risk neutral, i.e. that, in addition to (17.42), the following formula also holds, where Π_f is the foreign price of any asset traded on the foreign market

$$\Pi_f(t) = e^{-r_f(T-t)} E^P \left[\Pi_f(T) | \mathcal{F}_t \right]. \tag{17.43}$$

This seems innocent enough, but taken together these assumptions imply that

$$P = Q_d = Q_f. \tag{17.44}$$

Proposition 17.10 now tells us that (17.44) **can never hold, unless** $\sigma_X = 0$, i.e. if and only if the exchange rate is deterministic.

At first glance this seems highly counter-intuitive, since the assumption about risk neutrality often is interpreted as an assumption about the (aggregate) attitude towards risk **as such**. However, from (17.42), which is an equation for objects measured in the domestic currency, it should be clear that risk neutrality is a property which holds only **relative to a specified numeraire**. To put it as a slogan, you may very well be risk neutral w.r.t. pounds sterling, and still be risk averse w.r.t. US dollars.

There is nothing very deep going on here: it is basically just the Jensen inequality. To see this more clearly let us consider the following simplified situation. We assume that $r_d = r_f = 0$, and we assume that the domestic market is risk neutral. This means in particular that the exchange rate itself has the following risk neutral valuation formula

$$X(0) = E[X(T)]. \tag{17.45}$$

Looking at the exchange rate from the foreign perspective we see that if the foreign market also is risk neutral, then it must hold that

$$Y(0) = E[Y(T)], \tag{17.46}$$

with $Y = 1/X$. The Jensen inequality together with (17.45) gives us, however,

$$Y(0) = \frac{1}{X(0)} = \frac{1}{E[X(T)]} \leq E\left[\frac{1}{X(T)}\right] = E[Y(T)]. \tag{17.47}$$

Thus (17.45) and (17.46) can never hold simultaneously with a stochastic exchange rate.

17.4 The Martingale Approach*

In this section we will derive the main results of foreign currency pricing theory using the martingale approach, and as can be expected this turns out to be both easier and more general than using the classical approach. We assume a filtered probability space $(\Omega, \mathcal{F}, P, \underline{\mathcal{F}})$ carrying a multidimensional Wiener process W, and we consider a domestic and a foreign market. The exchange rate process is denoted by X and the interpretation is again that

$$X_t = \frac{\text{units of the domestic currency}}{\text{unit of the foreign currency}}.$$

We allow the domestic short rate r^d, as well as the foreign short rate r^f, to be adapted random processes, and we denote the corresponding bank accounts by B^d and B^f respectively.

In this setting there will exist several martingale measures and several associated likelihood processes.

The domestic and foreign martingale measures are denoted by Q^d and Q^f respectively, and we define the following likelihood processes

$$L_t^d = \frac{dQ^d}{dP}, \quad \text{on } \mathcal{F}_t,$$

$$L_t^f = \frac{dQ^f}{dP}, \quad \text{on } \mathcal{F}_t,$$

$$L_t = \frac{dQ^f}{dQ^d}, \quad \text{on } \mathcal{F}_t.$$

The corresponding Wiener processes under Q^d and Q^f are denoted by W^d and W^f. The Girsanov kernels corresponding to L^d and L^f and L are denoted by φ^d, φ^f, and φ so the likelihood processes have the dynamics

$$dL_t^d = L_t^d \varphi_t^d dW_t, \tag{17.48}$$
$$dL_t^f = L_t^f \varphi_t^f dW_t, \tag{17.49}$$
$$dL_t = L_t \varphi_t dW_t^d, \tag{17.50}$$

and the corresponding **market prices of risk** processes are defined as

$$\lambda_t^d = -\varphi_t^d, \quad \lambda_t^f = -\varphi_t^f, \quad \lambda_t = -\varphi_t. \tag{17.51}$$

The domestic and foreign stochastic discount factors are denoted by D^d and D^f, so we have

$$D_t^d = e^{-\int_0^t r_s^d ds} L_t^d,$$
$$D_t^f = e^{-\int_0^t r_s^f ds} L_t^f.$$

Our task is now to find out how all these objects are related, and this is in fact quite easy. We fix an arbitrary exercise date T and consider an arbitrarily chosen foreign contingent claim Z^f. The claim denotes the amount of money in the **foreign** currency that the holder of the claim will receive at time T. If we interpret the foreign market as the US market and the domestic market as UK, then the claim Z^f will thus be denoted in dollars.

We will now compute the **domestic** price of the claim Z at time $t = 0$ in two different ways, and then we will compare the results.

We start by computing the arbitrage free price of Z^f at $t = 0$, expressed in the foreign currency. By (foreign) risk neutral valuation this is given by

$$\Pi^f\left[0; Z^f\right] = E^{Q^f}\left[e^{-\int_0^t r_s^f ds} Z^f\right].$$

By changing foreign currency to the domestic currency at time $t = 0$, the domestic arbitrage free price of Z^f is thus given by

$$\Pi^d\left[0; Z^f\right] = X_0 \Pi^f\left[0; Z^f\right] = X_0 E^{Q^f}\left[e^{-\int_0^t r_s^f ds} Z^f\right].$$

On the other hand, by changing from the foreign to the domestic currency at $t = T$, we can express the foreign claim Z^f at time T as the **equivalent domestic claim**.

$$Z^d = X_T Z^f.$$

By (domestic) risk neutral valuation, the domestic arbitrage free price of Z^d is given by

$$\Pi^d\left[0; Z^d\right] = E^{Q^d}\left[e^{-\int_0^t r_s^f ds} Z^d\right] = E^{Q^d}\left[e^{-\int_0^t r_s^d ds} X_T Z^f\right].$$

Given absence of arbitrage on the international market, the domestic prices at $t = 0$ of Z^f and Z^d must coincide, so we obtain

$$X_0 E^{Q^f}\left[e^{-\int_0^t r_s^f ds} Z^f\right] = E^{Q^d}\left[e^{-\int_0^t r_s^d ds} X_T Z^f\right].$$

We can now rewrite this, under the domestic martingale measure Q^d as

$$X_0 E^{Q^d}\left[L_T e^{-\int_0^t r_s^f ds} Z^f\right] = E^{Q^d}\left[e^{-\int_0^t r_s^d ds} X_T Z^f\right],$$

and since this holds for every T claim Z^f we conclude that

$$X_0 L_T e^{-\int_0^t r_s^f ds} = e^{-\int_0^t r_s^d ds} X_T.$$

We may now state the first main result.

Proposition 17.11 *Assuming absence of arbitrage on a liquid international market, the exchange rate process X is given by any of the following expressions.*

$$X_t = X_0 L_t e^{\int_0^t \left(r_s^d - r_s^f\right) ds}, \tag{17.52}$$

$$X_t = X_0 \frac{D_t^f}{D_t^d}. \tag{17.53}$$

where D^d and D^f are the domestic and the foreign stochastic discount factors respectively.

Proof The relation (17.52) follows directly from the previous calculations, and (17.53) follows from (17.52), the definition of the stochastic discount factors, and the fact that on $\mathcal{F}_t$ we have

$$L_t = \frac{dQ^f}{dQ^d} = \frac{dQ^f/dP}{dQ^d/dP} = \frac{dL_t^f}{dL_t^d}.$$

$\square$

We thus see that the exchange rate process is in fact (apart from the normalizing factor X_0) given by the ratio between the foreign and the domestic stochastic discount factors, and this can be used in order to obtain quite detailed information concerning the exchange rate dynamics. To fix notation, let us write the P dynamics of the exchange rate X as

$$dX_t = \alpha_t X_t dt + X_t \sigma_t dW_t, \tag{17.54}$$

where α and σ are adapted processes. We recall that the exchange rate volatility σ will be the same under equivalent measure transformations from P to Q^d and Q^f but that α will depend on the measure, through the Girsanov Theorem. We now have the following result.

Proposition 17.12 *The dynamics of X under the domestic martingale measure Q^d are given by*

$$dX_t = X_t \left(r_t^d - r_t^f \right) dt + X_t \sigma_t dW_t^d. \tag{17.55}$$

The exchange rate volatility process σ is given by the expression

$$\sigma_t = \lambda_t^d - \lambda_t^f, \tag{17.56}$$

where λ^d and λ^f are the domestic and foreign market prices of risk.

Proof The dynamics (17.55) follows from (17.52). The relation (17.56) follows from (17.52), the fact that $L_t = L_t^f/L_t^d$, the dynamics in (17.48)-(17.49), the definition (17.51), and the Itô formula. $\square$

17.5 Exercises

Exercise 17.1 Consider the European call on the exchange rate described at the end of Section 17.1. Denote the price of the call by $c(t, x)$, and denote the price of the corresponding put option (with the same exercise price K and exercise date T) by $p(t, x)$. Show that the put–call parity relation between p and c is given by

$$p = c - xe^{-r_f(T-t)} + Ke^{-r_d(T-t)}$$

Exercise 17.2 Compute the pricing function (in the domestic currency) for **binary option** on the exchange rate. This option is a T-claim, $\mathcal{Z}$, of the form

$$\mathcal{Z} = 1_{[a,b]}(X(T)),$$

i.e. if $a \leq X(T) \leq b$ then you will obtain one unit of the domestic currency otherwise you get nothing.

Exercise 17.3 Derive the dynamics of the domestic stock price S_d under the foreign martingale measure Q_f.

Exercise 17.4 Compute a pricing formula for the exchange option in (17.19 Use the ideas from Section 13.4 in order to reduce the complexity of the formula For simplicity you may assume that the processes S_d, S_f and X are uncorrelated

Exercise 17.5 Consider a model with the domestic short rate r_d and two for eign currencies, the exchange rates of which (from the domestic perspective) ar denoted by X_1 and X_2 respectively. The foreign short rates are denoted by r_1 and r_2 respectively. We assume that the exchange rates have P-dynamics given by

$$dX_i = X_i\alpha_i dt + X_i\sigma_i d\bar{W}_i, \quad i = 1, 2,$$

where $\bar{W}_1, \bar{W}_2$ are P-Wiener processes with correlation ρ.

   (a) Derive the pricing PDE for contracts, quoted in the domestic currency of the form $\mathcal{Z} = \Phi(X_1(T), X_2(T))$.

   (b) Derive the corresponding risk neutral valuation formula, and the Q_d dynamics of X_1 and X_2.

   (c) Compute the price, in domestic terms, of the "binary quanto contract" $\mathcal{Z}$ which gives, at time T, K units of foreign currency No. 1, if $a \leq X_2(T)$ b, (where a and b are given numbers), and zero otherwise. If you want t facilitate computations you may assume that $\rho = 0$.

Exercise 17.6 Consider the model of the previous exercise. Compute the price in domestic terms, of a quanto exchange option, which at time T gives you the option, but not the obligation, to exchange K units of currency No. 1 for 1 uni of currency No. 2.

   Hint: It is possible to reduce the state space as in Section 13.4.

17.6 Notes

The classic in this field is Garman and Kohlhagen (1983). See also Reiner (199: and Amin and Jarrow (1991).

18

BARRIER OPTIONS

The purpose of this chapter is to give a reasonably systematic overview of the pricing theory for those financial derivatives which are, in some sense, connected to the extremal values of the underlying price process. We focus on barrier options, ladders and lookbacks, and we confine ourselves to the case of one underlying asset.

18.1 Mathematical Background

In this chapter we will give some probability distributions connected with barrier problems. All the results are standard, see e.g. Borodin–Salminen (1997).

To start with some notational conventions, let $\{X(t); \ 0 \leq t < \infty\}$ be any process with continuous trajectories taking values on the real line.

Definition 18.1 *For any $y \in R$, the* **hitting time** *of y, $\tau(X, y)$, sometimes denoted by $\tau(y)$ or τ_y, is defined by*

$$\tau(y) = \inf \left\{ t \geq 0 \ | X(t) = y \right\}.$$

The X-process **absorbed at** *y is defined by*

$$X_y(t) = X(t \wedge \tau)$$

where we have used the notation $\alpha \wedge \beta = \min [\alpha, \beta]$.

The **running maximum** *and* **minimum** *processes, $M_X(t)$ and $m_X(t)$, are defined by*

$$M_X(t) = \sup_{0 \leq s \leq t} X(s),$$
$$m_X(t) = \inf_{0 \leq s \leq t} X(s),$$

where we sometimes suppress the subscript X.

We will be mainly concerned with barrier problems for Wiener processes, so naturally the normal distribution will play a prominent role.

Definition 18.2 *Let $\varphi(x; \mu, \sigma)$ denote the density of a normal distribution with mean μ and variance σ^2, i.e.*

$$\varphi(x; \mu, \sigma) = \frac{1}{\sigma\sqrt{2\pi}} \exp \left\{ -\frac{(x - \mu)^2}{2\sigma^2} \right\}.$$

The standardized density $\varphi(x; 0, 1)$ is denoted by $\varphi(x)$, and the cumulative distribution function of $\varphi(x)$ is as usual denoted by $N(x)$, i.e.

$$N(x) = \frac{1}{\sqrt{2\pi}} \int_{-\infty}^{x} e^{-\frac{1}{2}z^2} dz.$$

Let us now consider a Wiener process with (constant) drift μ and (constant) diffusion σ, starting at a point α, i.e.

$$dX(t) = \mu dt + \sigma dW_t, \qquad (18.1)$$
$$X(0) = \alpha. \qquad (18.2)$$

We are primarily interested in the one-dimensional marginal distribution for $X_\beta(t)$, i.e. the distribution at time t of the X-process, absorbed at the point β. The distribution of $X_\beta(t)$ is of course a mixed distribution in the sense that it has a point mass at $x = \beta$ (the probability that the process is absorbed prior to time t) and a density. This density has its support on the interval (β, ∞) if $\alpha > \beta$, whereas the support is the interval $(-\infty, \beta)$ if $\alpha < \beta$. We now cite our main result concerning absorption densities.

Proposition 18.3 *The density $f_\beta(x; t, \alpha)$ of the absorbed process $X_\beta(t)$, where X is defined by (18.1)–(18.2), is given by*

$$f_\beta(x; t, \alpha) = \varphi(x; \mu t + \alpha, \sigma\sqrt{t}) - \exp\left\{ -\frac{2\mu(\alpha - \beta)}{\sigma^2} \right\} \varphi(x; \mu t - \alpha + 2\beta, \sigma\sqrt{t}).$$

The support of this density is the interval (β, ∞) if $\alpha > \beta$, and the interval $(-\infty, \beta)$ if $\alpha < \beta$.

We end this section by giving the distribution for the running maximum (minimum) processes.

Proposition 18.4 *Consider the process X defined by (18.1)–(18.2), and let M (m) denote the running maximum (minimum) processes as in Definition 18. Then the distribution functions for $M(t)$ (m(t)) are given by the following expressions, which hold for $x \geq \alpha$ and $x \leq \alpha$ respectively.*

$$F_{M(t)}(x) = N\left(\frac{x - \alpha - \mu t}{\sigma\sqrt{t}} \right) - \exp\left\{ 2 \cdot \frac{\mu(x - \alpha)}{\sigma^2} \right\} N\left(-\frac{x - \alpha + \mu t}{\sigma\sqrt{t}} \right),$$

$$F_{m(t)}(x) = N\left(\frac{x - \alpha - \mu t}{\sigma\sqrt{t}} \right) + \exp\left\{ 2 \cdot \frac{\mu(x - \alpha)}{\sigma^2} \right\} N\left(\frac{x - \alpha + \mu t}{\sigma\sqrt{t}} \right).$$

18.2   Out Contracts

In this section we will undertake a systematic study of the relations between a "standard" contingent claim and its different "barrier" versions. This will provide us with some basic insights and will also give us a number of easy formulas to use when pricing various barrier contracts. As usual we consider the standard Black–Scholes model

$$dS = \alpha S dt + \sigma S d\bar{W},$$
$$dB = r B dt,$$

with fixed parameters α, σ and r.

We fix an exercise time T and we consider as usual a contingent claim $\mathcal{Z}$ of the form

$$\mathcal{Z} = \Phi\left(S(T)\right). \tag{18.3}$$

We denote the pricing function of $\mathcal{Z}$ by $F(t, s; T, \Phi)$, often suppressing the parameter T. For mnemo-technical purposes we will also sometimes use the notation $\boldsymbol{\Phi}(t, s)$, i.e. the pricing function (as opposed to the function defining the claim) is given in bold.

18.2.1   Down-and-out Contracts

Fix a real number $L < S(0)$, which will act as the barrier, and consider the following contract, which we denote by $\mathcal{Z}_{LO}$:

- If the stock price stays above the barrier L during the entire contract period, then the amount $\mathcal{Z}$ is paid to the holder of the contract.
- If the stock price, at some time before the delivery time T, hits the barrier L, then the contract ceases to exist, and nothing is paid to the holder of the contract.

The contract $\mathcal{Z}_{LO}$ is called the "down-and-out" version of the contract $\mathcal{Z}$ above, and our main problem is to price $\mathcal{Z}_{LO}$. More formally we can describe $\mathcal{Z}_{LO}$ as follows.

Definition 18.5 *Take as given a T-contract $\mathcal{Z} = \Phi(S(T))$. Then the T-contract $\mathcal{Z}_{LO}$ is defined by*

$$\mathcal{Z}_{LO} = \begin{cases} \Phi(S(T)), & \textit{if } S(t) > L \textit{ for all } t \in [0, T] \\ 0, & \textit{if } S(t) \leq L \textit{ for some } t \in [0, T]. \end{cases} \tag{18.4}$$

Concerning the notation, L as a **subscript** indicates a "down"-type contract, whereas the letter O indicates that we are considering an "out" claim. You may also consider other types of barrier specifications and thus construct a "down-and-in" version of the basic contract $\mathcal{Z}$. A "down-and-in" contract **starts** to exist the first time the stock price hits a lower barrier. Going on we may then consider up-and-out as well as up-and-in contracts. All these types will be given precise definitions and studied in the following sections.

In order to price $\mathcal{Z}_{LO}$ we will have use for the function Φ_L, which is the original contract function Φ in (18.3) "chopped off" below L.

Definition 18.6 *For a fixed function Φ the function Φ_L is defined by*

$$\Phi_L(x) = \begin{cases} \Phi(x), & \text{for } x > L \\ 0, & \text{for } x \leq L. \end{cases} \tag{18.5}$$

In other words, $\Phi_L(x) = \Phi(x) \cdot I\{x > L\}$, where I denotes the indicator function.

For further use we note that the pricing functional $F(t, S; \Phi)$ is linear in the Φ-argument, and that the "chopping" operation above is also linear.

Lemma 18.7 *For all reals α and β, and all functions Φ and Ψ, we have*

$$F(t, s; \alpha\Phi + \beta\Psi) = \alpha F(t, s; \Phi) + \beta F(t, s; \Psi),$$

$$(\alpha\Phi + \beta\Psi)_L = \alpha\Phi_L + \beta\Psi_L.$$

Proof   For F the linearity follows immediately from the risk neutral valuation formula together with the linearity of the expectation operator. The linearity of the chopping operation is obvious. $\square$

Our main result is the following theorem, which tells us that the pricing problem for the down-and-out version of the contract Φ is essentially reduced to that of pricing the nonbarrier claim Φ_L. Thus, if we can price a standard (nonbarrier) claim with contract function Φ_L then we can also price the down-and-out version of the contract Φ.

Theorem 18.8 (Pricing down-and-out contracts) *Consider a fixed T-claim $\mathcal{Z} = \Phi(S(T))$. Then the pricing function, denoted by F_{LO}, of the corresponding down-and-out contract $\mathcal{Z}_{LO}$ is given, for $s > L$, by*

$$F_{LO}(t, s; \Phi) = F(t, s; \Phi_L) - \left(\frac{L}{s}\right)^{\frac{2\tilde{r}}{\sigma^2}} F\left(t, \frac{L^2}{s}; \Phi_L\right). \tag{18.6}$$

Here we have used the notation

$$\tilde{r} = r - \frac{1}{2}\sigma^2.$$

Proof   Without loss of generality we may set $t = 0$ in (18.6). Assume then that $S(0) = s > L$, and recall that S_L denotes the process S with (possible) absorption at L. Using risk neutral valuation we have

$$
F_{LO}(0, s; \Phi) = e^{-rT} E_{0,s}^Q \left[\mathcal{Z}_{LO} \right] = e^{-rT} E_{0,s}^Q \left[\Phi(S(T)) \cdot I \left\{ \inf_{0 \le t \le T} S(t) > L \right\} \right]
$$

$$
= e^{-rT} E_{0,s}^Q \left[\Phi_L(S_L(T)) \cdot I \left\{ \inf_{0 \le t \le T} S(t) > L \right\} \right]
$$

$$
= e^{-rT} E_{0,s}^Q \left[\Phi_L(S_L(T)) \right].
$$

It remains to compute the last expectation, and we have

$$
E_{0,s}^Q \left[\Phi_L(S_L(T)) \right] = \int_L^\infty \Phi_L(x) h(x) dx,
$$

where h is the density function for the stochastic variable $S_L(T)$.
From standard theory we have

$$
S(T) = \exp \left\{ \ln s + \tilde{r} T + \sigma W(T) \right\} = e^{X(T)},
$$

where the process X is defined by

$$
dX(t) = \tilde{r} dt + \sigma dW(t),
$$
$$
X(0) = \ln s.
$$

Thus we have

$$
S_L(t) = \exp \left\{ X_{\ln L}(t) \right\},
$$

so we may write

$$
E_{0,s}^Q \left[\Phi_L(S_L(T)) \right] = \int_{\ln L}^\infty \Phi_L(e^x) f(x) dx,
$$

where f is the density of the stochastic variable $X_{\ln L}(T)$. This density is, however, given by Proposition 18.3 as

$$
f(x) = \varphi \left(x; \tilde{r} T + \ln s, \sigma \sqrt{T} \right)
$$
$$
- \exp \left\{ -\frac{2\tilde{r}(\ln s - \ln L)}{\sigma^2} \right\} \varphi \left(x; \tilde{r} T - \ln s + 2 \ln L, \sigma \sqrt{T} \right)
$$
$$
= \varphi \left(x; \tilde{r} T + \ln s, \sigma \sqrt{T} \right) - \left(\frac{L}{s} \right)^{\frac{2\tilde{r}}{\sigma^2}} \varphi \left(x; \tilde{r} T + \ln \left(\frac{L^2}{s} \right), \sigma \sqrt{T} \right).
$$

Thus we have

$$
\begin{aligned}
E_{0,s}^{Q}\left[\Phi_{L}(S_{L}(T))\right] &= \int_{\ln L}^{\infty} \Phi_{L}(e^{x}) f(x) dx \\
&= \int_{\ln L}^{\infty} \Phi_{L}(e^{x}) \varphi\left(x; \tilde{r}T + \ln s, \sigma\sqrt{T}\right) dx \\
&\quad - \left(\frac{L}{s}\right)^{\frac{2\tilde{r}}{\sigma^{2}}} \int_{\ln L}^{\infty} \Phi_{L}(e^{x}) \varphi\left(x; \tilde{r}T + \ln\left(\frac{L^{2}}{s}\right), \sigma\sqrt{T}\right) dx \\
&= \int_{-\infty}^{\infty} \Phi_{L}(e^{x}) \varphi\left(x; \tilde{r}T + \ln s, \sigma\sqrt{T}\right) dx \\
&\quad - \left(\frac{L}{s}\right)^{\frac{2\tilde{r}}{\sigma^{2}}} \int_{-\infty}^{\infty} \Phi_{L}(e^{x}) \varphi\left(x; \tilde{r}T + \ln\left(\frac{L^{2}}{s}\right), \sigma\sqrt{T}\right) dx.
\end{aligned}
$$

Inspecting the last two lines we see that the density in the first integral is the density of $X(T)$ under the usual martingale measure Q, given the starting value $S(0) = s$. The density in the second integral is, in the same way, the density (under Q) of $X(T)$, given the starting point $S(0) = L^{2}/s$. Thus we have

$$
E_{0,s}^{Q}\left[\Phi_{L}(S_{L}(T))\right] = E_{0,s}^{Q}\left[\Phi_{L}(S(T))\right] - \left(\frac{L}{s}\right)^{\frac{2\tilde{r}}{\sigma^{2}}} E_{0,\frac{L^{2}}{s}}^{Q}\left[\Phi_{L}(S(T))\right]
$$

which gives us the result.   □

We again emphasize the point of this result.

The problem of computing the price for a down-and-out claim reduces to the standard problem of computing the price of an ordinary (related) claim without a barrier.

For future use we also note the fact that down-and-out pricing is a linear operation.

Corollary 18.9 *For any contract functions Φ and Ψ, and for any real numbers α and β, the following relation holds.*

$$
F_{LO}(t, s; \alpha\Phi + \beta\Psi) = \alpha F_{LO}(t, s; \Phi) + \beta F_{LO}(t, s; \Psi).
$$

Proof The result follows immediately from Theorem 18.8 together with the linearity of the ordinary pricing functional F and the linearity of the chopping operation.   □

18.2.2   Up-and-out Contracts

We again consider a fixed T-contract of the form $\mathcal{Z} = \Phi\left(S(T)\right)$, and we now describe the up-and-out version of $\mathcal{Z}$. This is the contract which at the time of delivery, T, will pay $\mathcal{Z}$ if the underlying price process during the entire contract period has stayed below the barrier L. If, at some time during the contract period, the price process exceeds L, then the contract is worthless. In formal terms this reads as follows.

Definition 18.10 *Take as given the T-contract $\mathcal{Z} = \Phi\left(S(T)\right)$. Then the T-contract $\mathcal{Z}^{LO}$ is defined by*

$$
\mathcal{Z}^{LO} = \begin{cases} \Phi\left(S(T)\right), & \text{if } S(t) < L \text{ for all } t \in [0,T] \\ 0, & \text{if } S(t) \geq L \text{ for some } t \in [0,T]. \end{cases} \tag{18.7}
$$

The pricing functional for $\mathcal{Z}^{LO}$ is denoted by $F^{LO}(t, s; \Phi)$, or according to our earlier notational convention, by $\mathbf{\Phi}^{LO}(t, s)$.

L as a **super**script indicates an "up"-type contract, whereas the superscript O indicates that the contract is an "out" contract. As in the previous sections we will relate the up-and-out contract to an associated standard contract. To this end we need to define, for a fixed contract function Φ, the function Φ^L, which is the function Φ "chopped off" above L.

Definition 18.11 *For a fixed function Φ the function Φ^L is defined by*

$$
\Phi^L(x) = \begin{cases} \Phi(x), & \text{for } x < L \\ 0, & \text{for } x \geq L. \end{cases} \tag{18.8}
$$

In other words, $\Phi^L(x) = \Phi(x) \cdot I\left\{x < L\right\}$.

The main result of this section is the following theorem, which is parallel to Theorem 18.8. The proof is almost identical.

Theorem 18.12 (Pricing up-and-out contracts) *Consider a fixed T-claim $\mathcal{Z} = \Phi(S(T))$. Then the pricing function, F^{LO}, of the corresponding up-and-out contract $\mathcal{Z}^{LO}$ is given, for $S < L$, by*

$$
F^{LO}(t, s, \Phi) = F\left(t, s, \Phi^L\right) - \left(\frac{L}{s}\right)^{\frac{2\tilde{r}}{\sigma^2}} F\left(t, \frac{L^2}{s}, \Phi^L\right) \tag{18.9}
$$

where we have used the notation

$$
\tilde{r} = r - \frac{1}{2}\sigma^2.
$$

18.2.3 Examples

In this section we will use Theorems 18.8 and 18.12, together with the linearity lemma 18.7, to give a systematic account of the pricing of a fairly wide class of barrier derivatives, including barrier call and put options. Let us define the following standard contracts, which will be the basic building blocks in the sequel.

Definition 18.13 *Fix a delivery time T. For fixed parameters K and L define the claims ST, BO, H and C by*

$$ST(x) = x, \ \forall x \tag{18.10}$$

$$BO(x) = 1, \ \forall x \tag{18.11}$$

$$H(x; L) = \begin{cases} 1, \ if \ x > L \\ 0, \ if \ x \le L \end{cases} \tag{18.12}$$

$$C(x; K) = \max\left[x - K, 0\right]. \tag{18.13}$$

The contract ST (ST for "stock") thus gives the owner (the price of) one unit of the underlying stock at delivery time T, whereas BO is an ordinary zero coupon bond paying one at maturity T. The H-contract (H stands for the Heaviside function) gives the owner one if the value of the underlying stock exceeds L at delivery time T, otherwise nothing is paid out. The C-claim is of course the ordinary European call with strike price K. We note in passing that $H(x; L) = H_L(x)$.

We now list the pricing functions for the standard contracts above. The value of ST at time t is of course equal to the value of the underlying stock at the same time, whereas the value of BO at t is $e^{-r(T-t)}$. The value of C is given by the Black–Scholes formula, and the value of H is easily calculated by using risk neutral valuation. Thus we have the following result.

Lemma 18.14 *The contracts (18.10)–(18.13) with delivery time T are priced at time t as follows (with the pricing function in bold).*

$$\mathbf{ST}(t, s) = s,$$
$$\mathbf{BO}(t, s) = e^{-r(T-t)},$$
$$\mathbf{H}(t, s; L) = e^{-r(T-t)} N \left[\frac{\tilde{r}(T - t) + \ln\left(\frac{s}{L}\right)}{\sigma\sqrt{T - t}} \right],$$
$$\mathbf{C}(t, s; K) = c(t, s; K),$$

where $c(t, s; K)$ is the usual Black–Scholes formula.

We may now put this machinery to some use and start with the simple case of valuing a down-and-out contract on a bond. This contract will thus pay out 1 dollar at time T if the stock price is above the level L during the entire contract period, and nothing if the stock price at some time during the period is below or equal to L.

A direct application of Theorem 18.8 gives us the formula

$$F_{LO}\left(t, s; BO\right) = F\left(t, s; BO_L\right) - \left(\frac{L}{s}\right)^{\frac{2\tilde{r}}{\sigma^2}} F\left(t, \frac{L^2}{s}; BO_L\right).$$

Obviously we have $BO_L(x) = H(x; L)$ for all x so we have the following result.

Lemma 18.15 *The down-and-out bond with barrier L is priced, for $s > L$, by the formula*

$$\mathbf{BO}_{LO}(t, s) = \mathbf{H}(t, s; L) - \left(\frac{L}{s}\right)^{\frac{2\tilde{r}}{\sigma^2}} \mathbf{H}\left(t, \frac{L^2}{s}; L\right), \qquad (18.14)$$

where $\mathbf{H}(t, s; L)$ is given by Lemma 18.14.

We continue by pricing a down-and-out contract on the stock itself (no option is involved). Thus we want to compute $F_{LO}(t, s; ST)$ and Theorem 18.8 gives us

$$F_{LO}(t, s; ST) = F(t, s; ST_L) - \left(\frac{L}{s}\right)^{\frac{2\tilde{r}}{\sigma^2}} F\left(t, \frac{L^2}{s}; ST_L\right). \qquad (18.15)$$

A quick look at a figure gives us the relation

$$ST_L(x) = L \cdot H(x; L) + C(x; L).$$

Substituting this into (18.15) and using linearity (Lemma 18.7) we get

$$\begin{aligned}
\mathbf{ST}_{LO}&(t, s) \\
&= F_{LO}(t, s; ST) \\
&= F\left(t, s; LH(\star, L) + C(\star, L)\right) - \left(\frac{L}{s}\right)^{\frac{2\tilde{r}}{\sigma^2}} F\left(t, \frac{L^2}{s}; LH(\star; L) + C(\star; L)\right) \\
&= L \cdot F\left(t, s; H(\star; L)\right) - L \cdot \left(\frac{L}{s}\right)^{\frac{2\tilde{r}}{\sigma^2}} F\left(t, \frac{L^2}{s}; H(\star; L)\right) \\
&\quad + F\left(t, s; C(\star; L)\right) - \left(\frac{L}{s}\right)^{\frac{2\tilde{r}}{\sigma^2}} F\left(t, \frac{L^2}{s}; C(\star; L)\right).
\end{aligned}$$

Summarizing we have the following.

Lemma 18.16 *The down-and-out contract on the underlying stock is given by*

$$\mathbf{ST}_{LO}(t,s) = L \cdot \mathbf{H}\left(t,s;L\right) - L \cdot \left(\frac{L}{s}\right)^{\frac{2\tilde{r}}{\sigma^2}} \mathbf{H}\left(t,\frac{L^2}{s};L\right)$$

$$+ \mathbf{C}\left(t,s;L\right) - \left(\frac{L}{s}\right)^{\frac{2\tilde{r}}{\sigma^2}} \mathbf{C}\left(t,\frac{L^2}{s};L\right),$$

where **H** *and* **C** *are given by Lemma 18.14.*

We now turn to a more interesting example—a down-and-out European call with strike price K. From the main proposition we immediately have

$$F_{LO}\left(t,s;C(\star;K)\right) = F\left(t,s;C_L(\star;K)\right) - \left(\frac{L}{s}\right)^{\frac{2\tilde{r}}{\sigma^2}} F\left(t,\frac{L^2}{s};C_L(\star,K)\right),$$
(18.16)

and we have to treat the two cases $L < K$ and $L > K$ separately. The result is as follows.

Proposition 18.17 (Down-and-out call) *The down-and-out European call option is priced as follows.*
For $L < K$:

$$\mathbf{C}_{LO}(t,s;K) = \mathbf{C}(t,s;K) - \left(\frac{L}{s}\right)^{\frac{2\tilde{r}}{\sigma^2}} \mathbf{C}\left(t,\frac{L^2}{s};K\right).$$ (18.17)

For $L > K$:

$$\mathbf{C}_{LO}(t,s;K) = \mathbf{C}(t,s;K) + (L-K)\mathbf{H}(t,s;L)$$

$$- \left(\frac{L}{s}\right)^{\frac{2\tilde{r}}{\sigma^2}} \left\{ \mathbf{C}\left(t,\frac{L^2}{s};K\right) + (L-K)\mathbf{H}\left(t,\frac{L^2}{s};L\right)\right\}.$$
(18.18)

Proof   For $L < K$ it is easily seen (draw a figure) that $C_L(x,K) = C(x,K)$, so from (18.16) we get

$$\mathbf{C}_{LO}(t,s;K) = F\left(t,s;C(\star;K)\right) - \left(\frac{L}{s}\right)^{\frac{2\tilde{r}}{\sigma^2}} F\left(t,\frac{L^2}{s};C(\star,K)\right),$$

which proves (18.17).

For $L > K$ the situation is slightly more complicated. Another figure shows that

$$C_L(x;K) = C(x;L) + (L-K)H(x;L).$$

Putting this relation into (18.16), and using the linear property of pricing, we get (18.18). □

As we have seen, almost all results are fairly easy consequences of the linearity of the pricing functional. In Section 9.1 we used this linearity to prove the standard put–call parity relation for standard European options, and we can now derive the put–call parity result for down-and-out options.

Drawing a figure we see that $P(x;K) = K - x + C(x;K)$, so, in terms of the standard contracts, we have

$$P(x;K) = K \cdot BO(x) - ST(x) + C(x;K).$$

Using Corollary 18.9 we immediately have the following result. Note that when $L = 0$ we have the usual put–call parity.

Proposition 18.18 (Put–call parity) *The down-and-out put price* $\mathbf{P}_{LO}$, *and call price* $\mathbf{C}_{LO}$, *are related by the formula*

$$\mathbf{P}_{LO}(t,s;K) = K \cdot \mathbf{B}_{LO}(t,s) - \mathbf{ST}_{LO}(t,s) + \mathbf{C}_{LO}(t,s;K). \tag{18.19}$$

Here $\mathbf{B}_{LO}$ *and* $\mathbf{ST}_{LO}$ *are given by Lemmas 18.15 and 18.16, whereas* $\mathbf{C}_{LO}$ *is given by Proposition 18.17.*

We end this section by computing the price of a European up-and-out put option with barrier L and strike price K.

Proposition 18.19 (Up-and-out put) *The price of an up-and-out European put option is given by the following formulas.*
If $L > K$ then, for $s < L$:

$$\mathbf{P}^{LO}(t,s;K) = \mathbf{P}(t,s;K) - \left(\frac{L}{s}\right)^{\frac{2\tilde{r}}{\sigma^2}} \mathbf{P}\left(t,\frac{L^2}{s};K\right). \tag{18.20}$$

If $L > K$, then for $s < L$:

$$\mathbf{P}^{LO}(t,s;K) = \mathbf{P}(t,s;L) - (K-L)\mathbf{H}(t,s;L)$$

$$- \left(\frac{L}{s}\right)^{\frac{2\tilde{r}}{\sigma^2}} \left\{ \mathbf{P}\left(t,\frac{L^2}{s};L\right) - (K-L)\mathbf{H}\left(t,\frac{L^2}{s};L\right) \right\}$$

$$+ \left\{ 1 - \left(\frac{L}{s}\right)^{\frac{2\tilde{r}}{\sigma^2}} \right\} (K-L)e^{-r(T-t)}. \tag{18.21}$$

Proof If $L > K$ then $P^L(s;K) = P(s;K)$, and then (18.20) follows immediately from Proposition 18.12.

If $L < K$ then it is easily seen that

$$P^L(x) = P(x;L) + (K-L) \cdot BO(x) - (K-L) \cdot H(x;L).$$

Linearity and Proposition 18.12 give us (18.21). □

18.3   In Contracts

In this section we study contracts which will **start** to exist if and only if the price of the underlying stock hits a prespecified barrier level at some time during the contract period. We thus fix a standard T-claim of the form $\mathcal{Z} = \Phi\left(S(T)\right)$ and we also fix a barrier L. We start by studying the "down-and-in" version of $\mathcal{Z}$, which is defined as follows:

• If the stock price stays above the barrier L during the entire contract period, then nothing is paid to the holder of the contract.
• If the stock price, at some time before the delivery time T, hits the barrier L, then the amount $\mathcal{Z}$ is paid to the holder of the contract.

We will write the down-and-in version of $\mathcal{Z}$ as $\mathcal{Z}_{LI}$, and the formal definition is as follows.

Definition 18.20 *Take as given the T-contract $\mathcal{Z} = \Phi\left(S(T)\right)$. Then the T contract $\mathcal{Z}_{LI}$ is defined by*

$$\mathcal{Z}_{LI} = \begin{cases} 0, & \text{if } S(t) > L \text{ for all } t \in [0,T] \\ \Phi\left(S(T)\right), & \text{if } S(t) \leq L \text{ for some } t \in [0,T]. \end{cases} \tag{18.22}$$

The pricing function for $\mathcal{Z}_{LI}$ is denoted by $F_{LI}(t,s;\Phi)$, or sometimes by $\Phi_{LI}(t,s)$.

Concerning the notation, L as a **sub**script indicates a "down" contract whereas the subscript I denotes an "in" contract. Pricing a down-and-in contract turns out to be fairly easy, since we can in fact price it in terms of the corresponding down-and-out contract.

Lemma 18.21 (In–out parity)

$$F_{LI}(t,s;\Phi) = F(t,s;\Phi) - F_{LO}(t,s;\Phi), \quad \forall s.$$

Proof   If, at time t, you have a portfolio consisting of a down-and-out version of $\mathcal{Z}$ as well as a down-and-in version of $\mathcal{Z}$ (with the same barrier L) then obviously you will receive exactly $\mathcal{Z}$ at time T. We thus have

$$F(t,s;\Phi) = F_{LI}(t,s;\Phi) + F_{LO}(t,s;\Phi).$$

We can now formulate the basic result.

Proposition 18.22 (Pricing down-and-in contracts) *Consider a fixed T contract $\mathcal{Z} = \Phi\left(S(T)\right)$. Then the price of the corresponding down-and-in contract $\mathcal{Z}_{LI}$ is given by*

$$F_{LI}(t,s;\Phi) = F(t,s;\Phi^L) + \left(\frac{L}{s}\right)^{\frac{2\bar{r}}{\sigma^2}} F\left(t,\frac{L^2}{s};\Phi_L\right).$$

Proof From the equality $\Phi = \Phi_L + \Phi^L$ we have

$$F(t, s; \Phi) = F(t, s; \Phi_L) + F(t, s; \Phi^L).$$

Now use this formula, the lemma above, and Theorem 18.8. □

The treatment of "up-and-in" contracts is of course parallel to down-and-in contracts, so we only give the basic definitions and results. We denote the up-and-in version of $\mathcal{Z}$ by $\mathcal{Z}^{LI}$, and the definition of $\mathcal{Z}^{LI}$ is as follows:

- If the stock price stays below the barrier L during the entire contract period, then nothing is paid to the holder of the contract.
- If the stock price, at some time before the delivery time T, hits the barrier L, then the amount $\mathcal{Z}$ is paid to the holder of the contract.

Corresponding to Lemma 18.21, we have

$$F^{LI}(t, s; \Phi) = F(t, s; \Phi) - F^{LO}(t, s; \Phi), \quad \forall s, \tag{18.23}$$

and from this relation, together with the pricing formula for up-and-out contracts, we have an easy valuation formula.

Proposition 18.23 (Pricing up-and-in contracts) *Consider a fixed T-contract $\mathcal{Z} = \Phi(S(T))$. Then the price of the corresponding up-and-in contract $\mathcal{Z}^{LI}$ is given by*

$$F^{LI}(t, s; \Phi) = F(t, s; \Phi_L) + \left(\frac{L}{s}\right)^{\frac{2\tilde{r}}{\sigma^2}} F\left(t, \frac{L^2}{s}; \Phi^L\right).$$

We end this section by giving, as an example, the pricing formula for a down-and-in European call with strike price K.

Proposition 18.24 (Down-and-in European call) *For $s > L$ the down-and-in European call option is priced as follows.*
For $L < K$:

$$\mathbf{C}_{LI}(t, s; K) = \left(\frac{L}{s}\right)^{\frac{2\tilde{r}}{\sigma^2}} \mathbf{C}\left(t, \frac{L^2}{s}; K\right).$$

For $L > K$:

$$\mathbf{C}_{LI}(t, s; K) = \left(\frac{L}{s}\right)^{\frac{2\tilde{r}}{\sigma^2}} \left\{ \mathbf{C}\left(t, \frac{L^2}{s}; K\right) + (L - K)\mathbf{H}\left(t, \frac{L^2}{s}; L\right) \right\}$$
$$- (L - K)\mathbf{H}(t, s; L).$$

18.4   Ladders

Let us take as given

- A finite increasing sequence of real numbers

$$0 = \alpha_0 < \alpha_1 < \cdots < \alpha_N.$$

This sequence will be denoted by α.
- Another finite increasing sequence of real numbers

$$0 = \beta_0 < \beta_1 < \cdots < \beta_N.$$

This sequence will be denoted by β.

Note that the number N is the same in both sequences. The interval $[\alpha_n, \alpha_{n+1})$ will play an important role in the sequel, and we denote it by D_n, with D_N defined as $D_N = [\alpha_N, \infty)$. For a fixed delivery time T we will now consider a new type of contract, called the "(α, β)-ladder", which is defined as follows.

Definition 18.25 *The (α, β)-**ladder** with delivery time T is a T-claim $\mathcal{Z}$, described by*

$$\mathcal{Z} = \sum_{n=0}^{N} \beta_n \cdot I \left\{ \sup_{t \le T} S(t) \in D_n \right\}. \tag{18.24}$$

In other words, if the realized maximum of the underlying stock during the contract period falls within the interval D_n, then the payout at T is β_n. A typical ladder used in practice is the **forward ladder call** with strike price K. For this contract α is exogenously specified, and β is then defined as

$$\beta_n = \max \left[\alpha_n - K, 0 \right]. \tag{18.25}$$

The α-sequence in this case acts as a sequence of barriers, and the ladder call allows you to buy (at time T) the underlying asset at the strike price K, while selling it (at T) at the highest barrier achieved by the stock price during the contract period. The ladder call is intimately connected to the lookback forward call (see the next section), to which it will converge as the α-partition is made finer.

The general (α, β)-ladder is fairly easy to value analytically, although the actual expressions may look formidable. To see this let us define the following series of up-and-in contracts.

Definition 18.26 *For a given pair (α, β), the series of contracts $\mathcal{Z}_0, \ldots, \mathcal{Z}_N$ is defined by*

$$\mathcal{Z}_0 = \beta_0 \cdot I \left\{ \sup_{t \le T} S(t) \ge \alpha_0 \right\},$$

$$\mathcal{Z}_n = (\beta_n - \beta_{n-1}) \cdot I \left\{ \sup_{t \le T} S(t) \ge \alpha_n \right\}, \quad n = 1, \ldots, N.$$

The point of introducing the $\mathcal{Z}_n$-contracts is that we have the following obvious relation

$$\mathcal{Z} = \sum_{n=0}^{N} \mathcal{Z}_n.$$

Thus a ladder is simply a sum of a series of up-and-in contracts. We see that in fact $\mathcal{Z}_n$ is an up-and-in contract on $\beta_n - \beta_{n-1}$ bonds, with barrier α_n. Thus we may use the results of the preceding sections to value $\mathcal{Z}_n$. The result is as follows.

Proposition 18.27 (Ladder pricing formula) *Consider an (α, β)-ladder with delivery time T. Assume that $S(t) = s$ and that $M_S(t) \in D_m$. Then the price, $\Pi(t)$, of the ladder is given by*

$$\Pi(t) = \beta_m + \sum_{n=m+1}^{N} \gamma_n F^{\alpha_n I}(t, s; BO),$$

where $\gamma_n = \beta_n - \beta_{n-1}$, and

$$F^{\alpha_n I}(t, s; BO) = \left(\frac{\alpha_n}{s}\right)^{\frac{2\tilde{r}}{\sigma^2}} e^{-r(T-t)} + e^{-r(T-t)} N\left[\frac{\tilde{r}(T-t) + \ln\left(\frac{s}{\alpha_n}\right)}{\sigma\sqrt{T-t}}\right]$$

$$- e^{-r(T-t)} \left(\frac{\alpha_n}{s}\right)^{\frac{2\tilde{r}}{\sigma^2}} N\left[\frac{\tilde{r}(T-t) - \ln\left(\frac{s}{\alpha_n}\right)}{\sigma\sqrt{T-t}}\right].$$

Proof Exercise for the reader.   □

18.5 Lookbacks

Lookback options are contracts which at the delivery time T allow you to take advantage of the realized maximum or minimum of the underlying price process over the entire contract period. Typical examples are

$$S(T) - \min_{t \leq T} S(t) \qquad \text{lookback call}$$

$$\max_{t \leq T} S(t) - S(T) \qquad \text{lookback put}$$

$$\max\left[\max_{t \leq T} S(t) - K, 0\right] \qquad \text{forward lookback call}$$

$$\max\left[K - \min_{t \leq T} S(t), 0\right] \qquad \text{forward lookback put.}$$

We will confine ourselves to give a sketch of the pricing of a lookback put; for further results see the Notes below.

From general theory, the price of the lookback put at $t = 0$ is given by

$$\Pi(0) = e^{-rT} E^Q \left[\max_{t \leq T} S(t) - S(T) \right]$$

$$= e^{-rT} E^Q \left[\max_{t \leq T} S(t) \right] - e^{-rT} E^Q \left[S(T) \right].$$

With $S(0) = s$, the last term is easily obtained as

$$e^{-rT} E^Q \left[S(T) \right] = s,$$

and it remains to compute the term $E^Q \left[\max_{t \leq T} S(t) \right]$. To this end we recall that $S(t)$ is given by

$$S(t) = \exp \left\{ \ln s + \tilde{r} t + \sigma W(t) \right\} = e^{X(t)},$$

where

$$dX = \tilde{r} dt + \sigma dW,$$
$$X(0) = \ln s.$$

Thus we see that

$$M_S(T) = e^{M_X(T)},$$

and the point is of course that the distribution for $M_X(T)$ is known to us from Proposition 18.4. Using this proposition we obtain the distribution function, F, for $M_X(T)$ as

$$F(x) = N \left(\frac{x - \ln s - \tilde{r} T}{\sigma \sqrt{T}} \right) - \exp \left\{ \frac{2\tilde{r}(x - \ln s)}{\sigma^2} \right\} N \left(-\frac{x - \ln s + \tilde{r} T}{\sigma \sqrt{T}} \right),$$

for all $x \geq \ln s$. From this expression we may compute the density function $f = F'$, and then the expected value is given by

$$E^Q \left[\max_{t \leq T} S(t) \right] = E^Q \left[e^{M_X(T)} \right] = \int_{\ln s}^{\infty} e^x f(x) dx.$$

After a series of elementary, but extremely tedious, partial integrations we end up with the following result.

Proposition 18.28 (Pricing formula for lookback put) *The price, at $t = 0$, of the lookback put is given by*

$$\Pi(0) = -sN\left[-d\right] + se^{-rT} N \left[-d + \sigma\sqrt{T} \right] + s \frac{\sigma^2}{2r} N\left[d\right] - se^{-rT} \frac{\sigma^2}{2r} N \left[-d + \sigma\sqrt{T} \right],$$

where

$$d = \frac{rT + \frac{1}{2}\sigma^2 T}{\sigma \sqrt{T}}.$$

18.6   Exercises

In all exercises below we assume a standard Black–Scholes model.

Exercise 18.1 An "all-or-nothing" contract, with delivery date T, and strike price K, will pay you the amount K, if the price of the underlying stock exceeds the level L at some time during the interval $[0, t]$. Otherwise it will pay nothing. Compute the price, at $t < T$, of the all-or-nothing contract. In order to avoid trivialities, we assume that $S(s) < L$ for all $s \leq t$.

Exercise 18.2 Consider a binary contract, i.e. a T-claim of the form

$$\mathcal{X} = I_{[a,b]}(S_T),$$

where as usual I is the indicator function. Compute the price of the down-and-out version of the binary contract above, for all possible values of the barrier L.

Exercise 18.3 Consider a general down-and-out contract, with contract function Φ, as descibed in Section 18.2.1. We now modify the contract by adding a fixed "rebate" A, and the entire contract is specified as follows:

- If $S(t) > L$ for all $t \leq T$ then $\Phi(S(T))$ is paid to the holder.
- If $S(t) \leq L$ for some $t \leq T$ then the holder receives the fixed amount A.

Derive a pricing formula for this contract.
   Hint: Use Proposition 18.4.

Exercise 18.4 Use the exercise above to price a down-and-out European call with rebate A.

Exercise 18.5 Derive a pricing formula for a down-and-out version of the T contract $\mathcal{X} = \Phi(S(T))$, when S has a continuous dividend yield δ. Specialize to the case of a European call.

18.7   Notes

Most of the concrete results above are standard. For barrier options we refer to Rubinstein and Reiner (1991), and the survey in Carr (1995). Two standard papers on lookbacks are Conze and Viswanathan (1991), and Goldman *et al.* (1979). See also Musiela and Rutkowski (1997). The general Theorem 18.8 and its extensions were first published in Björk (1998).

19

STOCHASTIC OPTIMAL CONTROL

19.1 An Example

Let us consider an economic agent over a fixed time interval $[0, T]$. At time $t = 0$ the agent is endowed with initial wealth x_0 and his/her problem is how to allocate investments and consumption over the given time horizon. We assume that the agent's investment opportunities are the following:

- The agent can invest money in the bank at the deterministic short rate of interest r, i.e. he/she has access to the risk free asset B with

$$dB = rBdt. \qquad (19.1)$$

- The agent can invest in a risky asset with price process S_t, where we assume that the S-dynamics are given by a standard Black–Scholes model

$$dS = \alpha S dt + \sigma S dW. \qquad (19.2)$$

We denote the agent's relative portfolio weights at time t by u_t^0 (for the riskless asset), and u_t^1 (for the risky asset) respectively. His/her consumption rate at time t is denoted by c_t.

We restrict the consumer's investment–consumption strategies to be self-financing, and as usual we assume that we live in a world where continuous trading and unlimited short selling is possible. If we denote the wealth of the consumer at time t by X_t, it now follows from Lemma 6.4 that (after a slight rearrangement of terms) the X-dynamics are given by

$$dX_t = X_t \left[u_t^0 r + u_t^1 \alpha \right] dt - c_t dt + u_t^1 \sigma X_t dW_t. \qquad (19.3)$$

The object of the agent is to choose a portfolio–consumption strategy in such a way as to maximize his/her total utility over $[0, T]$, and we assume that this utility is given by

$$E \left[\int_0^T F(t, c_t) dt + \Phi(X_T) \right], \qquad (19.4)$$

where F is the instantaneous utility function for consumption, whereas Φ is a "legacy" function which measures the utility of having some money left at the end of the period.

A natural constraint on consumption is the condition

$$c_t \geq 0, \quad \forall t \geq 0, \qquad (19.5)$$

and we also have of course the constraint

$$u_t^0 + u_t^1 = 1, \quad \forall t \geq 0. \tag{19.6}$$

Depending upon the actual situation we may be forced to impose other constraints (it may, say, be natural to demand that the consumer's wealth never becomes negative), but we will not do this at the moment.

We may now formally state the consumer's utility maximization problem as follows:

$$\max_{u^0, \, u^1, \, c} E\left[\int_0^T F(t, c_t)dt + \Phi(X_T)\right] \tag{19.7}$$

$$dX_t = X_t \left[u_t^0 r + u_t^1 \alpha\right] dt - c_t dt + u_t^1 \sigma X_t dW_t, \tag{19.8}$$

$$X_0 = x_0, \tag{19.9}$$

$$c_t \geq 0, \quad \forall t \geq 0, \tag{19.10}$$

$$u_t^0 + u_t^1 = 1, \quad \forall t \geq 0. \tag{19.11}$$

A problem of this kind is known as a **stochastic optimal control problem**. In this context the process X is called the **state process** (or state variable), the processes u^0, u^1, c are called **control processes**, and we have a number of **control constraints**. In the next sections we will study a fairly general class of stochastic optimal control problems. The method used is that of **dynamic programming**, and at the end of the chapter we will solve a version of the problem above.

19.2 The Formal Problem

We now go on to study a fairly general class of optimal control problems. To this end, let $\mu(t, x, u)$ and $\sigma(t, x, u)$ be given functions of the form

$$\mu : R_+ \times R^n \times R^k \to R^n,$$
$$\sigma : R_+ \times R^n \times R^k \to R^{n \times d}.$$

For a given point $x_0 \in R^n$ we will consider the following **controlled** stochastic differential equation.

$$dX_t = \mu\left(t, X_t, u_t\right) dt + \sigma\left(t, X_t, u_t\right) dW_t, \tag{19.12}$$
$$X_0 = x_0. \tag{19.13}$$

We view the n-dimensional process X as a **state process**, which we are trying to "control" (or "steer"). We can (partly) control the state process X by choosing the k-dimensional **control process** u in a suitable way. W is a

d-dimensional Wiener process, and we must now try to give a precise mathematical meaning to the formal expressions (19.12)–(19.13).

Remark 19.2.1 In this chapter, where we will work under a fixed measure, all Wiener processes are denoted by the letter W.

Our first modelling problem concerns the class of admissible control processes. In most concrete cases it is natural to require that the control process u is adapted to the X process. In other words, at time t the value u_t of the control process is only allowed to "depend" on past observed values of the state process X. One natural way to obtain an adapted control process is by choosing a deterministic function $g(t, x)$

$$g : R_+ \times R^n \to R^k,$$

and then defining the control process u by

$$u_t = g(t, X_t).$$

Such a function g is called a **feedback control law** , and in the sequel we will restrict ourselves to consider only feedback control laws. For mnemo-technical purposes we will often denote control laws by $\mathbf{u}(t, x)$, rather than $g(t, x)$, and write $u_t = \mathbf{u}(t, X_t)$. We use boldface in order to indicate that $\mathbf{u}$ is a **function**. In contrast to this we use the notation u (italics) to denote the **value** of a control at a certain time. Thus $\mathbf{u}$ denotes a mapping, whereas u denotes a point in R^k.

Suppose now that we have chosen a fixed control law $\mathbf{u}(t, x)$. Then we can insert $\mathbf{u}$ into (19.12) to obtain the standard SDE

$$dX_t = \mu(t, X_t, \mathbf{u}(t, X_t)) \, dt + \sigma(t, X_t, \mathbf{u}(t, X_t)) \, dW_t. \qquad (19.14)$$

In most concrete cases we also have to satisfy some **control constraints**, and we model this by taking as given a fixed subset $U \subseteq R^k$ and requiring that $u_t \in U$ for each t. We can now define the class of **admissible control laws**.

Definition 19.1 *A control law $\mathbf{u}$ is called* **admissible** *if*

- $\mathbf{u}(t, x) \in U$ *for all $t \in R_+$ and all $x \in R^n$.*
- *For any given initial point (t, x) the SDE*

$$dX_s = \mu(s, X_s, \mathbf{u}(s, X_s)) \, ds + \sigma(s, X_s, \mathbf{u}(s, X_s)) \, dW_s,$$
$$X_t = x$$

has a unique solution.

The class of admissible control laws is denoted by $\mathcal{U}$.

For a given control law $\mathbf{u}$, the solution process X will of course depend on the initial value x, as well as on the chosen control law $\mathbf{u}$. To be precise we should therefore denote the process X by $X^{x,\mathbf{u}}$, but sometimes we will suppress x or $\mathbf{u}$. We note that eqn (19.14) looks rather messy, and since we will also have to deal with the Itô formula in connection with (19.14) we need some more streamlined notation.

Definition 19.2 *Consider eqn (19.14), and let ′ denote matrix transpose.*

- *For any fixed vector $u \in R^k$, the functions μ^u, σ^u and C^u are defined by*

$$\mu^u(t,x) = \mu(t,x,u),$$
$$\sigma^u(t,x) = \sigma(t,x,u),$$
$$C^u(t,x) = \sigma(t,x,u)\sigma(t,x,u)'.$$

- *For any control law $\mathbf{u}$, the functions $\mu^{\mathbf{u}}$, $\sigma^{\mathbf{u}}$, $C^{\mathbf{u}}(t,x)$ and $F^{\mathbf{u}}(t,x)$ are defined by*

$$\mu^{\mathbf{u}}(t,x) = \mu(t,x,\mathbf{u}(t,x)),$$
$$\sigma^{\mathbf{u}}(t,x) = \sigma(t,x,\mathbf{u}(t,x)),$$
$$C^{\mathbf{u}}(t,x) = \sigma(t,x,\mathbf{u}(t,x))\sigma(t,x,\mathbf{u}(t,x))',$$
$$F^{\mathbf{u}}(t,x) = F(t,x,\mathbf{u}(t,x)).$$

- *For any fixed vector $u \in R^k$, the partial differential operator $\mathcal{A}^u$ is defined by*

$$\mathcal{A}^u = \sum_{i=1}^{n} \mu_i^u(t,x)\frac{\partial}{\partial x_i} + \frac{1}{2}\sum_{i,j=1}^{n} C_{ij}^u(t,x)\frac{\partial^2}{\partial x_i \partial x_j}.$$

- *For any control law $\mathbf{u}$, the partial differential operator $\mathcal{A}^{\mathbf{u}}$ is defined by*

$$\mathcal{A}^{\mathbf{u}} = \sum_{i=1}^{n} \mu_i^{\mathbf{u}}(t,x)\frac{\partial}{\partial x_i} + \frac{1}{2}\sum_{i,j=1}^{n} C_{ij}^{\mathbf{u}}(t,x)\frac{\partial^2}{\partial x_i \partial x_j}.$$

Given a control law $\mathbf{u}$ we will sometimes write eqn (19.14) in a convenient shorthand notation as

$$dX_t^{\mathbf{u}} = \mu^{\mathbf{u}}dt + \sigma^{\mathbf{u}}dW_t. \tag{19.15}$$

For a given control law $\mathbf{u}$ with a corresponding controlled process $X^{\mathbf{u}}$ we will also often use the shorthand notation $\mathbf{u}_t$ instead of the clumsier expression $\mathbf{u}(t, X_t^{\mathbf{u}})$.

The reader should be aware of the fact that the existence assumption in the definition above is not at all an innocent one. In many cases it is natural to consider control laws which are "rapidly varying", i.e. feedback laws $\mathbf{u}(t,x)$ which are very irregular as functions of the state variable x. Inserting such an irregular control law into the state dynamics will easily give us a very irregular drift function $\mu(t, x, \mathbf{u}(t, x))$ (as a function of x), and we may find ourselves outside the nice Lipschitz situation in Proposition 5.1, thus leaving us with a highly nontrivial existence problem. The reader is referred to the literature for details.

We now go on to the objective function of the control problem, and therefore we consider as given a pair of functions

$$F : R_+ \times R^n \times R^k \to R,$$
$$\Phi : R^n \to R.$$

Now we define the **value function** of our problem as the function

$$\mathcal{J}_0 : \mathcal{U} \to R,$$

defined by

$$\mathcal{J}_0(\mathbf{u}) = E\left[\int_0^T F(t, X_t^{\mathbf{u}}, \mathbf{u}_t)dt + \Phi\left(X_T^{\mathbf{u}}\right)\right],$$

where $X^{\mathbf{u}}$ is the solution to (19.14) with the given initial condition $X_0 = x_0$.

Our formal problem can thus be written as that of maximizing $\mathcal{J}_0(\mathbf{u})$ over all $\mathbf{u} \in \mathcal{U}$, and we define the **optimal value** $\hat{\mathcal{J}}_0$ by

$$\hat{\mathcal{J}}_0 = \sup_{\mathbf{u} \in \mathcal{U}} \mathcal{J}_0(\mathbf{u}).$$

If there exists an admissible control law $\hat{\mathbf{u}}$ with the property that

$$\mathcal{J}_0(\hat{\mathbf{u}}) = \hat{\mathcal{J}}_0,$$

then we say that $\hat{\mathbf{u}}$ is an **optimal control law** for the given problem. Note that, as for any optimization problem, the optimal law may not exist. For a given concrete control problem our main objective is of course to find the optimal control law (if it exists), or at least to learn something about the qualitative behavior of the optimal law.

19.3   The Hamilton–Jacobi–Bellman Equation

Given an optimal control problem we have two natural questions to answer:

(a) Does there exist an optimal control law?

(b) Given that an optimal control exists, how do we find it?

In this text we will mainly be concerned with problem (b) above, and the methodology used will be that of **dynamic programming**. The main idea is to embed our original problem into a much larger class of problems, and then to tie all

hese problems together with a partial differential equation (PDE) known as the
Iamilton–Jacobi–Bellman equation. The control problem is then shown to be
quivalent to the problem of finding a solution to the HJB equation.

We will now describe the embedding procedure, and for that purpose we
hoose a fixed point t in time, with $0 \leq t \leq T$. We also choose a fixed point x in
he state space, i.e. $x \in R^n$. For this fixed pair (t, x) we now define the following
ontrol problem.

Definition 19.3 *The control problem* $\mathcal{P}(t, x)$ *is defined as the problem to max-
mize*

$$E_{t,x}\left[\int_t^T F(s, X_s^\mathbf{u}, \mathbf{u}_s)ds + \Phi\left(X_T^\mathbf{u}\right)\right], \qquad (19.16)$$

iven the dynamics

$$dX_s^\mathbf{u} = \mu\left(s, X_s^\mathbf{u}, \mathbf{u}(s, X_s^\mathbf{u})\right)ds + \sigma\left(s, X_s^\mathbf{u}, \mathbf{u}(s, X_s^\mathbf{u})\right)dW_s, \qquad (19.17)$$

$$X_t = x, \qquad (19.18)$$

nd the constraints

$$\mathbf{u}(s, y) \in U, \quad \forall (s, y) \in [t, T] \times R^n. \qquad (19.19)$$

Observe that we use the notation s and y above because the letters t and x
.re already used to denote the fixed chosen point (t, x).

We note that in terms of the definition above, our original problem is the
roblem $\mathcal{P}(0, x_0)$. A somewhat drastic interpretation of the problem $\mathcal{P}(t, x)$
; that you have fallen asleep at time zero. Suddenly you wake up, noticing
hat the time now is t and that your state process while you were asleep has
noved to the point x. You now try to do as well as possible under the circum-
tances, so you want to maximize your utility over the remaining time, given the
act that you start at time t in the state x.

We now define the **value function** and the **optimal value function**.

Definition 19.4

- *The* **value function**

$$\mathcal{J} : R_+ \times R^n \times \mathcal{U} \to R$$

  is defined by

$$\mathcal{J}(t, x, \mathbf{u}) = E\left[\int_t^T F(s, X_s^\mathbf{u}, \mathbf{u}_s)ds + \Phi\left(X_T^\mathbf{u}\right)\right]$$

  given the dynamics (19.17)–(19.18).
- *The* **optimal value function**

$$V : R_+ \times R^n \to R$$

is defined by

$$V(t, x) = \sup_{\mathbf{u} \in \mathcal{U}} \mathcal{J}(t, x, \mathbf{u}).$$

Thus $\mathcal{J}(t, x, \mathbf{u})$ is the expected utility of using the control law $\mathbf{u}$ over the time interval $[t, T]$, given the fact that you start in state x at time t. The optimal value function gives you the optimal expected utility over $[t, T]$ under the same initial conditions.

The main object of interest for us is the optimal value function, and we now go on to derive a PDE for V. It should be noted that this derivation is largely heuristic. We make some rather strong regularity assumptions, and we disregard a number of technical problems. We will comment on these problems later, but to see exactly which problems we are ignoring we now make some basic assumptions.

Assumption 19.3.1 *We assume the following.*

1. *There exists an optimal control law $\hat{\mathbf{u}}$.*
2. *The optimal value function V is regular in the sense that $V \in C^{1,2}$.*
3. *A number of limiting procedures in the following arguments can be justified.*

We now go on to derive the PDE, and to this end we fix $(t, x) \in (0, T) \times R^n$. Furthermore we choose a real number h (interpreted as a "small" time increment) such that $t + h < T$. We choose a fixed but arbitrary control law $\mathbf{u}$, and define the control law $\mathbf{u}^\star$ by

$$\mathbf{u}^\star(s, y) = \begin{cases} \mathbf{u}(s, y), & (s, y) \in [t, t + h] \times R^n \\ \hat{\mathbf{u}}(s, y), & (s, y) \in (t + h, T] \times R^n. \end{cases}$$

In other words, if we use $\mathbf{u}^\star$ then we use the arbitrary control $\mathbf{u}$ during the time interval $[t, t + h]$, and then we switch to the optimal control law during the rest of the time period.

The whole idea of dynamic programming actually boils down to the following procedure.

- First, given the point (t, x) as above, we consider the following two strategies over the time interval $[t, T]$:

  Strategy I. Use the optimal law $\hat{\mathbf{u}}$.

  Strategy II. Use the control law $\mathbf{u}^\star$ defined above.

- We then compute the expected utilities obtained by the respective strategies.

- Finally, using the obvious fact that Strategy I by definition has to be at least as good as Strategy II, and letting h tend to zero, we obtain our fundamental PDE.

We now carry out this program.

Expected utility for strategy I: This is trivial, since by definition the utility is the optimal one given by $\mathcal{J}(t, x, \hat{\mathbf{u}}) = V(t, x)$.

Expected utility for strategy II: We divide the time interval $[t, T]$ into two parts, the intervals $[t, t + h]$ and $(t + h, T]$ respectively.

- The expected utility, using Strategy II, for the interval $[t, t + h)$ is given by

$$
E_{t,x} \left[\int_t^{t+h} F\left(s, X_s^{\mathbf{u}}, \mathbf{u}_s\right) ds \right].
$$

- In the interval $[t + h, T]$ we observe that at time $t + h$ we will be in the (stochastic) state $X_{t+h}^{\mathbf{u}}$. Since, by definition, we will use the optimal strategy during the entire interval $[t + h, T]$ we see that the remaining expected utility at time $t + h$ is given by $V(t + h, X_{t+h}^{\mathbf{u}})$. Thus the expected utility over the interval $[t + h, T]$, conditional on the fact that at time t we are in state x, is given by

$$
E_{t,x} \left[V(t + h, X_{t+h}^{\mathbf{u}}) \right].
$$

Thus the total expected utility for Strategy II is

$$
E_{t,x} \left[\int_t^{t+h} F\left(s, X_s^{\mathbf{u}}, \mathbf{u}_s\right) ds + V(t + h, X_{t+h}^{\mathbf{u}}) \right].
$$

Comparing the strategies: We now go on to compare the two strategies, and since by definition Strategy I is the optimal one, we must have the inequality

$$
V(t, x) \geq E_{t,x} \left[\int_t^{t+h} F\left(s, X_s^{\mathbf{u}}, \mathbf{u}_s\right) ds + V(t + h, X_{t+h}^{\mathbf{u}}) \right]. \tag{19.20}
$$

We also note that the inequality sign is due to the fact that the arbitrarily chosen control law $\mathbf{u}$ which we use on the interval $[t, t + h]$ need not be the optimal one. In particular we have the following obvious fact.

Remark 19.3.1 We have equality in (19.20) if and only if the control law $\mathbf{u}$ is an optimal law $\hat{\mathbf{u}}$. (Note that the optimal law does not have to be unique.)

Since, by assumption, V is smooth we now use the Itô formula to obtain (with obvious notation)

$$
V(t + h, X_{t+h}^{\mathbf{u}}) = V(t, x) + \int_t^{t+h} \left\{ \frac{\partial V}{\partial t}(s, X_s^{\mathbf{u}}) + \mathcal{A}^{\mathbf{u}} V(s, X_s^{\mathbf{u}}) \right\} ds
$$

$$
+ \int_t^{t+h} \nabla_x V(s, X_s^{\mathbf{u}}) \sigma^{\mathbf{u}} dW_s. \tag{19.21}
$$

If we apply the expectation operator $E_{t,x}$ to this equation, and assume enoug[] integrability, then the stochastic integral will vanish. We can then insert th[] resulting equation into the inequality (19.20). The term $V(t, x)$ will cancel, lea[] ing us with the inequality

$$E_{t,x}\left[\int_t^{t+h}\left[F\left(s, X_s^{\mathbf{u}}, \mathbf{u}_s\right) + \frac{\partial V}{\partial t}\left(s, X_s^{\mathbf{u}}\right) + \mathcal{A}^{\mathbf{u}}V\left(s, X_s^{\mathbf{u}}\right)\right]ds\right] \le 0. \qquad (19.22[]$$

Going to the limit: Now we divide by h, move h within the expectation an[] let h tend to zero. Assuming enough regularity to allow us to take the lim[] within the expectation, using the fundamental theorem of integral calculus, an[] recalling that $X_t = x$, we get

$$F(t, x, u) + \frac{\partial V}{\partial t}(t, x) + \mathcal{A}^u V(t, x) \le 0, \qquad (19.23[]$$

where u denotes the value of the law $\mathbf{u}$ evaluated at (t, x), i.e. $u = \mathbf{u}(t, x)$.

Since the control law $\mathbf{u}$ was arbitrary, this inequality will hold for all choice[] of $u \in U$, and we will have equality if and only if $u = \hat{\mathbf{u}}(t, x)$. We thus have th[] following equation

$$\frac{\partial V}{\partial t}(t, x) + \sup_{u \in U}\left\{F(t, x, u) + \mathcal{A}^u V(t, x)\right\} = 0.$$

During the discussion the point (t, x) was fixed, but since it was chosen as a[] arbitrary point we see that the equation holds in fact for all $(t, x) \in (0, T)$ [] R^n. Thus we have a (nonstandard type of) PDE, and we obviously need som[] boundary conditions. One such condition is easily obtained, since we obvious[] (why?) have $V(T, x) = \Phi(x)$ for all $x \in R^n$. We have now arrived at our goa[] namely the Hamilton–Jacobi–Bellman equation, (often referred to as the HJ[] equation.)

Theorem 19.5 (Hamilton–Jacobi–Bellman equation) *Under Assumptio[] 19.3.1, the following hold:*

1. *V satisfies the Hamilton–Jacobi–Bellman equation*

$$\begin{cases} \dfrac{\partial V}{\partial t}(t, x) + \sup_{u \in U}\left\{F(t, x, u) + \mathcal{A}^u V(t, x)\right\} = 0, & \forall(t, x) \in (0, T) \times R^n \\ \qquad\qquad\qquad V(T, x) = \Phi(x), & \forall x \in R^n. \end{cases}$$

2. *For each $(t, x) \in [0, T] \times R^n$ the supremum in the HJB equation above [] attained by $u = \hat{\mathbf{u}}(t, x)$.*

Remark 19.3.2 By going through the arguments above, it is easily seen that we may allow the constraint set U to be time- and state-dependent. If we thus have control constraints of the form

$$u(t,x) \in U(t,x), \quad \forall t, x$$

then the HJB equation still holds with the obvious modification of the supremum part.

It is important to note that this theorem has the form of a **necessary** condition. It says that if V is the optimal value function, and if $\hat{u}$ is the optimal control, **then** V satisfies the HJB equation, and $\hat{u}(t,x)$ realizes the supremum in the equation. We also note that Assumption 19.3.1 is an *ad hoc* assumption. One would prefer to have conditions in terms of the initial data μ, σ, F and Φ which would guarantee that Assumption 19.3.1 is satisfied. This can in fact be done, but at a fairly high price in terms of technical complexity. The reader is referred to the specialist literature.

A gratifying, and perhaps surprising, fact is that the HJB equation also acts as a **sufficient** condition for the optimal control problem. This result is known as the **verification theorem** for dynamic programming, and we will use it repeatedly below. Note that, as opposed to the necessary conditions above, the verification theorem is very easy to prove rigorously.

Theorem 19.6 (Verification theorem) *Suppose that we have two functions $H(t,x)$ and $g(t,x)$, such that*

- *H is sufficiently integrable (see Remark 19.3.4 below), and solves the HJB equation*

$$\begin{cases} \dfrac{\partial H}{\partial t}(t,x) + \sup_{u \in U} \{F(t,x,u) + \mathcal{A}^u H(t,x)\} = 0, & \forall (t,x) \in (0,T) \times R^n \\ H(T,x) = \Phi(x), & \forall x \in R^n. \end{cases}$$

- *The function g is an admissible control law.*
- *For each fixed (t,x), the supremum in the expression*

$$\sup_{u \in U} \{F(t,x,u) + \mathcal{A}^u H(t,x)\}$$

is attained by the choice $u = g(t,x)$.

Then the following hold:

1. *The optimal value function V to the control problem is given by*

$$V(t,x) = H(t,x).$$

2. *There exists an optimal control law $\hat{u}$, and in fact $\hat{u}(t,x) = g(t,x)$.*

Remark 19.3.3 Note that we have used the letter H (instead of V) in the HJB equation above. This is because the letter V by definition denotes the optimal value function.

Proof Assume that H and g are given as above. Now choose an arbitrary control law $\mathbf{u} \in \mathcal{U}$, and fix a point (t, x). We define the process $X^{\mathbf{u}}$ on the time interval $[t, T]$ as the solution to the equation

$$dX_s^{\mathbf{u}} = \mu^{\mathbf{u}}\left(s, X_s^{\mathbf{u}}\right) ds + \sigma^{\mathbf{u}}\left(s, X_s^{\mathbf{u}}\right) dW_s,$$
$$X_t = x.$$

Inserting the process $X^{\mathbf{u}}$ into the function H and using the Itô formula we obtain

$$H(T, X_T^{\mathbf{u}}) = H(t, x) + \int_t^T \left\{ \frac{\partial H}{\partial t}(s, X_s^{\mathbf{u}}) + (\mathcal{A}^{\mathbf{u}} H)(s, X_s^{\mathbf{u}}) \right\} ds$$
$$+ \int_t^T \nabla_x H(s, X_s^{\mathbf{u}}) \sigma^{\mathbf{u}}(s, X_s^{\mathbf{u}}) dW_s.$$

Since H solves the HJB equation we see that

$$\frac{\partial H}{\partial t}(t, x) + F(t, x, u) + \mathcal{A}^u H(t, x) \leq 0$$

for all $u \in U$, and thus we have, for each s and P-a.s, the inequality

$$\frac{\partial H}{\partial t}(s, X_s^{\mathbf{u}}) + (\mathcal{A}^{\mathbf{u}} H)(s, X_s^{\mathbf{u}}) \leq -F^{\mathbf{u}}(s, X_s^{\mathbf{u}}).$$

From the boundary condition for the HJB equation we also have $H(T, X_T^{\mathbf{u}}) = \Phi(X_T^{\mathbf{u}})$, so we obtain the inequality

$$H(t, x) \geq \int_t^T F^{\mathbf{u}}(s, X_s^{\mathbf{u}}) ds + \Phi(X_T^{\mathbf{u}}) - \int_t^T \nabla_x H(s, X_s^{\mathbf{u}}) \sigma^{\mathbf{u}} dW_s.$$

Taking expectations, and assuming enough integrability, we make the stochastic integral vanish, leaving us with the inequality

$$H(t, x) \geq E_{t,x} \left[\int_t^T F^{\mathbf{u}}(s, X_s^{\mathbf{u}}) ds + \Phi(X_T^{\mathbf{u}}) \right] = \mathcal{J}(t, x, \mathbf{u}).$$

Since the control law $\mathbf{u}$ was arbitrarily chosen this gives us

$$H(t, x) \geq \sup_{\mathbf{u} \in \mathcal{U}} \mathcal{J}(t, x, \mathbf{u}) = V(t, x). \tag{19.24}$$

To obtain the reverse inequality we choose the specific control law $\mathbf{u}(t, x) = \mathbf{g}(t, x)$. Going through the same calculations as above, and using the fact that by assumption we have

$$\frac{\partial H}{\partial t}(t, x) + F^{\mathbf{g}}(t, x) + \mathcal{A}^{\mathbf{g}} H(t, x) = 0,$$

we obtain the equality

$$H(t, x) = E_{t,x}\left[\int_t^T F^{\mathbf{g}}(s, X_s^{\mathbf{g}})ds + \Phi(X_T^{\mathbf{g}})\right] = \mathcal{J}(t, x, \mathbf{g}). \tag{19.25}$$

On the other hand we have the trivial inequality

$$V(t, x) \geq \mathcal{J}(t, x, \mathbf{g}), \tag{19.26}$$

so, using (19.24)–(19.26), we obtain

$$H(t, x) \geq V(t, x) \geq \mathcal{J}(t, x, \mathbf{g}) = H(t, x).$$

This shows that in fact

$$H(t, x) = V(t, x) = \mathcal{J}(t, x, \mathbf{g}),$$

which proves that $H = V$, and that $\mathbf{g}s$ is the optimal control law.   □

Remark 19.3.4 The assumption that H is "sufficiently integrable" in the theorem above is made in order for the stochastic integral in the proof to have expected value zero. This will be the case if, for example, H satisifes the condition

$$\nabla_x H(s, X_s^{\mathbf{u}})\sigma^{\mathbf{u}}(s, X_s^{\mathbf{u}}) \in \mathcal{L}^2,$$

for all admissible control laws.

Remark 19.3.5 Sometimes, instead of a maximization problem, we consider a minimization problem. Of course we now make the obvious definitions for the value function and the optimal value function. It is then easily seen that all the results above still hold if the expression

$$\sup_{u \in U} \{F(t, x, u) + \mathcal{A}^u V(t, x)\}$$

in the HJB equation is replaced by the expression

$$\inf_{u \in U} \{F(t, x, u) + \mathcal{A}^u V(t, x)\}.$$

Remark 19.3.6 In the Verification Theorem we may allow the control constraint set U to be state and time dependent, i.e. of the form $U(t, x)$.

19.4   Handling the HJB Equation

In this section we will describe the actual handling of the HJB equation, and in the next section we will study a classical example—the linear quadratic regulator. We thus consider our standard optimal control problem with the corresponding HJB equation:

$$
\begin{cases}
\dfrac{\partial V}{\partial t}(t,x) + \sup_{u \in U} \{F(t,x,u) + \mathcal{A}^u V(t,x)\} = 0, \\[2mm]
\qquad\qquad\qquad\qquad V(T,x) = \Phi(x).
\end{cases}
\tag{19.27}
$$

Schematically we now proceed as follows:

1. Consider the HJB equation as a PDE for an unknown function V.
2. Fix an arbitrary point $(t,x) \in [0,T] \times R^n$ and solve, for this fixed choice of (t,x), the static optimization problem

$$
\max_{u \in U}\ [F(t,x,u) + \mathcal{A}^u V(t,x)].
$$

   Note that in this problem u is the only variable, whereas t and x are considered to be fixed parameters. The functions F, μ, σ and V are considered as given.
3. The optimal choice of u, denoted by $\hat{u}$, will of course depend on our choice of t and x, but it will also depend on the function V and its various partial derivatives (which are hiding under the sign $\mathcal{A}^u V$). To highlight these dependencies we write $\hat{u}$ as

$$
\hat{\mathbf{u}} = \hat{\mathbf{u}}\,(t,x;V).
\tag{19.28}
$$

4. The function $\hat{u}\,(t,x;V)$ is our candidate for the optimal control law, but since we do not know V this description is incomplete. Therefore we substitute the expression for $\hat{u}$ in (19.28) into the PDE (19.27), giving us the PDE

$$
\frac{\partial V}{\partial t}(t,x) + F^{\hat{\mathbf{u}}}(t,x) + \mathcal{A}^{\hat{\mathbf{u}}} V(t,x) = 0,
\tag{19.29}
$$

$$
V(T,x) = \Phi(x).
\tag{19.30}
$$

5. Now we solve the PDE above! (See the remark below.) Then we put the solution V into expression (19.28). Using the verification theorem 19.6 we can now identify V as the optimal value function, and $\hat{u}$ as the optimal control law.

Remark 19.4.1 The hard work of dynamic programming consists in solving the highly nonlinear PDE in step 5 above. There are of course no general analytic methods available for this, so the number of known optimal control problems with an analytic solution is very small indeed. In an actual case one usually tries to **guess** a solution, i.e. we typically make an **ansatz** for V, parameterized by a finite number of parameters, and then we use the PDE in order to identify the parameters. The making of an ansatz is often helped by the intuitive observation that if there is an analytical solution to the problem, then it seems likely that V inherits some structural properties from the boundary function Φ as well as from the instantaneous utility function F.

For a general problem there is thus very little hope of obtaining an analytic solution, and it is worth pointing out that many of the known solved control problems have, to some extent, been "rigged" in order to be analytically solvable.

19.5 The Linear Regulator

We now want to put the ideas from the previous section into action, and for this purpose we study the most well known of all control problems, namely the linear quadratic regulator problem. In this classical engineering example we wish to **minimize**

$$E \left[\int_0^T \{X_t'QX_t + u_t'Ru_t\} \, dt + X_T'HX_T \right],$$

(where $'$ denotes transpose) given the dynamics

$$dX_t = \{AX_t + Bu_t\} \, dt + C \, dW_t.$$

One interpretation of this problem is that we want to control a vehicle in such a way that it stays close to the origin (the terms $x'Qx$ and $x'Hx$) while at the same time keeping the "energy" $u'Ru$ small.

As usual $X_t \in R^n$ and $\mathbf{u}_t \in R^k$, and we impose no control constraints on u. The matrices Q, R, H, A, B and C are assumed to be known. Without loss of generality we may assume that Q, R and H are symmetric, and we assume that R is positive definite (and thus invertible).

The HJB equation now becomes

$$\begin{cases} \dfrac{\partial V}{\partial t}(t,x) + \inf_{u \in R^k} \{x'Qx + u'Ru + [\nabla_x V](t,x)\,[Ax + Bu]\} \\[2mm] \quad + \dfrac{1}{2} \sum_{i,j} \dfrac{\partial^2 V}{\partial x_i \partial x_j}(t,x)\,[CC']_{i,j} = 0, \\[2mm] V(T,x) = x'Hx. \end{cases}$$

For each fixed choice of (t,x) we now have to solve the static unconstrained optimization problem to minimize

$$u'Ru + [\nabla_x V](t,x)\,[Ax + Bu].$$

Since, by assumption, $R > 0$ we get the solution by setting the gradient equal to zero, thus giving us the equation

$$2u'R = -(\nabla_x V)B,$$

which gives us the optimal u as

$$\hat{u} = -\frac{1}{2}R^{-1}B'(\nabla_x V)'.$$

Here we see clearly (compare point 2 in the scheme above) that in order to use this formula we need to know V, and we thus try to make an educated guess about the structure of V. From the boundary value function $x'Hx$ and the quadratic term $x'Qx$ in the instantaneous cost function it seems reasonable to assume that V is a quadratic function. Consequently we make the following ansatz

$$V(t,x) = x'P(t)x + q(t),$$

where we assume that $P(t)$ is a deterministic symmetric matrix function of time, whereas $q(t)$ is a scalar deterministic function. It would of course also be natural to include a linear term of the form $L(t)x$, but it turns out that this is not necessary.

With this trial solution we have, suppressing the t-variable and denoting time derivatives by a dot,

$$\frac{\partial V}{\partial t}(t,x) = x'\dot{P}x + \dot{q},$$

$$\nabla_x V(t,x) = 2x'P,$$

$$\nabla_{xx} V(t,x) = 2P$$

$$\hat{u} = -R^{-1}B'Px.$$

Inserting these expressions into the HJB equation we get

$$x'\dot{P}x + \dot{q} + x'Qx + x'PBR^{-1}RR^{-1}B'Px + 2x'PAx$$

$$-2x'PBR^{-1}B'Px + \sum_{i,j} P_{ij}[CC']_{ij} = 0.$$

We note that the last term above equals $tr[C'PC]$, where tr denote the trace of a matrix, and furthermore we see that $2x'PAx = x'A'Px + x'PAx$ (this is just cosmetic). Collecting terms gives us

$$x'\left\{\dot{P} + Q - PBR^{-1}B'P + A'P + PA\right\}x + \dot{q} + tr[C'PC] = 0. \qquad (19.31)$$

If this equation is to hold for all x and all t then firstly the bracket must vanish, leaving us with the matrix ODE

$$\dot{P} = PBR^{-1}B'P - A'P - PA - Q.$$

We are then left with the scalar equation

$$\dot{q} = -tr[C'PC].$$

We now need some boundary values for P and q, but these follow immediately from the boundary conditions of the HJB equation. We thus end up with the following pairs of equations:

$$\begin{cases} \dot{P} = PBR^{-1}B'P - A'P - PA - Q, \\ P(T) = H. \end{cases} \tag{19.32}$$

$$\begin{cases} \dot{q} = -tr[C'PC], \\ q(T) = 0. \end{cases} \tag{19.33}$$

The matrix equation (19.32) is known as a **Riccati equation**, and there are powerful algorithms available for solving it numerically. The equation for q can then be integrated directly.

Summing up we see that the optimal value function and the optimal control law are given by the following formulas. Note that the optimal control is linear in the state variable.

$$V(t,x) = x'P(t)x + \int_t^T tr[C'P(s)C]ds, \tag{19.34}$$

$$\hat{\mathbf{u}}(t,x) = -R^{-1}B'P(t)x. \tag{19.35}$$

19.6 Optimal Consumption and Investment

19.6.1 A Generalization

In many concrete applications, in particular in economics, it is natural to consider an optimal control problem, where the state variable is constrained to stay within a prespecified domain. As an example it may be reasonable to demand that the wealth of an investor is never allowed to become negative. We will now generalize our class of optimal control problems to allow for such considerations.

Let us therefore consider the following controlled SDE

$$dX_t = \mu(t, X_t, u_t)\, dt + \sigma(t, X_t, u_t)\, dW_t, \tag{19.36}$$

$$X_0 = x_0, \tag{19.37}$$

where as before we impose the control constraint $u_t \in U$. We also consider as given a fixed time interval $[0, T]$, and a fixed domain $D \subseteq [0, T] \times R^n$, and the basic idea is that when the state process hits the boundary ∂D of D, then the activity is at an end. It is thus natural to define the **stopping time** τ by

$$\tau = \inf\{t \geq 0 \,|\, (t, X_t) \in \partial D\} \wedge T,$$

where $x \wedge y = \min[x, y]$. We consider as given an instantaneous utility function $F(t, x, u)$ and a "bequest function" $\Phi(t, x)$, i.e. a mapping $\Phi : \partial D \to R$. The control problem to be considered is that of maximizing

$$E\left[\int_0^\tau F(s, X_s^{\mathbf{u}}, \mathbf{u}_s)ds + \Phi\left(\tau, X_\tau^{\mathbf{u}}\right)\right]. \tag{19.38}$$

In order for this problem to be interesting we have to demand that $X_0 \in D$, and the interpretation is that when we hit the boundary ∂D, the game is over and we obtain the bequest $\Phi(\tau, X_\tau)$. We see immediately that our earlier situation corresponds to the case when $D = [0, T] \times R^n$ and when Φ is constant in the t-variable.

In order to analyze our present problem we may proceed as in the previous sections, introducing the value function and the optimal value function exactly as before. The only new technical problem encountered is that of considering a stochastic integral with a stochastic limit of integration. Since this will take us outside the scope of the present text we will confine ourselves to giving the results. The proofs are (modulo the technicalities mentioned above) exactly as before.

Theorem 19.7 (HJB equation) *Assume that*

- *The optimal value function V is in $C^{1,2}$.*
- *An optimal law $\hat{\mathbf{u}}$ exists.*

Then the following hold:

1. *V satisifies the HJB equation*

$$\begin{cases} \dfrac{\partial V}{\partial t}(t, x) + \sup_{u \in U} \{F(t, x, u) + \mathcal{A}^u V(t, x)\} = 0, & \forall(t, x) \in D \\ V(t, x) = \Phi(t, x), & \forall(t, x) \in \partial D. \end{cases}$$

2. *For each $(t, x) \in D$ the supremum in the HJB equation above is attained by $u = \hat{\mathbf{u}}(t, x)$.*

Theorem 19.8 (Verification theorem) *Suppose that we have two functions $H(t, x)$ and $g(t, x)$, such that*

- *H is sufficiently integrable, and solves the HJB equation*

$$\begin{cases} \dfrac{\partial H}{\partial t}(t, x) + \sup_{u \in U} \{F(t, x, u) + \mathcal{A}^u H(t, x)\} = 0, & \forall(t, x) \in D \\ H(t, x) = \Phi(t, x), & \forall(t, x) \in \partial D. \end{cases}$$

- *The function g is an admissible control law.*

- *For each fixed (t, x), the supremum in the expression*

$$\sup_{u \in U} \{F(t, x, u) + \mathcal{A}^u H(t, x)\}$$

is attained by the choice $u = g(t, x)$.

Then the following hold:

1. *The optimal value function V to the control problem is given by*

$$V(t, x) = H(t, x).$$

2. *There exists an optimal control law $\hat{\mathbf{u}}$, and in fact $\hat{\mathbf{u}}(t, x) = g(t, x)$.*

19.6.2   Optimal Consumption

In order to illustrate the technique we will now go back to the optimal consumption problem at the beginning of the chapter. We thus consider the problem of maximizing

$$E\left[\int_0^T F(t, c_t)dt + \Phi(X_T) \right], \tag{19.39}$$

given the wealth dynamics

$$dX_t = X_t \left[u_t^0 r + u_t^1 \alpha \right] dt - c_t dt + u^1 \sigma X_t dW_t. \tag{19.40}$$

As usual we impose the control constraints

$$c_t \geq 0, \quad \forall t \geq 0,$$
$$u_t^0 + u_t^1 = 1, \quad \forall t \geq 0.$$

In a control problem of this kind it is important to be aware of the fact that one may quite easily formulate a nonsensical problem. To take a simple example, suppose that we have $\Phi = 0$, and suppose that F is increasing and unbounded in the c-variable. Then the problem above degenerates completely. It does not possess an optimal solution at all, and the reason is of course that the consumer can increase his/her utility to any given level by simply consuming an arbitrarily large amount at every t. The consequence of this hedonistic behavior is of course the fact that the wealth process will, with very high probability, become negative, but this is neither prohibited by the control constraints, nor punished by any bequest function.

An elegant way out of this dilemma is to choose the domain D of the preceding section as $D = [0, T] \times \{x \mid x > 0\}$. With τ defined as above this means, in concrete terms, that

$$\tau = \inf \{t > 0 \mid X_t = 0\} \wedge T.$$

A natural objective function in this case is thus given by

$$E\left[\int_0^\tau F(t, c_t)dt\right],\tag{19.41}$$

which automatically ensures that when the consumer has no wealth, then all activity is terminated.

We will now analyze this problem in some detail. Firstly we notice that we can get rid of the constraint $u_t^0 + u_t^1 = 1$ by defining a new control variable w as $w = u^1$, and then substituting $1 - w$ for u^0. This gives us the state dynamics

$$dX_t = w_t\left[\alpha - r\right]X_t dt + (rX_t - c_t)\,dt + w_t\sigma X_t dW_t,\tag{19.42}$$

and the corresponding HJB equation is

$$\begin{cases} \dfrac{\partial V}{\partial t} + \sup_{c \geq 0, w \in R}\left\{F(t, c) + wx(\alpha - r)\dfrac{\partial V}{\partial x} + (rx - c)\dfrac{\partial V}{\partial x} + \dfrac{1}{2}x^2 w^2 \sigma^2 \dfrac{\partial^2 V}{\partial x^2}\right\} = 0, \\[2mm] V(T, x) = 0, \\[1mm] V(t, 0) = 0. \end{cases}$$

We now specialize our example to the case when F is of the form

$$F(t, c) = e^{-\delta t}c^\gamma,$$

where $0 < \gamma < 1$. The economic reasoning behind this is that we now have an infinite marginal utility at $c = 0$. This will force the optimal consumption plan to be positive throughout the planning period, a fact which will facilitate the analytical treatment of the problem. In terms of Remark 19.4.1 we are thus "rigging" the problem.

The static optimization problem to be solved w.r.t. c and w is thus that of maximizing

$$e^{-\delta t}c^\gamma + wx(\alpha - r)\frac{\partial V}{\partial x} + (rx - c)\frac{\partial V}{\partial x} + \frac{1}{2}x^2 w^2 \sigma^2 \frac{\partial^2 V}{\partial x^2},$$

and, assuming an interior solution, the first order conditions are

$$\gamma c^{\gamma - 1} = e^{\delta t}V_x,\tag{19.43}$$

$$w = \frac{-V_x}{x \cdot V_{xx}} \cdot \frac{\alpha - r}{\sigma^2},\tag{19.44}$$

where we have used subscripts to denote partial derivatives.

We again see that in order to implement the optimal consumption–investment plan (19.43)–(19.44) we need to know the optimal value function V. We therefore suggest a trial solution (see Remark 19.4.1), and in view of the shape of the instantaneous utility function it is natural to try a V-function of the form

$$V(t, x) = e^{-\delta t} h(t) x^{\gamma}, \tag{19.45}$$

where, because of the boundary conditions, we must demand that

$$h(T) = 0. \tag{19.46}$$

Given a V of this form we have (using $\cdot$ to denote the time derivative)

$$\frac{\partial V}{\partial t} = e^{-\delta t} \dot{h} x^{\gamma} - \delta e^{-\delta t} h x^{\gamma}, \tag{19.47}$$

$$\frac{\partial V}{\partial x} = \gamma e^{-\delta t} h x^{\gamma-1}, \tag{19.48}$$

$$\frac{\partial^2 V}{\partial x^2} = \gamma(\gamma - 1) e^{-\delta t} h x^{\gamma-2}. \tag{19.49}$$

Inserting these expressions into (19.43)–(19.44) we get

$$\hat{w}(t, x) = \frac{\alpha - r}{\sigma^2(1 - \gamma)}, \tag{19.50}$$

$$\hat{c}(t, x) = x h(t)^{-1/(1-\gamma)}. \tag{19.51}$$

This looks very promising: we see that the candidate optimal portfolio is constant and that the candidate optimal consumption rule is linear in the wealth variable. In order to use the verification theorem we now want to show that a V-function of the form (19.45) actually solves the HJB equation. We therefore substitute the expressions (19.47)–(19.51) into the HJB equation. This gives us the equation

$$x^{\gamma} \left\{ \dot{h}(t) + A h(t) + B h(t)^{-\gamma/(1-\gamma)} \right\} = 0,$$

where the constants A and B are given by

$$A = \frac{\gamma(\alpha - r)^2}{\sigma^2(1 - \gamma)} + r\gamma - \frac{1}{2} \frac{\gamma(\alpha - r)^2}{\sigma^2(1 - \gamma)} - \delta$$

$$B = 1 - \gamma.$$

If this equation is to hold for all x and all t, then we see that h must solve the ODE

$$\dot{h}(t) + A h(t) + B h(t)^{-\gamma/(1-\gamma)} = 0, \tag{19.52}$$

$$h(T) = 0. \tag{19.53}$$

An equation of this kind is known as a **Bernoulli equation**, and it can be solved explicitly (see the exercises).

Summing up, we have shown that if we define V as in (19.45) with h defined as the solution to (19.52)–(19.53), and if we define $\hat{w}$ and $\hat{c}$ by (19.50)–(19.51), then V satisfies the HJB equation, and $\hat{w}$, $\hat{c}$ attain the supremum in the equation. The verification theorem then tells us that we have indeed found the optimal solution.

19.7 The Mutual Fund Theorems

In this section we will briefly go through the "Merton mutual fund theorems", originally presented in Merton (1971).

19.7.1 The Case with No Risk Free Asset

We consider a financial market with n asset prices $S_1, \ldots, S_n$. To start with we do not assume the existence of a risk free asset, and we assume that the price vector process $S(t)$ has the following dynamics under the objective measure P.

$$dS = D(S)\alpha dt + D(S)\sigma dW. \tag{19.54}$$

Here W is a k-dimensional standard Wiener process, α is an n-vector, σ is an $n \times k$ matrix, and $D(S)$ is the diagonal matrix

$$D(S) = diag[S_1, \ldots, S_n].$$

In more pedestrian terms this means that

$$dS_i = S_i\alpha_i dt + S_i\sigma_i dW,$$

where σ_i is the ith row of the matrix σ.

We denote the investment strategy (relative portfolio) by w, and the consumption plan by c. If the pair (w, c) is self-financing, then it follows from the S-dynamics above, and from Lemma 6.4, that the dynamics of the wealth process X are given by

$$dX = Xw'\alpha dt - cdt + Xw'\sigma dW. \tag{19.55}$$

We also take as given an instantaneous utility function $F(t, c)$, and we basically want to maximize

$$E\left[\int_0^T F(t, c_t)dt\right]$$

where T is some given time horizon. In order not to formulate a degenerate problem we also impose the condition that wealth is not allowed to become negative, and as before this is dealt with by introducing the stopping time

$$\tau = \inf\{t > 0 \mid X_t = 0\} \wedge T.$$

Our formal problem is then that of maximizing

$$E\left[\int_0^\tau F(t,c_t)dt\right]$$

given the dynamics (19.54)–(19.55), and subject to the control constraints

$$\sum_1^n w_i = 1, \qquad\qquad (19.56)$$

$$c \geq 0. \qquad\qquad (19.57)$$

Instead of (19.56) it is convenient to write

$$e'w = 1,$$

where e is the vector in R^n which has the number 1 in all components, i.e. $e' = (1, \ldots, 1)$.

The HJB equation for this problem now becomes

$$\begin{cases} \dfrac{\partial V}{\partial t}(t,x,s) + \sup_{e'w=1,\ c\geq 0} \{F(t,c) + \mathcal{A}^{c,w}V(t,x,s)\} = 0, \\[2ex] \qquad\qquad\qquad\qquad\qquad V(T,x,s) = 0, \\[1ex] \qquad\qquad\qquad\qquad\qquad V(t,0,s) = 0. \end{cases}$$

In the general case, when the parameters α and σ are allowed to be functions of the price vector process S, the term $\mathcal{A}^{c,w}V(t,x,s)$ turns out to be rather forbidding (see Merton's original paper). It will in fact involve partial derivatives to the second order with respect to all the variables $x, s_1, \ldots, s_n$.

If, however, we assume that α and σ are deterministic and constant over time, then we see by inspection that the wealth process X is a Markov process, and since the price processes do not appear, neither in the objective function nor in the definition of the stopping time, we draw the conclusion that in this case X itself will act as the state process, and we may forget about the underlying S-process completely.

Under these assumptions we may thus write the optimal value function as $V(t,x)$, with no s-dependence, and after some easy calculations the term $\mathcal{A}^{c,w}V$ turns out to be

$$\mathcal{A}^{c,w}V = xw'\alpha\frac{\partial V}{\partial x} - c\frac{\partial V}{\partial x} + \frac{1}{2}x^2 w'\Sigma w\frac{\partial^2 V}{\partial x^2},$$

where the matrix Σ is given by

$$\Sigma = \sigma\sigma'.$$

We now summarize our assumptions.

Assumption 19.7.1 *We assume that*

- *The vector α is constant and deterministic.*
- *The matrix σ is constant and deterministic.*
- *The matrix σ has rank n, and in particular the matrix $\Sigma = \sigma\sigma'$ is positive definite and invertible.*

We note that, in terms of contingent claims analysis, the last assumption means that the market is complete. Denoting partial derivatives by subscripts we now have the following HJB equation

$$
\begin{cases}
V_t(t,x) + \sup_{w'e=1,\ c\geq 0} \left\{ F(t,c) + (xw'\alpha - c)V_x(t,x) + \frac{1}{2}x^2w'\Sigma w V_{xx}(t,x) \right\} = 0, \\
\hspace{8cm} V(T,x) = 0, \\
\hspace{8cm} V(t,0) = 0.
\end{cases}
$$

If we relax the constraint $w'e = 1$, the Lagrange function for the static optimization problem is given by

$$
L = F(t,c) + (xw'\alpha - c)V_x(t,x) + \frac{1}{2}x^2w'\Sigma w V_{xx}(t,x) + \lambda\left(1 - w'e\right).
$$

Assuming the problem to be regular enough for an interior solution we see that the first order condition for c is

$$
\frac{\partial F}{\partial c}(t,c) = V_x(t,x).
$$

The first order condition for w is

$$
x\alpha'V_x + x^2 V_{xx}w'\Sigma = \lambda e',
$$

so we can solve for w in order to obtain

$$
\hat{w} = \Sigma^{-1}\left[\frac{\lambda}{x^2 V_{xx}}e - \frac{xV_x}{x^2 V_{xx}}\alpha\right]. \tag{19.58}
$$

Using the relation $e'w = 1$ this gives λ as

$$
\lambda = \frac{x^2 V_{xx} + xV_x e'\Sigma^{-1}\alpha}{e'\Sigma^{-1}e},
$$

and inserting this into (19.58) gives us, after some manipulation,

$$
\hat{w} = \frac{1}{e'\Sigma^{-1}e}\Sigma^{-1}e + \frac{V_x}{xV_{xx}}\Sigma^{-1}\left[\frac{e'\Sigma^{-1}\alpha}{e'\Sigma^{-1}e}e - \alpha\right]. \tag{19.59}
$$

To see more clearly what is going on we can write this expression as

$$\hat{\mathbf{w}}(t) = g + Y(t)h, \tag{19.60}$$

where the fixed vectors g and h are given by

$$g = \frac{1}{e'\Sigma^{-1}e}\Sigma^{-1}e, \tag{19.61}$$

$$h = \Sigma^{-1}\left[\frac{e'\Sigma^{-1}\alpha}{e'\Sigma^{-1}e}e - \alpha\right], \tag{19.62}$$

whereas Y is given by

$$Y(t) = \frac{V_x(t, X(t))}{X(t)V_{xx}(t, X(t))}. \tag{19.63}$$

Thus we see that the optimal portfolio is moving stochastically along the one-dimensional "optimal portfolio line"

$$g + sh,$$

in the $(n-1)$-dimensional "portfolio hyperplane" Δ, where

$$\Delta = \{w \in R^n \,|e'w = 1\}.$$

We now make the obvious geometric observation that if we fix two points on the optimal portfolio line, say the points $w^a = g + ah$ and $w^b = g + bh$, then any point w on the line can be written as an affine combination of the basis points w^a and w^b. An easy calculation shows that if $w^s = g + sh$ then we can write

$$w^s = \mu w^a + (1 - \mu)w^b,$$

where

$$\mu = \frac{s - b}{a - b}.$$

The point of all this is that we now have an interesting economic interpretation of the optimality results above. Let us thus fix w^a and w^b as above on the optimal portfolio line. Since these points are in the portfolio plane Δ we can interpret them as the relative portfolios of two fixed mutual funds. We may then write (19.60) as

$$\hat{\mathbf{w}}(t) = \mu(t)w^a + (1 - \mu(t))w^b, \tag{19.64}$$

with

$$\mu(t) = \frac{Y(t) - b}{a - b}.$$

Thus we see that the optimal portfolio $\hat{\mathbf{w}}$ can be obtained as a "super portfolio" where we allocate resources between two fixed mutual funds.

Theorem 19.9 (Mutual fund theorem) *Assume that the problem is regular enough to allow for an interior solution. Then there exists a one-dimensional parameterized family of mutual funds, given by $w^s = g + sh$, where g and h are defined by (19.61)–(19.62), such that the following hold:*

1. *For each fixed s the relative portfolio w^s stays fixed over time.*
2. *For any fixed choice of $a = b$ the optimal portfolio $\hat{w}(t)$ is, for all values of t, obtained by allocating all resources between the fixed funds w^a and w^b i.e.*

$$\hat{w}(t) = \mu^a(t)w^a + \mu^b(t)w^b,$$
$$\mu^a(t) + \mu^b(t) = 1.$$

3. *The relative proportions (μ^a, μ^b) of the portfolio wealth allocated to w^a and w^b respectively are given by*

$$\mu^a(t) = \frac{Y(t) - b}{a - b},$$

$$\mu^b(t) = \frac{a - Y(t)}{a - b},$$

where Y is given by (19.63).

19.7.2 The Case with a Risk Free Asset

Again we consider the model

$$dS = D(S)\alpha dt + D(S)\sigma dW(t), \tag{19.65}$$

with the same assumptions as in the preceding section. We now also take as given the standard risk free asset B with dynamics

$$dB = rBdt.$$

Formally we can denote this as a new asset by subscript zero, i.e. $B = S_0$, and then we can consider relative portfolios of the form $w = (w_0, w_1, \ldots, w_n)'$ where of course $\sum_0^n w_i = 1$. Since B will play such a special role it will, however, be convenient to eliminate w_0 by the relation

$$w_0 = 1 - \sum_1^n w_i,$$

and then use the letter w to denote the portfolio weight vector for the risky assets only. Thus we use the notation

$$w = (w_1, \ldots, w_n)',$$

and we note that this truncated portfolio vector is allowed to take any value in R^n.

Given this notation it is easily seen that the dynamics of a self-financing portfolio are given by

$$dX = X \cdot \left\{ \sum_1^n w_i \alpha_i + \left(1 - \sum_1^n w_i \right) r \right\} dt - cdt + X \cdot w' \sigma dW.$$

That is,

$$dX = X \cdot w'(\alpha - re)dt + (rX - c)dt + X \cdot w' \sigma dW, \qquad (19.66)$$

where as before $e \in R^n$ denotes the vector $(1, 1, \ldots, 1)'$.

The HJB equation now becomes

$$\begin{cases} V_t(t, x) + \sup_{c \geq 0, w \in R^n} \{ F(t, c) + \mathcal{A}^{c,w} V(t, x) \} = 0, \\ V(T, x) = 0, \\ V(t, 0) = 0, \end{cases}$$

where

$$\mathcal{A}^c V = xw'(\alpha - re)V_x(t, x) + (rx - c)V_x(t, x) + \frac{1}{2}x^2 w' \Sigma w V_{xx}(t, x).$$

The first order conditions for the static optimization problem are

$$\frac{\partial F}{\partial c}(t, c) = V_x(t, x),$$

$$\hat{w} = -\frac{V_x}{xV_{xx}} \Sigma^{-1}(\alpha - re),$$

and again we have a geometrically obvious economic interpretation.

Theorem 19.10 (Mutual fund theorem) *Given assumptions as above, the following hold:*

1. *The optimal portfolio consists of an allocation between two fixed mutual funds w^0 and w^f.*
2. *The fund w^0 consists only of the risk free asset.*
3. *The fund w^f consists only of the risky assets, and is given by*

$$w^f = \Sigma^{-1}(\alpha - re).$$

4. *At each t the optimal relative allocation of wealth between the funds is given by*

$$\mu^f(t) = -\frac{V_x(t, X(t))}{X(t)V_{xx}(t, X(t))},$$

$$\mu^0(t) = 1 - \mu^f(t).$$

Note that this result is not a corollary of the corresponding result from the previous section. Firstly it was an essential ingredient in the previous results that the volatility matrix of the price vector was invertible. In the case with a riskless asset the volatility matrix for the entire price vector $(B, S_1, \ldots, S_n)$ is of course degenerate, since its first row (having subscript zero) is identically equal to zero. Secondly, even if one assumes the results from the previous section, i.e. that the optimal portfolio is built up from two fixed portfolios, it is not at all obvious that one of these basis portfolios can be chosen so as to consist of the risk free asset alone.

19.8   Exercises

Exercise 19.1 Solve the problem of maximizing logarithmic utility

$$E\left[\int_0^T e^{-\delta t} \ln(c_t)dt + K \cdot \ln(X_T)\right],$$

given the usual wealth dynamics

$$dX_t = X_t \left[u_t^0 r + u_t^1 \alpha\right] dt - c_t dt + u^1 \sigma X_t dW_t,$$

and the usual control constraints

$$c_t \geq 0, \quad \forall t \geq 0,$$
$$u_t^0 + u_t^1 = 1, \quad \forall t \geq 0.$$

Exercise 19.2 A **Bernoulli equation** is an ODE of the form

$$\dot{x}_t + A_t x_t + B_t x_t^\alpha = 0,$$

where A and B are deterministic functions of time and α is a constant.

If $\alpha = 1$ this is a linear equation, and can thus easily be solved. Now consider the case $\alpha = 1$ and introduce the new variable y by

$$y_t = x_t^{1-\alpha}.$$

Show that y satisfies the **linear** equation

$$\dot{y}_t + (1 - \alpha)A_t y_t + (1 - \alpha)B_t = 0.$$

Exercise 19.3 Use the previous exercise in order to solve (19.52)–(19.53) explicitly.

Exercise 19.4 The following example is taken from Björk *et al.* (1987). We consider a consumption problem without risky investments, but with stochastic prices for various consumption goods.

N = the number of consumption goods,

$p_i(t)$ = price, at t, of good i (measured as dollars per unit per unit time),

$p(t) = [p_1(t), \ldots, p_N(t)]'$,

$c_i(t)$ = rate of consumption of good i,

$c(t) = [c_1(t), \ldots, c_N(t)]'$,

$X(t)$ = wealth process,

r = short rate of interest,

T = time horizon.

We assume that the consumption price processes satisfy

$$dp_i = \mu_i(p)dt + \sqrt{2}\sigma_i(p)dW_i$$

where $W_1, \ldots, W_n$ are independent. The X-dynamics become

$$dX = rXdt - c'pdt,$$

and the objective is to maximize expected discounted utility, as measured by

$$E\left[\int_0^\tau F(t, c_t)dt\right]$$

where τ is the time of ruin, i.e.

$$\tau = \inf\{t \geq 0; X_t = 0\} \wedge T.$$

(a) Denote the optimal value function by $V(t, x, p)$ and write down the relevant HJB equation (including boundary conditions for $t = T$ and $x = 0$).

(b) Assume that F is of the form

$$F(t, c) = e^{-\delta t} \prod_{i=1}^{N} c_i^{\alpha_i}$$

where $\delta > 0$, $0 < \alpha_i < 1$ and $\alpha = \sum_1^N \alpha_i < 1$. Show that the optimal value function and the optimal control have the structure

$$V(t,x,p) = e^{-\delta t} x^\alpha \alpha^{-\alpha} G(t,p),$$
$$c_i(t,x,p) = \frac{x}{p_i} \cdot \frac{\alpha_i}{\alpha} A(p)^\gamma G(t,p),$$

where G solves the nonlinear equation

$$\begin{cases} \dfrac{\partial G}{\partial t} + (\alpha r - \delta)G + (1-\alpha)A^\gamma G^{-\alpha\gamma} + \sum_i^N \mu_i \dfrac{\partial G}{\partial p_i} + \sum_i^N \sigma_i^2 \dfrac{\partial^2 G}{\partial p_i{}^2} = 0, \\ G(T,p) = 0, \quad p \in R^N. \end{cases}$$

If you find this too hard, then study the simpler case when $N = 1$.

(c) Now assume that the price dynamics are given by GBM, i.e.

$$dp_i = p_i \mu_i dt + \sqrt{2} p_i \sigma_i dW_i.$$

Try to solve the G-equation above by making the **ansatz**

$$G(t,p) = g(t)f(p).$$

Warning: This becomes somwhat messy.

Exercise 19.5 Consider as before state process dynamics

$$dX_t = \mu(t, X_t, u_t)\, dt + \sigma(t, X_t, u_t)\, dW_t$$

and the usual restrictions for u. Our entire derivation of the HJB equation has so far been based on the fact that the objective function is of the form

$$\int_0^T F(t, X_t, u_t)dt + \Phi(X_T).$$

Sometimes it is natural to consider other criteria, like the expected **exponential utility** criterion

$$E\left[\exp\left\{\int_0^T F(t, X_t, u_t)dt + \Phi(X_T)\right\}\right].$$

For this case we define the optimal value function as the supremum of

$$E_{t,x}\left[\exp\left\{\int_t^T F(s, X_s, u_s)dt + \Phi(X_T)\right\}\right].$$

Follow the reasoning in Section 19.3 in order to show that the HJB equation for the expected exponential utility criterion is given by

$$
\begin{cases}
\dfrac{\partial V}{\partial t}(t,x) + \sup_{u}\left\{ V(t,x)F(t,x,u) + \mathcal{A}^u V(t,x) \right\} = 0, \\
\hspace{5cm} V(T,x) = e^{\Phi(x)}.
\end{cases}
$$

Exercise 19.6 Solve the problem to minimize

$$
E\left[\exp\left\{ \int_0^T u_t^2 \, dt + X_T^2 \right\} \right]
$$

given the scalar dynamics

$$
dX = (ax + u)dt + \sigma dW
$$

where the control u is scalar and there are no control constraints.
   Hint: Make the ansatz

$$
V(t,x) = e^{A(t)x^2 + B(t)}.
$$

Exercise 19.7 Study the general linear–exponential–qudratic control problem of minimizing

$$
E\left[\exp\left\{ \int_0^T \left\{ X_t'QX_t + u_t'Ru_t \right\} dt + X_T'HX_T \right\} \right]
$$

given the dynamics

$$
dX_t = \left\{ AX_t + Bu_t \right\} dt + CdW_t.
$$

Exercise 19.8 The object of this exercise is to connect optimal control to martingale theory. Consider therefore a general control problem of minimizing

$$
E\left[\int_0^T F(t, X_t^{\mathbf{u}}, \mathbf{u}_t)dt + \Phi\left(X_T^{\mathbf{u}} \right) \right]
$$

given the dynamics

$$
dX_t = \mu\left(t, X_t, u_t \right) dt + \sigma\left(t, X_t, u_t \right) dW_t,
$$

and the constraints

$$
\mathbf{u}(t,x) \in U.
$$

Now, for any control law $\mathbf{u}$, define the **total cost process** $C(t; \mathbf{u})$ by

$$C(t; \mathbf{u}) = \int_0^t F(s, X_s^{\mathbf{u}}, \mathbf{u}_s) ds + E_{t, X_t^{\mathbf{u}}} \left[\int_t^T F(s, X_s^{\mathbf{u}}, \mathbf{u}_s) dt + \Phi(X_T^{\mathbf{u}}) \right],$$

i.e.

$$C(t; \mathbf{u}) = \int_0^t F(s, X_s^{\mathbf{u}}, \mathbf{u}_s) ds + \mathcal{J}(t, X_t^{\mathbf{u}}, \mathbf{u}).$$

Use the HJB equation in order to prove the following claims.

(a) If $\mathbf{u}$ is an arbitrary control law, then C is a submartingale.

(b) If $\mathbf{u}$ is optimal, then C is a martingale.

19.9   Notes

Standard references on optimal control are Fleming and Rishel (1975) and Krylov (1980). A very clear exposition can be found in Øksendal (1998). For more recent work, using viscosity solutions, see Fleming and Soner (1993). The classical papers on optimal consumption are Merton (1969) and Merton (1971). For optimal trading under constraints, and its relation to derivative pricing see Cvitanić (1997) and references therein. See also the monograph by Korn (1997).

20

THE MARTINGALE APPROACH TO OPTIMAL INVESTMENT*

In Chapter 19 we studied optimal investment and consumption problems, using dynamic programming. This approach transforms the original stochastic optimal control problem into the problem of solving a nonlinear deterministic PDE, namely the Hamilton–Jacobi–Bellman equation, so the probabilistic nature of the problem disappears as soon as we have formulated the HJB equation.

In this chapter we will present an alternative method of solving optimal investment problems. This method is commonly referred to as "the martingale approach" and it has the advantage that it is in some sense more direct and more probabilistic than dynamic programming, and we do not need to assume a Markovian structure. It should be noted, however, that while dynamic programming can be applied to **any** Markovian stochastic optimal control problem, the martingale approach is only applicable to financial portfolio problems, and in order to get explicit results we also typically need to assume market completeness.

20.1 Generalities

We consider a financial market living on a stochastic basis $(\Omega, \mathcal{F}, \mathbf{F}, P)$, where P is the objective probability measure. The basis carries an n-dimensional P-Wiener process W, and the filtration $\mathbf{F}$ is the one generated by the W process so $\mathbf{F} = \mathbf{F}^W$.

The financial market under consideration consists of n non-dividend paying risky assets ("stocks") with price processes $S^1, \ldots, S^n$, and a bank account with price process B. The formal assumptions concerning the price dynamics are as follows.

Assumption 20.1.1 *We assume the following.*

- *The risky asset prices have P-dynamics given by*

$$dS^i_t = \alpha^i_t S^i_t dt + S^i_t \sigma^i_t dW_t, \quad i = 1, \ldots, n. \qquad (20.1)$$

Here $\alpha^1, \ldots, \alpha^n$ are assumed to be $\mathbf{F}$-adapted scalar processes, and $\sigma^i, \ldots, \sigma^n$ are $\mathbf{F}^W$-adapted d-dimensional row vector processes.

- *The short rate r is assumed to be constant, i.e. the bank account has dynamics given by*

$$dB_t = r B_t dt.$$

Remark 20.1.1 Note that we do not make any Markovian assumptions, so in particular the processes α and σ are allowed to be arbitrary adapted path dependent processes.Of particular interest is of course the Markovian case i.e. when α and σ are deterministic functions of t and S_t so $\alpha_t = \alpha_t(S_t)$ and $\sigma_t = \sigma_t(S_t)$.

Defining the stock vector process S by

$$S = \begin{pmatrix} S^1 \\ \vdots \\ S^n \end{pmatrix},$$

the rate of return vector process α by

$$\alpha = \begin{pmatrix} \alpha^1 \\ \vdots \\ \alpha^n \end{pmatrix},$$

and the volatility matrix σ by

$$\sigma = \begin{pmatrix} -\sigma^1- \\ \vdots \\ -\sigma^n- \end{pmatrix},$$

we can write the stock price dynamics as

$$dS_t = D(S_t)\alpha_t dt + D(S_t)\sigma_t dW_t,$$

where $D(S)$ denotes the diagonal matrix with $S^1, \ldots, S^n$ on the diagonal.

We will need an important assumption concerning the volatility matrix.

Assumption 20.1.2 *We assume that with probability one the volatility matrix $\sigma(t)$ is non-singular for all t.*

The point of this assumption is the following result, the proof of which is obvious.

Proposition 20.1 *Under the assumptions above, the market model is complete.*

20.2   The Basic Idea

Let us consider an investor with initial capital x and a utility function U for terminal wealth. For any self-financing portfolio, we denote the corresponding portfolio value process by X and our problem is to maximize expected utility

$$E^P\left[U(X_T)\right],$$

over the class of self-financing adapted portfolios with the initial condition $X(0) = x$.

In Chapter 19 we viewed this as a **dynamic** optimization problem and attacked it by using dynamic programming. A different way of formulating the problem is however as follows. Define $\mathcal{K}_T$ as the set of contingent T-claims which can be replicated by a self-financing portfolio with initial capital x. Then our basic problem can be formulated as the **static** problem

$$\max_{X_T} \quad E^P\left[U(X_T)\right]$$

subject to the **static** constraint

$$X_T \in \mathcal{K}_T.$$

In this formulation, the focus is not on the optimal portfolio strategy but instead on the terminal wealth X_T. We now have the following important observation, which follows immediately from the market completeness.

Proposition 20.2 *With assumptions as above, the following conditions are equivalent for any random variable* $X_T \in \mathcal{F}_T$.

$$X_T \in \mathcal{K}_T. \tag{20.2}$$

$$e^{-rT}E^Q\left[X_T\right] = x. \tag{20.3}$$

The implication of this simple observation is that we can now **decouple** the problem of determining the optimal terminal wealth profile from the problem of determining the optimal portfolio. Schematically we proceed as follows.

- Instead of solving the dynamic control problem, we solve the **static** problem

$$\max_{X_T \in \mathcal{F}_T} \quad E^P\left[U(X_T)\right] \tag{20.4}$$

subject to the budget constraint

$$e^{-rT}E^Q\left[X_T\right] = x, \tag{20.5}$$

where x is the initial wealth, and Q is the unique martingale measure.
- Given the optimal wealth profile $\hat{X}_T$, we can (in principle) compute the corresponding generating portfolio using martingale representation results.

20.3 The Optimal Terminal Wealth

The static problem (20.4) with the constraint (20.5) can easily be solved using Lagrange relaxation. We start by rewriting the budget constraint (20.5) as

$$e^{-rT}E^P\left[L_T X\right] = x,$$

where L is the likelihood process between P and Q, i.e.,

$$L_t = \frac{dQ}{dP}, \quad \text{on } \mathcal{F}_t.$$

We now relax the budget constraint to obtain the Lagrangian

$$\mathcal{L} = E^P\left[U(X)\right] - \lambda\left(e^{-rT}E^P\left[L_T X\right] - x\right),$$

so

$$\mathcal{L} = \int_\Omega \left\{U(X(\omega)) - \lambda\left[e^{-rT}L_T(\omega)X(\omega) - x\right]\right\} dP(\omega).$$

It now remains to maximize the unconstrained Lagrangian over X_T, but this is trivial: Since we have no constraints we can maximize $\mathcal{L}$ for each ω. The optimality condition is

$$U'(X_T) = \lambda e^{-rT}L_T$$

so the optimal wealth profile is given by

$$\hat{X}_T = F\left(\lambda e^{-rT}L_T\right), \tag{20.6}$$

where F is the functional inverse of the utility function U, so $F = (U')^{-1}$.

We do in fact have an explicit expression for the Radon–Nikodym derivative L_T above. From the price dynamics (20.1) and the Girsanov Theorem it is easily seen that the L dynamics are given by

$$dL_t = \left\{\sigma_t^{-1}\left(\mathbf{r} - \alpha_t\right)\right\}' dW_t,$$
$$L_0 = 1,$$

where $'$ denotes transpose, and $\mathbf{r}$ denotes the n-column vector with r in each component. We thus have the explicit formula

$$L_t = \exp\left\{\int_0^t \left\{\sigma_s^{-1}\left(\mathbf{r} - \alpha_s\right)\right\}' dW_s - \frac{1}{2}\int_0^t \left\|\sigma_s^{-1}\left(\mathbf{r} - \alpha_s\right)\right\|^2 ds\right\}, \tag{20.7}$$

where $'$ denotes transpose. We collect our results in a proposition.

Proposition 20.3 *Under the assumptions above, the optimal terminal wealth profile $\hat{X}_T$ is given by*

$$\hat{X}_T = F\left(\lambda e^{-rT}L_T\right). \tag{20.8}$$

The likelihood process L is given by (20.7), and the Lagrange multiplier λ is determined by the budget constraint (20.5). The function F is the inverse of the marginal utility function U'.

20.4 The Optimal Portfolio

In the previous section we saw that we could, in principle quite easily, derive a closed form expression from the optimal terminal wealth $\hat{X}_T$. The next step is to determine the optimal portfolio strategy, i.e. the portfolio which generates $\hat{X}_T$. The general idea for how to do this is in fact quite simple, although it may be difficult to carry it out in a concrete case. It relies on using the Martingale Representation Theorem and works as follows.

If we denote the vector of relative portfolio weights on the n risky assets by $u_t = (u_t^1, \ldots, u_t^n)$, then it is easy to see that the dynamics of the induced wealth process X are given by

$$dX_t = X_t u_t \alpha_t dt + X_t(1 - u_t \mathbf{1})r dt + X_t u_t \sigma_t dW_t,$$

where $\mathbf{1}$ denotes the column vector in R^n with 1 in every position. If we now define the normalized process Z as

$$Z_t = \frac{X_t}{B_t} = e^{-rt}X_t,$$

then we know from general theory that Z is a Q-martingale. From the Itô formula we have

$$dZ_t = Z_t u_t \{\alpha_t - r\mathbf{1}\} t + Z_t u_t \sigma_t dW_t,$$

and, since we know that the diffusion part is unchanged under a Girsanov transformation, the Q-dynamics of Z are

$$dZ_t = Z_t u_t \sigma_t dW_t^Q, \tag{20.9}$$

where W^Q is a Q-Wiener process. We can now proceed along the following lines, where $\hat{X}_T$ is given by Proposition 20.3.

1. Define the process Z by

$$Z_t = E^Q\left[e^{-rT}\hat{X}_T\middle|\mathcal{F}_t\right].$$

2. Since Z is a Q martingale it follows from the Martingale Representation Theorem 11.2 that Z has dynamics of the form

$$dZ_t = h_t dW_t^Q, \tag{20.10}$$

for some adapted process h.

3. Comparing (20.10) with (20.9) we can determine the portfolio strategy u, which generates $\hat{X}_T$ by solving the equation

$$Z_t u_t \sigma_t = h_t,$$

for every t. Since σ_t was assumed to be invertible for every t, this is easily done and we can now collect our results.

Proposition 20.4 *The vector process $\hat{u}$ of optimal portfolio weights on the risky assets is given by*

$$\hat{u}_t = \frac{1}{Z_t} h_t \sigma_t^{-1}, \tag{20.11}$$

where h is given, through the Martingale Representation Theorem, by (20.10).

We see that we can "in principle" determine the optimal portfolio strategy $\hat{u}$. For a concrete model, the result of Proposition 20.4 does, however, not lead directly to a closed form expression for $\hat{u}$. The reason is that the formula (20.11) involves the process h which is provided by the martingale representation theorem. That theorem, however, is an **existence** theorem, so we know that h exists, but we typically do not know what it looks like. To obtain closed form expressions, we therefore have to make some further model assumptions. In the next sections we will assume a particular form of the utility function U, while still not assuming a Markovian structure. We will study the three most important cases, namely power, logarithmic, and exponential utility.

20.5   Power Utility

The most interesting case is that of power utility. In this case the utility function is of the form

$$U(x) = \frac{x^\gamma}{\gamma},$$

for some non-zero $\gamma < 1$. We have

$$F(y) = y^{-\frac{1}{1-\gamma}}.$$

20.5.1   The Optimal Terminal Wealth Profile

From (20.6), and the expression for F above we obtain the optimal wealth profile as

$$X_T^* = \lambda^{-\frac{1}{1-\gamma}} \cdot e^{\frac{rT}{1-\gamma}} L_T^{-\frac{1}{1-\gamma}}. \tag{20.12}$$

The budget constraint (20.5) becomes

$$e^{-rT} \lambda^{-\frac{1}{1-\gamma}} e^{\frac{rT}{1-\gamma}} E^P \left[L_T^{-\beta} \right] = x, \tag{20.13}$$

with β defined by

$$\beta = \frac{\gamma}{1-\gamma}. \tag{20.14}$$

Solving for $\lambda^{-\frac{1}{1-\gamma}}$ in (20.13) and inserting this into (20.12) gives us the optimal wealth profile as

$$X_T^* = e^{rT} \frac{x}{H_0} \cdot L_T^{-\frac{1}{1-\gamma}},$$

where
$$H_0 = E^P \left[L_T^{-\beta} \right].$$

The optimal expected utility $V_0 = E^P \left[U\left(X_T^* \right) \right]$ can easily be computed as

$$V_0 = e^{r\gamma T} \frac{x^\gamma}{\gamma} H_0^{1-\gamma}. \tag{20.15}$$

We will now study H_0 in some detail. From (20.7) we obtain

$$L_T^{-\beta} = \exp \left\{ \int_0^T \beta \left\{ \sigma_t^{-1} \left(\alpha_t - \mathbf{r} \right) \right\}' dW_t + \frac{1}{2} \int_0^T \beta \| \sigma_t^{-1} \left(\alpha_t - \mathbf{r} \right) \|^2 dt \right\}.$$

This expression looks almost like a Radon-Nikodym derivative, and this observation leads us to define the P-martingale L^0 by

$$L_t^0 = \exp \left\{ \int_0^t \beta \left\{ \sigma_s^{-1} \left(\alpha_s - \mathbf{r} \right) \right\}' dW_s - \frac{1}{2} \int_0^t \beta^2 \| \sigma_s^{-1} \left(\alpha_s - \mathbf{r} \right) \|^2 ds \right\}$$

i.e. with dynamics
$$dL_t^0 = L_t^0 \beta \left\{ \sigma_t^{-1} \left(\alpha_t - \mathbf{r} \right) \right\}' dW_t.$$

We can thus write

$$L_T^{-\beta} = L_T^0 \exp \left\{ \frac{1}{2} \int_0^T \frac{\beta}{1-\gamma} \| \sigma_t^{-1} \left(\alpha_t - \mathbf{r} \right) \|^2 dt \right\}, \tag{20.16}$$

to obtain

$$H_0 = E^0 \left[\exp \left\{ \frac{1}{2} \int_0^T \frac{\beta}{1-\gamma} \| \sigma_t^{-1} \left(\alpha_t - \mathbf{r} \right) \|^2 dt \right\} \right]$$

where we integrate over the measure Q^0 defined through the likelihood process L^0.

For easy reference we collect the definitions Q and Q^0.

Definition 20.5

- *The risk neutral martingale measure Q is defined by*

$$\frac{dQ}{dP} = L_t, \quad on \ \mathcal{F}_t, \tag{20.17}$$

  with L given by

$$dL_t = L_t \left\{ \sigma_t^{-1} \left(\mathbf{r} - \alpha_t \right) \right\}' dW_t. \tag{20.18}$$

- The measure Q^0 is defined by

$$\frac{dQ^0}{dP} = L_t^0, \quad \text{on } \mathcal{F}_t,$$

with L^0 given by

$$dL_t^0 = L_t^0 \beta \left\{ \sigma_t^{-1} (\alpha_t - \mathbf{r}) \right\}' dW_t \qquad (20.19)$$

with

$$\beta = \frac{\gamma}{1 - \gamma}.$$

We also collect our results so far.

Proposition 20.6 *With definitions as above, the following hold:*

- *The optimal terminal wealth is given by*

$$\hat{X}_T = e^{rT} \frac{x}{H_0} L_T^{-\frac{1}{1-\gamma}}, \qquad (20.20)$$

where H_0 is defined by

$$H_0 = E^0 \left[\exp \left\{ \frac{1}{2} \int_0^T \frac{\beta}{1 - \gamma} \| \sigma_t^{-1} (\alpha_t - \mathbf{r}) \|^2 dt \right\} \right].$$

- *The optimal utility V_0 is given by*

$$V_0 = e^{r\gamma T} \frac{x^\gamma}{\gamma} H_0^{1-\gamma}.$$

20.5.2   The Optimal Wealth Process

We have already computed the optimal terminal wealth profile $\hat{X}_T$ above. and we can in fact also derive a surprisingly explicit formula for the entire optimal wealth process $\hat{X}$.

Proposition 20.7 *The optimal wealth process $\widehat{X}$ is given by*

$$\hat{X}_t = e^{rt} x \cdot \frac{H_t}{H_0} L_t^{-\frac{1}{1-\gamma}}, \qquad (20.21)$$

where

$$H_t = E^0 \left[e^{\frac{1}{2} \int_t^T \frac{\beta}{1-\gamma} \| \sigma_s^{-1} (\alpha_s - \mathbf{r}) \|^2 ds} \, \middle| \, \mathcal{F}_t \right]. \qquad (20.22)$$

Proof   From general theory we know that the wealth process (normalized with the bank account) of any self-financing portfolio will be a Q-martingale, so from (20.20) we have

$$e^{-rt}X_t^* = e^{-rT} \cdot e^{rT}\frac{x}{H_0} \cdot E^Q\left[L_T^{-\frac{1}{1-\gamma}}\middle|\mathcal{F}_t\right]. \tag{20.23}$$

Using the abstract Bayes' formula, we can write this as

$$\hat{X}_t = e^{rt}\frac{x}{H_0} \cdot \frac{E^P\left[L_T^{-\beta}\middle|\mathcal{F}_t\right]}{L_t},$$

and, using (20.16) and Bayes again, we have

$$E^P\left[L_T^{-\beta}\middle|\mathcal{F}_t\right] = E^P\left[L_T^0 e^{\frac{1}{2}\int_0^T \frac{\beta}{1-\gamma}\|\sigma_s^{-1}(\alpha_s-\mathbf{r})\|^2 ds}\middle|\mathcal{F}_t\right]$$

$$= L_t^0 E^0\left[e^{\frac{1}{2}\int_0^T \frac{\beta}{1-\gamma}\|\sigma_s^{-1}(\alpha_s-\mathbf{r})\|^2 ds}\middle|\mathcal{F}_t\right]$$

$$= L_t^0 e^{\frac{1}{2}\int_0^t \frac{\beta}{1-\gamma}\|\sigma_s^{-1}(\alpha_s-\mathbf{r})\|^2 ds} \cdot E^0\left[e^{\frac{1}{2}\int_t^T \frac{\beta}{1-\gamma}\|\sigma_s^{-1}(\alpha_s-\mathbf{r})\|^2 ds}\middle|\mathcal{F}_t\right]$$

$$= L_t^{-\beta} E^0\left[e^{\frac{1}{2}\int_t^T \frac{\beta}{1-\gamma}\|\sigma_s^{-1}(\alpha_s-\mathbf{r})\|^2 ds}\middle|\mathcal{F}_t\right] = L_t^{-\beta}H_t.$$

Plugging this into (20.23) we thus obtain

$$\hat{X}_t = e^{rt}\frac{x}{H_0}L_t^{-1}L_t^{-\beta}H_t = e^{rt}x\frac{H_t}{H_0}L_t^{-\frac{1}{1-\gamma}}.$$

$\square$

20.5.3   *The Optimal Portfolio*

We can also derive a reasonably explicit formula for the optimal portfolio. We need some notation so let us denote by μ_H and σ_H the relative drift and diffusion parts of the process H defined in (20.22), i.e.

$$dH_t = H_t\mu_H(t)dt + H_t\sigma_H(t)dW_t. \tag{20.24}$$

Furthermore, for any self-financing portfolio we denote by $u_t = (u_t^1,\dots u_t^n)$ the vector process of portfolio weights on the risky assets. This of course implies that the weight, u^B, on the bank account is given by $u_t^B = 1 - u_t\mathbf{1}$, where $\mathbf{1}$ denotes the n-column vector with a unit in each position.

Proposition 20.8 *The optimal portfolio weight vector process $\hat{u}$ is given by*

$$\hat{u}_t = \left(\frac{1}{1 - \gamma} \left\{ \sigma_t^{-1} \left(\alpha_t - \mathbf{r} \right) \right\}' + \sigma_H(t) \right) \sigma_t^{-1}.$$

i.e.

$$\hat{u}_t = \frac{1}{1 - \gamma} \left(\alpha_t - \mathbf{r} \right)' \left(\sigma_t \sigma_t' \right)^{-1} + \sigma_H(t) \sigma_t^{-1} \tag{20.25}$$

In particular, if α and σ are deterministic functions of time we have

$$\hat{u}_t = \frac{1}{1 - \gamma} \left(\alpha_t - \mathbf{r} \right)' \left(\sigma_t \sigma_t' \right)^{-1} \tag{20.26}$$

Proof   From standard portfolio theory it follows that the wealth process X o any self-financing portfolio has the dynamics

$$dX_t = X_t u_t \alpha_t dt + X_t (1 - u_t \mathbf{1}) r dt + X_t u_t \sigma_t dW_t, \tag{20.27}$$

implying that the discounted wealth process $Z_t = e^{-rt} X_t$ has dynamics

$$dZ_t = Z_t u_t \left(\alpha_t - \mathbf{r} \right) dt + Z_t u_t \sigma_t dW_t, \tag{20.28}$$

the point being that the portfolio u can be determined from the diffusion part o the Z-dynamics. From (20.21) we see that the optimal discounted wealth proces has the form

$$\hat{Z}_t = A H_t L_t^c,$$

where $A = x H_0^{-1}$ and $c = -(1 - \gamma)^{-1}$. Using (20.18) and (20.24) we easily obtai

$$d\hat{Z}_t = \hat{Z}_t \left(\ldots \right) dt + \hat{Z}_t \left\{ c \left\{ \sigma_t^{-1} \left(\mathbf{r} - \alpha_t \right) \right\}' + \sigma_H(t) \right\} dW_t,$$

where we do not care about the exact form of the dt term. Post-multiplying th diffusion part by the term $\sigma_t^{-1} \sigma_t$ and comparing with (20.28) allows us to identif the portfolio process $\hat{u}_t$ as the one in (20.25). If α and σ are deterministic, the H is also deterministic so $\sigma_H = 0$ and we have (20.26).

We thus see that in (20.25) the first term is the solution to a classical (deter ministic parameter) Merton problem. The second term represents the "hedgin, demand for parameter risk".

20.6   The Markovian Case

In the previous sections we obtained surprisingly explicit expressions for th optimal portfolio weights. The optimal portfolio formula (20.25) is however no completely explicit, since it is expressed in terms of the volatility σ_H which i determined by the process H defined in (20.22).

To obtain a more analytically tractable formula we need to make furthe assumptions, so in this section we assume a Markovian structure. For notationa simplicity we restrict ourselves to the scalar case.

Assumption 20.6.1 *We assume that, under P, the stock price dynamics are given by*

$$dS_t = S_t \alpha(t, S_t)dt + S_t \sigma(t, S_t)dW_t, \tag{20.29}$$

where mean rate of return $\alpha(t, s)$ and the volatility $\sigma(t, s)$ are deterministic functions. The short rate r is assumed to be constant.

Given this setup, the process H is now defined as

$$H_t = E^0 \left[e^{\frac{1}{2} \int_t^T \frac{\beta}{1-\gamma} \left(\frac{\alpha(u, S_u) - r}{\sigma(u, S_u)} \right)^2 du} \middle| \mathcal{F}_t \right]. \tag{20.30}$$

The likelihood process $L^0 = dQ^0/dP$ has the structure

$$dL_t^0 = L_t^0 \beta \left\{ \frac{\alpha(t, S_t) - r}{\sigma(t, S_t)} \right\} dW_t, \tag{20.31}$$

so the Q^0 dynamics of S are

$$dS_t = S_t \left\{ (1 + \beta)\alpha(t, S_t) - \beta r \right\} dt + S_t \sigma(t, S_t)dW_t^0, \tag{20.32}$$

where W^0 is Q^0 Wiener. We write this as

$$dS_t = S_t \alpha_0(t, S_t)dt + S_t \sigma(t, S_t)dW_t^0,$$

where

$$\alpha_0(t, s) = (1 + \beta)\alpha(t, s) - \beta r. \tag{20.33}$$

In this Markovian setting the process H is in fact of the form

$$H_t = H(t, S_t),$$

where, with a slight abuse of notation the left-hand side occurrence of H denotes a random process, whereas the right-hand side H denotes a deterministic function of (t, s). We then have the following Kolmogorov backward equation for H

$$\begin{cases} \dfrac{\partial H}{\partial t} + \alpha_0 \dfrac{\partial H}{\partial s} + \dfrac{1}{2}\sigma^2 \dfrac{\partial^2 H}{\partial s^2} + \dfrac{1}{2}\dfrac{\beta}{1-\gamma}\left(\dfrac{\alpha - r}{\sigma} \right)^2 H = 0 \\ \\ \qquad\qquad\qquad\qquad H(T, s) = 1 \end{cases}$$

and the volatility σ_H is given by

$$\sigma_H(t, s) = \frac{H_s(t, s)}{H(t, s)}\sigma(t, s),$$

where the lower index s denotes partial derivative. Inserting this into (20.25) we thus have the following explicit formula for the optimal portfolio, up to the solution of the PDE above.

$$\hat{u}(t, s) = \frac{1}{1 - \gamma}\frac{\alpha(t, s) - r}{\sigma^2(t, s)} + \frac{H_s(t, s)}{H(t, s)}.$$

20.7 Log Utility

In this case the utility function is given by

$$U(x) = \ln(x),$$

which implies that

$$F(y) = \frac{1}{y}.$$

From the point of view of local risk aversion, log utility is the limiting case of power utility when the risk aversion parameter γ tends to zero. We would thus intuitively conjecture that the solution to the log utility problem is obtained from the power utility case by setting γ to zero, and in fact this turns out to be correct. We have the following result, and since the calculations in this case are very simple we omit the proof.

Proposition 20.9 *For the log utility case, the following hold:*

- *The optimal wealth process $\hat{X}$ is given by*

$$\hat{X}_t = e^{rt}xL_t^{-1},$$

  where, as before, the likelihood process L is given by (20.18).
- *The optimal portfolio weight vector process $\hat{u}$ is given by*

$$\hat{u}_t = (\alpha_t - \mathbf{r})' (\sigma_t \sigma_t')^{-1}$$

Comparing these expressions with the power utility case we see that the log utility results are indeed obtained by setting γ to zero. We also note that for log utility there is no hedging demand for parameter risk in the optimal portfolio. This is intuitively expected from the interpretation of log utility as myopic.

In particular we see that results from the power case trivialize in the log case in the sense that $L^0 \equiv 1$, $Q^0 = P$, and $H \equiv 1$.

20.8 Exponential Utility

In this case we have

$$U(x) = -\frac{1}{\gamma}e^{-\gamma x},$$

and

$$F(y) = -\frac{1}{\gamma}\ln(y).$$

20.8.1   *The Optimal Terminal Wealth*

From (20.6) the optimal terminal wealth profile is given by

$$\hat{X}_T = -\frac{1}{\gamma}\ln(\lambda) + \frac{rT}{\gamma} - \frac{1}{\gamma}\ln(L_T).$$

The Lagrange multiplier is easily determined by the budget constraint

$$e^{-rT}E^Q\left[\hat{X}_T\right] = x,$$

and after some calculations we obtain the following result.

Proposition 20.10 *The optimal terminal wealth profile is given by*

$$\hat{X}_T = e^{rT}x + \frac{1}{\gamma}H_0 - \frac{1}{\gamma}\ln(L_T), \qquad (20.34)$$

where

$$H_0 = E^Q\left[\ln(L_T)\right].$$

We note that the constant H_0 can also be written as

$$H_0 = E^P\left[L_T\ln(L_T)\right],$$

which is the relative entropy of Q w.r.t. P.

20.8.2   *The Optimal Wealth Process*

As for power utility, the optimal wealth process $\hat{X}_t$ is determined by the general relation

$$e^{-rt}\hat{X}_t = E^Q\left[e^{-rT}\hat{X}_T\middle|\mathcal{F}_t\right].$$

Plugging in $\hat{X}_T$ from (20.34) into this expression gives us

$$\hat{X}_t = e^{rt}x + e^{-r(T-t)}\frac{1}{\gamma}\left\{E^Q\left[\ln(L_T)\right] - E^Q\left[\ln(L_T)\middle|\mathcal{F}_t\right]\right\}, \qquad (20.35)$$

and this can be written in even more explicit form. From (20.7) we have

$$\ln(L_t) = \int_0^t \varphi_s'dW_s - \frac{1}{2}\int_0^t \|\varphi_s\|^2 ds, \qquad (20.36)$$

where

$$\varphi_t = \sigma_t^{-1}\left\{\mathbf{r} - \alpha_t\right\}. \qquad (20.37)$$

Furthermore, the Girsanov Theorem tells us that we can write

$$dW_t = \varphi_t dt + dW_t^Q,$$

where W^Q is Q-Wiener. Plugging this into (20.36) gives us the expression

$$\ln(L_t) = \int_0^t \varphi_s' dW_s^Q + \frac{1}{2} \int_0^t \|\varphi_s\|^2 ds.$$

We thus easily obtain

$$E^Q\left[\ln(L_T)\right] = \frac{1}{2} E^Q\left[\int_0^T \|\varphi_s\|^2 ds\right].$$

We also have

$$E^Q\left[\ln(L_T)|\, \mathcal{F}_t\right] = \ln(L_t) + E^Q\left[\int_t^T \varphi_s' dW_s^Q + \frac{1}{2} \int_t^T \|\varphi_s\|^2 ds \,\bigg|\, \mathcal{F}_t\right]$$

$$= \ln(L_t) + \frac{1}{2} E^Q\left[\int_t^T \|\varphi_s\|^2 ds \,\bigg|\, \mathcal{F}_t\right],$$

and plugging this into (20.35) gives us our final expression for the optimal wealth process.

Proposition 20.11 *The optimal wealth process is given by*

$$\hat{X}_t = e^{rt}x + e^{-r(T-t)}\frac{1}{\gamma}\left\{H_0 - H_t - \ln(L_t)\right\}, \tag{20.38}$$

where

$$H_t = \frac{1}{2} E^Q\left[\int_t^T \|\sigma_s^{-1}(\alpha - \mathbf{r})\|^2 ds \,\bigg|\, \mathcal{F}_t\right]. \tag{20.39}$$

20.8.3   *The Optimal Portfolio*

As in the power utility case, we will identify the optimal portfolio from the (discounted) wealth dynamics (20.27)–(20.28). Defining, as before, the discounted optimal wealth as

$$Z_t = e^{-rt}\hat{X}_t,$$

we obtain from (20.38)

$$Z_t = a + B\left\{H_t + \ln(L_t)\right\},$$

where $A = x + e^{-rT}\frac{1}{\gamma}H_0$ and $B = -e^{-rT}\frac{1}{\gamma}$. We thus obtain the Z dynamics as

$$dZ_t = B\left\{dH_t + d\ln(L_t)\right\}.$$

From (20.39) it is clear the H is an Itô process with dynamics of the form

$$dH_t = \mu_H(t)dt + \sigma_H(t)dW_t.$$

From this, and (20.36) we have

$$dZ_t = (\ldots)\,dt + B\left\{\varphi'_t + \sigma_H(t)\right\}dW_t,$$

with φ defined by (20.37). Comparing this with (20.28) we can finally identify the optimal portfolio.

Proposition 20.12 *The optimal portfolio, in terms of the optimal weights on the risky assets, is given by*

$$\hat{u}_t = e^{-r(T-t)}\frac{1}{\gamma X_t}\left(\left\{\sigma_t^{-1}\left[\alpha_t - \mathbf{r}\right]\right\}' - \sigma_H(t)\right)\sigma_t^{-1},$$

where σ_H is obtained from the H dynamics as

$$dH_t = \mu_H(t)dt + \sigma_H(t)dW_t,$$

where H is defined by (20.39). In particular, if α and σ are deterministic functions of time, then

$$\hat{u}_t = e^{-r(T-t)}\frac{1}{\gamma X_t}\left[\alpha_t - r\right]\left(\sigma'_t\sigma_t\right)^{-1}.$$

20.9 Exercises

Exercise 20.1 In this exercise we will see how intermediate consumption can be handled by the martingale approach. We make the assumptions of Section 20.1 and the problem is to maximize

$$E^P\left[\int_0^T g(s,c_s)ds + U(X_T)\right]$$

over the class of self-financing portfolios with initial wealth x. Here c is the consumption rate for a consumption good with unit price, so c denotes consumption rate in terms of dollars per unit time. The function g is the local utility of consumption, U is utility of terminal wealth, and X is portfolio wealth.

(a) Convince yourself that the appropriate budget constraint is given by

$$E^Q\left[\int_0^T e^{-rs}c_s ds + e^{-rT}X_T\right] = x.$$

(b) Show that the first-order condition for the optimal terminal wealth and the optimal consumption plan are given by

$$\hat{c}_t = G(\lambda e^{-rt}L_t),$$
$$\hat{X}_X = F(\lambda e^{-rT}L_T),$$

where $G = (g')^{-1}$, $F = (U')^{-1}$, L is the usual likelihood process, and λ is a Lagrange multiplier.

Exercise 20.2 Consider the setup in the previous exercise and assume that $g(c) = \ln(c)$ and $U(x) = a\ln(x)$, where a is a positive constant. Compute the optimal consumption plan, and the optimal terminal wealth profile.

Exercise 20.3 Consider the log-optimal portfolio given by Proposition 20.9 as

$$X_t = e^{rt}xL_t^{-1}.$$

Show that this portfolio is the "P numeraire portfolio" in the sense that if Π is the arbitrage free price process for any asset in the economy, underlying or derivative, then the normalized asset price

$$\frac{\Pi_t}{X_t}$$

is a martingale under the objective probability measure P.

20.10   Notes

The basic papers for the martingale approach to optimal investment problems see Karatzas *et al.* (1987) and Cox and Huang (1989) for the complete market case. The theory for the (much harder) incomplete market case were developed in Karatzas *et al.* (1991), and Kramkov and Schachermayer (1999). A very readable overview of convex duality theory for the incomplete market case, containing an extensive bibliography, is given in Schachermayer (2002).

21

OPTIMAL STOPPING THEORY
AND AMERICAN OPTIONS*

21.1 Introduction

The purpose of this chapter is to give an introduction to the theory of optimal stopping problems in discrete and continuous time. Since optimal stopping theory is rather technical, it is impossible to provide a rigorous derivation of the theory within the framework of this book, so the entire discussion is somewhat informal. We present the main ideas and tools of optimal stopping theory, such as the Snell Envelope Theorem, the system of variational inequalities, and the associated free boundary value problem. The reader is then referred to the specialist literature in the Notes for more precise information.

21.2 Generalities

Let $(\Omega, \mathcal{F}, P, \underline{\mathcal{F}})$ be a filtered probability space in discrete or continuous time, where the filtration $\mathbf{F} = \{\mathcal{F}_t\}_{t \geq 0}$ satisfies the usual conditions. We recall the following definition.

Definition 21.1 *A nonnegative random variable τ is called an (optional)* **stopping time** *w.r.t. the filtration* $\mathbf{F}$ *if it satisfies the condition*

$$\{\tau \leq t\} \in \mathcal{F}_t \quad \text{for all } t \geq 0. \tag{21.1}$$

Intuitively this means that the random time τ is nonanticipative, in the sense that at any time t we can actually determine whether the instant τ in time has occurred or not. It is an easy exercise to show that in discrete time the condition (21.1) can be replaced by

$$\{\tau = n\} \in \mathcal{F}_n, \quad \text{for all } n = 0, 1, 2, \dots$$

Suppose now that we are given an integrable process Z and a fixed time horizon T (where it is allowed that $T = \infty$). We can then pose the problem of maximizing the expression

$$E\left[Z_\tau\right]$$

over the class of all stopping times τ, satisfying $0 \leq \tau \leq T$ with probability one.

An intuitive way of thinking about this is that we are playing a game where, at any time, we are allowed to push a red button which stops the game. If we push the button at time t then we will obtain the amount Z_t, and our objective is to play this game in such a way that, at time $t = 0$, the expected value of the game is maximized. For this reason we will sometimes refer to the process Z as the "reward process".

We can thus formulate our problem as

$$\operatorname*{maximize}_{0 \leq \tau \leq T} \; E\left[Z_\tau\right] \tag{21.2}$$

where it is understood that τ varies over the class of stopping times, and we say that a stopping time $\hat{\tau} \leq T$ is **optimal** if

$$E\left[Z_{\hat{\tau}}\right] = \sup_{0 \leq \tau \leq T} E\left[Z_\tau\right].$$

For a given problem, an optimal stopping time does not necessarily exist. However; for every ϵ there will always exist an ϵ-optimal stopping time τ_ϵ with the property that

$$E\left[Z_{\tau_\epsilon}\right] \geq \sup_{0 \leq \tau \leq T} E\left[Z_\tau\right] - \epsilon.$$

We now have a number of natural questions.

- Under what conditions does there exist an optimal stopping time $\hat{\tau}$?
- If $\hat{\tau}$ exists, how do you find it?
- Is $\hat{\tau}$ unique?
- How do you compute the optimal value $\sup_{0 \leq \tau \leq T} E\left[Z_\tau\right]$?

Below we will study these questions in discrete as well as in continuous time. In both cases we will use the same approach, namely that of dynamic programming. For references to the literature, see the Notes at the end of the text.

21.3 Some Simple Results

We start by noticing that in some (very rare) cases, an optimal stopping problem admits a trivial solution.

Proposition 21.2 *The following hold:*

1. *If Z is a submartingale, then late stopping is optimal, i.e. $\hat{\tau} = T$.*
2. *If Z is a supermartingale, then it is optimal to stop immediately i.e. $\hat{\tau} = 0$.*
3. *If Z is a martingale, then all stopping times τ with $0 \leq \tau \leq T$ are optimal.*

Proof Obvious. ☐

It is of course very seldom that one comes across one of these cases, one of the few exceptions being the American call on an underlying stock without dividends in Section 21.6.1. It is nevertheless useful to be able to recognize when these simple cases appear. The following result is obvious.

Proposition 21.3 *Assume that the process Z has dynamics*

$$dZ_t = \mu_t dt + \sigma_t dW_t, \tag{21.3}$$

where μ and σ are adapted processes and σ is square integrable. Then the following hold:

- *If $\mu_t \geq 0$, $P - a.s$ for all t, then Z is a submartingale.*
- *If $\mu_t \leq 0$, $P - a.s$ for all t, then Z is a supermartingale.*
- *If $\mu_t = 0$, $P - a.s$ for all t, then Z is a martingale.*

There are also a number of results connecting martingale theory to the theory of convex (or harmonic) functions. The reader will probably recall the following basic results for real valued functions.

Proposition 21.4 *The following hold:*

- *If f is linear and g is convex, then $g(f(x))$ is convex.*
- *If f is convex and g is convex and increasing, then $g(f(x))$ is convex.*
- *If f is concave and g is concave and increasing, then $g(f(x))$ is concave.*

The connection to martingale theory is as follows:

$$\text{martingale} \sim \text{linear function,}$$
$$\text{submartingale} \sim \text{convex function,}$$
$$\text{supermartingale} \sim \text{concave function.}$$

The connections are in fact much deeper, but this will do nicely for our purposes. We now have the following result, which is parallel to Proposition 21.4.

Proposition 21.5 *Given enough integrability, the following hold:*

1. *If Z is a martingale and g is convex, then $g(Z_t)$ is a submartingale.*
2. *If Z is a submartingale and g is convex and increasing, then $g(Z_t)$ is a submartingale.*
3. *If Z is a supermartingale and g is concave and increasing, then $g(Z_t)$ is a supermartingale.*

21.4 Discrete Time

Our method of attacking the problem (21.2) is to use Dynamic Programming. The idea is to embed the original problem (21.2) into a large class of problems, indexed by time, and then to connect these problems by means of a simple recursion. We will start by analyzing a fairly general problem, and later on we specialize to a Markovian framework.

21.4.1 The General Case

In order to emphasize that we are now working in discrete time we denote a typical point in time by n or k, rather than by s or t.

Definition 21.6 *Consider the optimal stopping problem (21.2) above.*

- *For any point in time n and a given stopping time τ with $n \leq \tau \leq T$ we define the* **value process** *$J(\tau)$ by*

$$J_n(\tau) = E\left[Z_\tau \,|\, \mathcal{F}_n\right]. \tag{21.4}$$

- *The* **optimal value process** *V is defined by*

$$V_n = \sup_{n \leq \tau \leq T} E\left[Z_\tau \,|\, \mathcal{F}_n\right], \tag{21.5}$$

where, for brevity of notation, we use "sup" to denote the essential supremum.

- *A stopping time which realizes the (essential) supremum in (21.5) is said to be* **optimal at** *n, and it will be denoted by $\hat{\tau}_n$.*

We now try to understand the nature of the optimal value process V, and to do this we consider a fixed time n. We then compare three different stopping strategies:

Strategy 1: We use the optimal stopping strategy $\hat{\tau}_n$.

Strategy 2: We stop immediately.

Strategy 3: We do not stop at time n. Instead we wait until time $n + 1$, and from time $n + 1$ we behave optimally, i.e. we use the stopping time $\hat{\tau}_{n+1}$.

Let us now compute the values of these strategies, and compare them.

- The value of Strategy 1 (henceforth S1) is obviously, and by definition, given by V_n.
- The value of S2 is equally obviously given by Z_n.
- For S3 we do not stop at time n. Instead we wait one step and we find ourselves at time $n + 1$. By definition we are assumed to behave optimally from $n + 1$ and onwards, so at time $n + 1$ the value of our strategy is given by V_{n+1}. The value of this, from the point of view of time n, is then (at least intuitively) given by the conditional expectation $E\left[V_{n+1} \,|\, \mathcal{F}_n\right]$. More formally we argue as follows. The value, at time n, of using $\hat{\tau}_{n+1}$ is by definition given by $E\left[Z_{\hat{\tau}_{n+1}} \,\big|\, \mathcal{F}_n\right]$. Using iterated expectations we then obtain

$$E\left[Z_{\hat{\tau}_{n+1}} \,\big|\, \mathcal{F}_n\right] = E\left[E\left[Z_{\hat{\tau}_{n+1}} \,\big|\, \mathcal{F}_{n+1}\right] \,\big|\, \mathcal{F}_n\right] = E\left[V_{n+1} \,|\, \mathcal{F}_n\right].$$

We now compare S1 with S2 and S3. Since S1 by definition is the optimal one, the value of this strategy is at least as high as the value of S2 and S3. We thus have the trivial inequalities

$$V_n \geq Z_n, \tag{21.6}$$

$$V_n \geq E\left[V_{n+1} \,|\, \mathcal{F}_n\right]. \tag{21.7}$$

We now make the simple but important observation that at time n we have only two possibilities for the optimal stopping time $\hat{\tau}_n$: It is either optimal to stop immediately, in which case we have $\hat{\tau}_n = n$ and $V_n = Z_n$, or else it is optimal not to stop at time n, in which case $\hat{\tau}_n = \hat{\tau}_{n+1}$ and $V_n = E\left[V_{n+1} \middle| \mathcal{F}_n\right]$. We thus have the equation

$$V_n = \max\left\{Z_n, E\left[V_{n+1} \middle| \mathcal{F}_n\right]\right\}.$$

We have thus more or less proved our first result.

Proposition 21.7 *The optimal value process V is the solution of the following backward recursion.*

$$V_n = \max\left\{Z_n, E\left[V_{n+1} \middle| \mathcal{F}_n\right]\right\}, \tag{21.8}$$
$$V_T = Z_T. \tag{21.9}$$

Furthermore, it is optimal to stop at time n if and only if $V_n = Z_n$. If stopping at n is not optimal, then $V_n > Z_n$ and $V_n = E\left[V_{n+1} \middle| \mathcal{F}_n\right]$.

Proof This is obvious from the arguments given above.   □

We note that the recursion above implicitly defines the optimal stopping strategy. We know that $V_n = Z_n$ if and only if it is optimal to stop at n, and that $V_n > Z_n$ if and only if it is optimal to continue. Thus the optimal stopping policy is to stop the first time the optimal value process equals the payoff process.

Proposition 21.8 *The following hold:*

- *An optimal stopping rule $\hat{\tau}$ at time $t = 0$ is given by*

$$\hat{\tau} = \min\left\{n \geq 0: V_n = Z_n\right\}. \tag{21.10}$$

- *For a fixed n an optimal stopping time $\hat{\tau}_n$ is given by*

$$\hat{\tau}_n = \min\left\{k \geq n: V_k = Z_k\right\}. \tag{21.11}$$

- *For any n we have*

$$V_{\hat{\tau}_n} = Z_{\hat{\tau}_n}. \tag{21.12}$$

Remark 21.4.1 Note that an optimal stopping time will always exist in discrete time when $T < \infty$. It does not, however, need to be unique. The stopping time in (21.10) is in fact the smallest optimal stopping time.

We will now study the optimal value process in some more detail. To do this we need some new definitions.

Definition 21.9 *Consider a fixed process Y.*

- *We say that a process X **dominates** the process Y if $X_n \geq Y_n$ $P - a.s.$ for all n.*
- *Assuming that $E\left[Y_n\right] < \infty$ for all $n \leq T$, the **Snell Envelope** S, of the process Y is defined as the smallest supermartingale dominating Y. More precisely: S is a supermartingale dominating Y, and if D is another supermartingale dominating Y, then $S_n \leq D_n$ $P - a.s.$ for all n.*

It is not obvious that the Snell envelope exists, but existence does in fact follow from the following result, the proof of which is left to the reader.

Proposition 21.10 *Let* $\{D^\alpha\}_{\alpha \in A}$ *be a family of supermartingales, indexed by* α. *The the process* X, *defined by*

$$X_n = \inf_{\alpha \in A} D_n^\alpha$$

is a supermartingale.

Using this result we can easily prove the existence of a Snell envelope.

Proposition 21.11 *Consider a process* Y *with* $E[Y_n] < \infty$ *for all* $n \leq T$. *Then there exists a Snell envelope for* Y.

Proof Define $\mathcal{D}$ as the family of supermartingales dominating Y. Now define S by

$$S_n = \inf_{D \in \mathcal{D}} D_n.$$

By the previous proposition, S will be a supermartingale. It will obviously dominate Y and by construction it will be minimal. □

Going back to the optimal value process V, we see from (21.6) that V dominates Z. Furthermore we see from (21.7) that V is a supermartingale, and in fact we have the following result.

Theorem 21.12 (The Snell Envelope Theorem) *The optimal value process* V *is the Snell envelope of the reward process* Z.

Proof Since V is a supermartingale dominating Z, in order to show that $V = S$ we only have to prove the minimality of V. Let us thus assume that X is a supermartingale dominating Z. We then have to show that $V_n \leq X_n$ for all n. For $n = T$ we have $V_T = Z_T$, and since X dominates Z we have $X_T \geq Z_T$, so obviously $X_T \geq V_T$. We then proceed by induction and thus assume that $X_{n+1} \geq V_{n+1}$. Since X is a supermartingale we have $X_n \geq E[X_{n+1}|\mathcal{F}_n]$ so by the induction assumption we have $X_n \geq E[V_{n+1}|\mathcal{F}_n]$. Furthermore we know that X dominates Z so we have $X_n \geq Z_n$, and we thus obtain the inequality

$$X_n \geq \max\{Z_n, E[V_{n+1}|\mathcal{F}_n]\}.$$

Using (21.8) we conclude that $X_n \geq V_n$. □

Since V is a supermartingale we have $E[V_{n+1}|\mathcal{F}_n] \leq V_n$, so V is decreasing in conditional average, and this has a rather clear economic interpretation in terms of missed opportunities. Indeed, if you are standing at n, then V_n is by definition the optimal expected value of the game. The expectation $E[V_{n+1}|\mathcal{F}_n]$ is the expected value of waiting until tomorrow, (and then using an optimal stopping strategy). If it *de facto* is optimal to stop already today, then obviously you lose something by waiting until tomorrow, and this loss is measured by the gap in the supermartingale inequality.

From this you also are led to expect that if it is **not** optimal to stop at time n, then $E[V_{n+1} | \mathcal{F}_n] = V_n$, i.e. the V process should be a martingale on the interval $[n, n+1]$. This intuition is formalized by the result below, that says that V is indeed a martingale until the optimal stopping time, but first we need another definition.

Definition 21.13 *For any process X, and any stopping time τ, the* **stopped process** X^τ *is defined by*

$$X_n^\tau = X_{n \wedge \tau}, \quad n = 0, 1, \ldots, T.$$

where we have used the notation $a \wedge b = \min\{a, b\}$.

We also need two small standard results, the proofs of which are left to the reader.

Proposition 21.14 *Assume the process X is a supermartingale on a finite time interval $[0, T]$. Then the following hold:*

- *If τ is a stopping time, then the stopped process X^τ is a supermartingale.*
- *If $E[X_T] = X_0$, then X is in fact a martingale.*

The basic result is now the following.

Proposition 21.15 *Consider a fixed n. Then the stopped process $V^{\hat{\tau}_n}$ is a martingale on the interval $[n, T]$.*

Proof WLOG (without loss of generality) we may assume that $n = 0$, and we denote the optimal stopping time $\hat{\tau}_0$ by $\hat{\tau}$. Since V is a supermartingale it follows that also $V^{\hat{\tau}}$ is a supermartingale, and it is enough to show that $V_0 = E\left[V_T^{\hat{\tau}}\right]$. This follows from the following equalities

$$V_0 = E[Z_{\hat{\tau}}] = E[V_{\hat{\tau}}] = E[V_{\hat{\tau} \wedge T}] = E\left[V_T^{\hat{\tau}}\right].$$

$\square$

21.4.2 Markovian Models

In this section we will restrict ourselves to Markovian models. This will lead to greater analytical tractability, and we consider the simplest possible model. More precisely we consider a model driven by a finite state Markov chain X on the state space $\mathcal{X} = \{1, \ldots, N\}$ and we assume that the optimal stopping problem is of the form

$$\max_{0 \leq \tau \leq T} E\left[\alpha^\tau g\left(X_\tau\right)\right], \tag{21.13}$$

where the discount factor α is a real number with $\alpha < 1$, and g is a mapping $g : \mathcal{X} \to R$.

We assume furthermore that X is time homogeneous with transition matrix $\mathbf{A}$, i.e.

$$\mathbf{A}_{i,j} = P(X_{n+1} = j \,|\, X_n = i) \tag{21.14}$$

In this setting, the optimal value process V_n at time n will be a deterministic function of X_n and with a slight abuse of notation we denote this function also by V_n so we have $V_n = V_n(X_n)$.

We now need to introduce some useful notational conventions. We start by noting that any real valued function f defined on $\mathcal{X}$, i.e. $f : \mathcal{X} \to R$ is completely specified by its values $f(1), \ldots, f(N)$ on $\mathcal{X}$. We can thus view f as a vector in R^N, and we will regard it as the column vector

$$f = \begin{bmatrix} f(1) \\ f(2) \\ \vdots \\ f(N) \end{bmatrix}.$$

We can also view X as a process living on the set of unit vectors in R^N, so that instead of writing $X_n = i$ we write $X_n = e_i$ where e_i is the $i : th$ unit column vector in R^N. This implies that, for a fixed n, we can write the random variable $f(X_n)$ as

$$f(X_n) = f^\star X_n,$$

where * denotes transpose. In particular, we can write a conditional expectation of the form $E[f(X_{n+1})|\, X_n]$ as

$$E[f(X_{n+1})|\, X_n] = g(X_n)$$

where the function g on vector form is given by

$$g = \mathbf{A}f.$$

With this notation, the recursion from Proposition 21.7 reads as follows.

Proposition 21.16 *The optimal value functions $V_1, \ldots, V_T$ are determined by the recursion*

$$V_n = \max\left[\alpha^n g, \mathbf{A}V_{n+1}\right],$$
$$V_T = \alpha^T g,$$

where the maximum is interpreted component wise.

In a model with discounted payoffs like the present one it is natural to slightly redefine the optimal value function. We thus define an alternative optimal value function W by

$$W_n = \alpha^{-n}V_n.$$

This simply means that the W function is the optimal value for the problem

$$\underset{n \leq \tau \leq T}{\text{maximize}} \ E\left[\alpha^{\tau-n} g(X_\tau) \middle| X_n\right]$$

and we have the recursion

$$W_n = \max\left[g, \alpha \mathbf{A} W_{n+1}\right], \tag{21.15}$$
$$W_T = g. \tag{21.16}$$

21.4.3 Infinite Horizon

We now relax the assumption of having a finite time horizon and consider the infinite horizon problem

$$\underset{\tau \geq 0}{\text{maximize}} \ E\left[\alpha^\tau g(X_\tau) \middle| X_0\right] \tag{21.17}$$

With some extra effort it can be shown that most of the results of the preceeding sections still hold, and we summarize as follows.

Proposition 21.17 *Define the optimal value function by*

$$V_n = \sup_{\tau \geq n} E\left[\alpha^\tau g(X_\tau) \middle| X_n\right].$$

Then the following hold:

- *The optimal value process $V_n(X_n)$ is the smallest supermartingale dominating the process $\alpha^n g(X_n)$.*
- *V satisfies the recursion*

$$V_n = \max\left[\alpha^n g, \mathbf{A} V_{n+1}\right] \tag{21.18}$$

- *The optimal stopping time $\hat{\tau}_n$ is given by*

$$\hat{\tau}_n = \inf\left\{k \geq n; \ V_k(X_k) = \alpha^k g(X_k)\right\}. \tag{21.19}$$

We note that as opposed to the finite horizon case, we no longer have a boundary value at T, so it is not clear how to carry out the infinite recursion (21.18). More about this later.

In the present setting we may express the proposition above in pure function-theoretic language. To do this we need a definition.

Definition 21.18 *A function sequence $\{f_0, f_1, f_2, \ldots\}$ where $f_n : \mathcal{X} \to R$, is called **excessive** if it satisfies the relation*

$$f_n \geq \mathbf{A} f_{n+1}, \quad n = 0, 1, \ldots \tag{21.20}$$

The sequence is called α-**excessive** if

$$f_n \geq \alpha \mathbf{A} f_{n+1}, \quad n = 0, 1, \ldots \tag{21.21}$$

We can now reformulate Proposition 21.17 as follows.

Proposition 21.19 *With notation as above, the optimal value function sequence V_n is the smallest excessive function sequence dominating the sequence $\alpha^n g$.*

In the infinite horizon setting, the alternative optimal value process W, defined in the previous section as

$$W_n = \sup_{\tau \geq n} E\left[\alpha^{\tau-n} g(X_\tau) \mid X_n\right] \tag{21.22}$$

is much nicer to handle than the function sequence V. The reason for this is that because of the assumed time homogeneity of the process X and the infinite horizon, the function $W_n(i)$ will in fact not depend on running time n. Thus we can write $W_n(i) = W(i)$ where W is the **optimal value function**, and from (21.15) we obtain the recursion

$$W = \max\left[g, \alpha \mathbf{A} W\right].$$

It is also clear from the time invariance, that the state space $\mathcal{X}$ will be divided into two regions, the **continuation region** C and the **stopping region** S such that whenever $X_n \in C$ it is optimal to continue the game, whereas we stop immediately if $X_n \in S$. We now have the following result.

Proposition 21.20 *For the infinite horizon case the following hold:*

- *The optimal value function sequence W_n is time invariant, so $W_n = W$ for $n = 1, 2, \ldots$, and in particular we have*

$$W(i) = \sup_{\tau \geq 0} E\left[\alpha^\tau g(X_\tau) \mid X_0 = i\right], \quad i = 1, \ldots, N. \tag{21.23}$$

- *W satisfies the recursion*

$$W = \max\left[g, \alpha \mathbf{A} W\right]. \tag{21.24}$$

- *The function W is the smallest α-excessive function dominating the function g.*
- *The continuation region $C \in \mathcal{X}$ is given by*

$$C = \{i \in \mathcal{X}; \ W(i) > g(i)\}. \tag{21.25}$$

- *The stopping region S is given by*

$$S = \{i \in \mathcal{X}; \ W(i) = g(i)\}. \tag{21.26}$$

- *An optimal stopping time is given by*

$$\hat{\tau} = \inf \left\{ k \geq 0; \ W(X_k) = g(X_k) \right\}. \tag{21.27}$$

As we noted above, it is not immediately clear how to compute the optimal value function W. We know that it satisfies the recursion (21.24) but it is not obvious how to solve this equation. The good news is that the W function can in fact be computed numerically with a very fast algorithm. To see this we recall that W is the smallest α-excessive function dominating g. W will therefore be the optimal solution of the following finite dimensional optimization problem

$$\underset{W}{\text{minimize}} \ \sum_{i=1}^{N} W(i) \tag{21.28}$$

subject to the constraints

$$W \geq g, \tag{21.29}$$

$$W - \alpha \mathbf{A} W \geq 0. \tag{21.30}$$

Here we can obviously replace the sum $\sum_{i=1}^{n} W(i)$ by any sum of the form $\sum_{i=1}^{n} c(i) W(i)$ where $c(1), \ldots, c(N)$ are positive.

The point is that the optimization problem above is a **Linear Programming Problem**. Using standard software this problem can be solved in a fraction of a second even for very large values of N.

21.5 Continuous Time

We now turn to the continuous time theory. As can be expected, this is technically more complicated than the discrete time theory, and we will only present some of the main ideas. We will often sweep technical problems under the carpet by assuming "enough regularity", and we refer the reader to the specialist literature for technical details and precise formulations.

21.5.1 *General Theory*

The setup in continuous time is that we consider a given semimartingale Z, on a finite time interval $[0, T]$, satisfying the integrability condition

$$\sup_{0 \leq \tau \leq T} E\left[|Z_\tau|\right] < \infty. \tag{21.31}$$

The problem to be solved is again the following:

$$\underset{0 \leq \tau \leq T}{\text{maximize}} \ E\left[Z_\tau\right]. \tag{21.32}$$

As before we embed this in a wider class of problems by defining the optimal value process V by

$$V_t = \sup_{t \leq \tau \leq T} E\left[Z_\tau | \mathcal{F}_t\right] \tag{21.33}$$

and we denote an optimal stopping time (which does not necessarily exist) for this problem by $\hat{\tau}_t$. The main results from discrete time now carry over to continuous time. The arguments are basically the same as in Section 21.4.1 but it should be noted that in continuous time there are a number of quite hard technical problems to handle. We do not go into these problems here, but refer the reader to the extremely well written Appendix D on optimal stopping in Karatzas and Shreve (1998).

We recall the definition of the Snell envelope.

Definition 21.21 *Consider a fixed process Y.*

- *We say that a process X **dominates** the process Y if $X_t \geq Y_t$ $P - a.s.$ for all $t \geq 0$.*
- *Assuming that $E[Y_t] < \infty$ the **Snell Envelope** S, of the process Y is defined as the smallest supermartingale dominating Y. More precisely: S is a supermartingale dominating Y, and if D is another supermartingale dominating Y, then $S_t \leq D_t$, $P - a.s.$ for all $t \geq 0$.*

As in discrete time we do have existence of a Snell envelope.

Proposition 21.22 *For any integrable semimartingale Y, the Snell envelope exists.*

The proof of this result is more complicated than in discrete time since we can no longer rely on the simple recursion results from Section 21.4.1. We thus have to use a different technique, and the reader is again referred to Karatzas and Shreve (1998). In continuous time there are also some other nontrivial technical complications. For example; since the optimal value process V is defined by $V_t = \sup_{t \leq \tau \leq T} E\left[Z_\tau | \mathcal{F}_t\right]$, where the *sup* denotes the essential supremum, this implies that for each fixed t, the process value V_t is only defined P-a.s. It is now a rather hard problem to show that we can choose a version of the V process which is cadlag, i.e. right continuous and with left limits.

The basic optimal stopping theorem mirrors the one in discrete time.

Theorem 21.23 (The Snell Envelope Theorem) *Given the integrability condition (21.31) the following hold:*

- *The optimal value process V is the Snell envelope of the payoff process Z.*
- *If there exists a (not necessarily unique) optimal stopping time, then the smallest one is given by*

$$\hat{\tau}_t = \inf\left\{s \geq t;\ V_s = Z_s\right\}. \tag{21.34}$$

- *For any fixed t, the stopped process $V^{\hat{\tau}_t}$ is a martingale on the interval $[t, T]$.*

21.5.2   *Diffusion Models*

We now specialize the general model of the previous section to a diffusion setting by considering the SDE

$$dX_t = \mu(t, X_t)dt + \sigma(t, X_t)dW_t. \tag{21.35}$$

For simplicity we assume that X is scalar, but the theory extends in an obvious way to vector valued SDEs. We also consider a given payoff function $\Phi(t, x)$, i.e. $\Phi : [0, T] \times R \to R$, and we study the optimal stopping problem

$$\max_{0 \le \tau \le T} E\left[\Phi(\tau, X_\tau)\right]. \tag{21.36}$$

We attack this problem by dynamic programming, i.e. we embed the original problem within a large class of problems indexed by t and x. We then connect these problems by a PDE, which in our case turns out to be a so-called **free boundary value problem**. It should again be emphasized that we are sweeping a number of technical problems (mostly concerning regularity) under the carpet.

Definition 21.24 *For a fixed $(t, x) \in [0, T] \times R$, and each stopping time τ with $\tau \ge t$, the* **value function** *J is defined by*

$$J(t, x; \tau) = E_{t,x}\left[\Phi(\tau, X_\tau)\right]. \tag{21.37}$$

The **optimal value function** *$V(t, x)$ is defined by*

$$V(t, x) = \sup_{t \le \tau \le T} E_{t,x}\left[\Phi(\tau, X_\tau)\right] = \sup_{t \le \tau \le T} J(t, x; \tau). \tag{21.38}$$

Here, as always, the lower index (t, x) indicates that the expected value is obtained by integrating over the measure induced by the SDE

$$\begin{aligned} dX_s &= \mu(s, X_s)ds + \sigma(s, X_s)dW_s, \\ X_t &= x. \end{aligned}$$

A stopping time which realizes the supremum for V above is called **optimal** *and will be denoted by $\hat{\tau}_{tx}$. For brevity we will often suppress the x and denote it by $\hat{\tau}_t$.*

We now go to the dynamic programming argument, and to this end we fix (t, x) and a "small" time increment h, where later on $h \to 0$. We now consider three strategies:

Strategy 1: We use the optimal stopping strategy $\hat{\tau}_t$.
Strategy 2: We stop immediately.
Strategy 3: We do not stop at time t. Instead we wait until time $t + h$, and from time $t + h$ we behave optimally, i.e. we use the stopping time $\hat{\tau}_{t+h}$.

We will now compare these strategies, but before doing this, we need some *ad hoc* assumptions.

Assumption 21.5.1 *We assume the following.*

- *There exists an optimal stopping time $\hat{\tau}_{t,x}$ for each (t, x).*
- *The optimal value function V is "regular enough". More precisely we assume that $V \in C^{1,2}$.*
- *All processes below are "integrable enough", in the sense that expected values exist, stochastic integrals are true (instead of being merely local) martingales, etc.*

Comparing the three strategies S1,S2, and S3 above, we have the following results.

- The value of S1 is obviously given by $V(t, x)$.
- The value of S2 is obviously given by $\Phi(t, x)$.
- The value of S3 is given (why?) by $E_{t,x}[V(t + h, X_{t+h})]$.

Since, by definition, S1 is better than (or equal to) S2 and S3 we have the inequalities

$$V(t, x) \geq \Phi(t, x), \tag{21.39}$$

$$V(t, x) \geq E_{t,x}[V(t + h, X_{t+h})]. \tag{21.40}$$

Remark 21.5.1 If h is "small enough" then it seems to be clear, at least intuitively, that one of S2 and S3 is always optimal. In general it could of course be the case that it is optimal to stop in the interior of the interval $[t, t + h]$, but as $h \to 0$, such a strategy will be indistinguishable from S2. In other words: **In the limit, one of the inequalities (21.39)–(21.40) will be an equality**.

From the Itô formula we have

$$V(t + h, X_{t+h}) = V(t, x) + \int_t^{t+h} \left(\frac{\partial}{\partial s} + \mathbf{A} \right) V(s, X_s) ds \tag{21.41}$$

$$+ \int_t^{t+h} \sigma(s, X_s) \frac{\partial V}{\partial x}(s, X_s) dW_s, \tag{21.42}$$

where $\mathbf{A}$ is the usual Itô operator defined by

$$\mathbf{A}f(t, x) = \mu(t, x)\frac{\partial f}{\partial x}(t, x) + \frac{1}{2}\sigma^2(t, x)\frac{\partial^2 f}{\partial x^2}(t, x). \tag{21.43}$$

Plugging (21.42) into (21.40) we obtain

$$V(t, x) \geq V(t, x) + E_{t,x}\left[\int_t^{t+h} \left(\frac{\partial}{\partial s} + \mathbf{A} \right) V(s, X_s) ds \right]$$

$$+ E_{t,x}\left[\int_t^{t+h} \sigma(s, X_s)\frac{\partial V}{\partial x}(s, X_s) dW_s \right],$$

and, using the fact that the expected value of the stochastic integral will vanish, we have

$$E_{t,x} \left[\int_t^{t+h} \left(\frac{\partial}{\partial s} + \mathbf{A} \right) V(s, X_s) ds \right] \leq 0.$$

We may now divide by h and let $h \to 0$ to obtain

$$\left(\frac{\partial}{\partial t} + \mathbf{A} \right) V(t, x) \leq 0.$$

We thus see that the optimal value function has the two properties

$$V(t, x) \geq \Phi(t, x), \qquad (21.44)$$

$$\left(\frac{\partial}{\partial t} + \mathbf{A} \right) V(t, x) \leq 0. \qquad (21.45)$$

The arguments above do, however, provide more information than this. From Remark 21.5.1 we draw the following conclusion.

- It is optimal to stop at (t, x) if and only if

$$V(t, x) = \Phi(t, x),$$

  in which case

$$\left(\frac{\partial}{\partial t} + \mathbf{A} \right) V(t, x) < 0.$$

- It is optimal to continue if and only if

$$V(t, x) > \Phi(t, x),$$

  in which case

$$\left(\frac{\partial}{\partial t} + \mathbf{A} \right) V(t, x) = 0.$$

If we thus define the **continuation region** C by

$$C = \{(t, x); \; V(t, x) > \Phi(t, x)\}, \qquad (21.46)$$

we see that the structure of the optimal stopping rule is that it is optimal to stop at (t, x) if and only if $(t, x) \in C^c$, where ^{c} denotes the complement.

If, on the other hand, $(t, x) \in C$, then it is optimal to continue, which implies that the inequality (21.45) will be an equality, thus giving us the relation

$$\left(\frac{\partial}{\partial t} + \mathbf{A} \right) V(t, x) = 0, \quad (t, x) \in C.$$

If we now collect our heuristic arguments we have the following (somewhat imprecise) result.

Proposition 21.25 *If the optimal value function V is regular enough, the following hold.*

$$V(T, x) = \Phi(T, x), \tag{21.47}$$

$$V(t, x) \geq \Phi(t, x), \quad \forall(t, x), \tag{21.48}$$

$$V(t, x) = \Phi(t, x), \quad (t, x) \in C^c, \tag{21.49}$$

$$\left(\frac{\partial}{\partial t} + \mathbf{A} \right) V(t, x) \leq 0, \quad \forall(t, x), \tag{21.50}$$

$$\left(\frac{\partial}{\partial t} + \mathbf{A} \right) V(t, x) = 0, \quad (t, x) \in C. \tag{21.51}$$

Here C^c denotes the complement of C. Furthermore, given (t, x), the optimal stopping time $\hat{\tau}_{t,x}$ is given by

$$\hat{\tau}_{t,x} = \inf \left\{ s \geq t; \ V(s, X_s) = \Phi(s, X_s) \right\}. \tag{21.52}$$

The big problem with our heuristic result above is that it is very hard to give reasonable conditions on μ, σ, and Φ which guarantee that V is regular enough. It may easily happen that, even for seemingly very natural choices of μ, σ, and Φ, V is not $C^{1,2}$, and in many cases V is not even C^1 in the x variable across the boundary ∂C. The moral of this is that if we want to study optimal stopping problems rigorously, then we need a much more complicated technical machinery, and the reader is referred to the specialist literature.

We can in fact reformulate Proposition 21.25 in the following way.

Proposition 21.26 *Given enough regularity, the optimal value function is characterized by the following relations.*

$$V(T, x) = \Phi(T, x), \tag{21.53}$$

$$V(t, x) \geq \Phi(t, x), \quad \forall(t, x), \tag{21.54}$$

$$\left(\frac{\partial}{\partial t} + \mathbf{A} \right) V(t, x) \leq 0, \quad \forall(t, x), \tag{21.55}$$

$$\max \left\{ V(t, x) - \Phi(t, x), \left(\frac{\partial}{\partial t} + \mathbf{A} \right) V(t, x) \right\} = 0, \quad \forall(t, x) \tag{21.56}$$

The point of this reformulation as a set of **variational inequalities** is that the continuation region C does not appear.

We note that from Proposition 21.25 above, it follows that on C the optimal value function solves a boundary value problem.

Proposition 21.27 *Assuming enough regularity, the optimal value function satisfies the following parabolic equation.*

$$\frac{\partial V}{\partial t}(t, x) + \mu(t, x) \frac{\partial V}{\partial x}(t, x) + \frac{1}{2} \sigma^2(t, x) \frac{\partial^2 V}{\partial x^2}(t, x) = 0, \quad (t, x) \in C,$$

$$V(t, x) = \Phi(t, x), \quad (t, x) \in \partial C.$$

The PDE above is known as a **free boundary value problem**, because of the fact that the domain C and its boundary ∂C are not given a priori but have to be determined as a part of the solution. Generally speaking, there is little hope of having an analytical solution of a free boundary value problem, so typically one has to resort to numerical schemes.

Remark 21.5.2 When trying to solve the free boundary value problem above, it is common to add the condition that V should be smooth, not only in the interior of C, but that it should also be C^1 at the boundary of C. This is called a **smooth fit condition**, and it is a largely heuristic condition, which does not necessarily hold. See Peskir and Shiryaev (2006) for details.

Although it is generally very hard to determine the continuation region C, there is an easily applicable partial result.

Proposition 21.28 *It is never optimal to stop at a point where*

$$\frac{\partial \Phi}{\partial t}(t,x) + \mu(t,x)\frac{\partial \Phi}{\partial x}(t,x) + \frac{1}{2}\sigma^2(t,x)\frac{\partial^2 \Phi}{\partial x^2}(t,x) > 0. \tag{21.57}$$

Expressed otherwise, we have

$$\left\{ (t,x); \; \left(\frac{\partial}{\partial t} + \mathbf{A}\right)\Phi(t,x) > 0 \right\} \subseteq C. \tag{21.58}$$

Proof   If the condition (21.57) is satisfied, then the process $\Phi(t, X_t)$ is a submartingale close to (t, x) and it is therefore optimal to continue.   □

We note that the inclusion in (21.58) is generally a strict one, i.e. it can be optimal to continue also at points outside the set in the left-hand side of (21.58).

21.5.3 *Connections to the General Theory*

The connections between the free boundary value formulation in the previous section and the general Snell theory are more or less obvious. The inequality (21.48) says that the optimal value process $V(t, X_t)$ dominates the reward process $\Phi(t, X_t)$, and (21.50) says that $V(t, X_t)$ is a supermartingale. The relation (21.51) or, alternatively, the free boundary value formulation, is a differential statement of the fact that the stopped optimal value process is a martingale.

21.6   American Options

We now specialize the theory to study the pricing of American options.

21.6.1 *The American Call Without Dividends*

We recall from Section 7.8 that for an American call on an underlying stock without dividends, early exercise is never optimal, so the American call price will in fact coincide with the European call price. In Section 7.8 we provided an elementary proof of this, but we can also use our formal theory to derive the same result. The optimal stopping problem is

$$\text{maximize} \quad E^Q \left[e^{-r\tau} \max\{S_\tau - K, 0\} \right] \qquad (21.59)$$
$$\substack{0 \leq \tau \leq T}$$

where the stock price dynamics under the risk neutral measure Q are given by

$$dS_t = rS_t dt + \sigma_t S_t dW_t. \qquad (21.60)$$

Here r is the short rate (assumed to be positive), and σ is an arbitrary adapted process. In terms of the general theory, this means that the reward process Z is given by

$$Z_t = e^{-rt} \max\{S_t - K, 0\} = \max\{e^{-rt}S_t - e^{-rt}K, 0\}.$$

We now note that, from arbitrage theory, the process $e^{-rt}S_t$ is a Q-martingale, whereas the "process" $e^{-rt}K$ is a deterministic decreasing function of time and hence a supermartingale. The process $e^{-rt}S_t - e^{-rt}K$ is thus a Q-submartingale. Since the mapping $x \longrightarrow \max\{x, 0\}$ is convex and increasing we see that the reward process Z is a convex and increasing function of a submartingale and thus, according to Proposition 21.5, Z is itself a submartingale. Hence the optimal stopping problem is trivial, with optimal stopping time given by $\hat{\tau} = T$.

21.6.2   The American Put Option

If we specialize the arguments from the previous sections to the case of an American put option with last exercise day T and strike price K, within a Black–Scholes model, this implies that we are considering an optimal stopping problem of the form

$$\text{maximize} \quad E^Q \left[e^{-r\tau} \max\{K - S_\tau, 0\} \right]. \qquad (21.61)$$
$$\substack{0 \leq \tau \leq T}$$

Here Q denotes the risk neutral measure, and the Q dynamics of S are again given by

$$dS_t = rS_t dt + S_t \sigma dW_t. \qquad (21.62)$$

Because of the discounting factor it is convenient to define a slightly modified optimal value function V by

$$V(t, x) = \sup_{t \leq \tau \leq T} E^Q_{t,x} \left[e^{-r(\tau - t)} \max\{K - S_\tau, 0\} \right].$$

With this notation we have the following basic result for the American put.

Proposition 21.29 *Assume that a sufficiently regular function $V(t, s)$, and an open set $C \subseteq R_+ \times R_+$, satisfies the following conditions.*

1. C has a continuously differentiable boundary b_t, i.e. $b \in C^1$ and $(t, b_t) \in \partial\, C$.
2. V satisfies the PDE

$$\frac{\partial V}{\partial t} + rs\frac{\partial V}{\partial s} + \frac{1}{2}s^2\sigma^2\frac{\partial^2 V}{\partial s^2} - rV = 0, \quad (t, s) \in C. \tag{21.63}$$

3. V satisfies the final time boundary condition

$$V(T, s) = \max\left[K - s, 0\right], \quad s \in R_+. \tag{21.64}$$

4. V satisfies the inequality

$$V(t, s) > \max\left[K - s, 0\right], \quad (t, s) \in C. \tag{21.65}$$

5. V satisfies

$$V(t, s) = \max\left[K - s, 0\right], \quad (t, s) \in C^c. \tag{21.66}$$

6. V satisfies the **smooth fit condition**

$$\lim_{s\downarrow b(t)} \frac{\partial V}{\partial s}(t, s) = -1, \quad 0 \le t < T. \tag{21.67}$$

Then the following hold:
- V is the optimal value function.
- C is the continuation region.
- The optimal stopping time is given by

$$\hat{\tau} = \inf\left\{t \ge 0;\ S_t = b_t\right\}. \tag{21.68}$$

There is of course also an alternative characterization of the optimal value function in terms of a set of variational inequalities.

There is a large literature on the American put, but there are no analytical formulas for the pricing function or the optimal boundary. For practical use, the following alternatives are available

- Solve the free boundary value problem numerically.
- Solve the variational inequalities numerically.
- Approximate the Black–Scholes model by a binomial model and compute the exact binomial American put price.

21.6.3   The Perpetual American Put

As we have seen, optimal stopping problems are notoriously difficult to solve analytically. One happy exception is (within the Black–Scholes model) the perpetual American put, i.e. an American put with infinite time horizon. This option is fairly simple to analyze, since the infinite horizon and the time invariance of the stock price dynamics implies that the option price as well as the optimal boundary are constant as functions of running time.

From economic arguments it is reasonable to expect that there exists a (constant) critical price b such that we exercise the option whenever $S_t \leq b$. Since the optimal value function (i.e. the pricing function) $V(t, s)$ in this case will be independent of running time t and thus of the form $V(t, s) = V(s)$ we see that the free boundary value problem for V reduces to the ODE

$$rs\frac{\partial V}{\partial s} + \frac{1}{2}s^2\sigma^2\frac{\partial^2 V}{\partial s^2} - rV = 0, \quad s > b. \tag{21.69}$$

We now want to find a function V and a real number b such that V and b satisfies (21.69). It is not hard to see that the general solution of the ODE is of the form

$$V(s) = As + Bs^{-\gamma}, \tag{21.70}$$

where γ is given by

$$\gamma = \frac{2r}{\sigma^2}. \tag{21.71}$$

Since V must be bounded as $s \to \infty$ (why?) it follows directly that $A = 0$. We then use the boundary condition and the smooth fit condition:

$$V(b) = K - b,$$
$$\frac{\partial V}{\partial s}(b+) = -1$$

From this we easily deduce the following result.

Proposition 21.30 *For a perpetual American put with strike K, the pricing function V and the critical price b are given by*

$$b = \frac{\gamma K}{1 + \gamma} \tag{21.72}$$

$$V(s) = \frac{K}{1 + \gamma}\left(\frac{b}{s}\right)^\gamma, \quad s > b. \tag{21.73}$$

21.7   Exercises

Exercise 21.1 Prove that, in discrete time, random time τ is a stopping time if and only if $\{\tau = n\} \in \mathcal{F}_n$ for all n.

Exercise 21.2 Construct a (trivial) example in continuous time, of an optimal stopping problem for which there is no optimal stopping time.

Exercise 21.3 Prove Proposition 21.2.

Exercise 21.4 Prove Proposition 21.3.

Exercise 21.5 Prove Proposition 21.4.

Exercise 21.6 Prove Proposition 21.5.

Exercise 21.7 Let f and g be concave functions. Show that h defined by $h(x) = \min\{f(x), g(x)\}$ is concave.

Exercise 21.8 Let X and Y be supermartingales. Show that Z defined by

$$Z_n(\omega) = \min\{X_n(\omega), Y_n(\omega)\}$$

is a supermartingale. Compare with the previous exercise and with the relations between martingale theory and convex theory given in Section 21.3.

Exercise 21.9 Prove Proposition 21.14.

Exercise 21.10 Assume a standard Black–Scholes model for the stock price and assume that $r = 0$. In this (highly unrealistic) case, one can easily solve the American put problem on a finite time hiorizon $[0, T]$. Do this.

Exercise 21.11 Consider an ODE of the form

$$f(s) + asf'(s) + bs^2 f''(s) = 0.$$

Introduce a new variable x by $x = \ln(s)$. Show that the ODE by this change of variable will be transformed into a linear ODE with constant coefficients. More precisely, find the ODE satisfied by the function F, defined by $F(x) = f(e^x)$, i.e. $f(s) = F(\ln s)$.

Exercise 21.12 Consider the ODE (21.69). Use the transformation in the previous exercise to show that the ODE has a general solution of the form (21.70).

Exercise 21.13 Prove Proposition 21.30.

21.8   Notes

The basic paper on the Snell envelope is Snell (1952). A standard reference is Shiryaev (2008), and the monograph Peskir and Shiryaev (2006) is an almost encyclopedic text on optimal stopping theory with finance applications. In Karatzas and Shreve (1998) there is a detailed discussion of American options, and Appendix D contains an extremely well written account of the Snell theory for continuous time processes. A precise and very readable introduction to optimal stopping problems can be found in Øksendal (1998).

22

BONDS AND INTEREST RATES

22.1 Zero Coupon Bonds

In this chapter we will begin to study the particular problems which appear when we try to apply arbitrage theory to the bond market. The primary objects of investigation are **zero coupon bonds**, also known as **pure discount bonds**, of various maturities. All payments are assumed to be made in a fixed currency which, for convenience, we choose to be US dollars.

Definition 22.1 *A* **zero coupon bond** *with* **maturity date** T, *also called a* T*-bond, is a contract which guarantees the holder 1 dollar to be paid on the date* T. *The price at time* t *of a bond with maturity date* T *is denoted by* $p(t, T)$.

The convention that the payment at the time of maturity, known as the **principal value** or **face value**, equals one is made for computational convenience. **Coupon bonds**, which give the owner a payment stream during the interval $[0, T]$ are treated below. These instruments have the common property, that they provide the owner with a deterministic cash flow, and for this reason they are also known as **fixed income** instruments.

We now make an assumption to guarantee the existence of a sufficiently rich and regular bond market.

Assumption 22.1.1 *We assume the following:*

- *There exists a (frictionless) market for* T*-bonds for every* $T > 0$.
- *The relation* $p(t, t) = 1$ *holds for all* t.
- *For each fixed* t, *the bond price* $p(t, T)$ *is differentiable w.r.t. time of maturity* T.

Note that the relation $p(t, t) = 1$ above is necessary in order to avoid arbitrage. The bond price $p(t, T)$ is thus a stochastic object with two variables, t and T, and, for each outcome in the underlying sample space, the dependence upon these variables is very different.

- For a fixed value of t, $p(t, T)$ is a function of T. This function provides the prices, at the fixed time t, for bonds of all possible maturities. The graph of this function is called "the bond price curve at t", or "the term structure at t". Typically it will be a very smooth graph, i.e. for each t, $p(t, T)$ will be differentiable w.r.t. T. The smoothness property is in fact a part of our assumptions above, but this is mainly for convenience. All models to be considered below will automatically produce smooth bond price curves.
- For a fixed maturity T, $p(t, T)$ (as a function of t) will be a scalar stochastic process. This process gives the prices, at different times, of the bond with

fixed maturity T, and the trajectory will typically be very irregular (like a Wiener process).

We thus see that (our picture of) the bond market is different from any other market that we have considered so far, in the sense that the bond market contains an infinite number of assets (one bond type for each time of maturity). The basic goal in interest rate theory is roughly that of investigating the relations between all these different bonds. Somewhat more precisely we may pose the following general problems, to be studied below:

- What is a reasonable model for the bond market above?
- Which relations must hold between the price processes for bonds of different maturities, in order to guarantee an arbitrage free bond market?
- Is it possible to derive arbitrage free bond prices from a specification of the dynamics of the short rate of interest?
- Given a model for the bond market, how do you compute prices of interest rate derivatives, such as a European call option on an underlying bond?

22.2 Interest Rates

22.2.1 Definitions

Given the bond market above, we may now define a number of interest rates, and the basic construction is as follows. Suppose that we are standing at time t, and let us fix two other points in time, S and T, with $t < S < T$. The immediate project is to write a contract at time t which allows us to make an investment of one (dollar) at time S, and to have a **deterministic** rate of return, determined at the contract time t, over the interval $[S, T]$. This can easily be achieved as follows:

1. At time t we sell one S-bond. This will give us $p(t, S)$ dollars.
2. We use this income to buy exactly $p(t, S)/p(t, T)$ T-bonds. Thus our net investment at time t equals zero.
3. At time S the S-bond matures, so we are obliged to pay out one dollar.
4. At time T the T-bonds mature at one dollar a piece, so we will receive the amount $p(t, S)/p(t, T)$ dollars.
5. The net effect of all this is that, based on a contract at t, an investment of one dollar at time S has yielded $p(t, S)/p(t, T)$ dollars at time T.
6. Thus, at time t, we have made a contract guaranteeing a **riskless** rate of interest over the **future interval** $[S, T]$. Such an interest rate is called a **forward rate**.

We now go on to compute the relevant interest rates implied by the construction above. We will use two (out of many possible) ways of quoting forward rates, namely as continuously compounded rates or as simple rates.

The **simple** forward rate (or **LIBOR** rate) L, is the solution to the equation

$$1 + (T - S)L = \frac{p(t, S)}{p(t, T)},$$

whereas the **continuously compounded** forward rate R is the solution to the equation

$$e^{R(T-S)} = \frac{p(t,S)}{p(t,T)}.$$

The simple rate notation is the one used in the market, whereas the continuously compounded notation is used in theoretical contexts. They are of course logically equivalent, and the formal definitions are as follows.

Definition 22.2

1. *The simple* **forward rate for** $[S,T]$ **contracted at** t, *henceforth referred to as the* **LIBOR** *forward rate, is defined as*

$$L(t; S, T) = -\frac{p(t,T) - p(t,S)}{(T-S)p(t,T)}.$$

2. *The simple* **spot rate for** $[S,T]$, *henceforth referred to as the* **LIBOR** *spot rate, is defined as*

$$L(S, T) = -\frac{p(S,T) - 1}{(T-S)p(S,T)}.$$

3. *The continuously compounded* **forward rate for** $[S,T]$ **contracted at** t *is defined as*

$$R(t; S, T) = -\frac{\log p(t,T) - \log p(t,S)}{T-S}.$$

4. *The* **continuously compounded spot rate,** $R(S,T)$, *for the period* $[S,T]$ *is defined as*

$$R(S, T) = -\frac{\log p(S,T)}{T-S}.$$

5. *The* **instantaneous forward rate with maturity** T, **contracted at** t, *is defined by*

$$f(t, T) = -\frac{\partial \log p(t,T)}{\partial T}.$$

6. *The instantaneous* **short rate at time** t *is defined by*

$$r(t) = f(t, t).$$

We note that spot rates are forward rates where the time of contracting coincides with the start of the interval over which the interest rate is effective i.e. $t = S$. The instantaneous forward rate, which will be of great importance below, is the limit of the continuously compounded forward rate when $S \to T$. It can thus be interpreted as the riskless rate of interest, contracted at t, over the infinitesimal interval $[T, T + dT]$.

We now go on to define the money account process B.

Definition 22.3 *The* **money account** *process is defined by*

$$B_t = \exp\left\{\int_0^t r(s)ds\right\},$$

i.e.

$$\begin{cases} dB(t) = r(t)B(t)dt, \\ B(0) = 1. \end{cases}$$

The interpretation of the money account is the same as before, i.e. you may think of it as describing a bank with a stochastic short rate of interest. It can also be shown (see below) that investing in the money account is equivalent to investing in a self-financing "rolling over" trading strategy, which at each time t consists entirely of "just maturing" bonds, i.e. bonds which will mature at $t+dt$.

As an immediate consequence of the definitions we have the following useful formulas.

Lemma 22.4 *For $t \leq s \leq T$ we have*

$$p(t,T) = p(t,s) \cdot \exp\left\{-\int_s^T f(t,u)du\right\},$$

and in particular

$$p(t,T) = \exp\left\{-\int_t^T f(t,s)ds\right\}.$$

If we wish to make a model for the bond market, it is obvious that this can be done in many different ways.

- We may specify the dynamics of the short rate (and then perhaps try to derive bond prices using arbitrage arguments).
- We may directly specify the dynamics of all possible bonds.
- We may specify the dynamics of all possible forward rates, and then use Lemma 22.4 in order to obtain bond prices.

All these approaches are of course related to each other, and we now go on to present a small "toolbox" of results to facilitate the analysis below. These results will not be used until Chapter 25, and the proofs are somewhat technical, so the next two subsections can be omitted at a first reading.

22.2.2 *Relations between $df(t,T)$, $dp(t,T)$ and $dr(t)$*

We will consider dynamics of the following form:

Short rate dynamics

$$dr(t) = a(t)dt + b(t)dW(t). \tag{22.1}$$

Bond price dynamics

$$dp(t,T) = p(t,T)m(t,T)dt + p(t,T)v(t,T)dW(t). \qquad (22.2)$$

Forward rate dynamics

$$df(t,T) = \alpha(t,T)dt + \sigma(t,T)dW(t). \qquad (22.3)$$

The Wiener process W is allowed to be vector valued, in which case the volatilities $v(t,T)$ and $\sigma(t,T)$ are row vectors. The processes $a(t)$ and $b(t)$ are scalar adapted processes, whereas $m(t,T)$, $v(t,T)$, $\alpha(t,T)$ and $\sigma(t,T)$ are adapted processes parameterized by time of maturity T. The interpretation of the bond price equation (22.2) and the forward rate equation (22.3) is that these are scalar stochastic differential equations (in the t-variable) for each fixed time of maturity T. Thus (22.2) and (22.3) are both infinite dimensional systems of SDEs.

We will study the formal relations which must hold between bond prices and interest rates, and to this end we need a number of technical assumptions, which we collect below in an "operational" manner.

Assumption 22.2.1

1. *For each fixed ω, t all the objects $m(t,T)$, $v(t,T)$, $\alpha(t,T)$ and $\sigma(t,T)$ are assumed to be continuously differentiable in the T-variable. This partial T-derivative is sometimes denoted by $m_T(t,T)$ etc.*
2. *All processes are assumed to be regular enough to allow us to differentiate under the integral sign as well as to interchange the order of integration.*

The main result is as follows. Note that the results below hold, regardless of the measure under consideration, and in particular we do **not** assume that markets are free of arbitrage.

Proposition 22.5

1. *If $p(t,T)$ satisfies (22.2), then for the forward rate dynamics we have*

$$df(t,T) = \alpha(t,T)dt + \sigma(t,T)dW(t),$$

where α and σ are given by

$$\begin{cases} \alpha(t,T) = v_T(t,T) \cdot v(t,T) - m_T(t,T), \\ \sigma(t,T) = -v_T(t,T). \end{cases} \qquad (22.4)$$

2. *If $f(t,T)$ satisfies (22.3) then the short rate satisfies*

$$dr(t) = a(t)dt + b(t)dW(t),$$

where

$$\begin{cases} a(t) = f_T(t,t) + \alpha(t,t), \\ b(t) = \sigma(t,t). \end{cases} \qquad (22.5)$$

3. *If $f(t,T)$ satisfies (22.3) then $p(t,T)$ satisfies*

$$dp(t,T) = p(t,T) \left\{ r(t) + A(t,T) + \frac{1}{2}\|S(t,T)\|^2 \right\} dt + p(t,T)S(t,T)dW(t),$$

where $\|\cdot\|$ denotes the Euclidean norm, and

$$\begin{cases} A(t,T) = -\displaystyle\int_t^T \alpha(t,s)ds, \\[2mm] S(t,T) = -\displaystyle\int_t^T \sigma(t,s)ds. \end{cases} \qquad (22.6)$$

Proof   The first part of the proposition is left to the reader (see the exercises). For the second part we integrate the forward rate dynamics to get

$$r(t) = f(0,t) + \int_0^t \alpha(s,t)ds + \int_0^t \sigma(s,t)dW(s). \qquad (22.7)$$

Now we can write

$$\alpha(s,t) = \alpha(s,s) + \int_s^t \alpha_T(s,u)du,$$

$$\sigma(s,t) = \sigma(s,s) + \int_s^t \sigma_T(s,u)du,$$

and, inserting this into (22.7), we have

$$r(t) = f(0,t) + \int_0^t \alpha(s,s)ds + \int_0^t \int_s^t \alpha_T(s,u)duds$$

$$+ \int_0^t \sigma(s,s)dW_s + \int_0^t \int_s^t \sigma_T(s,u)dudW_s.$$

Changing the order of integration and identifying terms we obtain the result.

For the proof of the third part we give a slightly heuristic argument. The full formal proof, see Heath *et al.* (1987), is an integrated version of the proof given here, but the infinitesimal version below is (hopefully) easier to understand. Using the definition of the forward rates we may write

$$p(t,T) = e^{Y(t,T)}, \qquad (22.8)$$

where Y is given by

$$Y(t,T) = -\int_t^T f(t,s)ds. \qquad (22.9)$$

From the Itô formula we then obtain the bond dynamics as

$$dp(t,T) = p(t,T)dY(t,T) + \frac{1}{2}p(t,T)\left(dY(t,T)\right)^2, \qquad (22.10)$$

and it remains to compute $dY(t,T)$. We have

$$dY(t,T) = -d\left(\int_t^T f(t,s)ds\right),$$

and the problem is that in the integral the t-variable occurs in two places: as th lower limit of integration, and in the integrand $f(t,s)$. This is a situation that i not covered by the standard Itô formula, but it is easy to guess the answer. Th t appearing as the lower limit of integration should give rise to the term

$$\frac{\partial}{\partial t}\left(\int_t^T f(t,s)ds\right)dt.$$

Furthermore, since the stochastic differential is a linear operation, we should b allowed to move it inside the integral, thus providing us with the term

$$\left(\int_t^T df(t,s)ds\right).$$

We have therefore arrived at

$$dY(t,T) = -\frac{\partial}{\partial t}\left(\int_t^T f(t,s)ds\right)dt - \int_t^T df(t,s)ds,$$

which, using the fundamental theorem of integral calculus, as well as the forwar rate dynamics, gives us

$$dY(t,T) = f(t,t)dt - \int_t^T \alpha(t,s)dtds - \int_t^T \sigma(t,s)dW_tds.$$

We now exchange dt and dW_t with ds and recognize $f(t,t)$ as the short rate $r(t)$ thus obtaining

$$dY(t,T) = r(t)dt + A(t,T)dt + S(t,T)dW_t,$$

with A and S as above. We therefore have

$$(dY(t,T))^2 = \|S(t,T)\|^2 dt,$$

and, substituting all this into (22.10), we obtain our desired result.   □

22.2.3 An Alternative View of the Money Account

The object of this subsection is to show (heuristically) that the risk free asse B can in fact be replicated by a self-financing strategy, defined by "rolling over just-maturing bonds. This is a "folklore" result, which is very easy to prove i discrete time, but surprisingly tricky in a continuous time framework.

Let us consider a self-financing portfolio which at each time t consists entirely of bonds maturing x units of time later (where we think of x as a small number). At time t the portfolio thus consists only of bonds with maturity $t + x$, so the value dynamics for this portfolio is given by

$$dV(t) = V(t) \cdot 1 \cdot \frac{dp(t, t+x)}{p(t, t+x)}, \qquad (22.11)$$

where the constant 1 indicates that the weight of the $t + x$-bond in the portfolio equals one. We now want to study the behavior of this equation as x tends to zero, and to this end we use Proposition 22.5 to obtain

$$\frac{dp(t, t+x)}{p(t, t+x)} = \left\{ r(t) + A(t, t+x) + \frac{1}{2} \|S(t, t+x)\|^2 \right\} dt + S(t, t+x) dW(t).$$

Letting x tend to zero, (22.6) gives us

$$\lim_{x \to 0} A(t, t+x) = 0,$$
$$\lim_{x \to 0} S(t, t+x) = 0.$$

Furthermore we have

$$\lim_{x \to 0} p(t, t+x) = 1,$$

and, substituting all this into eqn (22.11), we obtain the value dynamics

$$dV(t) = r(t)V(t)dt, \qquad (22.12)$$

which we recognize as the dynamics of the money account.

The argument thus presented is of course only heuristical, and it requires some hard work to make it precise. Note, for example, that the rolling over portfolio above does not fall into the general framework of self-financing portfolios, developed earlier. The problem is that, although at each time t, the portfolio only consists of one particular bond (maturing at $t + x$), over an arbitrary short time interval, the portfolio will use an infinite number of different bonds. In order to handle such a situation, we need to extend the portfolio concept to include measure valued portfolios. This is done in Björk *et al.* (1997a), and in Björk *et al.* (1997b) the argument above is made precise.

22.3   Coupon Bonds, Swaps and Yields

In most bond markets, there are only a relative small number of zero coupon bonds traded actively. The maturities for these are generally short (typically between half a year and two years), whereas most bonds with a longer time to maturity are coupon bearing. Despite this empirical fact we will still assume the existence of a market for all possible pure discount bonds, and we now go on to introduce and price coupon bonds in terms of zero coupon bonds.

22.3.1   Fixed Coupon Bonds

The simplest coupon bond is the **fixed coupon bond**. This is a bond which, at some intermediary points in time, will provide predetermined payments (coupons) to the holder of the bond. The formal description is as follows.

- Fix a number of dates, i.e. points in time, $T_0, \ldots, T_n$. Here T_0 is interpreted as the emission date of the bond, whereas $T_1, \ldots, T_n$ are the coupon dates.
- At time $T_i, i = 1, \ldots, n$, the owner of the bond receives the deterministic coupon c_i.
- At time T_n the owner receives the face value K.

We now go on to compute the price of this bond, and it is obvious that the coupon bond can be replicated by holding a portfolio of zero coupon bonds with maturities T_i, $i = 1, \ldots, n$. More precisely we will hold c_i zero coupon bonds of maturity T_i, $i = 1, \ldots, n-1$, and $K + c_n$ bonds with maturity T_n, so the price, $p(t)$, at a time $t < T_1$, of the coupon bond is given by

$$p(t) = K \cdot p(t, T_n) + \sum_{i=1}^{n} c_i \cdot p(t, T_i). \tag{22.13}$$

Very often the coupons are determined in terms of **return**, rather than in monetary (e.g. dollar) terms. The return for the ith coupon is typically quoted as a simple rate acting on the face value K, over the period $[T_{i-1}, T_i]$. Thus, if, for example, the ith coupon has a return equal to r_i, and the face value is K, this means that

$$c_i = r_i(T_i - T_{i-1})K.$$

For a standardized coupon bond, the time intervals will be equally spaced, i.e.

$$T_i = T_0 + i\delta,$$

and the coupon rates $r_1, \ldots, r_n$ will be equal to a common coupon rate r. The price $p(t)$ of such a bond will, for $t \leq T_1$, be given by

$$p(t) = K \left(p(t, T_n) + r\delta \sum_{i=1}^{n} p(t, T_i) \right). \tag{22.14}$$

22.3.2   Floating Rate Bonds

There are various coupon bonds for which the value of the coupon is not fixed at the time the bond is issued, but rather reset for every coupon period. Most often the resetting is determined by some financial benchmark, like a market interest rate, but there are also bonds for which the coupon is benchmarked against a nonfinancial index.

As an example (to be used in the context of swaps below), we will confine ourselves to discussing one of the simplest floating rate bonds , where the coupon rate r_i is set to the spot LIBOR rate $L(T_{i-1}, T_i)$. Thus

$$c_i = (T_i - T_{i-1})L(T_{i-1}, T_i)K,$$

and we note that $L(T_{i-1}, T_i)$ is determined already at time T_{i-1}, but that c_i is not delivered until at time T_i. We now go on to compute the value of this bond at some time $t < T_0$, in the case when the coupon dates are equally spaced, with $T_i - T_{i-1} = \delta$, and to this end we study the individual coupon c_i. Without loss of generality we may assume that $K = 1$, and inserting the definition of the LIBOR rate (Definition 22.2) we have

$$c_i = \delta \frac{1 - p(T_{i-1}, T_i)}{\delta p(T_{i-1}, T_i)} = \frac{1}{p(T_{i-1}, T_i)} - 1.$$

The value at t, of the term -1 (paid out at T_i), is of course equal to

$$-p(t, T_i),$$

and it remains to compute the value of the term $\frac{1}{p(T_{i-1}, T_i)}$, which is paid out at T_i.

This is, however, easily done through the following argument.

- Buy, at time t, one T_{i-1}-bond. This will cost $p(t, T_{i-1})$.
- At time T_{i-1} you will receive the amount 1.
- Invest this unit amount in T_i-bonds. This will give you exactly $\frac{1}{p(T_{i-1}, T_i)}$ bonds.
- At T_i the bonds will mature, each at the face value 1. Thus, at time T_i, you will obtain the amount

$$\frac{1}{p(T_{i-1}, T_i)}.$$

This argument shows that it is possible to replicate the cash flow above, using a self-financing bond strategy, to the initial cost $p(t, T_{i-1})$. Thus the value at t, of obtaining $\frac{1}{p(T_{i-1}, T_i)}$ at T_i, is given by $p(t, T_{i-1})$, and the value at t of the coupon c_i is

$$p(t, T_{i-1}) - p(t, T_i).$$

Summing up all the terms we finally obtain the following valuation formula for the floating rate bond

$$p(t) = p(t, T_n) + \sum_{i=1}^{n} [p(t, T_{i-1}) - p(t, T_i)] = p(t, T_0). \qquad (22.15)$$

In particular we see that if $t = T_0$, then $p(T_0) = 1$. The reason for this (perhaps surprisingly easy) formula is of course that the entire floating rate bond can be replicated through a self-financing portfolio (see the exercises).

22.3.3 *Interest Rate Swaps*

In this section we will discuss the simplest of all interest rate derivatives, the interest rate swap. This is basically a scheme where you exchange a payment stream at a fixed rate of interest, known as the **swap rate**, for a payment stream at a floating rate (typically a LIBOR rate).

There are many versions of interest rate swaps, and we will study the **forward swap settled in arrears**, which is defined as follows. We denote the principal by K, and the swap rate by R. By assumption we have a number of equally spaced dates $T_0, \ldots, T_n$, and payment occurs at the dates $T_1, \ldots, T_n$ (not at T_0). If you swap a fixed rate for a floating rate (in this case the LIBOR spot rate), then, at time T_i, you will receive the amount

$$K \delta L(T_{i-1}, T_i),$$

which is exactly $K c_i$, where c_i is the ith coupon for the floating rate bond in the previous section. At T_i you will pay the amount

$$K \delta R.$$

The net cash flow at T_i is thus given by

$$K \delta \left[L(T_{i-1}, T_i) - R \right],$$

and using our results from the floating rate bond, we can compute the value at $t < T_0$ of this cash flow as

$$K p(t, T_{i-1}) - K(1 + \delta R) p(t, T_i).$$

The total value $\Pi(t)$, at t, of the swap is thus given by

$$\Pi(t) = K \sum_{i=1}^{n} \left[p(t, T_{i-1}) - (1 + \delta R) p(t, T_i) \right],$$

and we can simplify this to obtain the following result.

Proposition 22.6 *The price, for $t < T_0$, of the swap above is given by*

$$\Pi(t) = K p(t, T_0) - K \sum_{i=1}^{n} d_i p(t, T_i),$$

where

$$d_i = R\delta, \quad i = 1, \ldots, n - 1,$$
$$d_n = 1 + R\delta.$$

The remaining question is how the swap rate R is determined. By definition it is chosen such that the value of the swap equals zero at the time when the contract is made. We have the following easy result.

Proposition 22.7 *If, by convention, we assume that the contract is written at* $t = 0$, *the swap rate is gven by*

$$R = \frac{p(0, T_0) - p(0, T_n)}{\delta \sum_1^n p(0, T_i)}.$$

In the case that $T_0 = 0$ *this formula reduces to*

$$R = \frac{1 - p(0, T_n)}{\delta \sum_1^n p(0, T_i)}.$$

22.3.4   *Yield and Duration*

Consider a zero coupon T-bond with market price $p(t, T)$. We now look for the bond's "internal rate of interest", i.e. the constant short rate of interest which will give the same value to this bond as the value given by the market. Denoting this value of the short rate by y, we thus want to solve the equation

$$p(t, T) = e^{-y \cdot (T-t)} \cdot 1,$$

where the factor 1 indicates the face value of the bond. We are thus led to the following definition.

Definition 22.8 *The continuously compounded* **zero coupon yield**, $y(t, T)$, *is given by*

$$y(t, T) = -\frac{\log p(t, T)}{T - t}.$$

For a fixed t, *the function* $T \longrightarrow y(t, T)$ *is called the (zero coupon)* **yield curve**.

We note that the yield $y(t, T)$ is nothing more than the spot rate for the interval $[t, T]$. Now let us consider a fixed coupon bond of the form discussed in Section 22.3.1 where, for simplicity of notation, we include the face value in the coupon c_n. We denote its market value at t by $p(t)$. In the same spirit as above we now look for its internal rate of interest, i.e. the constant value of the short rate, which will give the market value of the coupon bond.

Definition 22.9 *The* **yield to maturity**, $y(t, T)$, *of a fixed coupon bond at time* t, *with market price* p, *and payments* c_i *at* T_i *for* $i = 1, \ldots, n$, *is defined as the value of* y *which solves the equation*

$$p(t) = \sum_{i=1}^n c_i e^{-y(T_i - t)}.$$

An important concept in bond portfolio management is the "Macaulay duration". Without loss of generality we may assume that $t = 0$.

Definition 22.10 *For the fixed coupon bond above, with price p at t = 0, and yield to maturity y, the* **duration**, *D, is defined as*

$$D = \frac{\sum_1^n T_i c_i e^{-yT_i}}{p}.$$

The duration is thus a weighted average of the coupon dates of the bond where the discounted values of the coupon payments are used as weights, and it will in a sense provide you with the "mean time to coupon payment". As such it is an important concept, and it also acts a measure of the sensitivity of the bond price w.r.t. changes in the yield. This is shown by the following obvious result.

Proposition 22.11 *With notation as above we have*

$$\frac{dp}{dy} = \frac{d}{dy} \left\{ \sum_1^n c_i e^{-yT_i} \right\} = -D \cdot p. \tag{22.16}$$

Thus we see that duration is essentially for bonds (w.r.t. yield) what delta (see Section 9.2) is for derivatives (w.r.t. the underlying price). The bond equivalent of the gamma is **convexity**, which is defined as

$$C = \frac{\partial^2 p}{\partial y^2}.$$

22.4 Exercises

Exercise 22.1 A **forward rate agreement** (FRA) is a contract, by convention entered into at $t = 0$, where the parties (a lender and a borrower) agree to let a certain interest rate, $R^\star$, act on a prespecified principal, K, over some future period $[S, T]$. Assuming that the interest rate is continuously compounded, the cash flow to the lender is, by definition, given as follows:

- At time S: $-K$.
- At time T: $K e^{R^\star(T-S)}$.

The cash flow to the borrower is of course the negative of that to the lender.

(a) Compute for any time $t < S$, the value, $\Pi(t)$, of the cash flow above in terms of zero coupon bond prices.
(b) Show that in order for the value of the FRA to equal zero at $t = 0$, the rate $R^\star$ has to equal the forward rate $R(0; S, T)$ (compare this result to the discussion leading to the definition of forward rates).

Exercise 22.2 Prove the first part of Proposition 22.5.
   Hint: Apply the Itô formula to the process $\log p(t, T)$, write this in integrated form and differentiate with respect to T.

Exercise 22.3 Consider a coupon bond, starting at T_0, with face value K coupon payments at $T_1, \ldots, T_n$ and a fixed coupon rate r. Determine the coupon rate r, such that the price of the bond, at T_0, equals its face value.

Exercise 22.4 Derive the pricing formula (22.15) directly, by constructing a self-financing portfolio which replicates the cash flow of the floating rate bond.

Exercise 22.5 Let $\{y(0,T); T \geq 0\}$ denote the zero coupon yield curve at $t = 0$. Assume that, apart from the zero coupon bonds, we also have exactly one fixed coupon bond for every maturity T. We make no particular assumptions about the coupon bonds, apart from the fact that all coupons are positive, and we denote the yield to maturity, again at time $t = 0$, for the coupon bond with maturity T, by $y_M(0,T)$. We now have three curves to consider: the forward rate curve $f(0,T)$, the zero coupon yield curve $y(0,T)$, and the coupon yield curve $y_M(0,T)$. The object of this exercise is to see how these curves are connected.

(a) Show that

$$f(0,T) = y(0,T) + T \cdot \frac{\partial y(0,T)}{\partial T}.$$

(b) Assume that the zero coupon yield curve is an increasing function of T. Show that this implies the inequalities

$$y_M(0,T) \leq y(0,T) \leq f(0,T), \quad \forall T,$$

(with the opposite inequalities holding if the zero coupon yield curve is decreasing). Give a verbal economic explanation of the inequalities.

Exercise 22.6 Prove Proposition 22.11.

Exercise 22.7 Consider a **consol bond**, i.e. a bond which will forever pay one unit of cash at $t = 1, 2, \ldots$. Suppose that the market yield y is constant for all maturities.

(a) Compute the price, at $t = 0$, of the consol.
(b) Derive a formula (in terms of an infinite series) for the duration of the consol.
(c) Use (a) and Proposition 22.11 in order to compute an analytical formula for the duration.
(d) Compute the convexity of the consol.

22.5 Notes

Fabozzi (2009) and Sundaresan (2009) are standard textbooks on bond markets.

23

SHORT RATE MODELS

23.1 Generalities

In this chapter we turn to the problem of how to model an arbitrage free family of zero coupon bond price processes $\{p(\cdot, T); T \geq 0\}$.

Since, at least intuitively, the price, $p(t, T)$, should in some sense depend upon the behavior of the short rate of interest over the interval $[t, T]$, a natural starting point is to give an a priori specification of the dynamics of the short rate of interest. This has in fact been the "classical" approach to interest rate theory, so let us model the short rate, under the objective probability measure P, as the solution of an SDE of the form

$$dr(t) = \mu(t, r(t))dt + \sigma(t, r(t))d\bar{W}(t). \qquad (23.1)$$

The short rate of interest is the only object given a priori, so the only exogenously given asset is the money account, with price process B defined by the dynamics

$$dB(t) = r(t)B(t)dt. \qquad (23.2)$$

As usual we interpret this as a model of a bank with the stochastic short rate of interest r. The dynamics of B can then be interpreted as the dynamics of the value of a bank account. To be quite clear let us formulate the above as a formalized assumption.

Assumption 23.1.1 *We assume the existence of one exogenously given (locally risk free) asset. The price, B, of this asset has dynamics given by eqn (23.2), where the dynamics of r, under the objective probability measure P, are given by eqn (23.1).*

As in the previous chapter, we make an assumption to guarantee the existence of a sufficiently rich bond market.

Assumption 23.1.2 *We assume that there exists a market for zero coupon T-bonds for every value of T.*

We thus assume that our market contains all possible bonds (plus, of course, the risk free asset above). Consequently it is a market containing an infinite number of assets, but we again stress the fact that only the risk free asset is exogenously given. In other words, in this model the risk free asset is considered as the underlying asset whereas all bonds are regarded as derivatives of the "underlying" short rate r. Our main goal is broadly to investigate the relationship which must hold in an arbitrage free market between the price processes of bonds with different maturities. As a second step we also want to obtain arbitrage free prices for other interest rate derivatives such as bond options and interest rate swaps.

Since we view bonds as interest rate derivatives it is natural to ask whether the bond prices are uniquely determined by the given r dynamics in (23.1) and the condition that the bond market shall be free of arbitrage. This question, and its answer, are fundamental.

Question:

Are bond prices uniquely determined

by the P-dynamics of the short rate r?

Answer:

No!

For the reader who has studied Chapter 15, this negative result should be fairly obvious. The arguments below are parallel to those of Section 15.2, and the results are in fact special cases of the general results in Section 15.4. If you have already studied these sections you can thus browse quickly through the text until the term structure equation (23.2). In order to keep this part of the book self-contained, and since the discussion is so important, we will (with some apologies) give the full argument.

Let us start by viewing the bond market in the light of the meta-theorem 8.3.1. We see that in the present situation the number M of exogenously given traded assets **excluding** the risk free asset equals zero. The number R of random sources on the other hand equals one (we have one driving Wiener process). From the meta-theorem we may thus expect that the exogenously given market is arbitrage free but not complete. The lack of completeness is quite clear: since the only exogenously given asset is the risk free one we have no possibility of forming interesting portfolios. The only thing we can do on the a priori given market is simply to invest our initial capital in the bank and then sit down and wait while the portfolio value evolves according to the dynamics (23.2). It is thus impossible to replicate an interesting derivative, even such a simple one as a T-bond.

Another way of seeing this problem appears if we try to price a certain T-bond using the technique used in Section 7.3. In order to imitate the old argument we would assume that the price of a certain bond is of the form $F(t, r(t))$.

Then we would like to form a risk free portfolio based on this bond and on the underlying asset. The rate of return of this risk free portfolio would then, by an arbitrage argument, have to equal the short rate of interest, thus giving us some kind of equation for the determination of the function F. Now, in the Black–Scholes model the underlying asset was the stock S, and at first glance this would correspond to r in the present situation. Here, however, we have the major difference between the Black–Scholes model and our present model. The short rate of interest r is **not** the price of a **traded** asset, i.e. there is no asset on the market whose price process is given by r. Thus it is meaningless to form a portfolio "based on r". Since there sometimes is a lot of confusion on this point let us elaborate somewhat. We observe then that the English word "price" can be used in two related but different ways.

The first way occurs in everyday (informal) speech, and in this context it is not unusual (or unreasonable) to say that the short rate of interest reflects the price of borrowing money in the bank. In particular we often say that it is expensive to borrow money if the rate of interest is high, and cheap when the rate of interest is low.

The second (formalized) use of the word "price" occurs when we are dealing with price systems in the context of, for example, general equilibrium theory. In this setting the word "price" has a much more precise and technical meaning than in everyday language. Firstly a price is now measured in a **unit** like, say, pounds sterling. The short rate of interest, on the contrary, is measured in the unit $(time)^{-1}$, though for numerical reasons it is sometimes given as a precentage. Secondly the price of an asset tells you how many pounds sterling you have to pay for one unit of the asset in question. If, say, the price of *ACME INC.* stock is 230 pounds this means that if you pay 230 pounds then you will obtain one share in *ACME INC.* If, on the other hand, the short rate of interest is 11%, this does **not** mean that you can pay 11 (units of what?) in order to obtain one unit of some asset (what would that be?).

This does not at all imply that the everyday interpretation of the interest rate as "the price of borrowing money" is wrong. This aspect of the short rate already appears in fact in the equation, $dB = rBdt$, for the money account, where it is obvious that if r is high, then our debt to the bank grows at a high rate.

When we use the word "price" in this text it is exclusively as in the second formalized meaning above, and a sloppy usage will easily lead to nonsense and chaos.

To sum up:

- The price of a particular bond will **not** be completely determined by the specification (23.1) of the r-dynamics and the requirement that the bond market is free of arbitrage.
- The reason for this fact is that arbitrage pricing is always a case of pricing a derivative **in terms of** the price of some underlying assets. In our market we do not have sufficiently many underlying assets.

We thus fail to determine a unique price of a particular bond. Fortunately this (perhaps disappointing) fact does not mean that bond prices can take any form whatsoever. On the contrary we have the following basic intuition.

Idea 23.1.1

- *Prices of bonds with **different** maturities will have to satisfy certain **internal consistency relations** in order to avoid arbitrage possibilities on the bond market.*
- *If we take the price of **one** particular "benchmark" bond as given then the prices of **all other** bonds (with maturity prior to the benchmark) will be uniquely determined **in terms of** the price of the benchmark bond (and the r-dynamics).*

This fact is in complete agreement with the meta-theorem, since in the a priori given market consisting of one benchmark bond plus the risk free asset we will have $R = M = 1$ thus guaranteeing completeness.

23.2   The Term Structure Equation

To make the ideas presented in the previous section more concrete we now begin our formal treatment.

Assumption 23.2.1 *We assume that there is a market for T-bonds for every choice of T and that the market is arbitrage free. We assume furthermore that, for every T, the price of a T-bond has the form*

$$p(t,T) = F(t, r(t); T), \tag{23.3}$$

where F is a smooth function of three real variables.

Conceptually it is perhaps easiest to think of F as a function of only two variables, namely r and t, whereas T is regarded as a parameter. Sometimes we will therefore write $F^T(t, r)$ instead of $F(t, r; T)$. The main problem now is to find out what F^T may look like on an arbitrage free market.

Just as in the case of stock derivatives we have a simple boundary condition. At the time of maturity a T-bond is of course worth exactly 1 pound, so we have the relation

$$F(T, r; T) = 1, \quad \text{for all } r. \tag{23.4}$$

Note that in the equation above the letter r denotes a real variable, while at the same time r is used as the name of the stochastic process for the short rate. To conform with our general notational principles we should really denote the stochastic process by a capital letter like R, and then denote an outcome of R by the letter r. Unfortunately the use of r as the name of the stochastic process seems to be so fixed that it cannot be changed. We will thus continue to use r as a name both for the process and for a generic outcome of the process. This is somewhat sloppy, but we hope that the meaning will be clear from the context.

In order to implement the ideas above we will now form a portfolio consisting of bonds having different times of maturity. We thus fix two times of maturity

S and T. From Assumption 23.2.1 and the Itô formula we get the following price dynamics for the T-bond, with corresponding equations for the S-bond.

$$dF^T = F^T \alpha_T dt + F^T \sigma_T d\bar{W}, \tag{23.5}$$

where, with subindices r and t denoting partial derivatives,

$$\alpha_T = \frac{F_t^T + \mu F_r^T + \frac{1}{2}\sigma^2 F_{rr}^T}{F^T}, \tag{23.6}$$

$$\sigma_T = \frac{\sigma F_r^T}{F^T}. \tag{23.7}$$

Denoting the relative portfolio by (u_S, u_T) we have the following value dynamics for our portfolio.

$$dV = V \left\{ u_T \frac{dF^T}{F^T} + u_S \frac{dF^S}{F^S} \right\}, \tag{23.8}$$

and inserting the differential from (23.5), as well as the corresponding equation for the S-bond, gives us, after some reshuffling of terms,

$$dV = V \cdot \{u_T \alpha_T + u_S \alpha_S\} \, dt + V \cdot \{u_T \sigma_T + u_S \sigma_S\} \, d\bar{W}. \tag{23.9}$$

Exactly as in Section 7.3 we now define our portfolio by the equations

$$u_T + u_S = 1, \tag{23.10}$$

$$u_T \sigma_T + u_S \sigma_S = 0. \tag{23.11}$$

With this portfolio the $d\bar{W}$-term in (23.9) will vanish, so the value dynamics reduce to

$$dV = V \cdot \{u_T \alpha_T + u_S \alpha_S\} \, dt. \tag{23.12}$$

The system (23.10)–(23.11) can easily be solved as

$$u_T = -\frac{\sigma_S}{\sigma_T - \sigma_S}, \tag{23.13}$$

$$u_S = \frac{\sigma_T}{\sigma_T - \sigma_S}, \tag{23.14}$$

and substituting this into (23.12) gives us

$$dV = V \cdot \left\{ \frac{\alpha_S \sigma_T - \alpha_T \sigma_S}{\sigma_T - \sigma_S} \right\} \, dt. \tag{23.15}$$

Using Proposition 7.6, the assumption of no arbitrage now implies that this portfolio must have a rate of return equal to the short rate of interest. Thus we have the condition

$$\frac{\alpha_S \sigma_T - \alpha_T \sigma_S}{\sigma_T - \sigma_S} = r(t), \quad \text{for all } t, \text{ with probability } 1, \tag{23.16}$$

or, written differently,

$$\frac{\alpha_S(t) - r(t)}{\sigma_S(t)} = \frac{\alpha_T(t) - r(t)}{\sigma_T(t)}. \tag{23.17}$$

The interesting fact about eqn (23.17) is that on the left-hand side we have a stochastic process which does not depend on the choice of T, whereas on the right-hand side we have a process which does not depend on the choice of S. The common quotient will thus not depend on the choice of either T or S, so we have thus proved the following fundamental result.

Proposition 23.1 *Assume that the bond market is free of arbitrage. Then there exists a process λ such that the relation*

$$\frac{\alpha_T(t) - r(t)}{\sigma_T(t)} = \lambda(t) \tag{23.18}$$

holds for all t and for every choice of maturity time T.

Observe that the process λ is **universal** in the sense that it is the same λ which occurs on the right-hand side of (23.18) regardless of the choice of T. Let us now take a somewhat closer look at this process.

In the numerator of (23.18) we have the term $\alpha_T(t) - r(t)$. By eqn (23.5), $\alpha_T(t)$ is the local rate of return on the T-bond, whereas r is the rate of return of the risk free asset. The difference $\alpha_T(t) - r(t)$ is thus the **risk premium** of the T-bond. It measures the excess rate of return for the risky T-bond over the riskless rate of return which is required by the market in order to avoid arbitrage possibilities. In the denominator of (23.18) we have $\sigma_T(t)$, i.e. the local volatility of the T-bond.

Thus we see that the process λ has the dimension "risk premium per unit of volatility". The process λ is known as the **market price of risk**, and we can paraphrase Proposition 23.1 by the following slogan:

- **In a no arbitrage market all bonds will, regardless of maturity time, have the same market price of risk.**

Before we move on, a brief word of warning: the name "market price of risk" is in some sense rather appealing and reasonable, but it is important to realize that the market price of risk is **not** a price in the technical (general equilibrium) sense reserved for the word "price" in the rest of this text. We do not measure λ in SEK, and λ is not something which we pay in order to obtain some commodity. Thus the usage of the word "price" in this context is that of informal everyday language, and one should be careful not to overinterpret the **words** "market price of risk" by assuming that properties holding for price processes in general equilibrium theory also automatically hold for the process λ.

We may obtain even more information from eqn (23.18) by inserting our earlier formulas (23.6)–(23.7) for α_T and σ_T. After some manipulation we then obtain one of the most important equations in the theory of interest rates—the so-called "term structure equation". Since this equation is so fundamental we formulate it as a separate result.

Proposition 23.2 (Term structure equation) *In an arbitrage free bond market, F^T will satisfy the term structure equation*

$$\begin{cases} F_t^T + \{\mu - \lambda\sigma\}\, F_r^T + \frac{1}{2}\sigma^2 F_{rr}^T - rF^T = 0, \\ \qquad\qquad\qquad\qquad\qquad F^T(T,r) = 1. \end{cases} \qquad (23.19)$$

The term structure equation is obviously closely related to the Black–Scholes equation, but it is a more complicated object due to the appearance of the market price of risk λ. It follows from eqns (23.6), (23.7) and (23.18) that λ is of the form $\lambda = \lambda(t,r)$ so the term structure equation is a standard PDE, but the problem is that λ is not determined within the model. In order to be able to solve the term structure equation we must specify λ exogenously just as we have to specify μ and σ.

Despite this problem it is not hard to obtain a Feynman–Kač representation of F^T. This is done by fixing (t,r) and then using the process

$$\exp\left\{-\int_t^s r(u)du\right\} F^T(s,r(s)). \qquad (23.20)$$

If we apply the Itô formula to (23.20) and use the fact that F^T satisfies the term structure equation then, by using exactly the same technique as in Section 5.5, we obtain the following stochastic representation formula.

Proposition 23.3 (Risk neutral valuation) *Bond prices are given by the formula $p(t,T) = F(t,r(t);T)$ where*

$$F(t,r;T) = E_{t,r}^Q\left[e^{-\int_t^T r(s)ds}\right]. \qquad (23.21)$$

Here the martingale measure Q and the subscripts t,r denote that the expectation shall be taken given the following dynamics for the short rate.

$$dr(s) = \{\mu - \lambda\sigma\}\, ds + \sigma dW(s), \qquad (23.22)$$
$$r(t) = r. \qquad (23.23)$$

The formula (23.21) has the usual natural economic interpretation, which is most easily seen if we write it as

$$F(t,r;T) = E_{t,r}^Q\left[e^{-\int_t^T r(s)ds} \times 1\right]. \qquad (23.24)$$

We see that the value of a T-bond at time t is given as the expected value of the final payoff of one pound, discounted to present value. The deflator used is the natural one, namely $\exp\left\{-\int_t^T r(s)ds\right\}$, but we observe that the expectation is not to be taken using the underlying objective probability measure P. Instead we must, as usual, use the martingale measure Q and we see that we have different martingale measures for different choices of λ.

The main difference between the present situation and the Black–Scholes setting is that in the Black–Scholes model the martingale measure is uniquely determined. It can be shown (see Chapters 13 and 15) that the uniqueness of the martingale measure is due to the fact that the Black–Scholes model is complete. In the present case our exogenously given market is not complete, so bond prices will not be uniquely determined by the given (P-)dynamics of the short rate r. To express this fact more precisely, the various bond prices will be determined **partly** by the P-dynamics of the short rate of interest, and **partly** by market forces. The fact that there are different possible choices of λ simply means that there are different conceivable bond markets all of which are consistent with the given r-dynamics. Precisely which set of bond price processes will be realized by an actual market will depend on the relations between supply and demand for bonds in this particular market, and these factors are in their turn determined by such things as the forms of risk aversion possessed by the various agents on the market. In particular this means that if we make an *ad hoc* choice of λ (e.g. such as $\lambda = 0$) then we have implicitly made an assumption concerning the aggregate risk aversion on the market.

We can also turn the argument around and say that when the market has determined the dynamics of **one** bond price process, say with maturity T, then the market has indirectly specified λ by eqn (23.18). When λ is thus determined, all other bond prices will be determined by the term structure equation. Expressed in another way: all bond prices will be determined **in terms of** the basic T-bond and the short rate of interest. Again we see that arbitrage pricing always is a case of determining prices of derivatives **in terms of** some a priori given price processes.

There remains one important and natural question, namely how we ought to choose λ in a concrete case. This question will be treated in some detail, in Section 24.2, and the moral is that we must go to the actual market and, by using market data, infer the market's choice of λ.

The bonds treated above are of course contingent claims of a particularly simple type; they are deterministic. Let us close this section by looking at a more general type of contingent T-claim of the form

$$\mathcal{X} = \Phi(r(T)), \tag{23.25}$$

where Φ is some real valued function. Using the same type of arguments as above it is easy to see that we have the following result.

Proposition 23.4 (General term structure equation) *Let $\mathcal{X}$ be a contingent T-claim of the form $\mathcal{X} = \Phi(r(T))$. In an arbitrage free market the price $\Pi(t; \Phi)$ will be given as*

$$\Pi(t; \Phi) = F(t, r(t)), \tag{23.26}$$

SHORT RATE MODELS

where F solves the boundary value problem

$$\begin{cases} F_t + \{\mu - \lambda\sigma\} F_r + \frac{1}{2}\sigma^2 F_{rr} - rF = 0, \\ \qquad\qquad\qquad\qquad\qquad F(T,r) = \Phi(r). \end{cases} \tag{23.27}$$

Furthermore F has the stochastic representation

$$F(t,r;T) = E_{t,r}^Q \left[\exp\left\{ -\int_t^T r(s)ds \right\} \times \Phi(r(T)) \right], \tag{23.28}$$

where the martingale measure Q and the subscripts t, r denote that the expectation shall be taken using the following dynamics:

$$dr(s) = \{\mu - \lambda\sigma\} \, ds + \sigma dW(s), \tag{23.29}$$

$$r(t) = r. \tag{23.30}$$

23.3 Exercises

Exercise 23.1 We take as given an interest rate model with the following P-dynamics for the short rate.

$$dr(t) = \mu(t, r(t))dt + \sigma(t, r(t))d\bar{W}(t).$$

Now consider a T-claim of the form $\mathcal{X} = \Phi(r(T))$ with corresponding price process $\Pi(t)$.

(a) Show that, under any martingale measure Q, the price process $\Pi(t)$ has a local rate of return equal to the short rate of interest. In other words, show that the stochastic differential of $\Pi(t)$ is of the form

$$d\Pi(t) = r(t)\Pi(t) \, dt + \sigma_\Pi \Pi(t) \, dW(t).$$

(b) Show that the normalized price process

$$Z(t) = \frac{\Pi(t)}{B(t)}$$

is a Q-martingale.

Exercise 23.2 The object of this exercise is to connect the forward rates defined in Chapter 22 to the framework above.

(a) Assuming that we are allowed to differentiate under the expectation sign, show that

$$f(t,T) = \frac{E_{t,r(t)}^Q \left[r(T) \exp\left\{ -\int_t^T r(s)ds \right\} \right]}{E_{t,r(t)}^Q \left[\exp\left\{ -\int_t^T r(s)ds \right\} \right]}.$$

(b) Check that indeed $r(t) = f(t,t)$.

Exercise 23.3 (Swap a fixed rate vs. a short rate) Consider the following version of an interest rate swap. The contract is made between two parties, A and B, and the payments are made as follows:

- A (hypothetically) invests the principal amount K at time 0 and lets it grow at a fixed rate of interest R (to be determined below) over the time interval $[0, T]$.
- At time T the principal will have grown to K_A SEK. A will then subtract the principal amount and pay the surplus $K - K_A$ to B (at time T).
- B (hypothetically) invests the principal at the stochastic short rate of interest over the interval $[0, T]$.
- At time T the principal will have grown to K_B SEK. B will then subtract the principal amount and pay the surplus $K - K_B$ to A (at time T).

The **swap rate** for this contract is now defined as the value, R, of the fixed rate which gives this contract the value zero at $t = 0$. Your task is to compute the swap rate.

Exercise 23.4 (Forward contract) Consider a model with a stochastic rate of interest. Fix a T-claim $\mathcal{X}$ of the form $\mathcal{X} = \Phi(r(T))$, and fix a point in time t, where $t < T$. From Proposition 23.4 we can in principle compute the arbitrage free price for $\mathcal{X}$ if we pay at time t. We may also consider a **forward contract** (see Section 7.6.1) on $\mathcal{X}$ **contracted at** t. This contract works as follows, where we assume that you are the buyer of the contract.

- At time T you obtain the amount $\mathcal{X}$ SEK.
- At time T you pay the amount K SEK.
- The amount K is determined at t.

The **forward price for** $\mathcal{X}$ **contracted at** t is defined as the value of K which gives the entire contract the value zero at time t. Give a formula for the forward price.

23.4 Notes

The exposition in this chapter is standard. For further information, see the notes at the end of the next chapter.

24

MARTINGALE MODELS FOR THE SHORT RATE

24.1 Q-dynamics

Let us again study an interest rate model where the P-dynamics of the short rate of interest are given by

$$dr(t) = \mu(t, r(t))dt + \sigma(t, r(t))d\bar{W}. \tag{24.1}$$

As we saw in the previous chapter, the term structure (i.e. the family of bond price processes) will, together with all other derivatives, be completely determined by the general term structure equation

$$\begin{cases} F_t + \{\mu - \lambda\sigma\} F_r + \dfrac{1}{2}\sigma^2 F_{rr} - rF = 0, \\ \qquad\qquad\qquad\qquad\qquad F(T, r) = \Phi(r), \end{cases} \tag{24.2}$$

as soon as we have specified the following objects.

- The drift term μ.
- The diffusion term σ.
- The market price of risk λ.

Consider for a moment σ to be given a priori. Then it is clear from (24.2) that it is irrelevant exactly how we specify μ and λ *per se*. The object, apart from σ, that really determines the term structure (and all other derivatives) is the term $\mu - \lambda\sigma$ in eqn (24.2). Now, from Proposition 23.4 we recall that the term $\mu - \lambda\sigma$ is precisely the drift term of the short rate of interest under the martingale measure Q. This fact is so important that we stress it again.

Result 24.1.1 *The term structure, as well as the prices of all other interest rate derivatives, are completely determined by specifying the* **r-dynamics** **under the martingale measure** Q.

Instead of specifying μ and λ under the objective probability measure P we will henceforth specify the dynamics of the short rate r directly under the martingale meaure Q. This procedure is known as **martingale modeling**, and the typical assumption will thus be that r under Q has dynamics given by

$$dr(t) = \mu(t, r(t))dt + \sigma(t, r(t))dW(t), \tag{24.3}$$

where μ and σ are given functions. From now on the letter μ will thus always denote the drift term of the short rate of interest under the martingale measure Q.

In the literature there are a large number of proposals on how to specify the Q-dynamics for r. We present a (far from complete) list of the most popular models. If a parameter is time dependent this is written out explicitly. Otherwise all parameters are constant.

1. Vasiček
$$dr = (b - ar)\,dt + \sigma dW, \quad (a > 0), \tag{24.4}$$

2. Cox–Ingersoll–Ross (CIR)
$$dr = a\,(b - r)\,dt + \sigma\sqrt{r}dW, \tag{24.5}$$

3. Dothan
$$dr = ardt + \sigma rdW, \tag{24.6}$$

4. Black–Derman–Toy
$$dr = \Theta(t)rdt + \sigma(t)rdW, \tag{24.7}$$

5. Ho–Lee
$$dr = \Theta(t)dt + \sigma dW, \tag{24.8}$$

6. Hull–White (extended Vasiček)
$$dr = (\Theta(t) - a(t)r)\,dt + \sigma(t)dW, \quad (a(t) > 0), \tag{24.9}$$

7. Hull–White (extended CIR)
$$dr = (\Theta(t) - a(t)r)\,dt + \sigma(t)\sqrt{r}dW. \quad (a(t) > 0). \tag{24.10}$$

24.2 Inversion of the Yield Curve

Let us now address the question of how we will estimate the various model parameters in the martingale models above. To take a specific case, assume that we have decided to use the Vasiček model. Then we have to get values for a, b, and σ in some way, and a natural procedure would be to look in some textbook dealing with parameter estimation for SDEs. This procedure, however, is unfortunately completely nonsensical and the reason is as follows.

We have chosen to model our r-process by giving the Q-dynamics, which means that a, b and σ are the parameters which hold under the martingale measure Q. When we make observations in the real world we are **not** observing r under the martingale measure Q, but under the objective measure P. This means that if we apply standard statistical procedures to our observed data we will not get our Q-parameters. What we get instead is pure nonsense.

This looks extremely disturbing but the situation is not hopeless. It is in fact possible to show that the diffusion term is the same under P and under Q, so "in principle" it may be possible to estimate diffusion parameters using P-data. (The reader familiar with martingale theory will at this point recall that a Girsanov transformation will only affect the drift term of a diffusion but not the diffusion term.)

When it comes to the estimation of parameters affecting the drift term of r we have to use completely different methods.

From Section 15.6 we recall the following moral:

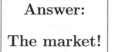

Thus, in order to obtain information about the Q-drift parameters we have to collect price information from the market, and the typical approach is that of **inverting the yield curve** which works as follows. (See the more detailed discussion in Section 15.6.)

- Choose a particular model involving one or several parameters. Let us denote the entire parameter vector by α. Thus we write the r-dynamics (under Q) as

$$dr(t) = \mu(t, r(t); \alpha)dt + \sigma(t, r(t); \alpha)dW(t). \qquad (24.11)$$

- Solve, for every conceivable time of maturity T, the term structure equation

$$\begin{cases} F_t^T + \mu F_r^T + \dfrac{1}{2}\sigma^2 F_{rr}^T - rF^T = 0, \\ \qquad\qquad\qquad F^T(T, r) = 1. \end{cases} \qquad (24.12)$$

In this way we have computed the theoretical term structure as

$$p(t, T; \alpha) = F^T(t, r; \alpha).$$

Note that the form of the term structure will depend upon our choice of parameter vector. We have not made this choice yet.

- Collect price data from the bond market. In particular we may today (i.e. at $t = 0$) observe $p(0, T)$ for all values of T. Denote this **empirical term structure** by $\{p^\star(0, T);\ T \geq 0\}$.
- Now choose the parameter vector α in such a way that the theoretical curve $\{p(0, T; \alpha);\ T \geq 0\}$ fits the empirical curve $\{p^\star(0, T);\ T \geq 0\}$ as well as possible (according to some objective function). This gives us our estimated parameter vector $\alpha^\star$.

- Insert $\alpha^\star$ into μ and σ. Now we have pinned down exactly which martingale measure we are working with. Let us denote the result of inserting $\alpha^\star$ into μ and σ by $\mu^\star$ and $\sigma^\star$ respectively.
- We have now pinned down our martingale measure Q, and we can go on to compute prices of interest rate derivatives, like, say, $\mathcal{X} = \Gamma(r(T))$. The price process is then given by $\Pi(t;\Gamma) = G(t, r(t))$ where G solves the term structure equation

$$\begin{cases} G_t + \mu^\star G_r + \dfrac{1}{2}[\sigma^\star]^2 G_{rr} - rG = 0, \\ \qquad\qquad G(T, r) = \Gamma(r). \end{cases} \tag{24.13}$$

If the above program is to be carried out within reasonable time limits it is of course of great importance that the PDEs involved are easy to solve. It turns out that some of the models above are much easier to deal with analytically than the others, and this leads us to the subject of so called **affine term structures**.

24.3 Affine Term Structures

24.3.1 Definition and Existence

Definition 24.1 *If the term structure* $\{p(t,T);\ 0 \le t \le T,\ T > 0\}$ *has the form*

$$p(t, T) = F(t, r(t); T), \tag{24.14}$$

where F has the form

$$F(t, r; T) = e^{A(t,T) - B(t,T)r}, \tag{24.15}$$

and where A and B are deterministic functions, then the model is said to possess an **affine term structure** *(ATS).*

The functions A and B above are functions of the two real variables t and T, but conceptually it is easier to think of A and B as being functions of t, while T serves as a parameter. It turns out that the existence of an affine term structure is extremely pleasing from an analytical and a computational point of view, so it is of considerable interest to understand when such a structure appears. In particular we would like to answer the following question:

- For which choices of μ and σ in the Q-dynamics for r do we get an affine term structure?

We will try to give at least a partial answer to this question, and we start by investigating some of the implications of an affine term structure. Assume then that we have the Q-dynamics

$$dr(t) = \mu(t, r(t))dt + \sigma(t, r(t))dW(t), \tag{24.16}$$

and assume that this model actually possesses an ATS. In other words we assume that the bond prices have the form (24.15) above. Using (24.15) we may easily compute the various partial derivatives of F, and since F must solve the term structure equation (23.19), we thus obtain

$$A_t(t,T) - \{1 + B_t(t,T)\} r - \mu(t,r)B(t,T) + \frac{1}{2}\sigma^2(t,r)B^2(t,T) = 0. \quad (24.17)$$

The boundary value $F(T,r;T) \equiv 1$ implies

$$\begin{cases} A(T,T) = 0, \\ B(T,T) = 0. \end{cases} \quad (24.18)$$

Equation (24.17) gives us the relations which must hold between A, B, μ and σ in order for an ATS to exist, and for a certain choice of μ and σ there may or may not exist functions A and B such that (24.17) is satisfied. Our immediate task is thus to give conditions on μ and σ which guarantee the existence of functions A and B solving (24.17). Generally speaking this is a fairly complex question, but we may give a very nice partial answer. We observe that if μ and σ^2 are both **affine** (i.e. linear plus a constant) functions of r, with possibly time dependent coefficients, then eqn (24.17) becomes a separable differential equation for the unknown functions A and B.

Assume thus that μ and σ have the form

$$\begin{cases} \mu(t,r) = \alpha(t)r + \beta(t), \\ \sigma(t,r) = \sqrt{\gamma(t)r + \delta(t)}. \end{cases} \quad (24.19)$$

Then, after collecting terms, (24.17) transforms into

$$A_t(t,T) - \beta(t)B(t,T) + \frac{1}{2}\delta(t)B^2(t,T)$$
$$- \left\{ 1 + B_t(t,T) + \alpha(t)B(t,T) - \frac{1}{2}\gamma(t)B^2(t,T) \right\} r = 0. \quad (24.20)$$

This equation holds for all t, T and r, so let us consider it for a fixed choice of T and t. Since the equation holds for all values of r the coefficient of r must be equal to zero. Thus we have the equation

$$B_t(t,T) + \alpha(t)B(t,T) - \frac{1}{2}\gamma(t)B^2(t,T) = -1. \quad (24.21)$$

Since the r-term in (24.20) is zero we see that the other term must also vanish, giving us the equation

$$A_t(t,T) = \beta(t)B(t,T) - \frac{1}{2}\delta(t)B^2(t,T). \quad (24.22)$$

We may thus formulate our main result.

Proposition 24.2 (Affine term structure) *Assume that μ and σ are of the form*

$$\begin{cases} \mu(t,r) = \alpha(t)r + \beta(t), \\ \sigma(t,r) = \sqrt{\gamma(t)r + \delta(t)}. \end{cases} \quad (24.23)$$

Then the model admits an ATS of the form (24.15), where A and B satisfy the system

$$\begin{cases} B_t(t,T) + \alpha(t)B(t,T) - \dfrac{1}{2}\gamma(t)B^2(t,T) = -1, \\ \qquad\qquad\qquad\qquad\qquad B(T,T) = 0. \end{cases} \quad (24.24)$$

$$\begin{cases} A_t(t,T) = \beta(t)B(t,T) - \dfrac{1}{2}\delta(t)B^2(t,T), \\ A(T,T) = 0. \end{cases} \quad (24.25)$$

We note that eqn (24.24) is a Riccati equation for the determination of B which does not involve A. Having solved eqn (24.24) we may then insert the solution B into eqn (24.25) and simply integrate in order to obtain A.

An interesting question is if it is only for an affine choice of μ and σ^2 that we get an ATS. This is not generally the case, but it can fairly easily be shown that if we demand that μ and σ^2 are time independent, then a necessary condition for the existence of an ATS is that μ and σ^2 are affine. Looking at the list of models in the previous section we see that all models except the Dothan and the Black–Derman–Toy models have an ATS.

24.3.2 A Probabilistic Discussion

There are good probabilistic reasons why some of the models in our list are easier to handle than others. We see that the models of Vasiček, Ho–Lee and Hull–White (extended Vasiček) all describe the short rate using a **linear** SDE. Such SDEs are easy to solve and the corresponding r-processes can be shown to be normally distributed. Now, bond prices are given by expressions like

$$p(0,T) = E\left[\exp\left\{ -\int_0^T r(s)ds \right\} \right], \quad (24.26)$$

and the normal property of r is inherited by the integral $\int_0^T r(s)ds$ (an integral is just a sum). Thus we see that the computation of bond prices for a model with a normally distributed short rate boils down to the easy problem of computing the expected value of a log-normal stochastic variable. This purely probabilistic program can in fact be carried out for all the linear models above (the interested reader is invited to do this), but it turns out that from a computational point of view it is easier to solve the system of equations (24.24)–(24.25).

In contrast with the linear models above, consider for a moment the Dothan model. This model for the short rate is the same as the Black–Scholes model for the underlying stock, so one is easily led to believe that computationally this is the nicest model conceivable. This is, however, not the case. For the Dothan model the short rate will be log-normally distributed, which means that in order to compute bond prices we are faced with determining the distribution of an integral $\int_0^T r(s)ds$ of log-normal stochastic variables. It is, however, a sad fact that a sum (or an integral) of log-normally distributed variables is a particularly nasty object, so this model leads to great computational problems. It also has the unreasonable property that the expected value of the money account equals plus infinity.

As for the Cox–Ingersoll–Ross model and the Hull–White extension, these models for the short rate are roughly obtained by taking the square of the solution of a linear SDE, and can thus be handled analytically (see the exercises for a simplified example). They are, however, quite a bit messier to deal with than the normally distributed models. See the notes.

From a computational point of view there is thus a lot to be said in favour of a linear SDE describing the short rate. The price we have to pay for these models is again the Gaussian property. Since the short rate will be normally distributed this means that for every t there is a positive probability that $r(t)$ is negative, and this is unreasonable from an economic point of view. For the Dothan model on the other hand, the short rate is log-normal and thus positive with probability 1. It is also possible to show that the Cox–Ingersoll–Ross model will produce a strictly positive short rate process. See Rogers (1995) for a discussion on these problems.

We end this section with a comment on the procedure of calibrating the model to data described in the previous section. If we want a complete fit between the theoretical and the observed bond prices this calibration procedure is formally that of solving the system of equations

$$p(0, T; \alpha) = p^\star(0, T) \quad \text{for all } T > 0. \tag{24.27}$$

We observe that this is an infinite dimensional system of equations (one equation for each T) with α as the unknown, so if we work with a model containing a finite parameter vector α (like the Vasiček model) there is no hope of obtaining a perfect fit. Now, one of the main goals of interest rate theory is to compute prices of various derivatives, like, for example, bond options, and it is well known that the price of a derivative can be very sensitive with respect to the price of the underlying asset. For bond options the underlying asset is a bond, and it is thus disturbing if we have a model for derivative pricing which is not even able to correctly price the underlying asset.

This leads to a natural demand for models which **can** be made to fit the observed bond data completely, and this is the reason why the Hull–White model has become so popular. In this model (and related ones) we introduce an infinite dimensional parameter vector α by letting some or all parameters be time dependent. Whether it is possible to actually solve the system (24.27) for a concrete model such as the Hull–White extension of the Vasiček model, and how this is to be done in detail, is of course not clear a priori but has to be dealt with in a deeper study. We carry out this study for the Hull–White model in the next section.

It should, however, be noted that the introduction of an infinite parameter, in order to fit the entire initial term structure, has its dangers in terms of numerical instability of the parameter estimates.

There is also a completely different approach to the problem of obtaining a perfect fit between today's theoretical bond prices and today's observed bond prices. This is the Heath–Jarrow–Morton approach which roughly takes the observed term structure as an initial condition for the forward rate curve, thus automatically obtaining a perfect fit. This model will be studied in the next chapter.

24.4 Some Standard Models

In this section we will apply the ATS theory above, in order to study the most common affine one factor models.

24.4.1 *The Vasiček Model*

To illustrate the technique we now compute the term structure for the Vasiček model

$$dr = (b - ar)\, dt + \sigma dW. \qquad (24.28)$$

Before starting the computations we note that this model has the property of being **mean reverting** (under Q) in the sense that it will tend to revert to the mean level b/a. The equations (24.24)–(24.25) become

$$\begin{cases} B_t(t,T) - aB(t,T) = -1, \\ \quad\quad\quad B(T,T) = 0. \end{cases} \qquad (24.29)$$

$$\begin{cases} A_t(t,T) = bB(t,T) - \dfrac{1}{2}\sigma^2 B^2(t,T), \\ A(T,T) = 0. \end{cases} \qquad (24.30)$$

Equation (24.29) is, for each fixed T, a simple linear ODE in the t-variable. It can easily be solved as

$$B(t,T) = \dfrac{1}{a}\left\{1 - e^{-a(T-t)}\right\}. \qquad (24.31)$$

Integrating eqn (24.30) we obtain

$$A(t,T) = \dfrac{\sigma^2}{2}\int_t^T B^2(s,T)ds - b\int_t^T B(s,T)ds, \qquad (24.32)$$

and, substituting the expression for B above, we obtain the following result.

Proposition 24.3 (The Vasiček term structure) *In the Vasiček model, bond prices are given by*

$$p(t,T) = e^{A(t,T) - B(t,T)r(t)},$$

where

$$B(t,T) = \frac{1}{a}\left\{1 - e^{-a(T-t)}\right\},$$

$$A(t,T) = \frac{\{B(t,T) - T + t\}\left(ab - \frac{1}{2}\sigma^2\right)}{a^2} - \frac{\sigma^2 B^2(t,T)}{4a}.$$

For the Vasiček model, there is also an explicit formula for European bond options. See Proposition 24.9 below.

24.4.2 The Ho–Lee Model

For the Ho–Lee model the ATS equations become

$$\begin{cases} B_t(t,T) = -1, \\ B(T,T) = 0. \end{cases}$$

$$\begin{cases} A_t(t,T) = \Theta(t)B(t,T) - \frac{1}{2}\sigma^2 B^2(t,T), \\ A(T,T) = 0. \end{cases}$$

These are easily solved as

$$B(t,T) = T - t,$$

$$A(t,T) = \int_t^T \Theta(s)(s-T)ds + \frac{\sigma^2}{2}\cdot\frac{(T-t)^3}{3}.$$

It now remains to choose Θ such that the theoretical bond prices, at $t = 0$, fit the observed initial term structure $\{p^\star(0,T); T \geq 0\}$. We thus want to find Θ such that $p(0,T) = p^\star(0,T)$ for all $T \geq 0$. This is left as an exercise, and the solution is given by

$$\Theta(t) = \frac{\partial f^\star(0,t)}{\partial T} + \sigma^2 t,$$

where $f^\star(0,t)$ denotes the observed forward rates. Plugging this expression into the ATS gives us the following bond prices.

Proposition 24.4 (The Ho–Lee term structure) *For the Ho–Lee model, the bond prices are given by*

$$p(t,T) = \frac{p^\star(0,T)}{p^\star(0,t)}\exp\left\{(T-t)f^\star(0,t) - \frac{\sigma^2}{2}t(T-t)^2 - (T-t)r(t)\right\}.$$

For completeness we also give the pricing formula for a European call on an underlying bond. We will not derive this result by solving the pricing PDE (this is in fact very hard), but instead we refer the reader to Chapter 26 where we will present a rather general option pricing formula (Proposition 26.11). It is then an easy exercise to obtain the result below as a special case.

Proposition 24.5 (Bond options) *For the Ho–Lee model, the price at* t, *of a European call option with strike price* K *and exercise date* T, *on an underlying* S-*bond, we have the following pricing formula:*

$$c(t, T, K, S) = p(t, S)N(d) - p(t, T) \cdot K \cdot N(d - \sigma_p), \qquad (24.33)$$

where

$$d = \frac{1}{\sigma_p} \log \left\{ \frac{p(t, S)}{p(t, T)K} \right\} + \frac{1}{2}\sigma_p, \qquad (24.34)$$

$$\sigma_p = \sigma(S - T)\sqrt{T}. \qquad (24.35)$$

24.4.3 The CIR Model

The CIR model is much more difficult to handle than the Vasiček model, since we have to solve a Riccati equation. We cite the following result.

Proposition 24.6 (The CIR term structure) *The term structure for the CIR model is given by*

$$F^T(t, r) = A_0(T - t)e^{-B(T-t)r},$$

where

$$B(x) = \frac{2(e^{\gamma x} - 1)}{(\gamma + a)(e^{\gamma x} - 1) + 2\gamma},$$

$$A_0(x) = \left[\frac{2\gamma e^{(a+\gamma)(x/2)}}{(\gamma + a)(e^{\gamma x} - 1) + 2\gamma} \right]^{2ab/\sigma^2},$$

and

$$\gamma = \sqrt{a^2 + 2\sigma^2}.$$

It is possible to obtain closed form expressions for European call options on zero coupon bonds within the CIR framework. Since these formulas are rather complicated, we refer the reader to Cox–Ingersoll–Ross (1985b).

24.4.4 The Hull–White Model

In this section we will make a fairly detailed study of a simplified version of the Hull–White extension of the Vasiček model. The Q-dynamics of the short rate are given by

$$dr = \{\Theta(t) - ar\} dt + \sigma dW(t), \qquad (24.36)$$

where a and σ are constants while Θ is a deterministic function of time. In this model we typically choose a and σ in order to obtain a nice volatility structure whereas Θ is chosen in order to fit the theoretical bond prices $\{p(0,T);\ T > 0\}$ to the observed curve $\{p^\star(0,T);\ T > 0\}$.

We have an affine structure so by Proposition 24.2 bond prices are given by

$$p(t,T) = e^{A(t,T)-B(t,T)r(t)}, \tag{24.37}$$

where A and B solve

$$\begin{cases} B_t(t,T) = aB(t,T) - 1, \\ B(T,T) = 0. \end{cases} \tag{24.38}$$

$$\begin{cases} A_t(t,T) = \Theta(t)B(t,T) - \dfrac{1}{2}\sigma^2 B^2(t,T), \\ A(T,T) = 0. \end{cases} \tag{24.39}$$

The solutions to these equations are given by

$$B(t,T) = \frac{1}{a}\left\{1 - e^{-a(T-t)}\right\}, \tag{24.40}$$

$$A(t,T) = \int_t^T \left\{\frac{1}{2}\sigma^2 B^2(s,T) - \Theta(s)B(s,T)\right\} ds. \tag{24.41}$$

Now we want to fit the theoretical prices above to the observed prices and it is convenient to do this using the forward rates. Since there is a one-to-one correspondence (see Lemma 22.4) between forward rates and bond prices, we may just as well fit the theoretical forward rate curve $\{f(0,T);\ T > 0\}$ to the observed curve $\{f^\star(0,T);\ T > 0\}$, where of course $f^\star$ is defined by $f^\star(t,T) = -\frac{\partial \log p^\star(t,T)}{\partial T}$. In any affine model the forward rates are given by

$$f(0,T) = B_T(0,T)r(0) - A_T(0,T), \tag{24.42}$$

which, after inserting (24.40)–(24.41), becomes

$$f(0,T) = e^{-aT}r(0) + \int_0^T e^{-a(T-s)}\Theta(s)ds - \frac{\sigma^2}{2a^2}\left(1 - e^{-aT}\right)^2. \tag{24.43}$$

Given an observed forward rate structure $f^\star$ our problem is to find a function Θ which solves the equation

$$f^\star(0,T) = e^{-aT}r(0) + \int_0^T e^{-a(T-s)}\Theta(s)ds - \frac{\sigma^2}{2a^2}\left(1 - e^{-aT}\right)^2, \quad \forall T > 0. \tag{24.44}$$

One way of solving (24.44) is to write it as

$$f^\star(0,T) = x(T) - g(T), \tag{24.45}$$

where x and g are defined by

$$\begin{cases} \dot{x} = -ax(t) + \Theta(t), \\ x(0) = r(0), \end{cases}$$

$$g(t) = \frac{\sigma^2}{2a^2}\left(1 - e^{-at}\right)^2 = \frac{\sigma^2}{2}B^2(0,t). \tag{24.46}$$

We now have

$$\Theta(T) = \dot{x}(T) + ax(T) = f_T^\star(0,T) + \dot{g}(T) + ax(T)$$
$$= f_T^\star(0,T) + \dot{g}(T) + a\left\{f^\star(0,T) + g(T)\right\}, \tag{24.47}$$

so we have in fact proved the following result.

Lemma 24.7 *Fix an arbitrary bond curve $\{p^\star(0,T); \ T > 0\}$, subject only to the condition that $p^\star(0,T)$ is twice differentiable w.r.t. T. Choosing Θ according to (24.47) will then produce a term structure $\{p(0,T); \ T > 0\}$ such that $p(0,T) = p^\star(0,T)$ for all $T > 0$.*

By choosing Θ according to (24.47) we have, for a fixed choice of a and σ, determined our martingale measure. Now we would like to compute the theoretical bond prices under this martingale measure, and in order to do this we have to substitute our choice of Θ into eqn (24.41). Then we perform the integration and substitute the result as well as eqn (24.40) into eqn (24.37). This leads to some exceedingly boring calculations which (of course) are left to the reader. The result is as follows.

Proposition 24.8 (The Hull–White term structure) *Consider the Hull–White model with a and σ fixed. Having inverted the yield curve by choosing Θ according to (24.47) we obtain the bond prices as*

$$p(t,T) = \frac{p^\star(0,T)}{p^\star(0,t)}\exp\left\{B(t,T)f^\star(0,t) - \frac{\sigma^2}{4a}B^2(t,T)\left(1 - e^{-2at}\right) - B(t,T)r(t)\right\}, \tag{24.48}$$

where B is given by (24.40).

We end this section by giving, for the Hull–White, as well as for the Vasiček model, the pricing formula for a European call option with time of maturity T and strike price K on an S-bond, where of course $T < S$. We denote this price by $c(t,T,K,S)$. At the present stage the reader is not encouraged to derive the formula below. In Chapter 26 we will instead present a technique which will greatly simplify computations of this kind, and the formula will be derived with relative ease in Section 26.6 (see Proposition 26.13). Note that the bond prices $p(t,T)$ and $p(t,S)$ below do not have to be computed at time t, since they can be observed directly on the market.

Proposition 24.9 (Bond options) *Using notation as above we have, both fo* *the Hull–White and the Vasiček models, the following bond option formula:*

$$c(t, T, K, S) = p(t, S)N(d) - p(t, T) \cdot K \cdot N(d - \sigma_p), \qquad (24.49)$$

where

$$d = \frac{1}{\sigma_p} \log \left\{ \frac{p(t, S)}{p(t, T)K} \right\} + \frac{1}{2}\sigma_p, \qquad (24.50)$$

$$\sigma_p = \frac{1}{a} \left\{ 1 - e^{-a(S-T)} \right\} \cdot \sqrt{\frac{\sigma^2}{2a} \left\{ 1 - e^{-2a(T-t)} \right\}}. \qquad (24.51)$$

24.5 Exercises

Exercise 24.1 Consider the Vasiček model, where we always assume that $a > 0$

(a) Solve the Vasiček SDE explicitly, and determine the distribution of $r(t)$
    Hint: The distribution is Gaussian (why?), so it is enough to comput
    the expected value and the variance.

(b) As $t \to \infty$, the distribution of $r(t)$ tends to a limiting distribution. Shov
    that this is the Gaussian distribution $N[b/a, \sigma/\sqrt{2a}]$. Thus we see that
    in the limit, r will indeed oscillate around its mean reversion level b/a.

(c) Now assume that $r(0)$ is a stochastic variable, independent of the Wiene
    process W, and by definition having the Gaussian distribution obtaine
    in (b). Show that this implies that $r(t)$ has the limit distribution in (b)
    for all values of t. Thus we have found the stationary distribution for th
    Vasiček model.

(d) Check that the density function of the limit distribution solves the tim
    invariant Fokker–Planck equation, i.e. the Fokker–Planck equation witl
    the $\frac{\partial}{\partial t}$-term equal to zero.

Exercise 24.2 Show directly that the Vasiček model has an affine term struc
ture without using the methodology of Proposition 24.2. Instead use the charac
terization of $p(t, T)$ as an expected value, insert the solution of the SDE for r
and look at the structure obtained.

Exercise 24.3 Try to carry out the program outlined above for the Dotha
model and convince yourself that you will only get a mess.

Exercise 24.4 Show that for the Dothan model you have $E^Q[B(t)] = \infty$.

Exercise 24.5 Consider the Ho–Lee model

$$dr = \Theta(t)dt + \sigma dW(t).$$

Assume that the observed bond prices at $t = 0$ are given by $\{p^\star(0, T); \ T \geq 0\}$
Assume furthermore that the constant σ is given. Show that this model can b

itted exactly to today's observed bond prices with Θ as

$$\Theta(t) = \frac{\partial f^\star}{\partial T}(0, t) + \sigma^2 t,$$

where $f^\star$ denotes the observed forward rates. (The observed bond price curve is assumed to be smooth.)

Hint: Use the affine term strucuture, and fit forward rates rather than bond prices (this is logically equivalent).

Exercise 24.6 Use the result of the previous exercise in order to derive the bond price formula in Proposition 24.4.

Exercise 24.7 It is often considered reasonable to demand that a forward rate curve always has an horizontal asymptote, i.e. that $\lim_{T\to\infty} f(t, T)$ exists for all (The limit will obviously depend upon t and $r(t)$). The object of this exercise is to show that the Ho–Lee model is not consistent with such a demand.

(a) Compute the explicit formula for the forward rate curve $f(t, T)$ for the Ho–Lee model (fitted to the initial term structure).
(b) Now assume that the initial term structure indeed has a horizontal asymptote, i.e. that $\lim_{T\to\infty} f^\star(0, T)$ exists. Show that this property is not respected by the Ho–Lee model, by fixing an arbitrary time t, and showing that $f(t, T)$ will be asymptotically linear in T.

Exercise 24.8 The object of this exercise is to indicate why the CIR model is connected to squares of linear diffusions. Let Y be given as the solution to the following SDE.

$$dY = \left(2aY + \sigma^2\right) dt + 2\sigma\sqrt{Y}\,dW, \quad Y(0) = y_0.$$

Define the process Z by $Z(t) = \sqrt{Y(t)}$. It turns out that Z satisfies a stochastic differential equation. Which?

4.6   Notes

Basic papers on short rate models are Vasiček (1977), Hull and White (1990), Ho and Lee (1986), Cox et al. (1985), Dothan (1978), and Black et al. (1990). For extensions and notes on the affine term structure theory, see Duffie and Kan 1996). An extensive analysis of the linear quadratic structure of the CIR model can be found in Magshoodi (1996). The bond option formula for the Vasiček model was first derived by Jamshidian (1989). For examples of two-factor models see Brennan and Schwartz (1979) and Longstaff and Schwartz (1992).

25

FORWARD RATE MODELS

25.1 The Heath–Jarrow–Morton Framework

Up to this point we have studied interest models where the short rate r is the only explanatory variable. The main advantages with such models are as follows

- Specifying r as the solution of an SDE allows us to use Markov process theory, so we may work within a PDE framework.
- In particular it is often possible to obtain analytical formulas for bond prices and derivatives.

The main drawbacks of short rate models are as follows.

- From an economic point of view it seems unreasonable to assume that the entire money market is governed by only one explanatory variable.
- It is hard to obtain a realistic volatility structure for the forward rate without introducing a very complicated short rate model.
- As the short rate model becomes more realistic, the inversion of the yield curve described above becomes increasingly more difficult.

These, and other considerations, have led various authors to propose model which use more than one state variable. One obvious idea would, for example be to present an a priori model for the short rate as well as for some long rate and one could of course also model one or several intermediary interest rates. The method proposed by Heath–Jarrow–Morton is at the far end of this spectrum—they choose the entire forward rate curve as their (infinite dimensional) state variable.

We now turn to the specification of the Heath–Jarrow–Morton (HJM) frame work. We start by specifying everything under a given objective measure P.

Assumption 25.1.1 *We assume that, for every fixed $T > 0$, the forward rate $f(\cdot, T)$ has a stochastic differential which under the objective measure P is given by*

$$df(t, T) = \alpha(t, T)dt + \sigma(t, T)d\bar{W}(t), \tag{25.1}$$

$$f(0, T) = f^{\star}(0, T), \tag{25.2}$$

where $\bar{W}$ is a (d-dimensional) P-Wiener process whereas $\alpha(\cdot, T)$ and $\sigma(\cdot, T)$ are adapted processes.

Note that conceptually eqn (25.1) is one stochastic differential in the t-variable for each fixed choice of T. The index T thus only serves as a "mark" or "parameter" in order to indicate which maturity we are looking at. Also note that we use the observed forward rated curve $\{f^{\star}(0, T); \ T \geq 0\}$ as the initial condition

This will automatically give us a perfect fit between observed and theoretical bond prices at $t = 0$, thus relieving us of the task of inverting the yield curve.

Remark 25.1.1 It is important to observe that the HJM approach to interest rates is not a proposal of a specific **model**, like, for example, the Vasiček model. It is instead a **framework** to be used for analyzing interest rate models. Every short rate model can be equivalently formulated in forward rate terms, and for every forward rate model, the arbitrage free price of a contingent T-claim $\mathcal{X}$ will still be given by the pricing formula

$$\Pi(0; \mathcal{X}) = E^Q \left[\exp \left\{ - \int_0^T r(s)ds \right\} \cdot \mathcal{X} \right],$$

where the short rate as usual is given by $r(s) = f(s, s)$.

Suppose now that we have specified α, σ and $\{f^\star(0, T); \ T \geq 0\}$. Then we have specified the entire forward rate structure and thus, by the relation

$$p(t, T) = \exp \left\{ - \int_t^T f(t, s)ds \right\}, \tag{25.3}$$

we have in fact specified the entire term structure $\{p(t, T); \ T > 0, \ 0 \leq t \leq T\}$. Since we have d sources of randomness (one for every Wiener process), and an infinite number of traded assets (one bond for each maturity T), we run a clear risk of having introduced arbitrage possibilities into the bond market. The first question we pose is thus very natural: How must the processes α and σ be related in order that the induced system of bond prices admits no arbitrage possibilities? The answer is given by the HJM drift condition below.

Theorem 25.1 (HJM drift condition) *Assume that the family of forward rates is given by (25.1) and that the induced bond market is arbitrage free. Then there exists a d-dimensional column-vector process*

$$\lambda(t) = [\lambda_1(t), \ldots, \lambda_d(t)]'$$

with the property that for all $T \geq 0$ and for all $t \leq T$, we have

$$\alpha(t, T) = \sigma(t, T) \int_t^T \sigma(t, s)'ds - \sigma(t, T)\lambda(t). \tag{25.4}$$

In these formulas $'$ denotes transpose.

Proof From Proposition 22.5 we have the bond dynamics

$$dp(t, T) = p(t, T) \left\{ r(t) + A(t, T) + \frac{1}{2}||S(t, T)||^2 \right\} dt + p(t, T)S(t, T)d\bar{W}(t), \tag{25.5}$$

where

$$
\begin{cases}
A(t,T) = -\int_t^T \alpha(t,s)ds, \\
S(t,T) = -\int_t^T \sigma(t,s)ds.
\end{cases}
\tag{25.6}
$$

The risk premium for the T-bond is thus given by

$$
A(t,T) + \frac{1}{2}\|S(t,T)\|^2,
$$

and, applying Result 15.6.1, we conclude the existence of a d-dimensional column-vector process λ such that

$$
A(t,T) + \frac{1}{2}\|S(t,T)\|^2 = \sum_{i=1}^d S_i(t,T)\lambda_i(t).
$$

Taking the T-derivative of this equation gives us eqn (25.4).   □

25.2   Martingale Modeling

We now turn to the question of martingale modeling, and thus assume that the forward rates are specified directly under a martingale measure Q as

$$
df(t,T) = \alpha(t,T)dt + \sigma(t,T)dW(t),
\tag{25.7}
$$

$$
f(0,T) = f^\star(0,T),
\tag{25.8}
$$

where W is a (d-dimensional) Q-Wiener process. Since a martingale measure automatically provides arbitrage free prices, we no longer have a problem of absence of arbitrage, but instead we have another problem. This is so because we now have the following two different formulas for bond prices

$$
p(0,T) = \exp\left\{-\int_0^T f(0,s)ds\right\},
$$

$$
p(0,T) = E^Q\left[\exp\left\{-\int_0^T r(s)ds\right\}\right],
$$

where the short rate r and the forward rates f are connected by $r(t) = f(t,t)$. In order for these formulas to hold simultaneously, we have to impose some sort of consistency relation between α and σ in the forward rate dynamics. The result is the famous Heath–Jarrow–Morton drift condition.

Proposition 25.2 (HJM drift condition) *Under the martingale measure Q, the processes α and σ must satisfy the following relation, for every t and every $T \geq t$.*

$$
\alpha(t,T) = \sigma(t,T)\int_t^T \sigma(t,s)'ds.
\tag{25.9}
$$

Proof   A short and brave argument is to observe that if we start by modeling directly under the martingale measure, then we may apply Proposition 25.1 with $\lambda = 0$. A more detailed argument is as follows.

From Proposition 22.5 we again have the bond price dynamics

$$dp(t,T) = p(t,T)\left\{r(t) + A(t,T) + \frac{1}{2}||S(t,T)||^2\right\}dt + p(t,T)S(t,T)d\tilde{W}(t).$$

We also know that, under a martingale measure, the local rate of return has to equal the short rate r. Thus we have the equation

$$r(t) + A(t,T) + \frac{1}{2}||S(t,T)||^2 = r(t),$$

which gives us the result.   □

The moral of Proposition 25.2 is that when we specify the forward rate dynamics (under Q) we may freely specify the volatility structure. The drift parameters are then uniquely determined. An "algorithm" for the use of an HJM model can be written schematically as follows:

1. Specify, by your own choice, the volatilities $\sigma(t,T)$.
2. The drift parameters of the forward rates are now given by

$$\alpha(t,T) = \sigma(t,T)\int_t^T \sigma(t,s)'ds. \tag{25.10}$$

3. Go to the market and observe today's forward rate structure

$$\{f^\star(0,T); \ T \geq 0\}.$$

4. Integrate in order to get the forward rates as

$$f(t,T) = f^\star(0,T) + \int_0^t \alpha(s,T)ds + \int_0^t \sigma(s,T)dW(s). \tag{25.11}$$

5. Compute bond prices using the formula

$$p(t,T) = \exp\left\{-\int_t^T f(t,s)ds\right\}. \tag{25.12}$$

6. Use the results above in order to compute prices for derivatives.

To see at least how part of this machinery works we now study the simplest example conceivable, which occurs when the process σ is a deterministic constant. With a slight abuse of notation let us thus write $\sigma(t,T) \equiv \sigma$, where $\sigma > 0$. Equation (25.9) gives us the drift process as

$$\alpha(t,T) = \sigma\int_t^T \sigma ds = \sigma^2(T-t), \tag{25.13}$$

so eqn (25.11) becomes

$$f(t,T) = f^\star(0,T) + \int_0^t \sigma^2(T-s)ds + \int_0^t \sigma dW(s), \qquad (25.14)$$

i.e.

$$f(t,T) = f^\star(0,T) + \sigma^2 t\left(T - \frac{t}{2}\right) + \sigma W(t). \qquad (25.15)$$

In particular we see that r is given as

$$r(t) = f(t,t) = f^\star(0,t) + \sigma^2\frac{t^2}{2} + \sigma W(t), \qquad (25.16)$$

so the short rate dynamics are

$$dr(t) = \left\{ f_T(0,t) + \sigma^2 t \right\} dt + \sigma dW(t), \qquad (25.17)$$

which is exactly the Ho–Lee model, fitted to the initial term structure. Observe in particular the ease with which we obtained a perfect fit to the initial term structure.

25.3   The Musiela Parameterization

In many practical applications it is more natural to use time **to** maturity, rather than time **of** maturity, to parametrize bonds and forward rates. If we denote running time by t, time of maturity by T, and time to maturity by x, then we have $x = T - t$, and in terms of x the forward rates are defined as follows.

Definition 25.3 *For all $x \geq 0$ the forward rates $r(t,x)$ are defined by the relation*

$$r(t,x) = f(t,t+x). \qquad (25.18)$$

Suppose now that we have the standard HJM-type model for the forward rates under a martingale measure Q

$$df(t,T) = \alpha(t,T)dt + \sigma(t,T)dW(t). \qquad (25.19)$$

The question is to find the Q-dynamics for $r(t,x)$, and we have the following result, known as the Musiela equation.

Proposition 25.4 (The Musiela equation) *Assume that the forward rate dynamics under Q are given by (25.19). Then*

$$dr(t,x) = \{\mathbf{F}r(t,x) + D(t,x)\} dt + \sigma_0(t,x)dW(t), \qquad (25.20)$$

where

$$\sigma_0(t, x) = \sigma(t, t + x),$$

$$D(t, x) = \sigma_0(t, x) \int_0^x \sigma_0(t, s)' ds,$$

$$\mathbf{F} = \frac{\partial}{\partial x}.$$

Proof   Using a slight variation of the Itô formula we have

$$dr(t, x) = df(t, t + x) + \frac{\partial f}{\partial T}(t, t + x) dt,$$

where the differential in the term $df(t, t + x)$ only operates on the first t. We thus obtain

$$dr(t, x) = \alpha(t, t + x) dt + \sigma(t, t + x) dW(t) + \frac{\partial}{\partial x} r(t, x) dt,$$

and, using the HJM drift condition, we obtain our result.   □

The point of the Musiela parameterization is that it highlights eqn (25.20) as an infinite dimensional SDE. It has become an indispensible tool of modern interest rate theory.

25.4   Exercises

Exercise 25.1 Show that for the Hull–White model

$$dr = (\Theta(t) - ar) dt + \sigma dW$$

the corresponding HJM formulation is given by

$$df(t, T) = \alpha(t, T) dt + \sigma e^{-a(T-t)} dW.$$

Exercise 25.2 (**Gaussian interest rates**) Take as given an HJM model (under the risk neutral measure Q) of the form

$$df(t, T) = \alpha(t, T) dt + \sigma(t, T) dW(t)$$

where the volatility $\sigma(t, T)$ is a **deterministic** function of t and T.

(a) Show that all forward rates, as well as the short rate, are normally distributed.

(b) Show that bond prices are log-normally distributed.

Exercise 25.3 Consider the domestic and a foreign bond market, with bond prices being denoted by $p_d(t,T)$ and $p_f(t,T)$ respectively. Take as given a standard HJM model for the domestic forward rates $f_d(t,T)$, of the form

$$df_d(t,T) = \alpha_d(t,T)dt + \sigma_d(t,T)dW(t),$$

where W is a multidimensional Wiener process under the **domestic** martingale measure Q. The foreign forward rates are denoted by $f_f(t,T)$, and their dynamics, still under the domestic martingale measure Q, are assumed to be given by

$$df_f(t,T) = \alpha_f(t,T)dt + \sigma_f(t,T)dW(t).$$

Note that the same vector Wiener process is driving both the domestic and the foreign bond market. The exchange rate X (denoted in units of domestic currency per unit of foreign currency) has the Q dynamics

$$dX(t) = \mu(t)X(t)dt + X(t)\sigma_X(t)dW(t).$$

Under a foreign martingale measure, the coefficient processes for the foreign forward rates will of course satisfy a standard HJM drift condition, but here we have given the dynamics of f_f under the domestic martingale measure Q. Show that under this measure the foreign forward rates satisfy the modified drift condition

$$\alpha_f(t,T) = \sigma_f(t,T)\left\{\int_t^T \sigma_f'(t,s)ds - \sigma_X'(t)\right\}.$$

Exercise 25.4 With notation as in the exercise above, we define the **yield spread** $g(t,T)$ by

$$g(t,T) = f_f(t,T) - f_d(t,T).$$

Assume that you are given the dynamics for the exchange rate and the domestic forward rates as above. You are also given the spread dynamics (again under the domestic measure Q) as

$$dg(t,T) = \alpha_g(t,T)dt + \sigma_g(t,T)dW(t).$$

Derive the appropriate drift condition for the coefficient process α_g in terms of σ_g, σ_d and σ_X (but not involving σ_f).

Exercise 25.5 A **consol bond** is a bond which forever pays a constant continuous coupon. We normalize the coupon to unity, so over every interval with lenght dt the consol pays $1 \cdot dt$. No face value is ever paid. The price $C(t)$, at time t, of the consol is the value of this infinite stream of income, and it is obviously (why?) given by

$$C(t) = \int_t^\infty p(t,s)ds.$$

Now assume that bond price dynamics under a martingale measure Q are given by

$$dp(t, T) = p(t, T)r(t)dt + p(t, T)v(t, T)dW(t),$$

where W is a vector valued Q-Wiener process. Use the heuristic arguments given in the derivation of the HJM drift condition (see Section 22.2.2) in order to show that the consol dynamics are of the form

$$dC(t) = (C(t)r(t) - 1) \, dt + \sigma_C(t)dW(t),$$

where

$$\sigma_C(t) = \int_t^\infty p(t, s)v(t, s)ds.$$

25.5   Notes

The basic paper for this chapter is Heath *et al.* (1992). The Musiela parameterization was first systematically investigated in Musiela (1993), and developed further in Brace and Musiela (1994). Consistency problems for HJM models and families of forward rate curves were studied in Björk and Christensen (1999), Filipović (1999), and Filipović (2001). The question of when the short rate in a HJM model is in fact Markovian was first studied in Carverhill (1994) for the case of deterministic volatility, and for the case of a short rate depending volatility structure it was solved in Jeffrey (1995). The more general question when a given HJM model admits a realization in terms of a finite dimensional Markovian diffusion was, for various special cases, studied in Ritchken and Sankarasubramanian (1995), Cheyette (1996), Inui and Kijima (1998), Björk and Gombani (1999), and Chiarella and Kwon (2001). The necessary and sufficient conditions for the existence of finite dimensional Markovian realizations in the general case were first obtained, using methods from differential geometry, in Björk and Svensson (2001). This theory has then been developed further in Björk and Landén (2002), Filipović and Teichmann (2003), and Filipović and Teichmann (2004). A survey is given in Björk (2001). In Shirakawa (1991), Björk *et al.* (1995), Björk *et al.* (1997), and Jarrow *et al.* (1995) the HJM theory has been extended to more general driving noise processes. There is an extensive literature on defaultable bonds. See Merton (1974), Duffie and Singleton (1999), Leland (1994), Jarrow *et al.* (1997), Lando (2004), and Schönbucher (2003). Concerning practical estimation of the yield curve see Anderson *et al.* (1996).

26

CHANGE OF NUMERAIRE*

26.1 Introduction

Consider a given financial market (not necessarily a bond market) with the usual locally risk free asset B, and a risk neutral martingale measure Q. As noted in Chapter 10 a measure is a martingale measure only relative to some chosen numeraire asset, and we recall that the risk neutral martingale measure, with the money account B as numeraire, has the property of martingalizing all processes of the form $S(t)/B(t)$ where S is the arbitrage free price process of any (non-dividend paying) traded asset.

In many concrete situations the computational work needed for the determination of arbitrage free prices can be drastically reduced by a clever change of numeraire, and the purpose of the present chapter, which to a large extent follows and is inspired by Geman *et al.* (1995), is to analyze such changes. See the Notes for the more bibliographic information.

To get some feeling for where we are heading, let us consider the pricing problem for a contingent claim $\mathcal{X}$, in a model with a stochastic short rate r. Using the standard risk neutral valuation formula we know that the price at $t = 0$ of $\mathcal{X}$ is given by

$$\Pi\left(0; \mathcal{X}\right) = E^Q \left[e^{-\int_0^T r(s)ds} \cdot \mathcal{X} \right]. \tag{26.1}$$

The problem with this formula from a computational point of view is that in order to compute the expected value we have to get hold of the joint distribution (under Q) of the two stochastic variables $\int_0^T r(s)ds$ and $\mathcal{X}$, and finally we have to integrate with respect to that distribution. Thus we have to compute a double integral, and in most cases this turns out to be rather hard work.

Let us now make the (extremely unrealistic) assumption that r and $\mathcal{X}$ are independent under Q. Then the expectation above splits, and we have the formula

$$\Pi\left(0; \mathcal{X}\right) = E^Q \left[e^{-\int_0^T r(s)ds} \right] \cdot E^Q \left[\mathcal{X}\right],$$

which we may write as

$$\Pi\left(0; \mathcal{X}\right) = p(0, T) \cdot E^Q \left[\mathcal{X}\right]. \tag{26.2}$$

We now note that (26.2) is a **much** nicer formula than (26.1), since

- We only have to compute the single integral $E^Q\left[\mathcal{X}\right]$ instead of the double integral $E^Q \left[\exp\left\{ -\int_0^T r(s)ds \right\} \cdot \mathcal{X} \right]$.

- The bond price $p(0, T)$ in formula (26.2) does not have to be computed theoretically at all. We can **observe** it (at $t = 0$) directly on the bond market.

The drawback with the argument above is that, in most concrete cases, r and $\mathcal{X}$ are **not** independent under Q, and if $\mathcal{X}$ is a contingent claim on an underlying bond, this is of course obvious. What may be less obvious is that even if $\mathcal{X}$ is a claim on an underlying stock which is P-independent of r, it will still be the case that $\mathcal{X}$ and r will be dependent (generically) under Q. The reason is that under Q the stock will have r as its local rate of return, thus introducing a Q-dependence.

This is the bad news. The good news is that there exists a **general** pricing formula (see Proposition 26.8), a special case of which reads as

$$\Pi(0; \mathcal{X}) = p(0, T) \cdot E^T[\mathcal{X}]. \tag{26.3}$$

Here E^T denotes expectation w.r.t. the so called **forward neutral** measure Q^T, which we will discuss below. We will also discuss more general changes of numeraire.

26.2 Generalities

We now proceed to the formal discussion of numeraire changes, and we start by setting the scene.

Assumption 26.2.1 *We consider an arbitrage free market model with asset prices $S_0, S_1, \ldots, S_n$ where S_0 is assumed to be strictly positive.*

Sometimes, but not always, we will need to assume that all prices are Wiener driven.

Condition 26.2.1 *Under P, the S-dynamics are of the form*

$$dS_i(t) = \alpha_i(t)S_i(t)dt + S_i(t)\sigma_i(t)d\bar{W}(t), \quad i = 0, \ldots, n,$$

where the coefficient processes are adapted and W is a multidimensional standard P-Wiener process.

Remark 26.2.1 We do not necessarily assume the existence of a short rate and a money account. If the model admits a short rate and a money account they will as usual be denoted by r and B respectively.

From a mathematical point of view, most of the results concerning changes of numeraire are really special cases of the First Fundamental Theorem and the associated pricing formulas. Thus the difference between the present chapter and Chapter 10 is more one of perspective than one of essence. We now recall some facts from Chapter 10 and start with the Invariance Lemma.

Lemma 26.1 (Invariance lemma) *Let β be any strictly positive Itô process, and define the normalized process Z with numeraire β, by $Z = S/\beta$. Then h is S-self-financing if and only if h is Z-self-financing, i.e. with notation as in Chapter 10 we have*

$$dV^S(t; h) = h(t)dS(t) \tag{26.4}$$

if and only if

$$dV^Z(t; h) = h(t)dZ(t). \tag{26.5}$$

Proof Follows immediately from the Itô formula. □

We make two remarks on the Invariance Lemma.

- A process β satisfying the assumptions above is sometimes called a "deflator process".
- We have assumed that S and β are Itô processes. This is not important, and the Invariance Lemma does in fact hold also in a general semimartingale setting.
- Observe that at this point we do **not** assume that the deflator process β is the price process for a traded asset. The Invariance Lemma will hold for any positive process β satisfying the assumptions above.

From Chapter 10 (see summary in Section 10.7) we now recall the First Fundamental Theorem and the corresponding pricing formula.

Theorem 26.2 *Under the assumptions above, the following hold:*

- *The market model is free of arbitrage if and only if there exists a **martingale measure**, $Q^0 \sim P$ such that the processes*

$$\frac{S_0(t)}{S_0(t)}, \frac{S_1(t)}{S_0(t)}, \ldots, \frac{S_N(t)}{S_0(t)}$$

are (local) martingales under Q^0.

- *In order to avoid arbitrage, a T-claim X must be priced according to the formula*

$$\Pi(t; X) = S_0(t)E^0\left[\frac{X}{S_0(T)} \bigg| \mathcal{F}_t\right], \tag{26.6}$$

where E^0 denotes expectation under Q^0.

In most of our applications earlier in the book we have used the money account B as the numeraire, but in many applications the choice of another asset as the numeraire asset can greatly facilitate computations. A typical example when this situation occurs is when dealing with derivatives defined in terms of several underlying assets. Assume for example that we are given two asset prices S_1 and S_2, and that the contract X to be priced is of the form $X = \Phi(S_1(T), S_2(T))$, where Φ is a given **linearly homogenous** function. Using the standard machinery, and denoting the risk neutral martingale measure by Q^0 we would have to compute the price as

$$\Pi(t; X) = E^0 \left[e^{-\int_t^T r(s)ds} \Phi(S_1(T), S_2(T)) \middle| \mathcal{F}_t \right],$$

which essentially amounts to the calculation of a triple integral. If we instead use S_1 as numeraire, with martingale measure Q^1, we have

$$\Pi(t; X) = S_1(t)E^1 \left[\varphi(Z_2(T)) \middle| \mathcal{F}_t \right], \tag{26.7}$$

where $\varphi(z) = \Phi(1, z)$ and $Z_2(t) = S_2(t)/S_1(t)$. In this formula we note that the factor $S_1(t)$ is the price of the traded asset S_1 at time t, so this quantity does not have to be computed—it can be directly observed on the market. Thus the computational work is reduced to computing a single integral. We also note the important fact that in the Z economy we have **zero short rate**.

Example 26.3 As an example of the reasoning above, assume that, we have two stocks, S_1 and S_2, with price processes of the following form under the objective probability measure P.

$$dS_1(t) = \alpha_1 S_1(t)dt + S_1(t)\sigma_1 d\bar{W}(t). \tag{26.8}$$

$$dS_2(t) = \alpha_2 S_2(t)dt + S_2(t)\sigma_2 d\bar{W}(t), \tag{26.9}$$

Here $\alpha_1, \alpha_2 \in R$ and $\sigma_1, \sigma_2 \in R^2$ are assumed to be deterministic, and $\bar{W}$ is assumed to be a two dimensional standard Wiener process under P. We assume absence of arbitrage.

The T-claim to be priced is an **exchange option**, which gives the holder the right, but not the obligation, to exchange one S_2 share for one S_1 share at time T. Formally this means that the claim is given by $\mathcal{Y} = \max[S_2(T) - S_1(T), 0]$, and we note that we have a linearly homogeneous contract function. It is thus natural to use one of the assets as the numeraire, and we choose S_1. From Theorem 26.2, and using homogeneity, the price is given by

$$\Pi(t; \mathcal{Y}) = S_1(t)E^1 \left[\max[Z_2(T) - 1, 0] \middle| \mathcal{F}_t \right],$$

with $Z_2(t) = S_2(t)/S_1(t)$ and with E^1 denoting expectation under Q^1. We are thus in fact valuing a European call option on $Z_2(T)$, with strike price $K = 1$ in a world with zero short rate.

We now have to compute the Q^1 dynamics of Z_2, but this turns out to be very easy. From Itô, the P-dynamics of Z_2 are of the form

$$dZ_2(t) = Z_2(t)(\cdots)dt + Z_2(t)\{\sigma_2 - \sigma_1\}d\bar{W}(t)$$

where we do not care about the precise form of the dt-terms. Under Q^1 we know that Z_2 is a martingale, and since the volatility terms do not change under a Girsanov transformation we obtain directly the Q^1 dynamics as

$$dZ_2(t) = Z_2(t) \{\sigma_2 - \sigma_1\} \, dW^1(t) \qquad (26.10)$$

where W^1 is Q^1-Wiener. We can write this as

$$dZ_2(t) = Z_2(t)\sigma dW(t)$$

where W is a scalar Q^1-Wiener process and

$$\sigma = \|\sigma_2 - \sigma_1\|.$$

Using the Black–Scholes formula with zero short rate, unit strike price and volatility σ, the price of the exchange option is thus given by the formula

$$\Pi(t; X) = S_1(t) \{Z_2(t)N[d_1] - N[d_2]\} \qquad (26.11)$$

$$= S_2(t)N[d_1] - S_1(t)N[d_2], \qquad (26.12)$$

where

$$d_1 = \frac{1}{\sigma\sqrt{T-t}} \left\{ \ln\left(\frac{S_2(t)}{S_1(t)}\right) + \frac{1}{2}\sigma^2(T-t) \right\}$$

$$d_2 = d_1 - \sigma\sqrt{T-t}.$$

If, instead of using a two dimensional standard Wiener process, we model the stock price dynamics as

$$dS_1(t) = \alpha_1 S_1(t)dt + S_1(t)\sigma_1 d\bar{W}_1(t).$$

$$dS_2(t) = \alpha_2 S_2(t)dt + S_2(t)\sigma_2 d\bar{W}_2(t),$$

Where $\bar{W}_1$ and $\bar{W}_2$ are scalar P-Wiener with local correlation ρ, and thus σ_1 and σ_2 are scalar constants, then it is easy to see that the relevant volatility to use in the formula above is given by

$$\sigma = \sqrt{\sigma_1^2 + \sigma_2^2 - 2\rho\sigma_1\sigma_2}.$$

Note that we made no assumption whatsoever about the dynamics of the short rate. The result above thus holds for every possible specification of the short rate process.

We will give several other concrete examples below, but first we will investigate how we change from one choice of numeraire to another, i.e. how we determine the appropriate Girsanov transformation. This will be done in the next section.

Remark 26.2.2 Since there sometimes seems to be confusion around what is a *bona fide* choice of numeraire, let us recall some points in the derivation of the First Fundamental Theorem.

- In the basic version of the theorem (Theorem 10.9) we assumed that S_0 was a risk free **traded asset** with zero rate of return. It was a crucial ingredient in the proof that we were allowed to invest in this risk free asset.
- For the general case we used the **traded asset** S_0 as the numeraire. In the normalized economy this provided us with a **traded asset** Z_0 which was risk free with zero rate of return. The Invariance Lemma then allowed us to use the basic version of Theorem 10.9 to complete the proof.
- The point of these comments is that the Invariance Lemma is true for any deflator process β, but when it comes to the existence of martingale measures and pricing, we **must** use a numeraire which is the price process of a **traded asset without dividends**.
- In particular, if we want to use numeraires like
  - a nonfinancial index,
  - a forward or futures price process,
  - the price process of a traded asset with dividends,
  then we must carry out a careful separate analysis, since in these cases we do **not** have access to a standard version of the First Fundamental Theorem.

26.3 Changing the Numeraire

Suppose that for a specific numeraire S_0 we have determined the corresponding (not necessarily unique) martingale measure Q^0, and the associated dynamics of the asset prices (and possibly also the dynamics of other factors within the model). Suppose furthermore that we want to change the numeraire from S_0 to, say, S_1. An immediate problem is then to find the appropriate Girsanov transformation which will take us from Q^0 to Q^1, where Q^1 is the martingale measure corresponding to the numeraire S_1. This problem will for example turn up in connection with the LIBOR market models treated later in the book.

This problem is in fact quite easily solved, and to see this, let us use the pricing part of Theorem 26.2 for an arbitrary choice of T-claim X. We then have

$$\Pi\left(0; X\right) = S_0(0)E^0\left[\frac{X}{S_0(T)}\right], \qquad (26.13)$$

and also

$$\Pi\left(0; X\right) = S_1(0)E^1\left[\frac{X}{S_1(T)}\right]. \qquad (26.14)$$

Denoting by $L_0^1(T)$ the Radon–Nikodym derivative

$$L_0^1(T) = \frac{dQ^1}{dQ^0}, \quad \text{on } \mathcal{F}_T, \tag{26.15}$$

we can write (26.14) as

$$\Pi(0; X) = S_1(0)E^0 \left[\frac{X}{S_1(T)} \cdot L_0^1(T) \right], \tag{26.16}$$

and we thus have

$$S_0(0)E^0 \left[\frac{X}{S_0(T)} \right] = S_1(0)E^0 \left[\frac{X}{S_1(T)} \cdot L_0^1(T) \right], \tag{26.17}$$

for all (sufficiently integrable) T-claims X. We thus deduce that

$$\frac{S_0(0)}{S_0(T)} = \frac{S_1(0)}{S_1(T)} \cdot L_0^1(T),$$

so we obtain

$$L_0^1(T) = \frac{S_0(0)}{S_1(0)} \cdot \frac{S_1(T)}{S_0(T)},$$

which is our candidate as a Radon–Nikodym derivative. The obvious choice of the induced likelihood process is of course given by

$$L_0^1(t) = \frac{S_0(0)}{S_1(0)} \cdot \frac{S_1(t)}{S_0(t)}, \quad 0 \le t \le T.$$

This looks promising, since the process $S_1(t)/S_0(t)$ is a Q^0-martingale (why?), and we know that any likelihood process for the transition from Q^0 to Q^1 has to be a Q^0-martingale. In more formal terms we have the following proposition.

Proposition 26.4 *Assume that Q^0 is a martingale measure for the numeraire S_0 (on $\mathcal{F}_T$) and assume that S_1 is a positive asset price process such that $S_1(t)/S_0(t)$ is a true Q^0-martingale (and not just a local one). Define Q^1 on $\mathcal{F}_T$ by the likelihood process*

$$L_0^1(t) = \frac{S_0(0)}{S_1(0)} \cdot \frac{S_1(t)}{S_0(t)}, \quad 0 \le t \le T. \tag{26.18}$$

Then Q^1 is a martingale measure for S_1.

Proof We have to show that for every (sufficiently integrable) arbitrage free price process Π, the normalized process $\Pi(t)/S_1(t)$ is a Q^1-martingale. Now, if

Π is an arbitrage free price process then we know that Π/S_0 is a Q^0-martingale and for $s \leq t$ we have the following calculation, where we use the Abstract Bayes' Formula.

$$E^1\left[\frac{\Pi(t)}{S_1(t)}\bigg|\mathcal{F}_s\right] = \frac{E^0\left[L_0^1(t)\frac{\Pi(t)}{S_1(t)}\bigg|\mathcal{F}_s\right]}{L_0^1(s)} = \frac{E^0\left[\frac{S_0(0)}{S_1(0)}\cdot\frac{S_1(t)}{S_0(t)}\cdot\frac{\Pi(t)}{S_1(t)}\bigg|\mathcal{F}_s\right]}{L_0^1(s)}$$

$$= \frac{\frac{S_0(0)}{S_1(0)}\cdot E^0\left[\frac{\Pi(t)}{S_0(t)}\bigg|\mathcal{F}_s\right]}{L_0^1(s)} = \frac{\frac{S_0(0)}{S_1(0)}\cdot\frac{\Pi(s)}{S_0(s)}}{L_0^1(s)} = \frac{\Pi(s)}{S_1(s)}.$$

$\square$

Since we have determined the relevant likelihood process, we can identify the Girsanov kernel.

Proposition 26.5 *Assume absence of arbitrage and that Condition 26.2.1 is in force. Denote the corresponding Q^0-Wiener process by W^0. Then the Q^0-dynamics of the likelihood process L_0^1 are given by*

$$dL_0^1(t) = L_0^1(t)\left\{\sigma_1(t) - \sigma_0(t)\right\}dW^0(t). \tag{26.19}$$

Thus the Girsanov kernel φ_0^1 for the transition from Q^0 to Q^1 is given by the volatility difference

$$\varphi_0^1(t) = \sigma_1(t) - \sigma_0(t). \tag{26.20}$$

Proof The result follows immediately from applying the Itô formula to (26.18). $\square$

26.4 Forward Measures

In this section we specialize the theory developed in the previous section to the case when the new numeraire chosen is a bond maturing at time T. As can be expected this choice of numeraire is particularly useful when dealing with interest rate derivatives.

26.4.1 Using the T-bond as Numeraire

Suppose that we are given a specified bond market model with a fixed (money account) martingale measure Q. For a fixed time of maturity T we now choose the zero coupon bond maturing at T as our new numeraire.

Definition 26.6 *For a fixed T, the T-forward measure Q^T is defined as the martingale measure for the numeraire process $p(t, T)$.*

In interest rate theory we often have our models specified under the risk neutral martingale measure Q with the money account B as the numeraire. We then have the following explicit description Q^T.

Proposition 26.7 *If Q denotes the risk neutral martingale measure, then the likelihood process*

$$L^T(t) = \frac{dQ^T}{dQ}, \quad on \; \mathcal{F}_t, \; 0 \le t \le T$$

is given by

$$L^T(t) = \frac{p(t,T)}{B(t)p(0,T)}. \tag{26.21}$$

In particular, if the Q-dynamics of the T-bond are Wiener driven, i.e. of the form

$$dp(t,T) = r(t)p(t,T)dt + p(t,T)v(t,T)dW(t), \tag{26.22}$$

where W is a (possibly multidimensional) Q-Wiener process, then the L^T dynamics are given by

$$dL^T(t) = L^T(t)v(t,T)dW(t), \tag{26.23}$$

i.e. the Girsanov kernel for the transition from Q to Q^T is given by the T-bond volatility $v(t,T)$.

Proof The result follows immediately from Proposition 26.4 with $Q^T = Q^1$ and $Q^0 = Q$. □

Observing that $P(T,T) = 1$ we have the following useful pricing formula as an immediate corollary of Proposition 26.2.

Proposition 26.8 *For any T-claim X we have*

$$\Pi(t;X) = p(t,T)E^T[X|\mathcal{F}_t], \tag{26.24}$$

where E^T denotes integration w.r.t. Q^T.

Note again that the price $p(t,T)$ does not have to be computed. It can be observed directly on the market at time t.

A natural question to ask is when Q and Q^T coincide.

Lemma 26.9 *The relation $Q = Q^T$ holds if and only if r is deterministic.*

Proof Exercise for the reader. □

26.4.2 An Expectation Hypothesis

We now make a small digression to discuss the forward rate process $f(t, T)$. The economic interpretation of $f(t, T)$ is that this is the risk free rate of return which we may have on an investment over the infinitesimal interval $[T, T + dT]$ if the contract is made at t. On the other hand, the short rate $r(T)$ is the risk free rate of return over the infinitesimal interval $[T, T + dT]$, if the contract is made at T. Thus it is natural to view $f(t, T)$ (which can be observed at t) as an estimate of the future short rate $r(T)$. More explicitly it is sometimes argued that if the market expects the short rate at T to be high, then it seems reasonable to assume that the forward rate $f(t, T)$ is also high, since otherwise there would be profits to be made on the bond market.

Our task now is to determine whether this reasoning is correct in a more precise sense, and to this end we study the most formalized version of the argument above, known as the "unbiased expectation hypothesis" for forward rates. This hypothesis then says that in an efficient market we must have

$$f(t, T) = E\left[r(T)|\,\mathcal{F}_t\right], \tag{26.25}$$

i.e. the present forward rate is an unbiased estimator of the future spot rate. If we interpret the expression "an efficient market" as "an arbitrage free market" then we may use our general machinery to analyze the problem.

First we notice that there is no probability measure indicated in (26.25), so we have to make a choice.

Of course there is no reason at all to expect the hypothesis to be true under the objective measure P, but it is often claimed that it holds "in a risk neutral world". This more refined version of the hypothesis can then be formulated as

$$f(t, T) = E^Q\left[r(T)|\,\mathcal{F}_t\right], \tag{26.26}$$

where Q is the usual risk neutral martingale measure. In fact, also this version of the expectation hypothesis is in general incorrect, which is shown by the following result.

Lemma 26.10 *Assume that, for all $T > 0$ we have $r(T)/B(T) \in L^1(Q)$. Then, for every fixed T, the process $f(t, T)$ is a Q^T-martingale for $0 \le t \le T$, and in particular we have*

$$f(t, T) = E^T\left[r(T)|\,\mathcal{F}_t\right]. \tag{26.27}$$

Proof Using Proposition 26.24 with $X = r(T)$ we have

$$\Pi\left(t; X\right) = E^Q\left[r(T)e^{-\int_t^T r(s)ds}\,\Big|\,\mathcal{F}_t\right] = p(t, T)E^T\left[r(T)|\,\mathcal{F}_t\right].$$

This gives us

$$
\begin{aligned}
E^T\left[r(T)\middle|\mathcal{F}_t\right] &= \frac{1}{p(t,T)}E^Q\left[r(T)e^{-\int_t^T r(s)ds}\middle|\mathcal{F}_t\right] \\
&= -\frac{1}{p(t,T)}E^Q\left[\frac{\partial}{\partial T}e^{-\int_t^T r(s)ds}\middle|\mathcal{F}_t\right] \\
&= -\frac{1}{p(t,T)}\frac{\partial}{\partial T}E^Q\left[e^{-\int_t^T r(s)ds}\middle|\mathcal{F}_t\right] \\
&= -\frac{p_T(t,T)}{p(t,T)} = f(t,T).
\end{aligned}
$$

$\square$

We thus see that the expectation hypothesis is false also under Q, but true under Q^T. Note, however, that we have different Q^T for different choices of the maturity date T.

26.5 A General Option Pricing Formula

The object of this section is to give a fairly general formula for the pricing of European call options, and for the rest of the section we basically follow Geman *et al* (1995). Assume therefore that we are given a financial market with a (possibly stochastic) short rate r, and a strictly positive asset price process $S(t)$.

The option under consideration is a European call on S with date of maturity T and strike price K. We are thus considering the T-claim

$$
\mathcal{X} = \max\left[S(T) - K,\ 0\right],
\tag{26.28}
$$

and, for readability reasons, we confine ourselves to computing the option price $\Pi(t;\mathcal{X})$ at time $t = 0$.

The main reason for the existence of a large number of explicit option pricing formulas is that the contract function for an option is piecewise linear. We can capitalize on this fact by using a not so well known trick with indicator functions. Write the option as

$$
\mathcal{X} = \left[S(T) - K\right]\cdot I\left\{S(T) \geq K\right\},
$$

where I is the indicator function, i.e.

$$
I\left\{S(T) \geq K\right\} = \begin{cases} 1 \text{ if } S(T) \geq K \\ 0 \text{ if } S(T) < K. \end{cases}
$$

Denoting the risk neutral martingale measure by Q, we obtain

$$
\begin{aligned}
\Pi(0;\mathcal{X}) &= E^Q\left[B^{-1}(T)\left[S(T) - K\right]I\left\{S(T) \geq K\right\}\right]. \\
&= E^Q\left[e^{-\int_0^T r(s)ds}S(T)\cdot I\left\{S(T) \geq K\right\}\right] \\
&\quad - KE^Q\left[e^{-\int_0^T r(s)ds}\cdot I\left\{S(T) \geq K\right\}\right].
\end{aligned}
$$

In the first term above, we use the measure Q^S having S as numeraire, and for the second term we use the T-forward measure. From Theorem 26.2 and Proposition 26.8 we then obtain the following basic option pricing formula, which is a substantial extension of the standard Black–Scholes formula.

Proposition 26.11 (General option pricing formula) *Given the assumptions above, the option price is given by*

$$\Pi\left(0;\mathcal{X}\right) = S(0)Q^S\left(S(T) \geq K\right) - Kp(0,T)Q^T\left(S(T) \geq K\right). \qquad (26.29)$$

Here Q^T denotes the T-forward measure, whereas Q^S denotes the martingale measure for the numeraire process $S(t)$.

In order to use this formula in a real situation we have to be able to compute the probabilities above, and the standard condition which ensures computability turns out to be that volatilities should be deterministic. Hence we have the following assumption.

Assumption 26.5.1 *Assume that the process $Z_{S,T}$ defined by*

$$Z_{S,T}(t) = \frac{S(t)}{p(t,T)} \qquad (26.30)$$

has a stochastic differential of the form

$$dZ_{S,T}(t) = Z_{S,T}(t)m_{S,T}(t)dt + Z_{S,T}(t)\sigma_{S,T}(t)dW(t), \qquad (26.31)$$

where the volatility process $\sigma_{S,T}(t)$ is **deterministic**.

The crucial point here is of course the assumption that the row-vector process $\sigma_{S,T}$ is deterministic. Note that the volatility process as always is unaffected by a change of measure, so we do not have to specify under which measure we check the condition. It can be done under P as well as under Q.

We start the computations by writing the probability in the second term of (26.29) as

$$Q^T\left(S(T) \geq K\right) = Q^T\left(\frac{S(T)}{p(T,T)} \geq K\right) = Q^T\left(Z_{S,T}(T) \geq K\right). \qquad (26.32)$$

Since $Z_{S,T}$ is an asset price, normalized by the price of a T-bond, it is a Q^T martingale, so its Q^T-dynamics are given by

$$dZ_{S,T}(t) = Z_{S,T}(t)\sigma_{S,T}(t)dW^T(t). \qquad (26.33)$$

This is basically GBM, driven by a multidimensional Wiener process, and it is easy to see that the solution is given by

$$Z_{S,T}(T) = \frac{S(0)}{p(0,T)} \exp\left\{-\frac{1}{2}\int_0^T \|\sigma_{S,T}\|^2(t)dt + \int_0^T \sigma_{S,T}(t)dW^T(t)\right\}. \qquad (26.34)$$

In the exponent we have a stochastic integral and a deterministic time integral. Since the integrand in the stochastic integral is deterministic, an easy extension of Lemma 4.15 shows that the stochastic integral has a Gaussian distribution with zero mean and variance

$$\Sigma_{S,T}^2(T) = \int_0^T \|\sigma_{S,T}(t)\|^2 dt. \tag{26.35}$$

The entire exponent is thus normally distributed, and we can write the probability in the second term in (26.29) as

$$Q^T\left(S(T) \geq K\right) = N[d_2],$$

where

$$d_2 = \frac{\ln\left(\frac{S(0)}{Kp(0,T)}\right) - \frac{1}{2}\Sigma_{S,T}^2(T)}{\sqrt{\Sigma_{S,T}^2(T)}}. \tag{26.36}$$

Since the first probability term in (26.29) is a Q^S-probability, it is natural to write the event under consideration in terms of a quotient with S in the denominator. Thus we write

$$Q^S\left(S(T) \geq K\right) = Q^S\left(\frac{p(T,T)}{S(T)} \leq \frac{1}{K}\right) = Q^S\left(Y_{S,T}(T) \leq \frac{1}{K}\right), \tag{26.37}$$

where $Y_{S,T}$ is defined by

$$Y_{S,T}(t) = \frac{p(t,T)}{S(t)} = \frac{1}{Z_{S,T}(t)}.$$

Under Q^S the process $Y_{S,T}$ has zero drift, so its Q^S-dynamics are of the form

$$dY_{S,T}(t) = Y_{S,T}(t)\delta_{S,T}(t)dW^S(t).$$

Since $Y_{S,T} = Z_{S,T}^{-1}$, an easy application of Itô's formula gives us $\delta_{S,T}(t) = -\sigma_{S,T}(t)$. Thus we have

$$Y_{S,T}(T) = \frac{p(0,T)}{S(0)} \exp\left\{-\frac{1}{2}\int_0^T \|\sigma_{S,T}\|^2(t)dt - \int_0^T \sigma_{S,T}(t)dW^S\right\},$$

and again we have a normally distributed exponent. Thus, after some simplification,

$$Q^S\left(S(T) \geq K\right) = N[d_1],$$

where

$$d_1 = d_2 + \sqrt{\Sigma_{S,T}^2(T)}. \tag{26.38}$$

We have thus proved the following result.

Proposition 26.12 (Geman–El Karoui–Rochet) *Under the conditions given in Assumption 26.5.1, the price of the call option defined in (26.28) is given by the formula*

$$\Pi(0; \mathcal{X}) = S(0)N[d_1] - K \cdot p(0, T)N[d_2]. \tag{26.39}$$

Here d_2 and d_1 are given in (26.36) and (26.38) respectively, whereas $\Sigma_{S,T}^2(T)$ is defined by (26.35).

26.6 The Hull–White Model

As a concrete application of the option pricing formula of the previous section, we will now consider the case of interest rate options in the Hull–White model (extended Vasiček). To this end recall that in the Hull–White model the Q-dynamics of r are given by

$$dr = \{\Phi(t) - ar\} dt + \sigma dW. \tag{26.40}$$

From Section 24.3 we recall that we have an affine term structure

$$p(t, T) = e^{A(t,T) - B(t,T)r(t)}, \tag{26.41}$$

where A and B are deterministic functions, and where B is given by

$$B(t, T) = \frac{1}{a}\left\{1 - e^{-a(T-t)}\right\}. \tag{26.42}$$

The project is to price a European call option with exercise date T_1 and strike price K, on an underlying bond with date of maturity T_2, where $T_1 < T_2$. In the notation of the general theory above this means that $T = T_1$ and that $S(t) = p(t, T_2)$. We start by checking Assumption 26.5.1, i.e. if the volatility, σ_z, of the process

$$Z(t) = \frac{p(t, T_2)}{p(t, T_1)} \tag{26.43}$$

is deterministic. (In terms of the notation in Section 26.5 Z corresponds to $Z_{S,T}$ and σ_z corresponds to $\sigma_{S,T}$.)

Inserting (26.41) into (26.43) gives

$$Z(t) = \exp\left\{A(t, T_2) - A(t, T_1) - [B(t, T_2) - B(t, T_1)]r(t)\right\}.$$

Applying the Itô formula to this expression, and using (26.40), we get the Q-dynamics

$$dZ(t) = Z(t)\{\cdots\} dt + Z(t) \cdot \sigma_z(t)dW, \tag{26.44}$$

where

$$\sigma_z(t) = -\sigma[B(t, T_2) - B(t, T_1)] = \frac{\sigma}{a}e^{at}\left[e^{-aT_2} - e^{-aT_1}\right]. \tag{26.45}$$

Thus σ_z is in fact deterministic, so we may apply Proposition 26.12. We obtain the following result, which also holds (why?) for the Vasiček model.

Proposition 26.13 (Hull–White bond option) *In the Hull–White model (26.40) the price, at $t = 0$, of a European call with strike price K, and time of maturity T_1, on a bond maturing at T_2 is given by the formula*

$$\Pi\,(0;\mathcal{X}) = p(0, T_2)N[d_1] - K \cdot p(0, T_1)N[d_2], \tag{26.46}$$

where

$$d_2 = \frac{\ln\left(\frac{p(0,T_2)}{Kp(0,T_1)}\right) - \frac{1}{2}\Sigma^2}{\sqrt{\Sigma^2}}, \tag{26.47}$$

$$d_1 = d_2 + \sqrt{\Sigma^2}, \tag{26.48}$$

$$\Sigma^2 = \frac{\sigma^2}{2a^3}\left\{1 - e^{-2aT_1}\right\}\left\{1 - e^{-a(T_2-T_1)}\right\}^2. \tag{26.49}$$

We end the discussion of the Hull–White model, by studying the pricing problem for a claim of the form

$$\mathcal{Z} = \Phi(r(T)).$$

Using the T-bond as numeraire Proposition 26.8 gives us

$$\Pi\,(t;\mathcal{Z}) = p(t, T)E^T\left[\Phi\left(r(T)\right)\middle|\,\mathcal{F}_t\right], \tag{26.50}$$

so we must find the distribution of $r(T)$ under Q^T, and to this end we will use Theorem 26.5 (with Q as Q^0 and Q^T as Q^1). We thus need the volatility of the T-bond, and from (26.41)–(26.42) we obtain bond prices (under Q) as

$$dp(t, T) = r(t)p(t, T)dt + v(t, T)p(t, T)dW, \tag{26.51}$$

where the volatility $v(t, T)$ is given by

$$v(t, T) = -\sigma B(t, T). \tag{26.52}$$

Thus, using Theorem 26.5 and the fact that the money account B has zero volatility, the Girsanov kernel for the transition from Q to Q^T is given by

$$\varphi^T(t) = -\sigma B(t, T).$$

The Q^T-dynamics of the short rate are thus given by

$$dr = \left[\Theta(t) - ar - \sigma^2 B(t, T)\right]dt + \sigma dW^T, \tag{26.53}$$

where W^T is a Q^T-Wiener process.

We observe that, since $v(t,T)$ and $\Theta(t)$ are deterministic, r is a Gaussian process, so the distribution of $r(T)$ is completely determined by its mean and variance under Q^T. Solving the linear SDE (26.53) gives us

$$r(T) = e^{-a(T-t)} + \int_t^T e^{-a(T-s)}\left[\Theta(s) - \sigma^2 B(s,T)\right]ds \qquad (26.54)$$

$$+ \sigma \int_t^T e^{-a(T-s)}dW^T(s).$$

We can now compute the conditional Q^T-variance of $r(T)$, $\sigma_r^2(t,T)$, as

$$\sigma_r^2(t,T) = \sigma^2 \int_t^T e^{-2a(T-s)}ds = \frac{\sigma^2}{2a}\left\{1 - e^{-2a(T-t)}\right\}. \qquad (26.55)$$

Note that the Q^T-mean of $r(T)$, $m_r(t,T) = E^T\left[r(T)|\mathcal{F}_t\right]$, does not have to be computed at all. We obtain it directly from Lemma 26.10 as

$$m_r(t,T) = f(t,T),$$

which can be observed directly from market data.

Under Q^T, the conditional distribution of $r(T)$ is thus the normal distribution $N[f(t,T), \sigma_r(t,T)]$, and performing the integration in (26.50) we have the final result.

Proposition 26.14 *Given the assumptions above, the price of the claim* $X = \Phi(r(T))$ *is given by*

$$\Pi(t;X) = p(t,T)\frac{1}{\sqrt{2\pi\sigma_r^2(t,T)}}\int_{-\infty}^{\infty}\Phi(z)\exp\left\{-\frac{[z - f(t,T)]^2}{2\sigma_r^2(t,T)}\right\}dz, \qquad (26.56)$$

where $\sigma_r^2(t,T)$ *is given by (26.55).*

26.7 The General Gaussian Model

In this section we extend our earlier results, by computing prices of bond options in a general Gaussian forward rate model. We specify the model (under Q) as

$$df(t,T) = \alpha(t,T)dt + \sigma(t,T)dW(t), \qquad (26.57)$$

where W is a d-dimensional Q-Wiener process.

Assumption 26.7.1 *We assume that the volatility vector function*

$$\sigma(t,T) = [\sigma_1(t,T),\cdots,\sigma_d(t,T)]$$

*is a **deterministic** function of the variables t and T.*

Using Proposition 22.5 the bond price dynamics under Q are given by

$$dp(t, T) = p(t, T)r(t)dt + p(t, T)v(t, T)dW(t), \qquad (26.58)$$

where the volatility is given by

$$v(t, T) = -\int_t^T \sigma(t, s)ds. \qquad (26.59)$$

We consider a European call option, with expiration date T_0 and exercise price K, on an underlying bond with maturity T_1 (where of course $T_0 < T_1$). In order to compute the price of the bond, we use Proposition 26.12, which means that we first have to find the volatility σ_{T_1,T_0} of the process

$$Z(t) = \frac{p(t, T_1)}{p(t, T_0)}.$$

An easy calculation shows that in fact

$$\sigma_{T_1,T_0}(t) = v(t, T_1) - v(t, T_0) = -\int_{T_0}^{T_1} \sigma(t, s)ds. \qquad (26.60)$$

This is clearly deterministic, so Assumption 26.5.1 is satisfied. We now have the following pricing formula.

Proposition 26.15 (Option prices for Gaussian forward rates) *The price, at $t = 0$, of the option*

$$\mathcal{X} = \max\left[p(T_0, T_1) - K, 0\right]$$

is given by

$$\Pi\left(0; \mathcal{X}\right) = p(0, T_1)N[d_1] - K \cdot p(0, T_0)N[d_2], \qquad (26.61)$$

where

$$d_1 = \frac{\ln\left(\frac{p(0,T_1)}{Kp(0,T_0)}\right) + \frac{1}{2}\Sigma_{T_1,T_0}^2}{\sqrt{\Sigma_{T_1,T_0}^2}},$$

$$d_2 = d_1 - \sqrt{\Sigma_{T_1,T_0}^2},$$

$$\Sigma_{T_1,T_0}^2 = \int_0^{T_0} \|\sigma_{T_1,T_0}(s)\|^2 ds,$$

and σ_{T_1,T_0} is given by (26.60).

Proof   Follows immediately from Proposition 26.12.   □

26.8   Caps and Floors

The object of this section is to present one of the most traded of all interest rate derivatives—the cap—and to show how it can be priced.

An interest rate **cap** is a financial insurance contract which protects you from having to pay more than a prespecified rate, the **cap rate**, even though you have a loan at a floating rate of interest. There are also **floor** contracts which guarantee that the interest paid on a floating rate loan will never be below some predetermined **floor rate**. For simplicity we assume that we are standing at time $t = 0$, and that the cap is to be in force over the interval $[0, T]$. Technically speaking, a cap is the sum of a number of basic contracts, known as **caplets**, which are defined as follows.

- The interval $[0, T]$ is subdivided by the equidistant points

$$0 = T_0, T_1, \ldots, T_n = T.$$

  We use the notation δ for the length of an elementary interval, i.e. $\delta = T_i - T_{i-1}$. Typically, δ is a quarter of a year, or half a year.
- The cap is working on some **principal amount** of money, denoted by K, and the **cap rate** is denoted by R.
- The floating rate of interest underlying the cap is not the short rate r, but rather some market rate, and we will assume that over the interval $[T_{i-1}, T_i]$ it is the LIBOR spot rate $L(T_{i-1}, T_i)$ (see Section 22.2).
- Caplet i is now defined as the following contingent claim, paid at T_i,

$$\mathcal{X}_i = K\delta \max[L(T_{i-1}, T_i) - R, 0]. \tag{26.62}$$

We now turn to the problem of pricing the caplet, and without loss of generality we may assume that $K = 1$. We will also use the notation $x^+ = \max[x, 0]$, so the caplet can be written as

$$\mathcal{X} = \delta(L - R)^+,$$

where $L = L(T_{i-1}, T_i)$. Denoting $p(T_{i-1}, T_i)$ by p, and recalling that

$$L = \frac{1 - p}{p\delta},$$

we have

$$\mathcal{X} = \delta\left(L - R\right)^+ = \delta\left(L - R\right)^+ = \delta\left(\frac{1-p}{p\delta} - R\right)^+$$

$$= \left(\frac{1}{p} - (1 + \delta R)\right)^+ = \left(\frac{1}{p} - R^\star\right)^+ = \frac{R^\star}{p}\left(\frac{1}{R^\star} - p\right)^+,$$

where $R^\star = 1 + \delta R$. It is, however, easily seen (why?) that a payment of $\frac{R^\star}{p}\left(\frac{1}{R^\star} - p\right)^+$ at time T_i is equivalent to a payment of $R^\star\left(\frac{1}{R^\star} - p\right)^+$ at time T_{i-1}.

Consequently we see that a caplet is equivalent to $R^\star$ put options on an underlying T_i-bond, where the exercise date of the option is at T_{i-1} and the exercise price is $1/R^\star$. An entire cap contract can thus be viewed as a portfolio of put options, and we may use the earlier results of the chapter to compute the theoretical price.

A different approach to the pricing of caplets (and hence of caps) is to view the caplet claim in (26.62) as a formal option directly on the LIBOR rate, and noting that the LIBOR forward rate $L(t; T_i, T_{i+1})$ is a martingale under $Q^{T_{i+1}}$. This approach will be investigated in some detail in the chapter on LIBOR market models below.

26.9 The Numeraire Portfolio

We have seen above that if we choose the arbitrage free price process S^0 of any asset without dividends, then there exists a martingale measure $Q^0 \sim P$ such that the normalized asset price

$$\frac{\Pi_t}{S_t^0},$$

is a Q^0 martingale for every arbitrage free asset price Π. The measure Q^0 will obviously depend on the numeraire asset S^0 and a natural question to ask is whether there exists a numeraire asset with the property that $Q^0 = P$, i.e. an asset for which the associated martingale measure coincides with the objective probability measure. Such an asset is known in the literature as "the numeraire asset" or "the numeraire portfolio" and, at least in a complete market, it always exists. To see this we go back to Proposition 20.9 which gives us value process of the log optimal portfolio in a complete market setting as

$$X_t = e^{rt} x L_t^{-1},$$

where x is the initial wealth. Let us normalize by setting $x = 1$. We then have the following result.

Proposition 26.16 *If Π is the price process of any asset, underlying or derivative, then the process*

$$\frac{\Pi_t}{X_t},$$

where X is the value process of the log optimal portfolio, is a P-martingale. In particular, the price of any T-claim Z is given by the P-expectation

$$\Pi(t; Z) = X_t E^P\left[\left.\frac{Z}{X_T}\right| \mathcal{F}_t\right].$$

Proof By assumption we know that $e^{-rt}\Pi_t$ is a Q-martingale. This is equivalent to saying that

$$e^{-rt}\Pi_t L_t$$

is a P-martingale, where $L_t = dQ/dP$ on $\mathcal{F}_t$. From the definition of the log optimal portfolio above we have

$$\frac{\Pi_t}{X_t} = e^{-rt}\Pi_t L_t,$$

which proves the first part of the proposition. The second part follows trivially. □

26.10 Exercises

Exercise 26.1 Derive a pricing formula for European bond options in the Ho–Lee model.

Exercise 26.2 A Gaussian Interest Rate Model
Take as given a HJM model (under the risk neutral measure Q) of the form

$$df(t,T) = \alpha(t,T)dt + \sigma_1 \cdot (T-t)dW_1(t) + \sigma_2 e^{-a(T-t)}dW_2(t)$$

where σ_1 and σ_2 are constants.

(a) Derive the bond price dynamics.
(b) Compute the pricing formula for a European call option on an underlying bond.

Exercise 26.3 Prove that a payment of $\frac{1}{p}(A-p)^+$ at time T_i is equivalent to a payment of $(A-p)^+$ at time T_{i-1}, where $p = p(T_{i-1}, T_i)$, and A is a deterministic constant.

Exercise 26.4 Prove Lemma 26.9.

Exercise 26.5 Use the technique above in order to prove the pricing formula of Proposition 24.5, for bond options in the Ho–Lee model.

26.11 Notes

The first usage of a numeraire different from the risk free asset B was probably in Merton (1973), where however the technique is not explicitly discussed. The first to explicitly use a change of numeraire change was Margrabe (1978), who (referring to a discussion with S. Ross) used an underlying stock as numeraire in order to value an exchange option. The numeraire change is also used in Harrison and Kreps (1979), Harrison and Pliska (1981) and basically in all later works on the existence of martingale measures in order to reduce (as we did in Chapter 10) the general case to the basic case of zero short rate. In these papers the numeraire change as such is however not put to systematic use as an instrument for facilitating the computation of option prices in complicated models. In the context of interest rate theory, changes of numeraire were then used and discussed independently by Geman (1989) and (in a Gaussian framework) Jamshidian (1989), who both used a bond maturing at a fixed time T as numeraire. A systematic study of general changes of numeraire has been carried out by Geman, El Karoui and Rochet in a series of papers, and many of the results above can be found in Geman *et al.* (1995). For further examples of the change of numeraire technique, see Benninga *et al.* (2002).

27

LIBOR AND SWAP MARKET MODELS

n the previous chapters we have concentrated on studying interest rate models ased on *infinitesimal* interest rates like the instantaneous short rate and the nstantaneous forward rates. While these objects are nice to handle from a mathmatical point of view, they have two main disadvantages.

- The instantaneous short and forward rates can never be observed in real life.
- If you would like to calibrate your model to cap- or swaption data, then this is typically very complicated from a numerical point of view if you use one of the "instantaneous" models.

A further fact from real life, which has been somewhat disturbing from a heoretical point of view is the following:

- For a very long time, the market practice has been to value caps, floors, and swaptions by using a formal extension of the Black (1976) model. Such an extension is typically obtained by an approximation argument where the short rate at one point in the argument is assumed to be deterministic, while later on in the argument the LIBOR rate is assumed to be stochastic. This is of course logically inconsistent.
- Despite this, the market happily continues to use Black-76 for the pricing of caps, floors, and swaptions.

n a situation like this, where market practice seems to be at odds with academic vork there are two possible attitudes for the theorist: you can join them (the narket) or you can try to beat them, and since the fixed income market does ot seem to collapse because of the use of Black-76, the more realistic alternative eems to be to join them.

Thus there has appeared a natural demand for constructing logically consisent (and arbitrage free!) models having the property that the theoretical prices or caps, floors and swaptions produced by the model are of the Black-76 form. 'his project has in fact been carried out very successfully, starting with Miltersen t al (1997), Brace *et al* (1997) and Jamshidian (1998). The basic structure of he models is as follows:

- Instead of modeling instantaneous interest rates, we model discrete **market rates** like LIBOR rates in the LIBOR market models, or forward swap rates in the swap market models.
- Under a suitable choice of numeraire(s), these market rates can in fact be modeled log normally.

- The market models will thus produce pricing formulas for caps and floor (the LIBOR models), and swaptions (the swap market models) which are of the Black-76 type and thus conforming with market practice.
- By construction the market models are thus very easy to calibrate to mar ket data for caps/floors and swaptions respectively. They are then used to price more exotic products. For this later pricing part, however, we wil typically have to resort to some numerical method, like Monte Carlo.

27.1   Caps: Definition and Market Practice

In this section we discuss LIBOR caps and the market practice for pricing and quoting these intruments. To this end we consider a fixed set of increasing matu rities $T_0, T_1, \ldots, T_N$ and we define α_i, by

$$\alpha_i = T_i - T_{i-1}, \quad i = 1, \ldots N.$$

The number α_i is known as the **tenor**, and in a typical application we could for example have all α_i equal to a quarter of a year.

Definition 27.1 We let $p_i(t)$ denote the zero coupon bond price $p(t, T_i)$ and le $L_i(t)$ denote the LIBOR forward rate (see Section 22.2), contracted at t, for th period $[T_{i-1}, T_i]$, i.e.

$$L_i(t) = \frac{1}{\alpha_i} \cdot \frac{p_{i-1}(t) - p_i(t)}{p_i(t)}, \quad i = 1, \ldots, N. \tag{27.1}$$

We recall that a **cap** with **cap rate** R and **resettlement dates** $T_0, \ldots, T_N$ i a contract which at time T_i gives the holder of the cap the amount

$$X_i = \alpha_i \cdot \max \left[L_i(T_{i-1}) - R, 0 \right], \tag{27.2}$$

for each $i = 1, \ldots, N$. The cap is thus a portfolio of the individual **caplet** $X_1, \ldots, X_N$. We note that the forward rate $L_i(T_{i-1})$ above is in fact the spo rate at time T_{i-1} for the period $[T_{i-1}, T_i]$, and determined already at time T_{i-1} The amount X_i is thus determined at T_{i-1} but not payed out until at time T_i. We also note that, formally speaking, the caplet X_i is a call option on the underlying spot rate.

The market practice is to use the Black-76 formula for the pricing of caplets

Definition 27.2 (Black's Formula for Caplets) The Black-76 formula for the caplet

$$X_i = \alpha_i \cdot \max \left[L(T_{i-1}, T_i) - R, 0 \right], \tag{27.3}$$

is given by the expression

$$\mathrm{Capl}_i^{\mathrm{B}}(t) = \alpha_i \cdot p_i(t) \left\{ L_i(t) N[d_1] - R N[d_2] \right\}, \quad i = 1, \ldots, N, \tag{27.4}$$

where

$$d_1 = \frac{1}{\sigma_i \sqrt{T_i - t}} \left[\ln \left(\frac{L_i(t)}{R} \right) + \frac{1}{2} \sigma_i^2 (T - t) \right], \tag{27.5}$$

$$d_2 = d_1 - \sigma_i \sqrt{T_i - t}. \tag{27.6}$$

The constant σ_i is known as the **Black volatility** *for caplet No. i. In order to make the dependence on the Black volatility σ_i explicit we will sometimes write the caplet price as $Capl_i^B(t; \sigma_i)$.*

It is implicit in the Black formula that the forward rates are lognormal (under some probability measure), but until recently there was no firm theoretical base for the use of the Black-76 formula for caplets. One of the main goals of this chapter is precisely that of investigating whether it is possible to build an arbitrage free model object which produces formulas of the Black type for caplet prices.

In the market, cap prices are not quoted in monetary terms but instead in terms of **implied Black volatilities**, and these volatilities can furthermore be quoted as **flat volatilities** or as **spot volatilities** (also known as **forward volatilities**). They are defined as follows.

Let us consider a fixed date t, the fixed set of dates $T_0, T_1, \ldots, T_N$ where $t \leq T_0$, and a fixed cap rate R. We assume that, for each $i = 1, \ldots, N$, there is a traded cap with resettlement dates $T_0, T_1, \ldots, T_i$, and we denote the corresponding observed market price by $\mathbf{Cap_i^m}$. From this data we can easily compute the market prices for the corresponding caplets as

$$\mathbf{Capl_i^m}(t) = \mathbf{Cap_i^m}(t) - \mathbf{Cap_{i-1}^m}(t), \quad i = 1, \ldots, N. \tag{27.7}$$

with the convention $\mathbf{Cap_0^m}(t) = 0$. Alternatively, given market data for caplets we can easily compute the corresponding market data for caps.

Definition 27.3 *Given market price data as above, the implied Black volatilities are defined as follows.*

- *The implied* **flat volatilities** $\bar{\sigma}_1, \ldots, \bar{\sigma}_N$ *are defined as the solutions of the equations*

$$\mathbf{Cap_i^m}(t) = \sum_{k=1}^{i} \mathbf{Capl_k^B}(t; \bar{\sigma}_i), \quad i = 1, \ldots, N. \tag{27.8}$$

- *The implied* **forward** *or* **spot** *volatilities* $\bar{\sigma}_1, \ldots, \bar{\sigma}_N$ *are defined as solutions of the equations*

$$\mathbf{Capl_i^m}(t) = \mathbf{Capl_i^B}(t; \bar{\sigma}_i), \quad i = 1, \ldots, N. \tag{27.9}$$

A sequence of implied volatilities $\bar{\sigma}_1, \ldots, \bar{\sigma}_N$ *(flat or spot) is called a volatility* **term structure**. *Note that we use the same notation $\bar{\sigma}_i$ for flat as well as for spot volatilities. In applications this will be made clear by the context.*

Summarizing the formal definition above, the flat volatility $\bar{\sigma}_i$ is volatility implied by the Black formula if you use *the same* volatility for each caplet in the cap with maturity T_i. The spot volatility σ_i is just the implied volatility from caplet No. i. The difference between flat and forward volatilities is thus similar to the difference between yields and forward rates. A typical shape of the volatility term structure (flat or spot) for caps with, say, a three months tenor is that it has an upward hump for maturities around two–three years, but that the long end of the curve is downward sloping.

27.2 The LIBOR Market Model

We now turn from market practice to the construction of the so-called LIBOR market models. To motivate these models let us consider the theoretical arbitrage free pricing of caps. The price $c_i(t)$ of a caplet No. i is of course on the one hand given by the standard risk neutral valuation formula

$$\textbf{Capl}_i(t) = \alpha_i E^Q \left[e^{-\int_0^{T_i} r(s)ds} \cdot \max\left[L_i(T_{i-1}) - R, 0\right] \middle| \mathcal{F}_t \right], \quad i = 1, \ldots, N,$$

but it is much more natural to use the T_i forward measure to obtain

$$\textbf{Capl}_i(t) = \alpha_i p_i(t) E^{T_i} \left[\max\left[L_i(T_{i-1}) - R, 0\right] \middle| \mathcal{F}_t \right], \quad i = 1, \ldots, N, \quad (27.10)$$

where E^{T_i} denotes expectation under the Q^{T_i}. In order to have a more compact notation we will from now on denote Q^{T_i} by Q^i.

The focal point of the LIBOR models is the following simple result.

Lemma 27.4 *For every $i = 1, \ldots, N$, the LIBOR process L_i is a martingale under the corresponding forward measure Q^{T_i}, on the interval $[0, T_{i-1}]$.*

Proof We have

$$\alpha_i \cdot L_i(t) = \frac{p_{i-1}(t)}{p_i(t)} - 1.$$

The process 1 is obviously a martingale under any measure. The process p_{i-1}/p_i is the price of the T_{i-1} bond normalized by the numeraire p_i. Since p_i is the numeraire for the martingale measure Q^{T_i}, the process p_{i-1}/p_i is thus trivially a martingale on the interval $[0, T_{i-1}]$. Thus $\alpha_i L_i$ is a martingale and hence L_i is also a martingale.   ⬜

The basic idea is now to define the LIBOR rates such that, for each i, $L_i(T)$ will be lognormal under "it's own" measure Q^i, since then all caplet prices in (27.10) will be given by a Black type formula. In order to do this we consider the following objects as given a priori.

- A set of resettlement dates $T_0, \ldots, T_N$.
- An arbitrage free market bond with maturities $T_0, \ldots, T_N$.
- A k-dimensional Q^N-Wiener process W^N.

- For each $i = 1, \ldots, N$ a *deterministic* function of time $\sigma_i(t)$.
- An initial nonnegative forward rate term structure $L_1(0), \ldots, L_N(0)$.
- For each $i = 1, \ldots, N$, we define W^i as the k-dimensional Q^i-Wiener process generated by W^N under the Girsanov transformation $Q^N \to Q^i$.

Definition 27.5 *If the LIBOR forward rates have the dynamics*

$$dL_i(t) = L_i(t)\sigma_i(t)dW^i(t), \quad i = 1, \ldots, N, \qquad (27.11)$$

where W^i is Q^i-Wiener as described above, then we say that we have a discrete tenor **LIBOR market model** *with volatilities $\sigma_1, \ldots, \sigma_N$.*

From the definition above it is not obvious that, given a specification of $\sigma_1, \ldots, \sigma_N$, there exists a corresponding LIBOR market model. In order to arrive at the basic pricing formulas as quickly as possible we will temporarily ignore the existence problem, but we will come back to it below and thus provide the missing link.

27.3 Pricing Caps in the LIBOR Model

Given a LIBOR market model, the pricing of a caplet, and hence also a cap, is trivial. Since L_i in (27.11) is just a GBM we obtain

$$L_i(T) = L_i(t) \cdot e^{\int_t^T \sigma_i(s)dW^i(s) - \frac{1}{2}\int_t^T \|\sigma_i(s)\|^2 ds}.$$

Since σ_i is assumed to be deterministic this implies that, conditional on $\mathcal{F}_t$, $L_i(T)$ is lognormal, i.e. we can write

$$L_i(T) = L_i(t)e^{Y_i(t,T)},$$

where $Y_i(t,T)$ is normally distributed with expected value

$$m_i(t,T) = -\frac{1}{2}\int_t^T \|\sigma_i(s)\|^2 ds, \qquad (27.12)$$

and variance

$$\Sigma_i^2(t,T) = \int_t^T \|\sigma_i(s)\|^2 ds. \qquad (27.13)$$

Using these results and (27.10), a simple calculation gives us the pricing formula for caps. Alternatively we see that the expectation E^i for the cap price in (27.10) is just the call price, within the Black–Scholes framework, in a world with zero short rate on an underlying traded asset with lognormal distribution as above.

Proposition 27.6 *In the LIBOR market model, the caplet prices are given by*

$$\mathbf{Capl}_i(t) = \alpha_i \cdot p_i(t) \{L_i(t)N[d_1] - RN[d_2]\}, \quad i = 1, \ldots, N, \qquad (27.14)$$

where

$$d_1 = \frac{1}{\Sigma_i(t, T_{i-1})} \left[\ln\left(\frac{L_i(t)}{R}\right) + \frac{1}{2}\Sigma_i^2(t, T_{i-1}) \right], \qquad (27.15)$$

$$d_2 = d_1 - \Sigma_i(t, T_{i-1}), \qquad (27.16)$$

with Σ_i defined by (27.13).

We thus see that each caplet price is given by a Black type formula.

Remark 27.3.1 Sometimes it is more convenient working with a LIBOR model of the form

$$dL_i(t) = L_i(t)\sigma_i(t)dW^i(t), \quad i = 1, \ldots, N, \qquad (27.17)$$

where $\sigma_i(t)$ is a *scalar* deterministic function, W^i is a *scalar* Q^i-Wiener process. Then the formulas above still hold if we replace $\|\sigma_i\|^2$ by σ_i^2. We can also allow for correlation between the various Wiener processes, but this will not affect the pricing of caps and floors. Such a correlation *will* however affect the pricing of more complicated products.

27.4 Terminal Measure Dynamics and Existence

We now turn to the question whether there always exists a LIBOR market model for any given specification of the deterministic volatilities $\sigma_1, \ldots, \sigma_N$. In order to even get started we first have to specify all LIBOR rates $L_1, \ldots, L_N$ under **one** common measure, and the canonical choice is the **terminal measure** Q^N.

Our problem is then basically that of carrying out a two stage program.

- Specify all LIBOR rates under Q^N with dynamics of the form

$$dL_i(t) = L_i(t)\mu_i(t, L(t)) \, dt + L_i(t)\sigma_i(t)dW^N(t), \quad i = 1, \ldots, N. \quad (27.18)$$

  where $L(t) = [L_1(t), \ldots, L_N(t)]^\star$, and μ_i is some deterministic function.
- Show that, for some suitable choice of $\mu_1, \ldots, \mu_N$, the Q^N dynamics in (27.18) will imply Q^i dynamics of the form (27.11).

In order to carry out this program we need to see how W^N is transformed into W^i as we change measure from Q^N to Q^i. We do this inductively by studying the effect of the Girsanov transformation from Q^i to Q^{i-1}.

Remark 27.4.1 We have a small but irritating notational problem. LIBOR rates are typically denoted by the letter "L", but this is also a standard notation for a likelihood process. In order to avoid confusion we therefore introduce the notational convention that, *in this chapter only*, likelihood processes will be denoted by the letter η. In particular we introduce the notation

$$\eta_i^j(t) = \frac{dQ^j}{dQ^i}, \quad \text{on } \mathcal{F}_t \text{ for } i, j = 1, \ldots, N. \qquad (27.19)$$

In order to get some idea of how we should choose the Q^N drifts of the LIBOR rates in (27.18) we will now perform some informal calculations. We thus (informally) assume that the LIBOR dynamics are of the form (27.18) under Q^N and that they are also of the form (27.11) under their own martingale measure. From Proposition 26.4 we know that the Radon–Nikodym derivative η_i^j is given by

$$\eta_i^j(t) = \frac{p_i(0)}{p_j(0)} \cdot \frac{p_j(t)}{p_i(t)}, \tag{27.20}$$

and in particular

$$\eta_i^{i-1}(t) = a_i \cdot \frac{p_{i-1}(t)}{p_i(t)} = a_i \left(1 + \alpha_i L_i(t)\right), \tag{27.21}$$

where $a_i = p_i(0)/p_{i-1}(0)$. From this formula we can now easily compute the η_i^{i-1} dynamics under Q^i as

$$d\eta_i^{i-1}(t) = a_i \alpha_i dL_i(t). \tag{27.22}$$

Assuming (still informally) that the L_i-dynamics are as in (27.11), and using (27.1) we then obtain

$$d\eta_i^{i-1}(t) = a_i \alpha_i L_i(t) \sigma_i(t) dW^i(t) \tag{27.23}$$

$$= a_i \alpha_i \frac{1}{\alpha_i} \left(\frac{p_{i-1}(t)}{p_i(t)} - 1 \right) \sigma_i(t) dW^i(t) \tag{27.24}$$

$$= \eta_i^{i-1}(t) a_i \alpha_i \frac{1}{\eta_i^{i-1}(t)} \left(\frac{p_{i-1}(t)}{p_i(t)} - 1 \right) \sigma_i(t) dW^i(t) \tag{27.25}$$

Using (27.21) we finally obtain

$$d\eta_i^{i-1}(t) = \eta_i^{i-1}(t) \frac{\alpha_i L_i(t)}{1 + \alpha_i L_i(t)} \sigma_i(t) dW^i(t). \tag{27.26}$$

Thus the Girsanov kernel for η_i^{i-1} is given by

$$\frac{\alpha_i L_i(t)}{1 + \alpha_i L_i(t)} \sigma_i^\star(t), \tag{27.27}$$

so from the Girsanov Theorem we have the relation

$$dW^i(t) = \frac{\alpha_i L_i(t)}{1 + \alpha_i L_i(t)} \sigma_i^\star(t) dt + dW^{i-1}(t). \tag{27.28}$$

Applying this inductively we obtain

$$dW^i(t) = - \sum_{k=i+1}^{N} \frac{\alpha_k L_k(t)}{1 + \alpha_k L_k(t)} \sigma_k^\star(t) dt + dW^N(t), \tag{27.29}$$

and plugging this into (27.11) we can finally obtain the Q^N dynamics of L_i (see (27.30) below).

All this was done under the informal assumption that there actually existed a LIBOR model satisfying both (27.11) and (27.18). We can however easily turn the argument around and we have the following existence result.

Proposition 27.7 *Consider a given volatility structure σ_1, σ_N, where each σ_i is assumed to be boundeed, a probability measure Q^N and a standard Q^N-Wiener process W^N. Define the processes $L_1, \ldots, L_N$ by*

$$dL_i(t) = -L_i(t) \left(\sum_{k=i+1}^{N} \frac{\alpha_k L_k(t)}{1 + \alpha_k L_k(t)} \sigma_k(t) \sigma_i^\star(t) \right) dt + L_i(t)\sigma_i(t)dW^N(t),$$
(27.30)

for $i = 1, \ldots, N$ where we use the convention $\sum_N^N(\ldots) = 0$. Then the Q^i-dynamics of L_i are given by (27.11). Thus there exists a LIBOR model with the given volatility structure.

Proof   Given that (27.30) has a solution for $i = 1, \ldots, N$, and that the Girsanov kernel in (27.27) satisfies the Novikov condition, the proof consists of exactly the calculations above. As for the existence of a solution of (27.30), this is trivial for $i = N$ since then the equation reads

$$dL_N(t) = L_i(t)\sigma_N(t)dW^N(t),$$

which is just GBM and since σ_N is bounded a solution does exist. Assume now that (27.30) admits a solution for $k = i + 1, \ldots, N$. We can then write the $i : th$ component of (27.30) as

$$dL_i(t) = L_i(t)\mu_i\left[t, L_{i+1}(t), \ldots, L_N(t)\right] dt + L_i(T)\sigma_i(t)dW^N(t),$$

where the point is that μ_i does only depend on L_k for $k = i + 1, \ldots, N$ and not on L_i. Denoting the vector $(L_{i+1}, \ldots, L_N)$ by L_{i+1}^N we thus have the explicit solution

$$L_i(t) = L_i(0) \exp\left\{ \int_0^t \left(\mu_i\left[s, L_{i+1}^N(s)\right] - \frac{1}{2}\|\sigma_i\|^2(s) \right) ds \right\}$$
$$\times \exp\left\{ \int_0^t \mu_i\left[s, L_{i+1}^N(s)\right] dW^N(s) \right\},$$

thus proving existence by induction. It also follows by induction that, given an initial positive LIBOR term structure, all LIBOR rate processes will be positive. From this we see that the Girsanov kernel in (27.27) is also bounded and thus it satisfies the Novikov condition.   □

Remark 27.4.2 Sometimes it is more convenient working with a LIBOR model of the form

$$dL_i(t) = L_i(t)\sigma_i(t)dW_i(t), \quad i = 1, \ldots, N, \tag{27.31}$$

where $\sigma_i(t)$ is a *scalar* deterministic function, W_i is a *scalar* Q^i-Wiener process, and where we assume a given correlation structure $dW_i(t)dW_j(t) = \rho_{ij}$. This can easily be obtained by a small variation of the arguments above, and eqn (27.30) is then replaced by

$$dL_i(t) = -L_i(t)\left(\sum_{k=i+1}^{N}\frac{\alpha_k L_k(t)}{1+\alpha_k L_k(t)}\sigma_i(t)\sigma_k(t)\rho_{ik}\right)dt + L_i(t)\sigma_i(t)dW_i^N(t),$$

$$\tag{27.32}$$

where W_i^N is the Q^N-Wiener process generated by W_i under the Girsanov transformation $Q^i \to Q^N$.

27.5 Calibration and Simulation

Suppose that we want to price some exotic (i.e. not a cap or a floor) interest rate derivative, like a Bermudan swaption. performing this with a LIBOR model means that we typically carry out the followng two steps:

- Use implied Black volatilities in order to calibrate the model parameters to market data.
- Use Monte Carlo (or some other numerical method) to price the exotic instrument.

In this section we mainly discuss the calibration part, and only comment briefly on the numerical aspects. For numerics and simulation see the Notes.

Let us thus assume that, for the resettlement dates $T_0, \ldots, T_N$, we are given an empirical term structure of implied forward volatilities, $\bar{\sigma}_1, \ldots, \bar{\sigma}_N$ i.e. the implied Black volatilities for all caplets. For simplicity we assume that we are standing at time $t = 0$. Comparing the Black formula (27.4) with (27.14) we see that in order to calibrate the model we have to choose the deterministic LIBOR volatilities $\sigma_1(\cdot), \ldots, \sigma_N(\cdot)$, such that

$$\bar{\sigma}_i = \frac{1}{T_i}\int_0^{T_{i-1}} \|\sigma_i(s)\|^2 ds, \quad i = 1, \ldots, N. \tag{27.33}$$

Alternatively, if we use a scalar Wiener process for each LIBOR rate we must choose the scalar function $\sigma_i(\cdot)$ such that

$$\bar{\sigma}_i = \frac{1}{T_i}\int_0^{T_{i-1}} \sigma_i^2(s) ds, \quad i = 1, \ldots, N. \tag{27.34}$$

This is obviously a higly underdetermined system, so in applications it is common to make some structural assumption about the shape of the volatility functions. Below is a short and incomplete list of popular specifications. We use the formalism with a scalar Wiener process for each forward rate, and we recall that L_i lives on the time interval $0 \le t \le T_{i-1}$. We also introduce the temporary convention that $T_{-1} = 0$.

1. For each $i = 1, \ldots, N$, assume that the corresponding volatility is constant in time, i.e. that

$$\sigma_i(t) = \sigma_i, \quad \text{for } 0 \le t \le T_{i-1}.$$

2. For each $i = 1, \ldots, N$, assume that σ_i is piecewise constant, i.e. that

$$\sigma_i(t) = \sigma_{ij}, \quad \text{for } T_{j-1} < t \le T_j, j = 0, \ldots, i-1$$

3. As in item 2, but with the requirement that the volatility only depends on the number of resettlement dates left to maturity, i.e. that

$$\sigma_{ij} = \beta_{i-j}, \quad \text{for } T_{j-1} < t \le T_j, j = 0, \ldots, i-1$$

where $\beta_1, \ldots, \beta_N$ are fixed numbers.

4. As in item 2, with the further specification that

$$\sigma_{ij} = \beta_i \gamma_j, \quad \text{for } T_{j-1} < t \le T_j, j = 0, \ldots, i-1$$

where β_i and γ_j are fixed numbers.

5. Assume some simple functional parameterized form of the volatilities such as for example

$$\sigma_i(t) = q_i(T_{i-1} - t)e^{\beta_i(T_{i-1}-t)}$$

where $q_i(\cdot)$ is some polynomial and β_i is a real number.

Assuming that the model has been calibrated to market data, Mone Carlo simulation is the standard tool for computing prices of exotics. Since the SDEs (27.30) and (27.32) are too complicated to allow analytical solutions, we have to resort to simulation of discretized versions of the equations.

The simplest way to discretize (27.30) is to introduce a grid of length h and use the following recursive Euler scheme.

$$L_i((n+1)h) = L_i(nh) - L_i(nh)\left(\sum_{k=i+1}^{N} \frac{\alpha_k L_k(nh)}{1 + \alpha_k L_k(nh)}\sigma_i(nh)\sigma_k^\star(nh)\right)h$$

$$+ L_i(nh)\sigma_i(nh)\left\{W^N((n+1)h) - W^N(nh)\right\}, \tag{27.35}$$

However, from the point of view of numerical stability it is preferable to use a discretization of the SDE for $\ln(L_i)$. Using Itô we easily obtain

$$d\ln L_i(t) = -\left(\frac{1}{2}\sigma_i^2(t) + \sigma_i(t)\sigma_k^\star(t) \sum_{k=i+1}^{N} \frac{\alpha_k L_k(t)}{1+\alpha_k L_k(t)}\right) dt + \sigma_i(t)dW^N(t).$$
(27.36)

The point of this is that we now have a deterministic diffusion part, which leads to improved convergence of the corresponding discrete scheme

$$\ln L_i((n+1)h) = \ln L_i(nh) - h\left(\frac{1}{2}\sigma_i^2(nh) + \sum_{k=i+1}^{N} \frac{\alpha_k L_k(nh)}{1+\alpha_k L_k(nh)}\sigma_i(nh)\sigma_k^\star(nh)\right)$$

$$+\sigma_i(nh)\left\{W^N((n+1)h) - W^N(nh)\right\}. \tag{27.37}$$

27.6 The Discrete Savings Account

In the LIBOR models discussed above there exists a forward neutral martingale measure $Q^i = Q^{T_i}$ for each $i = 1, \ldots, N$, but so far we have not seen any risk neutral measure Q^B for the bank account B, (also known as the *savings account*) and in fact we have not even seen a bank account process in the model. A natural question is therefore to investigate whether the LIBOR model will automatically imply a money account process B, as well as a corresponding risk neautral measure Q^B.

In this context it is, however, not quite clear what one would mean with a bank account. Since we are working in continuous time, one possibility is to look for a continuous bank account of the form we have seen earlier in the book, i.e. one with dynamics

$$dB(t) = r(t)B(t)dt,$$

where r is the continuously compounded short rate. However, since we have modeled discrete forward rates it would be unnatural to mix those with a continuously compounded short rate, so the natural choice would be to look for a bank account which is resettled at the points $T_0, \ldots, T_N$.

In order to construct the bank account we recall that the essential property is that it should be riskless on a local time scale, i.e. riskless between T_n and T_N for each n. The obvious way to achieve this is by forming the discretely rebalanced self-financing portfolio specified by constantly rolling over the bond of the shortest remaining maturity. More formally, suppose that we are standing at T_0 and consider the following portfolio strategy:

1. At T_0 invest one unit of money into the T_1 bond.
2. At T_1 sell the T_1 bond and invest everything in the T_2 bond.
3. Repeat this procedure recursively until T_N.

Denoting the value of this self-financing portfolio by B we immediately have

$$B(T_N) = \frac{B(T_n)}{p(T_n, T_N)}, \quad n = 0, \dots, N - 1, \qquad (27.38$$

and using the relation $p(T_n, T_N) = [1 + \alpha_N L(T_n, T_N)]^{-1}$ we obtain the discrete B dynamics as

$$B(T_0) = 1, \qquad (27.39$$

$$B(T_N) = (1 + \alpha_N L(T_n, T_N)) \, B(T_n), \qquad (27.40$$

or, more explicitly

$$B(T_n) = \prod_{k=0}^{n-1} \frac{1}{p(T_k, T_{k+1})}, \qquad (27.41$$

alternatively

$$B(T_n) = \prod_{k=0}^{n-1} \left[1 + \alpha_{k+1} L(T_k, T_{k+1})\right], \qquad (27.42$$

We note that B is indeed locally risk free in the sense that $B(T_N)$ is known already at time T_n, i.e. as a discrete time process B is *predictable* in the sense o Appendix C.

We can now easily determine the martingle measure coresponding to the discrete saving account.

Proposition 27.8 *The Radon–Nikodym derivative for the change from Q^N to Q^B is given by*

$$\frac{dQ^B}{dQ^N} = p(0, T_N) B(T_N), \quad on \ \mathcal{F}_{T_N} \qquad (27.43$$

Proof   From Proposition 26.4 we have (on $\mathcal{F}_{T_N}$)

$$\frac{dQ^B}{dQ^N} = \frac{B(T_N)}{p(T_N, T_N)} \cdot \frac{B(0)}{p(0, T_N)},$$

and since $P(T_N, T_N) = 1$ and $B(0) = 1$ we have the result.   ☐

27.7   Swaps

We now move from the LIBOR Market Models to the the Swap Market Models Consider a fixed set of resettlement dates $T_0, T_1, \dots, T_N$, with the usual notation $\alpha_i = T_i - T_{i-1}$. From Section 22.3.3 we recall that in an interest rate **swap**, a set of floating rate payments (the *floating leg*) are exchanged for a set of fixed payments (the *fixed leg*). The terminology for swaps always refers to the fixed leg, so the holder of a **reciever swap** with **tenor** $T_N - T_n$ will, at the dates $T_{n+1}, \ldots, T_N$, receive the fixed leg and pay the floating leg. For a **payer swap** the payments go in the other direction. For short we will refer to this swap as a $T_n \times (T_N - T_n)$ swap. We now make this precise.

Definition 27.9 *The payments in a $T_n \times (T_N - T_n)$ payer swap are as follows:*

- *Payments will be made and received at $T_{n+1}, T_{n+2}, \ldots, T_N$.*
- *For every elementary period $[T_i, T_{i+1}]$, $i = n, \ldots, N - 1$, the LIBOR rate $L_{i+1}(T_i)$ is set at time T_i and the floating leg*

$$\alpha_{i+1} \cdot L_{i+1}(T_i), \tag{27.44}$$

is received at T_{i+1}.
- *For the same period the fixed leg*

$$\alpha_{i+1} \cdot K \tag{27.45}$$

is payed at T_{i+1}.

It is easy to see (exercise for the reader) that the arbitrage free value, at $t < T_n$, of the floating payment made at T_i is given by

$$p(t, T_i) - p(t, T_{i+1}),$$

so the total value of the floating side at time t for $t \leq T_n$ equals

$$\sum_{i=n}^{N-1} [p(t, T_i) - p(t, T_{i+1})] = p_n(t) - p_N(t)$$

The total value at time t of the fixed side equals

$$\sum_{i=n}^{N-1} p(t, T_{i+1})\alpha_{i+1}K = K \sum_{i=n+1}^{N} \alpha_i p_i(t),$$

so the net value $\mathbf{PS_n^N}(t; K)$ of the $T_n \times (T_N - T_n)$ payer swap at time $t < T_n$ is thus given by

$$\mathbf{PS_n^N}(t; K) = p_n(t) - p_N(t) - K \sum_{i=n+1}^{N} \alpha_i p_i(t). \tag{27.46}$$

From Section 22.3.3 we recall the following definition.

Definition 27.10 *The **par** or **forward swap rate** $R_n^N(t)$ of the $T_n \times (T_N - T_n)$ swap is the value of K for which $\mathbf{PS_n^N}(t; K) = 0$, i.e.*

$$R_n^N(t) = \frac{p_n(t) - p_N(t)}{\sum_{i=n+1}^{N} \alpha_i p_i(t)}. \tag{27.47}$$

The first crucial observation to make at this point is that in the formula for the par swap rate we can interpret the denominator $\sum_{i=n+1}^{N} \alpha_i p_i(t)$ as the value, at t of a traded asset, namely as a buy-and-hold portfolio consisting, for each i, of α_i units of the zero coupon bond maturing at T_i. This object is so important that we give it a separate name.

Definition 27.11 *For each pair n, k with $n < k$, the process $S_n^k(t)$ is defined by*

$$S_n^k(t) = \sum_{i=n+1}^{k} \alpha_i p(t, T_i). \tag{27.48}$$

S_n^k *is referred to as the* **accrual factor** *or as* **the present value of a basis point**.

With this terminology we can express the par swap rate as

$$R_n^N(t) = \frac{p_n(t) - p_N(t)}{S_n^N(t)}, \quad 0 \le t \le T_n. \tag{27.49}$$

In the market there are no quoted prices for different swaps. Instead there are market quotes for the par swap rates R_n^N, and we see that from these we can easily compute the arbitrage free price for a payer swap with swap rate K by the formula

$$\mathbf{PS_n^N}(t; K) = \left(R_n^N(t) - K \right) S_n^N(t). \tag{27.50}$$

27.8 Swaptions: Definition and Market Practice

The definition of a swaption (short for "swap option") is as follows.

Definition 27.12 *A $T_n \times (T_N - T_n)$* **payer swaption** *with* **swaption strike** *K is a contract which at the exercise date T_n gives the holder the right but not the obligation to enter into a $T_n \times (T_N - T_n)$ swap with the fixed swap rate K.*

We thus see that the payer swaption is a contingent T_n-claim X_n^N defined by

$$X_n^N = \max \left[\mathbf{PS}_n^N(T_n; K); 0 \right], \tag{27.51}$$

which, using (27.49), we can write as

$$X_n^N = \max \left[R_n^N(T_n) - K; 0 \right] S_n^N(T_n) \tag{27.52}$$

Expressed in the numeraire S_n^N, the swaption is thus formally a call option on R_n^N with strike price K. The market practice is to compute swaption prices by using a formal extension of the Black-76 formula and to quote prices in terms of the implied Black volatilities.

Definition 27.13 (Black's Formula for Swaptions) *The Black-76 formula for a $T_n \times (T_N - T_n)$ payer swaption with strike K is defined as*

$$\mathbf{PSN}_n^N(t) = S_n^N(t) \left\{ R_n^N(t)N[d_1] - KN[d_2] \right\}, \qquad (27.53)$$

where

$$d_1 = \frac{1}{\sigma_{n,N}\sqrt{T_n - t}} \left[\ln\left(\frac{R_n^N(t)}{K} \right) + \frac{1}{2}\sigma_{n,N}^2(T_n - t) \right] \qquad (27.54)$$

$$d_2 = d_1 - \sigma_{n,N}\sqrt{T_n - t}. \qquad (27.55)$$

*The constant $\sigma_{n,N}$ is known as the **Black volatility**. Given a market price for the swaption, the Black volatility implied by the Black formula is referred to as the **implied Black volatility**.*

As was the case with the Black formula for caps, the Black swaption formula has been used by the market for a long time, without any explicit coherent underlying model. Our task is thus to build an arbitrage free model with the property that the theoretical prices derived within the model have the structure of the Black-76 formula above.

27.9 The Swap Market Models

From (27.52) it is clear that the natural choice of numeraire for swaptions is the accrual factor S_n^N, and since the accrual factor has an intepretation as the value of a traded asset it is a bona fide choice of numeraire from the point of view of martingale measures. We now have the following simple but important result.

Lemma 27.14 *Denote the martingale measure for the numeraire S_n^k by Q_n^k. Then the forward swap rate R_n^k is a Q_n^k-martingale.*

Proof This follows immediately from the fact that R_n^k is the value of a self-financing portfolio (a long T_n bond and a short T_k bond), divided by the value of the self-financing portfolio S_n^k. □

Thus the forward swap rate, like the LIBOR rates earlier, is a martingale under a suitable choice of numeraire, and the accrual factor plays the same role for swap market models as the bond prices did for the LIBOR models. The basic idea in the swaption market model which we will discuss below is then simply to model the forward swap rates R_n^N lognormally as GBM under the appropriate measures.

Definition 27.15 *Given the resettlement dates T_0, T_1, T_N, consider a fixed subset $\mathcal{N}$ of all positive integer pairs (n, k) such that $0 \leq n < k \leq N$. Consider* *furthermore, for each* $(n,k) \in \mathcal{N}$, *a deterministic function of time* $\sigma_{n,k}(\cdot)$. *A* **swap market model** *with the volatilities* $\sigma_{n,k}$ *is then specified by assuming that the par swap rates have dynamics of the form*

$$dR_n^k(t) = R_n^k(t)\sigma_{n,k}(t)dW_n^k(t), \quad (n,k) \in \mathcal{N}, \tag{27.56}$$

where W_n^k *is (possibly multidimensional) Wiener under* Q_n^k.

Remark 27.9.1 Because of the interrelations between different par swap rates, we cannot model all possible swap rates R_n^k for $0 \leq n < k \leq N$ simultaneously, so in a concrete model we have to restrict ourselves to modeling only a subset $\mathcal{N}$ of all par swap rates. In a model with $N + 1$ maturity dates we can only hope to model N independent swap rates, and typical choices of $\mathcal{N}$ are given by the following examples:

- A **regular swap market model** is specified by modeling, a fixed N, the par swap rates $R_0^N, R_1^N, \ldots, R_n^N$ i.e.

$$\mathcal{N} = \{(0,N),(1,N),\ldots,(N-1,N)\}.$$

- A **reverse swap market model** is specified by modeling, for a fixed N, the swap rates $R_0^1, R_0^2, \ldots, R_0^N$ i.e.

$$\mathcal{N} = \{(0,1),(0,2),\ldots,(0,N)\}.$$

27.10   Pricing Swaptions in the Swap Market Model

Given a swap market model, the pricing of a $T_n \times (T_N - T_n)$ swaption is surprisingly trivial. Formula (26.6) immediately gives us the following pricing formula for the payer swaption (regardless of the specific form of the model).

$$\mathbf{PSN}_n^N(t) = S_n^N(t) \cdot E^{n,N} \left[\max \left[R_n^N(T_n) - K; 0 \right] \middle| \mathcal{F}_t \right]. \quad 0 \leq t \leq T_n, \tag{27.57}$$

Since R_n^N, defined in (27.56), is just GBM we obtain

$$R_n^N(T_n) = R_n^N(t) \cdot e^{\int_t^{T_n} \sigma_{n,N}(s)dW_n^N(s) - \frac{1}{2}\int_t^{T_n} \|\sigma_{n,N}(s)\|^2 ds}. \tag{27.58}$$

Furthermore, since σ_i is assumed to be deterministic this implies that, conditional on $\mathcal{F}_t$, $R_n^N(T_n)$ is lognormal, i.e. we can write

$$L_i(T_n) = R_n^N(t)e^{Y_n^N(t,T_n)},$$

where $Y_n^N(t, T_n)$ is normally distributed with expected value

$$m_n^N = -\frac{1}{2}\int_t^{T_n} \|\sigma_{n,N}(s)\|^2 ds, \tag{27.59}$$

and variance

$$\Sigma_{n,N}^2 = \int_t^{T_n} \|\sigma_{n,N}(s)\|^2 ds. \tag{27.60}$$

As for the LIBOR model, a simple calculation easily gives us the swaption pricing formula.

Proposition 27.16 *In the swap market model (27.56), the $T_n \times (T_N - T_n)$ payer swaption price with strike K is given by*

$$\mathbf{PSN}_n^N(t) = S_n^N(t) \left\{ R_n^N(t)N[d_1] - KN[d_2] \right\}, \tag{27.61}$$

where

$$d_1 = \frac{1}{\Sigma_{n,N}} \left[\ln\left(\frac{R_n^N(t)}{K}\right) + \frac{1}{2}\Sigma_{n,N}^2 \right] \tag{27.62}$$

$$d_2 = d_1 - \Sigma_{n,N}. \tag{27.63}$$

We thus see that each swaption price is given by a Black type formula.

Remark 27.10.1 Sometimes it is more convenient working with a swap market model of the form

$$dR_n^N(t) = R_n^N(t)\sigma_{n,N}(t)dW_n^N(t) \tag{27.64}$$

where $\sigma_{n,N}(t)$ is a *scalar* deterministic function, W_n^N is a *scalar* Q^i-Wiener process. Then the formulas above still hold if we replace $\|\sigma_{n,N}\|^2$ by $\sigma_{n,N}^2$. We can also allow for correlation between the various Wiener processes, but this will not affect the swaption prices. Such a correlation *will* however affect the pricing of more complicated products.

In this section we have modeled each par swap rate R_n^k as GBM under its own martingale measure Q_n^k, and this led to the Black formula for swaptions. In order to price more exotic products we will typically have to resort to numerical methods like Monte Carlo, and then there is a need to specify the dynamics of the relevant par swap rates under a single martingale measure. This will be done in the next two sections.

27.11   Drift Conditions for the Regular Swap Market Model

In a regular swap market model, we model R_n^N for a fixed N and $0 \le n \le N-1$, so the obvious choice of a common measure for all swap rates is Q_{N-1}^N, which is nothing else (why?) than the T_N-forward measure Q^{T_N}. Our problem is to determine the various drift terms, and since this is somewhat messy it turns out to be convenient to have T_{N+1} as the last payment date rather than T_N. We will thus model $R_0^{N+1}, \ldots, R_N^{N+1}$ and our problem is to determine the drift terms of these par swap rates under the terminal measure Q_N^{N+1}.

Since the diffusion term of R_n^{N+1} will be the same under Q_N^{N+1} as under Q_n^{N+1}, the Q_N^{N+1} dynamics of R_n^{N+1} are of the form

$$dR_n^{N+1} = \mu_n^{N+1} R_n^{N+1} dt + R_n^{N+1} \sigma_{n,N+1} dW_N^{N+1}, \qquad (27.65)$$

where W_N^{N+1} is a Q_N^{N+1} Wiener process, and our problem is to determine the drift term μ_n^{N+1}.

The determination of the par swap drifts involves solving a backward linear difference equation, and for completeness sake we now recall a general result for such equations.

Proposition 27.17 *The linear backward difference equation*

$$x_n = A_{n+1} x_{n+1} + b_{n+1}, \quad n = 0, \ldots, N-1, \qquad (27.66)$$

has the solution

$$x_n = \left(\prod_{j=n+1}^{N} A_j \right) x_N + \sum_{j=n}^{N-1} \left(\prod_{k=n+1}^{j} A_k \right) b_{j+1}, \qquad (27.67)$$

with the convention $\prod_{j=N+1}^{N} a_j = 1$.

Proof   Exercise for the reader.   □

We may now state and prove the drift condition.

Proposition 27.18 *Under the terminal measure Q_N^{N+1}, the R_n^{N+1} dynamics are of the form*

$$dR_n^{N+1} = \mu_n^{N+1} R_n^{N+1} dt + R_n^{N+1} \sigma_{n,N+1} dW_N^{N+1}, \qquad (27.68)$$

where the drift term is given by

$$\mu_n^{N+1} = -\sigma_{n,N+1} \varphi_n,$$

where

$$\varphi_n = \sum_{j=n}^{N-1} \frac{Z_{j+1}}{Z_n} \left[\prod_{k=n+1}^{j} (1 + \alpha_k R_k) \right] \alpha_{j+1} R_{j+1} \sigma_{j+1}^\star, \qquad (27.69)$$

and where Z_n is defined by

$$Z_n = \frac{S_n}{p_{N+1}}. \qquad (27.70)$$

Before going on with the proof we recall that we consider a regular swap market model for $R_0^{N+1}, R_1^{N+1}, \ldots, R_N^{N+1}$, and since the super index $N+1$ will be the same throughout the argument we henceforth suppress the superindex.

Instead of R_n^{N+1}, Q_n^{N+1}, and μ_n^{N+1} we will thus write R_n, Q_n, and μ_n and similarly for all other terms.

For easy reference we also recall the following relations

$$R_n = \frac{p_n - p_{N+1}}{p_n}, \tag{27.71}$$

$$S_n = \sum_{i=n+1}^{N+1} \alpha_i p_i, \tag{27.72}$$

$$dR_n = R_n \sigma_n dW_n, \tag{27.73}$$

where W_n is Q_n-Wiener.

Proof We start by noticing that $S_N = p_{N+1}$, so Q_N is in fact the T_{N+1} forward measure with numeraire p_{N+1}. From Proposition 26.4 we know that, with

$$L_n(t) = \frac{Q_n}{Q_N}, \quad \text{on } \mathcal{F}_t,$$

we have

$$L_n(t) = \gamma_n Z_n(t),$$

where

$$Z_n = \frac{S_n}{p_{N+1}}, \quad \gamma_n = Z_n^{-1}(0). \tag{27.74}$$

Since L_n is a Q_N martingale it must have Q_N dynamics of the form

$$dZ_n = Z_n \varphi_n^\star dW_N, \tag{27.75}$$

so from (27.73), (27.65), and Girsanov's Theorem it follows that

$$\mu_n = -\sigma_n \varphi_n. \tag{27.76}$$

It thus remains to determine the process φ_n and to do this we must determine the Z_n dynamics from (27.74). From (27.72) we have

$$S_n = S_{n+1} + \alpha_{n+1} p_{n+1},$$

so from (27.74) we have

$$Z_n = Z_{n+1} + \alpha_{n+1} \cdot \frac{p_{n+1}}{p_{N+1}}. \tag{27.77}$$

From (27.71) we have

$$p_{n+1} = R_{n+1} S_{n+1} + p_{N+1},$$

and plugging this into (27.77) gives us the recursion

$$Z_n = Z_{n+1} \left(1 + \alpha_{n+1} R_{n+1}\right) + \alpha_{n+1}. \tag{27.78}$$

From this formula, (27.65), and (27.75) we obtain the Q_N dynamics

$$dZ_n = Z_{n+1} \left(1 + \alpha_{n+1} R_{n+1}\right) \varphi^\star_{n+1} dW_N + Z_{n+1} \alpha_{n+1} R_{n+1} \sigma_{n+1} dW_N, \tag{27.79}$$

where we have used the fact that, under Q_N, Z_n has zero drift. We thus have

$$dZ_n = Z_n \frac{Z_{n+1}}{Z_n} \left\{ \left(1 + \alpha_{n+1} R_{n+1}\right) \varphi^\star_{n+1} + \alpha_{n+1} R_{n+1} \sigma_{n+1} \right\} dW_N, \tag{27.80}$$

so from (27.75) we obtain the following recursion for φ_n.

$$\begin{cases} \varphi^\star_n = \frac{Z_{n+1}}{Z_n} \left\{ \left(1 + \alpha_{n+1} R_{n+1}\right) \varphi^\star_{n+1} + \alpha_{n+1} R_{n+1} \sigma_{n+1} \right\} \\ \varphi^\star_N = 0. \end{cases} \tag{27.81}$$

From Proposition 27.17 we obtain the solution

$$\varphi^\star_n = \sum_{j=n}^{N-1} \left(\prod_{k=n+1}^{j} a_k \right) b_{j+1},$$

where

$$a_k = \frac{Z_k}{Z_{k-1}} \left(1 + \alpha_k R_k\right), \quad b_{j+1} = \frac{Z_{j+1}}{Z_j} \alpha_{j+1} R_{j+1} \sigma_{j+1}.$$

A simple caclulation gives us

$$\prod_{k=n+1}^{j} a_k = \frac{Z_j}{Z_n} \prod_{k=n+1}^{j} \left(1 + \alpha_k R_k\right)$$

and we are done. $\qquad\qquad\qquad\qquad\qquad\qquad\qquad\qquad\qquad\square$

27.12 Concluding Comment

It can be shown that, given a swap market model, the LIBOR rates will *not* be lognormal. Thus LIBOR market models and swap market models are in general incompatible.

27.13 Exercises

Exercise 27.1 Prove that the arbitrage free value at $t \leq T_n$ of the T_{i+1} claim

$$\alpha_{i+1} \cdot L_{i+1}(T_i)$$

is given by

$$p(t, T_i) - p(t, T_{i+1}).$$

Exercise 27.2 Convince yourself that the swap measure Q^N_{N-1} equals the forward measure Q^{T_N}.

Exercise 27.3 Show that the arbitrage free price for a payer swap with swap rate K is given by the formula

$$\mathbf{PS^N_n}(t; K) = \left(R^N_n(t) - K\right) S^N_n(t).$$

Exercise 27.4 Prove Proposition 27.17.

27.14   Notes

The basic papers on the LIBOR and swap market models are Miltersen *et al.* (1997), Brace *et al.* (1997), and Jamshidian (1997). Since these basic papers vere published there has appeared a huge literature on the subject. Very readable accounts can be found in Hunt and Kennedy (2000), Pelsser (2000), and the almost encyclopedic Brigo and Mercurio (2007).

28

POTENTIALS AND POSITIVE INTEREST

The purpose of this chapter is to present two approaches to interest rate theory which are based directly on stochastic discount factors, while also relating bond prices to the theory of probabilistic potential theory. A very appealing aspect of these approaches is that they both generate **positive term structures**, i.e. systems of bond prices for which the induced interest rates are all positive.

28.1 Generalities

As a general setup we consider a standard filtered probability space $(\Omega, \mathcal{F}, \mathbf{F}, P)$ where P is the objective measure. We assume, as usual, that the market is pricing all assets, underlying and derivative, using a fixed martingale measure Q (with the money account as the numeraire.

We denote the likelihood process for the transition from the objective measure P to the martingale measure Q by L, i.e.

$$L_t = \frac{dQ_t}{dP_t},$$

where subindex t denotes the restriction of P and Q to $\mathcal{F}_t$. From Section 10.6 we recall that the **stochastic discount factor** Z is defined by

$$Z_t = e^{-\int_0^t r_s ds} \cdot L_t, \tag{28.1}$$

and that the short rate can be recovered from the dynamics of Z by the formula

$$dZ_t = -r_t Z_t + dM_t, \tag{28.2}$$

where M is a martingale defined by $M_t = B_t^{-1} L_t$.

We also recall that for any T-claim Y, the arbitrage free price process is given by

$$\Pi(t; Y) = \frac{E^P[Z_T Y \mid \mathcal{F}_t]}{Z_t},$$

so, in particular, bond prices are given by the formula

$$p(t, T) = \frac{E^P[Z_T \mid \mathcal{F}_t]}{Z_t}. \tag{28.3}$$

We now have the following important result.

Proposition 28.1 *Assume that the short rate is strictly positive and that the economically natural condition*

$$\lim_{T\to\infty} p(0,T) = 0 \qquad (28.4)$$

is satisfied. Then the stochastic discount factor Z is a probabilistic **potential**, *i.e.*

- *Z is a non-negative supermartingale.*
- *$E[Z_t] \to 0$ as $t \to \infty$.*

Proof   Assuming a positive short rate, we see from (28.1) that Z is a non-negative martingale multiplied by a decreasing process, so Z is clearly a super-martingale. The second condition follows directly from (28.4).   □

Conversely one can show that any potential will serve as a stochastic discount factor. The moral is thus that modeling bond prices in a market with positive interest rates is equivalent to modeling a potential, and in the next sections we will describe two ways of doing this.

28.2   The Flesaker–Hughston Framework

Given a stochastic discount factor Z and a positive short rate we may, for each fixed T, define the process $\{X(t,T); \ 0 \le t \le T\}$ by

$$X(t,T) = E^P\left[Z_T | \mathcal{F}_t\right], \qquad (28.5)$$

and thus, according to (28.3) write bond prices as

$$p(t,T) = \frac{X(t,T)}{X(t,t)}. \qquad (28.6)$$

We now have the following result.

Proposition 28.2 *For each fixed t, the mapping $T \longrightarrow X(t,T)$ is smooth, and in fact*

$$\frac{\partial}{\partial T} X(t,T) = -E^P\left[r_T Z_T | \mathcal{F}_t\right]. \qquad (28.7)$$

Furthermore, for each fixed T, the process

$$X_T(t,T) = \frac{\partial}{\partial T} X(t,T)$$

is a negative P-martingale satisfying

$$X_T(0,T) = p_T(0,T), \quad \textit{for all } T \ge 0.$$

Proof Using the definition of Z and the Itô formula, we obtain

$$dZ_s = -r_s Z_s ds + B_s^{-1} dL_s,$$

so

$$Z_T = Z_t - \int_t^T r_s Z_s ds + \int_t^T B_s^{-1} dL_s$$

Since L is a martingale, this gives us

$$E^P [Z_T | \mathcal{F}_t] = Z_t - E^P \left[\int_t^T r_s Z_s ds \,\bigg|\, \mathcal{F}_t \right].$$

Differentiating this expression w.r.t. T gives us (28.7). The martingale property follows directly from (28.7) and since $r > 0$ it is clear that X_T is negative. The relation $X_T(0, T) = p_T(0, T)$ follows from (28.6). □

We can now state the basic result from Flesaker–Hughston, but first we need a formal definition.

Definition 28.3 *We say that* **the term structure is positive** *if the following conditions hold.*

- *For all t and T we have*

$$\frac{\partial}{\partial T} p(t, T) \leq 0.$$

- *For all t we have*

$$\lim_{T \to \infty} p(t, T) = 0.$$

It is clear that in a positive term structure all forward rates are positive. We can now state the basic result from Flesaker–Hughston.

Theorem 28.4 *Assume that the term structure is positive. Then there exists a family of positive martingales $M(t, T)$ indexed by T and a positive deterministic function Φ such that*

$$p(t, T) = \frac{\int_T^\infty \Phi(s) M(t, s) ds}{\int_t^\infty \Phi(s) M(t, s) ds}. \tag{28.8}$$

The M family can, up to multiplicative scaling by the Φ function, be chosen as

$$M(t, T) = -X_T(t, T) = E^P [r_T Z_T | \mathcal{F}_t], \tag{28.9}$$

where X is defined by (28.5). In particular, Φ can be chosen as

$$\Phi(s) = -p_T(0, s), \tag{28.10}$$

in which case the corresponding M is normalized to $M(0, s) = 1$ for all $s \geq 0$.

Proof   A positive term structure implies that $X(t,T) \to 0$ as $T \to \infty$, so we have

$$X(t,T) = -\int_T^\infty X_T(t,s)ds,$$

and thus we obtain from (28.6)

$$p(t,T) = \frac{\int_T^\infty X_T(t,s)ds}{\int_t^\infty X_T(t,s)ds}. \tag{28.11}$$

If we now define $M(t,T)$ by

$$M(t,T) = -X_T(t,T), \tag{28.12}$$

then (28.8) follows from (28.11) with $\Phi \equiv 1$. The function Φ is only a scale factor which can be chosen arbitrarily, and the choice in (28.10) is natural in order to normalize the M family. Since X_T is negative, M is positive and we are done.   □

There is also a converse of the result above, due to Jin and Glasserman.

Proposition 28.5 *Consider a given family of positive martingales $M(t,T)$ indexed by T and a positive deterministic function Φ, such that the condition*

$$\int_0^\infty \Phi(s)M(t,s)ds < \infty,$$

is satisfied $P - a.s.$ for all t. Then the specification

$$p(t,T) = \frac{\int_T^\infty \Phi(s)M(t,s)ds}{\int_t^\infty \Phi(s)M(t,s)ds}. \tag{28.13}$$

will define an arbitrage free positive system of bond prices. Furthermore, the stochastic discount factor Z generating the bond prices is given by

$$Z_t = \int_t^\infty \Phi(s)M(t,s)ds. \tag{28.14}$$

Proof   Using the martingale property of the M family, as well as the positivity of M and Φ we obtain

$$E^P\left[Z_T|\,\mathcal{F}_t\right] = \int_T^\infty E^P\left[\Phi(s)M(T,s)|\,\mathcal{F}_t\right]ds = \int_T^\infty \Phi(s)M(t,s)ds$$

$$\leq \int_t^\infty \Phi(s)M(t,s)ds = Z_t.$$

We thus see that Z is a supermartingale. From the formula above we have in particular that

$$\lim_{T\to\infty} E^P\left[Z_T\right] = \lim_{T\to\infty} \int_T^\infty \Phi(s)M(0,s)ds = 0,$$

so Z is indeed a potential and can thus serve as a stochastic discount factor. The induced bond prices are thus given by

$$p(t,T) = \frac{E^P\left[Z_T|\mathcal{F}_t\right]}{Z_t},$$

and the calculation above shows the induced term structure given by (28.13). It is left to the reader to prove that the term structure is positive.   □

We can also easily compute forward rates.

Proposition 28.6 *With bond prices given by (28.13), forward rates are given by*

$$f(t,T) = \frac{\Phi(T)M(t,T)}{\int_T^\infty \Phi(s)M(t,s)ds}, \tag{28.15}$$

and the short rate has the form

$$r_t = \frac{\Phi(t)M(t,t)}{\int_t^\infty \Phi(s)M(t,s)ds} \tag{28.16}$$

Proof   The proof is left as an exercise to the reader.   □

The most used instance of a Flesaker–Hughston model is the so-called **rational model**. In such a model we consider a given positive martingale K and two deterministic positive functions $\alpha(t)$ and $\beta(t)$. We then define the M family by

$$M(t,T) = \alpha(T) + \beta(T)K(t). \tag{28.17}$$

With this specification of M it is easily seen that bond prices will have the form

$$p(t,T) = \frac{A(T) + B(T)K(t)}{A(t) + B(t)K(t)} \tag{28.18}$$

where

$$A(t) = \int_t^\infty \Phi(s)\alpha(s)ds, \quad B(t) = \int_t^\infty \Phi(s)\beta(s)ds.$$

We can specialize this further by assuming K to be of the form

$$K(t) = e^{\int_0^t \gamma(s)dW_s - \frac{1}{2}\int_0^t \gamma^2(s)ds}$$

where γ is deterministic. Then K will be a lognormal martingale, the entire term structure will be analytically very tractable, and α and β can be chosen in order to fit the initial observed term structure.

28.3 Changing Base Measure

The arguments above do not at all depend upon the fact that P was assumed to be the objective probability measure. If instead we work with another base measure $P^0 \sim P$, we will of course have a Flesaker–Hughston representation of bond prices of the form

$$p(t, T) = \frac{\int_T^\infty \Phi(s) M^0(t, s) ds}{\int_t^\infty \Phi(s) M^0(t, s) ds}. \tag{28.19}$$

where $M^0(t, T)$ is a family of positive P^0 martingales, and the question is how M^0 relates to M.

Proposition 28.7 *With notation as above, we have*

$$M^0(t, T) = \frac{M(t, T)}{R_t^0}, \tag{28.20}$$

where

$$R_t^0 = \frac{dP^0}{dP} \quad on \ \mathcal{F}_t. \tag{28.21}$$

Proof From (28.9) we have, modulo scaling, the relation

$$M(t, T) = E^P \left[r_T B_T^{-1} L_T \middle| \mathcal{F}_t \right]$$

where $L_T = dQ/dP$ on $\mathcal{F}_T$. On the other hand we also have

$$M^0(t, T) = E^0 \left[r_T B_T^{-1} L_T^0 \middle| \mathcal{F}_t \right].$$

where $L_T^0 = dQ/dP^0$ on $\mathcal{F}_T$. Using the Bayes formula we obtain

$$M^0(t, T) = E^0 \left[r_T B_T^{-1} L_T^0 \middle| \mathcal{F}_t \right] = \frac{1}{R_t^0} E^P \left[r_T B_T^{-1} L_T^0 R_T^0 \middle| \mathcal{F}_t \right].$$

Using the fact that

$$L_T^0 R_T^0 = \frac{dQ}{dP^0} \cdot \frac{dP^0}{dP} = \frac{dQ}{dP} = L_T,$$

we thus have

$$M^0(t, T) = \frac{1}{R_t^0} E^P \left[r_T B_T^{-1} L_T \middle| \mathcal{F}_t \right] = \frac{M(t, T)}{R_t^0}.$$

$\square$

28.4   Decomposition of a Potential

In Section 28 we saw that any SDF generating a positive term structure is a potential, so from a modeling point of view it is natural to ask how one can construct potentials from scratch. The main result used is the following.

Proposition 28.8 (Decomposition of a potential) *In Wiener driven setting, the following hold:*

1. *Let A be an increasing adapted process such that A_∞ is integrable, and define the martingale M by*

$$M_t = E^P\left[A_\infty | \mathcal{F}_t\right]. \tag{28.22}$$

   Then the process Z, defined by

$$Z_t = -A_t + M_t, \tag{28.23}$$

   is a potential.

2. *Conversely, if Z is a potential then it admits a representation as*

$$Z_t = -A_t + M_t, \tag{28.24}$$

   where A is an increasing adapted process with $A_\infty \in L^1$, and M is the martingale defined by

$$M_t = E^P\left[A_\infty | \mathcal{F}_t\right]. \tag{28.25}$$

Remark 28.4.1 The result above is valid also without the assumption of a Wiener driven framework. In the general case A should be **predictable** rather than merely adapted. Loosely speaking, predictability means that we require that $A_t \in \mathcal{F}_{t-}$ for all t.

Proof   The proof of the first part is trivial and left to the reader as an exercise. The proof of the second part is much more difficult. It relies on the Doob–Meyer decomposition and the reader is referred to the literature. See Protter (2004).

The point of this, for our purposes, is that by specifying an increasing adapted process A with $A_\infty < \infty$, we can generate a potential Z by the formula

$$Z_t = E^P\left[A_\infty | \mathcal{F}_t\right] - A_t, \tag{28.26}$$

and then use Z as our SDF. In particular we may define A as

$$A_t = \int_0^t a_s ds \tag{28.27}$$

for some adapted nonnegative process a. Then we easily obtain

$$Z_t = E^P\left[\int_0^\infty a_s ds \Big| \mathcal{F}_t\right] - \int_0^t a_s ds = \int_t^\infty E^P\left[a_s | \mathcal{F}_t\right] ds. \tag{28.28}$$

We can now connect this to the Flesaker–Hughston framework. The family of processes $X(t, T)$ defined in (28.5) will, in the present framework, have the form

$$X(t, T) = E^P[Z_T | \mathcal{F}_t] = E^P\left[\int_T^\infty E^P[a_s | \mathcal{F}_T]\, ds\, \middle|\, \mathcal{F}_t\right]$$

$$= \int_T^\infty E^P\left[E^P[a_s | \mathcal{F}_T]\, \middle|\, \mathcal{F}_t\right] ds = \int_T^\infty E^P[a_s | \mathcal{F}_t]\, ds, \quad (28.29)$$

so we have proved the following result.

Proposition 28.9 *Assume that* a *is a nonnegative adapted process and define the potential* Z *by (28.26) - (28.27). Then, modulo scaling, the basic family of Flesaker–Hughston martingales are given by*

$$M(t, T) = -\frac{\partial}{\partial T} X(t, T) = E^P[a_T | \mathcal{F}_t]. \quad (28.30)$$

28.5 The Markov Potential Approach of Rogers

As we have seen above, in order to generate an arbitrage free bond market model it is enough to construct a potential to act as stochastic discount factor (SDF), and in the previous section we learned how to do this using the decomposition (28.22)–(28.23). In this section we will present a systematic way of constructing potentials along the lines above, in terms of Markov processes and their resolvents. The ideas are due to Rogers (1997), and we largely follow his presentation.

We consider a time homogeneous Markov process X under the objective measure P, with infinitesimal generator $\mathcal{G}$. The reader unfamiliar with general Markov process theory can, without loss of good ideas, consider the case when X is a diffusion of the form

$$dX_t = \mu(X_t)dt + \sigma(X_t)dW_t, \quad (28.31)$$

where μ and σ do not depend on running time t. In this case $\mathcal{G}$ is the usual Itô partial differential operator

$$\mathcal{G} = \mu(x)\frac{\partial}{\partial x} + \frac{1}{2}\sigma^2(x)\frac{\partial^2}{\partial x^2} \quad (28.32)$$

For any positive real valued, and sufficiently integrable, function g, and any positive real number α, we can now define the process A in the decomposition (28.23) as

$$A_t = \int_0^t e^{-\alpha s} g(X_s)ds, \quad (28.33)$$

where the exponential is introduced in order to allow at least all bounded functions g. In terms of the representation (28.27) we thus have

$$a_t = e^{-\alpha t} g(X_t), \tag{28.34}$$

and a potential Z is, according to (28.28), obtained as

$$Z_t = \int_t^\infty e^{-\alpha s} E^P \left[g(X_s) \mid \mathcal{F}_t \right] ds = E^P \left[\int_t^\infty e^{-\alpha s} g(X_s) ds \mid \mathcal{F}_t \right], \tag{28.35}$$

so we have

$$Z_t = -\int_0^t e^{-\alpha s} g(X_s) ds + M_t, \tag{28.36}$$

where M is the martingale

$$M_t = E^P \left[\int_0^\infty e^{-\alpha s} g(X_s) ds \mid \mathcal{F}_t \right].$$

Using the Markov assumption we have in fact

$$Z_t = E^P \left[\int_t^\infty e^{-\alpha s} g(X_s) ds \mid X_t \right], \tag{28.37}$$

and this expression leads to a well known probabilistic object.

Definition 28.10 *For any nonnegative α the **resolvent** R_α is an operator, mapping a bounded measurable real valued function g into the real valued function $[R_\alpha g]$ defined by the expression*

$$[R_\alpha g](x) = E_x^P \left[\int_0^\infty e^{-\alpha s} g(X_s) ds \right] \tag{28.38}$$

where subindex x denotes the conditioning $X_0 = x$.

We can now connect resolvents to potentials.

Proposition 28.11 *The potential Z defined by (28.37) can be expressed as*

$$Z_t = e^{-\alpha t} R_\alpha g(X_t). \tag{28.39}$$

Conversely, for any bounded nonnegative g, the process

$$Z_t = e^{-\alpha t} R_\alpha g(X_t) \tag{28.40}$$

is a potential.

Proof   Assume that Z is defined by (28.38). We then have, using the time invariance,

$$Z_t = E^P \left[\int_0^\infty e^{-\alpha(t+s)} g(X_{t+s}) ds \mid X_t \right] = e^{-\alpha t} E^P \left[\int_0^\infty e^{-\alpha s} g(X_{t+s}) ds \mid X_t \right]$$
$$= e^{-\alpha t} R_\alpha g(X_t).$$

This proves the first part of the statement. The second part follows from the calculations above. $\square$

If we define a potential Z as above, and use it as a stochastic discount factor, we can of course compute bond prices, and the short rate can easily be recovered.

Proposition 28.12 *If the stochastic discount factor Z is defined by (28.40) then bond prices are given by*

$$p(t, T) = e^{-\alpha(T-t)} \frac{E^P [R_\alpha g(X_T)| \mathcal{F}_t]}{R_\alpha g(X_t)} \tag{28.41}$$

and the short rate is given by

$$r_t = \frac{g(X_t)}{R_\alpha g(X_t)}. \tag{28.42}$$

Proof The formula (28.41) follows directly from the general formula (28.3). From (28.36) we have

$$dZ_t = -e^{-\alpha t} g(X_t) dt + dM_t,$$

and (28.42) now follows from (28.2) and (28.36). $\qquad\square$

One problem with this scheme is that, for a concrete case, it may be very hard to compute the quotient in (28.42). To overcome this difficulty we will use the following standard result.

Proposition 28.13 *With notation as above we have essentially*

$$R_\alpha = (\alpha - \mathcal{G})^{-1}. \tag{28.43}$$

The phrase "essentially" above indicates that the result is "morally" correct, but that care has to be taken concerning the domain of the operators. We now provide a proof sketch for the diffusion case, i.e. when the X process satisfies an SDE of the form (28.31). The proof of the general case is similar, the only difference being that the Itô formula has to be replaced by the Dynkin formula. As usual we assume that all objects are well defined and "integrable enough".

Proof The proof is very straightforward. Suppressing the upper index P in E^P start by writing

$$R_\alpha g(x) = E_x \left[\int_0^\infty e^{-\alpha t} g(X_t) dt \right] = \int_0^\infty E_x \left[e^{-\alpha t} g(X_t) dt \right].$$

It is now natural to define the process Y by

$$Y_t = e^{-\alpha t} g(X_t),$$

and we easily obtain

$$dY_t = \left\{ -\alpha Y_t + e^{-\alpha t} \mathcal{G} g(X_t) \right\} dt + e^{-\alpha t} g'(X_t) \sigma(X_t) dW_t.$$

Using the Itô formula one readily verifies (see the exercises) that Y can be written as

$$
Y_t = e^{-\alpha t}Y_0 + \int_0^t e^{-\alpha(t-s)}e^{-\alpha s}\mathcal{G}g(X_s)ds + \int_0^t e^{-\alpha(t-s)}e^{-\alpha s}g'(X_s)\sigma(X_s)dW_s
$$

$$
= e^{-\alpha t}g(x) + e^{-\alpha t}\int_0^t \mathcal{G}g(X_s)ds + e^{-\alpha t}\int_0^t g'(X_s)\sigma(X_s)dW_s.
$$

Taking expectations we get

$$
E_x\left[e^{-\alpha t}g(X_t)\right] = E_x[Y_t] = e^{-\alpha t}g(x) + e^{-\alpha t}\int_0^t E_x[\mathcal{G}g(X_s)]\,ds
$$

and we now integrate this to obtain

$$
R_\alpha g(x) = E_x\left[\int_0^\infty e^{-\alpha t}g(X_t)dt\right]
$$

$$
= \int_0^\infty e^{-\alpha t}g(x)dt + \int_0^\infty e^{-\alpha t}\left(\int_0^t E_x[\mathcal{G}g(X_s)]\,ds\right)dt
$$

$$
= \frac{g(x)}{\alpha} + \int_0^\infty E_x[\mathcal{G}g(X_s)]\left(\int_s^\infty e^{-\alpha t}dt\right)ds
$$

$$
= \frac{g(x)}{\alpha} + \frac{1}{\alpha}E_x\left[\int_0^\infty e^{-\alpha s}\mathcal{G}g(X_s)ds\right].
$$

We thus have

$$
\alpha R_\alpha g = Ig + R_\alpha \mathcal{G}g,
$$

where I is the identity operator. Using the fact the R_α is linear we can write this as

$$
R_\alpha\left[\alpha - \mathcal{G}\right]g = Ig,
$$

and since this holds for all g we have in fact shown that $R_\alpha = (\alpha - \mathcal{G})^{-1}$.　□

We now go back to the short rate formula (28.42) and, using the identity $R_\alpha = (\alpha - \mathcal{G})^{-1}$, we see that with $f = R_\alpha g$ we have

$$
\frac{g(X_t)}{R_\alpha g(X_t)} = \frac{(\alpha - \mathcal{G})f(X_t)}{f(X_t)},
$$

where it usually is a trivial task to compute the last quotient.

This led Rogers to use the following scheme.

1. Choose a Markov process X, a real number α, and a function $f \geq 0$.
2. Define g by

$$
g = (\alpha - \mathcal{G})f
$$

3. Choose α (and perhaps the parameters of f) such that g is nonnegative.

4. Now we have $f = R_\alpha g$, and the short rate can be recaptured by

$$r(t) = \frac{(\alpha - \mathcal{G})f(X_t)}{f(X_t)}$$

In this way Rogers produces a surprising variety of concrete analytically tractable nonnegative interest rate models, and exchange rate models can also be treated within the same framework.

For illustration we consider the simplest possible example of a potential model, where the underlying Markov process is an n-dimensional Gaussian diffusion of the form

$$dX_t = -AX_t dt + dW_t. \tag{28.44}$$

In this case we have

$$\mathcal{G}f(x) = \frac{1}{2}\Delta f(x) - \nabla f(x)Ax \tag{28.45}$$

where Δ is the Laplacian and ∇f is the gradient viewed as a row vector. We now define f by

$$f(x) = e^{cx}$$

for some row vector $c \in R^n$. We immediately obtain

$$g(x) = (\alpha - \mathcal{G})f(x) = f(x)\left(\alpha - \frac{1}{2}\|c\|^2 + cAx\right).$$

The corresponding short rate is given by

$$r_t = \alpha - \frac{1}{2}\|c\|^2 + cAX_t, \tag{28.46}$$

so we have a Gaussian multifactor model.

We end this section by connecting the Rogers theory to the Flesaker–Hughston framework, and this is quite straightforward. Comparing (28.30) to (28.34) we have

$$M(t,T) = e^{-\alpha T} E^P\left[g(X_T)|\,\mathcal{F}_t\right]. \tag{28.47}$$

8.6   Exercises

Exercise 28.1 Prove that the term structure constructed in Proposition 28.5 is positive.

Exercise 28.2 Prove proposition 28.6.

Exercise 28.3 Prove the first part of Proposition 28.8.

Exercise 28.4 Assume that the process Y has a stochastic differential of th form

$$dY_t = \{\alpha Y_t + \beta_t\} dt + \sigma_t dW_t,$$

where α is a real number whereas β and σ are adapted processes. Show that Y can be written as

$$Y_t = e^{\alpha t} Y_0 + \int_0^t e^{\alpha(t-s)} \beta_s ds + \int_0^t e^{\alpha(t-s)} \sigma_s dW_s.$$

Exercise 28.5 Without the normalizing function Φ, we can write the forward rates in a Flesaker–Hughston model as

$$f(t,T) = \frac{M(t,T)}{\int_T^\infty M(t,s)ds}.$$

A natural way of modeling the positive martingale family $M(t,T)$ is to write

$$dM(t,T) = M(t,T)\sigma(t,T)dW_t$$

for some chosen volatility structure σ, where σ and W are d-dimensional. Show that in this framework the forward rate dynamics are given by

$$df(t,T) = f(t,T)\{v(t,T) - \sigma(t,T)\} v^\star(t,T)dt + f(t,T)\{\sigma(t,T) - v(t,T)\} dW_t$$

where $\star$ denotes transpose and

$$v(t,T) = \frac{\int_T^\infty M(t,s)\sigma(t,s)ds}{\int_T^\infty M(t,s)ds}$$

Exercise 28.6 This exercise describes another way of producing a potentia. Consider a fixed random variable $X_\infty \in L^2(P,\mathcal{F}_\infty)$. We can then define a mar tingale X by setting

$$X_t = E^P\left[X_\infty | \mathcal{F}_t\right].$$

Now define the process Z by

$$Z_t = E^P\left[(X_\infty - X_t)^2 \Big| \mathcal{F}_t\right]$$

(a) Show that

$$Z_t = E^P\left[X_\infty^2 | \mathcal{F}_t\right] - X_t^2.$$

(b) Show that Z is a supermartingale and that Z is, in fact, a potential.

The point of this is that the potential Z, and thus the complete interest rat model generated by Z, is fully determined by a specification of the single randor variable X_∞. This is called a "conditional variance model". See the Notes.

28.7   Notes

The Flesaker–Hughston fractional approach was developed in Flesaker and Hughston (1996) and Flesaker and Hughston (1997), but using completely different arguments from those above. In this chapter we basically follow Jin and Glasserman (2001). The Rogers potential theory approach was first presented in Rogers (1994). The general potential approach is developed further using conditional variance models and Wiener chaos in Brody and Hughston (2004), and in Hughston and Rafailidis (2005). A completely different, and more geometric, approach to modeling positive interest rates can be found in Brody and Hughston (2001) and Brody and Hughston (2002).

29

FORWARDS AND FUTURES

Consider a financial market of the type presented in the previous chapter, with an underlying factor process X, and with a (possibly stochastic) short rate r. (If r is stochastic we include it, for brevity of notation, as one component of X.) We assume that the market is arbitrage free, and that pricing is done under some fixed risk neutral martingale measure Q (with, as usual, B as numeraire).

Let us now consider a fixed **simple** T-claim $\mathcal{Y}$, i.e. a claim of the form $\mathcal{Y} = \Psi(X_T)$, and assume that we are standing at time t. If we buy $\mathcal{Y}$ and **pay today**, i.e. at time t, then we know that the arbitrage free price is given by

$$\Pi(t; \mathcal{Y}) = G(t, X_t; T, \mathcal{Y}), \tag{29.1}$$

where the pricing function G is given by

$$G(t, x; T, \mathcal{Y}) = E_{t,x}^Q \left[\mathcal{Y} \cdot \exp\left\{ -\int_t^T r(s)ds \right\} \right], \tag{29.2}$$

and the payment streams are as follows:

1. At time t we pay $\Pi(t; \mathcal{Y})$ to the underwriter of the contract.
2. At time T we receive $\mathcal{Y}$ from the underwriter.

There are two extremely common variations of this type of contract, namely **forwards** and **futures**. Both these contracts have the same claim $\mathcal{Y}$ as their underlying object, but they differ from our standard contract above by the way in which payments are made.

29.1 Forward Contracts

We will start with the conceptually easiest contract, which is the forward contract. This is an agreement between two parties to buy or sell a certain underlying claim at a fixed time T in the future. The difference between a forward contract and our standard claims studied so far is that for a forward contract all payments are made at time T. To be more precise we give a definition.

Definition 29.1 *Let $\mathcal{Y}$ be a contingent T-claim. A* **forward contract** *on $\mathcal{Y}$* **contracted at** *t, with* **time of delivery** *T, and with the* **forward price** *$f(t; T, \mathcal{Y})$, is defined by the following payment scheme.*

- *The holder of the forward contract receives, at time T, the stochastic amount $\mathcal{Y}$ from the underwriter.*

- *The holder of the contract pays, at time T, the amount $f(t; T, \mathcal{Y})$ to the underwriter.*
- *The forward price $f(t; T, \mathcal{Y})$ is determined at time t.*
- *The forward price $f(t; T, \mathcal{Y})$ is determined in such a way that the price of the forward contract equals zero, at the time t when the contract is made.*

Forward markets are typically not standardized, so forward contracts are usually traded as OTC ("over the counter") instruments. Note that even if the value of a specific forward contract equals zero at the time t of writing the contract, it will typically have a nonzero market value which varies stochastically in the time interval $[t, T]$.

Our immediate project is to give a mathematical formalization of the definition above, and to derive a theoretical expression for the forward price process $f(t; T, \mathcal{Y})$. This turns out to be quite simple, since the forward contract itself is a contingent T-claim ξ, defined by

$$\xi = \mathcal{Y} - f(t; T, \mathcal{Y}).$$

We are thus led to the following mathematical definition of the forward price process.

Definition 29.2 *Let $\mathcal{Y}$ be a contingent T-claim as above. By the **forward price process** we mean a process $f(t; T, \mathcal{Y})$ of the form $f(t; T, \mathcal{Y}) = f(t, X_t; T, \mathcal{Y})$, where f is some deterministic function, with the property that*

$$\Pi\left(t; \mathcal{Y} - f(t, X_t; T, \mathcal{Y})\right) = 0. \tag{29.3}$$

Writing the forward price as $f(t, X_t; T, \mathcal{Y})$ formalizes the fact that the forward price is determined at t, given the information that is available at that time.

We now have the following basic formula for the forward price process.

Proposition 29.3 *The forward price process is given by any of the following expressions.*

$$f(t; T, \mathcal{Y}) = \frac{\Pi(t; \mathcal{Y})}{p(t, T)}, \tag{29.4}$$

$$f(t; T, \mathcal{Y}) = f(t, X_t; T, \mathcal{Y}), \tag{29.5}$$

where

$$f(t, x; T, \mathcal{Y}) = \frac{1}{p(t, T)} E_{t,x}^{Q}\left[\mathcal{Y} \cdot \exp\left\{-\int_{t}^{T} r(s)ds\right\}\right], \tag{29.6}$$

$$f(t, x; T, \mathcal{Y}) = E_{t,x}^{T}\left[\mathcal{Y}\right]. \tag{29.7}$$

Proof   Using (29.3) and risk neutral valuation we immediately have the following identities, where we write $f(t, x)$ instead of $f(t, x; T, \mathcal{Y})$

$$0 = \Pi\left(t; \mathcal{Y} - f(t, X_t)\right) = E^Q_{t, X_t}\left[\left[\mathcal{Y} - f(t, X_t)\right] \cdot \exp\left\{-\int_t^T r(s)ds\right\}\right]$$

$$= E^Q_{t, X_t}\left[\mathcal{Y} \cdot \exp\left\{-\int_t^T r(s)ds\right\}\right] - E^Q_{t, X_t}\left[f(t, X_t) \cdot \exp\left\{-\int_t^T r(s)ds\right\}\right]$$

$$= \Pi\left(t; \mathcal{Y}\right) - f(t, X_t)E^Q_{t, X_t}\left[\exp\left\{-\int_t^T r(s)ds\right\}\right]$$

$$= \Pi\left(t; \mathcal{Y}\right) - f(t, X_t)p(t, T).$$

This immediately gives us (29.4)–(29.6). The relation (29.7) then follows from (29.6).   □

Note that when dealing with forward contracts there is some risk of conceptual confusion. If we fix t, T and $\mathcal{Y}$, and let s be a fixed point in time with $t \leq s \leq T$, then there will be two different prices.

1. The forward price $f(s; T, \mathcal{Y})$ which is paid to the underwriter at time T for a forward contract made at time s.
2. The (spot) price, at time s, of a fixed forward contract, entered at time t, and with time T of delivery. This spot price is easily seen to be equal to

$$\Pi\left(s; \mathcal{Y}\right) - p(s, T)f(t; T, \mathcal{Y}).$$

29.2   Futures Contracts

A futures contract is very much like a forward contract in the sense that it is an agreement between two parties to buy or sell a certain claim at a prespecified time T in the future. The principal difference between the two contracts lies in the way in which payments are being made. We first give a verbal definition of the futures contract.

Definition 29.4 *Let $\mathcal{Y}$ be a contingent T-claim. A* **futures contract** *on $\mathcal{Y}$, with* **time of delivery** T*, is a financial asset with the following properties.*

(i) *At every point of time t with $0 \leq t \leq T$, there exists in the market a quoted object $F(t; T, \mathcal{Y})$, known as the* **futures price** *for $\mathcal{Y}$ at t, for delivery at T.*

(ii) *At the time T of delivery, the holder of the contract pays $F(T; T, \mathcal{Y})$ and receives the claim $\mathcal{Y}$.*

(iii) *During an arbitrary time interval $(s, t]$ the holder of the contract receives the amount $F(t; T, \mathcal{Y}) - F(s; T, \mathcal{Y})$.*

(iv) *The spot price, at any time t prior to delivery, of obtaining the futures contract, is by definition equal to zero.*

A rough way of thinking about a futures contract is to regard it as a forward contract where the payments are made continuously in time in the way described above, rather than all payments being made at time T. As the forward price increased, you would then get richer, and as the forward price decreased you would lose money. The reason that this way of looking at the futures contract is not entirely correct is the fact that if we start with a standard forward contract, with its associated forward price process f, and then introduce the above payment scheme over time, this will (through supply and demand) affect the original forward price process, so generically we will expect the futures price process F to be different from the forward price process f. The payment schedule above is known as "marking to market"; it is organized in such a way that the holder of a futures position, be it short or long, is required to keep a certain amount of money with the broker as a safety margin against default.

Futures contracts, as opposed to forward contracts, are traded in a standardized manner at an exchange. The volumes in which futures are traded over the world are astronomical, and one of the reasons for this is that on many markets it is difficult to trade (or hedge) directly in the underlying object. A typical example is the commodity market, where you actually have to deliver the traded object (tons of copper, timber, or ripening grapes), and thus are not allowed to go short. In these markets, the futures contract is a convenient financial instrument which does not force you to physically deliver the underlying object, while still making it possible for you to hedge (or speculate) against the underlying object.

We now note some properties of the futures contract.

- From (ii) and (iv) above it is clear that we must have

$$F(T; T, \mathcal{Y}) = \mathcal{Y}. \tag{29.8}$$

  Thus there is really no economic reason to actually deliver either the underlying claim or the payment at time T. This is also an empirical fact; the vast majority of all futures contracts are closed before the time of delivery.
- If you enter a futures contract a time t with a corresponding futures price $F(t; T, \mathcal{Y})$, this does **not** mean that you are obliged to deliver $\mathcal{Y}$ at time T at the price $F(t; T, \mathcal{Y})$. The only contractual obligation is the payment stream defined above.
- The name futures **price** is therefore somewhat unfortunate from a linguistic point of view. If today's futures price is given by $F(t; T, \mathcal{Y})$ (with $t < T$) this does not mean that anyone will ever pay the amount $F(t; T, \mathcal{Y})$ in order to obtain some asset. It would perhaps be more clear to refer to $F(t; T, \mathcal{Y})$ as the futures **quotation**.
- Since, by definition, the spot price of a futures contract equals zero, there is no cost or gain of entering or closing a futures contract.
- If the reader thinks that a futures contract conceptually is a somewhat complicated object, then the author is inclined to agree.

We now turn to the mathematical formalization of the futures contract, and is should by now be clear that the natural model for a futures contract is an asset with dividends.

Definition 29.5 *The* **futures contract** *on an underlying T-claim $\mathcal{Y}$ is a financial asset with a price process $\Pi(t)$ and a dividend process $D(t)$ satisfying the following conditions.*

$$D(t) = F(t; T, \mathcal{Y}). \tag{29.9}$$

$$F(T; T, \mathcal{Y}) = \mathcal{Y}. \tag{29.10}$$

$$\Pi(t) = 0, \quad \forall t \leq T. \tag{29.11}$$

It now remains to investigate what the futures price process looks like. This turns out to be quite simple, and we can now prove the main result of the section.

Proposition 29.6 *Let $\mathcal{Y}$ be a given contingent T-claim, and assume that market prices are obtained from the fixed risk neutral martingale measure Q. Then the following hold:*

- *The futures price process is given by*

$$F(t; T, \mathcal{Y}) = E^Q_{t, X_t}[\mathcal{Y}]. \tag{29.12}$$

- *If the short rate is deterministic, then the forward and the futures price processes coincide, and we have*

$$f(t; T, \mathcal{Y}) = F(t; T, \mathcal{Y}) = E^Q_{t, X_t}[\mathcal{Y}]. \tag{29.13}$$

Proof From Proposition 16.14, it follows that the discounted gains process

$$G^Z(t) = \frac{\Pi(t)}{B_t} + \int_0^t \frac{1}{B_s} dF(s; T, \mathcal{Y})$$

has the representation

$$dG^Z_t = h_t dW_t$$

for some adapted process h. In our case we furthermore have $\Pi(t) = 0$ for all t, so we obtain the representation

$$\frac{1}{B_t} dF(t; T, \mathcal{Y}) = h_t dW_t.$$

Multiplying by B_t on both sides we get

$$dF(t; T, \mathcal{Y}) = B_t h_t dW_t,$$

which implies that $F(t; T, \mathcal{Y})$ is a Q-martingale. Using the martingale property, the fact that we are in a Markovian framework (see Lemma 5.9), and (29.10), we obtain

$$F(t; T, \mathcal{Y}) = E^Q_{t, X_t}[F(T; T, \mathcal{Y})] = E^Q_{t, X_t}[\mathcal{Y}],$$

which proves the first part of the assertion. The second part follows from the fact that $Q^T = Q$ when the short rate is deterministic (see Lemma 29.9). □

29.3   Exercises

Exercise 29.1 Suppose that S is the price process of a nondividend paying asset. Show that the forward price $f(t,x;T,\mathcal{Y})$ for the T-claim $\mathcal{Y} = S_T$ is given by

$$f(t,x;T,S_T) = \frac{S_t}{p(t,T)}.$$

Exercise 29.2 Suppose that S is the price process of a dividend paying asset with dividend process D.

(a) Show that the forward price $f(t,x;T,S_T)$ is given by the cost of carry formula

$$f(t,x;T,S_T) = \frac{1}{p(t,T)}\left(S_t - E_{t,x}^Q\left[\int_t^T \exp\left\{-\int_t^s r(u)du\right\}dD_s\right]\right).$$

Hint: Use the cost of carry formula for dividend paying assets.

(b) Now assume that the short rate r is deterministic but possibly time-varying. Show that in this case the formula above can be written as

$$f(t,x;T,S_T) = \frac{S_t}{p(t,T)} - E_{t,x}^Q\left[\int_t^T \exp\left\{-\int_s^T r(u)du\right\}dD_s\right].$$

Exercise 29.3 Suppose that S is the price process of an asset in a standard Black–Scholes model, with r as the constant rate of interest, and fix a contingent T-claim $\Phi(S(T))$. We know that this claim can be replicated by a portfolio based on the money account B, and on the underlying asset S. Show that it is also possible to find a replicating portfolio, based on the money account and on futures contracts for $S(T)$.

29.4   Notes

For a wealth of information on forwards and futures, see Hull (1997) and Duffie (1989).

Appendix A

MEASURE AND INTEGRATION*

The purpose of this appendix is to give an introduction to measure theory and to the associated integration theory on general measure spaces.

A.1 Sets and Mappings

Let X be an arbitrary set. We then say that X is **finite** if it contains only finitely many elements. If X is not finite, we say that it is **infinite**. We will use the notation $f : X \to Y$ to denote a function (or "mapping") f which takes values in Y and which has domain X. If we apply the f to an element $x \in X$, we denote the function value by $f(x)$.

Definition A.1 *Let X and Y be sets and let*

$$f : X \to Y$$

be a given mapping.

1. *The mapping f is **injective** if, for all x and z in X it holds that*

$$x = z \quad \Rightarrow \quad f(x) = f(z).$$

2. *The mapping f is **surjective** if, for all $y \in Y$, there exists an $x \in X$ such that*

$$y = f(x).$$

3. *The mapping f is **bijective** if it is both injective and surjective*
4. *The **image** of X under f, is denoted by $Im(f)$, and defined by*

$$Im(f) = \{f(x); \quad x \in X\}.$$

5. *For any set $B \subseteq Y$, the **inverse image** or **pullback** of B under f, is denoted by $f^{-1}(B)$, and defined by*

$$f^{-1}(B) = \{x; \quad f(x) \in B\}.$$

*We also say that B is **lifted** to $f^{-1}(B)$.*
6. *In particular, for every $y \in Y$ we write*

$$f^{-1}(y) = \{x; \quad f(x) = y\}.$$

7. *For any set $A \subseteq X$ the* **direct image** *of B under f is denoted by $f(A)$, and defined by*

$$f(A) = \{f(x); \quad x \in A\}.$$

Note that the inverse image of a set always exists (although it could be the empty set) even if the function f does not have an inverse. For our purposes the inverse image concept is much more important than the direct image. The following very useful result shows that the set algebraic operations are preserved under the inverse image.

Proposition A.2 *The following relations always hold:*

1. *For any $A, B \subseteq Y$ we have*

$$f^{-1}(A \cap B) = f^{-1}(A) \cap f^{-1}(B).$$

2. *For any $A, B \subseteq Y$ we have*

$$f^{-1}(A \cup B) = f^{-1}(A) \cup f^{-1}(B).$$

3. *For any $B \subseteq Y$ we have*

$$f^{-1}(B^c) = \left[f^{-1}(B)\right]^c.$$

where ^{c} denotes the complement.

4. *For any indexed collection $\{B_\gamma\}_{\gamma \in \Gamma}$ of sets in Y we have*

$$f^{-1}\left(\bigcap_{\gamma \in \Gamma} B_\gamma\right) = \bigcap_{\gamma \in \Gamma} f^{-1}(B_\gamma).$$

5. *For any indexed collection $\{B_\gamma\}_{\gamma \in \Gamma}$ of sets in Y we have*

$$f^{-1}\left(\bigcup_{\gamma \in \Gamma} B_\gamma\right) = \bigcup_{\gamma \in \Gamma} f^{-1}(B_\gamma).$$

Proof   We leave the proof to the reader.   □

We define the set of **natural numbers** as the set $N = \{1, 2, ...\}$, and the set of integers Z as $Z = \{0, \pm 1, \pm 2, ...\}$. Using N we can give a name to the "smallest" type of infinite set.

Definition A.3 *An infinite set X is* **countable** *if there exists a bijection*

$$f : N \to X.$$

If X is infinite but not countable, it is said to be **uncountable**.

Note that in our definition a countable set is always infinite. The intuitive interpretation of this is that a countable set has "as many" elements as N, whereas an uncountable set has "more" elements than N. If X is countable we may, for each $n \in N$ define $x_n \in X$ by $x_n = f(n)$. Since f is a bijection we can thus write X as

$$X = \{x_1, x_2, x_3, \ldots\},$$

so we see that in this sense we can really count off the elements in X, one-by-one.

A countable set is thus an infinite set, but in a sense it is "almost finite", and thus very easy and nice to handle. In mathematics in general and in particular in probability theory, the difference between countable and uncountable sets is crucial, and therefore it is important to be able to tell if a set is countable or not. The following result is a good start in that direction.

Proposition A.4 *The set Q of rational numbers is countable.*

Proof   It is enough to show that the set Q_+ of positive rational numbers is countable, and we do this by first representing each rational number p/q by the integer lattice point $(p, q) \in R^2$. We now prove that this set of integer lattice points is countable by simply presenting a scheme for counting them.

The scheme begins with $(1, 1), (2, 1), (1, 2), (1, 3), (2, 2), (3, 1), (4, 1), (3, 2),$ and if the reader draws a two dimensional graph of this scheme, she will easily see how to continue.   □

This simple idea can be extended considerably.

Proposition A.5 *Assume that we are given a countable family $\{X_n\}_{i=1}^{\infty}$ of sets, where each set X_n is countable. Then the union $\bigcup_{i=1}^{\infty} X_n$ is countable.*

Proof   Because of the countability assumption, the set X_i can be written as $\{x_{i1}, x_{i2}, x_{i3}, \ldots\}$, so the set X_i can be bijectively mapped into the integer lattice points of the form $(i, 1), (i, 2), (i, 3), \ldots$. Thus the union $\bigcup_{i=1}^{\infty} X_n$ can be mapped bijectively onto the entire set of positive integer lattice points in R^2 and we have already proved that this set is countable.   □

The most important example of an uncountable set is the set of real numbers.

Proposition A.6 *The set R of real numbers is uncountable.*

Proof   Omitted.   □

A.2   Measures and Sigma Algebras

Let X be a set and let us denote the class of all subsets of X by 2^X. More formally we thus see that 2^X, commonly known as **the power set of** X, is a set, the elements of which are subsets of X.

We now want to formalize the idea of a mass distribution on X, and the reader may think of a large plate (the set X) with mashed potatoes on it. For every subset $A \subseteq X$ we would now like to define the nonnegative real number $\mu(A)$ as "the amount of mashed potatoes which lies on the set A" or "the measure of A". However, when one tries to formalize this intuitively simple notion, one encounters technical problems, and the main problem is the fact that in the generic situation, there exist subsets $A \subseteq X$ which are so "nasty" that it is mathematically impossible to define $\mu(A)$. Typically we are therefore forced to define the measure $\mu(A)$ only for certain "nice" subsets $A \subseteq X$. These "nice" sets are called "measurable sets", and the technical concept needed is that of a **sigma algebra** (or σ-algebra). In order to define this concept, let $\mathcal{F}$ be a family of subsets of X, i.e. $\mathcal{F} \subseteq 2^X$.

Definition A.7 *A family $\mathcal{F}$ of subsets of X is a σ-algebra if the following hold:*

1.
$$\emptyset \in \mathcal{F}.$$

2.
$$A \in \mathcal{F} \quad \Rightarrow \quad A^c \in \mathcal{F}.$$

3.
$$A_n \in \mathcal{F}, \quad \text{for } n = 1, 2, \ldots \quad \Rightarrow \quad \bigcup_{i=1}^{\infty} A_n \in \mathcal{F}.$$

4.
$$A_n \in \mathcal{F}, \quad \text{for } n = 1, 2, \ldots \quad \Rightarrow \quad \bigcap_{i=1}^{\infty} A_n \in \mathcal{F}.$$

Thus a σ-algebra contains the empty set, and is closed under complement, countable unions and countable intersections. In fact, it is only necessary to require that $\mathcal{F}$ is closed under complements and countable unions (see the exercises). Note that the conditions (3) and (4) only concerns **countable** unions.

Trivial examples of σ-algebras are

$$\mathcal{F} = 2^X, \quad \mathcal{F} = \{\emptyset, X\}.$$

Definition A.8 *A pair $(X, \mathcal{F})$ where X is a set and $\mathcal{F}$ is a σ-algebra on X is called a* **measurable space**. *The subsets of X which are in $\mathcal{F}$ are called $\mathcal{F}$-measurable sets .*

We are now in a position to define the concept of a (nonnegative) measure.

Definition A.9 *A finite measure μ on a measurable space (X, μ) is a mapping*

$$\mu : \mathcal{F} \to R_+,$$

such that

1.
$$\mu(A) \geq 0, \quad \forall A \in \mathcal{F}.$$

2.
$$\mu(\emptyset) = 0.$$

3. *If $A_n \in \mathcal{F}$ $\forall n = 1, 2, \dots$ and $A_i \cap A_j = \emptyset$ for $i = j$, then*

$$\mu \left(\bigcup_{n=1}^{\infty} A_n \right) = \sum_{n=1}^{\infty} \mu(A_n).$$

The intuitive interpretation of (2) is obvious; there is no mass on the empty set. If A and B are disjoint set, it is also obvious that the mass on $A \cup B$ equals the sums of the masses on A and B. The condition (3) above is an extension of this property to the case of an infinite collection of sets, and is known as the **sigma-additivity** of the measure.

Generally speaking, it is a hard problem to construct non-trivial measures, and we will come back to this below. In our applications, we will typically be given a measure which is defined a priori.

Definition A.10 *A **measure space** is a triple $(X, \mathcal{F}, \mu)$, where μ is a measure on the measurable space $(X, \mathcal{F})$.*

A.3 Integration

Let $(X, \mathcal{F}, \mu)$ be a measure space, and let $f : X \to R$ be a given function. The object of the present section is to give a reasonable definition of the formal expression

$$\int_X f(x) d\mu(x), \qquad (A.1)$$

and we do this in a couple of simple steps.

Definition A.11 *For an arbitrary $A \subseteq X$ the **indicator function** I_A is defined by*

$$I_A(x) = \begin{cases} 1, & \text{if } x \in A, \\ 0, & \text{if } x \in A^c. \end{cases}$$

If $f = c \cdot I_A$ where c is a real number and A is measurable, then there is a very natural definition of (A.1), namely

$$\int_X f(x) d\mu(x) = \int_X c \cdot I_A(x) d\mu(x) = c \cdot \mu(A), \qquad (A.2)$$

i.e.

the "area under the graph of f" = "the base" $\cdot$ "the heigth" = $\mu(A) \cdot c$.

Observe that we must demand that A is $\mathcal{F}$-measurable, since otherwise the right-hand side of (A.2) is not defined. This also gives us a natural definition of linear combinations of indicator functions.

Definition A.12 *A mapping* $f : X \to R$ *is* **simple** *if it can be written as*

$$f(x) = \sum_{i=1}^{n} c_n \cdot I_{A_n}(x), \tag{A.3}$$

where $A_1, \ldots, A_n$ *are measurable and* $c_1, \ldots, c_n$ *are real numbers.*

Definition A.13 *For a simple function, as in (A.3), the integral is defined by*

$$\int_X f(x) d\mu(x) = \sum_{i=1}^{n} c_n \cdot \mu(A_n).$$

We now want to extend this integral concept to functions which are not simple. Let us therefore consider an arbitrary nonnegative function. The intuitive idea is now to carry out the following program:

- Approximate f from below by simple functions, i.e find simple f_n, $n = 1, 2, \ldots$, such that $f_n(x) \uparrow f(x)$ for all x.
- Define the integral of f as the limit of the integrals of the approximating simple functions, i.e.

$$\int_X f(x) d\mu(x) = \lim_n \int_X f_n(x) d\mu(x).$$

The problem with this natural idea is the fact that not all functions can be well approximated by simple functions, so we cannot define the integral for an arbitrary function.

Instead we have to be contented with defining the integral concept (A.1) for those functions f which **can** be approximated by simple functions. This is the class of **measurable** functions, and the formal definition is as follows.

Definition A.14 *A function* $f : X \to R$ *is* $\mathcal{F}$**-measurable** *if, for every interval* $I \subseteq R$ *it holds that* $f^{-1}(I) \in \mathcal{F}$, *i.e. if it holds that*

$$\{x \in X; f(x) \in I\} \in \mathcal{F},$$

for all intervals I. *We will often write this as* $f \in \mathcal{F}$.

When testing if a given function is measurable, the following result is often of great use.

Proposition A.15 *The following properties are equivalent:*

1.

$$f \text{ is } \mathcal{F}\text{-measurable.}$$

2.

$$\{x \in X; f(x) < \alpha\} \in \mathcal{F}, \quad \forall \alpha \in R.$$

3.
$$\{x \in X; f(x) \leq \alpha\} \in \mathcal{F}, \quad \forall \alpha \in R.$$

4.
$$\{x \in X; f(x) > \alpha\} \in \mathcal{F}, \quad \forall \alpha \in R.$$

5.
$$\{x \in X; f(x) \geq \alpha\} \in \mathcal{F}, \quad \forall \alpha \in R.$$

Proof   Use Proposition A.2.   □

The following important result shows that measurability is preserved under the most common operations.

Proposition A.16 *Assume that f and g are measurable on a measurable space $(X, \mathcal{F})$. Then the following hold:*

1. *For all real numbers α and β the functions*
$$\alpha f + \beta g, \quad f \cdot g$$
   are measurable.
2. *If $g(x) = 0$ for all x, then*
$$\frac{f}{g}$$
   is measurable.
3. *If $\{f_n\}_{n=1}^{\infty}$ is a (countable) sequence of measurable functions, then the functions*
$$\sup_n f_n, \quad \inf_n f_n, \quad \limsup_n f_n, \quad \liminf_n f_n,$$
   are measurable.

Proof   The proof is omitted.   □

We can now go on to define the integral of a nonnegative function on a measure space.

Definition A.17 *Let $f : X \to R$ be nonnegative and measurable on the measure space $(X, \mathcal{F}, \mu)$. The integral of f w.r.t. μ over X is then defined by*

$$\int_X f(x) d\mu(x) = \sup_\varphi \int_X \varphi(x) d\mu(x), \tag{A.4}$$

where the supremum is over the class of simple functions φ such that $0 \leq \varphi \leq f$.

We now want to extend this definition to functions which are not necessarily nonnegative. Let therefore f be an arbitrary measurable function. It then follows from Proposition A.16 that also $|f|$ is measurable, since we can write

$$f = f^+ - f^-,$$

where

$$f^+ = \max[f, 0], \quad f^- = \max[-f, 0].$$

Definition A.18 *A measurable function f is* **integrable**, *which we will write as* $f \in L^1(X, \mathcal{F}, \mu)$, *if*

$$\int_X |f(x)| d\mu(x) < \infty.$$

For an integrable function f, the integral over X is defined by

$$\int_X f(x) d\mu(x) = \int_X f^+(x) d\mu(x) - \int_X f^-(x) d\mu(x)$$

If A is any measurable set, the integral of f over A is defined by

$$\int_A f(x) d\mu(x) = \int_X I_A(x) f(x) d\mu(x).$$

We will often write $\int_X f(x) d\mu(x)$ *as* $\int_X f(x) \mu(dx)$ *or as* $\int_X f d\mu$. *When the underlying measure space is unambiguous, we will write* L^1 *as shorthand for* $L^1(X, \mathcal{F}, \mu)$.

Example A.19 We now give a simple but important example of a measure space. Let X be the set of natural numbers and let $\mathcal{F}$ be the power set. On this space we now define the **counting measure** ν by

$$\nu(A) = \text{the number of points in } A. \tag{A.5}$$

In other words, the counting measure puts unit mass on every single natural number. We immediately see that on $(N, 2^N, \nu)$, *every* real valued function will be measurable, and a function f is integrable if and only if

$$\sum_{n=1}^{\infty} |f(n)| < \infty.$$

The integral of any $f \in L^1$ is easily seen to be given by

$$\int_X f(x) d\mu(x) = \sum_{n=1}^{\infty} f(n).$$

Thus we see that our integration theory also allows us to treat ordinary sums as integrals.

We now have some very natural properties of the integral. The proof is not trivial and is omitted.

Proposition A.20 *The following relations hold:*

1. *For any* $f, g \in L^1(X, \mathcal{F}, \mu)$ *and any real numbers* α *and* β *it holds that*

$$\int_X (\alpha f(x) + \beta g(x)) \, d\mu(x) = \alpha \int_X f(x) d\mu(x) + \beta \int_X g(x) d\mu(x).$$

2. *If $f(x) \le g(x)$ for all x, then*

$$\int_X f(x)d\mu(x) \le \int_X g(x)d\mu(x).$$

3. *For any function in L^1 it holds that*

$$\left| \int_X f(x)d\mu(x) \right| \le \int_X |f(x)|\, d\mu(x).$$

One of the most striking properties of the integral concept defined above is the surprising ease with which it handles convergence problems. The three basic results are as follows.

Theorem A.21 (The Fatou Lemma) *Let $\{f_n\}_{n=1}^{\infty}$ be a sequence of measurable functions such that*

$$f_n \ge 0, \quad n = 1, 2, \ldots$$

and

$$\lim_{n \to \infty} f_n(x) = f(x), \quad \forall x \in X,$$

for some limit function f. Then

$$\int_X f(x)d\mu(x) \le \liminf_n \int_X f_n(x)d\mu(x).$$

Theorem A.22 (Monotone Convergence) *Let $\{f_n\}_{n=1}^{\infty}$ be a sequence of measurable functions such that*

1. *The sequence is nonnegative, i.e.*

$$f_n \ge 0, \quad n = 1, 2, \ldots$$

2. *The sequence is increasing, i.e. for all x we have*

$$f_1(x) \le f_2(x) \le \ldots \le f_n(x) \le f_{n+1}(x) \le \ldots$$

Then, defining the function f by

$$f(x) = \lim_n f_n(x),$$

it holds that

$$\int_X f(x)d\mu(x) = \lim_n \int_X f_n(x)d\mu(x).$$

Theorem A.23 (The Lebesgue Dominated Convergence Theorem)
Let $\{f_n\}_{n=1}^{\infty}$ be a sequence of measurable functions such that

$$f_n(x) \to f(x)$$

for some limit function f. Suppose that there exists a nonnegative function $g \in L^1$ such that,

$$|f_n(x)| \leq g(x), \quad \forall n, \ \forall x \in X.$$

Then

$$\int_X f(x) d\mu(x) = \lim_n \int_X f_n(x) d\mu(x).$$

A.4 Sigma-Algebras and Partitions

The purpose of this section is to give some more intuition for the measurability concept for functions. We will do this by considering the simplest case of a sigma-algebra, namely when it is generated by a *partition*.

Definition A.24 *A* **partition** $\mathcal{P}$ *of the space* X *is a finite collection of sets* $\{A_1, A_2, \ldots, A_n\}$ *such that*

1. *The sets cover* X, *i.e.*

$$\bigcup_{i=1}^{n} A_i = X,$$

2. *The sets are disjoint, i.e.*

$$i = j \quad \Rightarrow \quad A_i \cap A_j = \emptyset.$$

The sets $A_1, \ldots A_n$ *are called the* **components** *of* $\mathcal{P}$, *and the sigma-algebra consisting of all possible unions (including the empty set) of the components in* $\mathcal{P}$ *is denoted by* $\sigma(\mathcal{P})$. *This sigma-algebra is called* **the sigma-algebra generated by** $\mathcal{P}$.

We now have a result which shows (in this restricted setting) what measurability for a function "really means".

Proposition A.25 *Let* $\mathcal{P}$ *be a given partition of* X. *A function* $f : X \to R$ *is* $\sigma(\mathcal{P})$-*measurable if and only if* f *is constant on each component of* $\mathcal{P}$.

Proof First assume that f is measurable, and consider a fixed but arbitrarily chosen real number y. Since f is measurable we know that $f^{-1}(y)$ is in $\sigma(\mathcal{P})$ so it is a union of some of the components of $\mathcal{P}$. If the union is nonempty this means precisely that $f = y$ on that union, so in particular it takes the constant value y on all components in the union. The converse is trivial. $\square$

The sigma-algebras that we are going to consider later on in the text, are in general **not** generated by partitions. They are typically much more complicated, so the proposition above is of little "practical" interest. The point of the discussion concerning partitions is instead that when you **informally think about** sigma-algebras, it is very fruitful to have this simple case at the back of your head.

As an example, we see directly from Proposition A.25 why we must restrict ourselves to integrating measurable functions only. The problem with a non-measurable function is that the function is varying too wildly compared with the fine structure of the sigma-algebra. In particular this implies that a non-measurable function cannot be well approximated by simple functions.

It is also very instructive to see exactly what goes wrong when we try to integrate nonmeasurable functions. Even for a nonmeasurable function f we can of course in principle define the integral by (A.4), but this integral will not have the nice properties in Proposition A.20. See the exercises for concrete examples.

A.5   Sets of Measure Zero

Consider again a measure space $(X, \mathcal{F}, \mu)$. If $N \in \mathcal{F}$ and $\mu(N) = 0$, we say that N is a **null set**. If a certain property holds for all $x \in X$ except for on a null set, then we say that the property holds **almost everywhere** (w.r.t. μ), and in shorthand we write "μ-a.e.". For example: if we write

$$f \geq 0, \quad \mu - a.e.$$

this means that there exists a null set N such that $f(x) \geq 0$ for all $x \in N^c$. It is easy to see that if f and g are integrable, and $f = g$, almost everywhere, then for every $A \in \mathcal{F}$ we have

$$\int_A f d\mu = \int_A g d\mu.$$

In fact, there is an important converse of this statement, which shows that you can test whether two functions are equal almost everywhere or not, by testing their integrals. We omit the proof.

Proposition A.26

- *Assume that f and g are integrable and that*

$$\int_A f d\mu = \int_A g d\mu,$$

  for every $A \in \mathcal{F}$ Then $f = g$, μ-a.e.
- *Assume that f and g are integrable and that*

$$\int_A f d\mu \geq \int_A g d\mu,$$

  for every $A \in \mathcal{F}$ Then $f \geq g$, μ-a.e.

A.6 The L^p Spaces

Let p be a real number with $1 \le p < \infty$. We define the function class $L^p\left(X, \mathcal{F}, \mu\right)$ as the class of measurable functions f such that

$$\int_X |f(x)|^p d\mu(x) < \infty,$$

and for $f \in L^p$ we define the L^p-**norm** $\|f\|_p$ by

$$\|f\|_p = \left(\int_X |f(x)|^p d\mu(x)\right)^{1/p}.$$

For $p = \infty$ the norm is defined by

$$\|f\|_\infty = ess \; sup|f| = \inf\left\{M \in R; \; |f| \le M, \; a.e.\right\}.$$

The two main inequalities for L^p spaces are the Minkowski and the Hölder inequalities.

Proposition A.27 *The following hold for $1 \le p \le \infty$.*

1. *The Minkowski inequality:*

$$\|f + g\|_p \le \|f\|_p + \|g\|_p.$$

2. *The Hölder inequality:*

$$\int_X |f(x)g(x)| d\mu(x) \le \|f\|_p \cdot \|g\|_q.$$

where p and q are **conjugate** *i.e. $1/p + 1/q = 1$.*

From the Minkowski inequality it follows that if we identify functions which are equal almost everywhere, then L^p is a normed vector space. If $\{f_n\}$ is a sequence of functions in L^p and f is a function in L^p such that

$$\|f_n - f\| \to 0, \quad \text{as } n \to \infty,$$

then we say that f_n converges to f in L^p and we write

$$f_n \overset{L^p}{\to} f.$$

Definition A.28 *A sequence $\{f_n\}_n$ of functions in L^p is a* **Cauchy sequence** *if, for all $\epsilon < 0$ there exists an integer N such that*

$$\|f_n - f_M\| < \epsilon,$$

for all $n, m \ge N$.

It is easy to see (prove this) that if f_n converges to some f in L^p then $\{f_n\}_n$ is Cauchy. The converse is not necessarily true for generally normed spaces, but it is in fact true for the L^p spaces.

Proposition A.29 *Every L^p space, for $1 \leq p \leq \infty$, is* **complete** *in the sense that every Cauchy sequence converges to some limit point. In other words: if $\{f_n\}$ is a Cauchy sequence in L^p, then there exists a (unique) element $f \in L^p$ such that $f_n \to f$ in L^p.*

We will mainly be dealing with L^1 and L^2, and for L^2 there is furthermore an inner product, which is the natural generalization of the scalar product on R^n.

Definition A.30 *For any two elements f and g in L^2 we define the* **inner product** *(f, g) by*

$$(f, g) = \int_X f(x) \cdot g(x) d\mu(x).$$

It is easy to see the inner product is bilinear (i.e. linear in each variable) and that the inner product is related to the L^2 norm by

$$\|f\|_2 = \sqrt{(f, f)}.$$

The vector space structure, the inner product and the completeness of L^2, ensures that L^2 is a *Hilbert space*.

A.7   Hilbert Spaces

Hilbert spaces are infinite dimensional vector spaces which generalize the finite dimensional Euclidian spaces R^n.

Definition A.31 *Consider a real vector space* **H** *A mapping $(\ ,\ ): \mathbf{H} \times \mathbf{H} \to R$, is called an* **inner product** *on* **H** *if it has the following properties:*

- *It is bilinear, i.e. for any $\alpha, \beta \in R$ and $f, g, h \in \mathbf{H}$*

$$(\alpha f + \beta g, h) = \alpha(f, h) + \beta(g, h)$$

   and

$$(h, \alpha f + \beta g) = \alpha(h, f) + \beta(h, g).$$

- *It is symmetric, i.e.*

$$(f, g) = (g, f), \quad \forall f, g \in \mathbf{H}.$$

- *It is positive definite, i.e.*

$$(f, f) \geq 0, \quad \text{for all } f \in \mathbf{H} \text{ with equality if and only if } f = 0.$$

The inner product generalizes the standard scalar product on R^n and in particular it induces a *norm* and the concept of *orthogonality*.

Definition A.32

- For any $f \in \mathbf{H}$ the **norm** of f is denoted by $\|f\|$ and defined by

$$\|f\| = \sqrt{(f,f)}.$$

- Two vectors $f, g \in \mathbf{H}$ are said to be **orthogonal** if $f, g) = 0$. We write this as $f \perp g$.
- For any linear subspace $M \in \mathbf{H}$ we define its **orthogonal complement** $M^\perp$ as

$$M^\perp = \{f \in \mathbf{H}; \ f \perp M\}.$$

We interpret $\|f\|$ as "the length of f", and the following result shows that the norm concept really is a norm in the technical sense of satisfying the triangle inequality.

Proposition A.33

- For all $f, g \in \mathbf{H}$ the Cauchy-Schwartz inequality holds, i.e.

$$\|(f,g)\| \le \|f\| \cdot \|g\|.$$

- The norm $\| \cdot \|$ satisfies the **triangle inequality**, i.e. for any $f, g \in \mathbf{H}$ we have

$$\|f + g\| \le \|f\| + \|g\|.$$

Proof   To prove the Cauchy–Schwartz inequality we note that for all $f, g \in \mathbf{H}$ and $s \in R$ we have $(f - sg, f - sg) = \|f - sg\|^2 \ge 0$. We thus have $\|f\|^2 + \|g\|^2 - 2s(f, g) \ge 0$. Minimizing this over all real numbers s and plugging in the optimal s in the inequality gives us the Cauchy inequality. To prove the triangle inequality, write $\|f + g\|^2$ as $(f + g, f + g)$ and expand using the bilinearity and Cauchy–Schwartz. □

A vector space with an inner product is called an *inner product space*, and on such a space we may use the induced norm to define the concept of a Cauchy sequence and of completeness (as for the L^p spaces above).

Definition A.34 *A* **Hilbert space** *is an inner product space which is complete under the induced norm* $\| \cdot \|$.

We note that $L^2(X, \mathcal{F}, \mu)$ above is a Hilbert space and it is in fact the most important example of a Hilbert space. The single most important result for Hilbert spaces is probably the projection theorem. The proof is omitted.

Theorem A.35 *Assume that* $\mathbf{M}$ *is a closed linear subspace of a Hilbert space* $\mathbf{H}$.

- Assume that f is a fixed vector in $\mathbf{H}$. Consider the optimization problem

$$\min_{g \in \mathbf{M}} \|f - g\|.$$

  Then there exists a unique solution $\hat{g}$ and it is characterized by the condition that

$$f - \hat{g} \perp \mathbf{M}.$$

- *We have the decomposition of* $\mathbf{H}$ *as*

$$\mathbf{H} = M \oplus M^{\perp}.$$

The direct sum *sign* $\oplus$ *means that* $\mathbf{H} = M + M^{\perp}$ *and that* $M \cap M^{\perp} = \{0\}$.

The optimal $\hat{g}$ above is called the **orthogonal projection** of f onto $\mathbf{M}$. We see that the optimal "error vector" $f - \hat{g}$ is perpendicular to the subspace $\mathbf{M}$, exactly like the situation in R^n.

Definition A.36 *A linear mapping* $F : \mathbf{H} \to R$ *is called a* **linear functional**. *For any* $f \in \mathbf{H}$ *we sometimes write* Ff *rather than* $F(f)$. *A linear functional is said to be* **bounded** *if there exists a constant* K *such that*

$$|F(f)| \le K \|f\|, \quad \forall f \in \mathbf{H}.$$

It is relatively easy to see that a linear functional is bounded if and only if it is continuous. It is also easy to see that if we choose a fixed $f \in \mathbf{H}$ and define the mapping $F : \mathbf{H} \to R$ by

$$Fg = (f, g), \quad \forall f \in \mathbf{H}, \tag{A.6}$$

then F is a bounded linear functional. The next result shows that **all** bounded linear functionals on a Hilbert space are of this form.

Theorem A.37 (Riesz Representation Theorem)
Assume that

$$F : \mathbf{H} \to R$$

is a bounded linear functional. Then there exists a unique $g \in \mathbf{H}$ *such that*

$$Ff = (f, g), \quad \forall g \in \mathbf{H}.$$

Proof   Define M by $M = ker[F] = \{f \in \mathbf{H}; \ Ff = 0\}$. The M is a closed subspace and we can decompose $\mathbf{H}$ as $\mathbf{H} = M + M^{\perp}$. From the definition of M it is clear that F restricted to $M^{\perp}$ is linear with trivial kernel. It is thus a vector space isomorphism between $M^{\perp}$ and R, so $M^{\perp}$ has to be one-dimensional and we can write $M^{\perp} = Rg_0$ for some $g_0 \in M^{\perp}$. Now define g by

$$g = \frac{Fg_0}{\|g_0\|^2} g_0.$$

Then $(g_0, g) = Fg_0$ so by linearity we have $Ff = (f, g)$ for all $f \in M^{\perp}$ and hence (exactly why?) also for all $f \in \mathbf{H}$. $\square$

Note that we have to assume that the linear functional F is *bounded* i.e. continuous. On a finite dimensional Euclidian space R^n, *all* linear functionals are continuous, but on a Hilbert space there may exist linear functionals which are not continuous. It is only for the continuous ones that we have the Riesz representation above.

A.8   Sigma-Algebras and Generators

As usual we consider some basic space X. Let S be some a priori given class of subsets of X, i.e. $S \subseteq 2^X$, where S is not assumed to be a sigma-algebra. The question is whether there is some natural way of extending S to a sigma-algebra. We can of course always extend S to the power algebra 2^X, but in most applications this is going too far, and instead we would like to extend S in some *minimal* way to a sigma-algebra. This minimal extension can in fact always be achieved, and intuitively one is easily led to something like the following argument:

- Assume for example that S is not closed under complement formation. Then we extend S to S_1 by adjoining to S all sets which can be written as complements of sets in S. Thus S_1 is closed under complements.
- If S is a sigma-algebra then we are finished. If it is not, then assume for example that it is not closed under countable unions. We then extend S_1 to S_2 by adjoining to S_1 all countable unions of sets in S_1. Thus S_2 is closed under countable unions.
- It can now very well happen that S_2 is not closed under complement formation (or under countable intersections). In that case we extend S_2 to S_3 by adjoining to S_2 all complements of sets in S_2.
- And thus we go on ...

In this way it perhaps seems likely that "at last" we will obtain the (unique?) minimal extension of S to a sigma-algebra. Unfortunately the method is not constructive (unless of course X is finite) so we need a more indirect method.

Proposition A.38 *Let $\{\mathcal{F}_\alpha;\ \alpha \in A\}$ be an indexed family of sigma-algebras on some basic set X, where A is some index set, i,e. for each $\alpha \in A$ $\mathcal{F}_\alpha$ is a sigma-algebra. Define $\mathcal{F}$ by*

$$\mathcal{F} = \bigcap_{\alpha \in A} \mathcal{F}_\alpha.$$

Then $\mathcal{F}$ is a sigma-algebra.

Proof   The proof is left to the reader as an exercise.   □

We can now go back to our family S above.

Proposition A.39 *Let S be an arbitrary family of subsets of X. Then there exists a unique minimal extension of S to a sigma-algebra. More precisely, there exists a $\mathcal{G} \subseteq 2^X$ such that*

- $\mathcal{G}$ *extends S, i.e. $S \subseteq \mathcal{G}$.*
- $\mathcal{G}$ *is a sigma-algebra on X.*
- $\mathcal{G}$ *is minimal, i.e. if $\mathcal{F}$ is any sigma-algebra on X such that $S \subseteq \mathcal{F}$, then $\mathcal{G} \subseteq \mathcal{F}$.*

Proof   Define $\mathcal{G}$ by

$$\mathcal{G} = \bigcap \mathcal{F}$$

where the intersection is taken over all sigma-algebras $\mathcal{F}$ such that $\mathcal{S} \subseteq \mathcal{F}$. It follows from Proposition A.38 that $\mathcal{G}$ is a sigma-algebra, it obviously extends $\mathcal{S}$ and from the construction we easily see (why?) that it is minimal.   □

Definition A.40

- *The sigma-algebra $\mathcal{G}$ in the previous proposition is called* **the sigma-algebra generated by** *$\mathcal{S}$, and we write*

$$\mathcal{G} = \sigma\{\mathcal{S}\}.$$

- *The family $\mathcal{S}$ is called a* **generator system** *for $\mathcal{G}$.*
- *If $\{\mathcal{F}_\gamma;\ \gamma \in \Gamma\}$ is an indexed family of sigma-algebras on X, we denote by*

$$\bigvee_{\gamma \in \Gamma} \mathcal{F}_\gamma$$

the smallest sigma-algebra which contains each $\mathcal{F}_\gamma$.

- *If $\{f_\gamma;\ \gamma \in \Gamma\}$ is an indexed family of real valued functions on X, we denote by*

$$\mathcal{G} = \sigma\{f_\gamma;\ \gamma \in \Gamma\},$$

the smallest sigma-algebra $\mathcal{G}$ such that f_γ is measurable for each $\gamma \in \Gamma$.

It is important to understand that even if the elements in a generator system $\mathcal{S}$ are "simple" (in some sense), the sigma-algebra generated by $\mathcal{S}$ can be very complicated.

We first give some rather trivial examples.

1. If X is the interval $[0, 1]$ and $\mathcal{S} = \{[0, 1/2]\}$ it is easy to see that $\sigma\{\mathcal{S}\} = \{X, \emptyset, [0, 1/2], (1/2, 1]\}$.
2. If $X = N$ and $\mathcal{S}$ is the class of all singleton sets of N, i.e. $\mathcal{S} = \{\{n\};\ n \in N\}$, then $\sigma\{\mathcal{S}\} = 2^N$.

We now come to the single most important sigma-algebra.

Definition A.41 *If the set X is given by $X = R^n$ then we define the* **Borel algebra** *$\mathcal{B}(R^n)$ as the sigma-algebra which is generated by the class of open sets on R^n. The elements on the Borel algebra are called Borel sets.*

The Borel algebra is an extremely complicated object and the reader should be aware of the following facts.

- There is no "constructive" definition of the Borel algebra. In other words, it is not possible to give anything like a concrete description of what "the typical Borel set" looks like.
- The Borel algebra is strictly included in the power algebra. Thus there exists subsets of R^n which are not Borel sets.

- However, all subsets of R^n which ever turn up "in practice" are Borel sets. Reformulating this, one can say that it is enormously hard to construct a set which is not a Borel set. The pedestrian can therefore, and without danger, informally regard a Borel set as "an arbitrary subset" of R^n.

There are a large number of alternative ways of generating the Borel algebra. By recalling that a set is open if and only if its complement is closed it is easily seen that the Borel algebra is also generated by the class of all closed sets. Below is a list of some of the most common generator systems for the Borel algebra on R. The extensions to R^n are obvious.

Proposition A.42 *The Borel algebra $\mathcal{B}(R)$ can be defined in any of the following ways:*

$$\mathcal{B}(R) = \sigma\{open\ sets\},$$
$$\mathcal{B}(R) = \sigma\{closed\ sets\},$$
$$\mathcal{B}(R) = \sigma\{intervals\ of\ the\ type\ (a,b]\},$$
$$\mathcal{B}(R) = \sigma\{intervals\ of\ the\ type\ (a,b)\},$$
$$\mathcal{B}(R) = \sigma\{intervals\ of\ the\ type\ [a,b]\},$$
$$\mathcal{B}(R) = \sigma\{intervals\ of\ the\ type\ [a,b)\},$$
$$\mathcal{B}(R) = \sigma\{intervals\ of\ the\ type\ (-\infty,b)\},$$
$$\mathcal{B}(R) = \sigma\{intervals\ of\ the\ type\ (-\infty,b]\},$$
$$\mathcal{B}(R) = \sigma\{intervals\ of\ the\ type\ [a,\infty)\},$$
$$\mathcal{B}(R) = \sigma\{intervals\ of\ the\ type\ (a,\infty)\},$$
$$\mathcal{B}(R) = \sigma\{all\ intervals\}.$$

At first glance it seems impossible to prove any results at all about the Borel algebra, since we do not have a constructive definition of it. The reason that we have any control over the class of Borel sets is the fact that it is the *minimal* extension of the class of all intervals, and this can be seen in the following useful alternative characterization of the class of measurable functions.

Proposition A.43 *Let $(X, \mathcal{F})$ be a measurable space and let $f : X \to R$ be a given function. Then f is $\mathcal{F}$-measurable if and only if $f^{-1}(B) \in \mathcal{F}$ for every Borel set $B \subseteq R$.*

Proof   If $f^{-1}(B) \in \mathcal{F}$ for every Borel set $B \subseteq R$, then f is measurable since in particular it lifts intervals back to measurable sets. Assume now that f is measurable. We then have to show that f lifts arbitrary Borel sets to $\mathcal{F}$-measurable sets. To do this, define the class $\mathcal{G}$ of subsets of R by

$$\mathcal{G} = \{B \subseteq R;\ f^{-1}(B) \in \mathcal{F}\}.$$

The class $\mathcal{G}$ is thus the class of "good" subsets of R which do lift back to measurable sets on X. We now want to prove that every Borel set is a good set, i.e. that

$\mathcal{B} \subseteq \mathcal{G}$. Now, using Proposition A.2 it is not hard to prove (do this!) that $\mathcal{G}$ is a sigma-algebra. Since f was assumed to be measurable, it lifts intervals back to measurable sets, so $\mathcal{G}$ does in fact contain all intervals Thus $\mathcal{G}$ is a sigma-algebra containing all intervals, but since the Borel algebra is the smallest sigma-algebra containing all intervals it must hold that $\mathcal{B} \subseteq \mathcal{G}$ which was what we wanted to prove. $\qquad\square$

A particularly important example of a measurable space is $(R, \mathcal{B}(R))$, and a real valued function $f : R \to R$ which is measurable w.r.t $\mathcal{B}(R)$ is called **Borel measurable** or a **Borel function**. The following result shows that there are plenty of Borel functions.

Proposition A.44 *Every continuous function $f : R^n \to R$ is Borel measurable.*

Proof This follows immediately from the fact that a function is continuous if and only if it lifts open sets to open sets. $\qquad\square$

From Proposition A.16 it follows that every function that we can construct, by starting with continuous functions and then using the standard algebraic operations and limiting procedures, will be a Borel function. It does in fact requires a considerable amount of creativity to construct a function which is not a Borel function, so the reader can with very little danger interpret "a Borel function" as "an arbitrary function".

As an important consequence of Proposition A.43 we see that measurability is preserved under composition with Borel functions.

Proposition A.45 *Assume that $f : X \to R$ is a $\mathcal{F}$-measurable mapping, and that $g : R \to R$ is a Borel function. Then the composite mapping $h = g \circ f$ defined by $h(x) = g(f(x))$ is $\mathcal{F}$-measurable.*

Proof Easy exercise for the reader. $\qquad\square$

.

A.9 Product Measures

Let $(X, \mathcal{F}, \mu)$ and Let $(Y, \mathcal{G}, \nu)$ be two measure spaces. We now want to construct a measure on the product space $X \times Y$ along the same lines as when we construct the area measure on R^2 from the length measure on R.

Definition A.46 A measurable rectangle *is a set $Z \subseteq X \times Y$ of the form*

$$Z = A \times B,$$

where $A \in \mathcal{F}$ and $B \in \mathcal{G}$. the **product sigma-algebra** *$\mathcal{F} \otimes \mathcal{G}$ is defined by*

$$\mathcal{F} \otimes \mathcal{G} = \sigma \left\{ measurable\ rectangles \right\}.$$

There is now a natural definition of the measure of a measurable rectangle, namely $\lambda(A \times B) =$ "the base times the height"$= \mu(A) \cdot \nu(B)$. Thus we have defined a product measure on the class of measurable rectangles, and the following result shows that this measure can in fact be extended to the entire product sigma-algebra.

Proposition A.47 *There exists a unique measure λ on $\{X \times Y, \mathcal{F} \otimes \mathcal{G}\}$ such that*

$$\lambda(A \times B) = \mu(A) \cdot \nu(B),$$

for every measurable rectangle $A \times B$. This measure is called the **product measure** *and denoted by $\lambda = \mu \times \nu$.*

We end this section by formulating a very useful result which shows that instead of integrating w.r.t. the product measure we can perform iterated integrals.

Theorem A.48 (The Fubini Theorem) *Consider the product measure space $\{X \times Y, \mathcal{F} \otimes \mathcal{G}, \mu \times \nu\}$ and let $f : X \times Y \to R$ be a measurable mapping. Assume* **either** *that f is integrable over $X \times Y$ or that f is nonnegative. Then we have*

$$\int_{X \times Y} f d(\mu \times \nu) = \int_X \left[\int_Y f(x,y) d\nu(y) \right] d\mu(x) = \int_Y \left[\int_X f(x,y) d\mu(x) \right] d\nu(y).$$

Note that included in the Fubini Theorem is the statement that the function

$$x \longrightarrow \int_Y f(x,y) d\nu(y)$$

is $\mathcal{F}$-measurable, and correspondingly for the other integral.

The Fubini Theorem may of course be extended to any finite product space.

A.10 The Lebesgue Integral

On the class of intervals on R we have a natural length measure m defined by

$$m([a,b]) = b - a.$$

The obvious question is whether this length measure can be extended to a proper measure on the Borel algebra. That this is indeed the case is shown by the following highly nontrivial result.

Proposition A.49 *On the measurable space $(R, \mathcal{B})$ there exists a unique measure m with the property that for any interval $[a,b]$*

$$m([a,b]) = b - a.$$

This measure is called the (scalar) **Lebesgue measure**, and by taking products we can easily form the n-dimensional Lebesgue measure on R^n.

Equipped with the Lebesgue measure we can now start integrating real valued functions defined on the real line. We know that all continuous functions are Borel measurable, and at this point we could encounter a problem, since for continuous functions we also have the Riemann integral. If a function f is continuous and if A is a finite interval we can form two integrals, namely

$$\int_A f(x)dm(x), \quad \text{(Lebesgue)},$$

and

$$\int_A f(x)dx, \quad \text{(Riemann)},$$

and if we are unlucky these integral concepts could differ. Happily enough, it can be proved that whenever the Riemann integral is well defined, it will coincide with the Lebesgue integral. The advantage of using the Lebesgue integral instead of the Riemann integral is that the Lebesgue theory allows us to integrate all Borel functions, whereas the Riemann integral only allows us to integrate Riemann integrable functions (which is a much smaller class). Furthermore, a pointwise convergent sequence of nonnegative Riemann integrable functions may converge to a limit function for which the Riemann integral is not even defined, whereas the class of Borel functions is closed under pointwise convergence.

A.11   The Radon–Nikodym Theorem

One of the big breakthroughs in arbitrage pricing came from the realization that absence of arbitrage is very closely connected to the existence of certain absolutely continuous measure transformations. The basic mathematical tool is the Radon–Nikodym Theorem which we will prove below, and although our prime application will be in the context of probability theory, we present the theory for arbitrary finite measures.

Definition A.50 *Consider a measurable space* $(X, \mathcal{F})$ *on which there are defined two separate measures* μ *and* ν

- *If, for all* $A \in \mathcal{F}$, *it holds that*

$$\mu(A) = 0 \quad \Rightarrow \quad \nu(A) = 0, \tag{A.7}$$

  then ν *is said to be* **absolutely continuous** *with respect to* μ *on* $\mathcal{F}$ *and we write this as* $\nu << \mu$.
- *If we have both* $\mu << \nu$ *and* $\nu << \mu$, *then* μ *and* ν *are said to be* **equivalent** *and we write* $\mu \sim \nu$.
- *If there exists two events,* A *and* B *such that*
  - $* \ A \cap B = \emptyset$
  - $* \ \mu(B) = 0, \quad and \quad \nu(A) = 0.$
  Then μ *and* ν *are said to be mutually* **singular**, *and we write* $\mu \perp \nu$.

We now give some simple examples of these concepts.

Example A.51

- The simplest example of absolute continuity occurs when X is finite or at most countable, say $X = N$, and $\mathcal{F} = 2^X = 2^N$. Every measure μ on N is of course determined by its point masses $\mu(n)$, $n \in N$, and the relation $\nu << \mu$ simply means that

$$\mu(n) = 0 \quad \Rightarrow \quad \nu(n) = 0.$$

- Let μ be "Poisson(c)-measure", defined by its point masses on the natural numbers, as

$$\mu(n) = e^{-c}\frac{c^n}{n!}, \quad n \in N,$$

and let ν be Lebesgue measure on the positive real line. Then, viewed as measures on $(R, \mathcal{B}(R))$, we have $\mu \perp \nu$ since μ puts all its mass on N whereas ν puts all its mass on $R \cap N^c$.

Consider a fixed measure space $(X, \mathcal{F}, \mu)$, and let $f : X \to R$ be a nonnegative measurable mapping in $L^1(X, \mathcal{F}, \mu)$. We can then define a new measure ν on $(X, \mathcal{F})$, by setting

$$\nu(A) \overset{def}{=} \int_A f(x)d\mu(x), \quad A \in \mathcal{F}. \tag{A.8}$$

It now follows fairly easily that ν is a measure on $(X, \mathcal{F}, \mu)$ and from the definition it also follows directly that $\nu << \mu$ on $\mathcal{F}$. Thus (A.8) provides us with a way of constructing measures which are absolutely continuous w.r.t. the base measure μ, and a natural question is whether *all* measures which are absolutely continuous w.r.t. μ are obtained in this way. The affirmative answer to this question is given by the following central result.

Theorem A.52 (The Radon–Nikodym Theorem) *Consider the measure space $(X, \mathcal{F}, \mu)$, where we assume that μ is finite, i.e. that $\mu(X) < \infty$. Assume that there exists a measure ν on $(X, \mathcal{F})$ such that $\nu << \mu$ on $\mathcal{F}$. Then there exists a nonnegative function $f : X \to R$ such that*

$$f \text{ is } \mathcal{F}\text{-measurable.} \tag{A.9}$$

$$\int_X f(x)d\mu(x) < \infty, \tag{A.10}$$

$$\nu(A) = \int_A f(x)d\mu(x), \quad \text{for all } A \in \mathcal{F}. \tag{A.11}$$

The function f is called the **Radon–Nikodym derivative** *of ν w.r.t μ. It is uniquely determined μ-a.e. and we write*

$$f(x) = \frac{d\nu(x)}{d\mu(x)}, \tag{A.12}$$

or alternatively

$$d\nu(x) = f(x)d\mu(x). \tag{A.13}$$

Proof   We sketch a proof which is due to von Neumann. Define a new measure λ by setting $\lambda(A) = \mu(A) + \nu(A)$, for all $A \in \mathcal{F}$. For any $g \in L^2(\lambda)$ we can define the linear mapping $\Phi : X \to R$ by

$$\Phi(g) = \int_X g(x) d\nu(x),$$

and by the triangle and Cauchy–Schwartz inequalities we have

$$|\Phi(g)| = \left| \int_X g d\nu \right| \leq \int_X |g| d\nu \leq \int_X |g| d\lambda \leq \sqrt{\lambda(X)} \cdot \|g\|_{L^2(\lambda)}.$$

Thus, from the Riesz Representation Theorem there exists an $f \in L^2(\lambda)$ such that $\Phi(g) = (g, f)$ for all $g \in L^2(\lambda)$, i.e.

$$\int_X g d\nu = \int_X g f d\lambda, \quad \forall g \in L^2(\lambda). \tag{A.14}$$

By choosing $g = I_A$ for arbitrary $A \in \mathcal{F}$ and using the fact that $0 \leq \nu(A) \leq \lambda(A)$ we see that $0 \leq f \leq 1$. We now write (A.14) as

$$\int_X g d\nu = \int_X g f d\nu + \int_X g f d\mu,$$

i.e.

$$\int_X g(1 - f) d\nu = \int_X g f d\mu, \quad \forall g \in L^2(\lambda). \tag{A.15}$$

Since this holds for all $g \in L^2(\lambda)$ and in particular for all indicator functions, we can write this on "differential form" (see the exercises for a justification of this) as

$$(1 - f) d\nu = f d\mu.$$

It is now tempting to multiply through by $(1 - f)^{-1}$ to obtain

$$d\nu = \frac{f}{(1 - f)} d\mu,$$

and thus to define the Radon–Nikodym derivative by $f/(1 - f)$, but the problem is of course what happens when $f = 1$. Define therefore A by $A = \{x \in X; \ f(x) = 1\}$, and set $g = I_A$. From (A.15) we obtain

$$\int_A f d\mu = \int_A (1 - f) d\nu = 0,$$

and (since $f \geq 0$) this implies that $\mu(A) = 0$. We now use the assumption that $\nu << \mu$ to deduce that also $\nu(A) = 0$, so we can safely write

$$d\nu = \frac{f}{(1 - f)} d\mu,$$

and we see that the Radon–Nikodym derivative is in fact given by

$$\frac{d\nu}{d\mu} = \frac{f}{(1-f)}.$$

□

Example A.53 Going back to Example A.51 we consider the case when $X = N$, and $\mathcal{F} = 2^N$, and we recall that the relation $\nu << \mu$ means that

$$\mu(n) = 0 \quad \Rightarrow \quad \nu(n) = 0.$$

Thus, given μ and ν with $\nu << \mu$, the problem of finding a Radon–Nikodym derivative f will in this case boil down to the problem of finding an f such that

$$\nu(n) = f(n)\mu(n), \quad \forall n \in N. \tag{A.16}$$

We see that for those n where $\mu(n) = 0$ we can solve (A.16) by defining $f(n)$ as

$$f(n) = \frac{\nu(n)}{\mu(n)},$$

so the only problem occurs when $\mu(n) = 0$. However, from the absolute continuity it follows that $\nu(n) = 0$ whenever $\mu(n) = 0$, so for those n equation (A.16) becomes

$$0 = f(n) \cdot 0$$

and we see that for those n we can define f arbitrarily, say by putting $f(n) = 17$. Consequently f is not uniquely defined, but we see that the set where it is not uniquely defined (i.e. for those n where $\mu(n) = 0$) has μ measure zero.

It is important to realize that the concept of absolute continuity is defined relative to the given sigma-algebra. If, for example, $\mathcal{G} \subseteq \mathcal{F}$ then it could well happen that $\mu << \nu$ on $\mathcal{G}$ while it does not hold that $\mu << \nu$ on $\mathcal{F}$. A trivial example is given by setting $X = \{1, 2, 3\}$, and defining

$$\mathcal{F} = 2^X \quad \mathcal{G} = \{X, \emptyset, \{1\}, \{2, 3\}\}$$

and

$$\mu(1) = 2, \quad \mu(2) = 0, \quad \mu(3) = 2,$$
$$\nu(1) = 8, \quad \nu(2) = 5, \quad \nu(3) = 13.$$

Here we obviously do **not** have $\nu << \mu$ on $\mathcal{F}$, since $\mu(2) = 0$ while $\nu(2) = 0$. We do however, have $\nu << \mu$ on $\mathcal{G}$ with () Radon–Nikodym derivative given by

$$f(n) = \begin{cases} 4 \text{ for } n = 1, \\ 9 \text{ for } n = 2, \\ 9 \text{ for } n = 3. \end{cases}$$

(Note in particular that f is $\mathcal{G}$-measurable.)

We thus see that if we enlarge the sigma-algebra we may lose absolute continuity, but if $\nu << \mu$ on some measurable space $(X, \mathcal{F})$ and $\mathcal{G} \subseteq \mathcal{F}$, then $\nu << \mu$ also on $\mathcal{G}$.

A.12   Exercises

Exercise A.1 Prove Proposition A.2.

Exercise A.2 Which of the properties stated in Proposition A.2 are still valid (and which are not necessarily valid) if we replace f^{-1} with f in expressions like $f^{-1}(a \cup B)$ etc.?

Exercise A.3 Show that in the definition of a sigma-algebra, the closedness property under countable intersections in fact follows from the other defining properties.

Exercise A.4 Let μ be a measure. Show formally, using the axioms of a measure, that the following relations hold for all measurable sets A and B.

$$\mu(A \cup B) = \mu(A) + \mu(B) - \mu(A \cap B),$$
$$B \subseteq A \Rightarrow \mu(A \cap B^c) = \mu(A) - \mu(B).$$

Exercise A.5 Let X be a finite set $X = \{x_1, \ldots, x_K\}$ and define $\mathcal{F}$ as the power algebra 2^X. Let furthermore μ be a measure on $(X, \mathcal{F})$ and define p_n by $p_n = \mu(\{x_n\})$, i.e. p_n denotes the mass on the point x_n. Let f be any real valued nonnegative function, and show in detail, by using Definition A.17 that

$$\int_X f(x)d\mu(x) = \sum_{i=1}^{K} f(x_n)p_n.$$

Exercise A.6 Define X by $X = [0, 2]$ and define $\mathcal{F}$ by $\mathcal{F} = \{\emptyset, \Omega, [0, 1), [1, 2]\}$. Define a measure μ by setting

$$\mu([0, 1)) = 1, \quad \mu([1, 2]) = 1, \mu([0, 2]) = 2,$$

and define the functions $f, g : X \to R$ by $f(x) = x$ and $g(x) = 2 - x$.

(a) Show that f and g are not measurable.
(b) Despite the fact that neither f nor g is measurable we now define

$$\int_X f(x)d\mu(x) \stackrel{def}{=} \sup \int_X \varphi(x)d\mu(x),$$

where the supremum is taken over all nonnegative measurable simple functions φ such that $\varphi \leq g$. We make the corresponding definition for g. Now compute and compare $\int_X f d\mu$, $\int_X g d\mu$ and $\int_X (f + g)d\mu$.

Exercise A.7 The object of this exercise is to show that a measurable function can be well approximated by simple functions. Let therefore $f : X \to R$ be a nonnegative measurable function on some measurable space $(X, \mathcal{F})$, and also assume that there exists some constant M such $0 \leq f(x) \leq M$ for all $x \in X$. Show that for every n there exists a simple function f_n such that $f(x) \leq f_n(x) \leq f(x) + 1/n$ for all $x \in X$.

Hint: Consider sets of the form $\{x \in X; k/n \leq f(x) \leq (k + 1)/n\}$.

Exercise A.8 Continuing the exercise above, show that there exists an increasing sequence of simple functions f_n such $f_n(x) \uparrow f(x)$ for all $x \in X$.

Exercise A.9 Fill in the details in the proof of Proposition A.33.

Exercise A.10 Prove proposition A.38.

Exercise A.11 Describe the sigma-algebra on R which is generated by the class of all singleton sets, i.e. of all sets of the form $\{x\}$, where $x \in R$.

Exercise A.12 Prove Proposition A.45 by using Proposition A.43.

Exercise A.13 Let $\{\mathcal{F}_n;\ n = 1, 2, \ldots\}$ be a sequence of sigma-algebras on some common space X. Does it always hold that

$$\mathcal{G} \overset{def}{=} \bigcup_{i=1}^{\infty} \mathcal{F}_n$$

is a sigma-algebra? What if the sequence is increasing?

Exercise A.14 Consider two measures μ and ν with $\nu << \mu$. For any functions $g \in L^1(\nu)$ and $f \in L^1(\mu)$ we define the "differential equality"

$$g d\nu = f d\mu, \qquad\qquad\qquad\qquad\qquad\qquad (A.17)$$

as being shorthand for

$$\int_A g(x) d\nu(x) = \int_A f(x) d\mu(x), \quad \forall A \in \mathcal{F}.$$

(a) Prove that

$$f = \frac{d\nu}{d\mu} \quad \Leftrightarrow \quad d\nu = f d\mu$$

(b) Show that for any $h \in L^1(g d\nu)$ it holds that

$$g d\nu = f d\mu \quad \Rightarrow \quad h g d\nu = h f d\mu$$

(c) Assume that $\lambda << \nu << \mu$ and prove the "chain rule"

$$\frac{d\lambda}{d\mu} = \frac{d\lambda}{d\nu} \cdot \frac{d\nu}{d\mu}.$$

(d) Assuming $\nu \sim \mu$, prove that

$$\frac{d\mu}{d\nu} = \left(\frac{d\nu}{d\mu} \right)^{-1}.$$

A.13   Notes

Royden (1988) gives a very clear and readable presentation of measure theory, and also treats point set topology and basic functional analysis.

Appendix B

PROBABILITY THEORY*

A probability space is simply a measure space $(\Omega, \mathcal{F}, P)$ where the measure P has the property that it has total mass equal to unity, i.e.

$$P(\Omega) = 1.$$

The underlying space Ω often is referred to as the **sample space**, and the elements of the sigma-algebra $\mathcal{F}$ are called **events**.

B.1 Random Variables and Processes

In this section we will discuss random variables and random processes.

Definition B.1 *A **random variable** X is a mapping*

$$X : \Omega \to R$$

such that X is $\mathcal{F}$-measurable.

Remark B.1.1 As the reader probably has observed, the letter X, which in the previous chapter was used to designate a measure space, is now used as the name of a random variable. This is an unfortunate clash of notation, but since both uses of the letter X is standard within its respective area of application we will simply accept this. There is however no risk of confusion: from now on the measure space will always be a probability space, and thus denoted by Ω. The only use of X will be as a name for a random variable or a random process

The interpretation of a random variable is as follows:

- Somewhere, hidden from us, a point $\omega \in \Omega$ in the sample space is "randomly" chosen by, say, the God of Chance.
- We are not allowed to observe ω directly, but we are allowed to observe measurements on the sample space, i.e. we can observe the real number $X(\omega)$, which gives us partial information about ω.

Definition B.2 *The **distribution measure** μ_X for a random variable X is a measure on $(R, \mathcal{B})$ defined by*

$$\mu_X(B) = P(\{\omega \in \Omega; \ X(\omega) \in B\}), \quad B \in \mathcal{B},$$

i.e.

$$\mu_X(B) = P(X^{-1}(B)).$$

*The (cumulative) **distribution function** of X is denoted by F_X and defined by*

$$F_X(x) = P(\{\omega \in \Omega; \ X(\omega) \leq x\}).$$

Note that since X is assumed to be measurable, the event $\{\omega \in \Omega;\ X(\omega) \in B\}$ is in $\mathcal{F}$ so its P measure is well defined. We will often write this event as $\{X \in B\}$ and then the definition of the distribution measure becomes

$$\mu_X(B) = P(X \in B),$$

and the distribution function can be written as

$$F_X(x) = P(X \le x), \quad x \in R.$$

We now go on to introduce the measure theoretic definition of an expected value.

Definition B.3 *For any* $X \in L^1(\Omega, \mathcal{F}, P)$ *its* **expected value**, *denoted by* $E[X]$, *is defined by*

$$E[X] = \int_\Omega X(\omega)dP(\omega).$$

For $X \in L^2$ *the* **variance** *is defined by*

$$Var[X] = E\left[(X - E[X])^2\right].$$

We note that the definition above gives the expected value and the variance as integrals over the (abstract) sample space Ω. The following result connects these formulas to the standard elementary formulas where expectations and variances are computed as integrals over the real line.

Proposition B.4 *Let* $g : R \to R$ *be a Borel function such that the composite random variable* $g(X)$ *is integrable. Then we have*

$$E[g(X)] = \int_\Omega g(X(\omega))\, dP(\omega) = \int_R g(x)d\mu_X(x).$$

Proof   We leave the proof as an exercise. See the exercises for hints.   □

We note that the first equality above holds by definition. The point of the result is thus the second equality. The careful reader notes (with satisfaction) that, by Proposition A.45, the measurability of $g(X)$ is guaranteed.

In order to convince the reader that the framework above really is of some value we will now prove a useful result which shows that in some cases an expected value can be computed in terms of an ordinary Lebesgue integral.

Proposition B.5 *Let* X *be a nonnegative random variable. Then it holds that*

$$E[X] = \int_0^\infty P(X \ge t)\, dt.$$

Proof   By using the Fubini Theorem we have

$$E[X] = \int_\Omega X(\omega)dP(\omega) = \int_\Omega \left[\int_0^{X(\omega)} 1 \cdot dt \right] dP(\omega)$$

$$= \int_\Omega \left[\int_0^\infty I\{t \le X(\omega)\} \cdot dt \right] dP(\omega) = \int_0^\infty \left[\int_\Omega I\{t \le X(\omega)\} \, dP(\omega) \right] dt$$

$$= \int_0^\infty \left[\int_{A_t} dP(\omega) \right] dt,$$

where the event $A_t = \{X \ge t\}$. We thus have

$$E[X] = \int_0^\infty P(A_t)dt = \int_0^\infty P(X \ge t) \, dt.$$

$\square$

We now go on to the concept of a random process.

Definition B.6 *A random process on the probability space* $(\Omega, \mathcal{F}, P)$ *is a mapping*

$$X : R_+ \times \Omega \to R,$$

such that for each $t \in R_+$ *the mapping*

$$X(t, \cdot) : \Omega \to R,$$

is $\mathcal{F}$*-measurable.*

We interpret $X(t, \omega)$ as "the value at time t given the outcome ω", and we will also use the alternative notation $X_t(\omega)$.

Note the following:

- For each fixed t the mapping

$$\omega \longrightarrow X(t, \omega),$$

  which we also denote by X_t, is a **random variable**.
- For each $\omega \in \Omega$ the mapping

$$t \longrightarrow X(t, \omega)$$

  is a **deterministic function of time**. This function, which we may draw as a graph, is called the **realization** or **trajectory** of X for the outcome ω. When we observe a random process over time (like the evolution of a stock price) we thus see the trajectory of a single ω.

In the definition above we have defined processes only on the time interval $0 \le t < \infty$, but we can of course consider processes defined on just a subinterval or on the integers (a "discrete time process").

B.2 Partitions and Information

Consider a sample space Ω and a given partition $\mathcal{P} = \{A_1, \ldots A_K\}$ of Ω. We can now give an intuitive interpretation of $\mathcal{P}$ in *information terms* along the following lines:

- Someone (the God of Chance?) chooses a point ω in the sample space. We do not know exactly which point has been chosen.

- What we do get information about, is exactly which component of $\mathcal{P}$ that ω belongs to. More formally one can think of this as an experiment where we are allowed to observe the random variable Y defined by

$$Y(\omega) = \sum_{i=1}^{K} n \cdot I_{A_n}(\omega).$$

If we observe $Y(\omega) = n$ then we know with certainty that ω lies in A_n.

We thus see that having access to a certain partition can be interpreted as having access to a certain amount of information. We note that the trivial partition $\mathcal{P} = \{\Omega\}$ corresponds to "no information at all". The other extreme case occurs when Ω is finite, say $\Omega = \{\omega_1, \ldots, \omega_N\}$, and the partition is given by $\mathcal{F} = \{\{\omega_1\}, \{\omega_2\}, \ldots, \{\omega_N\}\}$. This case corresponds to "full information".

In some cases we may even compare the informational content in two separate partitions. Consider, as an example, the space $\Omega = [0, 1]$ with two partitions

$$\mathcal{P}_1 = \{A_1, A_2, A_3, A_4\},$$

where

$$A_1 = \left[0, \frac{1}{3}\right), \quad A_2 = \left[\frac{1}{3}, \frac{1}{2}\right), \quad A_3 = \left[\frac{1}{2}, \frac{3}{4}\right), \quad A_4 = \left[\frac{3}{4}, 1\right]$$

and

$$\mathcal{P}_2 = \{B_1, B_2, B_3\},$$

where

$$B_1 = \left[0, \frac{1}{3}\right), \quad B_2 = \left[\frac{1}{3}, \frac{3}{4}\right), \quad B_3 = \left[\frac{3}{4}, 1\right].$$

It is now natural to say that $\mathcal{P}_1$ *contains more information* than $\mathcal{P}_2$ since the partition $\mathcal{P}_1$ has been obtained by subdividing some of the components of $\mathcal{P}_2$ into smaller pieces. There is thus a natural partial order relation between different partitions of a given sample space, and in the example above we say that $\mathcal{P}_1$ is *finer* than $\mathcal{P}_2$.

Definition B.7 *For a given sample space Ω, a partition $\mathcal{S}$ is said to be **finer** than a partition $\mathcal{P}$ if every component in $\mathcal{P}$ is a union of components in $\mathcal{S}$.*

The interpretation of this is of course that "$\mathcal{S}$ contains more information than $\mathcal{P}$".

Consider again the sample space Ω and some given but otherwise arbitrary mapping $f : \Omega \to R$. For simplicity we assume that f only takes finitely many values, and we denote these values by $x_1, x_2, \ldots, x_K$. The interpretation is that f is a measurement on Ω and that we gain knowledge about the (unknown) sample point ω by observing the measurement $f(\omega)$. We now note that f generates a natural partition $\mathcal{P}(f)$ defined by

$$\mathcal{P}(f) = \{A_1, \ldots A_K\},$$

where

$$A_n = \{\omega \in \Omega; \ f(\omega) = x_n\}, \quad n = 1, 2, \ldots K.$$

i.e.

$$A_n = f^{-1}(x_n), \quad n = 1, 2, \ldots K.$$

It is then natural to interpret the partition $\mathcal{P}(f)$ as "the information generated by f", since by observing f we can exactly tell in which component of $\mathcal{P}(f)$ that ω lies.

We also see that given the information in $\mathcal{P}(f)$, i.e. given information about in which components ω lies, we can exactly determine the value $f(\omega)$. The reason for this is of course that f is constant on each component on $\mathcal{P}(f)$ and we can easily generalize this observation to the following definition and lemma.

Definition B.8 *A given mapping $f : \Omega \to R$ is called measurable w.r.t a partition $\mathcal{P}$ if and only if it is constant on the components of $\mathcal{P}$.*

Lemma B.9 *Take as given a sample space Ω, a finite valued mapping $f : \Omega \to R$ and a partition $\mathcal{P}$. If f is $\mathcal{P}$-measurable then the value of f is completely determined by the information in $\mathcal{P}$ in the sense that if we know in which component of $\mathcal{P}$ it is located, then we know the function value $f(\omega)$.*

Consider again the sample space Ω and a finite valued mapping $f : \Omega \to R$. If we also are given another mapping $g : R \to R$ and define $h : \Omega \to R$ by $h(\omega) = g(f(\omega))$, then it is obvious that h generates less information than f, i.e. that $\mathcal{P}(f)$ is finer than $\mathcal{P}(h)$, which also can be expressed by saying that h is constant on the components in $\mathcal{P}(f)$, i.e. h is $\mathcal{P}(f)$-measurable. There is also a converse of this result which will have important generalizations later on in the text.

Proposition B.10 *Consider a fixed Ω and two finite valued mappings $f : \Omega \to R$ and $h : \Omega \to R$. Assume that h is $\mathcal{P}(f)$-measurable. Then there exists a function $g : R \to R$ such that $h = g \circ f$.*

Proof   Exercise for the reader.   □

B.3   Sigma-algebras and Information

Let us again consider the sample space Ω and a given partition $\mathcal{P}$. We note the following facts:

- The partition $\mathcal{P}$ generates a natural sigma-algebra, namely $\sigma\{\mathcal{P}\}$.
- From $\sigma\{\mathcal{P}\}$ we can easily reconstruct the original partition $\mathcal{P}$, since the components of $\mathcal{P}$ are precisely the *atoms* in $\sigma\{\mathcal{P}\}$, i.e. the sets in $\sigma\{\mathcal{P}\}$ which have no proper subsets (apart from $\emptyset$) in $\sigma\{\mathcal{P}\}$.
- If $\mathcal{F}$ and $\mathcal{S}$ are two partitions, then

$$\mathcal{S} \quad \text{is finer than} \quad \mathcal{P}$$

if and only if

$$\mathcal{P}\subseteq\mathcal{S}.$$

- For any mapping $f : \Omega \to R$ it holds that

$$f \text{ is } \mathcal{P}\text{-measurable}$$

if and only if

$$f \text{ is } \sigma\{\mathcal{P}\}\text{-measurable}.$$

As long as we are working with finite partitions it is thus logically equivalent if we work with partitions or if we work with the corresponding sigma-algebras. From a technical point of view, however, the sigma-algebra formalism is superior to the partition formalism, since a sigma-algebra is closed under the usual set theoretic operations. Furthermore; our development of measure theory demands that we have a sigma-algebra as the basic object. Thus, even if the intuitive information concept is perhaps most natural to formulate within the partition framework, it turns out that the sigma-algebra formalism is vastly superior in the long run. It should also be emphasized that the equivalence between partitions and sigma-algebras only holds when the partition is finite. In the general case, there is simply no alternative to the sigma-algebra formalism.

We will therefore, henceforth, formalize the intuitive information concept in terms of sigma-algebras, and in particular we will interpret the relation

$$\mathcal{G}\subseteq\mathcal{F}$$

between two sigma-algebras $\mathcal{G}$ and $\mathcal{F}$ as

" $\mathcal{G}$ contains less information than $\mathcal{F}$."

Let us again take a sample space Ω as given, and consider a mapping Ω: $X \to R$. We recall an earlier definition:

Definition B.11 *The sigma-algebra $\sigma\{X\}$ is defined as the smallest sigma-algebra $\mathcal{F}$ such that X is $\mathcal{F}$-measurable.*

We will refer to $\sigma\{X\}$ as "the sigma-algebra generated by X". Technically speaking it is the intersection of all sigma-algebras $\mathcal{G}$ such that X is $\mathcal{G}$-measurable, but we can in fact give a more explicit representation.

Proposition B.12 *We have the representation*

$$\sigma\{X\} = \left\{X^{-1}(B);\ B \in \mathcal{B}(R)\right\}.$$

Proof Exercise for the reader. □

Definition B.13 *Let $\mathcal{K}$ be an arbitrary family of mappings from Ω to R. Then $\sigma\{\mathcal{K}\}$ is defined as the smallest sigma-algebra $\mathcal{G}$ such that X is $\mathcal{G}$-measurable for all $X \in \mathcal{K}$.*

We now have a general result for sigma-algebras, which is parallel to Proposition B.10 for partitions. The proof is not easy and therefore omitted.

Proposition B.14 *Let $X_1, \ldots, X_N$ be given mappings $X_n : \Omega \to R$, and assume that a mapping $Z : \Omega \to R$ is $\sigma\{X_1, \ldots, X_N\}$-measurable. Then there exists a Borel function $f : R^N \to R$ such that for all $\omega \in \Omega$ we have*

$$X(\omega) = f\left(X_1(\omega), \ldots X_N(\omega)\right).$$

This proposition thus formalizes the idea that if a random variable X is measurable w.r.t. a certain sigma-algebra then "the value of the variable is completely determined by the information contained in the sigma-algebra".

We now pass on to random processes, and note that every random process generates an entire family of interesting sigma-algebras.

Definition B.15 *Let $\{X_t;\ t \geq 0\}$ be a random process, defined on the probability space $(\Omega, \mathcal{F}, P)$. We then define the **sigma-algebra generated by X over the interval $[0, t]$** by*

$$\mathcal{F}_t^X = \sigma\{X_s;\ s \leq t\}.$$

The intuitive interpretation is that "$\mathcal{F}_t^X$ is the information generated by observing X over the time interval $[0, t]$". There is in general no very explicit description of $\mathcal{F}_t^X$, but it is not hard to show that $\mathcal{F}_t^X$ is generated by all events of the form $\{X_s \in B\}$ for all $s \leq t$ and all Borel sets B.

If Z is a random variable then, based on the discussions above, we interpret the statement

"Z is $\mathcal{F}_t^X$-measurable"

as

"Z is a function of the entire X-trajectory over the interval $[0, t]$."

From the definition it is immediately clear that

$$s \leq t \quad \Rightarrow \quad \mathcal{F}_s^X \subseteq \mathcal{F}_t^X,$$

so every random process X will in this way generate an increasing family of sigma-algebras. We now generalize this concept.

Definition B.16 *A* **filtration** $\underline{\mathcal{F}} = \{\mathcal{F}_t\}_{t\geq0}$, *sometimes written as* $\mathbf{F} = \{\mathcal{F}_t\}_{t\geq0}$, *on the probability space* $(\Omega, \mathcal{F}, P)$ *is an indexed family of sigma-algebras on* Ω *such that*

- $$\mathcal{F}_t \subseteq \mathcal{F}, \quad \forall t \geq 0.$$

- $$s \leq t \quad \Rightarrow \quad \mathcal{F}_s^X \subseteq \mathcal{F}_t^X.$$

Given a filtration $\underline{\mathcal{F}}$ *as above, the sigma algebra* $\mathcal{F}_\infty$ *is defined as*

$$\mathcal{F}_\infty = \bigvee_{t\geq0} \mathcal{F}_t.$$

A filtration thus formalizes the idea of a nondecreasing information flow over time. We now introduce one of the most basic concepts for stochastic processes.

Definition B.17 *Consider a given filtration* $\underline{\mathcal{F}} = \{\mathcal{F}_t\}_{t\geq0}$ *on some probability space, and a random process* X *on the same space. We say that the process* X *is* **adapted** *to the filtration* $\underline{\mathcal{F}}$ *if*

$$X_t \in \mathcal{F}_t, \quad \forall t \geq 0.$$

The interpretation of this definition is that "For every fixed t, the process value X_t is completely determined by the information $\mathcal{F}_t$ that we have access to at time t". Alternatively we can say that "an adapted process does not look into the future". We note in passing that the process X is always adapted to the **internal filtration** $\mathcal{F}_t^X$ generated by X.

Example B.18 Let Z be any random process with continuous trajectories, and define the filtration $\underline{\mathcal{F}}$ as the internal filtration $\mathcal{F}_t = \mathcal{F}_t^Z$. The following processes are adapted:

$$X_t = sup_{s\leq t}|Z_s|,$$

$$X_t = Z_{t/2},$$

$$X_t = \int_0^t Z_s ds.$$

The processes

$$X_t = Z_{t+1},$$

$$X_t = \int_0^{t+2} Z_s ds$$

are **not** adapted.

In a typical financial application, the filtration $\mathcal{F}$ is generated by the observed asset prices. A natural requirement for a portfolio strategy is that the portfolio decision that is taken at time t, is only allowed to depend upon the public information that we have access to at time t (by observing asset prices). The formalization of this idea is to demand that the portfolio strategy should be adapted.

B.4   Independence

We consider again a given probability space $(\Omega, \mathcal{F}, P)$, and recall the standard definition of independent events.

Definition B.19 *Two events $A, B \in \mathcal{F}$ are* **independent** *if*

$$P(A \cap B) = P(A) \cdot P(B).$$

We now generalize this definition to sigma-algebras, random variables and processes.

Definition B.20

- *Two sigma-algebras $\mathcal{G}, \mathcal{H} \subseteq \mathcal{F}$ are independent if*

$$P(G \cap H) = P(G) \cdot P(H),$$

  for all $G \in \mathcal{G}$ and all $H \in \mathcal{H}$.
- *Two random variables X and Y are independent if the sigma-algebras $\sigma\{X\}$ and $\sigma\{Y\}$ are independent.*
- *Two stochastic processes X and Y are independent if the sigma-algebras $\sigma\{X_t;\ t \geq 0\}$ and $\sigma\{Y_t;\ t \geq 0\}$ are independent.*
- *An indexed family $\{\mathcal{G}_\gamma;\ \gamma \in \Gamma\}$ of sigma-algebras, where $\mathcal{G}_\gamma \in \mathcal{F}$ for each $\gamma \in \Gamma$ are mutually independent if*

$$P\left(\bigcap_{i=1}^{n} G_n\right) = \prod_{i=1}^{n} P(G_n),$$

  for every finite sub collection $G_1, \ldots, G_n$ where $G_i \in \mathcal{G}_{\gamma_i}$ and where $\gamma_i = \gamma_j$ for $i = j$. The extension to random variables and processes is the obvious one.

We note that two random variables X and Y are independent if and only if

$$P(X \in B_1\ \&\ Y \in B_2) = P(X \in B_1) \cdot P(Y \in B_2),$$

for all Borel sets B_1 and B_2.

We now formulate and sketch the proof of a very useful result.

Proposition B.21 *Suppose that the random variables X and Y are independent. Assume furthermore that X, Y, and XY are in L^1. Then we have*

$$E[X \cdot Y] = E[X] \cdot E[Y]. \tag{B.1}$$

Proof　We do the proof in several steps.

1. Choose arbitrary $A \in \sigma\{X\}$ and $B \in \sigma\{Y\}$. Then we have

$$E[I_A \cdot I_B] = E[I_{A\cap B}] = \int_{A\cap B} dP(\omega) = P(A \cap B)$$
$$= P(A) \cdot P(B) = E[I_A] \cdot E[I_B].$$

Thus the proposition holds for indicator functions.

2. From the previous item and from the linearity of the integral it follows that (B.1) holds for all simple functions (check this in detail).

3. In the general case we can WLOG (without loss of generality) assume that X and Y are nonnegative. In that case there exist (see the exercises) sequences $\{X_n\}$ and $\{Y_n\}$ of simple random variables such that

$$X_n \uparrow X, \quad X_n \in \sigma\{X\},$$
$$Y_n \uparrow Y, \quad Y_n \in \sigma\{Y\}.$$

From item 2 above we have

$$E[X_n \cdot Y_n] = E[X_n] \cdot E[YN].$$

Now we let $n \to \infty$ and use the Monotone Convergence Theorem.　□

We also have the following simple but useful corollary.

Corollary B.22 *If X and Y are independent random variables, and if f and g are Borel functions, then $f(X)$ and $g(Y)$ are independent. In particular, if $f(X), g(Y)$ and $f(X)g(Y)$ are in L^1, then*

$$E[f(X) \cdot g(Y)] = E[f(X)] \cdot E[g(Y)].$$

Proof　Exercise for the reader.　□

B.5　Conditional Expectations

Apart from the concept of independence, the most important concept in probability theory is that of conditional expectation. We will need to treat this concept in its most general (but also most useful) version, namely that of a conditional expectation given a sigma-algebra. We start, however, with a more elementary discussion in order to motivate the more abstract arguments later on.

Consider a fixed probability space $(\Omega, \mathcal{F}, P)$, and suppose that A and B are events in $\mathcal{F}$ with $P(B) = 0$. We recall the elementary definition of conditional probability.

Definition B.23 *The probability of A, conditional on B is defined by*

$$P(A|B) = \frac{P(A \cap B)}{P(B)}.$$
(B.2)

The intuition behind this definition is as follows:

- The probability for any event A is the fraction of the total mass which is located on A, so

$$P(A) = \frac{P(A)}{P(\Omega)}.$$

- When we condition on B, we **know** that B has happened. Thus the effective sample space is now B rather than Ω. This explains the normalizing factor in the nominator of (B.2).

- The only part of A that can occur if we know that B has occured is precisely $A \cap B$.

What we are looking for is now a sensible definition of the object

$$E[X|\mathcal{G}],$$

where X is a random variable and $\mathcal{G}$ is a sigma-algebra included in $\mathcal{F}$. The interpretation should be that $E[X|\mathcal{G}]$ is "the expectation of X given that we have access to the information in $\mathcal{G}$". It is not trivial to formalize this rather vague notion, so we start with some heuristics.

We therfore recall that the unconditional expected value is given by

$$E[X] = \int_{\Omega} X(\omega)P(d\omega),$$

i.e. $E[X]$ is a weighted average of the values of X, where we have used the "probabilities" $P(d\omega)$ as weights.

Suppose now that we have obtained information about the outcome of the random experiment, in the sense that we know that sample point ω is in the set B. The natural definition of the expected value of X given B is then obtained by taking the weighted average of X over the new effective sample space B. We must of course normalize the probability measure so that we have total mass equal to unity on the new space B. Thus we normalize the probabilities as

$$\frac{P(d\omega)}{P(B)},$$

and we may thus define the object $E[X|B]$.

Definition B.24 *Suppose $B \in \mathcal{F}$ with $P(B) > 0$, and that $X \in L^1(\Omega, \mathcal{F}, P)$. Then "the conditional expectation of X given B" is defined by*

$$E[X|B] = \frac{1}{P(B)} \int_B X(\omega)dP(\omega).$$

We now consider a slightly more general case, where we are given a finite partition $\mathcal{P} = \{A_1, \ldots, A_K\}$ with $A_n \in \mathcal{F}$ for $n = 1, \ldots, K$. Having access to the information contained in $\mathcal{P}$ is, according to our earlier discussion, equivalent to knowing exactly in which of the components $A_1, \ldots, A_K$ that the outcome ω lies. Now consider the following schedule:

- Someone (the God of Chance?) chooses 'randomly" a point ω in the sample space. We do not know exactly which point has been chosen.
- We are informed about in exactly which component of the partition that ω lies.
- As soon as we know in which component ω lies, say for example in A_n, then we can compute the conditional expectation of X given A_n according to the formula above.

From this we see that exactly which conditional expectation that we will compute, will depend on in which component that ω lies. We may therefore define a mapping from Ω to the real line by

$$\omega \longrightarrow E[X|A_n], \quad \text{if } \omega \in A_n,\ n = 1, \ldots, K.$$

This leads us to the following definition.

Definition B.25 *With assumptions as above, and also assuming that $P(A_n) > 0$ for all n, we define $E[X|\mathcal{P}]$, "the conditional expectation of X given the information in $\mathcal{P}$" by*

$$E[X|\mathcal{P}](\omega) = \sum_{n=1}^{K} I_{A_n}(\omega) E[X|A_n], \tag{B.3}$$

i.e.

$$E[X|\mathcal{P}](\omega) = \frac{1}{P(A_n)} \int_{A_n} X dP, \quad \text{when } \omega \in A_n. \tag{B.4}$$

We note that the object $E[X|\mathcal{P}]$ is not a real number but a mapping from Ω to R, i.e. it is a **random variable**. We also note that, by definition, $E[X|\mathcal{P}]$ is constant on each component of $\mathcal{P}$, i.e. it is $\sigma\{\mathcal{P}\}$-measurable.

We would now like to extend the definition above to the case when we condition on a general sigma-algebra, and not only on a finite partition. This is however not entirely straightforward, and a major problem with the definition above is that we had to assume that $P(A_n) > 0$ for all n, since otherwise we divide by zero in (B.4). We therefore have to take a more indirect approach, and start by listing some important properties of the conditional expectation above.

Proposition B.26 *Assume that $(\Omega, \mathcal{F}, P)$, X and $\mathcal{P}$ are as above. Define the sigma-algebra $\mathcal{G} \subseteq \mathcal{F}$ by $\mathcal{G} = \sigma\{\mathcal{P}\}$. Then the conditional expectation $E[X|\mathcal{P}]$ is characterized as the unique random variable Z on $(\Omega, \mathcal{F}, P)$ with the following properties:*

(i) *Z is $\mathcal{G}$ measurable.*

(ii) *For every* $\in \mathcal{G}$ *it holds that*

$$\int_G Z(\omega)dP(\omega) = \int_G X(\omega)dP(\omega).$$

Proof   Exercise for the reader.   □

The point of this result is that it characterizes the conditional expectation in a way which does not require the components of $\mathcal{P}$ to have strictly positive probabilities. In fact, the conditions (i)–(ii) above can be formulated for *any* sigma-algebra $\mathcal{G}$ even if $\mathcal{G}$ is *not* generated by a finite partition. This is the starting point for our final definition of conditional expectations.

Definition B.27 *Let* $(\Omega, \mathcal{F}, P)$ *be a probability space and* X *a random variable in* $L^1(\Omega, \mathcal{F}, P)$. *Let furthermore* $\mathcal{G}$ *be a sigma-algebra such that* $\mathcal{G} \subseteq \mathcal{F}$. *If* Z *is a random variable with the properties that*

(i) Z *is* $\mathcal{G}$-*measurable.*

(ii) *For every* $G \in \mathcal{G}$ *it holds that*

$$\int_A Z(\omega)dP(\omega) = \int_A X(\omega)dP(\omega). \tag{B.5}$$

Then we say that Z *is the* **conditional expectation of** X **given the sigma-algebra** $\mathcal{G}$. *In that case we denote* Z *by the symbol*

$$E\left[X|\,\mathcal{G}\right].$$

The price that we have to pay for this very general definition of conditional expectation is that we have a nontrivial existence problem, since it is not immediately clear that in the general case there will always exist a random variable Z as above. We note that X itself will obviously always satisfy (i), but in the general case it will not satisfy (ii). We do however have an existence results, and the proof is a nice application of the Radon–Nikodym Theorem.

Theorem B.28 *Let* $(\Omega, \mathcal{F}, P)$, X *and* $\mathcal{G}$ *be as in Definition B.27. Then the following hold:*

- *There will always exist a random variable* Z *satisfying conditions (i)–(ii) above.*
- *The variable* Z *is unique, i.e. if both* Y *and* Z *satisfy (i)–(ii) then* $Y = Z$, P-*a.s.*

Proof   Define the measure ν on $(\Omega, \mathcal{G})$ by

$$\nu(G) \stackrel{def}{=} \int_G X(\omega)dP(\omega).$$

Trivially we then have $\nu \ll P$ and we see directly by inspection that   if we define Z by

$$Z = \frac{d\nu}{dP}, \quad \text{on } \mathcal{G},$$

then Z will be $\mathcal{G}$-measurable and it will have the property that

$$\nu(G) = \int_G Z dP,$$

i.e

$$\int_G Z dP = \int_G X dP,$$

for all, $G \in \mathcal{G}$. □

In passing we note that if $\mathcal{G}$ is the trivial sigma-algebra $\mathcal{G} = \{\Omega, \emptyset\}$ then it follows directly from the definition above (prove this!) that

$$E[X|\mathcal{G}] = E[X].$$

We now have some natural and simple rules for calculating conditional expectations.

Proposition B.29 *The following hold:*

$$X \le Y \quad \Rightarrow \quad E[X|\mathcal{G}] \le E[Y|\mathcal{G}], \quad P\text{-}a.s., \tag{B.6}$$

$$E[\alpha X + \beta Y|\mathcal{G}] = \alpha E[X|\mathcal{G}] + \beta E[Y|\mathcal{G}], \quad \forall \alpha, \beta \in R. \tag{B.7}$$

Proof The relation (B.6) follows more or less directly from Proposition A.26. In order to prove (B.7) we *define* Z by $Z = \alpha E[X|\mathcal{G}] + \beta E[Y|\mathcal{G}]$. Then Z is obviously $\mathcal{G}$-measurable and we only have to show that for every $G \in \mathcal{G}$ we have

$$\int_G (\alpha E[X|\mathcal{G}] + \beta E[Y|\mathcal{G}]) dP = \int_G (\alpha X + \beta Y) dP.$$

Using the definition of the conditional expectation and linearity, the right-hand side of the above becomes

$$\int_G (\alpha E[X|\mathcal{G}] + \beta E[Y|\mathcal{G}]) dP = \alpha \int_G E[X|\mathcal{G}] dP + \beta \int_G E[Y|\mathcal{G}] dP$$

$$= \alpha \int_G X dP + \beta \int_G Y dP = \int_G (\alpha X + \beta Y) dP.$$

□

One of the most important and frequently used properties of conditional expectation is the rule of iterated expectations.

Proposition B.30 *Assume the setting above and also assume that the sigma-algebra $\mathcal{H}$ satisfies $\mathcal{H} \subseteq \mathcal{G} \subseteq \mathcal{F}$. Then the following hold:*

$$E\left[E\left[X|\mathcal{G}\right]|\mathcal{H}\right] = E\left[X|\mathcal{H}\right], \tag{B.8}$$

$$E\left[X\right] = E\left[E\left[X|\mathcal{G}\right]\right]. \tag{B.9}$$

Proof   We start by noting that (B.9) is a special case of (B.8) since $E[X] = E\left[X|\mathcal{H}\right]$ where $\mathcal{H}$ is the trivial sigma-algebra. In order to prove (B.8) we define Z by $Z = E\left[X|\mathcal{H}\right]$. We now have to show that Z is $\mathcal{H}$-measurable and that for all events $H \in \mathcal{H}$ we have

$$\int_H Z dP = \int_H E\left[X|\mathcal{G}\right] dP. \tag{B.10}$$

The measurability is immediately clear (why?). As for (B.10) we note that since $\mathcal{H} \subseteq \mathcal{G}$ we have $H \in \mathcal{H} \Rightarrow H \in \mathcal{G}$ so

$$\int_H E\left[X|\mathcal{G}\right] dP = \int_H X dP = \int_H E\left[X|\mathcal{H}\right] dP = \int_H Z dP.$$

$\square$

Suppose now that X is $\mathcal{G}$-measurable. We have earlier said that the intuitive interpretation of this is that X is uniquely determined by the information contained in $\mathcal{G}$. When we condition on $\mathcal{G}$ this should imply that we know X and thus can treat it as deterministic (conditionally on $\mathcal{G}$). This intuition is formalized by the following result, where we leave the proof as an exercise.

Proposition B.31 *I X is $\mathcal{G}$-measurable and if X,Y and XY are in L^1, then*

$$E\left[X|\mathcal{G}\right] = X, \quad P\text{-}a.s. \tag{B.11}$$

$$E\left[XY|\mathcal{G}\right] = X \cdot E\left[Y|\mathcal{G}\right], \quad P\text{-}a.s. \tag{B.12}$$

There is a Jensen inequality also for conditional expectations.

Proposition B.32 *Assume that $f : R \to R$ is convex and that X and $f(X)$ are integrable. Then*

$$f\left(E\left[X|\mathcal{G}\right]\right) \leq E\left[f(X)|\mathcal{G}\right], \quad P - a.s.$$

Assume that X and Y are defined on the same space $(\Omega, \mathcal{F}, P)$. Then we can define the conditional expectation of Y, given X.

Definition B.33 *For any integrable Y and for any X we define*

$$E\left[Y|X\right] \overset{def}{=} E\left[Y|\sigma\{X\}\right].$$

Since $E[Y|X]$ by this definition automatically is $\sigma\{X\}$-measurable, Proposition B.14 guarantees that there exists a Borel function g such that

$$E[Y|X] = g(X), \quad P-a.s. \tag{B.13}$$

using this g we may now define conditional expectations on the distribution side instead of on the Ω side.

Definition B.34 *We define the object $E[Y|X = x]$ by*

$$E[Y|X = x] = g(x), \quad x \in R,$$

where g is given by (B.13).

From the law of iterated expectations and Proposition B.4 we obtain the following result, which should be well known from elementary probability theory.

Proposition B.35 *If μ_X denotes the distribution measure for X then, for any random variable Y:*

$$E[Y] = \int_R E[Y|X = x]\, d\mu_X(x).$$

If X and $\mathcal{G}$ are independent, i.e. if $\sigma\{X\}$ and $\mathcal{G}$ are independent sigma-algebras, then it seems reasonable to expect that $\mathcal{G}$ does not contain any information about X. The technical formulation of this intuition is as follows.

Proposition B.36 *Assume that X is integrable, and that X and $\mathcal{G}$ are independent. Then*

$$E[Y|X] = E[Y].$$

Proof   Left as an exercise.   □

It is well known that $E[X]$ is the optimal mean square deterministic predictor of X. The corresponding result for conditional expectations is as follows.

Proposition B.37 *Let $(\Omega, \mathcal{F}, P)$ be a given probability space, let $\mathcal{G}$ be a sub-sigma-algebra of $\mathcal{F}$ and let X be a square integrable random variable. Consider the problem of minimizing*

$$E\left[(X - Z)^2\right]$$

where Z is allowed to vary over the class of all square integrable $\mathcal{G}$ measurable random variables. The optimal solution $\hat{Z}$ is then given by

$$\hat{Z} = E[X|\mathcal{G}].$$

Proof   Left to the reader. See the exercises for a hint.   □

In geometrical terms this means that $E[X|\mathcal{G}]$ is the orthogonal projection (in $L^2(\Omega, \mathcal{F}, P)$) of X onto the closed subspace $L^2(\Omega, \mathcal{G}, P)$. For square integrable random variables one may in fact use this as the definition of the conditional expectation. This definition can then be extended from L^2 to L^1 by continuity, since L^2 is dense in L^1.

B.6   Equivalent Probability Measures

In this section we discuss absolute continuity and equivalence for the particular case of probability measures. The results in this section will be heavily used in Chapter 10.

Let therefore P and Q be probability measures on $(\Omega, \mathcal{F})$. We immediately have the following simple result.

Lemma B.38 *For two probability measures P and Q, the relation $P \sim Q$ on $\mathcal{F}$ holds if and only if*

$$P(A) = 1 \quad \Leftrightarrow \quad Q(A) = 1, \quad for\ all\ A \in \mathcal{F}. \tag{B.14}$$

Proof   Exercise for the reader.   □

In the context of probability measures we thus notice that although two equivalent measures P and Q may assign completely different probabilities to a fixed event A, but all events which are impossible under P (i.e. $P(A) = 0$) are also impossible under Q. Equivalently, all events which are certain under P (i.e. $P(A = 1)$), are also certain under Q. It also follows directly (prove this!) from the definition that if an event A has strictly positive P-probability, then it also has strictly positive Q-probability (and vice versa).

From the Radon–Nikodym Theorem we know that $Q << P$ on the probability space $(\Omega, \mathcal{F})$ if and only if there exists $\mathcal{F}$-measurable mapping $L : \Omega \to R_+$ such that

$$\int_A dQ(\omega) = \int_A L(\omega) dP(\omega) \tag{B.15}$$

for all $A \in \mathcal{F}$. Since Q is a probability measure L must also have the property that

$$\int_\Omega L dP = 1,$$

i.e

$$E^P[L] = 1.$$

In other words, the Radon–Nikodym derivative L is a nonnegative random variable with $E^P[L] = 1$, and it is often referred to as the **likelihood ratio** between Q and P. Written in terms of expected values, it follows from (B.15) that, for any random variable $X \in L^1(Q)$ we have

$$E^Q[X] = E^P[L \cdot X]. \tag{B.16}$$

Suppose now that $Q << P$ on $\mathcal{F}$ and that we also have a smaller sigma-algebra $\mathcal{G} \subseteq \mathcal{F}$. We then have two Radon–Nikodym derivatives; $L^{\mathcal{F}}$ on $\mathcal{F}$, and $L^{\mathcal{G}}$ on $\mathcal{G}$, and these are typically not equal, since $L^{\mathcal{F}}$ will generically not be $\mathcal{G}$-measurable. The following result shows how they are related.

Proposition B.39 *Assume that $Q << P$ on $\mathcal{F}$ and that $\mathcal{G} \subseteq \mathcal{F}$. Then the Radon–Nikodym derivatives $L^{\mathcal{F}}$ and $L^{\mathcal{G}}$ are related by*

$$L^{\mathcal{G}} = E^P \left[L^{\mathcal{F}} \middle| \mathcal{G} \right]. \tag{B.17}$$

Proof   We have to show that $E^P \left[L^{\mathcal{F}} \middle| \mathcal{G} \right]$ is $\mathcal{G}$-measurable (which is obvious) and that, for any $G \in \mathcal{G}$,

$$\int_G dQ = \int_G E^P \left[L^{\mathcal{F}} \middle| \mathcal{G} \right] dP.$$

This, however, follows immediately from the trivial calculation

$$\int_G dQ = \int_G L^{\mathcal{F}} dP = \int_G E^P \left[L^{\mathcal{F}} \middle| \mathcal{G} \right] dP,$$

where we have used the fact that $G \in \mathcal{G} \subseteq \mathcal{F}$.   □

Example B.40 To see an example of the result above let $\Omega = \{1, 2, 3\}$ and define

$$\mathcal{F} = 2^{\Omega} \quad \mathcal{G} = \{\Omega, \emptyset, \{1\}, \{2, 3\}\}$$

and

$$\begin{array}{lll} P(1) = 1/4, & P(2) = 1/2, & P(3) = 1/4, \\ Q(1) = 1/3, & Q(2) = 1/3, & Q(3) = 1/3. \end{array}$$

We see directly that

$$L^{\mathcal{F}}(1) = 3/4, \quad L^{\mathcal{F}}(2) = 3/2, \quad L^{\mathcal{F}}(3) = 3/4,$$

and it is obvious that $L^{\mathcal{F}}$ is not $\mathcal{G}$-measurable. Since $P(\{2, 3\}) = 3/4$, and $Q(\{2, 3\}) = 2/3$, the local scale factor on $\{2, 3\}$ is $9/8$, so $L^{\mathcal{G}}$ is given by

$$L^{\mathcal{G}}(1) = 3/4, \quad L^{\mathcal{G}}(2) = 9/8, \quad L^{\mathcal{G}}(3) = 9/8,$$

and we also have the simple calculation

$$E^P \left[L^{\mathcal{F}} \middle| \{2, 3\} \right] = \frac{P(2) L^{\mathcal{F}}(2) + P(3) L^{\mathcal{F}}(3)}{P(2) + P(3)} = \frac{9}{8}.$$

The formula (B.16) gives us expectations under Q in terms of expectations under P, and a natural question is how conditional expected values under Q are related to conditional expectations under P. The following very useful result, known as the "Abstract Bayes' Formula" solves this problem.

Proposition B.41 (Bayes' Theorem) *Assume that X is a random variable on $(\Omega, \mathcal{F}, P)$, and let Q be another probability measure on $(\Omega, \mathcal{F})$ with Radon–Nikodym derivative*

$$L = \frac{dQ}{dP} \quad on \ \mathcal{F}.$$

Assume that $X \in L^1(\Omega, \mathcal{F}, Q)$ and that $\mathcal{G}$ is a sigma-algebra with $\mathcal{G} \subseteq \mathcal{F}$. Then

$$E^Q [X | \mathcal{G}] = \frac{E^P [L \cdot X | \mathcal{G}]}{E^P [L | \mathcal{G}]}, \quad Q\text{-a.s.} \tag{B.18}$$

Proof   We start by proving that

$$E^Q\left[X|\mathcal{G}\right]\cdot E^P\left[L|\mathcal{G}\right]=E^P\left[L\cdot X|\mathcal{G}\right],\quad P-a.s. \tag{B.19}$$

We show this by proving that for an arbitrary $G\in\mathcal{G}$ the P-integral of both sides coincide. The left-hand side becomes

$$\int_G E^Q\left[X|\mathcal{G}\right]\cdot E^P\left[L|\mathcal{G}\right]dP=\int_G E^P\left[L\cdot E^Q\left[X|\mathcal{G}\right]|\mathcal{G}\right]dP$$

$$=\int_G L\cdot E^Q\left[X|\mathcal{G}\right]dP$$

$$=\int_G E^Q\left[X|\mathcal{G}\right]dQ=\int_G XdQ.$$

Integrating the right-hand side we obtain

$$\int_G E^P\left[L\cdot X|\mathcal{G}\right]dP=\int_G L\cdot XdP=\int_G XdQ.$$

Thus (B.19) holds P-a.s. and since $Q\ll P$ also Q-a.s. It remains to show that $E^P\left[L|\mathcal{G}\right]=0$ Q-a.s. but this follows from the calculation

$$Q\left(E^P\left[L|\mathcal{G}\right]=0\right)=\int_{\{E^P[L|\mathcal{G}]=0\}}dQ=\int_{\{E^P[L|\mathcal{G}]=0\}}LdP$$

$$=\int_{\{E^P[L|\mathcal{G}]=0\}}E^P\left[L|\mathcal{G}\right]dP=0.$$

$\square$

B.7   Exercises

Exercise B.1 Prove Proposition B.4 by carrying out the following steps.

- Prove the proposition in the case when $g=I_A$ where A is an arbitrary Borel set.
- Prove that the proposition holds when g is a simple function.
- You can WLOG assume that g is nonnegative (why?), so now approximate g by simple functions.

Exercise B.2 Prove Proposition B.10.

Exercise B.3 Prove Proposition B.12.

Exercise B.4 Prove Corollary B.22.

Exercise B.5 Prove Proposition B.26.

Exercise B.6 Prove (B.6) by using Proposition A.26.

Exercise B.7 Prove Proposition B.31 by first proving it when X is an indicator function, then extend by linearity to simple functions and at last by approximating X with a sequence of simple functions.

Exercise B.8 Prove Proposition B.31 by the following steps:
- Choose a fixed X.
- Show that for any $A \in \sigma\{X\}$ you have $E[I_A|\mathcal{G}] = E[I_A]$.
- Extend by linearity to simple $\sigma\{X\}$-measurable functions and at last by approximating X with a sequence of simple functions.

Exercise B.9 Let $h : R \to R$ be a function such that $h \geq 0$, $h' \geq 0$ and $h(0) = 0$. Assume that X is a nonnegative random variable. Prove that

$$E[h(X)] = \int_0^\infty h'(t)P(X \geq t)dt.$$

Exercise B.10 Prove Proposition B.36 by starting with the case when $X = I_A$ and then do the usual steps.

Exercise B.11 Prove Proposition B.37 by going along the following lines:
- Prove that the "estimation error" $X - E[X|\mathcal{G}]$ is orthogonal to $L^2(\Omega, \mathcal{G}, P)$ in the sense that for any $Z \in L^2(\Omega, \mathcal{G}, P)$ we have

$$E[Z \cdot (X - E[X|\mathcal{G}])] = 0.$$

- Now prove the proposition by writing

$$X - Z = (X - E[X|\mathcal{G}]) - (E[X|\mathcal{G}] - Z)$$

and use the result just proved.

B.8   Notes

For the mathematician, Durrett (1996) is a very good standard reference on probability theory. For the economist (and also for many mathematicians) the text by Jacod and Protter (2000) is the perfect, and amazingly far reaching, reference.

Appendix C

MARTINGALES AND STOPPING TIMES*

C.1 Martingales

Let $(\Omega, \mathcal{F}, P, \underline{\mathcal{F}})$ be a filtered probability space, and let X be a random process in continuous or discrete time.

Definition C.1 *The process X is an $\underline{\mathcal{F}}$-martingale if*

1. *X is $\underline{\mathcal{F}}$-adapted.*
2. *$X_t \in L^1$ for each t.*
3. *For every s and t with $0 \leq s \leq t$ it holds that*

$$X_s = E\left[X_t | \mathcal{F}_s\right], \quad P-a.s.$$

If the equality sign is replaced by $\leq$ ($\geq$) then x is said to be a **submartingale** *(***supermartingale***).*

Note that the martingale property is always with respect to some given filtration. In all honesty it should be mentioned that while martingale theory in discrete time is a fairly straightforward activity, martingale theory in continuous time is sometimes rather complicated and there are lots of highly nontrivial technical problems. In order for the theory to work well in continuous time we typically want our processes to have right continuous trajectories with left limits, and we also need to assume that the filtration $\underline{\mathcal{F}}$ has some regularity properties. However, in almost all concrete situations these technical problems can be taken care of, so with almost no danger the reader can safely forget about the technicalities. For the rest of this book we simply ignore these problems. Below we only give proofs for the discrete time case. The proofs for the continuous time results are typically obtained by sampling the continuous time processes at discrete points in time and then performing a limiting argument.

It follows immediately from the definition, that a martingale is characterized by the property that the conditional expectations of a forward increment equals zero, i.e. that

$$E\left[X_t - X_s | \mathcal{F}_s\right] = 0, \quad \text{for all } s \leq t.$$

For martingales in discrete time, it is in fact enough to demand that the martingale property holds for one single time step.

Proposition C.2 *An adapted integrable discrete time process $\{X_n; \ n = 0, 1, \ldots\}$ is a martingale w.r.t the filtration $\{\mathcal{F}_n; \ n = 0, 1, \ldots\}$ if and only if*

$$E\left[X_{n+1} | \mathcal{F}_n\right] = X_n, \quad n = 0, 1, 2, \ldots$$

Proof Easy exercise.   □

Two of the most common types of martingales are the following.

Example C.3 Let Y be any integrable random variable on the filtered space $(\Omega, \mathcal{F}, P, \underline{\mathcal{F}})$, and define the process X by

$$X_t = E\left[Y|\mathcal{F}_t\right], \quad t \geq 0. \tag{C.1}$$

Then it is an easy exercise to see that X is an $\mathcal{F}_t$-martingale. In particular, this implies that **on a compact interval** $[0, T]$ any given martingale M is always generated by its final value M_T by the formula

$$M_t = E\left[M_T|\mathcal{F}_t\right], \quad 0 \leq t \leq T. \tag{C.2}$$

Note that this only holds on a finite closed interval. The more complicated case of an infinite or open interval will be discussed below.

Example C.4 If X is a process with independent increments on $(\Omega, \mathcal{F}, P, \underline{\mathcal{F}})$, and if also $E\left[X_t - X_s\right] = 0$, for all s, t, then X is a martingale.

Example C.5 Let $\{Z_n; \ n = 1, 2, \ldots\}$ be a family of independent integrable random variables, and define the discrete time process X by

$$X_n = \sum_{i=1}^{n} Z_i, \tag{C.3}$$

the X is a martingale w.r.t. the filtration $\mathcal{F}^X$.

There is a close connection between martingale theory, the theory of convex functions, and the theory of harmonic functions. The correspondence is as follows:

Martingale theory	**Convex theory**	**Harmonic theory**
martingale	linear function	harmonic function
submartingale	convex function	subharmonic function
supermartingale	concave function	superharmonic function

We will not go deeper into this, but from convexity theory we recognize directly the structure of the following result.

Proposition C.6 Let X be a process on $(\Omega, \mathcal{F}, P, \underline{\mathcal{F}})$.

- If X is a martingale and if $f : R \to R$ is a convex (concave)function such that $f(X_t)$ is integrable for all t, then the process Y defined by

$$Y_t = f(X_t),$$

is a submartingale (supermartingale).

- If X is a submartingale and if $f : R \to R$ is a convex nondecreasing function such that $f(X_t)$ is integrable for all t, then the process Y defined by

$$Y_t = f(X_t),$$

is a submartingale.

Proof   Jensen's inequality for conditional expectations.   □

On every **finite** interval $[0, T]$, every martingale X is of the form

$$X_t = E\left[X_T | \mathcal{F}_t\right],$$

and a natural question is if **every** martingale X also on the infinite interval $[0, \infty]$ has a representation of this form, i.e. if there always exists some random variable X_∞ such that

$$X_t = E\left[X_\infty | \mathcal{F}_t\right]. \tag{C.4}$$

In general the answer is no, and a symmetric random walk on the integers is a typical counter example. In order to have a representation of the form (C.4) one needs some further integrability of X. We will not prove the most general (and hard) version of the results but for completeness' sake we will cite the most general convergence theorem without proof.

Theorem C.7 *Suppose that X is a submartingale satisfying the condition*

$$\sup_{t \geq 0} E\left[X_t^+\right] < \infty.$$

Then there exists a random variable Y such that $X_t \to Y$, P-a.s.

We now move to the more manageable quadratic case.

Definition C.8 *A martingale X is called* **square integrable** *if there exists a constant M such that*

$$E\left[X_t^2\right] \leq M, \quad \text{for all } t \in [0, \infty).$$

We now have the following nice result.

Proposition C.9 (Martingale Convergence) *Assume that x is a square integrable martingale. Then there exists a random variable, which we denote by X_∞, such that $X_t \to X_\infty$ in L^2 and P-a.s. as $t \to \infty$. Furthermore we have the representation*

$$X_t = E\left[X_\infty | \mathcal{F}_t\right], \quad \text{for all } t \geq 0. \tag{C.5}$$

Proof   Since $x \longrightarrow x^2$ is convex, the process X_t^2 is a submartingale, which implies that the mapping $m_t = E\left[X_t^2\right]$ is nondecreasing. The assumption that X is square integrable is thus equivalent to the existence of a real number $c < \infty$

such that $m_t \uparrow c$. We will now prove L^2-convergence by showing that X_t is Cauchy in L^2. We have

$$
\begin{aligned}
E\left[(X_t - X_s)^2\right] &= E\left[X_t^2 - 2X_sX_t + X_s^2\right] \\
&= E\left[E\left[X_t^2 - 2X_sX_t + X_s^2 \,\middle|\, \mathcal{F}_s\right]\right] \\
&= E\left[X_t^2\right] - 2E\left[X_s E\left[X_t \,\middle|\, \mathcal{F}_s\right]\right] + E\left[X_s^2\right] \\
&= E\left[X_t^2\right] - E\left[X_s^2\right] = m_t - m_s.
\end{aligned}
$$

Since $m_t \to c$ it follows that m_t is Cauchy and thus that X_t is Cauchy in L^2. Since L^2 is complete this implies the existence of a random variable $Y \in L^2$ such that $X_t \to Y$ in L^2. The almost sure convergence then follows from Theorem C.7 In order to prove (C.5) it is enough (why?) to show that for every s and every $A \in \mathcal{F}_s$ we have

$$
\int_A X_s dP = \int_A Y dP,
$$

and this follows easily from the fact that for every $t > s$ the martingale property implies that

$$
\int_A X_s dP = \int_A X_t dP.
$$

If now $t \to \infty$, it follows (how?) from the L^2-convergence that, as $t \to \infty$, we have

$$
\int_A X_t dP \to \int_A Y dP.
$$

$\square$

C.2 Discrete Stochastic Integrals

In this section we discuss briefly the simplest type of stochastic integration, namely integration of discrete time processes. This will thus serve as an introduction to the more complicated Wiener case later on, and it is also important in its own right. The cental concept here is that of a predictable process.

Definition C.10 *Consider a filtered space $(\Omega, \mathcal{F}, P, \underline{\mathcal{F}})$ in discrete time, i.e. $n = 0, 1, 2, \ldots$*

- *A random process X is $\underline{\mathcal{F}}$-**predictable** if, for each n, X_n is $\mathcal{F}_{n-1}$ measurable. Here we use the convention $\mathcal{F}_{-1} = \mathcal{F}_0$.*
- *For any random process X, the **increment process** ΔX is defined by*

$$
(\Delta X)_n = X_n - X_{n-1}, \tag{C.6}
$$

with the convention $X_{-1} = 0$.

- *For any two processes X and Y, the* **discrete stochastic integral** *process $X \star Y$ is defined by*

$$(X \star Y)_n = \sum_{k=0}^{n} X_k (\Delta Y)_k. \tag{C.7}$$

Instead of $(X \star Y)_n$ we will sometimes write $\int_0^n X_s dY_s$.

Note that a predictable process is "known one step ahead in time". The reason why we define ΔX by "backward increments" is that in this way ΔX is adapted, whenever X is.

The main result for stochastic integrals is that when you integrate a predictable process X w.r.t. a martingale M, the result is a new martingale.

Proposition C.11 *Assume that the space $(\Omega, \mathcal{F}, P, \underline{\mathcal{F}})$ carries the processes X and M where X is predictable, M is a martingale, and $X_n (\Delta M)_n$ is integrable for each n. Then the stochastic integral $X \star M$ is a martingale.*

Proof   Left as an exercise to the reader.   □

C.3   Likelihood Processes

Martingale theory is closely connected with absolutely continuous measure transformations and arbitrage theory. This will be discussed in detail in Chapter 10 and here we will only state some basic facts.

We consider a filtered probability space $(\Omega, \mathcal{F}, P, \underline{\mathcal{F}})$ on a compact interval $[0, T]$. Suppose now that L_T is some nonnegative integrable random variable in $\mathcal{F}_T$. We can then define a new measure Q on $\mathcal{F}_T$ by setting

$$dQ = L_T dP, \quad \text{on } \mathcal{F}_T,$$

and if

$$E^P [L_T] = 1,$$

the new measure will also be a probability measure.

From its definition, L_T will be the Radon–Nikodym derivative of Q w.r.t. P on $\mathcal{F}_T$ so $Q << P$ on $\mathcal{F}_T$. Hence we will also have $Q << P$ on $\mathcal{F}_t$ for all $t \leq T$ and thus, by the Radon–Nikodym Theorem, there will exist a random process $\{L_t;\ 0 \leq t \leq T\}$ defined by

$$L_t = \frac{dQ}{dP}, \quad \text{on } \mathcal{F}_t. \tag{C.8}$$

The L process is known as the **likelihood process** for the measure transformation from P to Q and it has the following fundamental property, which will be used frequently.

Proposition C.12 *With assumptions as above, the likelihood process L, defined by (C.8) is a $(P, \underline{\mathcal{F}})$-martingale.*

Proof The statement follows directly from Proposition B.39. □

Using the likelihood process, we can also characterize a Q-martingale in terms of the P measure.

Proposition C.13 *A process M is a Q-martingale if and only if the process $L \cdot M$ is a P-martingale.*

Proof Exercise for the reader. □

C.4 Stopping Times

Consider again a filtered space $(\Omega, \mathcal{F}, P, \underline{\mathcal{F}})$ and a martingale X on the space. A natural question, which we will encounter in connection with American options, is whether the martingale property also holds when the deterministic times are replaced by stochastic times, i.e. whether we always have the equality

$$E\left[X_T \middle| \mathcal{F}_S\right] = X_S, \qquad (C.9)$$

where S and T are random times with $S \leq T$. It is rather clear that we cannot expect a strong theory unless we restrict the study to those random times which in some sense are adapted to the information flow given by the filtration. These are the so-called *stopping times*.

Definition C.14 *A **stopping time** w.r.t. the filtration $\underline{\mathcal{F}}$ is a nonnegative random variable T such that*

$$\{T \leq t\} \in \mathcal{F}_t, \quad \text{for every } t \geq 0. \qquad (C.10)$$

A stopping time is thus characterized by the fact that at any time t we can, based upon the information available at t, decide whether T has occurred or not. This definition may seem a bit abstract, but in most concrete situations it is very easy to see whether a random time is a stopping time or not. A typical example of a stopping time is obtained if X is an adapted discrete time process and we define T as a *hitting time* i.e. we define T by

$$T \stackrel{def}{=} \inf\{n \geq 0; \ X_n \in A\},$$

where $A \subseteq R$ is some Borel set. T is thus the first time when X enters into the set A, and intuitively it is obvious that we can decide whether the event $\{T \leq n\}$ has occurred, based upon observations of X at the times $0, 1, 2, \ldots, n$. Thus T is a stopping time, and we obtain a formal proof by choosing a fixed n and noting that

$$\{T(\omega) \leq n\} = \{X_t(\omega) \in A, \text{ for some } t \leq n\} = \bigcup_{t=0}^{n} \{X_t \in A\}.$$

Since X is adapted we have $\{X_t \in A\} \in \mathcal{F}_t \subseteq \mathcal{F}_n$, so $\{T \leq n\} \in \mathcal{F}_n$.

A typical example of a random time which is **not** a stopping time is given by

$$T(\omega) = \sup \{n \geq 0; \ X_n \in A\}.$$

In this definition, T is thus the *last* time that X visits A, and it is again intuitively obvious that in the generic case we cannot decide whether T has occurred or not based upon the basis of observations upon $X_0, X_1, \ldots X_n$ since this would imply that at time n we already know if X will visit A or not at some time in the future.

In order to be able to even formulate the equality (C.9) we must define what we mean by the expression $\mathcal{F}_T$ for a stopping time T. Intuitively the interpretation is of course that $\mathcal{F}_T = $ "the information generated by the flow $\underline{\mathcal{F}}$ up to the random time T", but it is not obvious how to formalize this in mathematical terms. The generally accepted definition is the following.

Definition C.15 *Let T be an $\underline{\mathcal{F}}$ stopping time. The sigma-algebra $\mathcal{F}_T$ is defined as the class of events satisfying*

$$A \in \mathcal{F}_\infty, \tag{C.11}$$
$$A \cap \{T \leq t\} \in \mathcal{F}_t, \quad \text{for all } t \geq 0. \tag{C.12}$$

We now have some natural results.

Proposition C.16 *Let S and t be stopping times on the filtered space $(\Omega, \mathcal{F}, P, \underline{\mathcal{F}})$, and let X be an adapted process, which in the continuous time case is assumed to have trajectories which are either left- or right-continuous. Define $\vee$ and $\wedge$ by $x \vee y = \max [x, y]$ and $x \wedge y = \min [x, y]$ for any real number, and define $S \vee T$ by $(S \vee T)(\omega) = S(\omega) \vee T(\omega)$. Then the following hold.*

- *If $S \leq T$, P-a.s. then $\mathcal{F}_S \subseteq \mathcal{F}_T$.*
- *$S \vee T$ and $X \wedge T$ are stopping times.*
- *If T is P-a.s. finite or if X_∞ is well defined in $\mathcal{F}_\infty$, then X_T is $\mathcal{F}_T$-measurable.*

Proof The first two items are left as easy exercises, and we prove the third item only for the discrete time case. To show that X_T is $\mathcal{F}_T$-measurable we have to show that $\{X_T \in B\} \in \mathcal{F}_T$ for every Borel set B, so we thus have to show that for every n we have $\{X_T \in B\} \cap \{T \leq n\} \in \mathcal{F}_n$. We obtain

$$\{X_T \in B\} \cap \{T \leq n\} = \{X_T \in B\} \cap \bigcup_{k=0}^{N} \{T = k\} = \bigcup_{k=0}^{N} (\{X_k \in B\} \cap \{T = k\}) \tag{C.13}$$

Since X is adapted and T is a stopping time, $\{X_k \in B\}$ and $\{T = k\}$ are in $\mathcal{F}_k$ which is included in $\mathcal{F}_n$. $\square$

We now prove that the martingale property is stable under stopping.

Proposition C.17 *Let X be a martingale and let T be a stopping time. Then the* **stopped process** X^T*, defined by*

$$X_t^T = X_{T \wedge t}, \tag{C.14}$$

is a martingale.

Proof   We only give the proof for the discrete time case. For this we define the process h by $h_n = I\{n \le T\}$, $n = 0, 1, 2 \ldots$, where I denotes the indicator of the event within the bracket. Now, $\{n \le T\} = \{T < n\}^c = \{T \le n - 1\}^c$. Since T is a stopping time we thus see that $h_n \in \mathcal{F}_{n-1}$ so h is predicatable. Furthermore we have the obvious equality

$$X_n^T = \sum_{k=0}^n h_k (\Delta X)_k$$

so from Proposition C.11 we see that X^T is a martingale. $\square$

We finish by stating a fairly general version of the "optional sampling theorem" which shows that the martingale property is preserved under random sampling, but we only give the proof for a simple special case.

Theorem C.18 (The Optional Sampling Theorem) *Assume that X is a martingale satisfying*

$$\sup_{t \ge 0} E\left[X_t^2\right] \le \infty$$

Let S and T be stopping times such that $S \le T$. Then

$$E\left[X_T \mid \mathcal{F}_S\right] = X_S, \quad P-a.s. \tag{C.15}$$

If X is a submartingale satisfying the same integrability condition then (C.15) holds with $=$ replaced by $\ge$.

Proof   We will be content with proving the result in discrete time and for the case when X is a martingale, the submartingale case being a bit harder. From Proposition C.9 it follows that there exists an integrable random variable Y such that

$$X_n = E\left[Y \mid \mathcal{F}_n\right], \quad n = 0, 1, \ldots \tag{C.16}$$

It is thus enough (why?) to show that for any stopping time T we have

$$E\left[Y \mid \mathcal{F}_T\right] = X_T,$$

i.e. we have to show that for every $A \in \mathcal{F}_T$ we have

$$\int_A Y \, dP = \int_A X_T \, dP.$$

By writing A as $A = \bigcup_n (A \cap \{T = n\})$, noting that $A \cap \{T = n\} \in \mathcal{F}_n$, and using (C.16) we obtain

$$\int_A Y \, dP = \sum_{n=0}^{\infty} \int_{A \cap \{T=n\}} Y \, dP = \sum_{n=0}^{\infty} \int_{A \cap \{T=n\}} X_n \, dP = \int_A X_T \, dP.$$

$\square$

C.5 Exercises

Exercise C.1 Show that for any integrable random variable Y on a filtered space $(\Omega, \mathcal{F}, P, \underline{\mathcal{F}})$, the process X defined by

$$X_t = E[Y | \mathcal{F}_t], \quad t \geq 0,$$

is a martingale.

Exercise C.2 Let $\{Z_n\}$ be a sequence of i.i.d. (independent identically distributed) random variables with finite exponential moments of all orders. Define the function $\varphi : R \to R$ by

$$\varphi(\lambda) = E\left[e^{\lambda Z_n}\right],$$

and define the process X by

$$X_n = \frac{e^{\lambda S_n}}{[\varphi(\lambda)]^n}, \quad \text{where} \quad S_n = \sum_{k=1}^{n} Z_k.$$

Prove that X is an $\mathcal{F}_n$-martingale, where $\mathcal{F}_n = \sigma\{Z_i; \ i = 1, \ldots, n\}$.

Exercise C.3 Prove that, for any stopping time T, $\mathcal{F}_T$, defined by (C.10) is indeed a sigma-algebra.

Exercise C.4 Prove Proposition C.11.

Exercise C.5 Prove Proposition C.6.

Exercise C.6 Show that in discrete time, the defining property $\{T \leq t\} \in \mathcal{F}_t$ for a stopping time, can be replaced by the weaker condition

$$\{T = n\} \in \mathcal{F}_n, \quad \text{for all } n.$$

Exercise C.7 Prove the first two items in Proposition C.16.

Exercise C.8 A Wiener process W is a continuous time process with $W_0 = 0$, continuous trajectories, and Gaussian increments such that for $s < t$ the increment $W_t - W_s$ is normally distributed with mean zero and variance $t - s$.

Furthermore the increment $W_t - W_s$ is independent of $\mathcal{F}_s$, where the filtration is the internal one generated by W.

(a) Show that W is a martingale.

(b) Show that $W_t^2 - t$ is a martingale.

(c) Show that for any real number λ

$$e^{\lambda W_t - \frac{1}{2}\lambda t}$$

is a martingale.

(d) For $b < 0 < a$ we define the stopping time T as the first time that W hits one of the "barriers" a or b, i.e.

$$T = \inf \left\{ n \geq 0; \ X_n = a, \text{ or } X_n = b \right\}.$$

Define p_a and p_b as

$$p_a = P\left(W \text{ hits the } a \text{ barrier before hitting the } b \text{ barrier,}\right)$$
$$p_b = P\left(W \text{ hits the } b \text{ barrier before hitting the } a \text{ barrier,}\right)$$

so $p_a = P(W_T = a)$ and $p_b = P(W_T = b)$. Use the fact that every stopped martingale is a martingale to infer that $E[W_T] = 0$, and show that

$$p_a = \frac{-b}{a - b}, \quad p_b = \frac{a}{a + b}.$$

You may without proof use the fact that $P(T < \infty) = 1$.

(e) Use the technique above to show that

$$E[T] = |ab|.$$

(f) Let T be as above and let $b = -a$. Use the Optional Sampling Theorem, Proposition C.17 and item (iii) above to show that the Laplace transform $\varphi(\lambda)$ of the distribution of T is given by

$$\varphi(\lambda) = E\left[e^{-\lambda T}\right] = e^{-a\sqrt{2\lambda}}, \quad \lambda \geq 0.$$

Exercise C.9 Prove Proposition C.13.

Hint: Use the Bayes' Formula (B.18).

REFERENCES

Amin, K. and Jarrow, R. (1991). Pricing Foreign Currency Options under Stochastic Interest Rates. *Journal of International Money and Finance*, **10** 310–329.

Anderson, N., Breedon, F., Deacon, M., Derry, A., and Murphy, G. (1996) *Estimating and Interpreting the Yield Curve*. Wiley, Chichester.

Barone-Adesi, G. and Elliott, R. (1991). Approximations for the Values of American Options. *Stochastic Analysis and Applications*, **9**, 115–131.

Benninga, S., Björk, T., and Wiener, Z. (2002). On the Use of Numeraires in Option Pricing. *Journal of Derivatives*, **10**(2) 43–58.

Bingham, N.H.. and Kiesel, R. (2004). *Risk Neutral Valuation* (2nd edn). Springer, Berlin.

Björk, T. (1998). *Arbitrage Theory in Continuous Time*. Oxford University Press, Oxford.

Björk, T. (2001). A Geometric View of Interest Rate Theory. In *Option Pricing, Interest Rates and Risk Management*. (ed. E. Jouini, J. Cvitanic and M. Musiela). Cambridge University Press, Cambridge.

Björk, T. and Christensen, B. (1999). Interest Rate Dynamics and Consistent Forward Rate Curves. *Mathematical Finance*, **9**(4), 323–348.

Björk, T., Di Masi, G., Kabanov, Y., and Runggaldier, W. (1997). Towards a General Theory of Bond Markets. *Finance and Stochastics*, **1**, 141–174.

Björk, T. and Gombani, A. (1999). Minimal Realizations of Interest Rate Models. *Finance and Stochastics*, **3**(4), 413–432.

Björk, T., Kabanov, Y., and Runggaldier, W. (1995). Bond Market Structure in the Presence of a Marked Point Process. *Mathematical Finance*, **7**(2), 211–239.

Björk, Tomas and Landén, C (2002). On the Construction of Finite Dimensional Realizations for Nonlinear Forward Rate Models. *Finance and Stochastics*, **6**(3), 303–331.

Björk, T. and Svensson, L. (2001). On the Existence of Finite Dimensional Realizations for Nonlinear Forward Rate Models. *Mathematical Finance*, **11**(2), 205–243.

Black, F. (1976). The Pricing of Commodity Contracts. *Journal of Financial Economics*, **3**, 167–179.

Black, F., Derman, E., and Toy, W. (1990). A One-Factor Model of Interest Rates and its Application to Treasury Bond Options. *Financial Analysts Journal*, **33** 33–39.

Black, F. and Scholes, M. (1973). The Pricing of Options and Corporate Liabilities. *Journal of Political Economy*, **81**, 659–683.

Brace, A., Gatarek, D., and Musiela, M. (1997). The Market Model of Interest Rate Dynamics. *Mathematical Finance*, **7**, 127–154.

Brace, A. and Musiela, M. (1994). A Multifactor Gauss Markov Implementation of Heath, Jarrow, and Morton. *Mathematical Finance*, **4**, 259–283.

Brennan, M.J. and Schwartz, E.S. (1979). A Continuous Time Approach to Pricing Bonds. *Journal of Banking and Finance*, 133–155.

Brigo, D. and Mercurio, F. (2007). *Interest Rate Models* (2nd edn). Springer, Berlin, Heidelberg.

Brody, D.C. and Hughston, L.P. (2001). Interest Rates and Information Geometry. *Proc. Roy. Soc. London A*, **457**, 1343–1363.

Brody, D.C. and Hughston, L.P. (2002). Entropy and Information in the Interest Rate Term Structure. *Quantitative Finance*, **2**, 70–80.

Brody, D.C. and Hughston, L.P. (2004). Chaos and Coherence: A New Framework for Interest Rate Modelling. *Proc. Roy. Soc. Lond. A*, **460**, 85–110.

Carr, P. (1995). Two Extensions to Barrier Option Valuation. *Applied Mathematical Finance*, **2**, 173–209.

Carverhill, A. (1994). When is the Spot Rate Markovian? *Mathematical Finance*, **4**, 305–312.

Cheyette, O. (1996). Markov Representation of the Heath-Jarrow-Morton Model. Preprint. BARRA Inc.

Chiarella, C. and Kwon, O.K. (2001). Forward Rate Dependent Markovian Transformations of the Heath–Jarrow–Morton term structure model. *Finance and Stochastics*, **5**, 237–257.

Cochrane, J. (2001). *Asset Pricing*. Princeton University Press, Princeton, N.J.

Conze, A. and Viswanathan, R. (1991). Path Dependent Options: The Case of Lookback Options. *Journal of Finance*, **46**, 1893–1907.

Cox, J.C. and Huang, C.F. (1989). Optimal Consumption and Portfolio Choice when Asset Prices Follow a Diffusion Process. *Journal of Economic Theory*, **49**, 33–83.

Cox, J., Ingersoll, J., and Ross, S. (1985). A Theory of the Term Structure of Interest Rates. *Econometrica*, **53**, 385–407.

Cox, J., Ross, S., and Rubinstein, M. (1979). Option Pricing: A Simplified Approach. *Journal of Financial Economics*, **7**, 229–264.

Cox, J. and Rubinstein, M. (1992). *Options Markets*. Prentice Hall, Englewood Cliffs, N.J.

Cvitanić, J (1997). Optimal Trading under Constraints. In *Financial Mathematics, Springer Lecture Notes in Mathematics, Vol 1656* (ed. W. Runggaldier). Springer Verlag, Berlin, Heidelberg, New York.

Dana, R. and Jeanblanc, M. (2003). *Financial Markets in Continuous Time*. Springer Verlag, Berlin, Heidelberg, New York.

Davis, M.H.A. (1997). Option Pricing in Incomplete Markets. In *Mathematics of Derivative Securities* (ed. M. Demptster and S. Pliska), pp. 216–266. Cambridge University Press, Cambridge.

Delbaen, F. (1992). Representing Martingale Measures when Asset Prices are Continuous and Bounded. *Mathematical Finance*, **2**, 107–130.

Delbaen, F and Schachermayer, W (1994). A General Version of the Fundamental Theorem of Asset Pricing. *Matematische Annalen*, **300**, 463–520.

Delbaen, F. and Schachermayer, W. (1998). The Fundamental Theorem for Unbounded Processes. *Matematische Annalen*, **312**, 215–250.

Dellacherie, C. and Meyer, P.A. (1972). *Probabilités et Potentiel*. Hermann, Paris.

Doob, J.L. (1984). *Classical Potential Theory and its Probabilistic Counterpart*. Springer Verlag, New York.

Dothan, M. (1978). On the Term Structure of Interest Rates. *Journal of Financial Economics*, **6**, 59–69.

Duffie, D. (1989). *Futures Markets*. Prentice Hall, Englewood Cliffs, NJ.

Duffie, D. (2001). *Dynamic Asset Pricing Theory, 3rd ed.* Princeton University Press.

Duffie, D. and Huang, C. (1986). Multiperiod Securities Markets with Differential Information. *Journal of Mathematical Economics*, **15**, 283–303.

Duffie, D. and Kan, R. (1996). A Yield Factor Model of Interest Rates. *Mathematical Finance*, **6**(4), 379–406.

Duffie, D. and Singleton, K. (1999). Modeling Term Structures for Defaultable Bonds. *Review of Financial Studies*, **12**, 687–720.

Durrett, R. (1996). *Probability*. Duxbury Press, Belmont.

Elliott, R.J. (1982). *Stochastic Calculus and Applications*. Springer Verlag, New York.

Fabozzi, F. (2009). *Bond Markets, Analysis, and Strategies* (7th edn). Prentice Hall, Englewood Cliffs, N.J.

Filipović, D. (1999). A Note on the Nelson-Siegel Family. *Mathematical Finance*, **9**(4), 349–359.

Filipović, D. (2001). *Consistency Problems for Heath-Jarrow-Morton Interest Rate Models*. Springer Lecture Notes in Mathematics, Vol. 1760. Springer Verlag., Berlin, Heidelberg.

Filipović, D. and Teichmann, J. (2003). Existence of Invariant Manifolds for Stochastic Equations in Infinite Dimension. *Journal of Functional Analysis*, **197**, 398–432.

Filipović, D. and Teichmann, J. (2004). On the Geometry of the Term Structure of Interest Rates. *Proceedings of the Royal Society*, **460**, 129–167.

Fleming, W. and Rishel, R. (ed.) (1975). *Deterministic and Stochastic Optimal Control*. Springer Verlag, Berlin Heidelberg New York.

Fleming, W. and Soner, M. (ed.) (1993). *Controlled Markov Processes and Viscosity Solutions*. Springer Verlag, New York.

Flesaker, B. and Hughston, L. (1996). Positive Interest. *RISK Magazine*, **9** 46–49.

Flesaker, B. and Hughston, L. (1997). International Models for Interest Rates and Foreign Exchange. *Net Exposure*, **3**, 55–79.

Föllmer, H. and Sondermann, D. (1986). Hedging of Non-redundant Contingent Claims under Incomplete Information. In *Contributions to Mathematical Economics* (ed. W. Hildenbrand and A. Mas-Colell). North-Holland, Amsterdam.

Frittelli, M. (2000). The Minimal Entropy Martingale Measure and the Valuation Problem in Incomplete Markets. *Mathematical Finance*, **10**, 215–225.

Garman, M. and Kohlhagen, S. (1983). Foreign Currency Option Values. *Journal of International Money and Finance*, **2**, 231–237.

Geman, H. (1989). The Importance of the Forward Neutral Probability in a Stochastic Approach of Interest Rates. Working paper, ESSEC.

Geman, H., El Karoui, N., and Rochet, J.-C. (1995). Changes of Numéraire, Changes of Probability Measure and Option Pricing. *Journal of Applied Probability*, **32**, 443–458.

Gerber, H. and Shiu, E. (1994). Option Pricing by Esscher Transforms. *Transactions of the Society of Actuaries*, **46**, 51–92.

Geske, R. and Johnson, H. (1984). The American Put Option Valued Analytically. *Journal of Finance*, **39**, 1511–1524.

Goldman, M., Sosin, H., and Gatto, M. (1979). Path Dependent Options: "Buy at the High and Sell at the Low". *Journal of Finance*, **34**, 1111–1126.

Hansen, L. and Jagannathan, R. (1991). Implications of Security Market Data for Models of Dynamic Economies. *Journal of Political Economy*, **99**, 225–262.

Harrison, J. and Kreps, J. (1979). Martingales and Arbitrage in Multiperiod Markets. *Journal of Economic Theory*, **11**, 418–443.

Harrison, J. and Pliska, S. (1981). Martingales and Stochastic Integrals in the Theory of Continuous Trading. *Stochastic Processes & Applications*, **11**, 215–260.

Heath, D., Jarrow, R., and Morton, A. (1992). Bond Pricing and the Term Structure of Interest Rates: A New Methodology for Contingent Claims Valuation. *Econometrica*, **60**, 77–105.

Ho, T. and Lee, S. (1986). Term Structure Movements and Pricing Interest Rate Contingent Claims. *Journal of Finance*, **41**, 1011–1029.

Hughston, L.P. and Rafailidis, A. (2005). A Chaotic Approach to Interest Rate Modelling. *Finance and Stochastics*, **9**, 43–65.

Hull, J. (2003). *Options, Futures, and Other Derivatives* (5th edn). Prentice Hall, Englewood Cliffs, N.J.

Hull, J. and White, A. (1987). The Pricing of Options on Assets with Stochastic Volatilities. *Journal of Finance*, **42**, 281–300.

Hull, J. and White, A. (1990). Pricing Interest–Rate–Derivative Securities. *Review of Financial Studies*, **3**, 573–592.

Hunt, P. and Kennedy, J. (2000). *Financial Derivatives in Theory and Practice*. Wiley, Chichester.

Inui, K. and Kijima, M. (1998). A Markovian Framework in Multi-Factor Heath–Jarrow–Morton models. *Journal of Financial and Quantitative Analysis*, **33**, 423–440.

Jacod, J. and Protter, P. (2000). *Probability Essentials*. Springer Verlag, Berlin Heidelberg.

Jacod, J. and Shiryaev, A.N (1987). *Limit Theorems for Stochastic Processes*. Springer Verlag, Berlin.

Jamshidian, F. (1989). An Exact Bond Option Formula. *Journal of Finance*, **44**, 205–209.

Jamshidian, F. (1997). Libor and Swap Market Models and Measures. *Finance and Stochastics*, **1**, 293–330.

Jarrow, B., and Madan, D. (1995). Option Pricing Using the Term Structure of Interest Rates to Hedge Systematic Discontinuities in Asset Returns. *Mathematical Finance*, **5**, 311–336.

Jarrow, R., Lando, D., and Turnbull, S. (1997). A Markov Model for the Term Structure of Credit Risk Spreads. *Review of Financial Studies*, **10**, 481–523.

Jeffrey, A. (1995). Single Factor Heath–Jarrow–Morton Term Structure Models based on Markov Spot Interest Rate Dynamics. *Journal of Financial and Quantitative Analysis*, **30**, 619–642.

Jin, Y. and Glasserman, P. (2001). Equilibrium Positive Interest Rates: A Unified View. *Review of Financial Studies*, **14**, 187–214.

Karatzas, I., Lehoczky, J., and Shreve, S. (1987). Optimal Portfolio and Consumption Decision for a "Small Investor" on a Finite Horizon. *SIAM Journal of Control and Optimization*, **26**, 1157–1186.

Karatzas, I., Lehoczky, J., Shreve, S., and Xu, G.L. (1991). Martingale and Duality Methods for Utility Maximization in an Incomplete Market. *SIAM Journal of Control and Optimization*, **29**, 702–730.

Karatzas, I. and Shreve, S. (1998). *Methods of Mathematical Finance*. Springer, New York Heidelberg Berlin.

Karatzas, I. and Shreve, S. (2008). *Brownian Motion and Stochastic Calculus* (2nd edn). Springer, New York Heidelberg Berlin.

Korn, R. (1997). *Optimal Portfolios*. World Scientific, Singapore.

Kramkov, D. and Schachermayer, W. (1999). The Asymptotic Elasticity of Utility Functions and Optimal Investments in Incomplete Markets. *Annals of Applied Probability*, **9**, 904–950.

Kreps, D. (1981). Arbitrage and Equilibrium in Economies with Infinitely Many Commodities. *Journal of Mathematical Economics*, **8**, 15–35.

Krylov, R. (1980). *Controlled Diffusion Processes*. Springer Verlag, New York.

Lando, D. (2004). *Credit Risk Modeling*. Princeton University Press, Princeton, N.J.

Leland, H. (1994). Risky Debts, Bond Covenants and Optimal Capital Structure. *Journal of Finance*, **49**, 1213–1252.

Leland, H. (1995). Option Pricing and Replication with Transaction Costs. *Journal of Finance*, **47**, 1283–1301.

Longstaff, F.A. and Schwartz, E.S. (1992). Interest Rate Volatility and the Term Structure. *Journal of Finance*, **40**, 1259–1282.

Magshoodi, Y. (1996). Solution of the Extended CIR Term Structure and Bond Option Valuation. *Mathematical Finance*, **6**, 89–109.

Margrabe, W. (1978). The Value of an Option to Exchange One Asset for Another. *Journal of Finance*, **33**, 177–186.

Merton, R. (1969). Lifetime Portfolio Selection under Uncertainty. The Continuous Time Case. *Review of Economics and Statistics*, **51**, 247–257.

Merton, R. (1971). Optimum Consumption and Portfolio Rules in a Continuous Time Model. *Journal of Economic Theory*, **3**, 373–413.

Merton, R. (1973). The Theory of Rational Option Pricing. *Bell Journal of Economics and Management Science*, **4**, 141–183.

Merton, R. (1974). On the Pricing of Corporate Debt: The risk Structure of Interest Rates. *Journal Of Finance*, **29**, 449–479.

Meyer, P.A. (1976). Un Cours sur les Integrales Stochastiques. In *Seminaire de Probabilites X*. Springer Verlag, Berlin Heidelberg.

Miltersen, K., Sandmann, K., and Sondermann, D. (1997). Closed Form Solutions for Term Structure Derivatives with Log-normal Interest Rates. *Journal of Finance*, **52**, 409–430.

Miyahara, Y. (1976). Canonical Martingale Measures of Incomplete Assets Markets. In *Proceedings of the Seventh Japan–Russia Symposium* (ed. S. Watanabe). World Scientific, Singapore.

Musiela, M. (1993). Stochastic PDE:s and Term Structure Models. Preprint.

Musiela, M. and Rutkowski, M. (1997). *Martingale Methods in Financial Modelling*. Springer-Verlag, Berlin.

Øksendal, B (1998). *Stochastic Differential Equations*. Springer-Verlag, Berlin.

Pelsser, A. (2000). *Efficient Methods of Valuing Interest Rate Derivatives*. Springer-Verlag, Berlin.

Peskir, G. and Shiryaev, A.N. (2006). *Optimal stopping and free boundary value problems*. Birkhäuser, Basel.

Protter, P. (2004). *Stochastic Integration and Differential Equations* (2nd edn). Springer-Verlag, Berlin.

Reiner, E. (1992). Quanto Mechanics. *RISK*, **5**, 59–63.

Rendleman, R. and Bartter, B. (1979). Two State Option Pricing. *Journal of Finance*, **34**, 1092–1110.

Revuz, D. and Yor, M. (1991). *Continuous Martingales and Brownian Motion*. Springer-Verlag, Berlin, Heidelberg.

Ritchken, P. and Sankarasubramanian, L. (1995). Volatility Structures of Forward Rates and the Dynamics of the Term Structure. *Mathematical Finance*, **5**(1), 55–72.

Rogers, L.C.G. (1994). The Potential Approach to the Term Structure of Interest Rates and Foreign Exchange Rates. *Mathematical Finance*, **7**, 157–176.

Royden, H.L. (1988). *Real Analysis* (3rd edn). Prentice Hall, New York.

Rubinstein, M. and Reiner, E (1991). Breaking Down the Barriers. *RISK*, **4**, 28–35.

Rudin, W. (1991). *Functional Analysis*. McGraw–Hill.

Schachermayer, W. (1994). Martingale Measures for Discrete Time Processes with Infinite Horizon. *Mathematical Finance*, **4**, 25–56.

Schachermayer, W. (2002). Optimal Investment in Incomplete Financial Markets. In *Mathematical Finance–Bachelier Congress 2000* (ed. H. Geman). Springer-Verlag, Berlin Heidelberg New York.

Schönbucher, P. (2003). *Credit Derivatives Pricing Models*. Wiley.

Schweizer, M. (1991). Option Hedging for Semimartingales. *Stochastic Processes and Their Applications*, **37**, 339–363.

Schweizer, M. (2001). A Guided Tour through Quadratic Hedging Approaches. In *Option Pricing, Interest Rates and Risk Mangement* (ed. E. Jouini). Cambridge University Press, Cambridge.

Shirakawa, H. (1991). Interest Rate Option Pricing with Poisson–Gaussian Forward Rate Curve Processes. *Mathematical Finance*, **1**, 77–94.

Shiryaev, A.N. (2008). *Optimal Stopping Rules* (2nd edn). Springer Verlag, Berlin Heidelberg.

Snell, J.L. (1952). Application of Martingale System Theorems. *Trans. Am. Math. Soc.*, **73**, 293–312.

Steele, J.M. (2001). *Stochastic Calculus and Financial Applications*. Springer Verlag, New York Berlin Heidelberg.

Sundaresan, S. (2009). *Fixed Income Markets and Their Derivatives* (3rd edn). Academic Press.

Vasiček, O. (1977). An Equilibrium Characterization of the Term Stucture. *Journal of Financial Economics*, **5**, 177–188.

INDEX